Salmon P. Chase

Salmon P. Chase

A Biography

JOHN NIVEN

New York   Oxford
OXFORD UNIVERSITY PRESS
1995

Oxford University Press

Oxford   New York   Toronto
Delhi   Bombay   Calcutta   Madras   Karachi
Kuala Lumpur   Singapore   Hong Kong   Tokyo
Nairobi   Dar es Salaam   Cape Town
Melbourne   Auckland

and associated companies in
Berlin   Ibadan

Library of Congress Cataloging-in-Publication Data
Niven, John.
Salmon P. Chase : a biography /
John Niven.
p.   cm.   Includes bibliographical references and index.
ISBN 0–19–504653–6
1. Chase, Salmon P. (Salmon Portland), 1808–1873.
2. Legislators—United States—Biography.
3. United States. Congress. Senate—Biography.
4. Judges—United States—Biography.
5. Governors—Ohio—Biography.
6. United States—Politics and government—1849–1877.
I. Title.   E415.9.V4N58 1995   977.1′03′092—dc20   94–14465

1 2 3 4 5 6 7 8 9

Printed in the United States of America
on acid-free paper

To the memory of my sister
Mary Ann Niven

Preface

"Salmon P. Chase is going to be a tough nut to crack," wrote John Hay to John G. Nicolay, his collaborator on the massive biography of Lincoln they were writing. After toiling for many years on a biography of Chase and an edition of his papers, I heartily concur with Hay's statement.

Chase was an exceedingly complex individual with many conflicting facets to his character. A moralist torn by ambition, he appeared before the courts of Cincinnati and Columbus defending slaves for social justice and for personal recognition. A realist in politics to a point, he exhibited this quality when he first became involved with the Ohio Liberty party, a fledgling abolitionist enterprise in 1840–41. At the time the Liberty party seemed a forlorn hope to most practical politicians, but Chase sensed its importance in a reform movement that was beginning to sweep the northern states on the issue of slavery. And he meant to capitalize on what he was certain would be an exciting future that would yield benefits to him yet at the same time satisfy a genuine desire to help his fellowman regardless of his color or his condition of servitude.

But with all his faults and all his virtues—which were many—Chase was preeminently a representative nineteenth-century man. He moved through those turbulent years as a majestic figure with an air of conscious superiority that many found repellent. Yet he performed invaluable public service in the drive to end slavery, in his financial policies as Secretary of the Treasury during the Civil War, in his role as Chief Justice of the Supreme Court during the turmoil of the Reconstruction years. And he played a constructive role as presiding officer over the impeachment trial of Andrew Johnson in the senate.

Despite his years of service as a distinguished American statesman, but few works have dealt with his life and career. In 1874, Robert B. Warden, over the objections of Chase's imperious daughter Kate Sprague, published a rambling part memoir, part opinionated biography that with all its weaknesses brought to light much important manuscript material. That same year one of Chase's private secretaries, Jacob Schuckers, published an authorized biography. Better organized than the Warden work, it too printed important letters and diary entries. In 1899, Albert Bushnell Hart brought out the first biography of Chase in the *American Statesman* series that met the critical standards of the day. But it was not until 1987, some 82 years later, that in his biography, *Salmon P. Chase, a Life in Politics*, Frederick Blue recreated the man and his career and documented his life from manuscript sources.

My work seeks to go beyond Chase's political adventures the better to explain his career as an eminent American, yet not slight his family life and the environment in which he acted and which acted on him as a proper setting for his career.

Numerous individuals and colleagues have helped me in researching and writing this book. First, I want to recognize the inestimable assistance I have received from my fellow editors on the Chase Papers project. They are James McClure, Leigh Johnsen, William Ferraro, and Steve Leiken. My deep appreciation goes to Henry Gibbons, Hans L. Trefousse, and Bennett H. Wall, who read all or portions of the manuscript. I have profited much from their invaluable criticism.

Support for the Chase Papers project from the National Historical Publications and Records Commission (NHPRC) and the National Endowment for the Humanities (NEH) helped me immeasurably during the research phase of this book. Thus I record here my deep appreciation to Roger Bruns, Gerald George, Mary Giunta, Kathryn Jacob, and Nancy Sahli of the NHPRC and to Douglas Arnold of the NEH. I wish also to thank John McDonough and Oliver Orr of the Manuscript Division and Mary Ison, Head, Reference Section, Prints and Photograph Division of the Library of Congress; Richard Baker, Historian of the U.S. Senate; Bernard R. Crystal, Curator of Manuscripts, the Butler Library, Columbia University; the Manuscript Department of the New York Historical Society; the Cincinnati Historical society; the Huntington Library; and the New York Public Library, for assistance in unearthing relevant documents; and Chase's great grandson, Edward Hoyt of Berkeley, California, who made available some valuable family documents.

I owe a debt of gratitude to Sheldon Meyer, who provided me with pertinent criticism of the manuscript. I am also indebted to Stephanie Sakson, whose rigorous and creative corrections have significantly improved the text, and to Joellyn Ausanka. Finally I wish to thank Lelah Mullican, who typed so many drafts of the manuscript that I have lost count.

Claremont, California
1994

J. N.

Contents

Salmon P. Chase

chapter 1

Threshold

At a few minutes before one o'clock on March 5, 1868, Chief Justice Salmon P. Chase and senior associate Justice Nelson, in their black judicial robes, met the deputation that would escort them to the Senate Chamber. The trial of Andrew Johnson, seventeenth President of the United States, for high crimes and misdemeanors, was about to begin. As the group moved out, Chase and Senator Samuel Pomeroy were in the lead, followed by Nelson and Senators Henry Wilson and Charles R. Buckalew, the lone Democrat. They walked the 100 feet or so from the Supreme Court chambers to the south central doors of the Senate. As soon as they appeared, the senators rose as a body, not out of any respect for Chase and Nelson, but because the Republican majority and the Democratic minority had agreed, for their own particular reasons, to clothe the proceedings with dignity, emulating the great Anglo-American state trials of the past.

Chase himself was equally eager to dramatize the event because he was conscious of his own singular importance in presiding over a trial of obvious historic importance. The contrast between him and his escort, Samuel Pomeroy, could not have been more sharply defined. As the procession moved slowly toward the Vice President's desk the crowded galleries and the senators themselves noted that the tall, stately Chase overtopped Pomeroy by a good four inches, noted also how his strong, chiseled features differed from those of the suave, smooth Pomeroy's much to that Kansas senator's disadvantage. There was little doubt in anyone's mind that Chase's appearance, his massive frame enhanced by his flowing robes, dominated the scene.[1]

Well aware of the image he wished to project, Chase was satisfied that he had struck just the right note at the onset of the proceedings. If the senators were anxious to clothe their actions with the semblance of a profound public act, Chase outdid them by focusing attention on himself and on the judicial role he symbolized. But with him it was not just the trappings of a state trial that the senators had in mind, but the preservation of basic constitutional principles—the distribution of powers between the three branches of the federal government, the executive, legislative, and judicial. For some time he had feared that this time-honored system might be so seriously modified that the government of the nation would be transformed into a parliamentary mode of rule. The checks and balances the founding fathers had made the cornerstone of public policy would be hustled on their way to extinction. Congress would possess supreme power not just in its legislative capacity but in executing and interpreting its own laws.

Chase had always been devoted to measured change, as he understood the needs of society. To his orderly mind, slavery, the abasement of human beings, had always been an alien force, a kind of radicalism, that threatened the existence of the Republic, and a grave affront to personal and public morality, a subversion of the Constitution and the Declaration of Independence. Now that slavery had been abolished and civil rights of the former bondsmen guaranteed by the thirteenth and in all likelihood the impending fourteenth Amendment to the Constitution, Chase was satisfied that their freedom and their security were well protected.

It was time to "bind up the nation's wounds," in Lincoln's words, not a time to replace armed combat with the continuation of a divisive cold war against the former enemy. To his mind now that the ruling oligarchy had been displaced the people of the South were basically as law-abiding as their northern counterparts. Believing as he did, he had coined the slogan "Universal Amnesty and Universal Suffrage."

Thus he deplored the unprecedented action of the Congress to remove a President, however impractical his stubborn stand against Congress on Reconstruction, however dogmatic his policies upholding white supremacy and old-fashioned states' rights. In impeaching and trying Johnson under the partisan passions of the moment, the radicals in Congress among whom he had counted his closest political friends were acting more stubbornly and more irresponsibly than the President.

At least Johnson had observed constitutional constraints even if he interpreted them literally, not so the small group of able and articulate radicals who had driven their moderate colleagues along the dangerous road of political revolution. Chase had come to believe that this minority was manipulating the majority of their fellow Congressmen, much as the prewar minority of southern slave owners had crushed the moderate unionists and precipitated the unimaginable death and devastation of Civil War.

As he repeated after Nelson the oath to "do impartial justice according to the Constitution and the laws" he was reenacting what amounted to a life-long belief that the stability of society rested on interacting social and moral imperatives. He would if he could interpose the dignity of his office and his status as a preeminent public man against the "madness of the hour," to protect the government, not just the executive branch but the Congress itself, against its own excesses and somehow keep the Court free and independent while it painstakingly moved to interpret the Constitution so as to protect the civil rights of both black and white citizens.

There was of course, another side to this exceedingly complex individual. Political goals were never far from his mind. Invariably they were not to be sought for their own sake but rather for the good of the country and for the highest of moral purposes, the freedom and equality of all mankind. Yet these lofty motives masked a thirst for office and power that was deeply ingrained in his character, rooted as they were in a troubled childhood and adolescence.

His uncle, Philander Chase, the Episcopal Bishop of Ohio, recognized this flaw in his character during those years when his nephew was a member of his household. He wrote his brother, Baruch, that Salmon's "temper is not good, tho' much modified by discipline. His genius [is] extraordinarily good. If he finds someone to govern and direct him aright, he will with God's blessing make one of the finest of men; if otherwise, he may make one of the worst."[2]

Salmon Portland Chase was born in Cornish, New Hampshire, on January 13, 1808, the eighth child of Ithamar and Janette Ralston Chase. Chase's father, a prosperous, hardworking, and well-respected farmer, was a leading citizen of the town that his grandfather founded.

The town itself was a self-contained community as New Hampshire villages and towns were at the beginning of the nineteenth century. Situated almost in the middle of New Hampshire's western border, it profited as a sort of rural entrepôt conveying the resources from the rich farmlands in the upper Connecticut River valley, by way of the river to the more thickly settled areas of Massachusetts, Connecticut, and through Long Island Sound to New York City. By New Hampshire standards, Cornish was a relatively prosperous community, where some of the frontier heritage still lingered. His father, older brothers, and sisters formed a tightly knit group that counted themselves the leading spirits of the community. Chase's numerous uncles were all well-educated members of the professions, lawyers, clergymen, and physicians. In fact Chase owed his pompous name (which he disliked intensely) to one of his uncles, also a Salmon, who had been the foremost lawyer in Portland, Maine.[3]

Many extended families like the Chases, isolated for the most part in remote, rural New England, were riven with emotional turmoil and individual controversy. The Ithamar Chase family, however, was free of such internal jealousy and hatred. The elder Chase seems to have had a genial and expansive nature that avoided local quarrels and rivalries. His neighbors looked up to him as a natural leader that was manifest through his election to a succession of offices.[4] As his son remarked many years after Ithamar's death, he had also been a Justice of the Peace with Honorable before his name and Esquire after it, titles in which his wife took pride.[5]

Ithamar Chase, the sixth child of Dudley and Alice Corbett Chase, was born in 1763 in Sutton, Massachusetts, which later became the center of agrarian discontent and the seat of Shays' Rebellion. The family had emigrated from England in 1640 and settled first in Newbury, Massachusetts before moving westward to Sutton. Samuel Chase, Salmon's great-grandfather, seeking better land and prospects, moved a hundred miles northwest to New Hampshire where he had found a wilderness meadow in the fertile valley of the Connecticut River. Chase and several associates purchased the land very cheaply from the original proprietors, who had acquired a large land grant from the royal Governor, Benning Wentworth. Samuel Chase laid out a town which he named Cornish after the county of Cornwall in Great Britain, ancestral home of the Chases.[6]

Samuel Chase's offspring were prolific and hardy. Only one of the fifteen children born in Dudley Chase's family died in infancy and the immediate family was extraordinarily long-lived. Samuel Chase died in 1800 at the age of ninety-three. Born during the reign of Queen Anne, he had seen in the course of his lifetime three wars with France and their Indian allies, the Revolutionary War, and the creation of a new nation. Salmon's older brother and sister remembered the old gentleman. Chase's paternal grandparents both lived in good health until their mid-eighties. Longevity persisted into his parent's generation when their average mortality exceeded seventy-five years.

That generation was also a precocious lot. Five of Ithamar's brothers attended Dartmouth College. And the sisters, though they had the benefit of only the rustic one-room school in Cornish, were not neglected. Their self-educated parents saw to it that they continued reading and studying with their brothers when at home and with the local clergyman. Ithamar's younger sister Alice, the most conscientious of the girls in the family, vied with her college-educated brothers in the translation of Latin and Greek.[7] Religious training of the strict Calvinist variety pervaded not just the Dudley Chase family but all of the settlers in Cornish, a regimen that Chase's children continued.

Salmon Chase was thus born into a household where work, self-improvement, and religion were interchangeable. The only departure from this ancestral norm, variation more of form than of substance, occurred before

Chase's birth. The youngest of the eight brothers, Philander, became converted to Episcopalianism while a student at Dartmouth. He embraced his
new faith with such fervor and determination that he managed not only to have
his parents and all of his siblings confirmed in the denomination but to raise
the necessary means for building an Episcopal church in Cornish.[8]

Chase's father, Ithamar, seems to have been less of a driven person than
his brothers. He did not attend college, but he was a highly successful farmer
who produced enough of a surplus in cereal grains, fodder, and animal products to provide a comfortable life for his large family.

Nature had bestowed beauty on the Cornish countryside. The fecundity
of the Chase women and the fertility of Ithamar's fields bred security for
young Salmon. But such comfort of a prosperous extended family did not
mean exemption from the never-ending cycle of farm work.

Like his older brothers and sisters, Salmon had to earn his keep as soon
as he was old enough to help in the fields or the barns. Moreover, winters in
that northern climate were long and harsh for man and beast alike. The Chase
homestead was a substantial structure that Ithamar built in the 1790s, but it
was drafty, heated only by an inefficient fireplace which served for cooking
along with a "bake kettle and a Dutch oven." Fare was coarse and monotonous during the windswept, snow-driven winters. All-too-short summer
months brought significant improvement and variety to the family diet. Fresh
meat, though lean and tough by modern standards, garden vegetables, and
some orchard fruit were plentiful, but of little variety. Chase's younger sister,
Helen, remembered that her brother gave her the first peach she had ever
eaten when he returned from Ohio in 1823. She was then eight years old.[9]

Chase's mother, Janette Ralston Chase, was a resolute woman who was
determined that her children improve on whatever natural gifts she observed
in them. She was the second daughter of Scottish immigrants, who had come
to Massachusetts in the mid-eighteenth century and migrated to Keene, New
Hampshire, a market town some fifty miles south of Cornish. Janette Chase's
father, Alexander Ralston, for many years had prospered and when she married Ithamar was the richest man in town.

Protected and loved by a large and caring family in comfortable circumstances, young Chase enjoyed a secure early childhood. But when he reached
the age of eight, a series of tragic and difficult circumstances befell his family
during the harsh winter and very late spring of 1816.

Ithamar Chase, who for so many years had farmed his acres in Cornish
and who had provided a good living for his large family, suddenly decided to
make a drastic change in occupation. Attracted by what he heard were large
profits to be made in the glass business because of the war, which cut off these
essential imports, Ithamar sold out his holdings in Cornish and went into
partnership with Ebeneezer Brewer and William M. Bond, both part-time

manufacturers in Keene. During the fall of 1815 he moved the family to that town and into a spacious yellow-painted tavern on Main Street, owned by his father-in-law.[10]

The fledgling business of Chase, Brewer, and Bond was unable to withstand the flood of cheaper, better British glass goods that began pouring into the American market not long after the Treaty of Ghent in February, 1815. But equally damaging to their business was the failure of the local market following the year of 1816, during which killing frosts extending into the short New England growing season brought near famine to the countryside and inspired a heavy migration to the west.

Young Chase could have been only dimly aware of these extreme difficulties, but tensions in the household must have colored his remembrances of his first formal schooling which he said was held "in a dark room with a great many boys in it."[11] Tragedy stalked these early years and economic misfortune clouded the family's life. Such grim intrusions were interconnected and had a profound influence on the boy.

The elder Chase, so recently a well-to-do farmer and manufacturer and accustomed to providing a "comfortable" living standard for his family, accustomed also to being a leading figure in his hometown of Cornish and in state affairs, was now faced with financial ruin in another town, which though only about fifty miles distant from his home place was still an alien community. He could not claim the status he took for granted in Cornish except through his wife's connections. With the collapse of his financial fortunes, involving as it did a substantial portion of the property his father-in-law had deeded to his wife, Ithamar Chase, for the first time in his life, became a victim of despair that weakened his robust constitution. In August 1817, he suffered a massive stroke. For several days he was in a coma until the end was judged near. Then the children were called to his bedside. "How still the room was," Chase remembered, "except the heavy breathing and the ominous rattle. He could not speak to us, and we stood mute and sobbing. Soon all was over. We had no father . . . the light was gone out of our home."[12] Ithamar Chase was fifty-three years old. He left his widow in straitened circumstances with eight dependent children.[13]

His father's death made a lasting impression on the sensitive lad. But what must have been equally upsetting was the abrupt removal of the household (the second time in less than a year) from the big, comfortable yellow tavern in the middle of town to a nondescript farmhouse on the outskirts of Keene, almost all that was left of Janette's property. The move required a change in schools for the younger Chases, which again meant new acquaintances and the usual childhood difficulties to be faced in what for them was a new and troubling environment. Nor was young Salmon given time to adjust to his new situation. His mother felt that he, of all her children, deserved a better education than he was receiving in the district school. She made an arrangement with a friend of her husband's, Josiah Dunham, to board and educate the boy.

Dunham conducted a school at Windsor, Vermont, just across the New Hampshire border from Cornish. For those times in rural New England Dunham and his school enjoyed a high reputation. Like a good many proprietors and teachers of New England schools, he combined his pedagogical activities with local affairs and farming. He had also dabbled in politics and had at one time been a newspaper editor. Chase soon discovered that in the attic of Dunham's home there were a number of Federalist newspapers he had received in exchanges. The otherwise strict schoolmaster gave the boy access to them. Although Chase's mother had already cautioned him that newspapers "were not to be implicitly relied on for the truth," years later he maintained that his perusal of Dunham's papers awakened an interest in politics and in the role of political parties.[14]

Under Dunham's tutelage Chase began a systematic study of Latin, which he continued on his return to Keene, for further study with the Reverend Zedekiah Barstow, an accomplished classicist.[15] The next two years were comparatively uneventful for young Chase. He remained in Keene perfecting his Latin, beginning Greek, and gaining a sound grip of mathematics, including Euclidean geometry, under Barstow's tutelage. He also contributed to the family economy by doing his share of farm work. This stable interlude in his young life came to an end during the winter of 1820.

Chase's mother convinced her brother-in-law Philander to take young Salmon into his household and be responsible for his education. Philander Chase had just become Episcopalian Bishop of Ohio and was conducting a boy's school in Worthington, Ohio, which supplemented the scanty income he received from his pastoral duties.

Possibly because of financial problems, possibly because she felt Chase needed a father figure, Janette Chase had decided to enlist the Bishop's aid. Of certain influence on her decision was that her oldest son, twenty-three-year-old Alexander, a practical geologist, with a neighbor, Charles Schoolcraft, were leaving for the west to join a government-sponsored expedition into Michigan and Wisconsin under the territorial governor and Indian agent Lewis Cass.

Alexander and Schoolcraft would look after young Salmon for most of a trip, which posed some danger and meant long miles of travel over rough, undeveloped territory where human habitation was sparse. The decision must have been a painful and difficult one for Janette Chase, but it does suggest the reliance the family placed upon the formidable self-confident Bishop. Philander Chase, too, had gained some renown as an educator and like all of his surviving brothers was an accomplished classicist.[16]

For the twelve-year-old boy, a trip to the mysterious west seemed a great adventure. Grossly exaggerated tales of the wondrous sights and the incredible fertility of the Ohio region had been seeping into New England, still scarcely recovered from the devastating "winter" of famine 1816–17, its merchant and banker class still reeling from the panic and depression of 1819–20.

Young Chase, of course, had absorbed uncritically the Ohio lore that emanated from the scattered Yankee settlements in the Western Reserve, so named because of Connecticut's colonial charter claim to the region.[17] He read all that he could find about the new state, which was precious little, primarily gleaned from Jedediah Morse's *Gazetteer.*

Chase could not remember specific events of the trip over Vermont's Green Mountains in early April 1820. The route he, his brother, and Schoolcraft took, however, was clearly etched in his memory. By stage they traveled through Bennington and from there to Albany. Pushing westward the little group reached Buffalo in late April where they had planned to board the one steam vessel that plied Lake Erie, the *Walk-in-the-Water,* their destination the village of Cleveland. But the little 135-foot vessel was still ice-bound in Black Rock, a tiny port near Buffalo. Forced to remain in town until the ice broke up, Alexander Chase and Schoolcraft took the opportunity of visiting Niagara Falls, but for some reason left Salmon behind. In an early example of his adventurous, independent spirit, Salmon would not be deprived of the experience. With another young companion he walked to the falls. The awesome splendor of Niagara dazzled young Chase. He never forgot the experience, nor the warm reception he got from his brother and Schoolcraft, whom he met just below the falls. "But," said Chase, "they took charge of me, and got me back to Buffalo much easier than I got to the Falls."[18]

Toward the end of April, the ice broke up on the Niagara River. Jedediah Rogers, master of the *Walk-in-the-Water,* made ready to embark for Cleveland and Detroit. Forty cords of hardwood were stowed on her open deck for fuel. Provisions for twenty-nine paying passengers, the Chases and Schoolcraft among them, were stowed in the hold beneath the main cabin. Captain Rodgers got up steam that powered her chattering, reciprocating engine for a trial at her berth. He inspected the wrought-iron linkages to the paddle wheels on her port and starboard beam. Satisfied that her engine and wheels were in operating condition, he sent word for the passengers to come aboard. Saturday morning, May 6, the *Walk-in-the-Water* got under way.

Assigned a bunk in the main cabin, Chase was awakened by the engine's start-up sounds that shook the flimsy craft. With the wonder and curiosity of youth he rushed on deck to observe the departure. On shore he saw fifteen yoke of oxen hitched to a tow line assisting the weak engine buck the current that flowed from Lake Erie to the Niagara River. As soon as the *Walk-in-the-*

Water had crept below the river mouth, the tows were cast off and sails set on her two stubby masts as Rodgers set his course for Cleveland. Belching volumes of smoke from her lofty stovepipe stack, she gained more steerage way from her sails than from her inefficient engine. The weather was fair with a light breeze, but it still took the *Walk-in-the-Water* some sixty hours to make the 200-mile trip.[19]

At about five o'clock in the early evening of Monday, May 8, Chase caught his first glimpse of Cleveland. It was not much to see: a hamlet with a population of about 500 people, dwellings straggled across the heavily wooded bluffs that rose abruptly from the lake. Captain Rogers dropped his anchor a hundred yards offshore since there was no harbor. Small boats conveyed the passengers to the settlement at the mouth of the shallow meandering Cuyahoga River.[20]

An arrangement had been made to board young Chase with a fellow New Englander, "Judge" Barber, until he could find transportation south to Worthington, the Bishop's home, 125 miles southwest of Cleveland. Here Chase's brother and Schoolcraft parted company with Salmon and returned to the ship for passage to Detroit.

After a week or so at Judge Barber's, means were found to take Chase to Medina, a frontier settlement, twenty-five miles southwest of Cleveland. Again the New England network would provide him with a shelter on the way to Worthington. Judge Barber had learned that a circuit-riding Episcopal minister who lived in Medina would accompany the boy. And since Bishop Chase had organized a convention of all Episcopal ministers throughout the state to be held at Worthington, the Judge assumed there would be delegations passing through Medina en route to Worthington. Chase described his domicile at Medina as "one of the primitive log cabins of the country—one or two rooms below—a single room above, where all the children slept, with coarse curtains for partitions."[21]

Judge Barber's assumption proved correct. After a week's stay in Medina, two young clergymen bound for the convention arrived and were willing to have Chase join them for the hundred-mile journey to Worthington. The route south was but a winding trail through a dense wilderness. Vehicles, even farm wagons, could not work their way through it. The clergymen had two horses, thus the three travelers had to take turns riding. By this means it took four days to reach Worthington. They spent the nights at cabins along the way. It was young Chase's turn to walk when they reached Worthington and there, on the one and only muddy street of the village, he found the Bishop conversing with a friend.[22]

Bishop Chase was a huge, imposing figure well over six feet in height. In the words of a contemporary, "Large and heavy in stature as he was, he was remarkably light and graceful in his movements, and, when not ruffled with opposition or displeasure, exceedingly agreeable, polished and finished in his manner."[23]

Although young Chase instantly recognized him, he knew little about him personally and that knowledge he had gained from his mother and other older members of his immediate family. The Bishop was a very active person who had spent much of his early life wandering from one town to another in New England, the middle Atlantic states, and the Deep South. In fact, he was always on the move, seeking new challenges and new opportunities. He would deny it, of course, and explain his restlessness as evidence of God's will, but besides being a prodigious worker, he was supremely ambitious to make his mark in religious circles.[24]

When Salmon saw him on the main street of Worthington, Philander Chase was forty-four years old, in the prime of physical vigor. An Episcopal Bishop for just over a year, he combined organizational and missionary work with administration. He also managed the new Episcopal Academy in Worthington, boasting a two-story brick building. Bishop Chase owned a 150-acre farm near the village.

It is probable that he had offered Chase's mother a home and education for her son in return for his services as a farm hand. In any event, young Salmon's year and a half at Worthington was a period of intense physical and intellectual labor as well as of mental torment. Despite Bishop Chase's title and his great responsibilities, he remained a poor man who had to keep up the appearances of his office but at the same time depended largely on his own labor for support. He received a small income from the school, from the Episcopal church, and from the five parishes then in existence. The household was never far from poverty. "The Episcopal revenue," recalled Chase, "was scanty, the Church in Ohio weak. Most of its members were farmers. Of those who were not, few had considerable incomes."[25]

The panic and subsequent Depression of 1819 had fallen with crushing weight on the frontier economy of Ohio. Prices for surplus commodities that the farmers raised had been driven to ruinous lows, making them scarcely worth harvesting beyond family needs. Newly cleared farms were being foreclosed as the Bank of the United States began calling in its paper from what few state banks existed, they in turn seeking desperately for liquidity as they pressed for redemption of the mortgages and notes they held. For individuals like the Bishop whose living standard depended largely on outside income, these times proved even more precarious than usual. Salmon Chase described the primitive barter economy: "No good roads; no accessible markets; no revenue and poor chance therefore for salaries."[26]

Bishop Chase's duties frequently took him away from home, but he set up a regimen for his nephew that combined hard labor on the farm with intense study at the Academy. "Out of school I did chores," said Chase, "took the grain to the mill and brought back meal or flour; milked the cows; drove them to and from pasture; took wool to the carding factory over on the Scioto . . . built fires and brought in wood in the winter time; helped gather sugarwater maple syrup and make sugar when winter first turned to spring; helped plough and sow in the later spring."[27]

All of this labor was accomplished under the censorious eye of the Bishop on his return from his travels. Like many boys, particularly those on the verge of adolescence, Chase was forgetful and not a little rebellious. For his slightest departure from the daily routine, however, the Bishop resorted to a variety of punishments ranging from thrashing to confinement. But always he ratio-nalized such sessions that Salmon came to dread with homilies drawn from biblical example. At the same time, Bishop Chase exhorted his nephew to achieve excellence whether it be in exceeding his quota of farm chores or his translation of New Testament Greek. "My memories of Worthington, on the whole," said Chase, "are not pleasant. . . . I used to count the days and wish I could get home or go somewhere else and get a living by work."[28]

Yet the mixture of domestic tyranny and encouragement the Bishop prescribed did not crush Salmon's spirit. It did lead him to adopt devious means to escape his uncle's severe discipline so that a certain blending of morality and expediency became second nature to him. The Bishop himself quickly recognized Salmon's talents and his incipient temper. A harsh and unrelenting person when it came to any infractions of his many rules, he was also genuinely solicitous about his nephew's religious education. And he was successful in implanting an overweening religiosity in his young ward. After two years of struggling to maintain his family in what he felt was the proper style of an Episcopal Bishop and failing despite prodigious labor, Philander Chase abandoned the school at Worthington and accepted the presidency of Cincinnati College, which had been granted a charter in 1819 and seemed to present better prospects than the faltering Academy.[29]

Cincinnati was certainly booming in 1822 when Bishop Chase decided on his move. With a population of over 12,000 it had already gained renown as a center for the packing and distribution of pork products throughout the Ohio River valley and points south on the Mississippi River system. The magnificent location of the city on hills above the Ohio River which ultimately emptied into the Mississippi at Cairo, Illinois, provided natural waterborne access to Pittsburgh and the eastern seaboard and south to the cotton planta-tion consumers in the slave states. Eminently a practical man, Philander Chase saw much more opportunity for advancing the cause of the Church from a base in Cincinnati than from the more static prospects of central Ohio.[30]

The hundred-mile journey in the family carriage over the rudimentary road south was a test of everyone's endurance, but it especially tried the diligence and latent skills of young Salmon. Bishop Chase was convalescing from a serious illness when the family and servants, seven in all, started out. They had expected to spend the night at a tavern ten miles south of Columbus; when they reached it in the evening they found it crowded to capacity. Informed that they might obtain lodging in a cabin some miles distant, they moved on in the night. The road, with axle-deep mud and studded with tree stumps, required careful maneuvering. "In the course of an hour," Chase said, "the carriage was brought to a sudden halt by a stump too high for the wheels to go over. . . . Fortunately we had an ax and soon had cut levers from the saplings in the woods and with their help lifted first one axle then the other." Finally they reached the cabin, a rude log hut, occupied by a farmer, his wife, and several children. The farmer, as Chase remembered, had the drawn yellow features, long beard, and trembling hands characteristic of those recovering from malaria, or the ague, as it was commonly termed. The wife "was rough and imperious—evidently the mistress." But the couple took the Chase family in and gave one of their two beds in the common room to the Bishop and his wife. Young Chase and the others in the group found shelter in a lean-to shed.[31]

The difficulties of the journey thus far brought on a resurgence of the Bishop's sickness. During the night he became quite ill. Young Chase had to take charge, which he did quickly, quietly, and with an air of command. Into the woods he went where he cut a large quantity of dead wood, and brought it in to stoke a roaring fire. "To have been sick there, in such a place," he recalled, "so far from medical help was a distressing thought."[32] The heat together with Mrs. Chase's careful ministrations appeared to revive the Bishop's confidence. After a restorative sleep he awakened the following morning well enough to resume travel through the prairie and across the Scioto River to Cincinnati. Bishop Chase soon found adequate though scarcely commodious quarters in a small house on the northwest corner of Fifth Street and Lodge Alley. It was a tight fit with the seven individuals of the Chase family making do in a six-room cottage. That Chase remembered such incidents with startling clarity many years later testifies to the sharp impression those events made on him.

Despite his lack of consistent study, Chase was enrolled as a freshman in Cincinnati College. He found the curriculum to be unbelievably easy and the pedagogical discipline slack. The Latin and Greek he had studied in the many schools he attended and the exacting tutelage of his uncle more than made up for the academic demands of the new College. Chase raced through the first year and was well into the second year of instruction when the Bishop resigned his post to return east and travel to Great Britain on a fund-raising tour to endow a seminary he contemplated in Ohio.[33]

The old carriage was again pressed into service for a long trip. It had been a year since the Chases had left Worthington, but the road they took north and the weather all comported to make this journey far more comfortable and pleasant then the trip down to Cincinnati. Scarcely a night had passed when they had to stay in one of the crude frontier taverns or cabins. They now traveled in the older, eastern portion of the State where new but well-tended farms bespoke an air of stability and permanence. The Bishop, it seemed, had a friend or associate every thirty miles or so, who offered hospitality. But the more memorable places were at Chillicothe and Steubenville on the border of Virginia, Warren, and Ashtabula. From Warren to Ashtabula the carriage made the best headway of the trip as it bowled along on the only turnpike in the State, a graded dirt road largely free of rocks and stumps.[34]

At Ashtabula the Chases turned east and proceeded along the shore of Lake Erie, as that was the most level, unencumbered path. At times the horses made their way along the sandy beach, splashing through lake water up to their knees, drenching the travelers. It took three days for the party to reach Buffalo and four days more to cross New York to Kingston, a small town on the Hudson River south of Albany where they were lodged at the home of one of the Bishop's sisters.

Here Philander Chase gave his fifteen-year-old nephew four dollars and put him on the boat to Albany. On his own Salmon would travel the last 140 miles until he reached home in Keene. "My scanty purse did not contain enough," said Chase, "to pay stage fare." But with the confidence of youth, the wayfarer started off with little thought of any difficulties. "I walked, with occasionally a ride from some farmer going the same way." When he was about thirty-five miles from home, young Chase paid almost all of his remaining funds to the owner of a wagon for transport to Keene. Three days of slow, uncomfortable travel yet remained to cover this short distance. "It was dark before I entered the village," said Chase, "the man drove the wagon up the door. . . . [I] jumped out and giving him my last dollar, ran in, where mother and sisters, surprised and glad, gave me a most affectionate welcome."[35]

chapter 2

Trials and Triumphs

The New Hampshire Salmon Chase returned to in 1823 shocked the sensitive adolescent who had grown accustomed to the more exuberant life-style of the new west. In contrast to the booming, speculative economy of Cincinnati or the expansive settlements along the turnpike that connected Ashtabula with Steubenville, Chase's native state seemed to have gone backward in time. The depression that followed the panic of 1819 had, it is true, put a damper on western development but it had not checked perceptibly the influx of immigrants into Ohio from New York, Pennsylvania, Virginia, and Kentucky.

During their return trip east, the Chases encountered a constant procession of farm families heading west, their few belongings packed on their wagons. In contrast New Hampshire had none of this fluidity, this intermixture of transplanted New Englanders, their crisp accents contrasting with the slow-speaking southerners that provided interest and variety for the observant youth. In his passage over the Green Mountains to his home in Keene, he noticed that that section of New England seemed to have suffered more from the depression than had the west. Everywhere along the way, young Chase saw evidence of abandoned farmsteads and an occasional empty, silent mill along a watercourse. Apart from abandoned farms and appearances of other economic hardship, the overall impression was that of a society still retaining signs of respectable stability. The villages and towns had a more permanent feel than the jerry-built lean-tos and cabins of central Ohio.[1]

Chase's family greeted him warmly. His widowed mother, nearly blind, but erect and slim carrying well her fifty years, his older sister Alice, his younger sister Helen, and younger brothers, Edward and William, were the only members of the immediate family still in Keene. Chase's older brothers and sisters were living in other New England towns. But the four dependent children and now a fifth to support stretched an already thin family budget to near the subsistence level.

Janette Chase had lived so long on the borderline of poverty, making do with her small inheritance, that she must have pondered how she could continue to maintain the genteel status of her family, which meant so much in small-town New England communities. She was determined, however, that Salmon—her eighth child, whom everyone thought had impressive gifts—should continue his education. She hoped that he could contribute something to the expenses she anticipated for college. Probably the efforts of the local Congregational minister and his former tutor, Zedekiah Barstow, led to Salmon being hired as teacher for a nearby district school. His salary was about eight dollars a month plus board with a farm family. Chase found his charges, boys and girls—some older than he—a trial from the outset. With exaggerated ideas of discipline and his own self-importance gained from his experiences under the Bishop's tight regime, Chase dispensed corporal punishment to his students too freely for their parents. The school committee discharged him rather peremptorily and Salmon found himself again at home in Keene.[2]

Chase's favorite Aunt Rachel, Mrs. Joseph Denison, eased the family purse by agreeing to house the precocious lad for a period of time during which he could further his studies at the Royalton Academy. Nathaniel Sprague, its proprietor, agreed to take Salmon as a student.[3] The Denisons made an arrangement with Sprague to prepare him for entrance to Dartmouth College. Accustomed to the Bishop's mastery of the classics, Chase thought Sprague's knowledge of Latin and Greek rather superficial. But for the first time in nearly four years, he enjoyed the security and comparative leisure of a well-run household and a loving aunt and uncle.[4] Despite his low opinion of Sprague's capabilities the year at Royalton sharpened his previous education. He was better prepared than most of the farm boys who were seeking entrance to Dartmouth, well in advance even of third-year students in residence.[5]

At Hanover, New Hampshire, where Chase presented himself for admittance, the examining professors were quick to acknowledge his training. After a few cursory questions they admitted him as a third-year student without qualification. Years later Chase still scoffed at the perfunctory examination. "One of the questions by the learned professor of mathematics amused me," said Chase. "He undertook to fathom my geographical attainments and asked 'Where do the Hottentots live?' I was tempted to answer in 'Hanover' but prudence restrained me."[6]

Dartmouth College in 1824 was slowly recovering from the assault a Jeffersonian Republican state government had made upon it. Regarded as an aristocratic institution the legislature canceled its charter and sought to convert it into a public college. Not five years before Chase's entrance, Daniel Webster had successfully defended Dartmouth's private status before the United States Supreme Court in the celebrated case of *Dartmouth v. Woodward*. But the college in the isolated rural village of Hanover was still mired in financial difficulties. With a student body of about 150 young men, its teaching staff was minuscule, the library inadequate even when compared with the scant holdings of other New England colleges.

Bennett Tyler, spirited defender of orthodox Calvinism in the Jonathan Edwards vein, had been president for two years when Chase became a member of the junior class. In the tight little world of New England Congregationalism Tyler was far more interested in theological disputes than heading a college. He cared much for the spiritual nature of his undergraduates and expended more energy promoting a religious revival in Hanover than in strengthening the financial condition of the institution. A few minor bequests were added to the endowment during Tyler's tenure, but it was not until the end of his administration after Chase had graduated that his successor began a campaign to raise funds for sorely needed buildings and equipment.[7]

Including the president and two tutors appointed for a one-year term, a faculty of eight found it difficult to cope with a heavy teaching load and maintain a modicum of discipline over the student body.[8] There were no serious student outbreaks during Chase's two years at Hanover, but there was a good deal of mischief and some open disrespect for the faculty. More than two-thirds of the student body were from New Hampshire and most of them came from backgrounds similar to Chase's. Tuition and board for the year was less than a hundred dollars, but a majority of the students including Chase found it hard to meet this modest obligation. District school jobs, as poorly paid as they were, provided the major source of income. Thus they were eagerly sought and competition was great. Chase's previous experience with district schools had been neither successful nor pleasant. Nevertheless he deeply resented it when a classmate, to whom he had mentioned an opening he was interested in, moved ahead and secured the position for another applicant.[9]

Yet Chase formed some close attachments with his fellow scholars and in a curious display of boyish emotion and self-confidence impulsively challenged the faculty and President Tyler for what he considered to be wrongful punishment of a classmate. Chase sought an interview with Tyler, which was granted. One can picture the scene: the tall awkward adolescent facing the rotund but far from placid president, each conscious of his own rectitude. As a cover for his nervousness, Chase opened the conversation, adopting a firmer manner than he actually felt. He was certain, he said, that his friend was "innocent of the charge against him." Tyler thought that the faculty was a better judge than a student. Chase replied, "Then I desire to leave college; for I don't wish to remain when a student is liable to such injustice." "Have you consulted your mother?" Tyler asked. "No," said Chase, "but I want a leave of absence that I might do so." "You can't have it," said Tyler. "Then sir," said Chase, "I must go without it." Although unaccustomed to being contradicted and especially by a student the strict clergyman finally did give ground and permit the leave. Considering Tyler's rigid personality and the grim pleasure he took in argument, his concession speaks much for young Chase's debating ability and courage plus a hint of future self-assurance in this instance on what he deemed high moral ground. Chase believed he scored a victory of sorts over a formidable adversary. "In respect to the gov't," he wrote, "their bark is always worse than their bite, tho' they can bite keenly enough too upon occasion."[10]

Chase returned home to a surprised and disapproving mother. After the sacrifices she had made in drawing upon her slender means to support her son at college, she was not that moved by his youthful stand on principles, but, as he recorded many years later, "she did not censure harshly." Chase's mother was more concerned about not hearing from her son as regularly as she wanted. And recognizing in him a tendency to chafe at anything that interfered with his expectations, she cautioned him to be more understanding. "You must learn to put up with such little disappointments," she wrote, "you must cut off some of the ten thousand things and bring them down to hundreds."[11] With her income, stretched very near the breaking point to support one son in college and another away at school, Mrs. Chase preached economy down to cutting costs even if "only a six pence a week," which she pointed out would amount to 26 shillings a year. But then in an apologetic vein she added, "I hear you say what a close calculator mother has become, but it is my dear children that makes me parsimonious, if I am so. I hope never to be recommended among the stingy."[12] Fortunately the suspension of Chase's friend was brief. The two young men returned to Dartmouth, and Chase, a superior student, was able easily to make up for the time lost. At the end of the term the faculty elected him to Phi Beta Kappa.[13]

Chase may have been critical of the course of study and of his instructors, but, within the limits of a sense of personal superiority, he enjoyed the fellowship and the social life of Dartmouth. In order to economize he boarded with a group of students who formed a cooperative arrangement to purchase and prepare food for daily meals. Cooperative study and socializing eventually led to the formation of a club. Chase either was not asked to join or decided against becoming a member, probably the latter.[14] For he had a rather low opinion of his classmates and tended to be quite circumspect in the friendships he made. "I doubt," he said archly, "whether it would be possible, to find a poorer set of intellects in any college in America."[15] Nor was Chase any more forgiving of the administration and faculty of Dartmouth. "I do not admire or approve," he wrote two years after his graduation, "the spirit of exclusive sectarianism which has long distinguished the gov't of the College."[16]

During his senior year a revival swept through the town of Hanover and the college. President Tyler was active in promoting it from the pulpit of the Congregational church in town and to the student body, required to attend chapel every morning, evening, and of course several hours on Sundays—whatever its members' denominational inclination. At first Chase was cool to the excitement of the revival. While not exactly critical of Tyler's efforts, he was not complimentary either. "I was taught not to believe much in the [efficacy of such things]," he wrote, "but I do not know enough concerning their effects to oppose them." Yet as a serious young man he was pleased at the improvement the revival made on the students. "Everyone appears sober," he said, "compared to last fall. . . . In the chapel this evening you might have heard a pin drop so attentive and silent were the students."[17]

Whatever impact the revival made upon the deeply felt religious impulses that his uncle the Bishop had surely fostered, it did prompt him to reexamine the idea of the ministry as a career. But Chase decided he was not ready then to settle down to the limited confines of a New Hampshire or Vermont town; nor was he convinced that a clerical profession satisfied the expectations of a budding but strong ambition. Chase's varied life until now, though it had its unsettling and disagreeable aspects, stimulated a youthful restlessness, a lively curiosity and a yearning to see other areas of the country, to experience other settings beyond the simplicity of his native heath. Meanwhile he must support himself on this quest of self-realization.

He had talked his situation over with the Reverend M. B. Chase, a distant cousin and the pastor of the Episcopal church in Hopkinton, where he visited after his graduation from Dartmouth.[18] But he made his own decision, though still a tentative one on how and where he would satisfy his immediate goals. "It was my purpose," said Chase, "to go South and teach for a time, and then pursue whatever profession might appear to me best." The Reverend supplied him with letters to clergymen acquaintances in New Jersey, Maryland, and Virginia.[19] Before coming to any decision, Chase visited his mother, who was now living with his sister, Hannah Skinner, in Reading, New Hampshire. Mrs. Chase listened to her son's rather vague plans for his future, and though a very practical woman, she offered no serious objections. On a gray March morning with a hint of a snow in the air, Chase took an early breakfast. Supplied with a small sum of money his mother was able to spare, her "blessing and sad yet hopeful heart, [he] left home for the world." The great adventure was about to begin.[20]

Chase caught the Albany stage at Windsor, Vermont, a dozen miles from Hopkinton, and started on the two-day journey across the Green Mountains. At Albany, he embarked on the steamboat for the overnight trip to New York City. By stage and steamboat he reached Philadelphia a few days later, where he sought out one of the pastors the Reverend Chase had recommended. There, to his astonishment, he found his Uncle Philander, who had just returned from a successful fund-raising trip to England.[21] After considering his nephew's plans, the Bishop suggested he visit a colleague in Swedesboro, New Jersey, who could advise him about the prospects of establishing a school there. Chase dutifully followed his uncle's advice but quickly learned that founding a successful school was not as easy as he had hoped. From Swedesboro he continued on to Maryland and Virginia. The same poor prospects were replicated.[22] A chastened, somewhat crestfallen Chase finally made his way to Washington to the boarding house of another uncle, Dudley Chase, then serving as a United States senator from Vermont. Dudley Chase saw to it that his nephew was settled at Mrs. Markland's boarding house, and he introduced him to Henry Clay and to some of his congressional colleagues. Chase's meager resources were running out, but with his uncle's approval, he placed an advertisement in the *Daily National Intelligencer* announcing the "opening of a select classical school in the western part of the City." Chase limited enrollment to twenty students. Classes would begin on January 9, 1827.[23] He listed as references his uncle, Henry Clay, and four members of Congress to whom he had been introduced.

Despite the impressive list of names, Chase's notice attracted no students. After several weeks the now despairing young man again solicited his uncle's aid. He was well aware that Dudley Chase was a warm supporter of the Adams administration. Would the senator use his influence to secure a government clerkship for his now near penniless nephew? The senator would not. "Salmon," he said, "I once obtained an office for a nephew of mine, and he was ruined by it. I then determined never to ask one for another." Thereupon he reached in his pocket for his purse, extracted some coins, and speaking in measured accents of heavy and cutting irony, he said, "I will give you fifty cents to buy a spade with, but I will not help to get you a clerkship."[24]

Somehow young Chase's educational background and his connections had reached a wider audience than had his notice in the *Intelligencer*. The pastor of St. John's Episcopal Church, the Reverend Dr. Hawley, gave Chase a letter of introduction to Alexander R. Plumley, who conducted a well-established school for both boys and girls in the District. Chase visited

Plumley, presented his letter and had a long chat with the schoolmaster and his wife. They both had heard of the young man and were impressed with Hawley's glowing testimonial. Chase's considerable abilities also claimed their attention. Plumley was discouraging about the prospects for another school, but soon after this meeting he decided that his school had become too large for him to conduct alone. No doubt weary of the disciplinary chores he had faced so long with the boys in his classes, he decided to split his school, retaining the girls for his own instruction and offering the boys' classes to Chase. The desperate young man saw providence in Plumley's offer. He immediately accepted, and gained a school with a dozen or more students.[25]

The school posed some curriculum and disciplinary problems from the outset which Plumley outlined; yet these were not deterrents. Chase had an established school with a student roster that included the sons of all the Cabinet members except Richard Rush, the Secretary of the Treasury. If he made a success of it—despite his previous failure as a schoolmaster—he could count on income from tuition of about $1000 a year. It was certainly not wealth beyond the dreams of avarice but a sum ample enough for a young man of Chase's spartan habits to live comfortably.

With his assured means of livelihood Chase moved from his cramped quarters at Mrs. Markland's where he shared a bedroom with a young physician to Mrs. Cook's boarding house on Pennsylvania Avenue and H Street. After a few months there he moved again to Mrs. King's on the corner of 18th and G Street. Now Chase at least had the privacy of a single room, although his accommodations were small and sparsely furnished.

The King family, which included two daughters of Chase's age, brightened his humdrum existence. And though diffident in his personal relationships at this time, he became friendly with several members of Congress who also boarded at the Kings'.[26] His social life, however, soon became closely involved with that of the Wirt family, not with his fellow boarders.

Among Chase's students were two sons of William Wirt, President Adams's Attorney General. Wirt's interest in his children's education led him to quiz the young schoolmaster from time to time on the course of study he was prescribing for his charges. As a matter of course Wirt himself or his sons invited Chase to social occasions at their home. To the tall, thin, awkward young man, the portly, genial Wirt with his literary and legal accomplishments, his open personality, his ready wit, and his obvious tender care for his family was in decided contrast to the reserved, sometimes harsh angularity that Chase had known in New England and during his residence with the Bishop. He found the Wirt family not just charming but warm and endearing.[27]

Mrs. Wirt was in her late forties, an imposing, gifted woman who had borne twelve children but still retained much of the beauty that had graced the social circles of Richmond, Virginia, at the turn of the century. Related to the

Washingtons, she was well educated and had enjoyed the comfortable, secure life that her prosperous merchant father provided for his family. She took an interest in young Chase, but was always careful not to let his obvious need for companionship transcend her carefully marked limits of familiarity. She was especially circumspect when it came to her four daughters, three of whom were attractive young women of marriageable age.[28]

If the Wirt household with its women formed a center for Chase's attention and an outlet for his social needs, the figure of William Wirt made a lasting impact on the self-conscious young man. Friend of Jefferson and Madison, highly regarded member of the Cabinet, leading lawyer in Washington, much quoted essayist, and biographer, Wirt quickly became Chase's model for his career. This man of many talents meant much more than just an exemplar, however. In many respects, Wirt represented the father figure he never had. And his easy, open nature was a decided contrast to the domestic cruelty and the constant emphasis on success that marked that other significant influence on Chase's formative years, his uncle the Bishop.

Soon after Chase established a social relationship with the Wirt family, he decided on a legal career. He asked William Wirt if he could study law with him. The Attorney General, though overburdened as he was with his official duties and his law practice, was too kind-hearted to rebuff him. He agreed to accept Chase as a student, but then was unable to devote much of his precious time to instruction. Wirt rarely examined his pupil. "Only once," recalled Chase, "did he put a question to me about my studies. He asked me one day while I was reading Blackstone if I understood him."[29]

But apart from the hospitality the Wirt family provided, Wirt's negligence regarding Chase's legal instruction was of little consequence. Chase himself was well aware of the basic sources law students were required to study and was supremely industrious. Before his legal apprenticeship with Wirt, Chase was already familiar with Jean Jacques Burlamaqui's works on natural law and politics, which he had studied in college and which many American law students found useful, as well as practical texts for basic application of legal theory to social needs. After school hours, Chase worked his way through an eclectic collection of specific law books such as Espinasse on pleadings, Cruise's digest of the common law, Sir James Dalrymple's antiquarian compilation of British feudal law, and of course Blackstone and Coke.[30]

Fortunately Chase was gifted with considerable powers of analysis or he would not have been able without direction to make any sense out of these thorny, discursive tomes. As it was he lamented his unsystematic study, and there is no doubt that while he had little or no practice in preparing legal forms and in such stock-in-trade law as contracts, he did gain a firm grasp of Anglo-American legal institutions, a knowledge far in advance of his fellow law students.

He set himself a formidable routine of work and study. As he explained to his friend Thomas Sparhawk, "all my time after three in the afternoon will be my own besides two or three hours in the morning and all of Saturdays. I shall then certainly be able to devote six hours per diem to professional study and may make some progress. I retire to bed at 11 o'clock and rise by daybreak."[31] All was not work and study, however.[32]

William Wirt and his family were far more important in developing Chase's still plastic personality than any formal law instruction could possibly provide. Chase was not exactly without connections when he made his home in Washington. His uncle Dudley, despite his New England insistence on individual initiative, was after all well known in official circles. The Bishop was a friend of Henry Clay and was an acquaintance of President Adams with whom he dined on occasion. He was also a respected though controversial figure in the upper reaches of the Episcopal hierarchy.[33] But the Wirt connection opened up additional doors to the young schoolmaster and law student. For the Wirts were much in demand at the teas, the balls, the receptions that made life bearable in the isolated capital city. And Chase always took time from his work-haunted regime to escort one or another of the Wirt women to these events.

Washington may have been a disorderly, dirty, unfinished city, or more properly a southern country town, whose thoroughfares were alternately ankle deep in mud or billowing with dust, but to Chase it was a fascinating place, quite the most cosmopolitan city that he had ever seen. With the insouciance of youth, he overlooked the open drains, the ramshackle houses and stores that were interspersed with government buildings or the solid brick and stone houses of local magnates and high government officials.

Chase always lamented that he did not make the most of his stay in the capital to advance his career. But he certainly entered with a gusto into whatever social life his friendship with the Wirts afforded. President Adams held evening soirees twice a month where he greeted his fellow citizens. Frequently Chase braved the multitudes who jammed the corridors of the White House.[34] On one occasion he accompanied New Hampshire Congressman Icabod Bartlett and found the crush so dense that he did not renew a visit until Adams's last open house on January 28, 1829.[35] On that evening he accompanied Elizabeth Wirt, one of the Wirt daughters, Elizabeth Cabell, and Mrs. Stephen Pleasanton, the rather forbidding wife of a Treasury official, who acted as chaperon.[36]

When their carriage reached the vicinity of the White House, they found the avenue leading to the gate of the grounds jammed with vehicles. They were delayed fifteen minutes in line until they reached the door. Because it had been learned that a supper would be served and that there would be dancing, the crowd was far greater than at the twice-monthly receptions.

The three rooms adjoining the as yet unfinished East Room had been thrown open and it was only with difficulty that Chase and his charges were able to move toward the buffet. As each group of guests helped themselves to food and drink and sought some place where they could gorge on the President's fare, so another group took their place and with not a little jostling and spilling. By midnight a chamber orchestra played "Home Sweet Home," signaling the end of the festivities. President Adams and his Cabinet members were either not present or had made an early departure; Chase made no mention of any dignitaries in his diary.

At other affairs he attended Chase faithfully recorded the doings of important guests. "I saw Mr. Van Buren moving about paying compliments and hunting for good opinion," he remarked at the wedding reception given by Tench Ringgold, United States Marshal for the District.[37] And he admired Mrs. Peter B. Porter, Kentucky-born wife of the Secretary of War, an imposing woman who had the happy faculty of putting her guests at their ease but at the same time maintaining a certain distance that she felt requisite to the respect owed the wife of a Cabinet officer. Her deportment and her shapely physical attributes rather dazzled Chase. "If ever I should be joined 'for better or worse' I would desire to be united to one like Mrs. Porter and having the added and more precious ornament of pure religion."[38]

A week or so later, Chase attended another evening party at the Porter residence. In the center of one of the reception rooms Daniel Webster commanded the attention of all as he talked earnestly with a group of young ladies. While Chase watched from the fringe of the crowd, he saw Webster toss off a glass of whiskey "not without some involuntary grimace, which attracted the notice of Mrs. Porter." When she asked Webster if there was anything wrong, he explained that he had thought the glass of spirits he had downed was Madeira. The servant who passed around liquid refreshments had mistakenly brought in whiskey in place of wine.[39]

If Chase had been put off by the great man's human indulgences, his faith in Webster was completely restored after listening to him argue an important case before the Supreme Court. Webster's "language," said Chase, "is rich and copious, his manner dignified and impressive; his voice deep and sonorous, and his sentiments high and often sublime." Chase left the Court with the feeling that if he could even begin to match Webster's command of legal argument "day and night should testify to my toils."[40]

But Chase was not so charitable about other members of Congress whom he saw in action or inaction on the floors of the Senate and House chambers. Still a bit of the censor when observing human conduct, he was troubled by the lack of decorum in the chambers when Congress was in session. "It would astonish you," he wrote, "to see the indifference manifested, while a member addressed the House, by his brother members. One is [stretched] out in full length upon a sofa, a handkerchief spread over his face . . . another is marching to and fro behind the Speaker's chair . . . some members are writing letters or reading newspapers, some are stupidly gazing upon the orator."[41]

And so time passed, if not always pleasantly, at least at a varied and interesting pace between his teaching duties, his studies, and a full social life. He still managed some light reading and composing verses for the Wirt women. But after March 4, 1829, and the inauguration of a new President, Andrew Jackson, Chase's lifestyle changed for the worse. The Wirts, the Porters, and other members of the outgoing Adams administration left Washington.

A gloomy Chase went to the auction of the Wirt family household effects and roamed the rooms recalling with emotion the pleasant times he had enjoyed there and especially the security this hospitable household had extended to a lonely young man. Chase visited the Wirts on several occasions at their new home in Baltimore, but the atmosphere was never quite the same as it had been on those warm spring evenings in Washington when he read his romantic poetry to the young ladies in the flower-scented garden on which Mrs. Wirt bestowed so much care.[42]

On his last visit to the Wirts in Baltimore, Chase recorded in his diary that "It was not as it was wont to be. Some of the family was sick, others did not appear, and they who did seemed changed. Perhaps, it was but the picturing of my fancy, but I fear not."[43] The loss of this anchor seemed devastating to the earnest, overworked Chase, but again to be thrown on his own was entirely beneficial. It provided him with the initiative he needed to bear down even harder on his legal studies.

Wirt's commitment to human rights for Indians and slaves reinforced Chase's humanitarian concerns. But the baleful image of the Bishop could not be banished from Chase's memory, nor could its impact on his character be tempered. For Chase would always carry with him the Bishop's constant insistence on success and religiosity, his repeated emphasis on works and a dogma deeply ingrained that means were never dishonorable for ends that were honorable. Conversely, the influence of William Wirt would be lasting too. It would form the bright side of Chase's character, his life-long struggle for human rights, his care and generosity for his numerous family, his deep love for his wives, his remorse at their premature deaths, and the devotion he paid to his daughters.

Chase remained in what was for him an empty and featureless Washington. He had harsh things to say about Jackson's inauguration and especially his policies on removal of officeholders. He relished the gossip on the Peggy Eaton affair, which provided him with an interesting diversion from his solitary existence and his sharply curtailed social life. Curiosity impelled him to attend one of Jackson's public receptions. He came away with a different impression of the new President than he had expected. "He is rather above the ordinary stature and has a graceful figure," Chase said, ". . . General Jackson is not a man of mind. In his manners he is graceful and agreeable and much excels his predecessor in the art of winning golden opinions from all sorts of men." Chase then closed his diary account with an oraculor remark that foreshadowed a latent power of observation and analysis. "General Jackson's career, should be attentively observed by the political student who is endeavoring from the book of human affairs to glean the lessons of political experience."[44]

When Chase made these comments he had been admitted to the Washington bar and was preparing to take up residence in Cincinnati.[45] He had faced the oral examination with trepidation, as he realized that he had not received any substantial training from Wirt. On the other hand he had been systematic in his study and most conscientious in keeping to a daily schedule. Where he was lacking was in the short duration of his legal study. The policy of the Maryland bar, extended to the District, required three years of study under a recognized lawyer before one could stand for the exam. Chase had but two years of study with Wirt, but he hoped he would be able to count on the courses of constitutional law, philosophy, and jurisprudence he had taken in college.

He appeared before the venerable legal scholar and judge of the District of Columbia Court, William Cranch, and his colleagues on December 7, 1829. The date for examination was set for December 9, but to Chase's consternation was postponed until Monday the 14th. On that morning, he and five other aspirants waited their turn for examination. Cranch, who was one of the innumerable friends of the ubiquitous Bishop and who knew Chase socially, did not adopt an adversarial pose which was frequent on such occasions. But he was a thorough examiner. Chase answered his questions for the most part correctly. However, when the judge asked Chase about his legal training, he confessed that he did not have the required three years. Cranch said, "We think, Mr. Chase, that you must study another year and present yourself again for examination."[46]

Chase must have been dismayed but he resolved to make an appeal for extenuation. He had already decided whatever the outcome of the examination to try his luck in the West. "Please your honors," he addressed the court, "I have made arrangements to go the Western country and practice law." Cranch spoke briefly to his colleagues then turned to the clerk of the court and said, "Swear in Mr. Chase." Chase was one of three admitted to the bar that day. One was rejected outright and two others were given postponements. That night he wrote up the events of the day in his diary: "So I am now an attorney-at-law. I have a profession. Let me not dishonor it."[47]

Well before his bar exam Chase had been making inquiry about possible locations in the West. He spoke with the new Associate Justice of the U.S. Supreme Court, John McLean, whose family residence was in Cincinnati. And in February he sought out one of the Ohio senators, Jacob Burnet.

The Judge, as Burnet was called from his services on the Ohio supreme court, was a small, swarthy individual with a grim set to his face and a habit of speaking with portentous gravity.[48] Chase found little evidence of intellectual ability in Burnet and noted his peculiar manner of conversation. But he was an original settler of Ohio, long a resident of Cincinnati, and well connected with the bar of that bustling city. His advice was not to be taken lightly. Burnet said that the Cincinnati bar "was crowded as it is everywhere . . . . Still, Cincinnati is growing rapidly. Population and wealth are increasing. Living is cheap. And on the whole, it offers to you stronger inducements than any other place in the West." Burnet's counsel simply reinforced Chase's decision to establish his law practice in Cincinnati.

He was familiar with the city where he had lived for almost a year when the Bishop was president of Cincinnati College. More important, he was attracted to it because of its reputation for rapid growth and its apparent potential for an aspiring young lawyer. That the city was just across the river from Covington, Kentucky, a slave state, did not deter Chase. After all, he had spent three years in Washington, which was also slave territory. And though even then Chase had strong antislavery opinions gained from his New England background and his association with William Wirt and his disgust with the slave mart in the District, he had become accustomed to living in a southern environment.

Moreover, Cincinnati had a large population of Yankees who shared Chase's attitudes and to whom he had entree from McLean, Burnet, and associates of the Bishop who were residents of the city. Taking it all into account, the practical aspects of starting a law practice in Cincinnati far outweighed any hesitation he might have had because of its proximity to the border states. As Chase himself remarked rather grandiloquently on the eve of his departure: "True, there was little to invite in the foreground of the picture. I was fully aware that I must pass through a long period of probation. . . . But in the background were deserved honor, eminent usefulness . . . and toil and labor vanished from the sight which was directed over and beyond them."[49] Chase sold his school to his classmate Hamilton Smith for a small advance and the remainder on installments, and prepared for the journey with all the resilience and great expectations of youth.[50]

chapter 3

The Young Professional

Early on Saturday morning, March 13, 1830, Chase arrived in Cincinnati after a long and uncomfortable trip of nine days from Washington. He had taken the stage through Hagerstown to the National Road at Cumberland, Maryland, and then on to Wheeling, Virginia. There had been a thaw and the horses' hoofs sank through the thin crust of the deeply rutted road. Progress was slow, tilting, jolting at times, and must have seemed interminable. The stage upset once, leaving Chase and his fellow passengers sprawled. Fortunately no one was hurt, but Chase resolved on the spot that nothing less than a railroad would tempt him to travel that route again, a promise to himself that he would not keep.[1]

There was some respite from the mud when the stage reached Cumberland and could roll along at four miles per hour on the National Road with its graded bed of crushed stone. At Wheeling Chase boarded the small Ohio River steamer the *Paragon*. Passage to Cincinnati was smooth but the living arrangements were cramped, noisy, and dirty. The steamboat was "only a paragon," wrote Chase in his diary, if "meanness of accommodation and slowness of motion constitute one."[2]

The Cincinnati Chase found when he left the *Paragon* had changed significantly from the town he had known in 1823. Then it had a population of about 12,000 who lived in some 3000 dwellings that meandered along the north bank of the Ohio for several miles.[3] Now, the population had more than doubled, and a city center was forming. The skyline of flat-topped three- and four-story brick buildings was being altered dramatically: Mrs. Frances Trollope, later a popular British travel writer and novelist, then seeking to recoup the family fortunes, was having built a curious and fanciful bazaar designed to resemble a Turkish mosque.

A dozen tall-funneled steamboats at a time were loading or unloading at the paved landing. Cincinnati had gained its prominence as a major port because the great sweep of the river to the southwest just above the city produced a deep semi-circular eddy which in previous spring floods had scoured out the banks into a large sheltered cove.

The city not only was the hub for various small factories but acted as an entrepôt for the shipment of commodities raised on the rich soil of the new Northwest and from those regions of Kentucky and Virginia that shared borders with Ohio. Already it had gained the nickname "Porkopolis" for its slaughterhouse and packing establishments, which dressed, preserved, and barreled hogs. Salt pork, long a staple food in the era before refrigeration, was shipped in immense quantities from Cincinnati west to the Mississippi and then south for the plantation market, and east to Wheeling and Pittsburgh for distribution to Pennsylvania and the greater New York population centers.[4]

The fastidious Mrs. Trollope, who had settled temporarily in Cincinnati just before Chase arrived in the city, found the holding pens, slaughterhouses, and packing plants offensive in both appearance and odor. With casual disregard for health and cleanliness, butchers dumped blood and offal of slaughtered hogs into nearby streams that flushed the debris into the Ohio. These streams, all within the city boundaries, frequently ran red with blood. The city had no drains and household garbage was commonly tossed onto the unpaved streets as had been the custom and the necessity of urban development since the cities of western Europe took form in medieval times. The pigs that brought Cincinnati fame and fortune also acted as the new city's sanitation department, a common feature in all the larger towns and cities of the Republic. They were everywhere, roaming the streets on their perpetual quest for provender.[5]

Ubiquitous pigs disgusted Mrs. Trollope but not Chase. He had grown up in rural New Hampshire and Ohio; he was fresh from Washington which like Cincinnati had its share of pig population. The odors that permeated the streets and the byproducts of the packing industry that one saw everywhere neither concerned Chase nor offended his senses. Rather he was struck anew by the bustle and the expansiveness, the western flavor of the city. He found his room at the Washington Hotel, much more spacious than hotel rooms in the east, "much larger than I needed," he said, "for I am but six feet by one or two and the chamber was at least ten by six."[6]

The steamboat landing that slanted downward sixty to seventy feet and extended half a mile along the river's edge captured his interest. And he paid particular attention to the numerous steam-powered cotton spinning and weaving factories and engine works that stood close to each other on Front Street and filled the still air of a Saturday morning with a cacophony. As he surveyed that busy scene he decided—as many had said before him and many would say later—that labor, not material assets determined all worth. "The raw material is worthless till it is wrought," he wrote. "Labor must be applied before value can be created. . . ."[7]

Chase spent little time, however, surveying the city. He had a slender stock of funds that he had saved from his teaching career in Washington. He was in a hurry to stand for the Ohio bar and to begin a law practice that would support him. He had the usual letters to leading Cincinnati lawyers from Wirt, Burnet, and McLean.

Chase dined on his first day in Cincinnati with Daniel Caswell, one of the city's foremost lawyers. Joseph Benham, another leading member of the bar, was also present. Within a short time he became friendly with Cincinnati's richest citizen, Nicholas Longworth, the eccentric philanthropist who was even then adding to his fortune through shrewd speculation in Cincinnati real estate.[8]

Despite these influential acquaintances, Chase found that he had to be familiar with Ohio statute law and knew that he had to have experience in courtroom argument and procedure. He became a regular participant in the moot court that the faculty of Cincinnati College had organized, to provide just this kind of training to law students. Almost all students at first found the moot court experience difficult. Chase was no exception. Painfully shy, and with a slight speech impediment, he dreaded appearances that forced him to make extemporaneous arguments.[9]

Chase would never wholly overcome his self-consciousness in public speaking, but he realized that if he was to pursue a legal career, he had to gain enough confidence to make an impression in a courtroom before a jury as well as an audience. Courtroom sessions in those days of scant public entertainment always attracted a sizable group of spectators. Thus he rehearsed himself in his room on a regular basis, and by early June, 1830, when he applied for admission he had so far conquered his fear of public presentation that he was accorded a perfunctory examination and granted membership in the Ohio bar.[10]

Yet it was another three months of study and appearance at the moot court before he rented an office and began the practice of law. Nearing the end of his funds, not having received the agreed upon installment from Hamilton Smith for his share of the revenues of the school in Washington, he borrowed from one of his new friends.[11] The modest costs of renting and setting up an office—purchasing a desk, some chairs, and the necessary law books—all imposed financial pressures on the young man. After one month of practice in his new office on Third Street just off Main, Chase found that he had earned $15, "and perhaps shall be paid."[12]

With so much spare time on his hands, Chase redoubled his study of various books on law, some of which he had purchased, others borrowed. But he did not confine his reading to law, although his interest led him to works of a more practical and religious nature than to volumes of fiction or poetry. During that hot humid summer he studied Timothy Pitkin's *Statistical History of the United States,* which he admitted was written in a "dry but perspicuous style," among other information-laden works. He found time to do a line-by-line reading of the Old Testament Book of Psalms, finding, as he remarked, "new beauties and new glories at every perusal."[13]

His reading no doubt helped him through bouts of homesickness for his friends in Washington and his home in New Hampshire. Not study, outside reading, nor socializing could ease the pain of loneliness in this alien land. "I feel almost sorry," he wrote his friend Sparhawk in mid-June 1830, "that I ever left New England."[14]

However downcast Chase may have felt at times, he found other avenues for his youthful energy than solitary absorption in books and newspapers or writing in his diary. With an eye to improving his image as an educated young man, he was the moving spirit in establishing a lyceum in the city. The prospectus that Chase wrote and which was published in the *Cincinnati American* emphasized the diffusion of useful knowledge. Though the outline was not completely free of a patronizing tone, it did lay out a course of lectures that would appeal to self-improvement through papers and discussions.[15] Chase himself gave three talks on subjects that interested him. The first lecture commented on the scientific discoveries of Galileo, the second addressed the impact of machinery on society, and the third was about the life and career of Britain's chief justice Lord Brougham.[16] All were so well received that Chase decided to explore a further measure of local, even national visibility by seeking to have them published in an eastern journal, if possible.

Among the books and periodicals Chase read during these early months in Cincinnati were copies of the *Edinburgh Review* and the *North American Review,* that epitome of Bostonian bluestocking culture and *belles lettres.* The *Review* carried much intellectual prestige among the little group of educated Yankees in Cincinnati. Accordingly Chase edited his lyceum papers carefully, made clear copies, and sent them off to the inimitable Alexander Everett, who was then engaging in a second career as editor of the *Review.* Much to Chase's delight, Everett took two of his essays, the one on machinery and the one on Brougham. They appeared in the July 1831 and January 1832 issues of the *Review.*[17] Chase saw to it that copies were available to those he wished to impress. These youthful effusions were rather better than typical nonfiction pieces the American learned community was then publishing. Authors were primarily ministers, a sprinkling of college professors, and an occasional professional man. Their articles were prosy, didactic, dull, and frequently defective in argument, example, and fact.

Of Chase's two essays that the *North American Review* published, the Brougham piece is by far the better one. Its criticism of common law precedents, its comments on historical causation and on the influence of individuals as opposed to forces in the shaping of culture, and its discussion of slavery were for the time and considering Chase's youth quite original in argument. Both essays show that Chase had read widely and well. They indicate also considerable powers of analysis which would figure largely in his later career. But the style and the content especially of the essay on machinery are pretentious. Chase was advertising to the world and in particular to his Cincinnati audience that he was an educated person of culture, and a master of Latin and Greek.[18] Among his newfound friends, the young women were not that impressed. But their hearts may have missed a beat when they read in Miss Longworth's album Chase's tribute to her lineaments in these unheroic couplets. "Her lips like pomegranate seeds, but fewer; Her voice like Heaven's own music, rich and pure." At least he displayed a knowledge of fruit that was surely exotic by local standards. Then again he may have had a touch of fever when he penned the jingle.[19] For he was quite susceptible to winter complaints.

Chase was striving constantly and almost desperately to conquer his awkwardness in conversation at social occasions and on those infrequent public appearances when he appeared before judge, jury, and spectators at the Cincinnati Court House. Faithfully he recorded anecdotes he had heard especially those he thought had a humorous or moralistic turn which he might utilize in furthering his law practice or, as he hoped, eventually a political career. He still sought to model himself on Wirt, the eminent lawyer, the public man, the litterateur.

As a poet, Chase could never achieve anything better than contrived jingles in a romantic mode. But these hardy elegaics were meant for social occasions. In a more serious vein, he realized that it was not just the rich and well educated he wanted to impress, but the average Cincinnati citizen. Methodically he jotted down colloquialisms he remembered from his childhood in rural New Hampshire. As he noted in his diary, Yankee remarks, nicknames, and definitions "are so peculiar" yet so salted in everyday speech which he encountered "every day" that he decided to collect and preserve them for future use.[20]

Basically, however, Chase's first interest was the further education of the working men and the manufacturers of the city to what he deemed higher levels of intellectual activity than what the already established Mechanic's Institute provided. As he put it in his lyceum prospectus, he wanted his audiences to understand the principles and applications of the machinery with which they worked. "Thus the thousand accidents and losses that resulted from ignorance would be avoided with impressive benefits for both capital and labor, he wrote."[21]

Chase felt that if his lectures were to be a success, he had to present a formula that differed from the course the Mechanic's Institute sponsored, but at the same time he emphasized that his proposed lyceum was in no way in competition with a popular program. His cultural enterprise, he claimed, would provide broad-scale enrichment for all interested citizens. It was not to be confused with the specific educational program of the institute. Chase's careful balancing act proved to be successful. By January 1831, the Cincinnati lyceum had 131 regular members.

This high-minded endeavor was but a part of Chase's efforts to make a mark in Cincinnati society. He had been in the city less than a year when he began to think about starting a quarterly modeled on the *Southern Review*, which was now drifting into a regional format. He drafted a prospectus for what he called the *Western Review* and began a campaign for writers and subscribers. Among those he solicited for articles were such notables as well known Jacksonian editor Isaac Hill, despite his politics; and newly elected to the U.S. Senate from New Hampshire Daniel Webster, because of his politics; Edward Everett, noted theologue, Harvard professer, and Congressman; his brother Alexander, essayist and editor of the prestigious *North American Review;* and of course William Wirt.[22] Nor were the lyceum program and the *Review* the only projects that claimed his attention. He was also writing editorials for the *Cincinnati American* on a variety of subjects. It was not long after launching the lyceum, which Chase proudly proclaimed to be the first in the West, and drafting the prospectus for the *Western Review* that he decided to make a trip east where, he hoped, he would secure some clients who had investments in Cincinnati.

Before leaving, however, and ever solicitous of his career, he sought and received letters of introduction from Daniel Webster and other important figures. Though there is no precise account of his journey, he visited Boston, his mother in Hopkinton, his cousin in Philadelphia, and the Wirts in Baltimore.[23] One tangible result of his trip was that he persuaded his older sister Abigail and her husband Dr. Colby to relocate in Cincinnati.

Chase's mother was quite well at the time, although she had become blind. She hoped to accompany the Colbys to Cincinnati along with her youngest child Helen, a winsome young woman of seventeen. But in the early spring of 1832, Chase received letters from his sisters informing him of his mother's death on April 8. She was 59 years old and a vigorous, capable woman until near the end of her life, which was perhaps shortened by her addiction to snuff.[24] Oddly enough Chase made no mention of his mother's passing. Yet she had always comforted and supported him, in fact had bestowed more of her affection and her slender resources on him and his education than any of her other children. Chase seems to have been more concerned with the responsibilities for the care of younger members of his family than with any deep grief over his mother's passing.

His older brother Alexander was already showing signs of instability, of excessive drinking and general incapacity. Chase was now deemed head of the family. A practicing lawyer with seemingly improving prospects, his relatives looked to him for financial support. Still his driving ambition to succeed was disturbing to his perceptive older sister Abigail Colby. She reminded Chase of "the vanity of earthly things. I confess I almost tremble for you . . . your desire to distinguish yourself and apparent devotedness to those principles whose interests terminate in this life."[25]

Having squandered his small legacy from his mother's estate, his younger brother William began dunning Chase for money. William more closely resembled Chase in stature and appearance than any other member of the family. But there the similarity ended. William had grown into an irresponsible eighteen-year-old who had always done poorly in school and had been expelled from Waterville Academy for his errant ways.[26] Despite Abigail's censure of William—"because he is wicked"—Chase sent him small sums. Abigail wrote asking if he would become Helen's guardian. Though in need of money himself, Chase agreed to look after Helen, provided the executor of his mother's estate forwarded her portion immediately.[27]

The Colbys, Helen and Chase's older unmarried sister Alice, arrived in the late summer of 1832. Dr. Colby quickly established a practice and acquired a home on Sixth Street between Main and Walnut.[28] Chase moved in with his brother-in-law's family where he could enjoy the comforts of a home life. Now there were fewer lonely moments and longings during sultry summer days for the cool green hills of New Hampshire.

It was well that Dr. Colby was on the scene, for his medical skills were immediately pressed into service. The cholera epidemic that reached London in January 1831 had crossed the Atlantic and traveled west. By the summer of 1832 it was ravaging Cincinnati.[29] Before it finally subsided the disease had claimed hundreds of lives.[30] Chase himself became violently ill in December 1832 and very nearly died. Colby was in constant attendance and though his treatments were little better than standard practice for the time, Chase had confidence in his brother-in-law's professional skill, all important when ignorance largely ruled the medical profession.

A month before Chase was stricken, the daily death rate had climbed to 41. "The streets were quite deserted," recorded Chase, "and passerby's go to and fro all muffled up in scarves and great coats."[31] There is no doubt that the abysmal state of public health in Cincinnati and elsewhere was a ripe breeding ground for the disease. Chase, like other residents of Cincinnati, drank water from wells, many of which were polluted by the slaughterhouses in the hills above the city.

But the severity of his attack may have resulted in part because of Chase's physical condition, weakened from the grinding routine he set of study, work, religious devotions, and socializing that claimed a ten- to twelve-hour day, seven days a week. And during the fall of 1832, Chase drove himself unmercifully as he sought to build up his law practice. Bedridden with cholera for almost a month, he became so sick at times that he despaired of recovery. Yet even during bouts of fever-driven restlessness, he continued his study of legal and biblical texts and volumes of *Ohio Reports* that he kept by his bedside.[32] Not content with promoting the lyceum and taking on various editorial chores Chase had conceived the idea of bringing out a comprehensive new edition of the *Ohio Reports* up to 1833.

Ever since he had read the text of the Webster-Hayne debates in the *Annals of Congress,* Webster's declarations of flamboyant nationalism had appealed to him. But what really caught his attention were references Webster made to the Northwest Ordinance. He had followed up these comments with close study of the appendix in Nathan Dane's *Digest of American Law.* There, Dane had set forth his and Rufus King's role in the framing and the adoption of the ordinance.

As a New Englander Chase was proud that his fellow Yankees and not Jefferson were responsible for many of the specifics in that landmark legislation. Dane's argument and its proofs so impressed him that he copied them verbatim in his diary.[33] And it was those sections that dealt with education, free soil, and territorial governance that he considered to have endowed the Northwest with a legacy of progressive ideas on political and social issues. He was impressed with Dane's assertion that national sovereignty actually antedated the Declaration of Independence, confounding, as Chase saw it, Calhoun's nullification doctrine. But even more important to him was the principle of free soil that Rufus King had attached to the final draft of the ordinance.[34] Chase had been opposed to slavery since his residence in Washington where he had observed its baneful effects at first hand and had drafted a petition to Congress for the abolition of the institution in the District of Columbia.[35]

Thus inspired, he would include in the first volume of his *Ohio Statutes* a brief history of Ohio that would focus on the free-soil aspects of the Northwest Ordinance. Chase hoped that this ambitious project would advance his professional reputation, provide a public service, and at the same time be a profitable venture. His edition would also contain not just the laws of the territory and the state but also pertinent local ordinances, laws in force and amendments noted, laws repealed and dates of repeal. In short Chase would offer an accurate, up-to-date rendering along with a comprehensive commentary on the law in his references and notations that would enable lawyers, judges, local and state officers to find and to understand fully the laws of Ohio at any given time and circumstance. This in itself was a tremendously formidable undertaking that required research and close study of 38 volumes of general statutes not to mention important local ordinances that might warrant inclusion.[36]

Yet it was the preface that really interested Chase and claimed his major attention. With an innate sense of public relations, Chase had recognized the timeliness of such an essay, which would place the venerable ordinance in a new light. For he was determined to have volume one of the *Statutes* with its history of Ohio capitalize if at all possible on public opinion in the North during the uproar over the South Carolina nullification controversy.

A history of Ohio—never before done in entirety—could be a timely statement emphasizing Websterian nationalism as it applied to the state and by implication to all new territories that might become states. Chase had caught the stirrings of an antislavery movement, and he meant to emphasize what he considered to be the blessings of freedom not only for Ohio but for the entire Northwest. He did not have the financial resources to do the research or to interest a publisher. And he needed tangible public support before he could begin the task.

Accordingly, after his return from his trip east in the fall of 1831, he composed a detailed prospectus for his new three-volume edition of *Ohio Statutes*, which he circulated among members of the state legislature. No doubt he entrusted his prospectus to members whom he knew, probably those from Hamilton County in which Cincinnati was located. He may also have gotten letters of support from Senator Jacob Burnet and Supreme Court Justice John McLean.

At first his efforts seem to have succeeded beyond his expectations. While still sick and confined to his room he learned that the Ohio senate had passed a bill appropriating funds to purchase 200 copies. But the house refused to concur,and after some wrangle between the two bodies compromised on 100 copies. Official encouragement was far short of what Chase had hoped. It was barely sufficient for him to push on with the work. Then Chase's comfort and peace of mind were sadly disrupted when Dr. Colby himself became very ill with cholera. Chase was forced to move to a hotel, the Pearl Street House, but his change of residence did not interfere with his work schedule.[37]

By April 1833 Chase had made enough progress on the *Statutes* to begin research on the territorial history of Ohio. All through the summer and fall of that year he toiled on the project which he completed in January of 1834, an astonishing performance for less than a year of work. On the basis of the legislature's meager support, Corey and Fairchild, a Cincinnati printing concern, agreed to publish an edition of 1000 copies. The venture was not the financial success Chase had hoped but it added immensely to his legal reputation in Ohio and throughout the country. Chancellor James Kent and Supreme Court Justice Joseph Story, both renowned for their works in jurisprudence, praised Chase's work extravagantly. Kent even apologized for not having addressed the Northwest Ordinance in his *Commentaries*.[38]

When the last volume of the *Statutes* became available Chase's prospects had so improved that he was able to marry and begin a family. These early years in Cincinnati had been work-laden and anxious ones for the ambitious young man. At times he doubted whether all his labors would grant the success he so eagerly pursued. "I find the law is but a barren field," he had written his friend Hamilton Smith after more than a year of intense application. Again six months later he said, "My heart is sick when I think of my situation and reflect that it may be long before it will be changed for the better. . . . I have no influential and active friends who can give me business at once, and I am not formed by nature or habit to gain favour of the multitudes suddenly."[39] But perseverance, when combined with ability and assiduous labor not just in his practice but in community affairs, would soon pay off handsomely.

chapter 4

Upward Bound

Chase's socializing with Cincinnati's elite, while it satisfied some of his personal needs, had not brought him much business. His practice barely made enough to support him. After a year of struggling he was finally able to form a partnership with two leading lawyers, Edward King and Timothy Walker. Still shying away from court appearances, Chase handled the office work and drafted most of the correspondence. The arrangement did not work out. King was not well much of the time—he died in 1836—and he and Walker decided that the partnership could not bear the expense of a junior member not bringing in his share of new business.[1]

In November 1832 the partnership dissolved. Chase immediately entered into another partnership with Daniel T. Caswell. Caswell was not as eminent a member of the bar as either King or Walker, yet Chase had to purchase a share of the business. He gave a ninety-day note for $1,475.[2] The move, however, proved most beneficial to Chase and in due course would relieve him of all anxiety about his financial affairs. Caswell was the solicitor for the local branch of the Bank of the United States. Chase's new partnership carried with it an equal share in the branch's legal business. The branch was at the time the largest and most profitable bank in Cincinnati.

Jackson's hostility toward the central Bank of the U.S. in Philadelphia, though already manifest, had not as yet taken the form of direct action. More important than the steady income Chase would receive from this banking connection was the experience he would gain in the legal aspects of finance and the contacts he would make not merely in the Cincinnati business community but in other Ohio towns and cities and in the East, where he would represent Ohio creditors and debtors to eastern capitalists.

Chase's increasing law practice may have impressed the leading businessmen and the professional elite of Cincinnati, it did not at first improve his standing with the opposite sex. He was by no means indifferent to the charms of the young women he had known since his college days.[3] He had been attracted to Wirt's daughters, especially Catherine, but Mrs. Wirt did not encourage his romantic intentions, nor apparently did Catherine. He had at one time or another been fond of Emeline Webster, Daniel Webster's niece, and Adeline Hitchcock, a Hanover belle with whom he corresponded. He might have become seriously involved with Adeline but his native caution asserted itself after reflecting on the burdens marriage would place on his career. As he said to his Dartmouth classmate, "You must not think that either of us are in love, tho' perhaps I might be did not prudence point to long years of study and poverty and cry 'beware'".[4] This is not to say that Chase was innocent of the sexual role in human affairs or that this was simply an outburst of youthful emotion. He confessed that he was "not so strong a believer in woman's purity," but he qualified this comment with a remark typical of an educated young man's attitudes in the America of the 1820s and 1830s. "Man is always the seducer," he confided to his friend Smith, "woman the seduced and which is more guilty? If to the frailty of women we affix the name of reproach what name of infamy should the guilt of man be branded?"[5]

Chase avoided Cincinnati's solemn commemorative balls, where the young men and the young women met for country dancing and then dined separately, the feminine contingent on cakes and candies, the males on more robust fare.[6] He was much at the Longworths' for teas and dinners. There is no doubt that he was interested romantically in Catherine, Nicholas Longworth's daughter. But she seems not to have found Chase's attention anything more than a passing fancy.[7] Despite his youthful philosophizing about the "frailty" of women and his fear of giving hostages to fortune, he looked forward to marriage and a family. His sexual drive was strong, and as most young Americans at that time, he had grown up on farms and was familiar with the mechanics of sex. Prig he might have been but he was no prude.[8]

A combination of strict religious training and acute consciousness of his position in society and of his career forbade his seeking relief in casual encounters. In his relations with marriageable young women, he confessed that he was "astonishingly bashful about these matters. I can pay a compliment—utter a clever thing—round a tolerable period—but goodness! when it comes to anything like the real thing, how my heart pit-a-pats—how my tongue falters—how my nerves shake, how my arms dangle."[9]

Chase's social life revolved around serious discussions in hotel and boarding-house palors on such topics as revolutions, progress, and democracy, interspersed with horseback rides in the hills during spring and summer months and sleigh excursions in the winter. Almost always, young women of Cincinnati's educated elite and of New England heritage entered into his round of entertainment. Chase plied them with his poetry and must have bored some of them with his display of learning gleaned from articles he had read in British, American, and even French periodicals.

Chase studied French grammar and literature as assiduously as he polished up his Latin. He did not neglect his Bible or his prayer ritual on awaking in the morning and before bed at night. As a matter of course he read a number of Ohio and out-of-state newspapers. An ambitious lawyer, he saw the value of keeping current on the state of politics and politicians.[10] Poetry, prose, and a fair grasp of worldly knowledge aside, Chase made little headway with the young women of his circle until Catherine Garniss, daughter of a local capitalist, looked with favor on this dreadfully earnest young man.

Chase had known the Garnisses for several years when by accident they chose to board in Chase's hotel on Pearl Street. Their proximity led to a better acquaintance with their only daughter Catherine, or Kitty, as the family and friends called her. At first Chase found the family pretentious and boring. He took an instant dislike to Garniss, who at best was a difficult man of uncertain temper.[11] Obviously quite successful in a material sense, he struck Chase as a vulgar, social climber, "ambitious to lead the fashions here." Kitty he thought to be "an affected and shallow girl with little real delicacy or refinement of character." No doubt his impressions of her father carried over to the daughter, whom he decided had plain and far from delicate features.

Yet their proximity brought them frequently together. Chase was drawn almost he felt against his will to visit with the Garnisses. Again and again he called on the family and usually came away with the feeling that Garniss was a verbose, noisy dogmatist given to slanderous remarks about some of Chase's friends.[12]

Whatever he may have thought about the father, Chase had gradually come to appreciate the virtues of the daughter whose features now seemed quite lovely to him and whose understanding of religion and of literature were, he thought, superior to other young women he knew. Kitty responded to his overtures with a display of coquetry that Chase found charming. On one occasion in the spring of 1833 she told Chase she had dreamed of him the night before. She said that Chase had seen "a drop of water on her cheek and attempting to wipe it off discovered that she was rouged." When he "upbraided her with deception . . . she declared it was the first time she had ever used paint and was so upset she began to sob so loudly that her mother came in and woke her up."[13] Shortly after this incident Chase and Catherine Garniss set a date for their marriage and agreed that the Reverend Lyman Beecher would officiate.[14]

On March 4, 1834, Beecher married the young couple in the parlor of the Garnisses' spacious new home on the corner of Broadway and Fourth Street.[15] The Chases did not establish a household at once but took rooms at a nearby hotel. Chase's sister Helen lived with them and he continued to tutor her in French and in other subjects where he felt she was deficient. From the first the new bride resented Helen's presence. What might have put a strain on the marriage was resolved when Kitty found herself pregnant and persuaded Chase to take up residence with the Garnisses so that she could be close to her mother. Helen had, in the meantime, gone off to stay with relatives in New Hampshire.[16]

Kitty's pregnancy did not pose any apparent difficulties and on November 14, 1835, after a good many hours of painful labor she bore a daughter.[17] At first everything seemed normal, but in the evening Kitty suddenly became very ill. Chase described her condition as "delirious." He ran for his brother-in-law Dr. Colby, whose home was only a block away. After examining the incoherent Kitty, Colby decided that bleeding was necessary, but when he returned with his lancet, she had recovered. No further treatment would be undertaken that night.[18]

Over the next few days Kitty's condition seemed to improve. The household remained tense, however. Chase had a heated argument with his mother-in-law over the naming of the baby. It was finally decided in his favor to be Catherine Jane. As Kitty's recovery was now quite rapid Chase felt that he could travel east on business for Cincinnati's Lafayette bank. Recently he had been made counsel for the bank and had been asked to visit Philadelphia regarding important investments.

Now that Dr. Colby deemed Kitty to be out of danger, Chase broached the subject of his departure to her. "She seemed pleased with the idea of my going," said Chase, who added, "I should not get any compensation for going." Her reply must have gladdened his heart. "But you will get reputation by it," she said. He remained a trifle dubious until he was assured that Kitty wanted it this way. "She told me," said Chase, "to clothe myself warm, to take my overshoes—not to ride over the inclined plane etc." On the afternoon of November 21, 1835, he left town for Philadelphia.[19] Garniss kept Chase posted by means of the express mail service, which delivered his notes at stops along the way. They all pointed to a slow but steady recovery.

Chase quickly concluded his business and hurried home. When he reached Wheeling, Virginia, he learned that his wife had become critically ill.

The next day, another note announced her death. Chase was horror-stricken. He blamed himself for what he decided was a thoughtless decision to leave her for his own personal advancement. Had he been home, if he could not have saved her, at least he would have been with her during her last moments.[20]

So guilt-ridden was he that when he arrived home at midnight on Tuesday, December 6, and spied the black crepe on the Garnisses' door, he was "afraid to disturb her parents and determined to return to the boat. I walked several squares through the silent streets." Eventually Chase returned home. "I went upstairs," he said, "there lay my sweet wife." She was but little changed in features—but oh! the look of life was gone. Nothing was left but clay."[21]

For the next two days, until her burial on December 8, Chase, overcome with grief, remained almost continuously with the body. Although he would face many more shocks of death in his immediate family, he would never again indulge in such remorse. Even the little daughter Kitty had left did not alleviate his grief or his fruitless search for assigning blame to the Garnisses and to the many physicians called in who had diagnosed Kitty's condition correctly—peritonitis—but whose only remedy was repeated drawing of blood and large doses of calomel. After searching through several texts on childbirth, Chase became convinced that the physicians had killed his wife. They assuredly did not, but they hastened the process.[22]

Chase remained at the Garnisses' primarily for the benefit of the baby, though he deferred to Mrs. Garniss's wishes that the child should remain under her care. A relationship which had never been satisfactory began to erode. The crux of the problem for Chase now shifted from Garniss to his wife, who had become almost obsessive about the baby.

A distracted Chase finally wrote his sister Helen, pleading with her to return and help him with the care of little Catherine Jane.[23] He realized that it might be difficult for Helen because, as he explained, "feelings, habits of thought are all too dissimilar—too opposite I may say to allow a residence under the same roof with any prospect of comfort." Chase was in no condition to make any drastic change in his living conditions, but he was increasingly aware of his responsibilities toward his little daughter. And he hoped that Helen would act as a surrogate in his relations with his mother-in-law over the care of the child.[24]

Apart from Kitty's death other family problems were plaguing Chase at this time. His brother William had given up all thought of college. He had gone to Lockport, a small but growing town in western New York, where he lived with Chase's brother Edward. There, he read law with a local attorney. Early in 1835, William decided to try his luck in Cincinnati. For a time he clerked at Chase's law office and was admitted to the Ohio bar. A restless young man, he soon moved to St. Louis. There he indulged himself in liquor, gambling, and the sort of low company found around the taverns and oyster saloons of the city.[25] Throughout most of this period, he was a constant drain on Chase's resources as well as his peace of mind. By September 1836 Chase had had enough. He would not lend his brother any more money unless he changed his habits, but not before he had to accept a $3000 note that William had foolishly endorsed.[26]

Chase was able to meet his obligations and in addition lend money to a favorite cousin, James Denison, who was practicing law in New Orleans.[27] Chase's law practice and directorships in Cincinnati banks were now providing ample sums for his own support with enough of a surplus for investment and for assistance to the needy, if feckless members of his family.

Gradually Chase gained his composure after Kitty's death. A long held interest in political affairs provided a major anodyne. Politics was taking a timely turn in Ohio as two residents, William Henry Harrison, who lived but a few miles from Cincinnati, and Supreme Court Justice John McLean, currently residing at Columbus, were both candidates for the presidency on a favorite-son, anti-Jackson ticket. Chase was well acquainted with them. He and Kitty had boarded in the same house as the McLeans in Columbus, where Chase had gone for cases he was pleading before the federal district court.[28] At the time Harrison was clerk of the Cincinnati court of common pleas.

Chase had long been opposed to the Jackson administration for several reasons. As counsel for the Cincinnati branch of the Bank of the United States, self-interest made him a stalwart supporter of the institution against Jackson's attacks. His personal dislike of Jackson and his policies went back to Washington days and had been reinforced by his close association with Cincinnati's entrenched business community, which measured a man's worth by his social standing. Both Harrison and McLean had served in high government office. Harrison had the additional cachet of being a successful general in the War of 1812 and a popular Indian fighter. Politically, he was a stronger candidate than McLean, but Chase, with an eye to his own career, favored the Justice rather than the General.

His business before McLean's circuit court was already a source of income. An intriguing factor certainly for any aspiring politician was the impressive number of local officeholders that McLean had put in place when Postmaster General during the Monroe and Adams administrations. Most of them were still active politically and under obligation to the Justice. Chase and Jacob Burnet were members of the McLean Committee for Hamilton County.[29] Chase soon learned that he had backed the wrong man. McLean took himself out of the race. Then, a series of dramatic incidents occurred that shifted his attention away from the confusing political arena, but he would have to make a very risky move whose benefits, if they existed at all, were long-term.

A menacing threat to the social order had emerged in Cincinnati over the past few months in sporadic attacks on blacks and known abolitionists. In a particularly flagrant attempt to eradicate the one abolitionist press in the city, Chase became involved as a champion of law and order and free speech. He did so without much thought of the consequences to him personally in defending an unpopular cause in a city with strong southern ties.

Chase had taken no public stand on abolition, which had become a widely publicized movement since William Lloyd Garrison began effective agitation against slavery in 1829. A well-organized, well-led but tiny group of abolitionists furthered the message of emancipation through petitions to state legislatures and Congress and through antislavery papers established in many northern cities. The year of Chase's marriage witnessed the beginning of John Quincy Adams's presentation of abolition petitions in the House of Representatives. Usually couched in language that spared neither the character nor the motives of slaveholders, they provoked heated rejoinders from southern members.

Chase was of two minds about the movement. Community leaders on whom he depended for much of his law practice, men such as Nicholas Longworth and Josiah Lawrence, president of the Lafayette bank, were decidedly opposed to any agitation that disturbed their business connections or promoted civic unrest. On the other hand Chase cherished strong beliefs that slavery was an immoral institution that inhibited economic progress. Unlike most abolitionists he was especially concerned about the racial implications emancipated blacks might pose in a white-dominated culture.

His quandary, like that of many of his fellow countrymen, posed a conflict between idealism and realism, a posture that may have seemed equivocal to his abolitionist brother-in-law and neighbor, Dr. Colby. When translated into practical terms Chase found colonization the answer. It satisfied the conscience of moderate citizens but at the same time seemed to offer a practical answer in coping with a deep-seated white supremacist prejudice. Through Dr. Colby Chase had met many of the local opponents of slavery. He found them upright, religious people, well educated and from cosmopolitan backgrounds.[30] Still he avoided taking part in the looming controversy until a mob began forming to move against James G. Birney, who had begun publishing an antislavery weekly, the *Philanthropist*, in Cincinnati.[31]

During the spring and summer of 1835, Chase remained indifferent to the public outcry against Birney. He had not concerned himself with the debate over abolition that had raged for some time among the faculty and students at Lane Seminary in the Chestnut Hills section of Cincinnati. Lyman Beecher, the president of the seminary, led the conservative group that supported colonization as against emancipation. Chase's stance was similar to that of Beecher.

But there was too much tension in Cincinnati during the summer months of 1835 over the question of abolition for any resident of the city to maintain a neutral position. Birney, a Kentuckian who had been a prominent planter and slave owner in Alabama, was the activist who was disturbing the peace of Cincinnati's leading residents. A square-jawed, sturdy lawyer and gifted propagandist from a prominent Kentucky family, Birney had emancipated his slaves, moved to Ohio, and cast his lot with the American Anti-slavery Society.

Although Birney's tactics included lectures and political action, they also featured the publication of a newspaper that would carry the abolitionist message to a wider audience. Unlike Garrison and Wendell Phillips, the Boston radical abolitionists, Birney favored a moderate, peaceful approach that called for emancipation in accordance with natural right and freedom of expression for those who condemned slavery. Moderate or not, Birney's message was considered inflammatory especially in a city like Cincinnati, which bordered on a slave state and whose business interests were closely tied to the plantation market.[32] When Birney established his newspaper at the town of New Richmond, twenty miles from Cincinnati, his reputation as an extremist had preceded him there. Two of three leading newspapers in Cincinnati—the *Whig* and the *Republican*—almost immediately began a campaign based on rumor and hearsay that pictured Birney as a grave danger to the community.

Acting for an alarmed business community, the *Whig* called for a mass meeting at the courthouse on January 22. At the same time, word went out to organize a group which would take direct action against Birney and his family. Those interested should assemble on Front Street and then move on to the courthouse meeting. About 500 individuals crowded into the courtroom and listened to speeches by Mayor Samuel Davies, Methodist minister and the city's postmaster William Burke, and Chase's old acquaintance, Jacob Burnet, now a justice of the state supreme court.

Birney himself attended and startled the audience when he announced his presence and asked to be heard. His request was granted. For three-quarters of an hour he presented his case, calming the crowd that had been prepared to do him injury. Nothing untoward happened during the next six months, though the Cincinnati press continued to abuse Birney.[33] He in turn replied with vigor through the columns of the *Philanthropist* which in April he moved to Cincinnati, a much more convenient location. He rented for his editorial office rooms above the printing establishment of Achilles Pugh, on the corner of Main and Seventh streets. A Quaker, Pugh was sympathetic to Birney's aims and readily agreed to print the *Philanthropist*.[34]

Not long after the move, news spread through the city of the Texas revolt. Houston's victory over the Mexican army at San Jacinto brought a wave of pro-southern sentiment and patriotic froth. Those who would capitalize on such community spirit quickly organized the "Texas Aid Association," and to further their own ends singled out Birney and the Cincinnati Anti-slavery Society as scapegoats. During May and June, threats against Birney through letters and hand bills became more frequent and more strident. And finally on the evening of July 12, direct action was taken. Joseph Graham, a prominent commission merchant in the southern trade, organized a mob that broke into Pugh's shop, dismantled his press, and tore up an entire edition of the *Philanthropist* that was ready for circulation.[35]

Such vandalism frightened Pugh. Only after the Ohio Anti-slavery Society put up $2000 as security against mob-inspired disturbances was he willing to continue printing the paper.[36] It was now time for the leading citizens of the community again to take a public stand. Burnet, Burke, and Mayor Davies published a call for a mass meeting to be held on Saturday evening, July 23. Almost a thousand people crowded into Cincinnati's largest hall, where they heard heated remarks from some of the city's wealthiest citizens. Nicholas Longworth and Morgan Neville, both friends of Chase, were responsible for the incendiary comments that appeared in the *Whig* that the *Philanthropist* must be silenced, "peaceably if it could, forcibly, if it must." After approving a series of anti-abolition resolutions, the meeting named a committee of twelve to negotiate with Birney.[37]

On Monday, July 25, the citizen committee sent a note to Birney requesting a meeting for discussion of the course the *Philanthropist* was pursuing. Birney was out of town but other leading members of the anti slavery society agreed to meet at Dr. Colby's home. Jacob Burnet, Josiah Lawrence, an important Chase client, and Nicholas Longworth were the leading members of the committee that sought to negotiate the *Philanthropist* out of business.

Burnet spoke for the committee. His case against Birney and the *Philanthropist* was based squarely on the commercial interests of Cincinnati which he argued were dependent on the goodwill of the slave states the city served. Another committee member claimed he had specific information that the abolitionists were jeopardizing this trade. The antislavery men made no response but assured the citizen's committee they would publish their reply the next day in the *Philanthropist*. Birney, who had returned to the city, had his editorial written, printed, and ready for distribution. It was moderate in tone but he refused to back down. "We are not more the advocate of freedom for the slave," he wrote, "than we are of liberty for those who are yet free."[38]

On receipt of Birney's reply the citizen committee announced failure of its negotiations, implying that direct action should be taken. It issued a report that was sent to the leading papers in the city. Only Charles Hammond of the *Gazette*, a quirky lawyer turned editor, refused to publish it as an incitement to violence. Other papers gave it prominent display with bold headlines on their editorial pages. The violence that Hammond feared welled up soon after the papers were hawked in the streets. Orchestrated by a commission merchant in the southern trade and some Kentuckians who had crossed the river from Covington and Newport, the mob assembled at 6 p.m. before the Exchange Hotel on Front Street. There it was harangued about the evils of Birney and his paper. When worked up to an emotional high, the crowd moved off to the corner of Main and Seventh street and the *Philanthropist* office above Achilles Pugh's printing shop.

The door was easily forced, Pugh's press was quickly broken up. Books, desk, chairs, and other equipment in the editorial office were thrown out of the windows of the second story. The mob carried what was left of the press to the river's edge and threw it into the water. Its thirst for vandalism unslaked, the mob moved on to Pugh's house where nothing was found, then to Birney's home on Race Street. Ringleaders were intent on seizing the abolitionist editor, whom they would tar and feather and perhaps even murder. Birney, however, was out of town and so was another prominent abolitionist whose home they visited. Seemingly frustrated the ringleaders bound on vengeance directed the mob down Church Alley, the small black section of the city. There it vented its rage on the pitiful shanties of the black population. Fortunately, the hapless blacks had fled the city, fearing for their lives.

After four hours of willful destruction, Mayor Davies, who had been present, finally called a halt. "We have done enough for one night," he said. "As you can not punish the guilty without endangering the innocent, I advise you all to go home."[39] The next day was Sunday and again in the evening a small crowd collected at the Franklin House, where it was rumored Birney was staying.

Chase, who had of course followed events closely, learned that an attempt would be made on Birney's person. Horrified at the wanton destruction of property and fearing bloodshed, he hurried over to the Franklin House. Birney was not there. As Chase was about to leave the mob appeared at the front door of the hotel. He was in no mood to be intimidated, but stood at the door, barring entrance. Though thin, he was big-boned and muscular with a massive head. When charged with emotion, as he now was, he presented a truly formidable figure. Controlling his slight stammer, he clearly and firmly refused admittance. One of the ringleaders asked who he was. "Salmon P. Chase" was the reply. "You will pay for your actions," said another voice from the crowd. "I told him," said Chase, "that I could be found at any time." His voice and commanding presence caught the mood of the mob at just the right time and dampened its ardor. Since it was now quite late at night Mayor Davies talked the mob into breaking up.[40]

This incident and the fire and destruction the mob had wrought on Pugh's press and on the small free black community shocked Chase to action, but not sufficiently for him to abandon his rich, conservative clients. His major concern was the preservation of civil and property rights rather than human rights. In fact, some months after the mob smashed up Pugh's press, Chase assisted in a suit against Cincinnati residents who were identified as ringleaders. The antislavery society would eventually receive $1500 in damages.[41]

By now even Mayor Davies was concerned about the lawlessness that stalked the dirty streets of Cincinnati at night. An equally alarmed Charles Hammond, the *Gazette* editor, met with Chase, whom he knew had close ties with both the abolitionists and the business leaders of the city. Chase wrote a call for yet another mass meeting, to be held in the courthouse on Thursday evening, August 4. He pointed out that while slave owners' rights to claim fugitives should be respected according to federal and state law, the citizens of Cincinnati, both free blacks and whites, had civil rights guaranteed them under the First Amendment to the United States Constitution, Ohio's constitution, and the Northwest Ordinance. Together, Hammond and Chase drafted a set of resolutions for the meeting they had proposed. They condemned mob violence and pleaded for the rule of law. The call and the resolutions were published in the *Gazette* on Thursday morning.[42] When Chase and Hammond walked from Chase's office at Main and Sycamore to join the meeting, they confronted a crowd heading for the courthouse.

It was obvious that a mob atmosphere was again in the making. And when they managed to push their way through the motley throng in the antechamber of the courthouse they found that the meeting was already organized and in session. Chase heard his name called as a member of the committee, to report not on his and Hammond's resolutions but on a different set that condemned the abolitionists and held them responsible for the mob actions of the previous days. Chase met with other members of the committee in a separate room. He presented his and Hammond's resolutions, which were voted down. Over Chase's objections, the committee prepared a set of resolutions that was hastily approved. The only concession, if indeed a concession, was that the city government would cooperate in full with all parties to restore order.[43] A combination of firm action by the authorities against further violence, a realization in the business community that it risked too much in condoning anarchy in the streets, and the steadfast refusal of Birney and the abolitionists to be silenced finally brought some sort of order to Cincinnati. For the next year the *Philanthropist* continued to publish without serious incident; Birney continued to lecture without hindrance, though subject to abrasive rhetoric, catcalls, and occasional pelting with rotten vegetables.

Still mourning his dead wife, still occasionally quarreling with his mother-in-law, and still boarding with the Garnisses, Chase continued to be buried under the work of his expanding practice. Samuel Eels, a new partner, was in bad health. They came to an amicable termination in 1838. That year Chase took another partner with the improbable name of Flamen Ball, who seemed to meet Chase's requirements. Ball would be his partner for the remainder of his professional life.[44]

His sister Helen was some comfort to him when she arrived from New Hampshire in the spring of 1837. She acted as a buffer between Chase and his in-laws, a source of great relief to the overworked young lawyer. Helen was soon prospecting for a house so that her brother and her little niece would have more independence. Early the following year, she and Chase found what they wanted, a solid brick four-story residence two doors above the Garnisses on Broadway and Fourth Street. They were close enough to the grandparents who doted on little Catherine, yet could enjoy more privacy and less meddling from the Garnisses in family affairs.[45]

Meanwhile on the early afternoon of March 10, 1837, an event occurred that would have a profound effect on Chase's future. A troubled James Birney appeared at Chase's office. He was not his usual, genial self when he explained his mission.[46] His maid Matilda, a lovely young woman who was white in appearance but one of whose grandparents was a black slave, had been seized as a fugitive at Birney's home on Race Street. That very morning, a constable had appeared at his door with a warrant a magistrate had signed for her arrest. A notorious kidnapper, John M. Riley, had sworn out the complaint. He claimed to be the agent for Matilda's owner Larkin Lawrence, a Missouri citizen.

Birney related to Chase a strange, heart-wrenching tale that if accurate exposed the inadequacies of the federal Fugitive Slave Act and the anomaly of freedom and slavery separated only by geographic lines politicians had devised.[47] Legal fictions that determined where positive law either forbade or upheld the peculiar institution were called into question when Matilda's plight was exposed. As a well-trained, well-practiced lawyer, Birney understood these issues and all the paradoxes and hypocrisies they represented. But as an abolitionist, more or less a pariah in the community, and at the same time a possible defendant against the charge, punishable under Ohio law for harboring a fugitive, he was in no position to act as counsel for Matilda.[48]

Birney believed that Matilda was the natural daughter of her owner Lawrence. She had accompanied her father on a business trip east. He permitted her to pass as his daughter in public and in private. She seems to have been well enough educated and with sufficient poise to have been accepted in white society. And as she had related it to the Birneys, the trip had aroused in her strong desires for freedom. When the Lawrences arrived in Cincinnati en route to St. Louis she pleaded with her putative father for a certificate of freedom, which he refused to give. As soon as opportunity presented she left the boat and went to Church Alley, where she sought refuge with a black family. A black barber sheltered her until he learned that the boat carrying Lawrence had left for St. Louis.

Lawrence had not attempted to find her, nor had he publicized her escape in the papers. He may, however, had alerted known slave catchers in Cincinnati. Since it seemed safe, Matilda began clandestinely to seek employment. Her black protector directed her to known abolitionists, among whom Birney was the most prominent. Mrs. Birney, who was recovering from a difficult childbirth and was still confined to her house, hired her.

After Matilda gained the confidence of the family she explained her background and her predicament. Birney waited several weeks before he decided what to do. When there seemed to be no effort to reclaim her, he brought her into his household on a permanent basis. But Matilda was being watched, a fact borne out when a burly person claiming she was a fugitive tried to seize her on the street. She managed to elude him and fled to Birney's house.[49]

Birney was away at the time on one of his frequent lecture trips. On his return, he learned of the incident, which posed a serious problem for both Matilda and himself. Ohio and federal law required that fugitives be returned to their masters on proof of ownership and evidence of flight. Those such as Birney who harbored fugitives were subject to imprisonment or fine or both. Birney, because of his prominence, had been warned to keep clear of involvement. Aware of the penalties and concerned about Matilda, Birney made hasty preparations for her removal to safe quarters. He did not act fast enough. Nothing he could do prevented the constable from seizing Matilda as a fugitive in violation of the federal Fugitive Slave Act of 1793.

No sooner had the constable taken her away than Birney made a quick decision. Of the many lawyers in town who might render legal aid, Chase was his first choice, precisely because he occupied a middle ground between the fervent anti-abolitionists and those who were opposed to slavery everywhere. Besides, Chase had connections with wealthy citizens such as Nicholas Longworth and especially with judges who might hear the case directly or on an appeal. Chase was also well known as a young lawyer who presented thoroughly researched, eminently logical arguments. No legal mind in the state, it was thought, was as conversant with the state law as the editor of the justly appreciated *Ohio Statutes*.[50]

Chase listened carefully to Birney's account, agreed to take the case, and immediately applied to Judge David K. Este for a writ of habeas corpus on behalf of Matilda.[51] William Henry Harrison, then clerk of the Court of Common Pleas, issued the writ that was served on the sheriff. He released Matilda to stand trial before the very Judge Este who had granted the writ. No decent length of time was provided for preparation. Trial date was set the next day, March 11, 1837.

Chase was familiar with Birney's editorials on the federal Constitution and slavery which had appeared from time to time in the *Philanthropist*. As the acknowledged expert on the Ordinance of 1787, however, he had some ideas of his own. Yet he had little time to prepare a proper case. He, and Birney, spent the afternoon and evening framing a plea that they hoped would persuade Judge Este to rule against Matilda's fugitive status as claimed.

Over the months since the disturbances involving Birney and the *Philanthropist*, Chase had become more interested in the plight of fugitive slaves. Since his research on the Northwest Ordinance for his history of Ohio, he had been confronted with the arbitrariness of drawing imaginary lines such as the Ohio River, which separated freedom from slavery within an organic entity that was the United States.

Federalism, so useful in the government of a nation composed of so many diverse regions with so many differing entities, each with its own particular societies, interests, and cultures, imposed varying conditions on human rights. Was it a question of natural right versus local law and customs? When and where did natural right interpose itself between liberty and slavery? Was not freedom as adopted by one group of people, one segment of laws, facts, and governance as obligatory as slavery adopted by another similar set of laws, facts, and governance? What was property in one state and one section was not property in another. Was there a role for the federal government, and if so, how could it discriminate between so many anomalies?

Clearly, in Chase's mind, section 3 in Article IV of the federal Constitution—gave Congress plenary powers over the territories, powers that would designate whether slavery or freedom would prevail including any conditions on admission Congress might impose on a given territory prior to statehood. Thus under the Articles of Confederation Congress was setting a precedent when it assigned freedom to the Northwest territories, natural right or not. He was still faced with the quandary posed by federalism, the division of power between the states and the central government and its impact on civil and human rights. Chase had recourse to recent decisions of state courts. One group of precedents, oddly enough decisions of southern courts, declared slavery was a state right, governed by local law and custom. Other precedents laid down by northern courts brought some light to the murkiness surrounding the rights if any of fugitive slaves in a free state.[52]

The supreme court of New Jersey had held that in a free state a fugitive, whether a black slave or a white apprentice, could not under the federal Fugitive Slave Act be deprived of his liberty without being granted procedural rights,which included trial by jury as required by the New Jersey constitution.[53] Another recent case, that of *Commonwealth v. Aves*, was even more important to Chase's line of reasoning. Lemuel Shaw, highly respected chief justice of the Massachusetts supreme court, in speaking for the court had held that section 2 Article IV of the Constitution (the fugitive slave clause) was simply a declaration that rested on comity between states. He went on to declare the obvious principle that slavery was repugnant to natural right, justice, and humanity though still recognized by the law of nations.

But comity as he defined it applied solely to property that was everywhere recognized to be so irrespective of state and local law and customs. This was not the case of slave property, which was not recognized as such in many states of the Union. Comity did not extend to fugitives, and Massachusetts, though a free state, was bound to return them. He rendered no decision on slaves in transit.[54] Shaw's opinion had led Chase to British precedents, specifically to the Somerset case in *Howell's State Trials* and the British Chief Justice Mansfield's decision in that case which held that slavery existed only through positive law.[55] But neither Chase nor Birney had much time to do more than a quick scanning of precedents before they had to appear in court.[56]

Chase, his partner the ailing Samuel Eels, Birney, and Matilda made their way to the courthouse on the morning of March 11. A crowd awaited them, though it was Saturday and a work day. The news that the fate of an attractive fugitive female was to be decided no doubt added an element of spice. The fact that Birney himself might be tried for harboring a fugitive if Matilda was returned to her captors fueled interest in the proceedings.[57]

When Judge Este called upon Chase to begin his argument, the tall, awkward figure rose from the desk reserved for the defense and, after glancing at the prosecutors—three in number—began his argument. He opened with the familiar and customary effort to enlist the sympathy of the court by referring to Matilda who sat beside him as "a helpless and almost friendless women who sues for this protection," but then shifted his ground to "the legal and constitutional aspects of the case before the court." For the next three hours he spoke in a rather dry, conversational tone that was more of a lecture than an argument.[58]

The kernel of Chase's plea rested on Shaw's explication of the Somerset case.[59] "Slavery," Chase said, "is admitted, on all hands to be contrary to natural right. Whenever it exists at all, it exists only in virtue of positive law." "The right to hold a man," he asserted, his voice rising briefly and pausing for dramatic affect, "is a naked legal right. It is a right, which in its own value, can have no existence beyond the territorial limits of the state which sanctions it. . . ." "It vanishes," he continued, "when the master and the slave meet together where positive law interdicts slavery " But was not Ohio bound by its own laws and Article IV of the Constitution to return fugitives to the rightful owners? Chase had to answer in the affirmative, his contention being, however, that Matilda was not a fugitive. Her master had brought her to Cincinnati. He did not emphasize this point, however. Instead he argued that there was no act of Congress that authorized "the issuing of a state process in the name of the state, in any case whatever." In words that John Marshall or Daniel Webster might have uttered, Chase insisted that "the government of the United States, and the several State governments are entirely distinct and independent. Neither can control nor regulate the action of the other." A state officer acting under a state warrant had arrested Matilda for violation of a federal law. Thus his action was a violation of a state right. The Ohio fugitive statute of 1831 was appropriate to the case; but this law required that before anyone accused of being a fugitive slave could be carried out of the state, the owner had to prove his or her status and ownership before a judge or justice of the peace. Chase said that Riley had violated Matilda's procedural rights. But Chase and Birney were more interested in testing the constitutionality of the Fugitive Slave Act than in arguing for Matilda on technical grounds. For, as Chase pointed out, the Ordinance of 1787 abolished slavery in the Territory that became Ohio and documented procedural rights for all residents.[60]

Judge Este took only a few minutes to issue an order which Chase, Este, and Birney knew would be for the plaintiff. Disregarding evidence that Matilda was brought to Ohio, and was not fleeing from slavery, he remanded her to Riley's custody for transport south.[61] Seized by Riley and two accomplices the frightened woman was shipped out on the next steamboat for St. Louis.[62] Larkin never recovered her. She simply disappeared, in all likelihood sold in a slave mart.

Chase, however, gained considerable prominence from the case and the learned argument he made. What really mattered was that he put together in a cohesive pattern ideas and precedents regarding the anomalous position not just of fugitive slaves but of slavery itself in a nation that considered itself the epitome of liberty and equal rights. His argument would be further refined and expanded in later cases and on the political rostrum. All that he would ever accomplish in arguing fugitive slave cases and in setting the basic principles of free soil he enunciated in the Matilda case.

chapter 5

A Distant Shore

Chase's appearance in the Matilda case proved to be a turning point in his career. His lengthy argument probing the uncertain boundaries between federal and state relations and his eloquent discussion of natural right may not have satisfied the court, but it did gain him the respect of many thoughtful citizens in Cincinnati and elsewhere. He had his argument printed and circulated widely in pamphlet form.[1] Those who read it carefully could see that Chase was no abolitionist, but simply an earnest and learned individual who was pleading for human rights irrespective of color.

That Chase meant this message to be broadcast is obvious. He could have emphasized that Matilda was not a fugitive, that she had been brought to a free state. He could have argued that she had more white blood than a mulatto which according to Ohio law made her free.[2] These points might well have decided the case for Matilda. But rather than dwell on the fine points of statute law, Chase had laid the groundwork for an assault on the federal Fugitive Slave Act and an exposition of the Northwest Ordinance, which declared Ohio a free state.[3] Chase's motives were twofold. He courted an unfavorable decision from Judge Este because he sensed the political undercurrent that made states' rights and slavery issues that would eventually redound to his own advantage. He saw an opportunity to articulate an antislavery stance without being branded an abolitionist.[4] His timing was a bit premature, but his political sense put him on the right track.

More immediately important to Chase, however, was his close association with Birney, a temperate, able publicist for human rights, a person well versed in the law, an abolitionist but not of the inflammatory Garrisonian type. Chase and Birney got along well. Both men were lawyers; both were college-educated and came from similar class backgrounds. Both tended to be formal, even punctilious, in social relations, and both were well read not just in the law but in philosophy and history. Birney was more of an idealist than Chase, whose commitment to humanitarian causes balanced his drivingly ambitious nature, his tendency to emphasize the practical over the possible. Though Birney engaged in politics—in fact was a founder of the Liberty party—he always thought of himself as merely an instrument of social progress.

Yet the antislavery movement needed the pragmatic Chase as much as the self-sacrificial Birney to give it momentum and to propagate its goal of human rights. Binding them closer together in a common objective was the outcome of the Matilda case. Birney was immediately put on trial for violating the Ohio law of 1804 which forbade the harboring of a fugitive. Well satisfied with Chase's performance in the Matilda case, Birney asked him to act as his defense counsel with the understanding, of course, that Birney would assist in his own defense. Again the judge and the prosecutors were the same. This time, however, Chase argued effectively that Birney did not harbor a fugitive because Matilda had been brought to Cincinnati, had not escaped from servitude.

The courtroom was as crowded as before. Interest and excitement mounted when Chase put the controversial Birney on the stand. The carefully dressed, stocky Birney then took over his own defense, using the witness box as a pulpit for addressing not just the courtroom but the country at large. His voice even, though occasionally rising to emphasize points, Birney admitted that he had employed Matilda. In extenuation, he stoutly insisted she was a free woman, given the fact that she had been brought to a free state. Altogether Birney spoke for three hours. Chase in his questioning of Birney and in his summation spoke another two. He reinforced his client's testimony with elaborate use of precedent. Este's instructions from the bench were more of a rebuttal to Chase's and Birney's arguments than an explication of the law. When the jury found Birney guilty as charged in the indictment,[5] Este imposed a fine of $50, the maximum sum provided by law.[6]

Chase and Birney determined to take the case on a writ of error to the Ohio supreme court. Chase had noted a technical error in the indictment, which when presented he was confident would lead the court to reverse the conviction. But with Birney's approval, he decided not to bring this error to the attention of the bench. Rather he opted for maximum publicity by again basing his argument on the Ohio statute under which Birney had been convicted. "I maintain," said Chase, "that it is impossible in Ohio to commit the offense of harboring, or secreting a person being the property of another person." Citing the federal Constitution and the Ordinance of 1787 as the basis for his contention, he said that the statute in question "inflicts a penalty for violating a relation which can not exist constitutionally, must be repugnant to the constitution, and therefore void. The fugitive slave clause in the Ordinance and the Constitution speaks only of persons, not slaves, much less property; nor does it mention color, but simply asserts the master-servant relationship." He reverted also, to what would become a constant theme, that slavery, "wherever it exists is a creature of positive institutions. It has no support in natural right, on the contrary it is in direct derogation of natural right." Where municipal law did not protect it, slavery did not exist.

It seems plausible that Chase's argument impressed the justices because they took the extraordinary step of ordering his argument to be printed. But rather than answering Chase they decided to reverse the lower court's judgment on the very error in the indictment that Chase chose not to bring before them. In their decision they maintained that Birney could not have known whether Matilda was a slave or free person of color and the presumption favored freedom.[7]

Despite his outspoken opposition to slavery, Chase was at pains to deny that he was an abolitionist.[8] But he was unable to escape the stigma that his association with Birney and his role in the Matilda case fixed upon him. Still it did not effect his law business, which was flourishing even in the depth of the depression that followed the panic of 1837. Where the publicity caused some damage was the effect it had on his political aspirations, which he recognized and sought to rectify. He used a pseudonym when he wrote a brief essay attacking a report of the Ohio senate's judiciary committee that would selectively exclude persons of color in jury trials. For double insurance Chase had the editor preface his article with the phrase that the author was not an abolitionist.[9] Chase was seeking the Whig nomination for the state senate from Hamilton County at the time. His careful distinctions and his disclaimers were of no avail with the county convention, which turned down his bid on the grounds that he was an abolitionist.[10]

Chase had been opposed to Jacksonian Democracy since his Washington days. In 1832, Chase had preferred his old mentor William Wirt, who was running on the anti-Masonic ticket for President. Wirt was not given much of a chance for success against Jackson and Clay, who headed the National Republican ticket. Chase cast his vote for a general slate of electors that was pledged to vote for either Wirt or Clay, whichever proved to be the stronger candidate.[11]

Busy expanding his law practice and engaging in social and literary activities, Chase was more a spectator than a participant in politics, though he kept himself conversant with "men and measures" through his customary reading of half a dozen or so local and national newspapers. He did seek rather amateurishly to promote John McLean as the candidate of the emerging Whig party. In 1836 Chase cast his vote for Harrison, a fellow townsman who lived in the Cincinnati suburb of North Bend. He had known the General for a good many years, going back to his days as a student at Cincinnati College. Two of Harrison's sons were classmates.[12] Over the past four years, Chase had become more closely associated with Harrison, who acted as clerk of the court of common pleas.[13] The cheerful, neighborly Harrison with his ruddy cheeks, his ready stories of his military exploits, and his earthy humor had made him a favorite personage at the courthouse.[14]

Not that Harrison's political career and his popularity had escaped notice from the ambitious lawyers who traveled about the state or listened to the General's highly embroidered accounts of his battles against the British and the Indians. Author of a revised land purchase law when he was territorial delegate of the Northwest Territory in Congress, he was likewise considered the champion of the land-hungry West. Harrison's image as a military hero and his record in Congress made him the strongest of the Whig candidates in the West, ahead of such well-known national fixtures as Henry Clay and Daniel Webster. An early supporter of the General, Chase did not let his rebuff in his bid for the state senate weaken his support for the Whig cause. And he finally achieved political success of a modest sort when he was elected to the Cincinnati city council in 1840 on the Whig ticket.[15]

Membership in the council could assist one to political advancement and to business opportunities. In the progressive and expanding Cincinnati, council membership commanded considerable patronage in awarding bids for such urban projects as water works, street and sidewalk maintenance, licensing of businesses, and the like.[16] But the council could also be fatal to an emerging political career, if a member was not careful about his vote on controversial issues that affected the community directly. Discussions were heated when the council met weekly on the second floor of the new firehouse on Fourth Street.

Under the soft light of oil lamps (gas light would not be introduced in public buildings until 1843) Chase almost immediately found himself involved in a politically unpleasant decision on licensing taverns that dispensed liquor.[17] During that particular meeting of the council he had been quite vehement on the evils of drink and urged vigorously a refusal of the license. The council went along with him, but later that evening he had second thoughts about his role. "Ought I to vote for license," he asked himself, "to any tavern to retail intoxicating drinks?"[18]

While Chase did vote for some licenses during the year he served on the council, finally at one meeting he could not contain himself. Misjudging the strength of the growing temperance movement in the state, he flatly refused to endorse any more licenses, and "took some pains" to prevent the grant of a license to a new house proposed on Main Street. As he admitted later, "I don't know what the effect may be on me personally, but I believe I have done right."[19] When the news got out that Chase was a temperance man, a heavy vote was cast against him and he was defeated for re-election.[20] Chase's defeat was one of the few exceptions in a year that saw the Whigs triumph in most of the states. Ironically, Chase was more active than he had ever been campaigning for the Whig party.[21] In May 1840, at the beginning of the election excitement, Chase, happened to meet near his office on Broadway, Albert Hoyt, a portrait painter, who had been a freshman at Dartmouth when he was a graduating senior. Hoyt recognized Chase and in greeting him said that his reputation in Dartmouth circles had preceded him. Chase inquired what Hoyt's plans were. He had come, he explained, to paint Harrison's portrait on commission for the Boston Whig Association.[22] He planned to visit Harrison at his home the next day. Chase was presented with an opportunity to call on Harrison and an appropriate pretext for an informal visit. Accompanied by Hoyt, Eliza Ann, Chase's attractive second wife, and his niece Eliza Whipple, he arrived at North Bend about noon. If Chase had selected the two young and lovely women to impress Harrison (whose reputation as a womanizer was almost as widespread as his military exploits), he succeeded. The General insisted that they stay for dinner and acted as their personal guide for a visit to the new Whitewater canal, which ran through a 1600-foot-long tunnel bored through a nearby hill. Later, after one of Harrison's servants was slow and awkward in laying a fire, the General dismissed him and laid it himself.[23] The Chase party enjoyed itself. All were particularly taken with Harrison's friendly, modest demeanor. Chase himself had forged, he thought, a closer personal relationship with the Whig candidate, always useful to one who had political ambitions.

Six weeks later Chase was able to cement their relationship even more closely. In the late afternoon of July 1, he was standing outside of his office on Third Street, talking with a constituent, when he saw Harrison approaching them. The General stopped to greet them with what Chase described as a troubled look. "Do you know a person named Bailey?" he asked Chase. "Very well," said Chase, referring to Gamaliel Bailey, the new editor of the *Philanthropist,* who succeeded Birney when he moved to New York to head the American Anti-Slavery Society. "Would you," asked Harrison, his voice taking on an angry tone, "call on him . . . and inquire of him what foundation he had for the charges published against [me] yesterday morn'g in the *Philanthropist?*" Chase agreed. Harrison said that "he had never called on Dr. Bailey but once and had said nothing which would give color to the charges against him"—that he had been less than forthright on the slavery issue. Either later that evening or the next day Chase met with Bailey. He would not retract the articles that had aroused Harrison's anger.[24] Chase duly relayed Bailey's response.[25]

The sharp-eyed editor of the *Philanthropist* was far more skeptical of Harrison's stand on slavery than Chase. Both men had been deeply concerned by President Van Buren's comment in his inaugural address that he opposed any attempt of Congress to abolish slavery in the District of Columbia without the consent of Virginia and Maryland. Since his argument in the Matilda case, Chase had been a keen observer of what he took to be a coming issue and had along with Bailey concluded that the best way to halt what they felt was the encroachment of "the slavepower" was to concentrate on abolishing slavery in those areas where the Constitution conferred plenary powers on Congress— the District of Columbia, the territories, the internal slave trade, and the high seas. For Chase himself this policy was not only practical but constitutionally acceptable and would remove from his actions any taint of abolitionism. That it was more realistic than moralistic did not trouble him.

Chase and his newfound friends among the Cincinnati abolitionists deplored the open demagoguery of the Whig campaign. Chase also found Van Buren "a creature of the slave power," yet he had come to accept many of the Democratic party's principles. Suspension of specie payments by the banks, including those which were his clients in Cincinnati, shocked him. He now supported, though tacitly, Van Buren's subtreasury system. His tariff views had likewise undergone a change as he had come to understand the political power of the rural community.[26]

But he voted for Harrison because he thought the General would reverse Van Buren's policy on slavery in the District of Columbia. He also counted on his new friendship with Harrison to aid him politically. His was one of the flood of letters that engulfed President-elect Harrison's temporary lodgings in Washington seeking patronage favors during the weeks before his inauguration. Chase sought posts for his former law partner, Samuel Eels, his former father-in-law John P. Garniss, and a Major Clarkson. Chase took it upon himself to advise Harrison not to mention slavery in his inaugural, especially not to comment on it in the District of Columbia. "Slavery was not," he wrote, "a subject, on which Congress will be at all likely to act during your Presidency while it is a subject which cannot be touched without grievously offending one side or the other."[27]

None of Chase's nominations, if confirmed, would have helped him politically. Obviously he did not communicate his neutral stance on slavery to his antislavery friends. When he read Harrison's rambling inaugural and understood that the new President's position on slavery in the District was almost the same as Van Buren's, Chase decided that the Whig party was as hopeless as the Democrat on that issue. Bailey, the *Philanthropist* editor, had been right after all when he published those articles that doubted Harrison's honesty on the slavery question.

Chase had become very friendly with the earnest editor and his talented wife, Margaret. Almost the same age as Chase, Gamaliel Bailey was a small, thin person with dark hair, dark eyes, and a penchant for learned discussion on all current topics. To Chase he was a most appealing companion. Bailey also shared Chase's intense religiosity and his optimism about the future economic and social progress of the nation.

A physician by training, he had gone to sea as a sailor; before taking over the *Philanthropist* he had been a successful editor of the *Methodist Protestant,* a publication devoted to missionary activities and good works generally. During the winter of 1831, Bailey relinquished his position with the *Methodist.* He made his way west, settling eventually in Cincinnati where his father had opened a watch repair shop. He practiced medicine briefly in Cincinnati, but devoted much more of his time to journalism and to participation in the city's cultural activities. Before his arrival in Cincinnati, Bailey through Theodore Dwight Weld had been introduced to the abolitionists at Lane Seminary and to James G. Birney, who offered him a post as assistant editor of the *Philanthropist.*[28]

As Birney became more involved in his proselytizing activities he delegated virtually all editorial responsibility to Bailey. Within a year he became editor of the *Philanthropist* when Birney moved to New York in December 1837.[29] Freed from Birney's influence Bailey began to conduct the *Philanthropist* along broader paths that even hinted at abolitionist cooperation with whichever major party and its candidates in local elections supported emancipation, a stand that raised the suspicion of some important eastern abolitionists. Joshua Leavitt and Elizur Wright, influential abolitionist editors in Massachusetts and New York, were particularly caustic in their accusation that Bailey was drifting away from independent political action.[30]

Bailey was opposed to the movement favored by most of the eastern abolitionists who came from evangelical religious backgrounds. They aimed at organizing a new political party on one issue—abolition—or "one idea," as it came to be termed. Bailey felt and with good reason that such a party would attract a hopeless minority while it would alienate thousands of antislavery-leaning Whigs and Democrats. If slavery were ever to be abolished peacefully in the United States it had to be through the action of one or the other major parties and the conversion of enough southern states to support universal freedom. On these points Chase agreed wholeheartedly with the *Philanthropist* editor. But Bailey could not withstand the pressure of abolitionist leaders. He reluctantly supported the new Liberty party and its presidential candidate Birney. As he predicted, Birney received a mere 7000 votes nationwide, only 903 in Ohio.[31]

If Bailey was troubled at the course of the "one-idea" Liberty party, Chase was in a greater quandary. All of his connections with rich, conservative elements in Cincinnati society tended to keep him within the well-organized Whig fold. But Harrison's rejection of his advice on slavery, followed within a month by his death and the assumption of the Virginia slaveholder John Tyler to the presidency mocked the frequent assertions of Ohio Whigs that their party would not advance slaveholder interest.

Refused the Whig nomination for the state senate, defeated in his bid for a second term on the City Council, Chase despaired of any political future with the Whigs. Apart from personal grounds, his frustration emphasized the humanitarian aspect of his character. He reasoned that he should as a devout Christian seek to remove the sinful blemish of slavery from a nation that prided itself on its democracy. His understanding of the Declaration of Independence and his close study of *Elliot's Debates* at the Constitutional Convention of 1787 convinced him that the founding fathers had opposed slavery in principle. Jefferson's role in drafting the Declaration and his example that the authors of the Northwest Ordinance drew upon in establishing freedom as a precept brought all of these objectives together. Logically and legally slavery could be contained, a first step toward eventual emancipation.[32]

Chase recognized that the Liberty party had no organization. Cincinnati was solidly Democratic. Leading citizens whether Democrats or Whigs were sensitive to the economic and social pull of the slave states. Workingmen, many of whom were recent immigrants, were fearful of cheap black labor and were largely racist or, rather, white supremacist in outlook. The riots against Birney and the destruction of his abolitionist press provided Chase with ample evidence of alliance between leading citizens and the laboring classes. Civil rights and civil liberties Chase discovered were held cheaply, if at all by Cincinnati masses. Yet he had nowhere else to go politically except to the new Liberty party, as feeble as it was and as socially undesirable it was considered by many of Chase's clients and friends. While Chase pondered his political fate another fugitive slave incident claimed his attention and in all likelihood made his final decision to join the Liberty party.

Mary Towns had been a slave but had lived as a free woman for the previous ten years in Cincinnati where she married and had a family. She was suddenly seized for return to slavery in Kentucky. Before she could be sent out of the state Chase on his own responsibility appeared before Judge Nathaniel Read and secured a writ of habeas corpus. Chase could not have been very hopeful that he could convince the court that Mary Towns was a free person. The same Judge Read, who granted the writ, had been one of the prosecutors who had beaten him in both the Matilda and the Birney cases. Read harbored a personal dislike for Chase, which he had not bothered to conceal.[33]

Yet the Mary Towns case provided Chase with yet another forum and one free of political bias for placing his ideas before the legal system, the general public, and especially the abolitionists of the east. Mary Towns's seizure after so many years of quiet family life in Cincinnati shocked Chase. Should Read rule against his client, as Chase assumed he would, the judge would expose himself as being no better than any other kidnapper of fugitives, refusing to be swayed by the common instincts of humanity, the intent of the Declaration, and the Northwest Ordinance. Bailey's editorial page would exploit all of this in promoting the Liberty party. Characteristically Chase blended personal advantage with what he presumed to be the greater good.[34]

Word had gotten out that Chase was defending another fugitive slave. The upper gallery and the space outside of the bar in the courthouse was crowded when Chase made his way through the spectators to the lawyers' table directly in front of the bench. From previous skirmishes with Judge Read, Chase knew he was pitted against a fine legal mind, perhaps the keenest in the city. Outwardly giving the appearance of complete confidence, he waited for the formalities of the proceedings to begin. When his turn came Chase outlined his arguments that natural right ruled over state rights and that these conditions linked the Declaration with the Northwest Ordinance and the Constitution. But then he argued that Mary Towns's presumptive owner had not sworn in his affidavit that she had fled from slavery.[35]

Read handed down his decision two days later. He dismissed, as Chase thought he would, the natural right argument but surprisingly gave some credence to Chase's positive law contention. He accepted Chase's point that the slaveowner's affidavit did not declare Mary Towns to be a fugitive. She was therefore free because, he said, "liberty is the rule, involuntary servitude the exception" in Ohio.[36]

Shortly after the decision Chase sought to widen his acquaintance with the eastern abolitionists. Alvan Stewart, a leading proponent of independent political action and one of the more extreme advocates in the Liberty party of abolishing slavery everywhere through congressional action, seemed a likely candidate for conversion to Chase's more moderate, constitutionally acceptable program. In sending Stewart a copy of his arguments in the Towns and the Matilda cases, Chase pointed out that the positive law principle he had argued in the Matilda case and which the court denied was now accepted in the Mary Towns decision. "I then contended namely that persons deprived of liberty . . . unless proved to have been held to service and to have escaped from the state so held into Ohio, must be discharged. Thus a woman (Matilda) was sent into slavery under circumstances which in 1841 a woman was adjudged free."[37]

Neither the business community nor the labor force of Cincinnati applauded the Towns decision. Especially telling, as promoted by word of mouth and editorial opinion in two of the three major newspapers in Cincinnati, the *Whig* and the *Republican*, was the prediction that free-spending southerners who brought their slave servants with them would avoid Cincinnati. Bailey, of course, highlighted the case in the *Philanthropist*.[38]

Despite the spectacular growth of Cincinnati and the air of optimism it generated, the depression that began in 1837 became more pressing in the early forties. Unemployment and partial employment were endemic to most American cities. Hard times were if anything more acute in freewheeling Cincinnati, where an overbuilt financial and industrial complex was uniquely sensitive to economic downturns.

Business leaders and workingmen lived in a climate of apprehension, which could and did provoke violent incidents over the past four years. Civic unrest was frequently vented against blacks and abolitionists, who were accused of being the disruptive elements in a fragile economic and social order. Cincinnati's exposed position, separated only by a few hundred yards from a slave state, made the city particularly vulnerable to the mounting pressure of an increasingly defensive slave plantation system. There were of course racist undertones in the city's society. The black community numbered only about 2000 and was strictly segregated. But plenty of believers in the white community were more than willing to accept as truth rumors of miscegenation. Abolitionist male students at Lane Seminary who had been seen fraternizing with female blacks were a frequent source for these spurious allegations. It did not take long before the decision in the Mary Towns case brought another violent anti-black, anti-abolitionist episode.[39]

The sweltering summer heat following Read's decision was a time of physical discomfort for all. Heavy sultry weather that engulfed the city was to be expected and therefore endured, but it intensified feelings already frayed by wild rumors and ill-founded accusations. Ugly little incidents against blacks had been cropping up sporadically for weeks. Yet Chase and his friends did not expect a repetition of the 1837 riots. Toward the end of the summer, Chase left Cincinnati for the east. As usual he would combine business with visits to old friends, but he did not neglect political soundings. He had only been away a week or so when he read sketchy accounts of a major race riot in Cincinnati. Flamen Ball, his new partner, provided more details when his letter caught up with Chase.

Ball reported that the riot began when "three black loafers from the water front not residents of the city" assaulted a white woman. Passersby witnessed the attempt and chased the blacks away. No harm was done to the woman, but word of the incident provided the incentive for impromptu organizers to launch an attack on the black ghetto.

A mob of at least 2000 men gathered, many of them armed, and proceeded to Sixth, McAlister, and New streets, the black ghetto. They had with them a cannon which they had loaded with slugs and which they fired several times in such a way as to sweep both sides of each street. The blacks, many of whom were also armed, defended themselves. For three days there was anarchy in the streets, during which the *Philanthropist* press was again seized and destroyed, the office gutted. Fortunately no harm came to Bailey and his family even though mob leaders were demanding that he be lynched. The mayor sought to bring order but his pleas went unheeded.[40] Only until Governor Tom Corwin arrived with a hastily recruited militia force was order restored in the city.

Bailey and other known abolitionists in town, one of whom had his shop destroyed, for a time feared for their lives. State and city authorities were forced to execute the Black Laws, which had not been rigidly enforced for years. Each black had to prove his or her freedom or risk expulsion from the state. Blacks also had to post bonds as a guarantee of good behavior.[41]

In many respects this riot widened rather than circumscribed antislavery feeling. The grave assault on white as well as black civil rights and property rights led many to believe that a political conspiracy of slaveholders was indeed a fact, thus confirming for many citizens what the *Philanthropist* had been charging. Bailey was able to get out an edition of his paper printed on a borrowed press. In a lengthy editorial he insisted that he and other members of the new Liberty party were not "amalgamationists." Abolitionists as well as antislavery Whigs and Democrats in Ohio and elsewhere, many of whom differed from Bailey's political line, sent in substantial contributions for him to rebuild his press and office.[42]

By October, Chase was back in Cincinnati, the city still tense from public fear of armed blacks and a widespread, though completely erroneous belief that white abolitionists had armed them. Chase was disturbed at the silence of the upper classes, disgusted and dismayed by the failure of city authorities to take action against the inciters of the mob. "Indeed I see no reason why any law and liberty loving man should wish to come to this place," he wrote his friend Cleveland; "it is painful to witness occurrences like these: more painful to know that if not absolutely sanctioned, they are feebly if at all condemned by the leading men, the ministry of the gospel are almost dumb; the condition of the press while they condemn the mob, dare not vindicate the character or objects of those whom the mob assails."[43]

At the same time Chase noted that there was "a large amount of antislavery feeling in the city." Read's opinion in the Mary Towns case and the aftermath of the September riots convinced him that he must join his fortunes with the Liberty party. Chase, like Bailey, distrusted a third party dedicated so narrowly to total abolition everywhere in the nation. The decision to join his political fortunes with the Liberty party was a painful one. Still, it held out some unique possibilities.

During long evening conversations with Bailey and Samuel Lewis, another disillusioned antislavery Whig, the future may have seemed risky, but it
was not all that bleak. If somehow the party in Ohio could divorce itself from
the "one idea" platform of the eastern "immediatists" and broaden its objectives so as to attract antislavery men from the major parties, it could become an
independent force that could extract concessions from the political establishment.[44] Such a strategy differed quite radically from that used earlier, where
candidates for public office were quizzed about their outlook on slavery. If
deemed to give a satisfactory answer, abolitionists were urged to support them.
Too often those candidates once elected either ignored or disavowed their
promises. In a party like the Liberty party, however, small but concentrated on
objectives, continuous pressure could be imposed.[45]

Unfortunately for Chase his residence was in a community where the
Democrats were dominant, where abolition was weaker than anywhere else in
the state. The Whigs drew most of their strength from rural areas and especially from northeastern Ohio. There transplanted Yankees were more susceptible to the evangelical and moralistic appeals of the eastern abolitionists.[46]

Chase knew that Joshua Giddings and Benjamin Wade, his law partner,
just beginning his political career, were the acknowledged antislavery leaders
in populous northeastern Ohio, or what was known as the Western Reserve.
Both could count on solid Whig constituencies. Giddings, an intense, combative person, had made himself so irritating to his fellow congressmen in his
rasping defense of John Quincy Adams and the right of petition that they had
censured him for his conduct. He had promptly resigned only to be returned
in triumph to the next Congress. His partner Wade, a state senator from
Ashtabula County, was likewise a cantankerous individual of pronounced
antislavery views. He too was popular with the Whigs of the Western Reserve.[47]

As Chase assessed the situation during the summer and fall of 1841 he
concluded that the Liberty party must somehow be made more acceptable to
the Democratic leadership in his home area, yet without alienating the Giddings and the Wades. A cursory view would have concluded the task well-nigh
impossible. But a deeper, more thoughtful analysis would have disclosed some
areas of potential strength. Less than a month after the riot Chase pointed out
that "whether abolition is not properly speaking a political object, anti-slavery
is. Anti-slavery I understand to be hostility to slavery as a power antagonistic to
free labor, as an influence perverting our government from its true scope and
end, as an institution strictly local, but now escaped from proper limits and
threatening to . . . nullify whatever is most valuable in our political system."[48] On the national scene it was now obvious that President Tyler was
damaging seriously the structure of the Whig party. His strict constructionist,
states' rights views were in open conflict with Whig leaders such as Ohio's

Thomas Ewing and Kentucky's Henry Clay. The depression which the Whigs had so confidently and casually claimed they would lift was deeper and wider than it had been during Van Buren's term.

The Democratic party leadership was enmeshed in currency and banking quarrels, with the hard-money, subtreasury advocates contesting with the soft-money, pro-state-banking supporters. In Ohio the struggle was becoming particularly severe. Van Buren supporters, led by the two Democratic U.S. senators—handsome, persuasive William Allen and Benjamin Tappan, brother of Lewis Tappan, the rich New York abolitionist—commanded a majority of the party in the state. Samuel Medary, editor of the influential *Ohio Statesman,* backed them and promoted their hard-money views vigorously in his editorial columns.

No such charismatic leadership headed the Democratic party in Chase's home county, a distinct advantage to a perceptive would-be politician. And Chase was nothing if not perceptive. Thomas Morris, whom the Ohio legislature had recently refused to reelect to the U.S. Senate for his outspoken antislavery views, had been actually expelled from the Democratic party. He had been the only Democrat of status who resided in Cincinnati. An outspoken, pugnacious individual of Welsh ancestry, and transparent honesty, Morris could never be acceptable to the state Democratic leadership. He was now a member of the Liberty party, quite willing to join with Chase on the many points of Democratic doctrine which both men construed as Jeffersonian principles. He was no threat to Chase, who recognized that Morris's political career was finished. He was an important collaborator but no rival.

Thus sometime in the fall of 1841, Chase decided with some misgivings to cast his lot with the Liberty party. He had decided that if he could, he would move the party toward the Democracy. Its antislavery goal would remain uppermost, but issues such as hard money, free trade, and a federal government divorced from banks as well as slavery would attract antislavery Democrats even though such an approach risked the loss of "one idea" Liberty votes.

Chase had to pick his way carefully. He felt, and rightly so, that antislavery Whigs could not complain about such Jeffersonian notions as natural rights that were expounded in the Declaration of Independence. Nor in fact could the "one idea" men in the Liberty party be averse to basic Jeffersonian principles of human rights. But Whig tenets that emphasized Henry Clay's American system and Hamiltonian elitism Chase believed were incompatible with the idealism that underlay the Declaration and the Ordinance of 1787.

Chase's first tentative step in this direction came in late 1841.[49] On the cold clear morning of December 27 he caught the stage for Columbus, bowling along over the newly macadamized turnpike. Samuel Lewis, a Methodist preacher and educator, and Thomas Morris accompanied him. They arrived in Columbus on the 29th and, while still travel-stained, made their way to the First Baptist Church whose new, tall spire dominated the landscape. They were bound for Ohio's first state convention of the Liberty party, which was being held in the basement of the church.[50]

Soon after their arrival Leicester King called the delegates to order.[51] Chase must have found it reassuring to see such a celebrated businessman on the podium. King was the principal owner of the Pennsylvania and Ohio Canal, which linked Akron with the Pennsylvania and New York canal systems. He had broken with the Whig party that had twice elected him to the state senate. And he had earned the ire of the two major parties with his persistent attempts while a member of the legislature to repeal the discriminatory "Black Laws."[52]

For a new convert Chase was much in evidence, serving on three committees. Elected a member of the committee on committees, Chase had himself named to the important committee that would prepare the address and resolutions of the party. His hand was quite obvious in the resolutions that called for free labor as opposed to slave labor, and stated the federal Constitution to be an antislavery document. He was also responsible for the resolution which declared that "we expressly disclaim, in behalf of the general government, all right to interfere with slavery in the states where it exists."[53] Boldly Chase had taken issue with the eastern leadership of the Liberty party. This resolution charted the moderate course that he and Bailey had decided was most useful for bringing in converts. But it was sure to raise the suspicion if not the condemnation of easterners who found such a statement to be moral treason. An estimated 200 delegates from 36 Ohio counties were present and approved without any vocal dissent the party platform, which included a Chase-authored resolution that favored hard money though it masqueraded under the general phrase of currency reform.

By unanimous consent Leicister King was nominated for governor, but the convention made no nominations for other state officers. This planned omission underscored Chase's strategy that King, a well-known, well-liked individual, would provide a focus and a single rallying point. Before a well-knit organization was established, a full slate of nominees representing various locales and interests could be a distracting and possibly disruptive element.[54]

Chase did little active campaigning during the year following the convention. His legal business and family affairs occupied much of his time. He did venture forth to Butler County and made three speeches that cautiously broadened and defined the Columbus platform. Before an audience that for once was free of hecklers at the courthouse in Hamilton, he shared the platform with Dr. William H. Brisbane, formerly a rich Sea Island planter who had emancipated his slaves and become an abolitionist. Chase emphasized his belief that Congress had the power to abolish slavery in the territories and the

District of Columbia and should exercise it. He took a specific stand on the tariff, arguing for limited protection. Hard money, or "sound currency," as he phrased it, would be beneficial to free labor and farmers.[55] Chase had not as yet formulated precisely his political approach except that he agreed with Bailey that the Liberty party had to be made appealing to a broader audience without a compromise of principle.

Much of his free time was engaged in a letter-writing campaign which sought to bring important antislavery Whigs and Democrats into the Liberty party and in efforts to strengthen the party's statewide organization.[56] He discovered that the abolitionists, though divided into many quarreling factions, were united in their distrust of either political party.[57] Nor were the antislavery Whigs and Democrats any more comfortable with the new Liberty party. In a apologetic letter to Joshua Giddings Chase hoped that he would not use his influence to undermine antislavery strength in the Western Reserve. Giddings's reply gave Chase little grounds for optimism. He was "strongly opposed to a distinct political organization of anti-slavery friends." He did assure Chase that he would not make public statements to that effect.[58]

A growing problem for Chase was the fact that the Liberty party had nominated James G. Birney for President and Thomas Morris for Vice President the previous May. Birney was unacceptable to antislavery Whigs and Morris to antislavery Democrats. Many of those who might be weaned away from their parties on the state level were distrustful of supporting a third party on a national level. Chase recognized the difficulty Birney's nomination posed. He sought delicately to substitute a less controversial figure of national prominence for him.[59]

Birney was willing to withdraw his candidacy. But after saying this, he criticized Chase's efforts to nominate individuals who were not original abolitionists. He objected also to emphasizing economic issues at the expense of the moral issue of slavery. Chase managed to have Morris withdraw. Birney, however, remained a stumbling block.[60] "I am tired," Chase wrote Giddings, "of the cap in hand policy. I am unwilling to feel myself and my opinions to be contraband articles in my political party only to be tolerated because not safely to dispense with [*sic*]."[61] Having made this indignant statement, Chase persisted in pointing out the value of a third party that would be strong in the legislatures of the free states and in Congress, "to check the ruinous measures of one party and aiding and carrying out the beneficial propositions of another, without any bias in favor of either." Further he reminded Giddings that he opposed a national convention of the Liberty party because such an event would be regarded "rather as a meeting of the national Anti-slavery Society than as a convention of the Liberty party."[62]

From those backers of the Liberty party in the East came stern warnings that Chase and Bailey were seeking to destroy the identity and the goals of the

Ohio party by merging it with one of the two major parties. Birney was so worried about this apparent drift that he asked Chase to explain the party's position to Gerrit Smith, who along with the Tappans was the principal source of abolition funds. Chase, who did not know Smith personally, jumped at the chance to establish a relationship and to explain his objectives.

In a long letter to Smith he denied that the Ohio party would "fall back" into either major party. But at the same time he said that "we think it not advisable to incur any unnecessary odium." There was sufficient ill-will already, sufficient false allegations that the party represented a union of church and state whereas "most of us in fact believe that political bodies have nothing to do with ecclesiastical organizations." But speaking for the Ohio party, he wrote that he would like to see the churches "purified" of their neutral or proslavery stance.

Chase acknowledged that public opinion in the free states believed abolitionist agitation had caused a defensive reaction in the slave states which had set back emancipation. He would combat that image through the press and through other means of persuasion. He emphasized that the Ohio Liberty party, while always adhering to eventual emancipation, would never advocate interference in the domestic affairs of slave states. "We prefer," he said, "to let the burden of devising the best mode . . . of negro emancipation in the slave states, rest upon those states." Wherever the federal government has the power over domestic institutions, however, it should resist the encroachments of "the slave power." At the same time the party should act positively in abolishing slavery in the territories and in the District of Columbia, where it would serve as an example to be followed by state action itself.[63]

More succinctly Chase wrote Lewis Tappan that he thought the position of the eastern Liberty men was too narrow. He wanted the Liberty party to act as a reform agent that would root out what he charged was "the corruption in the major parties and in the churches," thus forming a new party. This organization would reassert "old and familiar but long neglected and dishonored principles."[64] Chase's explanations, definitions, and rhetoric, persuasive as they were, failed to disperse the cloud that hovered over his intentions. The eastern leadership group still distrusted his motives. Chase recognized this unpleasant truth but with supreme confidence in his strategy resolved to make it more emphatic at the Liberty party convention in December 1842.

chapter 6

To Recognize the Distinctions

Chase's political fortunes were far from hopeful, but his family life had improved after spending almost four years as a bereaved widower. His youngest sister Helen had acted as his housekeeper and provided a buffer between Chase and the Garnisses, who doted on little Catherine Jane.[1] Chase maintained cordial relations with the Garnisses, though it was good to have his own household. During this lengthy, lonesome period his older sister Abigail Colby died. She was barely thirty-nine years old.[2] Abigail had been close to Chase. Of all his sisters, she was the best-educated and together with her husband had introduced Chase to the abolitionist circle in Cincinnati.

Shortly after Abigail's death, the youthful Eliza Smith caught his eye. It is not known where they met, but the young lady had a deeply religious turn of mind which Chase found appealing. Her family could not claim high social standing, but her father owned valuable property in Cincinnati and seems to have been in comfortable circumstances.[3]

When the Garnisses learned that he planned to marry, they feared that it would put a strain on their relationship, especially on the care of their grandchild. Garniss himself pleaded with Chase not to have little Catherine Jane present at any of the wedding festivities where she might be exposed to illness.[4] Chase and the eighteen-year-old Eliza Ann Smith were married in September 1839. Susceptible to his former in-laws' entreaties, he allowed his little daughter to spend a good deal of time with her grandparents, unfortunately with fatal results.

A scarlet fever epidemic suddenly erupted in Cincinnati three months after Chase's marriage, but the city's medical fraternity deemed the disease to be a mild infection. Reassured, Chase took no special precautions to keep his daughter clear of possible contagion. More or less isolated at home, she did visit her grandparents despite the fact that Garniss was quite sick with what Chase called "an affection of the throat." Cincinnati physicians diagnosed scarlet fever. On 24 January 1840 his granddaughter became violently ill; the symptoms of scarlet fever soon appeared. After a few days of painful suffering she died.

Catherine Jane was a lively, loving child who reminded Chase of his beloved first wife. She got along well with her stepmother who, in Chase's words, "returned her love with all a mother's warmth." He added in a highly personal letter to his friend Cleveland: "We were very happy in each other and I had sometimes to wonder if there was another family so happy as mine."[5]

Chase was again grief-stricken; the Garnisses were equally distressed at the sudden death of their only grandchild.[6] If this loss were not enough, Chase had to bear the strain and worry that his feckless younger brother William imposed upon him and the appearance in Cincinnati of his oldest brother Alexander, sick and penniless.[7] William had married a young St. Louis woman who was a skilled milliner and set up a household.[8] Briefly William seems to have minded his ways. But about the time Chase's daughter fell ill, he received a letter from Lewis F. Thomas, a St. Louis acquaintance, relating a dreadful tale. William's family was in desperate straits. Money that Chase had sent his brother had been squandered at the gambling tables and taverns. Some of her former clients in St. Louis were trying to help Mrs. Chase, who had been for some time renting a room from a poor black woman. During several of the coldest days of the winter she had no food or firewood. As for William, frequently drunk and disorderly, his bad temper got him into scrapes at riverfront grog shops.

Through a St. Louis clergyman, Chase doled out small sums to help support his brother's family.[9] Concerned about his brother, Chase wrote a friend in Alton, Illinois, where William and his family moved and received a reply giving more evidence of his brother's shiftlessness and continued alcoholism. William's wife was expecting another child and as usual the family was poverty-stricken. Chase continued to do what he could though William remained a constant drain on his emotional and financial resources until he died in 1852. As for Alexander, Chase provided him with a home until his death in March of 1847.[10]

When Chase's daughter died, Eliza was two months' pregnant. As her time for confinement drew near, Chase became increasingly concerned about her health, recalling with anguish the suffering and death of his first wife. For more than a week, Chase said, in late July, "I have neglected to frame any plan, and though I have continued to read with some diligence I have omitted several duties, through forgetfulness." After dinner that day Chase had a long conversation with Eliza, whom he called "Lizzie." Heavily pregnant, Lizzie was well aware how life-threatening her coming delivery might be. She spoke of her confidence in God and was prepared for death should it come. Chase was so moved that he went to his Bible and reread the latter portion of the 119th Psalm where David testifies that he had followed the Lord's commandments and asks for deliverance. This was the third time Chase had reviewed the psalm in addition to his regular Bible reading, usually an hour set aside each day.[11]

Chase returned home from his office on the muggy evening of August 12, to find Lizzie in labor. Chase insisted on sending for her mother and Dr. Rives, who was now the family physician. Mrs. Smith arrived first, followed by the doctor and Mrs. Flamen Ball, the wife of Chase's partner. Chase wandered about the house, frequently praying that God spare his wife and child. After four hours of labor Lizzie gave birth to a daughter. Mrs. Ball brought him the news at 2 a.m. that the mother and child had passed safely through the ordeal.

After Chase had seen Lizzie and the child, he went into the library and read "a few pages in [Dr. John] Eberle's book on children,—a judicious treatise," he remarked before retiring. "The babe is pronounced pretty," said Chase. "I think it quite otherwise." The parents had already agreed on a name: "Catherine Jane Chase."[12] Chase greeted the year of 1841 with sadness and satisfaction. He still lamented the loss of his four-year-old daughter Catherine Jane. Lizzie's recuperation from childbirth was slow. By January her health seemed pretty much restored. "She has been safely delivered of a little daughter," Chase wrote, "who lives to be our common delight." The family would call her Kate. Lizzie's recovery, however, was only temporary.

On a May night almost nine months later Chase and his wife had a long conversation on serious topics of a family nature. She was not well and spoke of death and their shared faith in God. Chase was concerned about her health, but did not think she was in any danger. They had resumed marital relations and though still suffering from intermittent fever, Lizzie became pregnant again in the fall. When a second daughter was born on May 30, 1842, Chase was not overly concerned about Lizzie's delivery. The baby girl they named Elizabeth lived only three months. Chase recorded her brief existence with a terse note he wrote in his "Family Memoranda" book on August 30: "Lizzie Chase, daughter of S. P. Chase and E. A. C. born May 30, 1842; died August 30, 1842."[13]

Chase had been extremely busy during Lizzie's second pregnancy. He had established an extended list of correspondents among Liberty party leaders and antislavery Whigs and Democrats. On any pretext he initiated correspondence with political movers and shakers of known liberal persuasion. In addition he was seeking to organize the Liberty party in Ohio.

On the evening of April 22, 1842, Chase entertained at his home his friend and collaborator Samuel Lewis, James G. Birney, then on one of his speech-making trips to Ohio, and several other Liberty men. Speaking for himself and for the eastern abolitionist leadership, Birney criticized what he said were attempts to separate the Liberty party from the tag of abolitionism and thus avoid the onus that name carried. "I specified," said Birney, "the course of the *Philanthropist* but more particularly that of the Columbus *Freeman.*"

Chase and Lewis were guilty of what Birney charged. Neither, however, sought to rebut him, but agreed wholeheartedly with his comments. Chase even volunteered to write John Duffy of the *Freeman* (an early convert to his political strategy) in most explicit terms not to publish any hint of separation.[14] Another Liberty party person who was present took the opposite view that the party should "wholly disclaim all connection and sympathy with the abolitionists." All the others spontaneously upbraided him for his insensitivity and his apparent rejection of a worthy cause in which so many selfless individuals and organizations were engaged simply because it was politically unpopular. Chase led everyone in his righteous condemnation, despite the fact that he was even then seeking covertly to expunge the abolitionist label from the Ohio Liberty party.[15]

While his letters do not indicate any abandonment of moral principles they do underscore an increasing yen for practical politics as he cultivated his personal ties with Democratic party powers in Cincinnati. His law practice and his brothers' difficulties also commanded his attention and he continued with church affairs, education, and community enhancement projects. He taught Sunday school, was a school visitor, a member of the board of newly established Woodward College, and a deacon of St. Paul's Episcopal Church.[16] Chase may have been a busy man, but apart from his law practice, all of his diverse activities were aimed at his own advancement politically which he invariably rationalized as contributing to the benefit of humanity and the glory of God.

That the birth and death of his third daughter warranted no more than two sentences in one of Chase's journals seems a rather unusual turn for such an emotional person. True he may not have had time to record his feelings; but if one considers his past practice of venting his grief one must conclude that Chase's innermost thoughts lay elsewhere.

As he grew older and more successful he seems to have taken married life for granted. Of course the birth and death of infants were commonplace events in those days before the sources of infectious diseases were understood. Yet Chase's excessive mourning of his first wife and child, his deep concern, as expressed fully in his diary, over his second wife's first pregnancy and delivery, were not evident over the second birth and death in the summer of 1842. Even though Lizzie was in poor health after her confinement, Chase commented infrequently on her condition. Nor did he react in his diary or in his letters when Dr. Worcester, a close friend who examined Lizzie, diagnosed her as having tuberculosis.

Through palpating, stethoscopic, and sputum examinations Worcester detected tuberculosis in the upper lobe of each lung, but saw no evidence of ulceration. He gave sensible advice, rather unusual in those days of primitive medicine—a plain nutritious diet, daily exercise in the open air, sponging the chest with tepid water every morning and an occasional mild laxative. No narcotics, the doctor warned. The governing principle was to be the improvement of her general health. Worcester's treatment would remain a standard regimen for tuberculosis until the advent of sulfa drugs and antibiotics in the late 1930s, almost a hundred years later.[17]

Shortly after Chase received this alarming information Lizzie became pregnant for a third time. On April 1, when she was eight months' pregnant she suffered premature contractions along with a paroxysm of coughing. The pregnancy may have hastened her tuberculosis infection, but as so often happened with this insidious disease, Lizzie rallied. There was no mention of any further complication.

Early on the morning of June 16, Chase went to his office as usual. A message from his wife asking him to come home interrupted his work. He found Lizzie in labor which lasted about four hours when another daughter,— "a little stranger," as Chase described her—"was ushered into the world." They named her Elizabeth after her mother and her dead sister. Despite her weakened condition Lizzie again made a fairly quick recovery, which Chase recorded for a week or so.[18]

Chase seems to have concentrated his attention on three-year-old Kate. He noted that she was dosed with spirits of turpentine followed by castor oil, a harsh laxative for a small child. Kate was a lovely child, though already showing signs of assertiveness that Chase sought to control by subjecting her to measured scolding, punctuated by object lessons of good behavior.[19] Apart from the few sentences he wrote in his journal during the first couple of weeks after little Lizzie's birth, he made no further mention of her or her mother for that matter. Chase records daily visits of friends and neighbors, books he read, sermons he heard, law business, and comments on his own health—"good and my appetite excellent and I am prone to eat too much at meals."[20] On July

24, thirteen months after her birth, Chase wrote another terse comment in his "Family Memoranda": "Lizzie Chase 2nd, daughter of S. P. Chase and E. Chase, born June 1, 1843; died July 24, 1844."[21]

Lizzie was in poor health, but the crisp fall weather seems to have brought on another remission. In late December she and her brother traveled by carriage to Columbus in easy stages.[22] Nor is there any further mention of his wife's illness over the next two months as she gradually became weaker from the developing tuberculosis infection.

In February 1845, he confided to his friend Cleveland that he thought Lizzie was dying and asked if he would look after Lizzie's fifteen-year-old sister for an undetermined stay. He added that she had an income of from $400 to $500 a year from her father's estate but that he would make up any difference.[23] Lizzie rallied again. Chase decided that she was well enough to accompany him on his usual summer business trip. In early July, Chase, Lizzie, little Kate, and his two sisters, Alice and Helen, headed north for Columbus, Cleveland, and points east. At Buffalo, however, Lizzie became desperately ill. Chase immediately canceled his appointments and returned to Cincinnati.[24] For the next two months Lizzie's health continued to decline. Bedridden, sleepless from constant coughing and hemorrhaging, her breathing gradually became more labored until she relapsed into a coma early on September 29 and died a few hours later.[25]

Again in his "Family Memoranda" Chase wrote the few lines that recorded Lizzie's death.[26] Five weeks later he did interrupt his busy routine to say, "I resume my journal after a long intermission, during which the saddest affliction has fallen upon me. I have recorded its details on separate sheets which with other intervening events I may yet note in this book." He never added any account of his wife's last illness, nor have the separate sheets he alluded to ever been found.[27]

At the time of Lizzie's death, Chase was preparing a lengthy pamphlet which he planned to give wide distribution not just among Liberty party leaders but also leading individuals in the major parties without respect to their views on slavery. Some were proponents of slavery, some ardent antislavery men, some moderate, and even some who had made no public expression on the issue. Included on his list were most members of the new Thirtieth Congress.[28] The pamphlet consisted of Chase's argument expanded and corrected in a case that had attracted national attention. It involved John Van Zandt, a local farmer, an abolitionist, and a member of Ohio's underground railroad, who had been charged with violating the federal Fugitive Slave Act.

The case began when a federal marshall served Van Zandt with a writ to appear before the district court of Ohio.[29] Chase and Thomas Morris, joint counsel, knew all the details of Van Zandt's involvement, which would certainly convict him of breaking the Fugitive Slave Law, yet they were still optimistic about the trial, which win or lose, would publicize the antislavery cause. In the light of the recent *Prigg v. Pennsylvania* decision, the Fugitive Slave Act superseded state legislation on the subject. Van Zandt's actions provided an excellent opportunity for Chase and Morris to challenge the statute and to reinterpret the fugitive slave provision of the Constitution.

The day after Chase had engaged in earnest and somewhat duplicitous conversation with Birney and other Liberty party members on April 22, about the direction of the Liberty party in Ohio, nine slaves crossed the river from Kentucky to Ohio and made their way to Walnut Hills near the Lane Seminary. John Van Zandt, a farmer who had left Kentucky some years before because of his hatred of slavery, met the small party of fugitives as he was returning to his home about twenty miles north of Cincinnati.[30]

Van Zandt had loaded his covered wagon with early spring vegetables on the 20th and the next day sold them at Cincinnati's Central Market.[31] He spent the night with a friend in Walnut Hills and set forth for home very early between 2:30 and 3:00 in the morning.[32] Just north of Walnut Hills, Van Zandt encountered the party of fugitives. One of their members asked him if he would convey them to Lebanon or Springborough, thirty to thirty-five miles north of Cincinnati.[33]

Two professional man hunters, Hargrave and Hefferman, tracked Van Zandt's movements because of his known sympathies and affiliations, waiting for him to make a move. Once Van Zandt accepted the fugitives, he asked one of their members to handle the reins and joined the others in the wagon.

They had proceeded some seven miles north of Walnut Hills and crossed into Warren County when Hargrave and Hefferman, both on horseback, planted themselves in front of the wagon. One of them dismounted and seized the reins of Van Zandt's wagon whereupon Andrew, the driver, and another fugitive who was riding with him jumped to the ground and made off. Andrew was never found but his companion returned voluntarily to remain with the group. By this time several other individuals surrounded the wagon. One of them asked Van Zandt if "he knew the colored persons in his wagon were not free." He replied, "They ought to be free." To another he said: "They are as free by nature as you are."[34] Hargrave and Hefferman, aided by others, whom they enlisted for small sums, rushed their prey across the river to Covington, Kentucky. Their owner, Wharton Jones, reclaimed them and paid the man-hunters $450 for their services.[35]

After the federal marshall appeared at Van Zandt's farm charging him with harboring fugitives, a violation of federal law, the old farmer made his way to Chase's office, where he explained his predicament. He asked Chase to represent him, doubtless pointing out that he was too poor personally to pay any legal fees. If Van Zandt's home indicated his financial condition, he was not so poor as he professed. His dwelling was a solid stone four-story structure with two chimneys at either end of a two-story wing and porch.[36] Chase dismissed the matter of payment because he recognized at once that in representing Van Zandt he would define the very approach he had denied he was following the night before. Such a case would help remove the stigma of abolitionist from Ohio's Liberty party and advance the claim that states' rights protected human liberty.

Chase was certain that antislavery opinion was on the rise in Ohio and he knew that the kidnapping of fugitives was generally repugnant to many of his fellow residents of Hamilton County. He had already earned the reputation of being the "Attorney General for Runaway Negroes," and he had been studying precedents in common law, British and American statute law, and the debates in the Constitutional Convention of 1787, edited by Jonathan Elliot. He had also made a close study of Madison's *Notes* and Yates's *Minutes*. Nevertheless, Chase decided to improve his standing with the Liberty party leadership by having Thomas Morris act as co-counsel. He too, agreed to serve without pay.[37]

Chase had crystallized much of his thinking on the technical legal aspects that the problem of fugitive slaves posed and that arose from slaves in transit through free states. Collateral issues were the legal implications from actions taken to help slaves escaping to freedom. Since his defeats in the Matilda and the Birney cases, he had become more assured than ever that he would secure partial vindication of his contentions. Judge Read's acceptance of some of his arguments a year earlier in the Mary Towns case gave him hope that fugitives had some protection in a free state.

Although Lizzie had been almost nine months' pregnant at the time, Chase had found the Van Zandt case too alluring to be turned down for family reasons. Of course he could always withdraw should Lizzie have any serious complications. More than relief over his wife's safe confinement and his newborn daughter's welfare prompted Chase's delight over their reasonably quick recovery.

Tempting also was the fact that the Van Zandt case would be a federal action and that Humphrey Howe Leavitt, the District Court Judge, and Justice John McLean on Circuit would hear the case. They were well enough known in Ohio and elsewhere to give Chase the additional visibility he craved. He must have assumed that the verdict would go against Van Zandt because precedents including *Somerset* and *Aves* either did not deal with fugitive slaves or held against them. But he thought he could develop a good foundation for appeal to the Supreme Court of the United States, where again his longtime friend McLean would be one of those sitting in judgment.

Chase was well aware of McLean's political instincts, his broad interpretation of the Northwest Ordinance, and his judicial rulings on slaves in transit while a justice of the Ohio supreme court. He knew also that McLean had concurred with the majority in the recent *Prigg v. Pennsylvania,* which held that the federal Fugitive Slave Law was constitutional and superseded state legislation on the subject. Yet Chase took due note of McLean's phrase that "in a state where slavery is allowed, every colored person is presumed to be a slave and on the same principle in a non-slaveholding state every person is presumed to be free without regard to color".[38] Chase also estimated the length of time the case would take before the U.S. Supreme Court might accept it for review. Considering the state of national politics, where the Tyler administration seemed bent on destroying its own party, much could happen over the next three or four years.

An old farmer, stooped and thin, Van Zandt was a pathetic figure. He could be expected to gain the sympathy of a jury, even an Ohio jury, which might be antiblack but was usually antislavery. Chase was much better prepared than he had been in the Matilda and the Mary Towns cases. As in his earlier fugitive slave trials Chase's main concern was not with the fate of the defendants. Of course he would seek acquittal, but he reserved most of his telling arguments and his display of learning for an appeal to the Supreme Court on the constitutionality of the federal Fugitive Slave Law. Much would depend on McLean's charge to the jury in the Circuit Court action.

Chase was now thirty-five years old, in his physical prime, a well-ripened lawyer whose years of systematic study and many appearances before the courts of Ohio had sharpened a formidable legal talent. He had conquered his initial shyness in public speaking and argument. Always sure of his own powers, self-critical to a fault, he had long since decided that if he were to make a name for himself, he must rely not on the humor and the folksiness that western lawyers used with such affect before country juries. Rather he would adopt a carefully cultivated, dignified bearing where his analytical skills and his intellectual precocity would influence judges and the charges they made to juries. Chase had also put on weight. In accordance with the presence he wished to project he made strenuous efforts to improve his posture and general appearance. The Chase who appeared before Judges Leavitt and McLean must have presented a striking figure, six feet two inches tall, big-boned and well-muscled, clean-shaven and immaculately dressed. The only outward blemishes were his near-sightedness which he sought to conceal by eschewing glasses in public and a tendency toward premature baldness.

When the case began Chase appeared to be in perfect control of himself and his material. Opening for the defense, he alternately faced the two judges and the jury, whose sympathy he sought to arouse. Initially, he asserted that Van Zandt had not been aware of the status of the blacks.[39] Utilizing the language of the Fugitive Slave Act itself he argued that Van Zandt did not "harbor" or "conceal" his passengers. He simply offered them a lift. Witnesses to the affair testified that although Van Zandt did not conceal the slaves he had to know they were fugitives. Morris joined Chase in successfully attacking their credibility.[40] They pointed out that the slave hunters had not taken the alleged fugitives before a federal judge or magistrate residing within the boundaries of the place where the violation took place, as the act required. Nor had the kidnappers given either written or verbal notice to Van Zandt that the blacks were fugitives.

Having thus offered a brief defense of his client against punitive damages, Chase banished Van Zandt and quickly moved to the higher and broader ground that had originally impelled him to take the case, the constitutionality of the Fugitive Slave Law. He raised all the points and precedents he had employed in the Matilda and Towns cases but much more elaborately, citing decisions made in slave states that the institution was local in character and protected only by state and municipal laws.[41]

He had refined his argument that the Ordinance of 1787 decreed freedom for residents of Ohio, quoting McLean's own decision and state law reinforcing that interpretation while ignoring any implications favoring slavery that might be drawn from the document. His contention here, a rather weak one, was that the fugitive slave provision in the Ordinance applied only to slaves escaping from the original thirteen states. Kentucky was not one of the original states.[42]

Chase's line of argument again emphasized the decisions of Lord Mansfield in the Somerset case and of Lemuel Shaw in *Commonwealth v. Aves*, both of which declared that any person brought to a free state or nation was conferred freedom irrespective of race or previous condition of bondage. Lord Mansfield had added that slavery could be introduced only by positive law, a point Chase had raised in the Matilda case.[43] Shaw explicitly excepted fugitive slaves from this dictum. In utilizing these precedents Chase relied on Mansfield and Shaw, whose opinions he cited out of context. The Somerset case supplied Chase with a precedent that insisted on due process, a factor not included in the Fugitive Slave Law. He quoted Shaw's comment that "slavery is a relation founded in force, not a right, existing where it does exist, by force of positive law and not recognized as founded in national right."[44]

Chase alluded to the positive law doctrine he had advanced in the Matilda case, but had not then, as he did now, cite his sources and elaborate upon them. He also relied on Shaw for his definition of the fugitive slave clause in Article IV of the Constitution. Chase maintained that the clause established only the principle of comity between states. It was for the states themselves to decide how they would handle fugitives, whether they be white apprentices or black slaves. The Act of 1793 was unconstitutional because nowhere in the enumerated powers of Congress was there a fugitive slave provision.

The primary purpose of the framers was to create a national government.

A secondary principle "was to adjust and settle certain matters of right and duty between the states . . . . The clause in relation to fugitives from service is nothing but a covenant or a contract. It had nothing, whatever, to do with the creation of a government, and it conferred no powers, whatever, upon the government created by other provisions."[45]

Chase made all of his now familiar arguments that the Northwest Ordinance conferred freedom on all residents in Ohio, and gave his restrictive definition of its fugitive slave provision. His voice rising and the tempo of his remarks measured, he said: "The very moment a slave passes beyond the jurisdiction of the state, in which he was held as such, he ceases to be a slave; not because any law or regulation of the state which he enters confers freedom upon him, but because he continues to be a man and leaves behind him the law of force, which made him a slave."

Chase's emotional appeal to natural right was made strictly for its value as publicity for him and for the Liberty party.[46] Only by the broadest implication was it relevant to Van Zandt's plight or the constitutionality of the Act of 1793. His comment did summarize in eloquent terms what would become free-soil doctrine and would influence the dissenting opinion in the Dred Scott case. "What is a slave?" he had asked rhetorically and then answered his own question: "A slave is a person held as property, by legalized force, against natural right. . . . The law, which enables one man to hold his fellow man, as a slave, making the private force of the individual effective for that purpose by aid of the public force of the community must necessarily, be local and municipal in character."[47]

Chase's learned three-hour argument drew upon the Bible, Shakespeare, Cicero, Madison's *Notes, Elliot's Debates,* and a wealth of state and national judicial precedents, yet he failed to move the jury. Rather, they accepted in the main McLean's charge and the argument of the attorneys who acted for the plaintiff, Wharton Jones. In charging the jury, however, McLean did agree with some of Chase's contentions.[48]

He told the jury that if the slaves had come into Ohio with Jones's consent or in any other way "except as fugitives from labor, and came into the possession" of Van Zandt, then the slave owner had no rights to reclaim them or to receive compensation for Andrew, the slave who escaped. More important, McLean accepted Chase's argument and reiterated his own position in the Prigg case that in Ohio and all free states every person is presumed free "without regard to color." The two judges also made their disagreement on the constitutionality of the Act of 1793, a matter of record so that Chase and Morris could appeal the verdict to the Supreme Court.[49]

Van Zandt was convicted on all counts and fined $1500. Morris now dropped out of the case, providing Chase with an opportunity to select a more impressive public figure as co-counsel, preferably one who was not an abolitionist or a prominent member of the Liberty party, but who was no truckler to the slavery interest. As soon as Chase learned of the verdict and the decision on appeal of the circuit court, he contacted William H. Seward and Thaddeus Stevens, who shared Chase's reputation as defenders of slaves. After some delay during which the cautious Seward weighed the political consequences of appearing as counsel in a fugitive slave case, he agreed to serve without pay.[50]

Seward was a better fit than Stevens. As governor of New York, the small, red-haired, large-nosed Seward was one of the more prominent Whigs in the North known to oppose slavery on a matter of principle. He had recently gained extensive visibility when he refused to extradite to Virginia three individuals accused of abetting the escape of slaves.

Seward and Chase had never met. But the New York governor had been one of Chase's choices to replace Birney as the presidential candidate on the Liberty ticket.[51] He was also one of the leading mainline Whig politicians whom Chase wished to cultivate. For whatever his protests to the contrary, when Birney or other Liberty party leaders taxed him with subverting the original aim of universal emancipation for political advantage, Chase always sought to place the party in a bargaining position with either of the major parties that would grant the more substantial concessions. He was careful to deflect any suspicion the abolitionist leaders might have regarding his ultimate intentions. Chase wrote Tappan in early February 1844 that he expected gains from Seward's cooperation in the Van Zandt case, "though I think he has lost much of his moral force by binding himself to Clay."[52] With their political antennae attuned to the political frequencies that were being broadcast after Polk's election to the presidency, Chase and Seward were unconcerned about any extended delay in the hearing of their case."[53]

On several occasions in the past at least one of the three—Seward, Chase, or the Kentucky senator James Morehead, who was acting for Jones—were in Washington and prepared to appear. Chief Justice Taney, however, who controlled the docket, saw to it that other cases took precedence. In some exasperation Seward noted that the Van Zandt case was numbered 78 and that the Court had reached only 55. He was dubious about whether he could be present at the next session of the Court.[54] Finally in mid-December, 1846, the Justices discussed Van Zandt in conference.

The impressive McLean—whose features resembled those of George Washington and whose bearing was just as reserved and distant with his colleagues—took the lead. He addressed all of his colleagues as they sat around the polished mahogany table in the court's cramped conference room, but he reserved particular attention to the Chief Justice, who as usual was smoking a black Spanish cigar.[55]

McLean's frosty dignity may have put off other members of the Court even in closed and intimate surroundings such as this, but they respected his industry, learning, and political connections. His opinion carried weight especially since his concurring decision in the *Prigg* case. "I proposed to them," he wrote Chase, "that you should be permitted to argue the case at the bar if you choose." After McLean completed his remarks, Taney objected to any oral argument.[56] As a matter of course, the Chief Justice reserved to himself the disposition of cases. He cited the general rule the Court had adopted on hearing cases that the same constitutional question would not be argued again in Court.[57] He thought that the Prigg case had settled all constitutional points on that aspect of the Fugitive Slave Law, and he carried all of the Court except McLean with him.

Obviously in some heat McLean wrote that he "would never again make any estimate or *guess* on what the court will do." He advised Chase to file a written brief rather than go to the expense of traveling to Washington, only to find that the Court would not hear him or any of the other principals in the case.[58] Chase had already prepared such a document. Over the years since he had appeared for Van Zandt in the crowded Cincinnati courtroom, he had improved it significantly with additional precedents and strengthening of various points.

The 108-page brief Chase published was a cogent, scholarly argument which at times reached rhetorical brilliance. "No Legislature is omnipotent," he wrote in burning phrases. "No Legislature can make right wrong; or wrong right. No Legislature can make light, darkness; or darkness light. No Legislature can make men things; or things men." The brief must surely rank as one of the more penetrating examinations of the legal and constitutional anomalies that slavery presented in a republic where human rights were restricted to privileged whites who saw no contradiction when they trumpeted democracy and virtue to the world.[59] It was of no help to Van Zandt, who died during the lengthy court proceedings, or his heirs, who had to pay the fine when the Supreme Court upheld the circuit court decision.

Seward's argument was also an able one, but confined to the technical aspects of the case, though he too declared that slavery "is an open violation of the personal rights guaranteed to the people by the constitution." Ever the careful politician, his rhetoric was far more subdued than Chase's. After all he had much more to lose if he indulged in ringing antislavery phrases.[60] No mean judge of political personalities, Seward saw in Chase a useful surrogate in the West and sought to enlist his services. Still somewhat naive in the ways of practical politics, Chase on his side tried to entice Seward into the Liberty party.[61] Other antislavery Whigs—notably, Joshua Giddings, Washington Hunt, and Cassius Clay—now recognized Chase's leadership role in Ohio's Liberty party.[62]

While the Van Zandt case was making its slow way through the crowded docket of the Supreme Court, Chase acted as counsel for the defendant in another important slave case, that of *State v. Hoppess*. On the evening of January 22, 1845, Chase interrupted his customary evening reading and hurried off to the office of Judge Read, who had so often in the past presided over Chase's fugitive slave cases.

Chase explained what facts he had about a slave named Samuel Watson, who, with the agent of his master, Henry Hoppess, had been traveling from Arkansas to Virginia and had spent the day in Cincinnati. Their steamer, the *Ohio Belle*, was moored to the landing at Cincinnati when Watson disappeared. Hoppess found him standing on Front Street about 100 yards from the landing. Someone, probably an abolitionist who kept a close watch on the river traffic, saw Hoppess take Watson back to the steamboat. That individual reported the incident to Chase, who immediately sought a writ of habeas corpus from Read, who was now a state supreme court judge.[63] Read issued the writ which was served on Hoppess before the *Ohio Belle* cast off.[64]

Read disliked Chase as a person but respected him as a lawyer. A Democrat and very much the politician on and off the bench, he responded to what he understood was public opinion; and after considerable study of the state and federal fugitive slave legislation had come a long way since his successful rebuttal of Chase and Birney in the Matilda case.[65] Though Chase had lost his natural-rights argument in the Mary Towns case, Read had agreed with Chase's argument that slavery was purely a local institution. Chase was hopeful that he would convince Read in the habeas corpus hearing and rescue Watson from slavery.

Watson represented a far stronger defense than Van Zandt. He was clearly not a fugitive from a slave state and when arrested he was on the soil of a free state. This time Chase was concerned primarily with Ohio law. He had compelling evidence that the *Ohio Belle* was tied up to the Cincinnati landing when Watson left the vessel. Nor had Watson resisted when Hoppess forced him to return to the steamboat. There had been no escape from a slave state.[66] Chase alluded briefly to the Constitution and the Fugitive Slave Law when he raised the issue of Fifth Amendment procedural rights for Watson as a person. He followed this up with a persuasive argument on riparian rights, contending that Ohio jurisdiction reached to the middle of the river. He even traced his boundary to the historic low-water marks on the north shore of the Ohio river to support his claim. But the principal thrust of his argument as it had been over the past four years was that slavery was a local institution, merely a certifiable creature of municipal law. Freedom was a national concept and universal in character.

Chase made a compelling argument, but he underestimated Read's hairsplitting qualities and his ambition to maintain his reputation for legal scholarship.[67] In answering Chase he admitted that slavery was an oppressive, morally unjust institution maintained by force. It did grievous harm to America's free institutions. But because of the compromise on slavery in the Constitution and because of "peculiar circumstances" that he defined as the racial charac-teristics of the black minority as opposed to the white majority, it had to be tolerated until the states themselves got rid of it presumably through coloniza-tion.

Read then addressed himself to what he regarded as the crux of the case, the navigation of the Ohio River. He made no allusion to riparian rights, nor to the fact that Watson had been brought to Ohio voluntarily and that he was therefore not a fugitive. He had changed his mind, however, since the Matilda case about the right of a master to bring a slave into Ohio and keep him enslaved. In support of this argument the learned judge sought to make a precise definition of where slavery ended and freedom began on the Ohio River. Comity as well as freedom of navigation placed the entire river from bank to bank under the jurisdiction of both free and slave states. As far as being tied up to the Ohio shore, Read—in an exercise of implied powers worthy of Alexander Hamilton,—found this simply a means to accomplish the end of open navigation. Watson was returned to slavery, but Read's accep-tance of Chase's opinion that slavery was a local and artificial condition which inflicted a moral wrong was a distinct victory for the antislavery cause.[68]

Chase was disappointed in the result. He had hoped the court would free Watson. The black community leaders in Cincinnati overlooked the eccen-tricities in Read's opinion and even poor Watson's fate. They deemed, and properly so, that the broader points of Read's conversion were of great impor-tance to their security in Ohio and a future at least partially free of legal and judicial stigma.

In a touching gesture A. J. Jordan, the pastor of the African American Baker Street church, collected enough donations from his impoverished con-gregation to present Chase with an inscribed sterling silver pitcher for his part in the Hoppess case. The sacrifice was patent because it must have cost members of his small congregation many days of labor.[69] In accepting the gift Chase made a memorable reply: "Every law on the statute book," he said, "so wrong and mean that it can not be executed, or felt, if executed to be oppres-sive and unjust, tends to the overthrow of all law, by separating in the minds of the people, the idea of law from the idea of right." "I am only one of a great number," he continued, with more emotion than he usually displayed as he spoke to his small audience of earnest blacks dressed in their best clothes, "who adopt the opinion that in a country of democratic institutions, there is no reliable security for the right of any, unless the right of all are also secure.[70] True democracy makes no inquiry about the color or the skin, or the place of nationality or any other similar circumstance of condition." Having thus ex-pressed himself so eloquently, he could not let this occasion go by without spreading the word as far and wide as he could. He had the brief speeches and his own reply recorded and printed as a pamphlet for distribution not just to abolitionist and antislavery men and strict party leaders in the North but also in the South.[71]

Chase gained much from the Hoppess and the Van Zandt cases. His association with Seward was an important event. Seward was a national figure, Chase's reputation was largely local. Even in abolitionist circles he could not claim more than a passing acquaintance with leading individuals outside Ohio. The reaction to his pamphlets, sent to a good many members of the Thirtieth Congress (not failing to omit such southern firebands as Robert Barnwell Rhett of South Carolina and of course John C. Calhoun) spread his name for good or for ill far and wide.

Chase no doubt expected to fail in his attack on the Fugitive Slave Law, since he knew how reluctant the Supreme Court had been over the years to declare an Act of Congress unconstitutional. His judicial failures, however, were personal victories for him and for the antislavery cause in the North.

He had even found his connection with the abolitionists financially profitable. When Birney left for the East, Lewis and Arthur Tappan turned over all of their substantial western business to Chase.[72] He was careful however, not to alienate his other Cincinnati business commitments.[73]

Chase had sustained many personal tragedies during the 1840s, but at the same time he had become not just a prosperous western lawyer but one of the leading, if not the most articulate antislavery voices in the nation. His rise had been rapid yet not without arousing suspicions and sustaining reverses. He had gained some important, lasting friendships and had incurred some lasting enemies in his persistent drive to gain stature and status for himself as an incident to furthering the antislavery cause.

chapter 7

Climbing the Slippery Pole

On a overcast morning in late November 1845, Chase rose early, "as usual of late before sunrise."[1] After washing and dressing, he went to the library and began again to write in his diary, as he said, "after a long intermission, during which the saddest affliction has fallen upon me." He was referring to Lizzie's death and with these painful thoughts in mind he breakfasted with his sister Alice and little Kate. As soon as Vina, the black maid, cleared the table, Chase reached for one of his Bibles, kept always close at hand, and sought a lesson that he thought would help relieve his somber mood.[2] He indulged little self-pity when he chose the book of Job but there was also the hope of deliverance after Job's confession of his sins and his acceptance of God's will.[3] Little Kate "listened and seemed to be pleased, probably with the solemn rhythms," said Chase; "for she certainly can understand very little. . . ." Vina had taken her place at the table, but not the other two household servants, both of whom were Roman Catholic, "and one of them a German unacquainted with our language," as Chase remarked.[4]

Apart from his personal afflictions, Chase was finding life much more comfortable. The new omnibus appeared before his door at regular hours, carrying him downtown to his office and returning him home. In the winter after a heavy snowfall obstructed the streets, a large passenger sleigh replaced the coach.[5] His law practice was prospering. He had several capable and

enterprising law students who did most of the routine clerical work, performed research tasks, and pushed Chase's emerging political career.

The way had not been easy as Chase picked his way among the various
factions in the abolitionist movement. Four years had passed since he had seen
a political future for himself and the cause of human rights in capitalizing on
what he shrewdly detected as the beginnings of a broad-spectrum reform
movement. He had devoted considerable time in his work-crowded schedule
to making himself known not only to western and eastern abolitionist leaders
but to newspaper editors and politicians of both major parties in Ohio and
elsewhere.

Once Chase decided to pursue antislavery politics, he laid out his personal strategy with care and precision. He translated his undoubted literary
talent into captivating promotional campaigns. He employed his legal and
logical skills on fugitive slave cases that earned respect even from those who
watched his burgeoning career with some skepticism about his vaunted moral
principles. These doubts had arisen from his untiring efforts to convert the
Ohio Liberty party into a political force that would embrace other issues
besides emancipation and thus enhance its bargaining power with the major
parties in what had become very close elections.

And above all as an inborn publicist he was much concerned with purging
the Liberty party of its abolitionist label. He had early recognized that particular tag to be a detriment to any successful political effort. But he denied, when
pressed, that disassociation of the Liberty party from the abolitionist name was
in any way a lessening of commitment to the goal of emancipation.

Chase had early decided that a third party would never achieve either his
own political agenda or the social justice program he envisaged. He leaned
toward the Democratic party rather than the Whig as the best vehicle for
reform. "Equal rights and equal privileges for all men," he wrote Giddings,
"is forever in the mouths of all democrats. Will you say this is pretense and
hypocritical profession? Why not rather impute it to the ignorance of the
proper application of these principles to slavery as it exists in this country."[6]

Chase's assessment blended both the practical and the ideal. Cincinnati
was solidly Democratic; but equally important was a belief, confirmed after
years of intense study, that Jeffersonian idealism was basically much more
appropriate to the abolitionist objective than the Whig program of economic
development through national planning, which a strong central government
would devise and execute. Even his views on slavery comported with Jeffersonian states' rights doctrine. His arguments on fugitive slave cases consistently
proclaimed slavery to be the creature of local custom and law.

Congressional supremacy, which the Whigs preached, violated the federal compact when it involved the central government in supporting the internal slave trade and the institution of slavery in the District of Columbia, the

territories, and on the high seas. Slavery must be "denationalized," or divorced from national public policy.[7] Unlike William Lloyd Garrison and other like-minded abolitionist leaders, Chase insisted that the Constitution was not a proslavery document. A stout opponent of the decision in the Prigg case, Chase argued that the fugitive slave clause in the Constitution was subject to state power, not federal; in addition, without noting any inconsistency in his basic premise, he argued that the Fifth Amendment, a limitation on federal power, not state, guaranteed judicial procedural rights to all persons, which included blacks. For Chase always demanded a proper constitutional setting.[8] By now his political instincts were sufficiently developed for him to understand that presenting such arguments in legal briefs was quite different from asserting them in party platforms where one could be branded subversive in contravening majority public opinion on a given topic.

National politics seemed to present Chase and others of antislavery convictions with a sterling opportunity. But at the same time it made their approach even more difficult with the abolitionist leadership, because of fears that the Liberty party would be sacrificed on the altar of expediency. With some trepidation Bailey, Lewis, and Chase continued to hew to their line that the Democracy offered a better opportunity for eventual emancipation than the Whiggery.[9]

Chase's efforts to remove Birney from the Liberty ticket ran into a storm of disapproval from eastern leaders such as Joshua Leavitt, editor of the influential abolitionist paper the *Emancipator*. From that encounter and kindred experiences he learned that one must be very careful with abolitionists, who dealt in moral absolutes. They were a querulous, changeable lot, suspicious and with good reason of political parties. Coming from an evangelistic tradition—many of them Protestant ministers—they were accustomed to exhortation and moral persuasion through the religious press, pamphlets, books, and lectures. Most considered themselves missionaries carrying God's will to a heathen nation.[10] Leavitt, a corpulent, excitable ex-Congregational minister, mirrored the inconsistency of the eastern Liberty party leadership. Leavitt made no secret of his contempt for Chase's program, which he considered an abandonment of principle for political gain. Nor was Chase as tactful as he might have been in dealing with Leavitt.[11] And a year later as the presidential campaign of 1844 was just getting under way, Leavitt was as defiant as ever in rejecting Chase's tactics. Leavitt wrote Birney, "I have no thought of yielding a hair's breadth to the supposed designs of C[hase]. We will not consent that our former nomination should go for nothing at the bidding of a clique of Cincinnati lawyers."[12]

Despite Birney's nativistic posture and his record as a loser, Leavitt and others persisted in blocking Chase's determination to cast off Birney and to make the Liberty party a stronger force nationally.[13] Birney's son William joined a chorus of opponents to Chase and Lewis's ill-fated attempt to change the name of the Liberty party to that of the "True Democrat."[14]

Whether Birney should continue to lead the party was not the only problem for the Cincinnati realists. Wealthy Gerrit Smith, a major source of revenue for the abolitionist movement, was openly critical of any move that would involve the party in social and economic questions not directly related to slavery.[15] But more dangerous to the future of the Liberty party in Chase's mind were not the strictures of Leavitt or Smith but what he detected to be a latent strain of disunionism, even anarchy, that permeated abolitionist thought and strategy.

He was deeply troubled by the clause in the platform adopted at the Liberty Convention in Buffalo that openly committed all party members to disobey the Fugitive Slave Law that the Supreme Court had recently upheld in the Prigg decision. The convention approved a resolution of John Pierepont, a Unitarian minister, that declared the clause to be "utterly null and void as forming no part of the constitution of the United States, whenever we are called upon or sworn to support it."[16] Chase had opposed Garrison's stand that the Constitution was a proslavery document not to be considered a lawful instrument. But just when the Liberty party was gaining an extended organization in the free states, it was most discouraging to find what seemed to be a majority of its members upholding many Garrisonian ideas. Chase took some comfort from the former Lane Seminarian, now antislavery lawyer Henry B. Stanton, who wrote: "Garrison is an artful Jacobin and a genuine Robespierre with few followers."[17]

Chase had already come under fire for his address to the Southern and Western Liberty Convention, held in Cincinnati on June 11 and 12, 1845. Before an enthusiastic audience that crowded into the Tabernacle, Chase had dissected both of the major parties. But his obvious leaning toward the Democrats and his references to the "true Democracy" acted as a tocsin to the sensitive ears of leading abolitionists and also outraged many antislavery Whigs.

He had been careful to distinguish between the leadership of the Democratic party and its principles. "Our reverence for Democratic principles is the precise measure of our detestation of those who are permitted to shape the action of the Democratic party," he told the 2000 delegates, who represented all of the midwestern states and territories as well as western Virginia, Pennsylvania, Kentucky, Rhode Island, New York, and Massachusetts.

As Chase surveyed the dense crowd of perspiring delegates he knew he had chosen the right track when he made his painful decision in 1841. The enthusiasm he could feel rising from the audience that greeted his remarks on "true democracy" temporarily carried him away to indulge in a partisan attack on the Whigs. Whatever the Whig party concedes to antislavery, he declared, "must be reluctantly conceded. Its natural position is conservative. Its natural line of action is to maintain things as they are. Its natural bond of union is regard for interests rather than for rights." Strong words these, anathema to antislavery and traditional Whigs everywhere. If taken as it was by many eastern abolitionists as well as those in the state it provided clear evidence of Chase's partiality to the Democratic party.[18]

For the time being, it appears that he had given up on Giddings and other antislavery Whigs in the state after several years of careful cultivation. He seems also to have been willing to risk his always tenuous relationship with the eastern abolitionist leadership, whose political inclinations if anything leaned toward the Whig party. Seward was just one of the important antislavery Whigs who described Chase's political animadversions as unjust. In a thoughtful but measured rebuke not without a partisan tinge, he explained that "there can be, but two permanent parties. The one will be and must be the Locofoco party. And that always was, and is, and must be, the slavery party. Its antagonist of course must be, always, as it always was and is, an anti-slavery party *more or less. . . .*"[19]

No doubt the political scene as it was unfolding during the summer and fall of 1845 had influenced Chase's swing toward the Van Buren Democracy. He could not have known the extent of the so-called New York Barnburner's antipathy toward the new Polk administration. But from his reading of the press, both northern and southern, he could see that the Barnburner or Van Buren wing of the Democracy had been thrust aside at the party's convention,which nominated Polk for the presidency. Silas Wright, Van Buren's faithful lieutenant, had rejected the vice presidential nomination, but had then apparently united the party in New York. He had been nominated and elected governor of the Empire State. The New York vote had been crucial to Polk's victory over Henry Clay. And Wright's candidacy had been largely responsible. To Chase's disgust, Birney had again been the Liberty party candidate in 1844. He polled 65,000 votes, which may have helped defeat Clay in New York. But the Liberty vote in Ohio had not come up to Chase's expectations. And he blamed Birney and the eastern Liberty men for the disappointing result.[20]

The makeup of Polk's cabinet, which had excluded partisans of both Calhoun and Van Buren, had been public news for some time. Chase was well aware that both statesmen were disenchanted with the new administration. Annexation of Texas had been a fait accompli despite opposition from Clay and Van Buren, both of whom feared sectional repercussions.[21] The Liberty party had opposed annexation in the face of majority public opinion, which supported territorial expansion under the slogan of Manifest Destiny. During the summer of 1845 the new Polk administration began moving toward a settlement of the Oregon territory boundary with Great Britain. More significant for those who feared the expansion of slave territory were moves made by the administration to extend the Texas boundary westward and to acquire California from Mexico.

In Ohio Chase had been seeking indirectly to make the Liberty party more attractive to Democratic leaders. He did not attend the Liberty Convention at Columbus in early 1844, but he wrote the resolutions that were adopted. One of his associates reported that the editor of the Columbus *Ohio Statesmen*, Samuel Medary, Van Buren's chief spokesman in the state, was present. "He treated us with respect," said Chase's correspondent, "has contempt for J.C. Calhoun, and his southern followers. Look out for a revolution next year in the Democratic ranks—they must abandon the south or loose [*sic*] the north."[22]

Rebuffed by antislavery, or conscience Whigs, as they were called, Chase sought vainly to capture Democrats such as Jacob Brinkerhoff, a well-respected congressman from Richland County just south of the Ohio Western Reserve. Brinkerhoff, too, resisted Chase's blandishments. But Chase's tilt toward the Democracy seemed to be the right tactic when John P. Hale, a Democratic congressman from New Hampshire, publicly denounced the annexation of Texas and the Polk administration's policy of expansionism at the expense of Mexico. A strong-featured, humorous, fiercely independent lawyer, Hale had thought he could capitalize on the growing antislavery mood he sensed among his constituents. Franklin Pierce, then chairman of the New Hampshire Democratic Central Committee, and his associates—all stalwart defenders of the Polk administration—quickly moved to silence Hale.

In a series of moves that gladdened Chase's heart, a group of antislavery Democrats met and formerly nominated Hale for reelection. Framing what they called an "Independent Democrat" ticket, they denounced the annexation of Texas and the administration's policy of territorial expansion in the Southwest. Liberty party men everywhere applauded these actions. Joining with the recusant Democrats, the New Hampshire Liberty party endorsed Hale.[23] Since New Hampshire congressmen were elected at large, Hale polled enough votes to block one of the regular Democratic candidates. Even ultra-abolitionists of the Garrison stripe now urged support for Hale. The quixotic Leavitt in his paper the *Emancipator* echoed the general attitude of eastern abolitionists that Massachusetts and other eastern states must be "New Hampshireized." The New Hampshire Liberty party now did what Chase had always secretly hoped the Ohio party would do: it merged with the Hale Democrats in an amalgamation that styled itself the New Hampshire Alliance.[24] There followed some hard bargaining with the Whig establishment. The Alliance agreed to support the Whig candidate for governor in return for that party's support of Hale's election to the U.S. Senate, which was assured when the Alliance swept the New Hampshire legislature in March, 1846.[25]

Chase lost no time in introducing himself to the independent Democrat. Before any formal merger of the Liberty party and the antislavery Democrats in New Hampshire, Chase wrote the triumphant Hale: "Now it seems to me quite useless to have two organizations, contending for the same objects. I am well persuaded moreover that the Liberty party can accomplish little as such, except indirectly."[26] Ever the wily politician Hale was in no hurry to establish communications with Chase. His letter remained unanswered.

Meanwhile Joshua Giddings was making a series of speeches in New England that called for an antislavery union of all political groups with himself at its head.[27] It was galling for Chase to have Giddings coopt his own program. A further frustration came when the former Whig congressman Edward S. Hamlin launched a new journal in Cleveland which he named the *True Democrat,* the very name Chase had suggested and which had brought such criticism from eastern Liberty men. In a conversation with Theodore Foster, editor of the Michigan Anti-slavery Society's paper *The Signal of Liberty,* Hamlin boasted that the Ohio conscience Whigs were using Chase's strategy.[28]

If these obstacles were not enough, Chase decided that Cassius Clay, the colorful Kentucky editor and politician, could not be trusted either. An overly sensitive and tactless Chase read what he decided was a slur on the Liberty party and on blacks in Clay's *True American.* Chase wrote Clay an indignant letter complaining about his attitude only to receive a sharp reply defending his independence as an editor while denying that he meant to impugn the Liberty party.[29] Chase's thoughtless criticism of an editor and an editor whom he had counted on to lead the struggle for emancipation in the slave states would seldom be repeated in the future. This particular transgression can be explained only by the unsettling activities of Giddings and the antislavery Whigs in the state aimed at himself and his allies Samuel Lewis and Gamaliel Bailey.

Few aspiring reformers and politicians were as knowledgeable as Chase about the power of the press, about the importance of publicity for himself and for the cause. In fact he was already involved in discussions with the abolitionist poet John Greenleaf Whittier, Lewis Tappan, and the Reverend Amos A. Phelps, the anti-Garrisonian agitator, regarding the establishment of an antislavery paper in Washington.[30] Bailey and Joshua Leavitt were the most prominent candidates for the editorship.[31] There was no doubt about Chase's choice. Bailey and his wife Margaret were among Chase's closest friends in Cincinnati. He enjoyed his evenings at their home or his where the discussions ranged over the problems of the world, and especially Daniel O'Connell's Repeal movement to gain Irish home rule.

Chase and Bailey were in complete agreement on strategy for the Liberty party, not just in Ohio but in other states. And as no mean writer himself, Chase admired Bailey's clear, epigrammatic style, his courage, and his industry. Moreover, Bailey was in financial straits. He had renamed his paper the *Herald Philanthropist* and made it a daily while still retaining its weekly edition. His subscription list and advertising revenue, always precarious, did not warrant the expansion. The Tappans helped out with a subsidy as did other well-to-do antislavery men including Chase. But it was simply not enough. Overwork and concerns about his family's welfare were undermining the high-strung editor's health, all of which was apparent to Bailey's principal backers. A change of scene, a national arena for the display of his undoubted talents, was certainly in order.[32]

Leavitt was also experiencing financial difficulties and was anxious for the post. However, he had so embroiled himself in the factional disputes that bedeviled the antislavery cause that many considered him too controversial for such an important post. His frequent absences from his editorial desk had diminished the quality and the influence of the *Emancipator*. The Tappans, who would be the principal backers of the new paper, resented Leavitt's abrasiveness and his caustic remarks in the *Emancipator* about their position on the moralistic concerns of abolition.[33] An exasperated Lewis Tappan asked rhetorically, "How, for instance, can Garrison and Leavitt unite . . . considering the bitter spirit that prevails?".

When Bailey was offered and accepted the editorship of the new paper, which was to be named the *National Era,* Leavitt was deeply disappointed. Concerned that the *Era* would cut into the circulation of his paper, he sought Chase's support for taking over the *Herald Philanthropist*. Chase was sympathetic to Leavitt's plight but wary about his position on political action in Ohio. He was not encouraging to the distracted editor.[34] Stanley Matthews, a trusted assistant, good journalist, and dedicated antislavery man, assumed the editorial direction of the paper.[35]

In January 1847 Bailey moved with his family to Washington, where he took charge of the *Era.* Well financed, the new publishing venture would emphasize the realistic approach to abolition that he and Chase had long sought for the Liberty party. In addition Bailey would score slavery as a national, not a sectional problem. The *Era* would carry this message to the South, where both men hoped it would encourage public opinion in the slave states eventually to throw off the yoke of slavery.[36]

Bailey's move came at just the right time for launching an antislavery daily in Washington. The Mexican American war, which most Whigs, many Van Buren Democrats, and the Liberty party opposed, was proving a serious political problem to the Polk administration despite the successes of the American army in the field.

On a hot August evening six months earlier, an appropriation bill to provide funds for negotiating a peace settlement with Mexico was before the House. A portly Democratic congressman from Pennsylvania, David Wilmot, gained the floor and offered a rider to the bill which would exclude slavery from any territory that might be gained from Mexico.

For some time a small group of northern Democratic congressman had been looking for a proper time to present such a provision which they had purposely copied from Jefferson's Ordinance of 1787. The group consisted of Van Buren Democrats who were as much motivated in embarrassing the Polk administration as they were in containing slavery. Wilmot had been a member of the group, but without consulting them he introduced the proviso that ever after bore his name, to the irritation of his colleagues, who had hoped to call it the Jefferson Proviso.[37]

The appropriation bill with Wilmot's rider passed the House, but was defeated in the Senate by a combination of proslavery southern votes, both Democratic and Whig, and administration Democrats. From then throughout the next decade, it was repeatedly offered and passed in the House and as repeatedly rejected by the Senate.

Thomas Jefferson may have been the actual author of the proviso, but Wilmot and others working with him were indebted to one of Chase's basic arguments for free soil first broached in the Matilda case and underscored in all of his subsequent fugitive slave defenses. The Van Buren Democrats' acceptance of the proviso and their break with the conservative administration Democrats in New York during the summer of 1847 was the major move that confirmed Chase's strategy for the Liberty party.

Silas Wright, Van Buren's closest political associate and since the ex-President's retirement from active politics leader of the Barnburner Democracy in New York, had been defeated in his bid for reelection to the governorship. Wright had openly supported the proviso. His defeat, the result of sabotage from the conservative, or "Hunker" wing of the Democracy, brought into the open the smoldering feud between the two factions. Wright's death in August of 1847 not only deprived the Barnburners of their gifted leader but widened the rift in the party. The Hunkers seized the initiative when the New York Democrats met at Syracuse for their state convention shortly after Wright's death. Outvoted by the Hunker majority, the Barnburners walked out of the convention. Under the leadership of John Van Buren, the ex-President's magnetic son, plans were undertaken to make the break final at yet another convention to be held at Herkimer in the fall of that year.[38]

Meanwhile Giddings and Hamlin had not been particularly successful in their efforts to concentrate Ohio antislavery sentiment in the Whig party. In the post-Wilmot euphoria, Giddings invited Chase to attend a Whig-inspired antislavery conference in Columbus. Chase turned him down with the most direct disclosure of his political preferences he had yet made. He could not he said accept a Whig antislavery platform "because I do not concur in Whig views of public policy either as an antislavery man or as simply a citizen." Chase declared that he opposed a high tariff, a recharter of the now defunct Bank of the United States, (a whig priority), or any system of government support for corporate banking.[39]

Without consulting Giddings Chase spoke with Tom Corwin, leader of the Ohio Whigs and a national figure of eminence since his spectacular speech opposing the Mexican War. Corwin explained that the Whig party could never accept Giddings's platform without losing its southern wing. Satisfied that Giddings had little backing from mainline Whigs, Chase was now ready to meet with him.[40] Giddings was not so easily caught, nor would he forgo his Whig affiliation.[41] Sensing that he would remain within the Whig fold, Chase decided that he had little to worry about the Liberty party being coopted, or of Giddings wresting the initiative from him.

Chase was more sure of himself than he had ever been since he had decided to stake his political future on the antislavery cause. He was right with himself and right with God, always important to Chase. Whatever he may have felt about the Mexican War and the Polk administration he could not deny that the economic depression which had ground on for almost ten years had finally worked its way out. Cincinnati was booming again and Chase's income had improved along with it. His income from his law practice alone for the first six months of 1845 was $3,405 after office expenses.[42]

Less than a year after Lizzie's death, Chase married the dark-haired, dark-eyed Sarah Belle Dunlop Ludlow. Belle, as she was called, was the daughter of James C. Ludlow, an abolitionist and one of the city's leading citizens. She was also the niece by marriage of John McLean which brought Chase into a family connection with the politically minded justice before whom he had appeared so many times in fugitive slave cases. Chase had also supported McLean's political ambitions from time to time and was even now prepared to back him for the presidency on a Liberty ticket.

Chase and Belle were married on November 6, 1846, at the McLean's residence on Fourth Street. In an outward display of his new affluence and his never failing help for family members in need he employed his nephew Ithamar Chase Whipple to supervise the construction of a large brick home with two wings, near the McLean residence.[43]

Of all Chase's wives, Belle's interests and tastes were more in the artistic than in the religious mode. She had considerable talent for sketching and for watercolor painting, which also revealed a sense of humor and a whimsical view of the world. One must conclude that she lightened Chase's all-too-serious approach to life and brought a bit of laughter and lightness into his heavy work-driven existence. There were fewer references of intensive self criticism and of supplication to an angry God in his journals and letters to intimate friends.

Belle, who quickly became pregnant, seemed to be in reasonable health, which eased Chase's mind after the illness connected with childbirth that lead to the death of his two former wives. But Chase experienced three tragic episodes during the early spring of 1847 that renewed a sense of grief. His older brother Alexander, who had looked after Chase when just a lad on his journey west, became seriously ill in early March of 1847. Diagnosed with a serious heart disease, Alexander, who had lived with Chase for some time, continued to decline and became bedridden.[44] Three weeks after the diagnosis, Chase rose and in what had become routine with him went to his brother's room before breakfast. "He seemed much as usual but weaker," Chase observed. He had not finished breakfast when he heard Alexander "breathing hard." "Hastened upstairs—at first thought him asleep, but soon began to fear he was dying . . . the result proved too well founded; he expired in a few moments at about nine o'clock. . . ."[45]

An even greater blow to Chase was the death of his dear friend and family physician Dr. Noah Worcester. Not a month after he had diagnosed Alexander Chase's fatal disease, he became desperately ill with tuberculosis, which apparently had been in remission for some time.[46] Within five days he was dead. "I never knew a franker or sincerer man," said Chase. "Emphatically he was faithful but true. I love him as a brother; and have now no friend left for whom I feel the same attachment."[47] Chase had many acquaintances and some good friends, but few really close relationships with men or with women for that matter. Over a long, busy career, only four men and two women apart from his wives were really close to Chase: Worcester, who died when Chase was still a young man; Cleveland and Hamilton Smith, college chums, one a fine classics scholar, abolitionist, and academic, the other a successful businessman in Louisville; and Gamaliel Bailey, the intense, gifted editor first of the *Philanthropist* and then the *Era* in Washington. Of the women, Susan Walker, a Cincinnati bluestocking and confirmed abolitionist, shared many of Chase's innermost thoughts. Charlotte Eastman, widow of a Wisconsin congressman, enjoyed a near physical relationship with him later in life. Cold, dignified, distant in many ways, once he had thrown off his apparent diffidence Chase could be a very warm and even humorous companion with his small group of close friends.

And always he was a devoted family man not just to his own children and wives but to his extended family, which included in-laws from all three marriages. Seventeen days after Dr. Worcester's funeral, Edmund Smith, his brother-in-law from his second marriage, whom he had helped financially and had counseled in various ways, also died of tuberculosis.[48] As Chase had noted a few weeks before Edmund's death, "He is much wasted by consumption and cannot survive very long."[49] Surrounded as he was with this most communicable, insidious disease, Chase seems never to have been infected. He did have occasional bouts of malaria, suffered from headaches, and complained of numbness in his head from time to time, but, considering his work schedule and his peripatetic life, he enjoyed good health.[50]

chapter 8

"Free Soil, Free Labor and Free Men"

Chase's social life and to some extent his legal business had become secondary to a passion for politics. After the Wilmot debates, antislavery gained in acceptance. The division in the Democratic party and the end of the Mexican American War fueled the movement. Chase now bent every effort to head off any Liberty party nomination for the Presidency in 1848. Most of the eastern leadership except Bailey and Lewis Tappan were insisting on a nomination. Their favorite candidate, if not Birney, was John P. Hale, recently elected to the United States Senate from New Hampshire and one of the few distinct antislavery members of that body. Chase tried to dampen the Hale enthusiasm indirectly. He pointed out to his eastern colleagues that the new senator's ability to further antislavery goals should not be jeopardized by formal identification with the Liberty party.[1]

Meanwhile Chase busied himself extending his own and the party's influence in the press. When Cassius Clay, the bombastic antislavery editor of the Lexington, Kentucky, *True American*, enlisted in the army during the Mexican American War, Chase managed to place an associate, John C. Vaughan, as editor of the paper.[2] Vaughan was a peppery South Carolinian, a lawyer who had become a zealous opponent of slavery.[3] He had been associ-

ate editor of the largest Whig paper in Cincinnati, the *Gazette*. There, however, his editorial talents and his devotion to the Liberty party had been effectively muzzled. Judge John C. Wright, the editor of the *Gazette*, was an
"ultra conservative" to antislavery men.[4] At the *Herald Philanthropist*, editor
Stanley Matthews had not regarded his as a permanent job. He was anxious
to forgo the burdens of the paper and to resume his law practice with a
sideline in politics.[5] Well aware of Matthews's state of mind Chase was on the
lookout for a long-term replacement. Vaughan ranked high among the possibilities.

Another important goal of Chase's overall strategy was to advance his
standing and that of the Liberty party among the antislavery Whigs everywhere, but especially in Ohio where political rivals included Giddings, Benjamin Wade, his brother Edward, and mainline Whigs such as the old veterans
Corwin and Ewing.

For the time being Vaughan could prove a key player in Chase's strategy.
Nominally an antislavery Whig, Vaughan had links with the party establishment in Ohio and with Clay's small but increasing group in Kentucky. It had
not been lost on Chase that eastern Liberty party men such as Gerrit Smith,
Charles Sumner, and others of Whig background had been strong supporters
of Cassius Clay. To them he represented not simply an antislavery bastion in
the western slave states, but also a vigorous defender of Whig principles.
Despite Clay's openly racist stance Chase could play the political chameleon
when it seemed useful, though he always shrouded these color shifts in a
raiment of principle.[6]

Such a battle-scarred political veteran as Joshua Giddings, to whom
Chase relayed these sentiments, was "glad to see that we agree substantially
on all points made." Giddings considered Chase to be a Whig, his talk of "true
democracy" and "equal rights" merely rhetorical flourishes, until direct evidence of Chase's dealings with the Democratic leadership abruptly brought
him to his senses.[7] But even then Chase couched his political leanings on
Jeffersonian principles in the language of reform. To the end of his career he
sought to move the political process on to a broader course that would embrace not just emancipation for the slaves but emancipation of the free
workingmen and farmers from what he perceived to be elitist sponsored
special interest groups.

In this early phase of his political jousting, Chase's preference for the
Democratic party coincided with his understanding that the Declaration of
Independence, the Northwest Ordinance, and their links to the Constitution
formed the original intent of the Founding Fathers. His residence and his law
practice in Cincinnati meant that his politics had to be palatable to the Democratic machine in the city and the state yet not so overtly partisan as to alienate
rich Whiggish clients. In particular, he must reach out somehow to the Whig

leadership in the state and to important Whigs such as Seward and Washington Hunt in New York and Charles Francis Adams in Massachusetts, not to mention Gerrit Smith, the Tappans, and other Liberty party men in the East.[8] "Shall we stand apart," Chase asked Charles Sumner, "Whigs, Democrats and Liberty men and neutralize each other? Or shall we unite. I am for union. I care nothing for names (except abolitionist) all that I ask for is a platform and an issue, not buried out of sight. . . ."[9] In the post-Wilmot environment Chase had determined that the time was ripe for expanding the free-soil idea in the West and in the South. *"Laus Deo!"* he wrote Washington Hunt in February, 1847, noting that the proviso had again passed the House of Representatives with an increased majority. "It is a great triumph of freedom and right."[10]

Chase sent Vaughan on a fund-raising trip to New York and Massachusetts. The youthful editor met with Seward, Sumner, Greeley, and other antislavery Whigs as well as Liberty party men.[11] Vaughan's trip was successful in raising the necessary funds to maintain Clay's *True American.*[12] But after a short period the free-wheeling Vaughan moved to Louisville where he edited and published the *Examiner,*[13] an antislavery Whig paper. Finally he settled in Cleveland to assist Hamlin in publishing the *True Democrat* until Chase brought him back to Cincinnati.

In seeking to hold together the Liberty organization in Ohio under the unremitting pressure exerted by the established parties, Chase had worked diligently inside as well as outside the state to forestall a national convention that would make a Liberty presidential nomination. He was quite certain the New York Barnburners would launch a Free Soil ticket after their rebuff at Syracuse at the hands of the Hunkers, who had gained control of the Democratic party convention. His assumption was further confirmed when the Barnburners met at Herkimer, New York, in October, 1847, where they emphatically endorsed the Wilmot Proviso. They made no nomination but Chase believed they would.

That the Whigs would nominate the popular Mexican War hero Zachary Taylor at their convention in Baltimore seemed a foregone conclusion. Taylor was a southerner, a planter, and a large slaveholder. Antislavery Whigs were already being thrown into confusion, and Chase was facing a painful dilemma. Would the Whigs as a national party break apart on a sectional basis? Would the revolt of the New York Barnburners expand beyond the borders of the Empire State?[14] National politics were in such a flux that it seemed more imperative than ever for the Liberty party to adopt a wait-and-see attitude.

Liberty party leadership had overruled Chase on the national convention issue. He now adopted a fallback position: defer the planned convention at Buffalo, make no nomination for President and Vice President, let Hale establish himself in the Senate before adding to his burdens with a Liberty nomination.[15] "I am still clearly of the opinion that we ought not to nominate this fall," he wrote Lewis Tappan. "The opinion is strengthened by the probability that Mr. Hale will be our candidate. By a nomination this fall we shall rob him of a great part of his moral power in the Senate, and perhaps make ourselves inconveniently responsible for his acts there."[16] At the same time Chase was in touch with Hale. "I wish you would to go into the Senate," he said, "as an Independent Democratic Senator, occupying very nearly the same relation to the Democratic Party, on the antislavery side of it, as Calhoun does on the pro-slavery side. . . ."[17] But Chase's homilies had slight impact on the eastern leadership. Hale, it was reported, would accept the nomination though reluctantly.[18]

In the late spring of 1847, Chase had concluded that the Liberty party would never be an effective political instrument. He knew that there were more antislavery men in the Whig party than in the Democracy. But at the same time he bemoaned the fact that Whig programs were "mere expedients."[19] Chase had enough trouble trying to circumvent the earnest efforts of several important Liberty leaders to nominate him for the vice presidency.[20] To an anxious politician who was despairing of a future for the Liberty party, such a losing proposition on a losing ticket, while it might bring brief publicity to him, could do nothing other than tarnish the career he had planned.[21]

With no feelings of confidence Chase, Stanley Matthews, and Samuel Lewis set forth to attend the Buffalo convention under the gray skies of an October day. His spirits were not improved by the miserable accommodations and sleeplessness he had to endure enroute. Everything went well from Cincinnati to Springfield, but then they endured a seven-hour stage ride to Bellefontaine, only 36 miles away. When Chase and his associates arrived there at 12:30 a.m., the only accommodation they could find was a crowded, "miserable" tavern, where they were compelled to sleep on the floor. "Some charitable people had compassion on me," he related, "and lent me a comforter and a pillow; and I spread the comforter on the floor and put the pillow on the back of a chair turned down and covered myself with my cloak and got on as well as I could."[22] The weary travelers finally reached Sandusky, where they were happy to find berths on the *Lexington*, understood to be the best and most comfortable lake steamer for points east and Buffalo.[23]

Physical arrangements for the convention were better than most similar meetings Chase had attended. And the weather also cooperated. It was bright and sunny when the Chase group found its way to the "Tabernacle," a huge tent especially made for religious revivals and shipped from Cincinnati. There they found 140 accredited delegates and another hundred or so "voluntary" delegates, the whole representing all of the northern states. To a professional politician the assortment of antislavery extremists of the "one idea" persuasion was daunting—evangelical ministers, those who wanted a nomination and those who did not, those who favored John P. Hale as the nominee and those who backed Gerrit Smith, those who would ban slavery everywhere and denounced the Constitution and those who looked to the Constitution as a means of fighting slavery. Into this motley assemblage Chase plunged.

He bore with him a sheaf of practical proposals. Active in the various conferences that were held outside the main tent, his ideas on strategy for the most part met with little support. Henry B. Stanton and Lewis Tappan, hitherto responsive to Chase's pragmatic posture, joined forces with the mercurial Leavitt to block him on the postponement of nominations. They and their followers did stand with Chase in beating back a resolution that reached the floor calling for emancipation everywhere in the states, the territories, and the District of Columbia. Accepting his defeat on the subject of nominations, Chase reluctantly agreed to support Hale and his old friend Leicester King, who had been nominated for Vice President. At least there were no Pierepont resolutions this time.[24]

Chase appears to have been concerned that Gerrit Smith and his extremists would break away from the party. Or, more harmful to the future, Smith could withhold his financial support or use it to support yet another antislavery faction. In a printed letter addressed to Chase and circulated widely Smith threatened just such a move after chiding him for blocking the convention resolution calling for abolition of slavery everywhere in the nation.[25]

Chase remained in the East for a week or so conferring with Liberty party leaders and antislavery men from both parties, visiting relatives in Lockport, and seeing clients.[26] That he was able to be absent for more than six weeks underscores the confidence he had in his partner Flamen Ball. After his eastern sojourn he left for another extended period in Columbus, where he went to defend fellow lawyer Francis D. Parish for violating the Fugitive Slave Law. Chase lost the case, as he had so often before. Parrish had to pay a $1000 fine.[27]

Presumably Belle wrote him about family affairs, but none of her letters for this period survived. Of course her infant daughter Janette Ralston, who was born on September 19, required constant attention and she herself was convalescent. Curiously Chase's correspondence with his wife made little mention of the new daughter whom the family would call Nettie. But Chase was anxious about Kate. "Tell little Kate," he said, "she must be very particular about keeping herself perfectly clean, never forgetting her teeth morning or evening."[28]

Back in Cincinnati, Chase found that most leading members of both major parties were clinging to their respective organizations and were ignoring the slavery issue. Samuel Medary, the hard-bitten Democratic editor of the Columbus *Statesman* and a Van Buren supporter, was swinging over to Lewis Cass, a party regular. The tears Medary claimed he had wept at the news of

Silas Wright's death now seemed more of the crocodile variety.[29] Chase had hoped that Medary, who was counted as the "dictator" of the Democratic party in Ohio, would bring the entire organization behind the Barnburner rebels in New York. He and close associates in Columbus had been cultivating Medary for some time. Chase found some legal business to do in Columbus when the Democratic convention assembled there in early January, 1848.[30] He tested the waters at the convention, fishing for any support among the delegates for the Wilmot Proviso. He soon discovered that the convention as a whole had little interest in containing slavery, or as he put it to Belle, will probably give the proviso "the go by."[31]

Chase's principal private contact with Medary and with others of the state Democratic leadership was the young, highly emotional but brilliant lawyer from Steubenville Edwin M. Stanton. Stanton, a graduate of Bishop Chase's Kenyon College, was obviously impressed with Chase, his intellectual and social background, his fame as a lawyer and a scholar of jurisprudence, and his ideas about the Democratic party and slavery.[32] Stanton stood in well with Medary and was a close friend of the Democratic traditionalist Clement L. Vallandigham, a newspaper editor and a successful lawyer.[33]

It did not surprise Chase especially during the winter of 1847–48 that Stanton's ties with the traditional Democracy were overcoming his antislavery views. But it was painful to hear after so many conversations in Chase's hotel room in Columbus and the letters that had passed between them.[34] Equally discouraging was the attitude of Jacob Brinkerhoff. An original supporter of the proviso, he bluntly informed Chase that he would remain with the Democratic party.[35]

As far as the Whigs were concerned, it was cold comfort to Chase that his uncle-in-law John McLean was finding the proviso to be useless in preventing the spread of slavery to the territories.[36] After the drubbing Chase had taken at the hands of the learned justice in the Parrish case, Chase was not impressed with McLean's antislavery credentials.[37] He had to respect McLean's standing with the Whigs, however, and his importance as a possible makeweight against Giddings in the state.[38] McLean also enjoyed considerable popularity in eastern Whig circles.[39] One thing was certain in Chase's mind. The Liberty party should reserve its nomination of Hale and King until after the conventions of the major parties so as to protect its independent status. And noting that Hale was neither known nor trusted in Ohio, Chase began a quiet promotion of McLean should a Liberty nomination for the presidency become necessary.[40]

Chase had made a short visit to Washington, where he had several long conversations with McLean. These satisfied him that the justice "was nearer right than any so prominent man of the old parties I know."[41] Even Hale's warm supporter, Joshua Leavitt, admitted that the senator "is less familiar with the facts of slavery than some of the old soldiers . . . not so thoroughly identified with the Liberty party as I might wish in his feelings. . . ."[42]

To gain postponement of the Liberty nomination Chase began a cautious approach to Giddings's prominent supporters, especially Edward S. Hamlin, editor and publisher of the *True Democrat* in Cleveland. He had sounded out Hamlin on calling a Liberty or People's convention in June right after the conventions of the major parties. Hamlin was positive and noted that the Wilmot Proviso was the only distinct issue for the campaign of 1848.[43]

Bolstered by this advice Chase acted quickly. He published a call for a "People's" convention to be held at Columbus in June, signed among others by Stanley Matthews and Samuel Lewis, and sent it forth to all known antislavery men in the state irrespective of party.[44] Significantly and purposefully, Chase omitted any mention of the Liberty party as he bid for broad antislavery support that would meld with the action of the Barnburners in New York. At the same time he would not dismiss his Liberty party connections or backing.

As he suspected politicians such as Brinkerhoff on the Democratic side refused to sign the call; nor would Joseph Root, an antislavery congressman from Ohio and Joshua Giddings on the Whig side agree to any nonparty convention.[45]

In late May the Democrats nominated Lewis Cass and William O. Butler, a Kentuckian and a minor war hero in the War of 1812 and the Mexican American War. Jacksonian stalwarts, both were exponents of "popular sovereignty," or "squatter sovereignty," as its traducers called it. Their solution to the slavery question was to let the inhabitants of a given territory decide for themselves whether to support or exclude slavery.

Cass's stand as expressed in his public letter to Tennessee senator A. O. P. Nicholson went against those free soilers like Chase and the Barnburners who held that Congress had plenary powers over the territories and must exercise them for freedom. Southern extremists such as Calhoun likewise opposed Cass's plan. They insisted that the national government must protect slavery wherever American sovereignty extended. When the Democratic convention in a vain attempt at compromise admitted both the Hunker and the Barnburner delegations from New York, assigning each half a vote—thus nullifying New York's say in the nominations—the Barnburners walked out.[46] As anticipated, the Whig convention in Baltimore nominated Zachary Taylor and Millard Fillmore, a New York straight-line Whig for Vice President. The platform stressed typical time-honored Whig themes, but was silent on the slavery extension issue.[47]

After their bolt from the regular Democratic convention, the Barnburner leadership decided on a convention to be held at Utica, New York, on June 22, 1848. Several leading antislavery men in Ohio and elsewhere advised Chase to postpone his convention until after Utica. Benjamin Tappan voiced his concern, arguing that the Ohio convention would then be in a better position to support the Utica candidate.[48]

On June 9, John Van Buren himself asked Chase to have the convention meet a day after Utica.[49] Van Buren assured Chase that the Barnburners would nominate a free-soil candidate. He recommended that the Columbus convention name a full electoral ticket and call a delegated convention in July or August to decide whom the free-soilers would support.[50]

Quite apart from the logistics concerned in changing the date Chase was wary of Van Buren's intentions. He felt he must protect himself against any imputation that the Ohio antislavery movement was subject to the dictation of the New York radical Democrats. He refused to change the date, but decided that one of his close associates should be present at the Utica convention. And he arranged for a meeting in Cincinnati after the Columbus convention at which the decisions of the Utica convention could be considered.

Chase was acting as shrewdly as any veteran of Martin Van Buren's Albany Regency. He was hopeful that if the Barnburners did nominate at Utica, the candidate would be someone who would run well with both conscience Whigs and Proviso Democrats. Chase still wanted McLean on the ticket, if not in first place at least for the vice presidency. His ideal ticket at this time was McLean and John Van Buren, a nice balance of West and East, Democrats and Whigs.[51] He was still exerting as much pressure as he could command to have Hale withdraw his Liberty candidacy.[52] Hale had always been a reluctant candidate. Finally he wrote Chase on June 14 that he was ready to withdraw if a union of all opponents of slavery extension could be managed.[53]

Chase realized that he was risking the loss of Liberty party support not merely in Ohio but in New York and Massachusetts.[54] Lewis Tappan, so often a supporter of Chase's strategy, was deeply distressed at Chase's call for a free-territory convention. "How could you, my dear sir," asked Tappan, "sign your name to such a call? How could Mr. Lewis and Mr. Matthews? Are we not bound to Mr. Hale and bound to the Liberty party?"[55] Nor could Chase expect significant defections from the Ohio Democracy.[56]

Speaking for the Whigs, William H. Seward remarked that the Barnburners will "save this state [New York] for us." Ever the prudent politician, he amended this statement in the same letter by asking his friend Thurlow Weed, "if the temper around me is at all like that of New England and Ohio and Indiana, what is to save us in those regions?"[57] Horace Greeley was more perceptive than Seward in judging public opinion, as Chase would eventually learn. "I have now waited twelve days," he wrote Giddings, "for such demonstrations of free soil sentiment as ought to have followed the Baltimore and Philadelphia nominations. The truth is there is no deep devotion to principle among any large portion of the American people."[58]

Aware that traditional party lines would probably hold, Chase neverthe-less was determined to push forward with his coalition of free soilers even if this meant dissolving the Liberty organization in Ohio. He had been heart-ened by the response to his call, which he estimated was returned with 3000 names.[59]

As he had drafted the call for the Columbus convention, so he wrote the resolutions, gave the principal address, and, in short, dominated the Colum-bus meeting where over 1000 antislavery men gathered on June 20, the date he had set. "Our convention," he wrote Hale, "was one of the largest, most intelligent and most enthusiastic and most resolved political assemblies I have ever attended in the state." He admitted that few proficient politicians or leaders of the two major parties attended. Yet the very next day Chase took the final step of advising the Liberty party delegation to bury their differences with the Democrats and the Whigs and join in a common effort to halt the expan-sion of slavery. Chase's inspiring address, the impassioned remarks of George Hoadly, Jr., one of Chase's young law partners, and other speakers elicited enthusiastic acceptance. The Liberty party in Ohio to all intents and purposes had ceased to exist as a distinct organization.

Chase carefully avoided any imputations that the free soilers in Ohio were simply the clones of the New York Barnburners. His actions at Colum-bus belied his intent, however. In effect he committed the free soilers to support the Utica nomination if one were made. He must have been dismayed when he learned on June 22 that Martin Van Buren would be the candidate. Yet he did not voice any misgivings at the ratifying convention that was held in Cincinnati on June 24. Before an audience of about 250, he spoke in gener-alities, denouncing Taylor and Cass and only alluding to Van Buren in passing as "the honest insistent champion of liberty." The major burden of organizing the meeting and reading the resolutions was passed on to Hoadly. Even though the tone of the proceedings was not as enthusiastic as he had hoped, he had hitched his personal fortunes and his plans for combatting slavery to the Barnburners. There was no turning back.[60]

Chase still hoped that he could persuade John McLean to be a candidate, that Martin Van Buren would not be a nominee, and that Hale would withdraw.[61] He already had the authoritative, seemingly unequivocal com-ment of Samuel Tilden, the cautiously astute New York lawyer and second only to John Van Buren and Benjamin F. Butler in the Barnburner leadership, that they would stand by the elder Van Buren at Buffalo. But concerned about free soil in Ohio and the hostility of his old Liberty party friends to Van Buren, Chase needed at least a good showing for McLean at Buffalo.

The perpetually ambitious McLean had toyed with the idea of control-ling the free-soil movement, which he recognized "was growing stronger . . . with a fortunate organization I am inclined to think Ohio and the other western states may be carried." But in the end he resisted Chase's pleadings and refused categorically to lend his name to the Buffalo convention.[62] Chase and his little network of activists in Ohio had no choice but to support Van Buren. They were comforted with Van Buren's public statements supporting the proviso and with Butler's assurances that, if elected Van Buren would not veto free soil for the District of Columbia.

Early in August, Chase, Belle, Kate, the infant Nettie, and a nursemaid set forth for Buffalo. On arrival Chase went directly to a Buffalo hotel, while the family proceeded on to Lockport, twenty miles away, where they would stay with Chase's brother Edward.

Chase was well aware, after years of urbane contention, that vocal and monied members of the Liberty party and associated abolitionists who formed the Liberty League considered Chase's free-soil position a betrayal of abolition's aims. Even Justice McLean criticized the proviso in terms that cast doubt on some of Chase's most telling arguments. Slavery, McLean said, as Chase had declared many times, was a local institution, and any national legislation either for or against slavery was inherently unconstitutional despite the territorial clause in the Constitution.[63] Needless to say Chase regarded such a position as a mere quibble, though on occasion he would denounce the Missouri Compromise as largely the product of "Dough Face" northern politicians who bowed to southern demands on similar grounds.

Chase had to take seriously anticipated attacks on his and Bailey's approach which he would make more palatable, but not too palatable to the white supremacist Barnburners. For the abolitionist audience, the proviso would be cast as a preliminary move on the road to eventual emancipation. But that distant goal could be achieved only through lawful means and with the gradual assent of the slave states themselves. Meanwhile the territories, the District of Columbia, the high seas, and the domestic slave trade where Congress had the power to legislate would be reserved for free white labor. These were the arguments he had emphasized and would utilize again and again in his dialogue with the more radical emancipationists.

For a neophyte organization which still had not affirmed itself as a political party the free territory leaders had done a good job of spreading the word in the press and at local meetings. When Chase arrived in Buffalo a day or so before the convention's opening he found the great revival tent was being put up in the courthouse square to accommodate an anticipated 10,000 people. The imposing Universalist church nearby had been acquired for the meetings of accredited delegates, or "conferees," as they were listed.

Chase and Hoadly visited with Butler, John Van Buren, and Preston King, the shrewd, fat, and cheerful congressman from northern New York and one of the best tacticians in the House.[64] Chase and Hoadly now learned how sensitive the New Yorkers were to the language of any platform that would emerge from the convention. Since conscience Whigs in the person of Charles Francis Adams, Joshua Giddings, and Richard Henry Dana, Jr., were delegates, the radical Democrats feared a platform that raised the old questions of a Bank of the United States, federally funded and managed internal improvements, a high protective tariff, and the like. They were also concerned about the "one idea" Liberty Leaguers and those extremist Liberty party men who regarded the Wilmot Proviso as a betrayal of moral purpose and national rights for all irrespective of race or color.

When Chase walked over to the church the next day he found an estimated 450 conferees who promptly elected him president of the convention. From his vantage point at the lectern and surveying the group which he learned came from eighteen states, and included representatives from three slave states, Chase must have experienced a thrill of expectation before he got down to business.

He had arranged for Preston King to address the "conference," with the intent that King would interpret the resolutions that Chase had written so as to reassure the New Yorkers. King performed this task to perfection. After elaborating on the free-soil theme, he mentioned the need for homestead legislation—popular in the West—cheap postage, and economy in government. His round face glistening with sweat, King left the platform amid a storm of applause, having raised the emotions of the audience to a fever pitch. Chase took this opportunity to gain support for his resolutions with a minimum of vocal opposition.

Various attempts that the Liberty Leaguers and their allies made to rush through nominations, adopt a platform, and authenticate conferee credentials were defeated handily. On a voice vote the convention gave almost exclusive powers for framing a platform to the committee on resolutions. And chairmen of the various delegations were authorized to present authentic lists of official conferees. The general view of the assemblage was that after a platform had been reported and accepted then the vote would be taken for nominees.

Joshua Leavitt and Henry B. Stanton for the Liberty group, Chase for the Wilmot men, Preston King, John Van Buren, Tilden, and Butler for the Barnburners made up an informal platform committee. They met privately and worked out a deal that effectively scuttled the Liberty party and the Hale candidacy.[65] In return the Barnburners agreed to a platform that Chase had devised which was in more precise and specific language than the same points King had made. Two major changes were a resolution calling for a revenue tariff and a pledge that Van Buren's nomination must be made unanimous if possible.[66]

August 10 dawned hot and humid. Now the great tent was jammed with people representing all sorts of political persuasions and of course many of the idle and curious. Charles Francis Adams, son and grandson of Presidents, a

balding and stocky figure resembling his father, had been elected presiding
officer of this mass convention. Considering the assemblage, steamy atmosphere, noise and confusion, he managed adroitly to maintain a semblance of
order as orator after orator worked up the crowd.

Meanwhile, the serious work was being accomplished in the church. The
slight, nervous, but eloquent Benjamin F. Butler read the resolutions, letting
stand a closing phrase that Chase had written and that he thought "magnilo-
quent."[67] It brought the conferees to their feet in a surging torrent of emotion.
That rousing phrase, pleasing to the ear, would become not only the major
theme of the campaign but would be explained in political vocabulary for years
to come: "Free Soil, Free Labor and Free Men." The atmosphere in the tent
was even more electric as the sweltering multitude cheered each resolution
which Adams shouted out. And finally when he came to the end and in
measured tones repeated Chase's slogan, the crowd went into a frenzy. Even
the normally laconic Adams was caught up in the emotion of the moment. He
said later that he had never witnessed such a scene.[68]

After acceptance of the platform, the conferees at the church began the
process of nomination. Obviously there was a strong undercurrent of suspicion about Martin Van Buren and his previous role as the preeminent northern man of southern principles. McLean and Hale still had followers among
those who were not privy to the deal that had been made with the Barnburners.

Several conferees insisted on knowing about the availability of the various
candidates. Chase, speaking from the lectern, withdrew McLean's name from
consideration. Hale and Van Buren were now the only candidates. Chase
recognized Benjamin Butler, who spoke at length about Van Buren's virtues
and his dedication to free soil, which included the District of Columbia. As
arranged the energetic Henry B. Stanton gained the floor. But instead of
presenting the case for the reluctant Senator Hale, he said that he had permission from Hale to withdraw. To the roar of "Vote! Vote! Vote!" Chase called
for an informal ballot beginning geographically with Maine. The result was
244 votes for Van Buren, 183 for Hale. Giddings had 23 votes and Charles
Francis Adams 13.

Ignoring Stanton's withdrawal of Hale's name, the Liberty conferees
stood by him. It now befell Leavitt and Stanton to convince their Liberty
colleagues to vote for the ex-President. They met with Lewis and with other
Liberty leaders at the rear of the spacious area and managed to convince them
to cast Hale aside. The corpulent white-maned Leavitt, conscious of his role
in the proceedings, strode slowly to the lectern, which Chase turned over to
him. Exerting all the power of a voice conditioned by his years in the ministry,
Leavitt withdrew Hale on behalf of the Liberty party. He ended his brief
speech with the quaint phrase that the Liberty party was "not dead but trans-

lated," and moved a unanimous vote for Van Buren.[69] The voice vote that followed was as "unanimous as possible." In a manner of speaking the pledge had been redeemed. As a concession to the conscience Whigs who had supported Van Buren, the Convention nominated Adams for Vice President.

Chase had been tempted to push himself for the post, but his good sense asserted itself. He made no move to be a candidate. The mass meeting in the tent greeted the slate with the same enthusiasm it had voiced for the platform. There were complaints, of course. Lewis Tappan was very bitter, but Chase was pleased at the outcome and at his own role. He was in a much better frame of mind at the end of his journey than he had been at the beginning. He spent some time in Lockport and the surrounding area with his family for a brief rest.

Chase realized that he had suddenly leapt from relative obscurity to national prominence. Even those who opposed his free-soil convictions praised his conduct as chairman of the conferee's convention. His reputation as a dignified and judicious lawyer was complemented by the poise and confidence with which he dealt with national figures and seasoned political veterans such as Benjamin Butler and John Van Buren.[70] What they did not know at the time was that Chase, despite his noble rhetoric, had a mental reservation regarding the Free Soil party. Its objectives proved far too narrow for him. "I for one," he said three years later, "never dreamed of building up at Buffalo a mere free soil party; I had hoped and supposed that a platform of democratic principles would be occupied by a Democratic party with sufficient breadth and scope to take into regard all the great interests and obligations of the country." Free Soil to him was simply the reagent to purify the Democracy of its slavery connection and of its ties with powerful vested interests.[71]

There was one more chore and that was almost as important as the work he had done for the convention. He must stump the state for the new Free Soil party not just for the political candidates but for the state election. Chase's total experience in campaign speaking had been limited to a few speeches in nearby towns during the 1844 campaign and two or so in the Columbus area during July 1848.[72] To be sure he had made a number of lengthy addresses to large audiences at political meetings, his stirring remarks to the Free Soil convention being the must recent example. But extemporaneous comments to audiences which ranged from mid-morning speeches to farmers and day laborers at village crossroads to afternoon and evening performances before leading citizens in larger towns and cities were not the same thing.

Chase had to alter his style—direct, pungent, humorous for one group, serious, analytical, historical for another—not an easy task for such a self-conscious speaker. Problems with travel and with scheduling would be ever-present especially in the remote areas of the state. Chase had done circuit riding but most of his cases were either at the local and county courts or the federal district court in Columbus. The physical not to mention emotional demands of stump speaking in the concentrated time-span of a campaign could not be taken lightly. And except for his law students and partners and his small network of supporters, neither the manpower nor the money to mount a formidable campaign existed. In the enthusiasm that followed the Buffalo convention, Chase and others misread the grass-roots popularity of Free Soil.

Chase left Belle and the children at Lockport. He began his campaign in Ohio a few days after the Buffalo convention.[73] John C. Vaughan, who had moved to Cleveland, and James A. Briggs, a Cleveland businessman, lawyer, noted orator, and like Vaughan a former Whig, joined him on the campaign trail.[74] Chase opened his campaign at Empire Hall in Cleveland, Wednesday evening, August 16.

The next stop was Painesville, thirty miles away. Briggs supplied the buggy and drove with Chase on one side and Vaughan on the other. It was a close fit for the three large men. Briggs, an incessant talker, was a careless driver. Once or twice they nearly capsized.[75] The trip to Painesville was made under a driving rain. With his clothing still damp, Chase addressed an attentive audience for several hours extolling the virtues of Van Buren and Adams and lashing out at the slave power. Then it was sixteen miles to Orwell, where they spent the night. The next day it was another thirty-mile ride to Jefferson, where Chase spoke at great length. On Saturday the 19th he and Briggs denounced Taylor while they asserted why Free Soil must prevail at a large meeting in Warren, a prosperous market town deep in the Western Reserve of the state. Thereafter the three men crisscrossed eastern Ohio until the last day in August. From the very beginning of the tour Chase found "daily speaking and travelling hard work."[76] But he enjoyed the company of Vaughan and Briggs, at least when the Cleveland lawyer was "not letting the horses go anyway they pleased." Altogether the three men visited six counties. Chase had made ten speeches averaging two hours each, and had traveled 220 miles in six working days. Despite this killing routine, he said, "I feel quite as well as I did when I started incessant labor."[77]

After two weeks on the road, Chase felt optimistic about the campaign. He wrote the elder Van Buren in a letter crammed with advice that the party would carry Ohio. Leavitt was even more optimistic about Massachusetts.[78] Back in Cincinnati, a tired Chase was faced with orchestrating John Van Buren's whirlwind campaign in the state.[79] The magnetic, impulsive Van Buren made the task more difficult because of his penchant for canceling engagements at the last moment, postponing travel plans, and arriving late or not at all at meetings where increasingly restless audiences drifted away.[80]

Despite the color and the interest John Van Buren brought to the Ohio campaign, despite the strenuous personal efforts of Chase and other Free Soilers, the organization of the party was very weak. Complaints about not receiving promised campaign material including ballots poured into Chase's law office from party workers all over the state. Early optimism began to evaporate as election day approached. The Whigs especially had an effective organization and effective speakers in the colorful Corwin and the pungent and direct Ewing.[81] The result in Ohio was disappointing and especially so to Chase, who worked long and hard for success. Regular party lines had held, though the 35,000 votes cast for Van Buren mainly in northeastern Ohio were sufficient to give Taylor the state. The ex-President polled only 290,000 votes, about 10 percent of the votes cast. He did not receive one electoral vote, but politics in the United States would never be the same after the election of 1848.[82]

There were solid benefits for the party and for Chase. In the new legislature that would elect a United States senator, the Whigs and the Democrats were so evenly divided that the 11 Free Soilers who were elected held the balance of power.

Important for Chase's future was his newly established visibility, obvious to the leadership of the two major parties. He had also gained three valuable lieutenants, two in Columbus and one in Cincinnati. All were gifted editors and publishers, as well as sound political tacticians; two were from Whig backgrounds: Edward S. Hamlin, editor of the Columbus *True Democrat;* John C. Vaughan, whom Chase had placed on the *Democrat*'s staff as an associate editor; and the ex-Democrat Donn Piatt of the Cincinnati *Gazette.*[83] These younger men were attracted to Chase not because of any personal warmth that he projected but because of his earnestness, political ability, and sincerity, so they thought, in his zeal for the antislavery cause. At this point none of them could sense the driving ambition that lay concealed behind this dignified, cultivated man who seemed so open and so passionate for the cause.

chapter 9

Among the Great

Chase had thought that the Free Soil ticket would make a better showing in Ohio, yet he saw hope both for the cause and for his own future in the close vote between the two major parties.[1] If the eleven Free Soilers elected to the legislature voted as a bloc, they would hold the balance of power between the Whigs and the Democrats. But that "if," as Chase well knew, was a tenuous one. Almost all of the Free Soil vote came from the northeastern counties, the core of Whig strength in the state. The election of Zachary Taylor, a slaveholder and a southerner, had hurt the Whig party in that region. But Lewis Cass and his popular sovereignty theme had not endeared the Democratic party to conscience Whigs either.

Chase had gained some acceptance in Ohio for his role in the creation of the Free Soil party, more for his long record in support of antislavery objectives. He and Gamaliel Bailey had striven to inculcate the idea of utilizing the Liberty party to extract concessions from the major parties. Yet in doing so they had been accused of betraying moral issues, for bartering the Liberty party and the antislavery cause in Ohio for personal advancement. While Chase remained at the head of the Free Soil organization, this charge, like a faint, but poisonous fog, hovered over his every action, his every utterance in public and even in private conversation. Still he never quite understood how or why anyone should mistrust his motives. Supremely confident, he associated his own personal fortunes with the advancement of the cause. Immediately after the election he began to woo possible prospects among the conscience Whigs and antislavery Democrats.

Chase worked hard to weld the structure of the Free Soilers into a cohesive mass. His goal was the United States senatorship which the 1849 legislature would decide. He never gave a thought to the fact that the only political office he had ever won was a seat on the Cincinnati City Council, or that popular Democratic and Whig veterans, all of whom enjoyed national reputations, stood in his way. Chase recognized that there were issues, purely local ones with little or nothing to do with slavery, that were distracting both parties. He was eager to exploit them, all along ascribing his moves in this direction to be for the ultimate benefit of Free Soil.

Ohio, like many other new western states, had overburdened itself with public works projects. Despite the appearance of prosperity after the close of the Mexican American War, the burdensome state debt and an inadequate credit supply were the subjects of heated political controversy. Democratic solidarity was still threatened by division between hard-money and soft-money advocates. In general the Barnburners, or Van Buren wing, to which Chase had nailed his flag, followed a hard-money course. The majority, however, were or seemed to be on the soft-money side, as were most of the Whigs.[2]

Samuel Medary was the undoubted leader of the Ohio Democratic party. Originally a Van Buren partisan, Medary had cast aside this political attachment as easily as he had shaken off his financial beliefs, if they ever meant much to him.[3] He mobilized his organization behind Cass, who unfortunately was the losing candidate. Colorful, highly opinionated, Medary survived this defeat and, wearing his former allegiance lightly, went into the bidding for lucrative state offices and printing contracts.[4] Unlike the moralists among the abolitionists, Medary understood Chase as a practical politician. His motives were not of consequence to him.[5] Chase's Free Soil group, however, was another matter. Medary's unquenchable thirst to rule the state for power and profit made him open to bargaining.[6]

To Chase Medary was an important figure, whose price for support was as yet unknown.[7] More impressive were four individuals of national prominence with strong local constituencies: Thomas Corwin of Lebanon; Thomas Ewing, a Whig war-horse from the center of state; Joshua Giddings, the preeminent conscience Whig; and Democrat William Allen, the incumbent senator whose term was due to expire on March 4, 1849. In the background a presence always to be reckoned with was Justice McLean.[8]

These individuals were well known throughout the state as much for their appearance, their manner, and idiosyncrasies as for their political ability. All were big men; Giddings, known affectionately as "the Ashtabula Giant," stood six feet, two inches in height, weighed 225 pounds, and was known for his prodigious muscular strength.[9] In speech he was plain and direct, the epitome of the conscience Whig. Ewing, Chase's principal competitor, had spent his entire political career in the Whig party. Less outspoken than Giddings on the slavery issue, he was a favorite son among party regulars. He too was large-boned, but tended toward corpulence.[10] An eloquent speaker, he was rather taciturn in his demeanor, though reckoned to be a fine trial lawyer.[11] Chase shared a legal background with both of these Whig leaders, but only Ewing had enjoyed as he had the benefit of a higher education. They were self-made men, a trait much admired in the frontier West. William Allen, incumbent United States senator and the Democratic candidate, was tall and lean. Of the aspirants he was the most approachable. A hard-money man, he had been a supporter of Martin Van Buren until the Free Soil ticket emerged in 1848.[12] Then he cast his lot with Lewis Cass and supported Cass's position of popular sovereignty on the slavery issue.[13] Free Soilers and antislavery Democrats distrusted Allen. He could expect no support from Medary, who had become personally and politically hostile.[14] Allen was the weakest of Chase's opponents. Of these politicians Giddings posed the greatest threat because of his long-term antislavery stand, though his backing of Taylor had weakened him substantially. Corwin and Ewing had the same problem, but both men benefited from the strong statewide Whig organization and a host of well-edited Whig papers.

The Whig party, however, had damaged itself when the year before its legislative members took advantage of a temporary majority and without a quorum present gerrymandered Hamilton County, whose major population center was the city of Cincinnati. They had hoped to gain two members of the lower House by combining rural areas of the county to offset Cincinnati's Democratic majority. Chase himself regarded their action as unconstitutional.[15] Whether unconstitutional or not, the move had been foolish in the extreme. It provided durable grist for the Democratic press; it strengthened Democratic ranks against what was perceived as a concerted effort to discriminate against the rapidly growing cities and towns of the state for partisan advantage. Above all, Medary and his group saw the gerrymander as a serious challenge to their control of the legislature.[16]

Just before the 1849 legislative session was to convene in Columbus, the Whigs under the new apportionment law claimed the election of two representatives from Cincinnati.[17] So close was the statewide election between the two major parties that if the Whig candidates were seated and nine of the eleven Free Soilers voted with the Whigs, they would have a majority of two in joint session. The Whigs would organize the lower house of the state legislature, have a good chance to elect the United States senator, and control state officers and contracts. The Democratic candidates had their election certificates authenticated by the county clerk and two justices of the peace as provided by law.[18] The Free Soil contingent would determine who would be seated, a factor not lost on Chase and on Medary.

Well before the election, Chase had been working toward the U.S. Senate seat.[19] He lined up a small group of point men, all of whom had been or still were journalists.[20] Largely out of his own pocket he had provided the money which kept afloat the *Cincinnati Globe,* a Free Soil weekly. He had a hand in converting Hamlin's *True Democrat* to a Free Soil paper.[21] These journalists began a discreet campaign to push Chase's availability for the forthcoming U.S. Senate seat.[22]

Edward S. Hamlin had come under Chase's spell when he attended the Buffalo convention. An ambitious editor and a shrewd politician, he saw better opportunities in Chase's cause than in Giddings's, with whom he had been associated. Chase was eager to secure the assistance of such an energetic, politically wise individual, and incidentally to weaken Giddings whom he regarded as a major threat to his leadership of the Free Soil movement. Thus he was susceptible to Hamlin's pleas for financial support. Chase provided the funds necessary to establish the *Daily Standard* in Columbus. Hamlin was happy to edit the new Free Soil paper in the state's capital and leave Cleveland, where he said he had met "with a cruel contempt even bitter opposition."[23] And, finally, a younger member of Chase's law firm, Stanley Matthews, who had edited the *Herald Philanthropist* for a time after Bailey left for Washington, acted as Chase's liaison with antislavery Democrats.

Beyond their journalistic capabilities, Chase had chosen them for their political talents. Now at the outset of his career, he recognized the importance, even the necessity to have around him men who could promote his cause in the editorial columns of the partisan press under his control, editors who could also be counted on to advance the cause of Free Soil. Vaughan and Matthews had connections in the slave states and understood southern culture. These attributes Chase found attractive because they could propagate his belief that the these states would eventually emancipate their slaves without federal imposition.[24] A third member of the Chase team was Donn Piatt, formerly a lawyer and journalist, whose private income permitted him to indulge in politics and to write humorous public letters on political subjects to various Democratic journals.[25] This intimate little group made a nice political balance: with Piatt and Matthews formerly Democrats and Vaughan and Hamlin formerly Whigs, they covered the spectrum of political parties in the state.

Hamlin was the first of the Chase men to contact the newly elected Free Soil members of the legislature. "If they form their own caucus and act independently," Hamlin wrote Chase, "all would be well. But if Free Soil Whigs sympathize with Taylor Whigs, in the Legislature, and Free Soil

Democrats sympathize and unite with Cass Democrats, then our party will die."[26] Hamlin's analysis was all too true. The only Free Soiler who was elected as an independent and who was loyal to Chase was Dr. Norton S. Townshend, a thirty-four-year-old physician and ardent antislavery man. British by birth, self-taught until he entered medical school in New York, Townshend had been a Chase supporter since 1837 after hearing Chase's argument in the Matilda case.[27]

Vaughan was on hand when the conflicting parties sought to organize the legislature on December 6. His report was not encouraging. "When I came here," he wrote, "I found in a sense no Free Soil party. Our friends are not united; indeed they are opposed to each other; and as a result much idle talk passed around. . . . as for organization, as units of actions, there was none. . . ." Undeterred, the knowledgeable Vaughan persisted. He encouraged Free Soilers to share their suspicions with him and together with Hamlin managed to arrange a caucus which they all attended. Dr. Townshend, by virtue of his deeply felt, long-held convictions and his strong personality, managed to inspire confidence while infusing a sense of solidarity. "He is the soul of our band," said Vaughan.[28]

The Democrats made the first overture. Donn Piatt climbed the stairs to Chase's second-story office and relayed the news, which must have raised Chase's hopes, though he retained his usual composure. Piatt said his brother-in-law Judge Nathaniel Read, who Chase knew was in touch with Medary, had remarked that "the Free Soilers may have the Senator, if they will give the Democrats the other offices." Feigning indifference Chase said loftily that he "hoped the Free Soilers would act with conscientious regard to right and let the consequences take care of themselves."[29]

He was aware that there was suspicion of Democratic motives among the Free Soil contingent, a feeling especially strong among former Whigs. One of his contacts in Columbus, Eli Nichols, had told him that John Morse, a Free Soiler who had been a conscience Whig and was counted on as a Chase supporter, was skeptical of Democratic intentions. He wanted a written agreement that the Democrats would vote for the repeal of the Black Laws which discriminated against African Americans in the state and for Chase as U.S. senator before he would support the seating in the legislature's lower House of the Democratic claimants.[30] Nichols added that Morse would vote for "you or Giddings."[31] Information Chase was receiving daily from Columbus did not ease his anxiety. On December 17, he left for the state capital to take personal charge of his campaign.[32] Fortunately he had a legitimate cover for his activities. He was representing Lyman Beecher, who had brought suit against the trustees of Lane Seminary. Beecher had been ousted from his faculty post and was seeking reinstatement.[33]

From his room at the Neil House, a few blocks away from the state house,

Chase kept a close watch on developments in the legislature.[34] He had dinner with Townshend and an articulate young lawyer, Albert G. Riddle. Townshend had introduced Riddle to Chase as a conscience Whig and a member of the legislature who could be counted on to vote for Free Soil measures, especially the repeal of the Black Laws. Chase found Riddle "a promising and talented young man." He was hopeful that he had made a convert to his bid for the Senate and to a coalition he was seeking to build.

Chase and his associates sounded out both the Whigs and the Democrats. But after a caucus of the Free Soilers, which he attended the next evening, he concluded that the Whigs were in no mood to treat with them as a distinct unit on any useful terms. The caucus had been a spirited one during which Chase became quite certain of two things. Most of the Free Soilers were leaning toward the Whigs, and the Democratic leadership seemed far more open to a deal.[35] "There is reason to think," he wrote Belle, "that some of both parties will prefer me, but it is possible that I am not the choice of a majority of either. My location is unacceptable to some of the Free Soilers, all of whom are from the [Western] Reserve. And my political position is unacceptable to many of the Democrats. . . . " Chase closed his letter by saying that "as neither can elect alone, and as I am perhaps more acceptable to both, though not to each . . . I may be elected." No wonder he went to bed after the caucus with a severe headache that kept him awake most of the night.

During the next two days, Chase drafted a deal which he left in Hamlin's hands to be presented to Samuel Medary.[36] Included among Chase's requirements was a bill that would repeal the most objectionable of the Black Laws. If accepted it would be a hard bargain for Medary, but not without immediate gains. Some 25,000 blacks resided in the state, whose white population was almost 2 million.[37] Most blacks were concentrated in urban or urbanizing areas which the Democrats controlled.[38] It is not known what Medary's calculations were when he tentatively accepted Chase's proposals. Chase always believed that he and the Democratic leadership were more flexible because they had lost the national election.[39] Whether this cause influenced his decision, Medary may have figured that if the Black Laws were repealed and a public backlash developed, the legislature could reinstate them. Possibly he thought the laws were more symbolic than real or he may have sensed the growth of antislavery feeling in the aftermath of the national election. The laws that Chase's bill would revoke would permit blacks to enter the state without restriction. They could testify in court against whites and the state would underwrite segregated public schools. Blacks still could not vote, hold public office, sit on juries, or be eligible for poorhouse relief.[40]

But surely Medary was well aware that race prejudice was strong outside northeastern Ohio. Race riots in Cincinnati were still fresh in the minds of Ohioans and were still a possibility, though the prosperity following the Mexican American War had eased tensions. Other aspects of the deal were bound to outrage the Whigs and many Free Soilers: Democratic support of Chase's candidacy for the U.S. Senate, two state offices for Chase's lieutenants, Clerk of the House for Stanley Matthews, and head of the Board of Public Works for Hamlin. In return, enough Free Soilers would vote for the Hamilton County Democrats to give that party control of the legislature. They would support the Democratic candidate for speaker and would allocate the remainder of the state offices, which included the judges to the Democrats. Medary's press would receive the state printing. Chase exacted a high price from Medary considering that he could not count on complete Free Soil support.[41] Of some importance that would make Chase more palatable to the Democrats was his long-standing campaign to portray himself as an adherent to Jeffersonian states' rights and to what had become a Democratic canon: tariff for revenue only, hard money, and opposition to centralized banking.

Yet suspicion was always near the surface. When the first vote came up on the contesting seats, only Townshend of all the Free Soilers joined the Democrats. Chase was on the house floor at the time and angry Democrats immediately surrounded him, charging bad faith. They threatened, he said, "to go home and break up the Legislature." Chase in reassuring tones told them to "keep cool," and they finally agreed to delay any precipitous action. He lobbied hard the next day with Morse, Albert Riddle, and other Whig-leaning Free Soilers. He finally got an agreement from enough members to elect the Democratic candidate John G. Breslin to be Speaker, Stanley Matthews to be Clerk of the House, and Hamlin to the Board of Public Works.[42]

Chase was not present for this first test of the coalition he and Medary had put together. He was in his room at the Neil House, as he said, "busy at my argument" on the Lyman Beecher case. The triumphant Democrats organized the legislature.

Neither Chase nor any of his contingent was invited to their victory celebration at the American Hotel.[43] Was this a portent of the future? Would the Whigs muster enough support to block the Democratic candidates from Hamilton County, without passage of Chase's bills on the Black Laws and his election as senator? Would the Democrats hold to the remainder of the bargain?

Chase returned home on January 11 and remained in an agony of suspense for several weeks as his frail coalition began to fray. Many Democratic members were balking at repeal of the Black Laws.[44] Yet at the same time Chase received encouraging reports from Hamlin, who was in constant touch with Medary.[45] On January 20 Hamlin wrote that "the arrangement is pretty much made for Townshend and Morse to vote in Pugh and Pierce (Democratic House claimants) and the Black Laws are to be repealed."[46]

Chase's election to the Senate remained very much in doubt. The Whigs now had more than an inkling of the deal and began to shore up their defense against the Democratic candidates for Hamilton County and against Chase's election. They pushed for Giddings. Despairing of Townshend's vote, they brought heavy pressure on Morse, who began to waiver, despite the editorial defense of him and Townshend that Stanley Matthews and John Vaughan were publishing in the *Standard* and the *Globe*.[47]

Chase took other action to forestall Whig reprisals. He wrote Giddings a long letter arguing delicately that he would be of better service to the cause if he retained his congressional seat and thus helped in the election of another Free Soiler (obviously Chase) from Ohio. He noted that Corwin's term in the Senate would expire a year hence and that Giddings would be in line for it.

Chase was as frank as he felt he could be regarding the situation in Columbus. He recognized that the Free Soilers and the Democrats were not "harmonized," as he put it. He paraphrased the advice he gave them. "Some of you," he said, "have come from the Democratic party and naturally sympathize with your old associates and some from the Whig party and naturally sympathize with yours. Only he [Townshend] came from neither. Now why not meet together. Agree that no one shall be admitted (into caucus) who did not vote for Van Buren and Adams and does now fully identify himself with our own organization upon our national slate." Chase added that the straight-line Whigs would not vote for Giddings because they "wish a more conservative and less ultra man than you for Senator." He closed with a hint that he would step aside if he was assured Giddings would be elected.[48]

Bolstering this direct appeal to Giddings, Chase enlisted Dr. Bailey to use his influence on the congressman. Besides heading off any move by Giddings, Chase hungered for the radical congressman's assistance. "If Giddings would give me his support," said Chase, "it would probably ensure most of the Whig Free Soilers, and one or two Whigs perhaps to give me their votes, say eight in all."[49]

If the Giddings problem were not enough, Chase was fearful that Hamlin's new paper in Columbus would have to suspend publication. He judged that the *Standard*, which was pumping out daily arguments for Chase and defending Free Soilers loyal to him, was indispensable for his campaign. He was already contributing heavily to the weekly Cincinnati *Globe* and his secret support of Hamlin was substantial. Yet the *Standard's* Free Soil publisher—a close friend of McLean—was threatening to withdraw his financial aid. These drains on Chase's income were now severe, but as he wrote Hamlin, the *Standard* "must not be suffered to stop."[50]

Finally on January 26, Morse joined Townshend and the Democrats to seat the Democratic candidates from Hamilton County.[51] As expected, Whigs and Whig Free Soilers turned on Townshend and Morse, with a fervor that exceeded their fury at their votes for speaker and clerk. Riddle, who had voted with the Whigs, said, "What a terrible torrent has broken over and still dashes on our poor friends . . . especially Townshend. He maintained his imperturbable self possession and coolness. . . ."[52] Obviously the loss of state patronage was in part responsible, but since repeal of the Black Laws was generally supported in areas of Whig strength, it was the near certainty, as many believed, that Chase would be elected to the Senate that inspired the real anger of the Whigs.

Chase was still unsure about the eventual result, as well he might be, considering the bitter attacks upon him in the Whig press. Giddings's supporters could throw their votes to Ewing and enough Democrats might vote for Allen, the incumbent, to defeat him. "I am therefore in this singular predicament," he wrote Matthews, "tolerably certain that I am the choice of a very large majority of all who look earnestly to the permanency and success of the Free Democracy without any reasonable assurance from the supposed friends of the same cause in the Legislature."[53]

Concerned about the fate of the *Standard* and about the solidarity of the coalition, Chase left his comfortable home and his pregnant wife and along with Vaughan made the trying winter trip to Columbus, where he would take stock of the situation.[54] On the very cold morning of February 2, he took the train to Springfield. Except for the area around the hot wood stove, the car was freezing. Chase had provided himself with a heavy overcoat and two pairs of woolen socks, but he could not keep his feet warm. "I kept as near the stove as I could," he said, "at the expense of enduring its disagreeable heat." At Springfield, he and Vaughan took the stage to Columbus, where Chase found that he had to share a room with a stranger at the overcrowded American Hotel.[55]

By now the bills that Chase had drafted on blacks and fugitives had been introduced by Morse and Townshend. They had passed the house, a tribute to Chase's industry and his persistence. Eventually the senate concurred. But the apportionment bill was held up and that problem persisted until the state Constitutional Convention of 1850.[56] What Chase hoped would be a short trip became an extended one as leaders of both parties tried various expedients which put Chase's election at risk. McLean, Ewing, and Allen were now the leading threats after Giddings failed to command united Whig support.[57]

On Thursday, February 22, Chase's long and agonizing effort was resolved. With Hamlin keeping his own tally the legislature went into joint session. On the first ballot, Ewing led with 41 votes, Allen next with 27. Chase had 14, the two votes of Morse and Townshend and the remainder from Democrats. Not one Whig voted for him. Giddings received all nine of the remaining Free Soil Whigs. Eleven blank votes were cast and four went to other candidates.

On the second ballot, to the astonishment of the Whigs who expected defections, the coalition held together. All of the Democrats voted for Chase and one of Giddings's votes went over to him, giving him a plurality of 52 votes out of 106 cast. On the third ballot two additional Whig votes and two cast for other candidates elected Chase with 54 votes, a clear majority.[58] Chase was overjoyed at the result as he boarded the stage for home. But ominously for his future career, the Whig contingent and most of Giddings's supporters not only remained intact but were furious at what they regarded as a gross betrayal of high-minded morality.

Chase was not present at the victory celebration the Democrats held on Thursday evening. Nor had he heard about the splenetic response of the Whig leadership to his election, but he soon would as he prepared for his journey to Washington.[59] Waiting for him when he reached Cincinnati was a letter from Hamlin explaining that Riddle would lead the Whigs in what he described as "war on us."[60]

Chase hastened to placate Riddle with a long, persuasive letter in which he sought to cast his actions as not personally inspired, but made for the good of the cause. He also argued that the objectives of the Democratic party, aside from the issue of slavery, were much closer to Free Soil beliefs than those of the Whigs. It is significant that he did not mention his role in the repeal of the Black Laws and other social legislation which he himself had drafted. In these areas conscience Whigs and Free Soilers such as Riddle had given much needed support. And if there were to be any repercussions, the burden could be cast upon Townshend and Morse, who had introduced the legislation. The letter was artfully sincere, reflecting both sides of Chase's character. But this and other efforts at damage control would never completely erase the image from Whig minds of the high-minded Chase bargaining with such a cynical, patronage-hungry politician as Medary.[61]

Anxious to take his seat in time for the inauguration of the new President, Zachary Taylor, Chase wound up urgent office business in Cincinnati and assigned political chores to his young associates at home, in Columbus, and in other sections of the state. Chase took his niece, young Hannah Whipple, with him to Washington. After a series of travel problems Chase arrived in Washington too late for the inauguration on the evening of March 4.[62] But he was pleased to find Bailey waiting for him at the depot and ready to put him up at his home.

The next day Chase sought out Giddings to whom he had written from Cincinnati, hoping for a long talk. He was chagrined and no doubt concerned when he found that Giddings had left town for home. Hale and Corwin were on hand, however, for the special session of the Senate that convened on March 5. The amiable Free Soil senator called for Chase that morning and accompanied him to the Senate chamber. Hale introduced him to a number of his new colleagues. Among them were several southern slaveholders whose social and political views Chase had so often castigated. "They were," said Chase, "civil enough but I dare say wished in their hearts that I was anywhere other than in the chamber." Sam Houston was especially open and friendly. Chase noted that his linen was dirty and his dress careless.[63] Corwin presented Chase's credentials to Vice President Fillmore, who swore him in and then ushered Chase to his seat on the Democratic side between Houston and James Shields of Illinois.[64]

Chase was familiar with the Senate chamber, which he had visited many times. Now as a member of this august body, he surveyed his fellow members: the frail, intense Calhoun, the deep-browed Webster, and the ebullient Clay, all betraying signs of age, as were Benton and Houston. Active and agile Stephen A. Douglas, with his massive head and torso, moved about the chamber on his stubby legs. For the first time in many years, Chase's self-confidence deserted him. "I found myself among the most celebrated men of the country . . . [they] were all there; genuinely I felt myself insignificant."[65]

Chase took no part in the proceedings except to vote with the Democrats on confirmations of appointments. Much of the business was purely routine, which left Chase spare time to visit old acquaintances and the few political friends he had in Washington. He made it a point to call upon all the Ohio representatives, which included the one Free Soiler Joseph M. Root of Sandusky. He also did some prospecting for a house he could afford with the idea of setting up a permanent establishment for his family. He wrote Belle that Dr. Bailey's household, consisting of himself, wife, his father, five children, and four servants, had weekly expenses of about $40.[66] He thought his family expenses would be $50 a week, a sum that would include servants and one or two of Belle's relatives or members of his extended family, who lived with the Chases for various lengths of time in Cincinnati.[67]

Pleasant as these spring days were in the city of his young manhood, Chase had nagging concerns about his political future.[68] The Whig reaction to his election was most disturbing. In the heady moments of victory, Chase saw visions of himself leading an irresistible band of "Free" or "True Democrats," a new party that would arise like the mythical Phoenix from the ashes of Whig and Democratic Hunkerdom to dominate the political landscape. Broad-based, national not sectional, it would vitalize the old Jacksonian shibboleth of equal rights and sweep out entrenched privilege everywhere. The institution of slavery would eventually fall not by national or extra-legal action but by the slave states themselves as the free states cut loose their political support of the South.[69]

All these visionary ideas that Chase hoped would lead him eventually to the White House were put at grave risk if he could not bring about a fusion of hitherto warring parties and factions in his home state. And this meant, first of all, gaining control of the Free Soilers. Even this modest objective seemed in jeopardy.

Speaking for the Free Soil Whigs, Riddle would have nothing to do with the Democratic leadership in Ohio. Chase's long letter of explanation and persuasion had not mollified him. He accused the Democrats of obstructing his apportionment bill and indirectly charged Chase with bad faith in his alliances with Medary and the New York Barnburners, whom he did not trust. Giddings, too, was unhappy with the Medary compact and with the action of Townshend and Morse. Though he claimed, as had Riddle, that he stood by the Free Soil Buffalo platform, his response was Whiggish in tone and critical of Chase's role in the Senate election.[70]

On March 23, the special session adjourned. Shortly thereafter Chase began the tiresome journey west by train, stage, and steamboat to Cincinnati, where a host of problems had accumulated, the most time-consuming an important telegraph case in which Henry O'Reilly, a Rochester, New York, entrepreneur, was challenging the Morse patents and attempting to construct competing lines.[71]

More serious to Chase and his family was an outbreak of cholera in the city that seemed to be approaching the limits of the epidemic of 1832. "The number of cases reported," he wrote Sumner, "is no index to the real number, which is doubtless twice or thrice as great. . . ."[72] Returning from a business trip to Louisville on Sunday morning, July 1, he noticed the city authorities had coal fires burning at intersections along Broadway in what passed as a precaution against the disease. As he walked through the smoky streets, he thought it "a preposterous remedy for Cholera—giving an aspect of gloom to everything hardly to be surpassed."[73] In the long and dismal record of illness and death from infectious disease that had afflicted his immediate family, Chase was deeply concerned when little Katie became ill with cholera symptoms. And Belle, in the last stages of pregnancy, was increasingly uncomfortable while the heavy, humid heat of late June settled over this inland river city.[74]

Though Belle's delivery was expected at any time, and no one in the household was particularly in the best of health, Chase went off to Louisville for the court proceedings in the O'Reilly-Morse case.[75] Much to Chase's relief, Katie recovered and Belle gave birth on July 3 to another daughter without any complications. They named the infant Josephine Ludlow Chase.[76]

Satisfied that Belle, baby Josephine, and Katie were all recovering their health, Chase left for Sandusky, a bustling town near Cleveland, where he was to join John Van Buren for a Free Soil rally. He reached Sandusky on July 12 and put up at the Townshend House. When he awoke in the morning he had a

sharp attack of diarrhea, a forerunner of cholera that he thus far had successfully avoided. "I got into bed again," as he described his treatment, "and
covered myself up and took some camphor pellets—perspiration followed and
felt better—breakfasted very light." After a busy day where he combined
business with politics and apparently a restful night he met John Van Buren at
the wooden stand that had been erected in the square. Chase was to follow
Van Buren. While the handsome "Prince John" was in the midst of his rousing
speech, an embarrassed Chase felt the onset of another attack. He left the
stand quickly and was taken in hand by George Hoadley, Sr., the father of one
of Chase's political aides. Hoadley took him home.[77]

For a week he was seriously ill and could not be moved. Hoadley's family
sheltered him and provided nursing care. Dr. Williams, a homeopathic physician who was called in to treat the ailing senator, prescribed "phosphorous
globules." Despite heavy doses of this concoction Chase recovered rapidly. As
he explained to Belle when he was convalescing, "this morning I thought the
looseness of my bowels was returning upon me. It turned out nothing of
consequence. I have had a very decent operation—almost *au natural*."[78] By
the last week in July he was well enough to return home and resume his
customary crowded schedule.[79]

In his efforts to ease criticism of the means he used for his election,
Chase spent a good deal of time during the summer of 1849 writing letters to
conscience Whigs, Whig Free Soilers, and abolitionists explaining his position. He employed his usual skill with words and argument in making not just
an impressive case for his actions but in bidding for leadership of what he
dubbed the Free Democratic party. He viewed it as a coalition of all antislavery men with a reform emphasis and a reassertion of old Jeffersonian
values.

He cast his net for rural votes and traditional Democratic constituencies
when he voiced more positively his belief in a tariff for revenue only, sound
money on a specie basis, and always the time-tested doctrine of states' rights
especially when it applied to slavery.[80] He summed up his political ideas in a
letter to George Bradburn, the eccentric ex-Garrisonian minister, which was
brimming with stirring metaphors and glowing phrases. "I hope for the best
results from the organization of the fused elements of Libertyism and radical
Democracy," he wrote, "and progressive Whiggism in the free Democracy."
Chase's personal credo that he would reiterate time and again when asked
about his past affiliations with the Liberty party was: "I am *still* a Liberty man,
because I am a Democrat," a satisfying answer to some, a sophism to many
more, if they were accustomed to regular party discipline.[81] Chase made it
plain that he did not countenance any truck with Cass and orthodox Democrats then pushing for popular sovereignty in the territories.[82]

He was most concerned about rumors that the Barnburners and the

Hunkers in New York were reuniting on that issue.[83] His lofty rhetoric about political principle, which he indulged in his letters, had been a bit tarnished when a paper he prepared for the guidance of an Ohio legislator fell into Whig hands. They promptly accused him of placing state offices at auction.[84] The exposure was embarrassing but Chase regarded it as a passing phenomenon in the cut and thrust of practical politics. Much more alarming was evidence of widespread Whig bitterness toward him. He worried about Vaughan, who was now editor of the Columbus *True Democrat*. With the collapse of the *Globe* in Cincinnati, Vaughan's paper and the *Standard* in Columbus were the only presses with substantial subscription lists in the state that espoused Chase's Free Democracy.[85] Nor was he certain of the reliability of Morse and Giddings. Hamlin was engaged in an acrimonious dispute with the former publisher of the *Standard* that brought criticism from Judge McLean and many of the conscience Whigs.[86]

In mid-August Chase left these cares behind him when he went east, partially for business reasons but mainly for a personal evaluation of the political scene in New York and New England. Since the cholera epidemic had subsided the family seemed in good health. Without that particular worry, he left Cincinnati for Albany and New York City.[87] In Boston he talked Free Soil politics with Sumner and John Gorham Palfrey. In Portland, Maine, he had long conversations with William Pitt Fessenden, a leading conscience Whig.[88] Chase concluded his trip with a visit to Bailey in Washington, returning to Cincinnati on October 1.[89]

While in Washington Chase learned that though the Free Soilers in Ohio held their own in the state elections his friend and supporter Dr. Townshend had lost out to a Whig in his bid for the state senate. Elsewhere the regular Democrats deserted their erstwhile allies.[90] Even though Sumner had reassured him that John Van Buren, David Dudley Field, and John Bigelow, Bryant's associate editor of the New York *Evening Post*, were not deviating from the Buffalo platform, the future of Free Soil seemed grim.[91]

Chase was looking forward to the first session of the 31st Congress, though the Free Soil contingent was very small. It consisted of himself and Hale in the Senate; Giddings; Amos Tuck, the handsome lawyer-businessman from Exeter, New Hampshire, and a Dartmouth graduate; John W. Howe of Pennsylvania; and Joseph Root from Norwalk, Ohio, in the House. But many northern senators and representatives were known to be antislavery men. John A. Dix, a former Democratic senator and Free Soil candidate for the governorship of New York the past year, predicted a stormy session. "You are, to all appearances," he wrote, "to have your hands full this winter, with California asking for freedom and eight states prepared to secede if they are not permitted to extend the evil of slavery." Calhoun had set in motion the call for a southern convention at Nashville where secession might result if California came into the Union as a free state in accordance with President Taylor's recommendation.[92]

To his dismay, Chase was not invited to become a member of the Democratic caucus. He also found himself excluded from all important committees. All sorts of disturbing news came from home. Medary appeared ready to dissolve the coalition as he began to use his organization to test the solidity of the Free Soil front in the new legislative session.[93]

chapter 10

Mid-passage

Occasionally after an extremely busy workday, Chase would sit back in his law office and let his mind wander over events or incidents long past. One such Saturday evening in January 1849 he did some reminiscing after clients, callers, politicians, partners, and students had left him alone with his thoughts. As his eyes wandered over the shelves of law books, he imagined that learned jurists such as Coke, Littleton, Mansfield, Holt, and Blackstone were "looking down on me, not as full wigged and full robed judiciaries but as quaint elves with solemn faces, peering out from between dusty leaves."

These idle thoughts prompted Chase to speculate about the power of these great expounders of the law who had helped and hindered so many. "How many hearts have beat and throbbed almost bursting with expectancy of them! To some how late they came. Too late, indeed, when hope deferred had sickened and died, and substance wasted, health destroyed, and life lost. . . ." Continuing in this gloomy vein Chase arraigned the vagaries of an unfeeling world, where "successful knavery or cold and callous avarice, has won the trick of the cards of law, or obtained judgment for the penalty of his bond. . . ."[1]

Like so many others of New England birth and upbringing who had been educated for a purpose, whether the reform of society, the propagation of God's will, or the notion of Christian stewardship over the ownership and distribution of material gains, Chase hoped to do his bit in removing the disparities he saw all around him in human affairs. He could be and frequently was a generous soul who adhered to strict moral standards. While he had all the failings of his generation in viewing man's inhumanity to man through a vision that was more often than not an abstraction, unlike most of his contemporaries in the pulpit, in trade, or even in the law, he had everyday contact with the realities of life.

When at home in Cincinnati, the poor and the friendless, especially the blacks, sought him out. He always listened to their stories, many of which were heart-rending testimonials to an indifferent social order of get-ahead Americans where slavery, discrimination, and errant materialism were taken for granted. Beneath a dignified, cold demeanor, Chase was a sensitive, passionate individual. Emotional pressure when it accumulated behind the wall of willed control could be and usually was channeled in directions that brooked no opposition if personal and public concerns were involved.

While Chase made friends with some difficulty, he made enemies far more easily and they were long-lasting. Tactics that he thought reasonable and right were often clumsy and wrong. Yet he never seemed to be able to sort out the acceptable means to reconcile his ambitions with his goals. There was too much of Bishop Chase's insistence on success at whatever price in his makeup that surfaced at critical junctures in his career, too little of William Wirt's warm sensitivity to the feelings of colleagues and opponents alike; instead that was reserved for times when he was alone with his thoughts.

As he prepared for the winter trip to Washington he knew he must make his mark not just on the powerful figures who were now his colleagues there but on the folks at home. Many of them cordially despised him as a wire-puller, an individual with a paltry constituency of half a dozen noisy Free Soil legislators and not one-tenth of the eligible voters, a political upstart who did not deserve the eminent position he now occupied. Albert G. Riddle, the young Whiggish Free Soiler whom Chase had so assiduously courted, speaking for his fellow Free Soilers and regular Whigs, said that "Chase's election lost to him at once and forever the confidence of every Whig of middle age in Ohio. . . ."[2]

Concerned but not aware of the depth of hostility he would be leaving, he was wholly involved with his personal mission and he meant to achieve it whatever the political consequences. There was no doubt that he read the slavery and antislavery signals aright. He had of course studied Calhoun's recent "Southern Address" with its furious indictment of northern politicians, its charge of a conspiracy in the making that would free the slaves and set them up as masters over the southern whites. Chase had not needed Dix's warning that concerted efforts were in process to forge a sectional unity of the slave states bent on secession from the Union if California and the New Mexico territory were acknowledged to be free soil. Yet it would require a man far less sensitive of public opinion than Chase to recognize that antislavery lines were drawing closer in the free states.

The numbers of avowed Free Soil members of Congress may have been scant, but most northern legislators of both parties and of all political hues, variously nicknamed "dough faces," "northern men with southern principles," "hards," "softs," "silver greys," "cotton and conscience Whigs," "free," and "independent Democrats," all had varying degrees of reservations about the peculiar institution. Rather than with dismay at this swirling vortex of political persuasions, Chase looked forward with relish to impending developments, though he tended to discount the assertions that a constitutional crisis was imminent.

Chase envisaged a leadership role in purifying the Democratic party of its slavery taint as a step toward consolidating antislavery elements not just in the North but in the southern states. He foresaw the eventual entrance of "conscience" Whigs in a grand coalition that was based on the principles of the Declaration of Independence. Influenced by the ethnic diversity and conditions of the laboring population of his home city he broadened his perspective to include labor reform, the old Jacksonian opposition to monopoly, free trade, and hard money. Chase admitted that some of what he said and wrote for the press was heading in a sectional direction. But God and morality were on his side. Hard economic realities made slave labor the nemesis of free labor, slave plantation agriculture the antithesis of free homesteads, lords of the loom in the North the cognate of lords of the lash in the South. Monopoly, whether in banking, manufacturing, or transportation, was simply a fraud on the public, or the engrossing of the best in public and private lands for the benefit of the few, the detriment of the many. The slave plantation system was simply another name for monopoly in its most invidious form.

Surely with these grand ideas in mind, backed up with his constant study of European treatises on such subjects, his in-depth analysis of articles in numerous southern and northern journals and newspapers, his years of diligent work in jurisprudence, he should be able to make a mark quickly in the Senate. And he was well aware how important it was for him to achieve a reputation on which to build up his tiny constituency in Ohio beyond the usual approach of utilizing government patronage to assist in the organization and the shaping of public opinion.

This time his family would be with him. For a person who enjoyed creature comforts and who had so often in his busy life been deprived of them, family surroundings even in the unpleasant transient town of Washington were very important to him, as to most of his new colleagues. What Chase had not counted on was the effect on Belle and the children of the arduous trip, the cold, damp December weather, and the physical impact of dirt and disease in the ill-kept capital. Fearing and properly so the filthy streets and poor sanitation of Cincinnati as a prime cause of disease, he had purchased a farm in Clifton, a country suburb of that city, where Belle, who was prone to colds and bouts of fever, could enjoy the benefits of rural surroundings well removed from urban congestion. When it came to the sessions of Congress, some lasting eight or nine months, Chase could not bear the loneliness and the celibate existence of so long a period away from home. His personal needs overcame his caution. He lodged his family, which consisted of Belle, her sister Kate Ludlow, the little girls, and Catherine MacDonald, a nurse, in a suite at the National Hotel and set about prospecting for a more permanent home which he could rent.[3]

There was ample leisure time to scout for available rentals, because the House was deadlocked over the election of Speaker. Chase's Free Soil contingent was largely responsible, the immediate cause their insistence that the Wilmot Proviso be a test for any proposed legislation on the new territories acquired from Mexico. The Senate met briefly each day and adjourned while the voting went on in the House.

Chase was in comfortable circumstances. His salary and his income from his law practice and from investments (principally in Cincinnati real estate) totaled about $8000 a year. But financial demands upon him were heavy. He was supporting wholly or in part an extended family. He was still making contributions to newspaper supporters and underwriting the printing of pamphlets on various subjects for distribution. He wanted to maintain his home in Ohio and a comfortable Washington residence. Thus he had to be careful about his expenditures.[4]

Straining his budget and his peace of mind were additional heavy drains on his financial and particularly his emotional resources that unexpectedly surfaced in mid-December. Belle, who had contracted a heavy cold, suddenly developed what Chase described as "alarming pulmonary symptoms." Physicians in attendance diagnosed her condition as tuberculosis. Deeply concerned that Belle would go the same way as Lizzie, his second wife, Chase made arrangements for further diagnosis and treatment at a noted "Hydropathic Establishment" in Philadelphia. He placed nine-year-old Kate under the care of Miss Henrietta B. Haines, formidable head mistress of a fashionable school for young ladies in New York.[5] He took the rest of his immediate family with him north but after a few days at the Philadelphia sanitarium, he and Belle decided that more than "ordinary" treatment was indicated. They moved on to the Parkerville Institute near Woodbury, New Jersey, where the physician in charge—Dr. George S. Dexter, a renowned specialist in diseases of the lungs—prescribed a course of treatment which featured cod liver oil pellets, bed rest, and sponge baths. This regimen seems to have improved Belle's condition. Then Chase noticed "a sudden change for the worse. She rallied again," he wrote Hamlin, "and I hung between hope and despair." The disease as it often does in early stages went into remission.[6]

Chase was upset at having to be absent from the Senate, but he felt he had to be at his wife's side until material improvement occurred. He had gone to Philadelphia on the very day that the deadlocked House finally organized by electing Howell Cobb, the huge, cheerful Douglas Democrat from Georgia, as Speaker.[7] On January 2, 1850, Belle's condition had improved sufficiently for Chase to leave her and his daughters under the care of the nurse and his brother-in-law James Ludlow, who happened to be in the East at the time.[8] He hurried back to Washington on the night train from Philadelphia and went directly to the Senate chamber. He was determined to refuse the appointment he had been offered to the insignificant committee on Revolutionary claims. Earlier he had been excluded from membership in the Democratic caucus. Two calculated humiliations were galling.[9] On Hale's advice, however, he swallowed his pride and accepted the committee post.[10]

His disturbed mood was evident in his search for new quarters. Twice he made up his mind to accept rooms at various boarding houses only to cancel at the last minute before he eventually took lodgings in a house at the northeast corner of Third and B street, next to Gatsby's Hotel.[11] Torn between his concern for Belle and the children and his desire, indeed his imperative need, to make a speech in the Senate on the looming constitutional crisis over Texas and the Mexican cession, Chase sought a place on the agenda.

He wanted an early appearance despite the sound advice he had received from a friendly source not to speak "until you are quite sure you feel entirely at home in your place."[12] But he found that as a junior senator and an ostracized one at that he was relegated to a scheduled appearance in March, which for him was in the distant future. He could take part in the debate if he could catch the Vice President's eye over the Compromise measures that Clay had presented to the Senate, though even here his remarks were severely limited under the rules. Debate for the Compromise bills was to begin on Wednesday, January 23, and Chase was determined to participate. As he wrote Belle, "I wished I was better prepared or had a better opportunity of preparation, but I must do the best I can."[13]

Some days before he voiced his qualms about entering the arena where the giants of the day were making long, and to Chase's ear compelling speeches he had suddenly found himself under attack for a letter he had written to John Breslin many months before. The elderly, loquacious senator from South Carolina, Andrew Butler, after a lengthy rambling speech in which he accused the North of sectionalism that would tear the Union apart closed his remarks by asking the secretary of the Senate to read Chase's letter. It too was a long piece, but it simply declared Chase's long-held position that the Free Democracy which he espoused would seek all legitimate and constitutional means to halt slavery expansion into areas where Congress had exclusive control. What had aroused Butler's ire was Chase's frank definition of slavery as "the worst form of despotism": "the ownership of one man by another is the most absolute subjection known to human experience."

Chase rose to reply on a point raised in Butler's closing denunciation, but after a sentence or two of explanation Butler interrupted him as permitted under the rules, effectively closing him out in the exchange.[14] Eventually he gained the floor on debate over a petition praying for the dissolution of the Union. Surveying the assemblage, which included Calhoun, Chase calmly denied that he or any person who believed in the precepts of Free Democracy was committed to disunion as Butler and others had charged. He admitted that the Free Democracy "is sometimes sectional, but "I trust will not remain forever sectional."[15] His brief remarks were not especially pointed or eloquent. A touch of nervousness emphasized the throatiness of his voice and his slight lisp. But he appeared a majestic figure, handsome and seemingly self-assured, though he was tired out physically and emotionally drained by worry over Belle's condition.[16] When the Senate adjourned over the long weekend, Chase was on the night train to Philadelphia and the three-hour coach ride to Parkerville. He found Belle's health much improved but she remained seriously ill.[17]

Over the next two weeks, Chase traveled the wearing night train and carriage trip on long weekends, but always was in his Senate seat on Monday morning. Belle's condition claimed much of his thoughts, as he listened to Henry Clay's efforts to compromise the territorial issue between the North and South. His letters to Belle, and also his correspondence with Kate, teemed with advice and instruction. "Set the temperature of your room to be kept at 68 or 70," he told Belle, "put shoulder straps on your petticoat so as to keep them off your hips—when you ride out dress warm. Be careful of diet—Eat simple things well cooked."[18] Dr. Dexter's treatment, perhaps Chase's advice, but more likely a remission seems to have affected a cure.

By early February Belle had so far recovered that she felt well enough to return to Cincinnati. Chase wanted her to be with him in Washington, but was so relieved at what he took to be a permanent cure that he agreed to Belle's plans.[19] Improvement was slow and there were bouts of fever and the coughing up of blood even though the debilitating weakness that had come with the onset of the disease was no longer apparent.

During April, she remained with Chase in Washington.[20] Evidently plans had changed. For financial reasons and because he was satisfied that Belle would recover completely Chase instructed his law partner Flamen Ball and his nephew Ralston Skinner in Cincinnati to sell his home there and the furniture at auction.[21]

The companionship of Belle and the family made Washington a much more congenial place than it had been for the past four months. Belle's illness had taken a heavy toll but the sudden death of his oldest sister Hannah Whipple had shocked and grieved him. Seemingly in the best of health, she had suffered a massive heart attack and died instantly at the dinner table. She had been fifty-eight years old.[22] "Death has pursued me incessantly ever since I was twenty-five," wrote a disconsolate Chase.[23]

His sorrow was of short duration, however. He was so fascinated by the scenes in the Senate, the set speeches of Webster, Clay, Cass, Douglas, and other principals arguing for compromise, and the rejoinders of Calhoun, Seward, and Hale that even worry over Belle's illness receded to a minor place.

Calhoun intrigued Chase. He recalled his youthful admiration for the great Carolinian's logical discourse. Everyone knew that Calhoun was seriously, if not critically ill. His speech on the territorial question was looked upon as the ultimate demand of the South. Chase watched the sick statesman come into the chamber on the arm of Senator James M. Mason of Virginia. He listened while Mason read the speech, which he found a waste of time since he knew that the address had already been printed and would be for sale that very afternoon. Calhoun's threat of secession if the North did not give in on slavery in California and on the Texas boundary did not concern Chase. Like many of his northern colleagues, he dismissed it as the alarmist rhetoric that southerners had been voicing over the years.[24] When Calhoun died on March 31, Chase wrote, "Thus has terminated an uneasy, restless earnest life, a life which if he devoted to a noble cause would have been illustrious beyond that of any of our modern statesman. . . ."[25]

Webster's pro-Compromise stand, especially his great speech on March 7, disappointed Chase. When he concluded his remarks Chase heard him say in an undertone to Douglas, "You don't want anything more than that, do you?" Webster's sotto voce comment concerned Chase as much as the speech itself. The torrent of abuse that descended on Webster mainly from abolitionists Chase felt was deserved. But he still had a lingering fondness for "Black Dan" and a warm remembrance of the great speeches he had heard when he was young and Webster was in top form. "He was," Chase wrote Wendell Phillips, "in earlier manhood my father's friend. In my own commencing in public life he showed some personal kindness to me. While therefore I acquiesce in the justice of your stern judgments of his great apostasy, I acquiesce mournfully and wish for some drops of melting charity. . . ."[26]

As a matter of course Chase opposed Clay's "Omnibus Bill" and all eight separate bills it encompassed. As far as he could see it would be a reenactment of the Missouri Compromise, "sentiment for the north, substance for the south." There were many conferences with Seward and with Hale, as well as with Giddings and other antislavery members of the House. While agreeing with their positions, Chase was irked at the leadership these two senators assumed over the minority in opposition to the Compromise. He found Seward pretentious and except for his antislavery stand a doctrinaire Whig. Hale, with all of his ready wit and friendliness, always shied away when Chase proposed some concerted action. "Hale is a first rate guerillaist," Chase noted, "Seward is a Whig partizan, though perfect[ly] reliable on any vote where our questions are concerned. . . ."[27] Giddings on the other hand now generally fell in with Chase's plans and he sought to repay him by utilizing what influence he had in Ohio to push him for the senatorship when Corwin's term expired.

In rejecting the idea that a crisis threatened the Union Chase exalted in a struggle which Hamlin described as a "far more glorious one than that of our Revolution. Our father's weapons were *carnal,* ours spiritual, they fought for their *own* liberty, we are fighting for that *of others,* a poor despised, down trodden race."[28]

Political developments in Ohio increased Chase's frustration at his inability to play a more prominent role in the Senate debates. Hamlin and Hoadly kept him informed and the news was not good. Chase did not have a well-edited paper in Cleveland, Columbus, or Cincinnati to advance his fortunes. The *Standard* in Columbus was reliable, but in Hamlin's words, "a poor weak thing. The proprietors are good men but are harassed for funds and have not sufficient experiences to edit a central organ." Chase worried also about the Toledo *Weekly Republican*, which backed him politically. It too was in parlous financial condition.[29] He was willing to underwrite the *Standard* if Matthews or Hamlin would assume the editorship. Neither was willing, however.

Chase cast a covetous eye on the labor reform paper in Cincinnati, the *Nonpareil,* which he understood could be purchased.[30] Again, however, he ran up against the problem of securing an able editor, and nothing came of his efforts. Vaughan, who had been one of Chase's white hopes as much for his editorial and political ability as for his southern background and his links with the conscience Whigs, was now turning against Chase and aligning his paper the *True Democrat* with the regular Whig organization. Chase was alarmed and annoyed. He told Giddings that he would not fight a political battle with Vaughan. Furthermore, he would not enter into any alliance with the Whigs under any circumstances, "real or apparent."[31] Chase would not grant Vaughan, it would seem, the same freedom he claimed for his association with the Democratic party. That party in which he had such faith was even then deserting him and his cause in Ohio. The regular Democrats carried all before them in the state convention, including a resolution that endorsed the Compromise measures.

Despite this rebuff Chase wanted his handful of Free Democrats to cooperate with the party though they were never to retreat from their anti-extension principles. In the legislature, during the last session under the old constitution, surprisingly, temporary union was achieved between the organization Whigs and the Democrats long enough to cast out the few Free Soilers who held state office, excepting Hamlin, who managed to retain his post as president of the Board of Public Works.[32] The one bright shaft of light that penetrated the gloomy aspect of Chase's position in Ohio was the nomination and election of his close friend and ally Dr. Norton Townshend to Congress as a Free Democrat.[33]

Chase's political situation in Ohio continued to erode. Nor was his position any better in the country at large. Seward had already given a memorable speech in which he spoke of a "higher law" than the Constitution. The little New Yorker had, in effect, preempted the free soil position with respect to the new territories and the abolition of slavery in the District of Columbia. Moreover his influence with the Taylor administration had placed him and many of the mainline northern Whigs squarely on the Wilmot Proviso track.

Outside of Washington, public opinion was predominantly on Clay's and Webster's side. Chase found himself in the uncomfortable position of explaining just where his "Free Democracy" was going. Democratic leadership in the Congress, now that Calhoun's voice was stilled, was gravitating more and more to Douglas and to the excitable senator from Mississippi Henry S. Foote. Both men were cooperating with Clay in backing the Compromise.[34]

Such developments made it even more imperative that Chase reinforce his image as a defender of liberty and democracy with a forceful statement of these principles in a set speech. All during March he sought anxiously and continually to be allotted a time and date for extended remarks. He found that as a junior senator without regular party credentials he was in no position to push for a place on the Senate agenda. Finally on March 19, he managed to make a deal with the Virginia Senator Robert M. T. Hunter which would give him the floor a week later.

Sumner had been in touch with Chase throughout the debate. And now the Massachusetts mandarin poured out advice in a spate of letters.[35] Chase accepted some of Sumner's ideas, but he was obviously gunning for Douglas and Cass, who were calling the slavery question an abstraction. The geography and the climate of the new territory in their opinion placed absolute limits on the expansion of the institution.

Chase had pretty well all the points he wanted to make fixed in his mind when he rose on the morning of March 26. At the outset he declared that though democratic principles insisted upon the abolition of slavery wherever the Constitution gave Congress the power to do so, it was "equally clear . . . that we have no right to interfere with slavery by legislation beyond the sphere of our constitutional powers." This statement was pure Free Soil, pure

Chase doctrine. He emphasized a well-worn theme when he said, "We do have power to prevent its extension." Much of the remainder of his six-hour address given over two days to a near-empty chamber provided a digest of the history of opposition to slavery in the colonies and in the nation.[36] Toward the end of his speech, he shifted away from history to specific points.

Chase denied the often-repeated assertions of Douglas and other politicians that slavery could not extend into the Mexican cession because soil, climate, and aridity imposed physical limits. Peonage, which he likened to slavery, had flourished in Mexican territory before the war. He correctly pointed out that water stored in the heavy snows of the western mountain ranges of the new territories or from rivers like the Colorado, the Rio Grande, and many others remained untapped resources for irrigation that could sustain a slave plantation economy. As for climate, he pointed out that slavery had existed and still did exist in other inhospitable areas of the globe. Nor did he exclude mining from his list of ventures where slavery might be used to advantage.

Obviously Chase had done a good deal of research, but his address, an able one, lacked the resonance that would move thousands. Its emotional content was nil. Its telling arguments, however, and its core analysis made it one of richest presentations of the anti-extension forces.[37] As such it could and was used as a basic source for free-soil advocates around the nation. Important political thinkers such as Benjamin F. Butler of New York and even Horace Greeley, who had recently castigated Chase's role in his election to the Senate, praised the speech warmly.[38] Sumner arranged for its printing and publication in Boston in pamphlet form. After a grueling period of editing and polishing Chase gave the final draft the catchy title of "Union and Freedom Without Compromise" when he submitted it to the congressional printer for publication in the Appendix of the *Globe*.

Apart from this speech and some extended remarks he had made earlier, Chase's participation in the early stages of the great debate over the Mexican cession was minimal. It was confined to amendments, a brief statement on a fugitive slave petitions, and an unsuccessful attempt to smuggle through the Wilmot Proviso in which he changed the wording but not the meaning in an amendment to the New Mexico Territory bill.[39] Bitterly opposed as he was to any compromise, he denounced the Omnibus Bill as "the dodge and give bill." He disparaged the work of Foote, Douglas, Cass, Clay, and Webster, who forged the great Compromise measures.[40]

Family problems again intruded themselves. His baby daughter Josey, or Zoe, as she was later called, never a healthy child, became seriously ill.[41] Belle, Nettie, and Zoe were now in Northampton, Massachusetts, under the care of Chase's former in-laws, the Garnisses.[42] Belle's uncertain health was a grave concern to Chase. She felt well enough, but on occasion coughed up blood.

The physicians who examined her were divided in their opinions. Some thought the upper lobe of her right lung was affected. Others believed she would eventually overcome the disease.[43]

Perplexed and disturbed, Chase decided to seek yet another opinion. In July he took Belle and the family to New York, where Dr. Fitch, a noted specialist in pulmonary diseases, advised Chase to place Belle in another sanatorium at Morristown, New Jersey. After the move Belle's health improved dramatically.

Chase resumed his long weekend visits from Washington to Morristown, and the couple resumed sexual relations, which Dr. Fitch had said would not impair Belle's health even if she became pregnant. "I hope you are not," wrote Chase, "but it will not be any worse for you according to Dr. Fitch." A week later, noting that Belle had gained three to four pounds, he said, "I hope no 'little stranger' has anything to do with this increase in weight."[44]

A week later came the mournful news that little Zoe had died. She had been born with a heart defect and had struggled since birth. She was buried in Morristown without her father's presence; he was obligated to remain in the Senate. He wrote a consoling letter to Belle in which he said that he wanted Zoe's body to be sent eventually to Cincinnati for permanent burial, "where other little ones lie."[45]

Clay's "Omnibus Bill," up for its final vote in the closing days of July, was roundly defeated in the Senate only to have its provisions made into separate bills which, under the astute management of Stephen A. Douglas, passed through both Houses and received the signature of Millard Fillmore, who succeeded to the presidency on the death of Zachary Taylor. Chase, Seward, and Hale joined with the southern extremists to vote against all these measures. Moderate opinion prevailed, much to Chase's disgust. "I have no faith at all in this administration," he said, "I abhor the doctrines of the extreme south but I condemn Whig policy . . . I hate oppression but I despise truckling."[46]

chapter 11

Independent Democrat

The onset of Belle's illness and the expenses entailed made it difficult for Chase to find decent lodgings that were within his means. He was glad to move out of Dr. Bailey's busy household where he had temporary quarters and into Mrs. Galvin's boarding house on C Street nearby and close to the Capitol.[1] Chase's social life was as intermittent as his living conditions. Apart from formal dinners at the White House, any relief from his duties as a senator and his weekends in New Jersey centered around Dr. Bailey's Saturday evenings. The inimitable doctor and his equally inimitable wife Margaret presided over a salon in the European tradition.

From the beginning of its publication Bailey's *National Era* paid almost as much attention to the American literary scene as to the antislavery movement. John Greenleaf Whitter, the abolitionist Quaker poet, published most of his work in the *Era*. In fact, the *Era* was his chief financial support during these years.[2] Likewise, the *Era* carried short stories from the pens of Nathaniel Hawthorne, essays and serials of the popular female novelist Mrs. E. D. E. N. Southworth, Frederika Bremer, the Swedish writer who toured the United States in the early 1850s, and especially the journalist Sarah Jane Clarke, who wrote articles for the *Era* under the pen name of Grace Greenwood. Clarke, whom the Baileys employed for a time as a governess for their six children, was a permanent fixture in the household during much of

Chase's first term in the Senate. Later Bailey would publish Harriet Beecher Stowe's *Uncle Tom's Cabin* in installments.

Bailey's hospitality also extended to politicians and visiting European writers and intellectuals. He and his wife made no distinctions on party grounds for the invitations they sent out to members of Congress, though no proslavery Congressmen attended their soirées. Benton, Hale, Corwin, Seward, and even the cynical Thaddeus Stevens were guests. There was no liquor but plenty of coffee to stimulate the intellectual games the Baileys preferred such as charades, and the high-minded discussions of political theory, liberalism, reform, and kindred subjects.[3] Chase enjoyed these evenings very much. He always held his own in the word games that so often made up the after-dinner entertainment.[4]

Elizabeth Wirt, whom Chase had admired years before when he studied law with her father, was an occasional companion. Married to a naval officer, Louis M. Goldsborough, who was frequently absent from home on assignment in foreign waters, she sought out Chase as an escort to various affairs. He disliked the theater and most public amusements, but Elizabeth prevailed upon him to attend one of Jenny Lind's concerts. Chase paid seven dollars for the tickets and four dollars for a rented carriage, an exorbitant sum to him for an evening's entertainment. He wrote Belle that he was "amply repaid." Through his opera glasses he was able to see "the expression of the features; the light of the eyes, all the movements of the person . . . ." "She is not a large woman, but well made," he said, "good but not fine chest—a countenance expressing great sweetness. . . ."[5]

His restricted social life in Washington and concern over Belle focused his leisure hours on the children. Kate, who was domiciled in New York City under the tutelage of Miss Haines, claimed most of his attention. He wrote her at least once a week, letters which too often took on the demanding attitude the Bishop had once forced on him years before and which he had so resented. "You do not know how much I grieve," he wrote Kate, "whenever you deviate at all from the straight line of duty." Chase then wondered why Kate tended to lie, which he attributed to her "timidity and seriousness."[6]

He was determined to have his daughters excel in society and thus he placed a heavy emphasis on writing and on languages, particularly French.[7] He seems not to have concerned himself that Kate, who was a very sensitive child, might be desperately lonely without a mother's care and devotion. Her only parental contact was through letters which invariably dwelt on criticism and exhortation.[8] Miss Haines was an able teacher but a strict disciplinarian when it came to her charges. Nor was she a particularly warm or caring person. Even Nettie, who was only three years old at the time, came in for some scolding from her fretful father. "She is a dear sweet little creature—too much set on having her own way," said Chase, "and has rather too much temper."[9]

After Zoe's death, Belle's condition fluctuated between severe bouts of fever and hemorrhaging to comparatively good health. Chase moved Belle from Northampton to another sanitarium in southern New Jersey. By the fall of 1850, she was able to join Chase in Clifton, where he rented a house near McLean's home.[10] For once Chase was glad to leave Washington and his boarding house. The tedious speeches, debates, and even social gatherings at the Baileys' had begun to pall. As he confessed to Belle, Washington's "hot weather, late Senate sessions, and late dinners have already given me a bit of indigestion and a slight headache."[11]

Back home Belle was almost herself again and after a few months of further improvement decided on a trip to visit relatives in New Orleans and Texas. Chase reluctantly agreed. Not without misgivings, he resigned himself to another extended period of loneliness and celibacy. Belle, her sister Charlotte Ludlow Jones, and Nettie left Cincinnati in November.[12] Ten days later Chase and Kate were off to New York. He placed Kate in the care of Cordelia Austin, a relative of the Garnisses, for the holidays before she returned to Miss Haines's school. Chase was back in Washington for the second session of the Thirty-first Congress. Unable to find a boarding house to his taste, he took up residence at the National Hotel.[13]

His position in the Senate had not improved. In fact, when President Fillmore appointed his colleague Corwin to be Secretary of the Treasury, the Whig governor of Ohio, Seabury Ford, selected a bitter opponent of Chase, Thomas Ewing, to complete Corwin's term.[14] The Ewing appointment seems to have reinforced Chase's adherence to the Democratic party at home if not in Washington, where he remained excluded from the party caucus and important committee assignments. He still clung to his belief that he could reform the Democratic party in Ohio as a first step to its purification on the slavery issue in the North.

Not unmindful of his political future, Chase avoided any commitment to the Free Soil party. Without his support, the Ohio Free Soilers met in convention, nominated a slate of candidates, and retained their distinct organization. The Democrats were even more evasive than the Whigs on the Compromise issue except to blame their opponents for the passage of the unpopular Fugitive Slave Act. The result was a narrow Democratic victory with the election of an antislavery Democrat, Reuben Wood, to the governorship.

Though the Free Soil vote overall was not large, its concentration in more densely populated northeastern Ohio again gave it the balance of power in the legislature. Chase had been pleased at Ford's inaugural, where he seemed to follow a definite antislavery line. When Chase's ally John F. Morse was elected Speaker of the House by a Democratic-Free Soil alliance, Chase mistakenly thought that the coalition would hold and elect Giddings, his choice for the Senate. This was not to be. Followers of former Senator Allen managed to convince a number of the Democratic Free Soilers not to vote for Giddings. And he, as before, could not muster the Whig vote. With the Free Soilers split between those who followed Chase, those responsive to Allen's faction, and those who leaned toward the Whigs, the legislature was dead-locked for many ballots. Despite Hamlin and Chase's frantic efforts to bridge the schism, the Whigs not only held fast but attracted enough Free Soilers to elect Benjamin Wade, a rough, outspoken antislavery lawyer and former state senator to fill Ewing's seat.[15]

Chase tried to make light of Wade's election. After all, he was a staunch antislavery man, even though he had supported Taylor in the presidential campaign of 1848. But there was no concealing that the election was another setback to Chase's influence and his political aims.[16] As for Giddings, he had no use for Wade, his former law partner, but he was pleased at Chase's rebuff, and may very well have had a hand in it.[17]

Bad news from Ohio was balanced with good news from Massachusetts. After an exhausting and attenuated legislative session, Charles Sumner was elected senator to fill the seat Daniel Webster had vacated to become Fill-more's Secretary of State. Sumner's election was astonishingly similar to Chase's. It had been effected by a fusion of Democrats and Free Soilers and like Chase's by a majority of one vote. There was a decided difference, however: Sumner's antislavery base was far stronger in Massachusetts than was Chase's in Ohio.

Meanwhile Chase had inadvertently provided the opportunity for the articulate South Carolinian Robert Barnwell Rhett to explain in concrete terms the reasons for the South's stand on slavery. The closing session of the Thirty-first Congress was only ten days away from adjournment, yet Henry Clay and others continued to debate the consequences of the Compromise legislation. Chase was anxious to close debate on slavery so that several bills of a public nature in which he was interested, such as cheaper postage and rivers and harbors legislation, could be acted upon. He saw an opportunity to inject himself into the debate, and by way of introducing his subject, complained that the slavery issue was holding up public business.

Chase's comments brought the red-haired, vigorous Rhett to his feet and, claiming his privilege to reply, launched into a brief speech which opened Chase's eyes to the problems southerners faced over the dilemma of slavery. Paradoxically, Rhett shared Chase's views on the fugitive slave clause of the Constitution. Remarked Chase: "These southern ultras are altogether more honest than northern doughfaces. They believe slavery to be right most of them. And the rest believe it to be a necessity. They all agree in believing that the present state of races in the slave states, is best for both and indeed indispensable to the safety of both. Thus believing and holding also that the Constitution recognizes their right of property in slaves, their conclusions are natural enough."

Compromisers, or "Dough Faces," as Chase stigmatized them, declared that slavery was "a temporary institution, but use it as a means of gaining and retaining political power."[18] He disagreed with the southern ultras that slavery was a permanent institution but was beginning to be concerned about the racial and social consequences of emancipation. Chase's thinking was rather muddled on this point. Departing from his customary realistic approach, he decided that once universal emancipation was secured, the former slaves would naturally want to emigrate to more hospitable lands. Climate, he felt, and the racial intolerance of the overwhelming white majority had separated the whites and the blacks in society. Only through the coercion of slavery had the two races been brought into coexistence. Yet he opposed forced colonization because this abrogated the natural rights and the freedom of choice which the Declaration of Independence had proclaimed for all human beings.[19]

As if perplexities in politics at home and isolation in the Senate were not enough to test Chase's mental balance, he was again faced with family problems. Chase's unfortunate ne'er-do-well brother William died in St. Louis on November 30, leaving his family and his pregnant wife destitute. Though his finances were strained, Chase made some provision for William's family. "Thus I have lost my youngest brother: and of five brothers, myself and my brother Edward of Lockport, alone remain," he noted in his diary. "Of our family of ten, five and our father and mother also have departed. A few years and we shall follow."[20]

Belle had returned from Texas with her health seemingly restored. After a few months in Kentucky and Ohio, however, she again went into a rapid decline. Chase was in Washington when he learned from the family physician in Clifton that Belle was critically ill. She could not speak above a whisper. Her heart was obviously giving way, her pulse weak, her racking cough constant. He was enroute to Cincinnati when he received another alarming report and prepared for the worst. But when he reached home, Belle's condition had improved sufficiently for her to be up and about. Chase made plans to return to Washington when Belle's condition again changed dramatically. She died on January 13, 1852.[21]

Chase's grief was not of long duration. He returned to Washington immediately after Belle's funeral, leaving Nettie in the care of relatives.[22] One may surmise that Belle's illness, lasting as it had over two years, made her death a welcome relief. It had been a long-drawn-out emotional and financial drain that together with his living expenses left Chase deeply in debt. He now concentrated his attentions on his two daughters and threw himself into the swirling politics of Ohio and of the nation at large. Yet his own political future, always dubious seemed worse despite his best efforts to keep himself within the Democratic fold.

Chase's neutrality during the 1851 campaign had not endeared him to many Free Soilers. Nor was the regular Democratic organization attracted to his antislavery record. Fierce factional fights in Cincinnati had pretty well ruined Medary's leadership. Still laboring under the onus of the Compromise of 1850, the Whigs were losing ground steadily in northeastern Ohio, their area of greatest strength. As their numbers diminished, that of the Free Soilers increased, a trend not lost on Chase, though he persisted in calling himself a Democrat.

With no credit to their motives he and Hamlin had involved themselves in the struggle between those who supported ex-Senator William Allen and those who supported Samuel Medary. Chase, who always claimed a higher purpose in politics, allowed himself to be allied with Allen and the extreme Hunkers in the party to defeat his erstwhile supporter Medary. He had ready excuses for his action, but he had gained another powerful enemy.[23]

Nor could he ignore the furious indictment from the powerful editor of the *Tribune,* Horace Greeley, who castigated the means he had used to gain election to the Senate. Greeley wrote Chase that it was "the consumma-tion . . . of a series of outrages as gross as if Medary had been proclaimed governor elect and the state subjected to martial law in support of his preten-sions."[24] Greeley's philippic was highly partisan. And the Democratic state platform conformed generally with Chase's antislavery position. As he had written his friend Cleveland shortly after the Democratic state convention, "I am a democrat. I do not go for the abolition of slavery at all events and by all means. I never did."[25]

The nomination of Franklin Pierce and the adoption of a platform at the Baltimore convention supporting the Compromise compounded Chase's dif-ficulties. He found himself in the awkward position of defending the party and its nominations in Ohio but opposing the national candidate and platform. The Whigs in the state had backed Winfield Scott for the presidency before his nomination. But many of them balked at a platform that endorsed the Compromise legislation.[26] Without advice or encouragement from Chase, the Free Soilers, or Free Democrats, as they were now calling themselves, offered the only anti-Compromise alternative. They met in convention in early Feb-ruary and nominated John P. Hale for President and that hardy perennial Samuel Lewis for Vice President.[27]

Now Chase had to drop all pretenses. He could no longer pose as an interested but neutral party. Obviously he could not support the policy and candidates of the national Democratic party's pro-Compromise stand he had so vehemently opposed. On the other hand, if he openly supported the Free Democrats, he risked losing whatever support he might have from the party

regulars in the state. The strategy he finally decided upon was to style himself
an "Independent Democrat." He would not back Pierce or the Baltimore
platform.[28] As he had done years before, he wrote and talked with his old
associates in the free-soil movement, arguing that they should not run a
national ticket. Such a move, he warned, would be doomed to failure and
could only result in setting back the antislavery cause with voters, who would
treat the party and its candidates as a feeble, even contemptuous gesture and
no more. The proper course was to preserve its identity on the state level and
cooperate with either of the major parties who would be most acceptable to its
antislavery objectives.

When his efforts failed, Chase was forced to accept the call of the Free
Democratic Convention, which was scheduled to meet in Pittsburgh on August 11. No sooner had he made his position known than he was placed in the
embarrassing predicament of heading off his own nomination on the Free
Democratic ticket. Hale refused to be a candidate. He, Sumner, and other
radical antislavery men demanded that Chase head the ticket. Chase had
problems enough in Ohio without becoming a sacrifice to a party he believed
had nowhere to go. He wanted very much a second term in the Senate and he
could not achieve this by relying solely on the Free Democrats in the state. He
would not even attend the convention that nominated Hale against his wishes
and George W. Julian of Indiana for Vice President.[29]

Chase accepted the Free Democratic platform and agreed to support its
candidates, "as near to my idea of what is best, not having had the making of
this myself," he wrote, "but I think I shall not sink my individuality in this
organization which it seems to me must be temporary." "I propose rather," he
added, "to maintain my position as an Independent Democrat."[30] It was just
as well because there was a great deal of bitterness among Ohio Free Democrats regarding Chase, an attitude that soon displayed itself.[31]

In an effort to raise his waning fortunes, Chase stumped the state for
Hale and Julian.[32] His major effort, however, was directed toward the Western Reserve, where he made over a dozen speeches. All parties made strenuous efforts to carry the state. All parties also, for the first time, recognized the
importance of the immigrant vote, and prominent in the fulsome political
rhetoric were statements aired to please the Irish and the Germans such as
backing for free homestead legislation and a ten-hour day for workmen. The
Democrats won a substantial victory in the congressional election,[33] and carried the state for Pierce. A harbinger of the future was the strong showing of
the Free Democrats. Hale and Julian polled over 30,000 votes—only 3600
less than Van Buren's vote four years earlier.[34]

Chase's last-minute support of the Free Democratic ticket had not
helped remove a growing belief that he would sacrifice virtually any position
he had staked out in the past for his political advantage. These allegations

were not strictly fair, but the mistakes he had made in not standing by his old comrades marked him a political changeling.

Chase was in a somber mood when he left for Washington on November 22. At least his living conditions would be improved. Bailey had secured a house for him on C Street.[35] Chase was now able to entertain colleagues at dinners, where guests were Seward, Sumner, Benton, Preston King, and members of the Ohio congressional delegation, but not Wade. Chase held him responsible for his poor standing among Whigs and Free Democrats of Whig antecedents.[36]

Ohio not Washington claimed Chase's major attention during the short session of the Thirty-second Congress. Franklin Pierce's inaugural address simply confirmed Chase's negative opinion of the youthful President and the Democracy for which he stood.[37] There would be no equivocation this time about his support of the Free Democrats in Ohio. Despite temptations aplenty he was careful to keep himself clear of the strife that was besetting the Democrats in their jousting for federal patronage from the new administration.[38] Chase was still hopeful there would be another deadlock in the legislature that would reelect him to the Senate by a coalition of Free and regular Democrats.[39]

The Free Democrats had adopted a radical program calling for free trade, temperance legislation, a variety of measures of assistance to the workingmen, and even suffrage without qualifications for black males. These campaign resolutions went well beyond Chase's reform objectives, but he was happy to accept them. He sensed a deep groundswell for reform in society and was willing to stake his reputation on its eventual fulfillment.[40]

On the campaign trail again after Congress adjourned Chase hewed to familiar themes, opposition to slavery and to its extension into undeveloped territories and abolition wherever Congress controlled. He spoke in twenty counties, usually in the company of his old associate Samuel Lewis, now the Free Democratic candidate for governor.[41] In addition to oratory, Chase supplied Hamlin with his congressional record of accomplishment for projects of specific interest to Ohio, mainly public works bills, but also his efforts to have the federal government cede public lands to the states and various bills for the establishment of free homesteads for settlers.[42]

The Democrats gained a clear majority in the popular vote and in the legislature, though the Free Democrats polled the most votes ever, more than 50,000 out of 283,842 cast.[43] Chase was impressed with the increase in their vote and the election of his friend Townshend to the state senate.[44] However, his hopes for a closer vote between the Whigs and the Democrats were dashed by the very poor showing of the Whigs. Traditional Democratic strength far exceeded his calculations. Now there was no possibility that the Free Democrats who might have supported Chase's reelection to the Senate could bargain with Pierce administration Democrats. And Chase himself was even more isolated from that party because of his refusal to support the President and the national Democratic platform. "The Legislature is more completely old Line," he said, "than I thought possible: which assures me my walking papers. . . ."[45] He professed to be unconcerned about his future, mentioning to Hamlin that he had "no wish ever again to fill a public office."[46]

As he prepared to leave for Washington in November, 1853, his actions belied his words. After arranging for Nettie to spend the winter at Hillsboro, Ohio, with one of Belle's cousins and sending Kate again to Miss Haines's, Chase found time to write a very long public letter to a persistent critic of Chase's Independent Democracy, Alfred P. Edgerton, land speculator and main line Democrat.[47] In his letter, which was published and distributed widely as a pamphlet, Chase spelled out the Party's aims:

To denationalize slavery; to divorce the General Government from slavery; to rescue the Government and its administration from the control of the Slave Power; to put its example and influence perpetually and actively on the side of Freedom at home and abroad; to decentralize power; to substitute as far as possible, popular election of officials, such as postmasters and the like . . . to reform abuses; to economize expenditures; to cheapen postage; . . . to secure Homes for the Homeless and Land for the Landless; to encourage nations struggling with tyrants, by a noble example, by a generous sympathy, and, when practicable, by active aid; in short, to make the American Republic what our Fathers designed it should be—the country of Freemen,—the Refuge of the Oppressed,—the light of the world.[48]

Chase had scarcely settled himself in his new quarters on Capitol Hill when he learned that Stephen A. Douglas was preparing a bill to organize the Nebraska Territory along the lines of the Compromise Acts and the recent Baltimore platform of the Democratic party. This meant that Nebraska would be thrown open to popular sovereignty. The settlers, whoever they might be and regardless of whether they were genuine residents or not, would determine whether the territory would enter the Union as a free or a slave state.

On a superficial level popular sovereignty divorced the general government from slavery, an aim that Chase had so often demanded, but in shifting the burden of slavery or freedom to the local inhabitants, it was not denationalizing the institution. In a negative sense Douglas's bill simply ignored Congress's clear constitutional power to legislate whatever governance or other economic and social conditions it chose to impose on the territories. And for Chase this meant legislating free soil. His position on popular sovereignty was similar to that of Calhoun, their objectives, of course, being diametrically opposite, Calhoun for slavery, Chase for freedom.

The first session of the Thirty-third Congress was only twenty-eight days old when Douglas reported his Nebraska bill. In the previous session of

Congress, a bill for the organization of the territory with the Proviso attached had passed the House with but was defeated in the Senate. As soon as Chase read Douglas's bill, he realized that it was a controversial measure. Concerned, as he always was, about the power of the slave interest over the federal government, sensing a possible political conspiracy to extend slavery into the territories under the pretext of popular sovereignty, Chase began to do research on the geographic limits and the existing population of Nebraska.

There were also conferences with antislavery members of Congress, notably Sumner, Benton, Edward Wade, Joshua Giddings, and the imposing abolitionist Gerrit Smith, then serving his first and only term in the House. At dinner with Benton that elderly flamboyant with characteristic hyperbole told Chase that "Douglas has committed political suicide."[49]

A decision was quickly taken that the only way to delay the Douglas juggernaut and acquaint the nation with what they regarded as the enormity of the Nebraska bill was to draft a political document which would be published in as many of the major newspapers as possible. Once the document had made a maximum impression on those free state legislatures then in session they counted on them to pass resolutions condemning the bill as a blatant extension of slavery into hitherto free areas. Mass meetings in the free states would be encouraged. And efforts would be made to postpone action on the bill until their public education program could take hold. Finally Chase, who was now completely familiar with the Senate rules, would utilize the debate on the bill for comments and brief speeches on the floor. The group chose Chase as their point man in the savage encounters they expected from Douglas and those of the southern senators that were sure to support him. He had the least to lose politically should the document react against its authors (the Democratic majority in the Ohio legislature had already replaced him in the Senate), but his composure under strain, his powers of logical analysis, and his reputation were also factors.

It is fair to assume that Chase's keen understanding of the press and the value of this media to persuade northern leadership groups defined his strategy. It is understandable that he gave the document in its finished version the arresting title "Appeal of the Independent Democrats in Congress to the People of the United States."

Giddings agreed to prepare a draft that was completed during the week of January 16. Chase rewrote most of it, injecting phrases that cast Douglas as the instrument of a conspiracy that slave-state senators had concocted.[50] Then Douglas played directly into Chase's hands. With the "Appeal" drafted and ready for release, Douglas brought before the Senate on January 23 a new version of his original bill. As Chase listened to the clerk reading this redrawn proposed legislation, he must have been amazed that such a shrewd politician as Douglas should have allowed himself to front so openly for the slave interest. The new bill, like the old one, split the territory into two parts, the southern portion, named Kansas, the northern retaining the name Nebraska. The entire region came within the boundaries of the Louisiana Purchase and was north of the Missouri Compromise line.

Douglas's original bill had made no mention of the Missouri Compromise, but had contained the popular sovereignty principle of the Compromise of 1850. It had been taken by both its supporters and its detractors, however, as an implicit repeal of the Missouri Compromise. Now Douglas's new bill contained an explicit repeal of the Compromise which many articulate groups had venerated as a milestone in the short history of the young Republic.

No doubt Chase had a few words with Sumner before the clerk finished his reading. And they may have suspected that Seward and Archibald Dixon, a Whig senator from Kentucky who had been active in preliminary debates of the original bill, had enticed Douglas into dangerous areas in order to embarrass him and the Democratic party.[51] Whatever they thought, Chase was on his feet as soon as the reading ended. In his most plausible and courteous manner he asked Douglas to postpone debate so that the new bill could be studied in all its details. It was a perfectly reasonable request and Douglas, backed up by Cass, agreed when Sumner suggested a delay of one week.[52] Even as Sumner and Chase were asking for a delay the "Appeal" was being set in type in the composing room of the *Era*. It appeared the next day and immediately created a sensation in the tight little circle of official Washington. Studded with such inflammatory words and phrases as "a gross violation of a sacred pledge," a "criminal betrayal," and an "atrocious plot," it frankly accused Douglas by name of being the cat's-paw of Southern conspirators for his own personal ambition.[53]

Chase expected that Douglas would retaliate, but not with such vituperative abuse as he now charged upon him. Muzzled by his own motion from replying for one week, Douglas's rage was Olympian in the flow of violent language and raging epithets he directed at Chase. While "the little giant" worked himself up to a passion of explosive rhetoric, Chase stood behind his desk, a tall, handsome dignified figure confronting the furious Douglas. Several times he sought to interrupt the flow of invective from the scowling senator but to no avail. Eventually Douglas exhausted his stock of pejorative phrases. Chase gained the floor and in distinct contrast to the roaring voice and slang-ridden phrases of Douglas spoke in carefully chiseled language, denying many of the senator's allegations, correcting his carelessness on points of precedent and history with which he was most familiar.

In the exchange made before crowded galleries Chase's demeanor was deliberately aimed at creating the image of the controlled, cultivated gentleman replying to an ill-educated, ill-mannered irascible bully. "I did better than I anticipated in my reply to Douglas," he said, "I knew I could break down his positions: but I did not expect to come near satisfying myself. . . ."[54] Sumner followed Chase with a few words. When he sat down, Seward moved and carried an adjournment to the by now hushed assemblage.

It was not over by any means, for the pugnacious Douglas had been held up as a profligate retainer of the slave interest. That this was an unjust accusation made little or no difference either to the authors of the "Appeal" or to a growing northern audience that was coming around to the opinion that slave owners were controlling the nation for their own special interest. Douglas had made the greatest mistake of his political career and he knew it. The very depth of his rage was a clear indication of just how much Chase and his colleagues had injured his reputation. And neither side in the debate that continued into March would give ground.

Douglas raked up the Whig charge, given wide currency by Greeley in the *Tribune,* that Chase had entered into a corrupt bargain with the Democrats in Ohio for the senatorship. Repeatedly he scored Chase as an abolitionist, and through an ardent supporter, John B. Weller, a Chase-hating Ohio transplant to California, raised the issue of negrophobia.

What a startling contrast—Douglas, the moderate and the nationalist speaking to the race-conscious defenders of slavery in the South and the race-bigoted masses elsewhere. Chase, the radical, now the near-sectionalist, speaking to the conservative elites in the North, the ministers and the editors of the metropolitan press who feared for the disappearance of old landmarks such as the Missouri Compromise. Making the issues and their spokesmen more jumbled, Chase was defending the Missouri settlement, which privately he condemned, and whose import he had publicly denied for years, while Douglas was dismissing it as outmoded legislation, not relevant to the Nebraska settlement.[55] On March 2, Chase finally secured the floor for a set speech on the bill. For the past three days, he had pondered his reply and had accumulated a stack of notes. Yet he regarded his preparation as "very inadequate."

When he began speaking, however, his thoughts fell into place, and "was surprised to get off as well as [he] did in the actual delivery." His speech lasted for several hours and occupied most of the Senate's time over two days.[56] It was a thorough exposition of Chase's views on the Compromises of 1820 and 1850. The former he proclaimed to be a solemn "compact" between the free and the slave states, the latter simply a series of laws subject to repeal. The argument was clear and lucid, couched in language that was free of any abusive phrases or caustic personal allusions. After completing his remarks he successfully parried the attempts of Archibald Dixon and others to pin him down on his definitions. Nor did this effort conclude Chase's opposition to the bill.[57] He and other opponents of the measure fell back on stalling tactics through amendments that not only made copy for the press, but gained time for the "Appeal" to make its way through the northern states.[58]

By the last day of the debate Douglas admitted that he had been "hung" in effigy in Boston. Moderates of both parties were dismayed at the turn the debates had taken. Chase's galling attacks on Douglas and his supporters was the object of widespread criticism. But even those northern senators and congressmen who would not sign the "Appeal," such as Ben Wade and John P. Hale, openly associated themselves with it when they saw the impression it was making in the free states. Chase, himself, had not known at the time how the "Appeal" would take, whether it would be a sensation or simply be dismissed as the work of a lame duck who was an impractical idealist. But he put his best effort into it, and its reception in the North was most gratifying.[59] He considered the "Appeal" to be one of his greatest achievements. And it was in its own way every bit as important as the bill it denounced in precipitating the constitutional crisis that would come six years later.[60] Yet at the time the furor it raised throughout the country was unable to crack Douglas's majority in the Congress. On the dawn of March 4, after an intense all-night wrangle in the Senate, the bill passed. It had already cleared the House. A weary Chase and Sumner were startled as they made their way down the broad steps of the Capitol to hear the steady boom of cannon from the Navy Yard, a mile or so away. Chase turned to Sumner and said, "They celebrate a present victory, but the echoes they awake will never rest until slavery itself will die."[61]

chapter 12

An Uncertain Future

Sunday morning, March 25, 1855, was a busy one for ex-Senator Chase. Over breakfast at the Burnet House in Cincinnati, he discussed a fugitive slave case with a fellow lawyer, Judge Key. After that he read Thomas Hart Benton's speech on the government's policy toward the Indians. Ever seeking some issue that would identify him with man's inhumanity to man and thus solidify further his place in progressive politics, Chase made notes on what he called "horrible injustice" done the Indians. Later that day he would compose an editorial on this subject for the *Columbian,* the reform weekly in Columbus that Hamlin was now editing and he was helping to support. But the highlight of the day was the Reverend Doctor Boynton's sermon on "the necessity of death in the Christian economy" at the Second Congregational Orthodox church that the now ecumenical Episcopalian Chase attended frequently. The idea of supply and demand regulating one's tenure on earth appealed to Chase's notions of laissez-faire economy, even in spiritual matters. In the evening he again attended church, this time Christ Church and again liked the Reverend Clement Moore Butler's theme which utilized a turnpike metaphor to travel the "highway to redemption."[1]

Chase's careful reading of Benton's speech on the government's flawed Indian policy mocked the Reverend Butler's theme on redemption as he recalled his futile efforts to block Douglas's Kansas-Nebraska bill in the last

year of his senatorial term. The administration had moved rapidly to implement the act by providing a territorial government in Kansas. Andrew Reeder,
a political hack, was appointed governor. He and other lackluster members of
the territorial government left for Kansas in October, 1854.[2] They put in
motion the machinery to provide for a legislature and a constitution which they
took to be based on popular sovereignty principles. Foreseeing trouble in
Kansas, Chase began to follow carefully the events in the territory. His taste
for national prominence reinforced through his tenure in the Senate had
quickened an already driving ambition.

Over the past five years he had added to his small circle of political
operators, drawing them from his carefully selected law clerks and law students. These included, at one time or another, James W. Taylor, an attractive
upstate New Yorker, Stanley Matthews, George Hoadly, Jr., and Edward L.
Pierce, thin and spare, an excitable, self-important person whom Sumner had
brought to Chase's attention. All of these lawyers or aspiring lawyers had been
chosen as much for their writing abilities as for their intelligence and legal
aptitude. Loyalty to Chase and Chase's interest in politics counted much.[3]

Of Chase's law-office alumni, Stanley Matthews and Edward L. Pierce
had the longest standing relationship. Pierce, who shared Chase's views on
slavery, was a publicist.[4] Chase had brought him to Washington toward the
end of his Senate term where he acted as his private secretary.[5]

Once the "Appeal" was published in the *Era*, Chase sent Pierce back to
Cincinnati to work with Hamlin and others in organizing mass meetings of
protest against the Kansas-Nebraska bill.[6] Pierce carried with him an "Address" to the people of Ohio, largely a copy of the "Appeal," though Chase
had adapted it to the political situation in the state. Pierce was to have it
published in the Cincinnati *Gazette*, the Cincinnati *Times*, and the *Columbian*.
Equally solicitous of the reaction of the German community in Cincinnati to
his stand, he impressed upon Pierce that a copy of the "Address" be given to
Charles Reemelin, a leading member of Cincinnati's German establishment.

Reemelin had emigrated to the United States in 1832. Well educated, he
was also a practical business man who had entered the grocery business in
Cincinnati and retired in 1845 with a fortune. He was a good public speaker in
both German and English and in retirement had devoted himself to journalism and politics. For a time he owned the most popular German paper in the
Queen City, the *Volksblatt*, but soon turned over the editorial duties to Stephen Molitor, whose background interests and views paralleled his own. Both
men were Protestant Germans and both were devoted to the antislavery cause.
No radical, Reemelin did espouse liberal causes, labor reform, and those
Jacksonian precepts so close to Chase's heart—free trade, hard money, equal
rights for white and black residents of Ohio, opposition to monopoly in any
form, free public education, and prison reform. A close friend of Molitor,

Reemelin was a contentious individual who wrote many public letters and editorials that came close to espousing Chase's Independent Democracy. Reemelin had been a leading spirit in the writing of Ohio's new Constitution of 1850, which finally solved the districting problem not just for Hamilton County but throughout the state.[7] "If he and Molitor side with the Independent Democracy, we may hope for great things," Chase wrote Pierce.[8] From a strategic viewpoint it was essential to build up public opposition to the Kansas-Nebraska Act. Unless opposition become formidable and was sustained, the anti-extension mood in Ohio and elsewhere could evaporate as quickly as it rose.

Shrewdly, Chase charged his friends at home to capitalize on the wave of public indignation through renewed organizing activities on a broad scale. "No faith," he wrote Norton Townshend, "must be put in a mere anti-Nebraska movement. We must adhere to a Democratic organization such as will bring in the German strength."[9] Thus he sought also to improve his position with William Allen, whom he had defeated in the Senate election of 1849, but whom he had supported in the bitterly contested Democratic convention of 1852.[10] At this time Allen represented the Hunker element in the Ohio Democratic party; his conservatism and his fierce opposition to Medary seemed not to have influenced Chase's vaunted progressive pretensions. Nor did his betrayal of Medary (the man most responsible for his election to the Senate) concern this ambitious player in the mix of local politics. There were some mitigating factors.

When Chase cast his line out to Allen, the former senator had shed his Hunker skin for a full-scale attack on Douglas's Kansas-Nebraska bill.[11] Medary, on the other hand, had moved away from his brief flirtation with the progressive cause to back Douglas.[12] To be sure, Chase had an ulterior motive in his approach to Allen, for there was a possibility that the ex-senator would throw his influence behind Chase's reelection to the Senate. But his principal interest in attracting Allen and his following was to strengthen the Independent Democrat movement. The election of Chase's former law student and current Ohio attorney general George E. Pugh to fill Chase's seat after 79 ballots so upset Allen that he decided to retire from politics. He did not respond to Chase's overtures.[13]

Seeking to implement his grand design for a new party organized around his antislavery principles and his progressive reform ideas, Chase did not confine his attention to Ohio. He had certain evidence of division on the slavery issue in Connecticut which was about to elect a senator who would take over the seat of Truman Smith, a Whig regular. Chase enlisted Ichabod Codding, an abolitionist clergyman who traveled about the country lecturing on antislavery themes and who was then in Connecticut to do what he could in lobbying the legislature for the election of an Independent Democrat. Chase pointed out, as he had so often before, that the Whigs would be more prone to adopt an antislavery stance than the Democrats because they were not in power at Washington and therefore not dependent on slave-state support. Whether Codding exerted any influence or not, the Connecticut legislature elected Francis Gillette, formerly a Free Soiler of Whig antecedents. Unfortunately for Chase's plans Gillette would serve only for the remainder of Smith's term, nine months, and would drop out of politics altogether.[14]

As foreshadowed in his Codding letter Chase's political program had taken on a Whiggish cast. He was not quite ready for fusion, but he was all for cooperation between his Independent Democrats and the Whigs not only in Ohio but in Iowa and other western states. Chase had taken the measure of the anti-Nebraska mood when he addressed a well-attended, enthusiastic meeting at the Town Street Methodist Church in Columbus on March 22, 1854, just eighteen days after the passage of the Kansas-Nebraska bill.[15] Chase had seen other possibilities to gain more conscience Whig adherents. He noted how fiercely Lewis Campbell, a conscience Whig and a pugnacious lawyer from Hamilton, Ohio, had fought Douglas's bill in the House of Representatives. More than that Chase was impressed with the public acclaim Campbell achieved by his action.[16]

While Campbell's anti-Nebraska debate was at its height in Washington, Chase urged Hamlin to work out a deal with the Whigs where they would receive a member of the Board of Public Works in return for a judgeship for the Independent Democrats. "The Whigs are now where the old Democrats were four years ago opposed to a pro-slavery national administration," he said.[17] A similar message went out to James Grimes, the new governor of Iowa and a Dartmouth alumnus, who was firmly opposed to the expansion of slavery. Chase would not commit himself to those who were pressing for fusion between all of the political segments that were opposing the extension of slavery.[18] These were conscience Whigs, anti-Nebraska Democrats, and a new and menacing political organization, the Know-Nothings, an antiforeign movement that was spreading its intolerant gospel rapidly in the eastern free states, the border states, and the Northwest. None of these segments had congealed sufficiently for Chase to consider making a distinct move.[19]

Two events following close on each other reinforced his Whiggish tilt, though he was still dubious about fusion. Oran Follett, a conservative-minded editor from Sandusky who had long enjoyed the confidence of the Ohio Whig leadership, had recently taken over the *Ohio State Journal*. From a very nearly moribund newspaper in the state capital, Follett quickly transformed the *Journal* into the most influential anti-Nebraska Whig organ in the state.[20] The other event was a fusion convention that met on July 13, 1854, at Neil's new hall in Cleveland. Two of Chase's close associates, both ex-Democratic Free Soilers, participated in the deliberations and were responsible for a resolution declaring the Kansas-Nebraska Act "inoperative and void" in areas in which the Missouri Compromise established freedom. The meeting did not form a new party but it clearly aimed in that direction when it nominated the Free Soil Democrat Joseph P. Swan for the state supreme court and the Whig Jacob Blickensderfer for the Board of Public Works. Similar conventions with similar nominations and resolutions were held in Indiana and in Michigan.[21]

A fusion resolution at the Cleveland Convention that was bothersome to him was one that had a distinctly nativist pigment. Not explicitly Know Nothing, it could and was construed as reflecting the dominant Whig complexion of the delegates. If Chase's plans for his own future depended upon anti-Nebraska, Whig Know Nothing support, they also required his own free Democratic contingent and the support of anti-Nebraska Democrats, especially those in the German communities of Cincinnati and in the eastern and central areas of the state.

Native-born and foreign immigrants of German ancestry constituted over 10 percent of Ohio's population.[22] In a close election, their votes were crucial. Yet the Whig-inspired fusion ticket in the November election swept all before it in such overwhelming numbers that Chase knew he would somehow have to deal with the Know Nothings. He would have to devise a very delicate, very complicated formula that would retain a sizable foreign vote but not alienate native-born citizens. Until he had achieved a workable plan, he resisted Bailey's campaign for a new fusion party based exclusively on anti-Nebraska objectives. What was abundantly clear, however, was that most Ohioans very definitely opposed the Kansas-Nebraska Act.[23]

That Sunday five months later as Chase listened with close attention to the sermons of Boynton and of Butler he may have intuitively applied their supply and demand themes to the condition of Ohio politics, its economy, and his own political future. On the supply side there were too few politicians of national stature chasing the obvious popular demand to keep slavery and the blacks out of the as yet unsettled western territories. Yet inflated demand, while it was certainly there, was in a state of factional flux, presenting great opportunity but at the same time great dangers to any aspiring politician.

Was Know Nothingism a temporary phenomenon like the anti-Masonic movement of a bygone day? Or had it developed a more permanent organization reflecting a deep-seated trend that saw in immigration a greater threat to American values than slavery? Was it simply a revulsion of a Calvinist-oriented Protestant people toward an anti-democratic, hierarchical Roman Catholicism? Prejudice and intolerance were elements of American society that had existed long before the establishment of the Republic. As a well-read, well-educated man, Chase was aware of these dark undercurrents.

Instinctively he rejected Know Nothingism as he rejected slavery, but as an ambitious politician he would use the movement provided he could do so with a minimum of risk. Most of the Know Nothings in Ohio had been Whigs, a party that was now in the final stages of dissolution as a national organization. If Chase had any future in politics he had to have Know Nothing support. A difficult feat this would be under any circumstances because of the distrust and even hatred many of the former Whig leaders in the state harbored toward him. They had not forgotten his deal with the Democrats that ensured his election to the Senate five years before. They looked askance at his reform ideas, not merely his opposition to slavery and its extension but to his progressive agenda on other social issues.[24] While recognizing their animus Chase was bending every effort to placate would-be Know Nothings, to emphasize to them slavery's graver peril to free institutions.

This stance was one of the reasons why in those spring days a year earlier Chase objected to the term Republican for the new party that was being organized in neighboring states.[25] Chase and other anti-extension leaders in Ohio were also concerned about timing. They shied away from any distinctive name for a new party until at least one state election decided whether fusion was a genuine coalescing of all antislavery elements or simply a device of the Whigs, the Democrats, or the Know-Nothings to swallow up the original Free Soilers.[26] As late as September, 1854, Chase was opposed to the Republican label which he deemed a poor substitute for Independent Democrat.[27]

Another compelling reason for caution was that the German element dominant in Cincinnati, a majority solidly in the anti-Nebraska fold, was just as solidly opposed to the Know Nothings. Chase realized that he must stand for governor on some ticket that had a reasonable chance for success if he was to maintain the momentum he had initiated with his "Appeal." Reluctantly he came to the conclusion that he must jettison his Independent Democratic label and assume that of Republican.

The times were dicey for an aspiring politician. With Chase's background they were especially so, since he would have to knit together mutually suspicious, querulous, and discordant groups, each with its own organization, unique objectives, local champions. Out of this mass he must concoct an amalgam sufficiently binding for these mutually hostile parts to work as a unit against the extension of slavery.

Fusion with the Know Nothings, as the dominant force, even with anti-extension as a prime objective, was repugnant to Chase's cherished ideals of human rights. He believed that the Know Nothing thrust was too narrow for any sustaining political institution. Even as he deplored its intolerant nativism, Chase recognized its essential weakness as a political party. Yet he confessed to Hamlin his "uneasiness about the probable influence of the order on our movement." He still thought that it was "best not to say anything against them; what is objectionable may cure itself."[28] He had learned that some Know Nothing leaders were pushing Jacob Brinkerhoff, an anti-Nebraska Democrat, for the gubernatorial nomination. Oran Follet in the Columbus *State Journal* now came out for Brinkerhoff, providing Chase with sufficient evidence that the old-line Whigs in the Know Nothing party were still unforgiving.[29] Yet Chase judged that the anti-Nebraska surge which he had pioneered was so strong that it would swamp any lingering ill-will to him personally. He had taken part in the state campaign that had climaxed less than a month before with an overwhelming victory for the "People's" anti-Nebraska party. Even his home city, a Democratic stronghold for more than a decade, piled up unprecedented majorities for the fusion candidates.[30]

These tidings along with the Brinkerhoff movement precipitated Chase's decision to seek the People's or Republican nomination for governor. James M. Ashley, a broad-shouldered, self-taught lawyer, chaired a secret meeting of Chase supporters in October 1854 to prepare for the campaign of 1855.[31] News of the meeting got out, however, and an ever-cautious Chase felt compelled to offer a lame explanation when he disavowed to Follet his connection with it. "I never knew anything of any such conference until after it had been held," he said. Referring to it as an "accidental meeting," he added that he happened to be in Toledo the day after the convention. He admitted that he talked over the governorship with Ashley.[32]

Ashley's political career had been as checkered as his business affairs. The son of a peripatetic Campbellite minister, he had been brought up in a poor, highly religious family that had moved about Illinois, the Ohio Valley, Kentucky, and western Virginia. Variously a deck hand and stevedore on Mississippi river boats, a printer, and an editor, he finally became a lawyer but kept a drugstore on the side.

Ashley possessed in abundance character traits that made him attractive to Chase. He had a strong commitment to temperance, a growing popular force in Ohio; he was a dedicated antislavery man; he had been a Democrat; and he was an ambitious political organizer and publicist. Briefly a Know Nothing, Ashley parted from that organization and, indicative of his impulsive temperament, had become a fierce opponent of nativism in any form.

If Chase found in Ashley an interesting person whose background and editorial skills were useful to his political plans, Ashley found in Chase the political and social aims he espoused. His impoverished background and his unstable, dogmatic father from whom he had long since severed relations made the handsome, highly educated Chase a model figure he sought to emulate.[33]

As soon as Chase launched his candidacy in northwestern Ohio, a center of Know Nothing strength, he was immediately faced with a series of perplexing political questions. How and when to utilize the Know Nothings without compromising his integrity was the all-important question. Beyond the problems the temporary political climate posed, the situation in Kansas was playing into Chase's hands. The Pierce administration had bungled the Kansas settlement when it sent to the territory a weak team of administrators divided within itself on how to establish a territorial government. However inept these individuals, it was soon apparent that any effort to organize the territory on a popular sovereignty basis was doomed to failure. The reckless proslavery ex-senator from Missouri, David Atchison, was masterminding a concerted effort to defeat any organization on free territorial lines.[34]

Atchison had two objects in mind. He hoped to repair his political fortunes and to stave off the rapid decline of slavery in Missouri. He and others of like persuasion led a horde of Missourians across the Missouri River into neighboring Kansas whenever a crucial vote was to be taken. Opposing Atchison and his adventurers were those who hoped to settle permanently in Kansas. Small farmers mainly from free and slave states and emigrants from Illinois, Ohio, and Indiana predominated. There were also some New Englanders, though a distinct minority, who had come into Kansas under the sponsorship of a gifted promoter, Eli Thayer, who had formed the well-publicized, well-financed Massachusetts Emigrant Aid Society. Behind these contesting groups were the typical land speculators, among whom was Pierce's territorial governor Andrew H. Reeder. Eastern capitalists were also involved, and many had contributed handsomely to Thayer's company. Also in the rush to Kansas came lawyers, expectant politicians, and especially presumptive newspaper editors, as well as a cohort of reporters for eastern newspapers. Here was a vocal, contentious group ready to exploit any opportunity for publicity, politics, or profit.[35]

And the activities of slave-state partisans and their opponents quickly claimed national attention, providing opportunities for newspaper editors and politicians alike. When such vociferous elements of society combined on a single theme, the attention of the general public was bound to be concentrated on the territory. Kansas was fast providing a cutting edge between two opposing value systems.

As armed clashes, murders, and destruction of property escalated during the spring and summer of 1855, Chase made the most of this turmoil to elaborate on his charges of a conspiracy between the slave power and a subservient administration. He was certain that the Kansas trouble would override individual group interests and would focus attention upon the clash between slavery and freedom, not just in Kansas but in all the territories as yet unsettled. Although Chase believed Kansas would be the deciding factor, he was not that confident of his nomination for the governorship despite firm support from the more liberal antislavery Whigs and Democrats.[36] Characteristically, he sought more personal publicity to advance his cause. He had Pierce draft a sort of campaign biography, and he finally managed to have

Hamlin take over the *Columbian* after months of cajoling and a personal investment of substantial sums in the paper.[37]

Chase continued to correspond with Grimes of Iowa and Kinsley Bingham, the newly elected governor of Michigan. His letters to these influential westerners were aimed at promoting his national image. Like other perceptive politicians he recognized that a new party organization would arise out of the wreckage of the Whigs and the sudden emergence of the Know Nothings.[38]

Chase was in Washington attending the short session of the Thirty-third Congress and his last one as senator, but the speeches and debates did not claim his interest. His mind was on the unfolding political situation in Ohio. He was kept abreast of affairs there by the constant flow of correspondence that crossed his desk in the Senate, through conversations with political emissaries, and careful reading of the Ohio newspapers he received.[39] He was, as usual, much in the company of the Baileys. While he was not always in agreement with the editorial policy of the *Era*, he could not help but be influenced by the radical antislavery discussions that went on at Bailey's hospitable table.[40] He differed with the idealistic editor on how to deal with the Know Nothings. Bailey railed against the order, condemning its secrecy, and, among other indictments, accused it of dividing and weakening the antislavery movement with false issues.

But since the Ohio election, during the past fall Chase and Giddings, who were now acting together, were less worried than Bailey about the Know Nothings. They were nonetheless careful about cooperation with them.[41] George W. Julian, former Free Soil congressman from Ohio and an old acquaintance dating from the Van Buren Free Soil campaign, asked Chase what he thought about the order. Chase replied that as he had been and was still willing to cooperate with the Whigs and the "Old line" Democrats when they were willing to oppose the expansion of slavery, so he would cooperate with the Know Nothings when he could do so "honorably and without sacrifice of principle."[42] Principle or not he cautioned Hamlin to tone down his critical editorials on the Order in the *Columbian*. "Apart from its secrecy in which it shrouds itself," he wrote, "it is infinitely more respectable, for it does not contradict itself," a failing he charged upon the Democrats.[43]

Follett and Ashley, though opposites in political beliefs, had become indispensable to the success of the Chase candidacy. Chase needed Follett for his editorial influence and his Whig ties, Ashley because of his knowledge of Know Nothing organization, his firm adherence to Chase's Independent Democracy, his newspaper experience, his place of residence, and his personal devotion.

Well before Ashley's Toledo meeting Follett was inadvertently assisting Chase with important Whigs. To Thomas Ewing Follett wrote, "I know the cry of abolitionism is potent; and I know that the address ["the Appeal"] of Chase, Sumner, Giddings on the introduction of the Nebraska Bill, came near swamping us altogether. . . ."[44] In spite of the depth and the breadth of the anti-Nebraska sentiment that Chase's "Appeal" was generating, many of the old-line Whigs and the Whig Know Nothings continued to oppose him and the emerging "People's" or Republican organization. Compounding the political confusion were the sweeping victories of the Know Nothings in New Hampshire and Massachusetts.[45]

But then a dramatic and dangerous antiforeign riot in Cincinnati sent shock waves through the business communities of the state.[46] Chase was boarding at the Burnet House in downtown Cincinnati at the time.[47] He was devoting most of his energies and abilities to politics, rather than his law practice. Ball and the younger partners, including his nephew Ralston Skinner, were carrying on the legal business of the firm. Because it was municipal election day in Cincinnati, Chase had a special reason to be in his office on April 2. Only two parties, the Democratic and the Know Nothing, were offering slates for city officers. The candidates for mayor were both journalists. James J. Farran, editor of the *Enquirer*, was heading the Democratic (pro-German) ticket; James Taylor, editor of the *Times*, a virulent nativist paper, was the Know Nothing candidate. Chase knew both well. He mistrusted them politically, but he was careful not to make any public or even private comment on the election.[48] He must have been disgusted at the low depths in political billingsgate the campaign had plumbed. Yet he and many others were taken aback at the outbreak of violence that occurred on election day and continued for three days.

Anarchy reigned in the eastern wards of the city when a boatload of Kentuckians joined forces with Cincinnati nativists to assault the German wards. Spasmodic gunfire became a virtual barrage when the well-disciplined, well-armed Germans broke an assault on the defensive barricades they had thrown across the canal bridges to their section of town. Two of the attackers were killed and a score or more wounded before the mob retreated. All semblance of law and order disappeared from the streets of the city before passions ran their course and a shaky peace was restored. Farran and the Democratic slate were declared victors.

What upset Chase and his grand design for enlisting the discordant elements of Know Nothings, emigrants, former Democrats, and Whigs behind an anti-Nebraska banner was that the riot was directed against all foreigners irrespective of religious preference.[49] He was well aware of the latent antagonism against foreigners that had been present in Cincinnati since his arrival there in 1830. Like others in his professional class, he had assumed this attitude was a deeply felt prejudice against the Roman Catholic Church. While he himself as a high church Episcopalian was tolerant of Catholics, he had after all grown up in a Protestant world where Rome was generally considered the "whore of Babylon," a visible expression of European despotism.

It was no coincidence that he cultivated Charles Reemelin and Frederick Hassaurek as much for their influence among Cincinnati's German community and their journalistic abilities as for their anti-Catholicism.[50] For there is no doubt that Chase hoped to sustain a working relationship between the Protestant Germans and Irish and the Know Nothings. It had held together in the election the previous year when the "People's" or Republican party had swept the state as a protest against the Nebraska Act. This unlikely alliance had contributed mightily to the rebuke of the orthodox Democrats.

Unfortunately for Chase's planning the election day riot drove the German and Irish Protestants away from the Know Nothings. But, simultaneously, its challenge to civic order hurt the Know Nothing organization far more. Business classes and well-to-do farmers throughout the state who had leaned toward nativism now saw graphically how it could be employed with destructive effects on society.

The fact that there was considerable unemployment in Cincinnati and other urban centers and that jobless workingmen formed a major component in the mob actions deeply concerned the propertied classes, who counted among their ranks most of the Know Nothing leaders. Joseph Medill, editor of the Cleveland *Leader* and an outspoken Republican journalist, had caught the first tremors of Know Nothing disruption several months before the riot. "So long as the Know-Nothings refuse to admit Protestants naturalized in the councils and proscribe them the same as Catholics," he wrote Oran Follett, "they will be thrown off to the loco focos and so long as the order ignores the slavery question the antislavery men will refuse to cooperate with them." Medill, of emigrant stock himself, had been active in seeking common ground between emigrant Protestants and Know Nothings on an antislavery basis.[51] He claimed with some exaggeration that this movement controlled some thirty counties in Ohio. "Its leading men are Know Nothings," he said; "the object is to get control of the Know-Nothing orders . . . it works as a wheel within a wheel."[52]

Chase had made no mention of the riot in his correspondence, which remained conspicuously blank for that week. Nor did he comment on it much later when he furnished his campaign biographer with details of his life and career. Unusually responsive to local unrest and always a champion of law and order, he had learned from past experience to move carefully on what he perceived to be a delicate issue. He had already received hints that he not seek the Republican nomination for governor. Edward Wade, for instance, speaking for those Independent Democrats who had been Whigs, urged that Chase be a candidate for the state supreme court, advice that he rejected.[53] Another key to Chase's reticence was his belief that if the anti-Nebraska movement should lose the support of the Know Nothings in favor of a national party with a slaveholding wing, the consequences for him and for the entire movement would be disastrous. "The future had not a very satisfying look to me," he said, and added that "the Republican party seems to me not likely to last long."[54]

chapter 13

On the Campaign Trail

In the aftermath of the Cincinnati riot, it became apparent that the Brinkerhoff candidacy was a move the Whig Know Nothings were pushing to cut short Chase's political career or force him into their party. As Chase saw it this latter course was far more dangerous to the antislavery cause and to his own political ambitions.[1] Though Brinkerhoff had a fine antislavery record as a congressman (one of the authors of what became known as the Wilmot Proviso), this splenetic lawyer from Mansfield, in north-central Ohio, was one of the few Democratic political leaders in the state who had openly joined the Know Nothing organization.[2]

Spring verged on summer when Chase began to ease away from his cautious attitude toward the Know Nothings. His changing position was the result of evidence he received from supporters, former free-soil Whigs and Democrats, that they would stand firm against any fusion that left the Know Nothings the dominant party. More important, he had assurances from Thomas Spooner, an amiable Cincinnati neighbor who headed the Order, and from Lewis Campbell that the Know Nothings were not solidly behind Brinkerhoff, that they were beginning to fear the social consequences of nativism.

Chase's authorship of the "Appeal," his course in the Senate in seeking and garnering federal money for the state, his long association with antislavery causes, and his national prestige had blunted some Whig Know Nothing criticism of his past political actions. His association with Giddings gained him support in the greater Cleveland area and his early disavowal of Hamlin's diatribes against the Order in the *Columbian* also helped.[3] The apparent neutrality of those old Whig warhorses Ewing and Corwin was also a positive sign. Their confidant, Oran Follett, was anxious to promote fusion on a broad antislavery basis. But Joseph Medill, editor of the Cleveland *Herald*, the most influential Whig paper in Ohio's Western Reserve, sought to line up Follett as a move to discredit Chase at any early stage.[4]

After much twisting and turning Follett rejected Medill's advice and urged a fusion policy in the *Journal*, citing ample benefits for both the Know Nothings and Chase's Independent Democrats. Follett was in a strategic position to act as honest broker, if this term can be used for such a canny politician. Chairman of the People's, or Republican, central committee, he had been a conscience Whig. He and his predominantly Whiggish committee were indignant that the Know Nothings were apparently going ahead on an independent course. They were in effect ignoring the benefits of cooperation so abundantly manifest in the People's party triumph of the past year.[5] Nevertheless the committee authorized Follett to approach its Know Nothing counterpart and participate in any "secret" meetings it planned.

The Republican central committee had already set July 13, the anniversary of the Northwest Ordinance, as the date for its convention. An impression was gaining currency that the Democrats and the Know Nothings would await the results of the convention before they acted. Reflecting this attitude, the Republican committee reserved the right to defer its convention as events should indicate. Chase was alerted to its decisions. The indecisiveness of the party leaders prompted him and his followers to firm up their stand.[6] Even if the Know Nothings packed the Republican Convention, nominated their slate, and wrote the platform, Chase's faction was strong enough to give the state to the Democrats.[7]

Follett contacted members of the Know Nothing executive council and was invited along with two others of his own choice to attend a secret meeting in Cincinnati. He selected William Schouler, editor of the Cincinnati *Gazette*, and George A. Benedict of the Cleveland *Herald* as his colleagues. At one time or another they had endorsed nativist concepts and together with Follett himself represented three distinct areas of the state. The secret conclave met in Cincinnati during the last week of April in a room on Fourth Street which was being used during the day by the engineers and draughtsmen planning the construction of the Ohio and Mississippi Railroad.[8] These quarters were a part of an elaborate deception the Know Nothing leaders planned to preserve tactical secrecy.[9] On his arrival Follett noticed Lewis Campbell in the room and at once took a seat next to him. It had been arranged that Follett, representing the Republicans, would be the first speaker.

Prior to the meeting Follett had called on Chase in a vain effort to have him decline nomination. Thus when he addressed the meeting he knew that both Chase and Brinkerhoff were certain candidates. Surveying the soberly dressed individuals crammed in among the drafting tables and other office paraphernalia, Follett told his audience in no uncertain terms that Chase would be a candidate and that if they backed Brinkerhoff not only would the party be defeated, but the antislavery cause would suffer a very distinct setback in Ohio and elsewhere in the nation. He urged that they divide the ticket between the Republicans and the Know Nothings and adopt an anti-Nebraska platform when they met in convention. "Half a loaf is better than no bread," he said on concluding his remarks. Campbell followed with a similar message. Both men were questioned closely and it seemed apparent to them that no commitments would be made at this time.

But, to their astonishment, one of the Know Nothing members secured the floor. Obviously by pre-arrangement, he asked that a full ticket be made forthwith, a motion that was adopted with enthusiasm despite Follett's objections. Thereupon Follett nominated Brinkerhoff, whom he knew was the preferred candidate. As a Republican leader Follett's nomination was taken to be his party's recommendation. The Know Nothings were delighted to accept the supposed offer.[10] A Chase candidacy, they felt, if not scuttled was reduced merely to nuisance value.

Despite the elaborate attempts at secrecy that took on the trappings of comedy, before ten o'clock in the morning of the next day the supposed crippled candidate had learned all about the meeting in specific detail. Chase gathered that the Know Nothings were divided in their councils and, except for a cadre of Chase hating ex-Whigs, seemed to be placing antislavery above nativism. As Follett recalled, Chase "was active and aggressive. His Liberty friends as a class, were men of concentrated views and determined purpose."[11] Taking the high road with Follett, who complained that he was not being "open and fair," Chase denied the allegation. He saw no need for the Know Nothings to be "'divided and conquered,'" as Medill—who was now backing Chase—and Ashley were attempting.[12] His supporters, he insisted, had been and still were "ready for fair and honorable cooperation."[13]

Not a month after the secret meeting Brinkerhoff questioned whether "the peculiar friends of Mr. C[hase] have about made up their minds to rule or ruin." Still he dismissed Chase's group as a "corporal's guard" and looked forward to his nomination as a fusion candidate at the Republican convention on July 13.[14] Actually Chase's supporters were far more numerous and politically vigorous than any corporal's guard. A good many antislavery Protestant

Germans and Scotch-Irish, concerned about nativism, saw in Chase an appropriate alternative. The now faithful Giddings and Chase's political rival Ben Wade, representing free-soil Whigs, were backing Chase for much the same reasons. And the hard core of former Liberty party members and Free Soilers had reason to mistrust Chase's tactics in the past but not his antislavery principles.

All along Chase had maintained a relationship with two key Know Nothing leaders, Thomas Spooner and Lewis Campbell. With Campbell he had held out the prize of his support among his congressional friends to help elect him Speaker of the House. Spooner, too, who was clerk of the superior court in Cincinnati, was receptive to hints from Chase about higher office. The Know Nothing leadership, however, remained skeptical until they were able to gauge more accurately the results of the Republican convention. The state council decided not to formalize its nominations at a separate convention and went ahead with its plans to dominate the Republican convention. It would meet again in August to determine whether the Order would support the Republican candidate for governor, who the council hoped would not be Chase.

Follett too was not impressed with Chase's insistence on independent action and was determined to emphasize Republican leadership with Know Nothing support as a preliminary move toward fusion on an antislavery platform. He traveled to Mansfield, Brinkerhoff's home, and had a personal interview with the Know Nothing candidate. He asked Brinkerhoff for "a pledge not to withdraw from the canvas at the insistence of Mr. Chase's friends or of anybody else without consulting me." Follett explained the position of the Republican party, reiterating the split policy of half Republican, half Know Nothing as far as the candidates were concerned, and presumably the same ratio as it applied to the platform. Brinkerhoff gave the pledge and kept it.[15]

By now Chase had solidified fairly well his standing with Campbell and Spooner though not without some lengthy correspondence in which he categorically refused to participate in any fusion movement made on Know Nothing principles. At a meeting of the state council in Cleveland, the second week in June, Chase's spokespersons were in attendance. Campbell successfully blocked all efforts to make separate nominations.[16]

For some time Medill and Ashley had been working hard to split the Know Nothings by emphasizing the anti-Catholic, antislavery issues that would appeal to Protestant emigrants not just in Ohio but elsewhere.[17] Despite Chase's denial that he was not pursuing a divide-and-conquer course, he certainly knew of Ashley's and Medill's efforts in this direction and tacitly at least supported them. The Know Somethings, as their faction came to be known, organized a national convention in Cleveland that was held June 13–

15. Ashley was the moving spirit.[18] Of transcendent importance to the Know Somethings and to Chase's aspirations was the outcome of the National Council of the Know Nothings meeting in Philadelphia just before the Cleveland convention. There the order dropped its secrecy and adopted a new name, the American party. These cosmetic changes did not improve its fortunes. Quite the contrary: the party's leadership broke down completely after its southern members demanded a proslavery resolution for its recommendation to the state organizations and for its national platform. Northern members refused and when no compromise could be achieved seceded from the Council. Henceforth for a brief period the northern group would be known as the North Americans while the rump was known as the South Americans.

A good many of the seceding members had attended the Know Something convention where Chase's name, whenever mentioned, according to Ashley "'brought down the house'". Besides promoting Chase, the ebullient Ashley managed to secure a resolution for a committee of correspondence that would work with the Ohio North Americans on the slavery and Kansas issues while playing down nativism as far as the Protestant emigrants were concerned.[19] Ashley was made chairman of the committee which included the accommodating Schuyler Colfax of Indiana, an old friend of Chase.[20] The convention was broadly representative, having members from New York, Massachusetts, and Maine. Ashley's committee was empowered to work up a national organization on an anti-Nebraska platform. Chase was well content with the results of the Know Something convention. Presidential aspirations which he had been cultivating since his election to the Senate in 1849 now seemed more than a distant possibility.[21]

These developments confirmed Chase's rejection of Ashley's suggestion that a mass meeting of anti-Nebraska men should be held on July 4 in Columbus to stimulate enthusiasm for Chase's nomination at the Republican state convention eleven days later. Fearful that the Know Nothings would seize control of the convention, Ashley and others wanted Chase to edit a letter he had written to Dr. John Paul in December, 1854.[22] The letter was an eloquent anti-Nebraska statement, yet at the same time dealt in an evenhanded manner with the Know Nothings. It was explicit, however, in expressing personal opposition to the movement. "I cannot proscribe men on account of their birth," Chase had written. "I can not make religious faith a political test."[23]

Chase was a better judge of his own chances and of the declining fortunes of the Know Nothings than were his political lieutenants. He rejected their advice for a pre-convention meeting of his supporters as a sign of weakness. And he withheld any tampering with his letter to Paul until the political mist had cleared sufficiently for him to see the way.[24] As early as February 1855 when he was still in the Senate Chase had correctly predicted the future of the Know Nothing party. "There is a great struggle going on in the Know Nothing organization between the antislavery and the pro-slavery element," he had observed. "Be patient and time will separate the progressive from the conservative."[25]

As the date for what was now known as the fusion convention drew near, Chase became more confident of his nomination. He thought that the Know Nothings "will quietly acquiesce in the Democratic-Republican movement" and that he would be nominated on July 13.[26] From various quarters of the state he received optimistic reports. By his own count some forty to fifty newspapers were favoring his nomination.[27] He felt easy enough about his prospects to leave for the East in May, where he would improve his candidacy for a presidential nomination in 1856. He anticipated a new political organization would emerge out of the wreckage of the Whig and Know Nothing parties in combination with his own cherished Independent Democrats.

As usual he traveled to the northeast, visiting Kate in New York before going on to Washington in mid-May.[28] He had lengthy conversations with James S. Pike, a coming force in Maine politics and one of Greeley's most trusted reporters. In Washington, he stayed with the Baileys and talked with Montgomery Blair, Pierce's Secretary of State William L. Marcy, and several other Democratic and Republican politicians.[29] Yet, as he knew well, in politics one should never take anything for granted.

To be sure, Hamlin, Stone, and Ashley had seen to it that the immediate precincts of the Town Street Methodist Church where the fusion convention was convening on July 13 had a large crowd of Chase supporters through whom the delegates had to make their way to the meeting room. And the balconies were also thoughtfully filled with Chase advocates.[30] Chase was on hand trying to be as friendly and warm with the delegates as his dignified presence would allow. Though in reality a fusion convention, he was quite insistent that it be a Republican or as he preferred a Democratic-Republican convention. Follett, who was handling the new party's interests, thought along the same lines and was pushing earnestly for his "half and half" formula.[31] Much in evidence among the excited delegates was Giddings, his massive form overtopping the crowd. He, too, was maneuvering to bring the delegates behind Chase and to bring pressure on the platform committee to drop any plank that favored nativism implicitly or explicitly.

Hard-core Whig Know Nothings sought to block Chase by pushing for the nomination of Judge Swan, the successful "People's" candidate of the previous year. Another smaller group but one that could be threatening was made up of antislavery Whigs from Chase's hometown of Cincinnati. Lead by the earnest and able lawyer Rutherford B. Hayes, they distrusted Chase's motives.[32] Nor had the Brinkerhoff men given up his candidacy. In fact at one point when the tension in the chamber reached its highest point, it appeared that the convention might deadlock. Follett was the delegate who had the best

chance of breaking the impasse. He decided to cast his influence behind
Chase to forestall any bolt of Chase's Independent Democrats.

A nervous Chase had left the convention while the bargaining went on
and returned to his room at the Neil House.[33] Follett approached Brinkerhoff
and convinced him to withdraw in exchange for a Supreme Court judgeship.
Armed with this news Follett hurried to Chase's room. Brinkerhoff's
withdrawal meant certain nomination. Chase "seemed incredulous" until
Lewis Campbell appeared and confirmed the deal.[34]

Whether Chase was "incredulous" or not, he approved the slate whose
nominees were all prominent Know Nothings but who were also confirmed
anti-Nebraska men. And it was his insistence backed by Giddings and others
of Chase's group that the platform adopted had a thoroughgoing anti-
extension resolution. Chase was responsible also for the planks that demanded
a tariff for revenue only and liberal homestead laws. On the state level it called
for lower taxes on real estate and the enactment of more progressive banking
legislation. Chase saw to it that there was no mention of nativism.

He was nominated for governor on the first ballot with 220 votes to Judge
Swan's 102. Hiram Griswold, a last-minute candidate of the Know Nothings,
received only 42 votes.[35] Chase's gambit that the Cincinnati riot would compel the Know Nothing leadership to see the error of their ways had paid off.

Follett's formula of "half and half" prevailed but only on the ticket. Much
more important to Chase's future, the convention translated fusion into the
formal organization of the Republican party in Ohio despite his preference for
the Democratic name.[36] Chase had his nomination, which would be of great
assistance to him and to the new Republican party that was being formed in
other states.

The platform was a firm antislavery declaration with particular reference
to the territories but without any specific rebuke to nativism. The anomaly of a
free-soil champion heading a Know Nothing slate was not lost on the electorate, especially the Chase-hating former Whigs, even though the ticket favored them with six of the nine nominations. Opposition to the new party and
its leading nominee was spread thinly in Know Nothing regions throughout
the state, but it was highly concentrated in those counties that bordered on the
slave states of Kentucky and Virginia. In spite of Campbell's vigorous drilling
of his fellow Know Nothings in Hamilton County, its population center,
Cincinnati, and its immediate environs were intensely antagonistic to Chase.

The *State Journal*, Follett's paper in Columbus, was not exactly pleased
at his nomination either. An editorial that appeared four days after the convention summed up Follett's opinion. "Mr. Chase is rather a dark mixture," it
commented, "but you know some of the gredients ain't so black."[37] Similarly
Shouler's Cincinnati *Gazette* and the *Commercial* gave tepid support. Taylor's
Cincinnati *Times* was venomous in its charges upon Chase and the Know

Nothing leaders who had joined the Republicans. Preparations were made to hold a separatist mass meeting in mid-August. Everyone expected that a formal Know Nothing ticket would enter the campaign. Deeply concerned by strident accusations of betrayal, Thomas Spooner sought to head off a threatened bolt. He authored and distributed a circular to Know Nothing party members to abide by their leaders' pledges and support the ticket that had been openly chosen in a formal convention.[38]

Neither Chase nor any of his close friends had any doubt that a rough campaign lay ahead. There was to be no resting upon their oars after their stunning victory over a majority opponent. The stigma of the Know Nothing ticket had to be overcome by emphasizing the fact that Chase had never been a member of the order and that he and the platform stood for the new Republican party erected on Liberty party and Free Soil party principles. Chase had made that plain in his brief acceptance speech.[39] Despite the efforts of Spooner and other Know Nothing party chieftains who had gone for Chase, there was no stopping the momentum for the mass Know Nothing convention on August 9.

To Chase's consternation, the convention met at Columbus and was well attended. Delegates were in general agreement to run an American ticket in the October election. But the organizers had some differences of opinion on the choice of acceptable candidates. After the expenditure of much heated rhetoric, the convention finally settled on former governor Allen Trimble to head the ticket. It was obvious that the convention members were more opposed to Chase than to voicing nativist concerns. Trimble had been a prominent Whig, but was never formally a member of the Order, a test that had been fixed for any candidate it would support. All of the Republican nominees except Chase were endorsed, equally telling evidence of personal hostility. Trimble was over seventy years old, and beyond his call for old Whig principles he simply rehearsed in his acceptance remarks the by now hallowed grievance of mainline Whigs regarding Chase's political conduct.[40]

Meanwhile the Democrats had renominated William Medill as their candidate for governor. They had counted on a mass desertion of Know Nothings from the Republican party. But when fusion triumphed with Chase's nomination at the July 13 convention and a distinct Know Nothing party seemed to be fading as a political force, they changed their campaign approach. Instead of exploiting nativist themes, their presses and stump speakers began stressing sectional issues, in particular belaboring Chase as an abolitionist who would flood the state with blacks.

The Democratic leadership took some comfort from the Trimble candidacy and encouraged its opposition to Chase, whom they pictured as decidedly opposed to nativism. Naturally they downplayed the Kansas issue which for the moment was on hold as the Pierce administration had just appointed Wilson Shannon to replace Andrew Reeder as governor of that troubled territory. A former Democratic governor of Ohio, it was felt that Shannon should be given a chance.[41]

Chase left Ohio shortly after his nomination for his customary summer visit to the East, where he visited politicians, newspaper editors, and family—Kate in New York and relatives in Concord, New Hampshire. He had left the conduct of his campaign in the capable hands of Hamlin, Lewis Campbell, Thomas Spooner, and late convert Oran Follett.[42] Back in the state by mid-August, Chase prepared to take the stump on his own and his new party's behalf. He knew that if it were defeated—and there was a good possibility that this would occur—his own political career would be at an end. The anti-Nebraska momentum could not be sustained indefinitely if the Kansas issue was resolved. Comparing his election prospects with those of the previous year, Chase found the outlook rather grim. The Know Nothings had enough remaining strength to be an important if not crucial factor. And while most of them were antislavery, and the movement itself on the wane, he felt he had to be discreet on nativist issues but not so discreet that he alienated the foreign voters. Yet he had to reconcile himself to the possibility that the bulk of the naturalized citizens would vote for the Democratic candidate.[43]

He began his campaign on August 2 with the torrid heat of late summer in the Midwest beating down upon him.[44] He wore no hat to shield his balding, massive head or protect his clean-shaven face from the sun because he decided that any head covering would detract from the dignified bearing he wished to project. And though very near-sighted, he would never appear upon the public stage with glasses. It was always awkward for him when he had to read a passage or refer to notes.

At Zanesville on August 7 near the center of the state, having traveled the twenty-five miles by buggy from Newark where he had spoken the day before, he addressed a crowd in the town square. Then instead of resting he spent his leisure time dashing off letters to associates on campaign particulars and to influential editors with optimistic accounts of his receptions and audiences.[45]

The usual thorny problems came up that required deft handling. Chase had written a decidedly anti-Know Nothing letter to one of his German friends in Cincinnati, which he had marked private. But it found its way into the German press. Chase was told its publication was meant to curb the mounting belief in the German community that he was a Know Nothing. Naturally the letter not only called down upon him the acrimony of the Trimble group but also alarmed many of the former Know Nothings then backing Chase. In a hasty move to control the damage Chase had Campbell accompany him on the campaign trail. Campbell was an effective speaker and certainly his presence helped the campaign.[46]

From the beginning Chase had been most concerned about Cincinnati, not just for the Ohio campaign but because he thought a repudiation from his home city would weaken his national reputation. Writing from Wooster, Ohio, which he characterized the chief seat of the "Hunker Democracy," he complained rather bitterly to Schouler, editor of the not too friendly *Gazette*, about the personal attacks on him that the *Times* was making. In a reference to the anti-German election-day riots of April he spoke of the harm they had done to the city's image. "The mobs which they [the Know-Nothings] have excited," said Chase, "have done more to injure Cincinnati than all the abolition that was ever there."[47]

His advisors were worried about the northwestern counties. Although sparsely settled, they were a center of nativist agitation. Should Trimble carry them, his vote might throw the election to the Democrats.[48] With many misgivings Chase bowed to necessity and undertook the arduous task of stumping the area. "I was not a little uneasy," he wrote Kate, "when I came up into this sickly country lest I might get sick myself and be obliged to give up my appointments." His health stood up but he had not had such rough travel since he was a boy on the way to join his uncle the Bishop. He was thoroughly drenched crossing the Auglaise River in an open wagon. He was carried in a railroad handcar at night and nearly dumped in a canal when the drawbridge over the track happened to be open. He traveled in two canoes lashed together, canal boats, buggies, and once rented a horse and rode horseback from the town of Charloe to Defiance.[49]

Altogether Chase gave speeches in 57 different towns and cities that represented 49 counties.[50] Through it all, he concentrated his remarks on the Kansas issue and what he called the slave planter conspiracy. The Democrats, on other hand, stuck to local issues. They accused Chase of inordinate ambition, opportunism, and tacit Know Nothingism. Nor was he forthright, they charged, on state and local issues. Chase was less concerned about the Democratic charges than he was about the cohesiveness of his own coalition. The Know Nothing leaders worked hard for the Republican cause. Yet as Chase explained to Pierce, "I lost on both sides, on the American because not a member of the order and on the naturalized because of the Know-Nothings on the ticket."

When he wrote these words he was at home in Cincinnati and believed from early telegraphed returns that he had lost to Medill. But then as the vote from the towns and rural areas in the central counties and the Western Reserve started coming in, he began to have some hope that he had prevailed. Despite his strenuous and uncomfortable efforts in the northwest, he lost three of the counties there including Defiance and Auglaise.[51] By the end of the week his vote caught up and crept past Medill's. The final result gave Chase a plurality of about 16,000 votes over Medill, with Trimble polling over

24,000 votes.[52] Chase's slim victory in Ohio was the only bright spot for the Republicans amidst dismal performances in other states.

The fall elections in New York and Massachusetts registered Know Nothing triumphs; the Democrats swept Pennsylvania. In Illinois and Indiana they also showed renewed strength. Kansas seemed to have faded into the background with local issues and party organization predominating. For those Republican leaders in the East, Chase's triumph promoted him to leadership status.

But some, notably Bailey, were upset by his involvement with the Know Nothings. In a captious tone which he had never used before he scolded Chase. "The Americans on whom you bestowed approbation," he wrote, "are more Know Nothings than A.S. [antislavery]. They are trying to serve two masters."[53] In Boston, where Edward Pierce nervously scanned the returns from Ohio, the telegraph finally reported a 10,000 vote plurality for Chase.[54] On that same day another anxious observer, Charles Sumner, who was not given to political soothsaying, read the dispatches from Columbus that the Democrats had conceded and exclaimed, "Good! Good! Good!"[55]

chapter 14

As Others See Us

Chase arose early in his rooms at Kelsey's American Hotel in Columbus on January 14, 1856. Since his election in October he had spent considerable time reflecting on what he would say in his inaugural address as the first Republican governor of a major northern state. By now he was deeply involved in exploiting his victory for political advantage with Know Nothing Whigs and hesitant antislavery Democrats. He was particularly active in soliciting advice and support from the political sachems in the East, not the least of whom was Horace Greeley, whose New York *Tribune* had looked askance at Chase's relationship with the Know Nothings.[1]

He was not comfortable with his speech, which he knew was over-long. To satisfy the legislature and visitors in the gallery he had devoted more than half of the address to the mundane affairs of the state. The latter portion of his remarks that dealt with slavery and Kansas were much more to his taste.[2] As well it might have been. For it was that part of his address where he speculated on an impending collision between the free and slave states. He had fashioned this statement not just for his immediate listeners, but for an audience all over the North that would read extracts from the address in their local papers or study his words carefully when a full rendering was available in pamphlet form. His discussion of the slavery issue had to ring with such sincerity that the querulous could not accuse him of making such assertions for mere political gain.[3]

The governorship of Ohio was little more than an ornamental position. Chase would have no veto power and, beyond some patronage, little administrative authority. The governor could not even remove officers that had been elected with him or had been appointed to fixed terms. But it was, of course, the most visible office in the state and it furnished a platform for pronouncements on state and national affairs that carried with it a dignity and a force of significant publicity value. Chase meant to make the most of his advantageous position, but he was shrewd enough to have his statements on public concerns melded with what he perceived to be majority opinion in Ohio. He made sure that his recommendations to the legislature showed a firm grasp of the problems and possibilities that faced the state.

As his carriage rolled along High Street, he doubtless glanced at the huge edifice of the new capitol near his destination.[4] Like the evolving contours of Ohio's rapidly changing society, the new building was still unfinished, but the solid, unyielding structure seemed to reflect an underlying confidence in a bright future for the state. After more than sixteen years of spasmodic construction, convict laborers in their prison stripes were still putting into place huge blocks and slabs of granite quarried locally and anchoring the Doric columns that supported the roof and rotunda.[5]

The week before his inauguration, Chase had been busy with two measures of importance to him personally, an anti-Nebraska resolution and one opposing the Fugitive Slave Law, which he managed to guide through the legislature.[6] He was also lobbying for the election of Ben Wade to another six-year term in the United States Senate.[7] He thought the election of Wade certain, but then the American party's state council, meeting in Cincinnati, nominated Lieutenant Governor-elect Thomas H. Ford for senator and passed a raft of nativist resolutions. Wade's election looked uncertain.[8] At this point Chase could have derailed Wade's reelection, but the only substitute would have been the far more politically hazardous posture of supporting an American candidate. Wade eventually prevailed in the American-Republican caucus.[9]

Of greater importance to him than the Senate election was the initiative he quickly assumed in organizing the new Republican coalition into a national party. His first move in this direction (albeit a sectional one, though he did not see it that way) was to push for a national organization meeting. On December 10, he had written John P. Hale suggesting an informal gathering of the party leaders to meet in Pittsburgh on Washington's birthday, February 22, 1856.[10] There they would name a national committee and take whatever other steps were necessary to consolidate the loose coalition. Chase added that he had received encouragement from antislavery leaders to stand for the Republican nomination. Hale could not have been fooled by Chase's apparent modesty and feigned indifference. Chase meant to play a major role in the new party, but he had had enough experience with coalitions to keep all of his options open. Ashley and Alfred Stone, a leading American-Republican, had begun a campaign on his behalf.[11]

Chase certainly recognized the difficulties if not the outright danger that faced his career if a party composed of such discordant elements went into a national election campaign after less than a year of existence. Henry Wilson, formerly a Know Nothing-American, now a Republican senator from Massachusetts, feared that the party in his state and in others "will not recover from the effects of Know Nothings in time for the '56 election."[12] His letter was one of many Chase received from party workers in other states.

For some time Chase had been cultivating F. P. Blair and his two politically active sons, Francis Jr., or Frank, as he was called, and Montgomery. Chase had been in touch with Frank, a power in Missouri politics, and he kept himself cognizant of Montgomery's moves as counsel for Dred Scott.[13] This most interesting slave case would again test the constitutionality of Chase's theory that residence in free states and territories conferred freedom on a slave. Chase had been aware of the case since October 1854 when he received the pamphlet that Dred Scott's defenders issued giving details of the case up to that point in time. He offered his legal assistance "if necessary," but nothing came of his voluntary gesture.[14] Thus when Chase received an invitation from the elder Blair to attend a Christmas dinner party at Silver Spring to which a select group of Republican notables would be present, he was happy to accept.

When he arrived at the rambling mansion he found there his friend, Sumner, the New York congressman Preston King, and that handsome pliable politician from Massachusetts, Nathaniel P. Banks. Dr. Bailey rounded out the guest list. Chase may have wondered why Seward was not present. If he had he probably would have guessed that the New York senator was not ready to make any political commitment.

Some if not all of the guests knew that John Charles Fremont, the western explorer and Thomas Hart Benton's son-in-law, was being discussed as a possible candidate should the Republican party go into the impending presidential campaign.[15] Banks himself had been mentioned especially since his struggle for the Speakership of the House had been a central topic in the northern metropolitan dailies. When he appeared at the Blair party, his election was still in doubt after nearly a hundred ballots had been cast. The Massachusetts politician had had a variable but highly visible political past. Originally a Democrat, he had sensed the importance of the Know Nothings, openly embraced the movement, and was still nominally an American party member.

After one of Mrs. Blair's elaborate dinners, the guests settled down to a long evening of political discussion. It was decided that the new party should be launched nationally. And Chase was able to convince the group that a preliminary organization meeting should be held at Pittsburgh on February 22. One condition was imposed: the election of Banks to the speakership was "deemed an indispensable antecedent."[16]

After these decisions were made, the conversation centered on potential candidates. Thomas Hart Benton, who had taken a prominent part in the anti-extension movement, was quickly ruled out of the running. Blair suggested Fremont, no doubt to Chase's consternation, but he voiced no objection; nor did he oppose Blair's suggestion that Banks should be on the ticket to complete fusion on national lines with the North Americans.

Borrowing Follett's formula, Chase proposed that membership at Pittsburgh and later at the national convention (to be held either in Pittsburgh or Cincinnati) should be made up of half Americans and half Republicans. King referred to it as "the Ohio Plan"; it gained general agreement. Since Chase was the only one present who had been elected as a Republican to a major office, even that old political veteran Blair deferred to his ideas on party planning. Not so Gamaliel Bailey, who had feared all along what was coming to pass. He had had prior knowledge of the Ohio Plan and Chase's proposals for an organization meeting. He vigorously denounced the "half and half" strategy.

Bailey kept his own counsel during the discussion at Silver Spring on potential candidates, but everyone present knew that he was vehemently opposed to any avowed American on the Republican ticket. Well before the dinner meeting he had expressed his concerns to Chase that the professional politicians of the Banks type would either submerge the Republicans in the American party or renege on the lofty antislavery theme he wanted the coalition to emphasize. The Blair meeting simply confirmed for him a "regular plot that dates back many months."[17] He also considered Fremont a lightweight: "an amiable, honorable gentlemen, with a gift of exploration and adventure, but without knowledge of politics or political men."[18]

When his objections to the Ohio plan were politely brushed aside Bailey decided that if he could not change the composition of the new party he would seek to purge it of what he deemed were discordant elements. Without consulting Chase, he drafted a call for the Pittsburgh convention but changed the date from February 22 to March 26. After clearing the document with Republican members of Congress, he sent it to state party chairmen.[19]

King also reflected Bailey's concerns when he wrote Gideon Welles that the Pittsburgh meeting would be held sometime in March and explained further that "much as we are opposed to national conventions, our friends here and at Washington think there is no other way in which we can agree on a candidate." But, he added, everything was tentative. "Nothing definite will be reached," he said, "until the house is organized and our position there more clearly settled."[20]

While waiting for "the indispensable antecedent," as the Banks vote slowly edged toward a majority, Chase faced another uncertainty, the prospect of Judge McLean's continuing ambition. Lieut. Governor Ford and Lewis Campbell were both credited with boosting McLean as the American party's presidential candidate. Campbell was then vying with Banks for the Speakership. But Chase had not made good on his implied promise to use his influence with the Republican contingent in the House on Campbell's behalf.[21] Ford and Campbell had both been Whigs before they became Know Nothings. Banks had been a Democrat. Chase's tacit support of Banks would not be forgotten by the already sizable contingent of Chase-haters among Ohio Whig Republicans.[22]

On February 2, 1856, much of the uncertainty cleared up. Banks finally received enough combined Republican-American and anti-Nebraska Democratic votes to gain a majority of three over the regular Democratic candidate on the 133rd ballot.[23] With fusion seemingly an accomplished fact throughout the northern states Chase now saw the possibility of a Republican victory in the fall election. Accordingly he began to concentrate his support for the organization meeting in Pittsburgh and the nominating convention which he hoped would be held either in Cincinnati or Pittsburgh.

Chase urged his old friend Hiram Barney to attend the Pittsburgh meeting. Barney had been a progressive Ohio commissioner of education but had subsequently moved to New York City where he set up a law practice.[24] In a letter to Barney Chase said, "Of course I cannot be there myself," but he suggested that Barney consult with A. P. Stone, chairman of the Ohio State Republican Committee, and W. H. Gibson, the recently elected state treasurer.[25]

A deteriorating situation in Kansas strengthened Chase's conviction that the Republican party could prevail and if nominated he could be elected President. Alarming news had come from the territory of an impending invasion of Lawrence, the center of free-soil power. James Lane provided it and though this picturesque ex-congressman was a blatant opportunist who had supported the Kansas-Nebraska bill, Chase chose to accept his warning. Demagogue and mountebank Lane certainly was, but in this case ambition overcame any scruples Chase may have had about the accuracy of the report.[26]

As a western governor of a free state, Chase saw to it that Lane's warning and request for aid was given the widest possible circulation under his own imprimatur. In further preparation for the Pittsburgh meeting, Chase managed to keep his February 22 date and his fusion policy intact without alienating his friend Bailey, who withdrew his convention call.

In fact the date he had chosen worked smoothly with his plans because the American national convention was scheduled for the same day. Chase could portray himself and his fusion plans as free from American party interference at this point. He calmed Bailey's fears with an explicit statement that there would be no catering to the American party at Pittsburgh.[27] Chase was quite certain that the American party would divide again along sectional lines. Not trusting it to chance, he planned to have his own agents in Philadelphia to aid in a disruption that would make the North Americans an easily assimilated minority in the broader-based Republican party. He did not discuss this latter alternative with Bailey or with any of the eastern antinativists, but in emphasizing the separation of the two conventions he had also made fusion more attractive to powerful newspaper editors such as Horace Greeley.

Thomas Spooner, a devoted supporter of Chase who still retained his American party connection, Dr. John Paul, another Chase man from northwestern Ohio, and Lieut. Governor Ford attended the American convention in Philadelphia. James Ashley, Thomas Bolton of Cleveland, and Alfred Stone were Chase's trusted advocates at the Pittsburgh convention. The news both sets of delegates brought back to Columbus was generally favorable. Dr. Paul gave an account that the American party was so ridden with sectional divisions that it would not prove an obstacle to Republican dominance in a fusion context.[28] Chase was optimistic, though he admitted that the Americans were still "quite far away for us." A month later, the Ohio Council of the American party rejected Millard Fillmore, the party's candidate for President, and avowed themselves as opposing slavery in the territories.[29]

The Pittsburgh meeting seemed also to have positive overtones, but there was reason for concern. Rufus Spalding, an early associate of Chase, a former Democrat and Free Soiler, and an influential delegate on whom Chase counted for support, "astonished" Ashley when he openly pushed Justice McLean for eventual nomination. Chase had expected that the Blairs would advance Fremont's name, but the fact that McLean was talked of and among the Ohio delegates at that was very troublesome, especially after Chase had thought the state delegation was solid for him after his recent victory in the polls.[30] Although the Chase men worked hard to have Cincinnati chosen for the site of the nominating convention, their efforts were unavailing. Philadelphia was selected, a blow though not a significant one for Chase's chances.[31]

On the whole the informal convention validated Chase's strategy. His chief political manager, Alfred P. Stone, was made Ohio's representative on the Republican National Committee.[32] Had the Pittsburgh meeting been a regular nominating convention, Ashley told Chase, he would have been the choice by an overwhelming margin. Chase was satisfied that his candidacy had achieved a desired momentum. "It may be and probably is true that no candidate from our side can be elected, but it is not impossible and with faith and work we need not despair," he wrote Barney.[33] Chase's popularity was genuine enough to impress Ben Wade, who was even then intriguing against him.[34] But just when Chase was congratulating himself on a job well done the Seward-Weed influence emerged in the selection of Edwin D. Morgan, a wealthy New York merchant, to be their choice for chairman of the Republican National Committee.[35]

As the time set for the official nominating convention in Philadelphia on June 17 approached, Chase and his small group of boosters sought to skirt the anomalies they recognized could wreck his candidacy. McLean, Fremont, and Seward were serious impediments, McLean appearing to be the most formidable. Wade wrote from Washington that the majority of the Republican members of Congress were supporting the aged justice. And in Ohio, Chase was well aware that McLean stood much higher than he among former Whig leaders and some Free Soil Democrats too.[36]

But of more consequence to many Ohio Republicans was the conservative drift they perceived in the party. In the interest of fusion with the Americans Stone had been forced to agree that the term Republican be omitted from the call for the election of delegates. Suddenly there emerged evidence of tampering with this carefully worded document. The charge—which involved the substitution of one word—seemed inconsequential to most Republican leaders, but not to the sharp-eyed, suspicious Bailey and to the trained legal mind of Chase. The original document hammered out after exhausting and exhaustive sessions of the committee in Washington had used the word "exclusion" regarding slavery in the territories. A prominent moderate newspaper editor denounced that particular usage to Edwin Morgan with the plausible argument that "exclusion" connoted abolition; "extension," he maintained, was the proper word for all those moderate antislavery men who would contain slavery but not abolish it where it existed legally. Morgan agreed and "extension" replaced "exclusion."

When Chase read the call as altered, his reaction, while not as explosive as Bailey's, still reflected a concern that the party was in danger of losing its perspective should the conservatives bury the Kansas issue. A promising future seemed in doubt. Slavery had already been planted in Kansas and it was legal in the Utah Territory and in the vast unorganized New Mexico Territory. The definition was an abstraction to say the least, but in view of the existing situation and other concessions made, penetrating eyes and sensitive ears especially among abolitionists of the Gerrit Smith type whom Chase was courting at the time saw and heard another political conspiracy developing.[37]

"Politicians are always short sighted," said Chase after receiving Bailey's letter. "They now want to prepare our organization for a race by cutting off its feet to secure success by conciliating weakness and alienating strength."[38] Yet beyond agreeing with Bailey's and Stone's vehement objections, he let the matter subside while actively preparing to have his supporters ready to halt any breaking of bedrock principle for conservative American support. Always the realist, Chase may not have been too upset by such a trivial issue which could be settled at the nominating convention in June. But he was very worried about the McLean, Fremont, and what appeared to be an impending Seward candidacy.[39]

In late May, Chase was startled, as were his friends in Columbus and elsewhere, by two events that had widespread political effects. A rag-tag "army," or more properly a posse, under the ostensible control of a federal marshal, but actually directed by a proslavery sheriff, attacked the free-soil town of Lawrence. The marauders burned the Free State Hotel, destroyed the presses and the offices of the two free-state papers and committed other minor acts of vandalism before dispersing. One member of the invasion force was accidentally killed, and there were some minor injuries. On the very evening the telegraph carried the news of the Lawrence affair, it was reported from Washington that Sumner had been beaten savagely at his desk in the Senate. Preston Brooks, an unstable congressman, was retaliating for an offensive speech Sumner had made in which he castigated in unseemly terms his uncle, the venerable and courtly Senator Andrew Butler from South Carolina.

Chase was relieved when he learned that his friend was not in a life-threatening condition. At the same time he recognized what a politically potent affair the beating would become if taken up by the press in the free states.[40] Similarly the Lawrence attack which Lane had warned would occur had important political ramifications. Newspaper accounts in Ohio and in other free states exaggerated the raid far out of proportion. As regrettable as the attack had been it was scarcely the bloody affair that even the normally composed governor thought it to be. If the so-called "sack" of Lawrence and the Sumner caning energized the more radical side of the antislavery movement and hence improved Chase's political position, a chilling event that occurred two weeks after his inauguration opened him up to criticism from these same groups. Enough evidence emerged of brutality and insensitivity on the part of federal authorities in what became known as the Margaret Garner affair to attract widespread publicity.

Chase first learned about fugitive slave Margaret Garner from John Burgoyne, the probate judge of Hamilton County who had issued a writ of habeas corpus to remand her and her family, held under federal authority, to state jurisdiction. In a quandary over whether federal or state authority governed, the judge had immediately taken the train to Columbus and met with the governor for advice and possible action.

Chase must have been appalled as he listened to the account of one of the most heart-rending, if not the most technically difficult proceedings under the federal Fugitive Slave Law. Margaret Garner, her husband Simon Garner, her husband's father, also named Simon, and their four children—all fugitive slaves—had escaped from Boone County, Kentucky, crossed the Ohio River, and took refuge with Elijah Kite, a free black. A Kentucky posse abetted by Ohio slave catchers tracked the group to Kite's house. They secured a warrant for their arrest from the unsavory Fugitive Slave Law commissioner, John L. Pendery, a pettifogging Cincinnati lawyer, who invariably remanded fugitives to slavery for the double amount of the fees the law allowed.

Simon Garner, Jr., who was armed, resisted arrest in defense of himself and his family. One of the arresting force was wounded before the slaves were overpowered and chained. In the excitement of the fray Margaret, who had become hysterical, murdered her ten-year-old daughter, exclaiming that she would rather see all of her family dead than returned to slavery. She was restrained before she could harm her three remaining children. The Garners were then taken to the Hamilton County jail for temporary custody.

While in jail alert abolitionists secured a writ of habeas corpus for their return to state authority on a murder and accessory to murder charges. Here was a clear clash of federal and state authority that could involve the constitutionality of the Fugitive Slave Law as a violation of habeas corpus and of a state's police power. Yet Chase, ever the prudent lawyer, decided to let the Cincinnati courts follow their own course without interference from the executive authority of the state. And he so advised Burgoyne.

After a variety of legal procedures, the slaves, who had been indicted for murder under state law, were transferred to federal authority and hastened off to Kentucky where they were eventually sold in the slave marts of New Orleans.[41] The Garner family was never heard of again. Chase claimed that he had no power to halt the process and, further, that he could not foresee what in fact had happened. In extenuation, he said, "no one imagined that any judge could be found who would undertake to transfer by a proceeding in habeas corpus prisoners indicted under a state law to federal custody under the Fugitive Slave Act. . . . But such a judge was found, and such an abduction was perpetrated." Chase also confessed that he was new to the office of governor and "wholly without experience in its duties." He did seek to have Margaret and her family extradited from Kentucky to Ohio. But by the time Kentucky Governor Morehead had examined the papers and made a judgment to extradite, the slaves were out of the state.

The Margaret Garner case dogged Chase for years, and despite his able defense of his conduct, many of his followers and of course his traducers accused him of placing the niceties of the law above human rights.[42] Could Chase have intervened and brought about a different result?

The answer is a qualified yes. The legislature was in session and there is no doubt that had he acted to support Judge Burgoyne in any effort to resist removing the prisoners from his jurisdiction, he would have had legislative sanction. Holding the "supreme executive power" of the state, he could have personally gone to Cincinnati and asserted Ohio's right to hold the Garner family for trial on the murder charges. Despite the decision of the federal district judge Humphry Leavitt to remand the Garners to federal custody, other legal avenues were available that could have been pursued had Chase invoked the power of the state. But these would have been politically sensitive and controversial even in such an obviously criminal case.[43]

Judge Leavitt had cited McLean's circuit court decision in the Rosetta Armistead case as a precedent for his refusal to sanction the state court's writ. McLean had ruled that there should be no interference with a federal officer in the performance of his duties under a federal law.[44] His ruling had rebuked in no uncertain terms Chase and Rutherford B. Hayes, both of whom were representing the sheriff of Hamilton County on a contempt charge in another fugitive slave case.[45] Clearly this was not the time to be caught up in a legal dispute over federal versus state power with McLean, even though the New York *Tribune* and the abolitionist press had accused the Justice of being a captive of the slave interest. For McLean had emerged as Chase's most dangerous rival in Ohio for the presidential nomination.

Chase remained confident that the forthcoming Ohio Republican convention would elect a delegation unanimously committed to his candidacy.[46] He was to be disappointed, however. Led by Rufus Spalding, a sizable group of delegates rumored to be for McLean were elected delegates to the Philadelphia convention. Of the six delegates at large to the convention, none was instructed, but four were Chase men.[47] "Our friends," said a disgusted and alarmed Chase, "are not overpowered but out generaled. The [Ohio Republican] Convention, I have no doubt was two to one or nearly so in my favor. But our friends did not act with the skill and decision which was required."[48]

On the eve of the convention in Philadelphia, Chase had received both favorable and unfavorable information on the prospects of his nomination.[49] From what he could learn Seward had withdrawn as a candidate. It seemed apparent to him that a major contest would develop between McLean and Fremont.[50] McLean had removed the charge of subservience to the slave interests. In a public letter to Lewis Cass he declared that Congress had the power to prohibit slavery in the territories but not the power to establish the institution in those regions.[51]

Dr. Bailey had given up on Chase for both practical and idealistic reasons. The overworked, overwrought editor was deeply suspicious of Chase's connections with the American party. He had been for Seward, whose anti-nativist, antislavery views most approximated his own. But when Seward withdrew and Bailey was left with the bitter choice of Fremont or the aged

McLean, he reluctantly bowed to the pressure of Giddings, Thaddeus Stevens, and the persuasive Schuyler Colfax to back McLean. At the convention Giddings's earnest appeals in behalf of the Justice made a distinct impression on former Liberty and Free Soil delegates who might have supported Chase.[52] On the conservative side most of the skilled politicians and journalists mobilized for Fremont. These included former Democrats such as John Bigelow of the New York *Evening Post* and former Whigs such as Horace Greeley of the *Tribune,* who joined his erstwhile foe Thurlow Weed and the Blairs to work for Fremont.[53]

On Monday evening, June 17, Alfred Stone, delegate-at-large, managed to arrange a caucus of the 69 Ohio delegates at the Girard House, where most of them were staying.[54] All present regarded their action as extremely important, if not crucial to the nomination that would be made the following day. After some heated discussion Stone called the roll for delegate preference: 35 delegates indicated that Chase was their first choice, 34 would vote for either McLean or Fremont. Not Stone, Hoadly, Hamlin, nor any other Chase supporter made a vigorous effort to convert those delegates who opposed Chase's candidacy. When the word went out to other state delegations that Ohio was split almost evenly, whatever chance Chase may have had for the nomination quickly evaporated.

After Barney and Chase's brother Edward, a delegate from New York, learned of the caucus decision and Bailey's position they too gave up. In Barney's words they decided to "surrender with grace and make a virtue of necessity." Had Ohio been unanimous for Chase and "a tithe of the pains which were taken to urge Fremont had been employed for your nomination it would have been accomplished," said Barney.[55]

Possibly so, but Chase's nomination was beset with other, more serious problems than the lack of a competent team at Philadelphia. His chances were never bright. Anathema to many former Whigs who cherished their feeling of betrayal for past sins, Chase's opportunism was earnestly and persistently advertised wherever the powerful New York *Tribune* had influence. Nor were Weed and Seward about to lend any support to a man who would be a formidable rival in 1860, if, as Weed suspected, Fremont were defeated in the election.[56] They added their weight to that of such political fixers as the Blairs in backing Fremont. And Chase's long-held, well-known views on hard money and free trade were repugnant to powerful manufacturing interests in Pennsylvania, New York, and New England, not to mention his home state. At Chase's urging the Ohio legislature had enacted what was known as the "subtreasury law" just a few months before the convention. While this legislation appealed to former hard-money Democrats, it was looked upon with fear and loathing by the banking interests in Ohio and elsewhere. Many former Whigs and Whig Americans that made up the bulk of the Republican party saw this law as material evidence of Chase's dedication to Jacksonian credos in the face of the emerging Depression's acute shortage of money and credit.[57]

The McLean candidacy had acted as a spoiler, but not to the extent that Chase thought. The Justice himself was certain that had Chase not persisted in his candidacy, he would have been nominated. To the end of his life this former friend became Chase's deadly enemy. His bitterness was distilled in a comment he made some three years later. "Chase is the most unprincipled man politically that I have ever known," said McLean. "He is selfish beyond any other man, and I know from the bargain he has made in being elected to the Senate, he is ready to make any bargain to promote his interest."[58] McLean was not an objective observer and his verdict was far too harsh coming from someone who had been a political player since 1828.

In no effort to conceal his feelings Chase faulted the convention for ignoring men such as he, who, he said, "personified the great real issue before the country."[59] He had thought to the very end that he had a chance for the nomination even while he was composing his withdrawal letter for George Hoadly, Jr., to use at his discretion. He had just returned from Toledo where his sister Janette, or Jane, as the family called her, had died. She had been visiting her younger sister Helen Chase Walbridge when she was stricken. Jane was only fifty-three at the time and seemingly in good health. Chase hurried back from her deathbed, so that he could entrust his letter to Hoadly whom he knew would be passing through Columbus on his way to Philadelphia.[60]

As with all of his letters meant for public use, it was carefully thought out and carefully written for maximum publicity and favorable impact. In a succinct statement he condemned the Pierce administration's proslavery policies and arraigned the Democratic platform just adopted at Cincinnati as "slavery propagandism." A touch of bitterness crept into his statement when he wrote, "I can not look upon any nomination for any office, however exalted, if likely to prove prejudicial to it [the cause], as a calamity to be dreaded and avoided rather than as a distinction to be desired and sought."[61] Obviously he had in mind the untried Fremont or McLean, the perpetual candidate and regarded by many as an "old fossil."

Chase was already positioning himself for 1860. Yet he was deeply disappointed not so much by his defeat but by his lack of popularity among the convention delegates, considering the fact that he had been the first Republican to be elected governor of a major state.[62] After all in a political sense he had provided the successful formula that bridged the gap between the Americans and the Republicans.[63] He had established, he felt the broad-based coalition which could challenge the Democratic party on equal terms and contain any further extension of slavery.[64]

It took over a month before he congratulated Fremont on his nomination while reminding him that the free-soil principles in the platform on which he stood had been originated in Ohio some fifteen years earlier.[65] Nor did he join the host of early admirers and politicians who crowded the entrance hall of Fremont's New York home at 56 Ninth Street in Manhattan.[66]

Chase approved of the careful maneuvering which brought the North Americans behind the Republican ticket and foretold the complete dissolution of that party in Ohio and the free states. He wasted little remorse on Campbell or any of the former Americans. Even Spooner, who remained loyal and had performed valuable services, would be rewarded only with minor patronage when available. Lieut. Governor Ford would complain not a year after the fall election that "every living man, connected however remotely with the American organization in Ohio is dead with the Republicans."[67]

If Chase was chagrined at the lack of proper respect he felt he deserved from the leaders of the new party, he heartily supported the platform which reiterated almost all the antislavery ideas he had propounded over the years. It was forthright on the exclusion of slavery from the territories and wherever the federal government controlled, though there was no specific condemnation of the Fugitive Slave Law or of nativism in its call for equal rights.

After reading the antislavery resolutions he thought that the framers and the delegates had not "understood what broad principles they were avowing."[68] He was particularly struck by the inclusion of the due process language of the Fifth Amendment to the federal Constitution. Depending on one's point of view (in Chase's case the denial of the government's power to deprive a person of life, liberty, or property without due process), it meant that no slavery could exist in any territory. Calhoun had used the same argument years before to justify slaves as property wherever the power of the national government extended, a doctrine Taney would expose in the Dred Scott decision.

Chase was hopeful that the campaign would be conducted on a high and significant plane. The canvass never came up to his expectations. But in these early days of Republican party enthusiasm, he was resolved to take the stump for Fremont and William L. Dayton, his vice presidential running mate. A former New Jersey Whig, Dayton was clearly not a member of the group who had attended Gamaliel Bailey's evening soirées.

Yet Chase did not let his disappointment mar his relations with the Blairs, who had been most instrumental in the Fremont nomination. Both Montgomery and F. P. Blair, Sr., were on his list of appointments when he visited Washington in August. And Frank Jr., a newly elected congressman from Missouri, accompanied Chase to New York where he spent five days. At Chase's rooms in the St. Nicholas Hotel he had long conversations with the notable Boston minister Theodore Parker, with Barney, and with Bigelow before he began the journey west.[69]

The campaign had begun in earnest. Republican leaders were generally satisfied that their incongruous coalition was holding up well in the northern states against a well-organized Democratic party. Pennsylvania, Buchanan's home state, presented a serious problem, however. Henry B. Stanton gave vent to the consternation party workers felt when he said, "I know the Democracy of that thick headed, broad buttocked commonwealth." And then he went on to complain about party workers who were saying, "Everything is safe."[70]

Pennsylvania was not the only weak spot in the Republican offensive. New Jersey, Indiana, Illinois, and California, where the Douglas machine was well-knit and aggressive, were leaning toward Buchanan. And it was undeniable even in the early stages of the campaign that the angry talk of disunion that came out of the South was frightening to some potential Republican voters in key states.[71] The Democrats won the election but their margin of victory was surprisingly close.[72] Like other Republicans, Chase was impressed with the strength of the new party in the free states and with the size of Fremont's popular vote. Had Fillmore not been a candidate on the American ticket, the Republicans might have carried the election.[73]

Fremont's defeat could not have overburdened Chase. He had never had much enthusiasm for the "Pathfinder." And he must have taken some satisfaction that an impressive obstacle to his candidacy in 1860 was removed. Time, Chase believed, was on the Republican side: time to iron out organizational problems; time to improve his image as the proper leader of this new and vigorous political organization. Evidence of Chase's view of himself in this process and of his strategy for 1860 was his insistence on broadening the appeal of the party now that the American menace was under control. "Looking back on the Fremont campaign," he said, "it always seemed to me that our friends committed an act of positive injustice as well as impolicy in narrowing their issues during the campaign to the mere question of freedom or slavery for Kansas."[74]

Not that the situation in Kansas was to be ignored—far from it—but Chase wanted the party to use it as simply another glaring example of what was happening when a proslavery administration and a southern-dominated Supreme Court were determined to engulf first the territories, then eventually all the states in a consolidated slave republic. Nor would he muffle the moral outrage that slavery perpetrated on the nation. The denationalization of slavery, an objective that Chase had called for many times in the past, was a first step because, as he wrote Theodore Parker, "the faith and practice of the national government is on the side of freedom. . . ."[75]

Chase used strong language in his letter to Parker, but for once he was willing to express views deeply felt, which he believed would influence southerners, as well as racist northerners, to feel as he did about the inherent equality of man irrespective of color or economic condition or place of origin. In the Parker letter Chase vividly disclosed his sincere repugnance not just to servitude but to discrimination based on color and race. Unfortunately the means he would employ to attain the lofty goals he set forth were of small concern to this inordinately ambitious man. Ever since his "Appeal of the Independent Democrats" Kansas was fertile ground to be exploited, for his personal advancement and for the cause, always the cause. Chase's driving ambition to achieve his goal at any cost more than countered his many good and strong qualities. This character trait that reflected the darker side of his personality he was never able to control and was all too evident in his moves to gain the presidential nomination four years hence.

chapter 15

For the Good of the Party

Near-anarchy in Kansas had subsided in the early spring of 1857, but mutual suspicions remained. There were enough threats of violence, enough perplexing factors bedeviling that troubled territory to lend credence to claims that the Taney Court in the Scott case was a part of a great slaveholding conspiracy bent on encircling and destroying free institutions everywhere.

With the antislavery press in the free states still featuring Kansas, Chase stood ready to take whatever action he could lawfully and legitimately should events warrant it. There may have been precious little in a direct way, but the situation remained ripe for enhancing his political capital. Ohio citizens who had ventured into Kansas had been caught up in the turmoil. Several of them, imprisoned at the proslavery center of Lecompton, petitioned him for assistance. Chase promptly wrote Governor James Grimes of Iowa in an effort to bring him and whatever influence he could command to secure release of the prisoners. "Can you not send some able and respected lawyers into the territory and ascertain all the facts?" he asked. "Would it be out of the way for you to go yourself? You are the governor of the nearest Free State. . . ."[1] Apparently Grimes took no action, for Chase wrote a lengthy letter to the new territorial governor, John W. Geary, denouncing the proslavery Shawnee Mission legislature as having no legal basis and urging him to release the prisoners.

Geary replied that some had been tried, found guilty, and sentenced to prison terms because they had defied his Proclamation and attacked the pro-slave hamlet of Hickory Point. Others were awaiting trial. In the most respectful terms Geary refused to intervene in their cases, but indicated that he would welcome pardon petitions. He said that he had remitted the ball and chain during their confinement. Shortly afterward all of the prisoners either escaped or were acquitted.[2]

Chase claimed credit and properly so for his intervention.[3] However, he did not mention in any public or even private way that he had met with John Brown, who was on a fund-raising trip to finance what he represented as aid to the beleaguered free-territory forces. Chase was sufficiently impressed with Brown to write a strong note of recommendation as an endorsement on a letter of Charles Robinson, sometime free-territory "governor." Chase subscribed $25 to Brown's cause.[4] Since then he had followed Brown's murderous career in Kansas and noted his complicity in the Pottawatomie massacre of six innocent farmers. By the summer of 1857, when full details of Brown's activities became public, Chase disassociated himself from all connection with his enterprise.[5]

Chase featured Kansas in his message to the adjourned session of the Ohio legislature on January 5, 1857, but he saved his comments on that subject to the end of his long, statistical-studded state paper.[6] Of the many recommendations he made, two in particular stood out. He wanted a thorough revamping and improvement of the laws regarding the militia to bring it up to a better standard of reliability, organization, and discipline. Second, he urged that the laws regarding married women be liberalized so that they would have control of their own property. For his own purposes he used the message to remedy the defect in the Republican party's national platform on the granting of suffrage to foreign-born residents of the state. "Every citizen, native or naturalized, is entitled to absolute freedom and security in the exercise of it," he said.[7]

In his commentary on Kansas and slavery Chase followed familiar paths. "Slavery," as he put it, was contrary to "reason and natural justice. . . . Nothing short of positive law can sustain it." He said that emigrants from free states to Kansas were "practically disfranchised by odious test oaths" and also suffered destruction of property, bodily injury, and even murder yet received no protection from the federal government. Still, he thought that the worst was over and he looked forward to the peaceful entrance of Kansas into the Union as a free state.[8]

After receiving the message the legislature adjourned to make way for scores of workmen and decorators who moved into the chambers and the rotunda of the new state house. They were readying the building for the grand festivities planned for its dedication the next day. Halls were being decked with red, white, and blue bunting of the national colors, the red and white burgee of the state flag, along with evergreen boughs to complement the huge gaslit chandeliers suspended from the ceilings.[9]

Crowds were already forming to watch the practice drills of the Cleveland Grays and the State Fencibles on the ten acre grounds of the capitol.[10] Rooms in hotels and boarding houses were at a premium as thousands of visitors thronged the city to witness the celebration. A heavy snowstorm over the weekend and chilling temperatures had not dampened the holiday atmosphere. But the disagreeable weather brought with it additional discomfort for Chase, who was suffering from a painful attack of rheumatism. He had been, he said, "too lame and sore to go to church on Sunday."[11] By Monday he felt well enough to have his sleigh take him from his temporary quarters in P. T. Snowden's mansion on Washington Avenue to his old office.[12] From there he directed that copies of his printed message be conveyed to the legislature, and his furniture, books, and files be sent to his new chambers.[13] When he could spare the time between frequent interruptions he worked on the speech he would give in the new capitol.

Returning home he put the finishing touches on his address and had copies made for the Columbus and Cincinnati papers before bundling sixteen-year-old Katie and nine-year-old Nettie into the waiting sleigh. Escorted by a detachment of the Ohio military and his militia aide, Henry B. Carrington, they set out for the capitol. As they approached, they noticed that the building had been magnificently, illuminated, and saw hordes of people as an estimated 4000 moved on to the capitol grounds. To one observer the building and the crowd reminded him of "a mountainous illuminated ant hill and the living masses, outside and in, the occupants thereof."[14]

Chase and his daughters got as far as the capitol steps when they were so "hemmed in" that they quickly retreated to their sleigh and went across the avenue to Chase's old office. Eventually they were informed that the south door of the capitol was open and that a way had been made so that they could enter the building. As Chase, Nettie, and Katie moved through the rotunda they skirted a dense crowd of visitors that surrounded tables loaded down with hams and stewed oysters that a thoughtful state, sparing no expense, had provided free for the public. A reporter for the *State Journal* said that the crowd around the table "was as impenetrable as a Macedonian Phalanx."[15]

After the opening ceremonies, Chase was introduced. Extremely nearsighted, yet too vain about his public appearance to wear glasses, he had to hold his address close to his face and therefore was unable to communicate easily with the crowd. He much preferred stump speeches, where he could look directly at his audience and sense their rapport with him. But on occasions such as this one, where the address would be reprinted for the papers on the morrow, and an important statement was expected, he had to read his carefully prepared remarks. He later wrote in his diary: "Got through better than expected."[16]

Chase's speech, published in the Ohio papers and in the large metropolitan dailies outside of the state, reaffirmed the optimistic note he had cast in his address to the legislature. "We need not doubt," he concluded, "that faithful adherence to the principle which has brought us the elected position we now occupy, will advance to more conspicuous heights."[17]

Even as he said these comforting words there were signs of trouble ahead menacing to his political future and that of the party. Unknown to Chase, the state treasurer of the previous Democratic administration, John G. Breslin, had embezzled well over a half a million dollars of state funds. William H. Gibson, the Republican state treasurer and Breslin's brother-in-law, was covering up the fraud in the hope that the funds could be made up by what Breslin assured him was a successful speculation.

For some weeks before the state house dedication, Chase had been pondering whether he should again accept the Republican nomination for governor. If he decided to be a candidate he knew he would be nominated. He was, of course, flattered by such testimonials to his popularity and self-esteem so bruised by the Fremont nomination. But he had to make some cold, clear calculations on his prospects for election. Defeat at this point might cripple his career. "Indications are that I shall be compelled to be a candidate for reelection," he wrote Pierce. "I wish I could avoid this without seeming to shrink from a point of some danger, and without giving just occasion of dissatisfaction to any friends."[18] Throughout the early spring Chase acted like a candidate without committing himself. Uppermost in his mind now that the Kansas issue had faded into the background were naturalization laws that would be acceptable to the foreign-born citizens yet do away with suffrage abuses for partisan purposes. He was in touch with leading members of Cincinnati's German community on the politically thorny question of a residence requirement for suffrage.[19] As Chase sought to strike a balance between the demands of the foreign-born and the former Americans in his own party, the latent scandal in the state treasurer's office suddenly became public. Chase was faced with a political disaster.

He had traversed the state during May and June making speeches at college commencements and local celebrations of historical events.[20] On Wednesday, June 10, Chase was in Delaware, a town about an hour's train ride from Columbus, where he attended the commencement exercises of the new Ohio Wesleyan University. When he reached the depot for the return trip to Columbus he was met by Francis Wright, the state auditor, who bore alarming news of the Breslin embezzlement and the Gibson cover-up.

At its adjourned session in early 1857 the legislature had enacted new laws that provided for quarterly examinations of state funds and appointed a special committee to assist the auditor. Gibson's accounts were examined and his books balanced with temporarily borrowed funds. But Gibson found himself unable with the funds he had on hand to meet the semi-annual interest payments on state bonds that came due in July. He had no option but to make a clean breast to Wright of his complicity in the cover-up. Gibson did manage to convince the auditor that he had never converted any of the public funds to his own use.[21] Wright immediately telegraphed Christopher Wolcott, the attorney general, who was in Cincinnati, with an urgent message that he return to Columbus. Having taken this action, he boarded the train to Delaware and his fateful meeting with the governor.

Back in Columbus Chase took charge. He added his urgent request to that of Wright's that Wolcott return immediately. He had Wright telegraph Gibson, who was absent from the city, and learned that he would not return until the following day. He met with William Dennison, a leading Whig-Republican, prominent lawyer, and businessman whom he acquainted with the facts as far as he knew them, and asked him to be a special treasury examiner.[22] Scenting political problems of the first magnitude, the cautious Dennison refused the appointment.

Friday was a day of mounting anxiety for Chase.[23] Early in the morning with Dennison's note declining the appointment before him he met with Wright and Wolcott. By then they knew that Breslin had left the state and they feared Gibson would depart also. They agreed that if Gibson returned as promised he must be asked to resign. If he refused he was to be arrested and indicted for obstruction of justice. Chase contacted another potential examiner who also refused to serve. That evening Gibson appeared at the state house to Chase's vast relief. It was agreed that he would meet with the governor and other state officers at 7:30 the following morning. At that meeting Chase listened to Gibson's explanation. When the subject of resignation came up, the treasurer refused to consider it and there was disagreement on what should be done. All present were well aware that Gibson, an elected officer, could not be peremptorily removed from office.

Barely controlling his anger and his anguish, Chase decided that he had to confront Gibson alone and force him to resign. He adjourned the meeting but asked Gibson to remain. Composed but seething with repressed anger, Chase demanded Gibson's resignation. The tall, spare treasurer again refused until he had consulted his friends. He did, however, relinquish the keys to his safe and agreed on a further meeting after dinner.

When they met again, Chase pulled out all the stops. If Gibson did not resign the attorney general would have him arrested pending indictment, which would create a vacancy. The treasurer had maintained an air of injured innocence, but under Chase's stern words he collapsed completely and proffered his resignation. Moreover he agreed to help straighten out the tangled affairs of his office. Chase appointed Alfred Stone as Gibson's replacement, but he continued to experience difficulty in finding someone with the ability and the probity to act as a special examiner. He finally secured the services of a well-known, highly respected Democrat, Thomas Sparrow, who was willing to accept the politically sensitive job.

These details completed, Chase acted quickly in the money marts. The credit of the state was at stake if the interest on its bonds was not paid at the stipulated time. He immediately contacted the Ohio Insurance and Trust Company, a great New York financial house, for a loan of $150,000 which together with other existing state funds would meet the interest payments. He also sent Auditor Wright to New York to oversee the transaction, with the injunction: "Let nothing go, let nothing be admitted which can, by possibility, prejudice in the least the interests of the state."[24] He was immensely relieved when Wright telegraphed from New York on June 24 that the drafts on the state were paid and interest payments on the bonds provided for.[25]

A special legislative committee and Sparrow questioned Gibson closely but he managed to avoid criminal prosecution.[26] Later he would distinguish himself as a regimental commander in the Civil War. Chase sought to have Breslin extradited from Canada but no treaty existed between Great Britain and the United States where embezzlement was specified as an extraditable offense. Secretary of State Lewis Cass and Canadian Governor General Sir Edmund Head to whom Chase applied turned down his request.[27]

Through various means Chase and his financial advisors managed to secure enough funds to cover state debts just before the Ohio Insurance and Trust Company suspended payment on August 24, which was promptly followed by its bankruptcy. Shocked business communities in both Europe and the United States that had been riding high on the speculative boom following the Crimean War now experienced a severe panic in the money marts that quickly spread to the overextended manufacturing and railroad enterprises throughout the northern states.[28] Fortunately Ohio did not lose any of its funds in the collapse of the Ohio Insurance and Trust Company because the payment it had made to cover the interest on the state bonds very nearly equaled the amount that had been deposited with it for security. Paradoxically, the cashier of Ohio Trust, Edwin Ludlow, who arranged the loan, was in part responsible for the Bank's collapse. Like Breslin he too had been embezzling large sums from Ohio Trust's liquid assets.[29]

As soon as Chase had the facts of the Breslin fraud and the Gibson cover-up, he knew that his political future and that of the party was in grave danger. He knew also that now he had to be the party's candidate for reelection or face the consequences that the public would hold him and his administration responsible for the entire affair. To a person who prided himself on his honesty and who was indeed guiltless such a retreat was unthinkable. He would have to impress on the public mind that a Democrat acting with a Democratic administration had perpetrated the crime and that no Republican had pocketed any of the state funds. He was still left with the problem of Gibson. All he could do was admit Gibson's wrong and point to the fact that as soon as he learned of the cover-up he demanded and received Gibson's resignation. In a letter to Pierce Chase outlined his position. He did not want to run but could not see how he could avoid it. "The misconduct of Gibson will hurt us, but Breslin's misconduct will, I think, hurt our opponents more. But what a load to carry!"[30]

No sooner had the word gotten out about the scandal than Republican leaders deluged Chase with their advice and their fears. Former state supreme court justice Rufus Spalding, the not so loyal ex-Democrat, ex-Free Soiler, had been east and had talked with Preston King and other party leaders. "Gibson has given us a tremendous back-set," he wrote Chase, "you will be our candidate. Sound policy requires it, but you will risk much and must make up your mind to work."[31] From Cincinnati, Charles Reemelin, speaking for the German community, expressed alarm. Reemelin wanted Chase to call a special session of the legislature, a drastic move that he promptly rejected.[32]

With a sense of foreboding, but with a determination to do his best, Chase agreed to accept renomination. The Republican convention met in Columbus on Wednesday, August 12. Caleb Smith, a smooth and active courthouse lawyer whose political activities moved back and forth between Indiana and Ohio, presided. On hand were Wade and Giddings, personal enemies, but united in supporting the party. Smith was about to call the roll of districts for nominating the candidate for governor when Sampson Mason, a delegate from Clark County in central Ohio gained the floor. He arose he said to nominate Salmon P. Chase for the office of governor, and as he regarded it useless to go through the formality of a ballot, he moved that the nomination be made by acclamation. When Smith put the motion to a vote, all of the 250 delegates were on their feet and a roar of ayes reverberated through the hall.[33] After the ringing voice vote Smith called for the nomination of Lieut. Governor, but got no further than the naming of candidates when Chase himself appeared in the hall to more sustained applause and waving of handkerchiefs. The usually imperturbable Chase for once displayed emotion as he moved toward the dais. Never before had he ever experienced such an upsurge of enthusiasm.[34]

The warmth of the audience inspired him to make a short but heartfelt address in which he stressed the rights of the individual against the oppressive power of the state. He was of course referring to the Fugitive Slave Law. He roundly condemned the "slave power" for "arresting our Judges, Sheriffs and citizens . . . to answer for alleged crimes which have no existence in fact."[35] That evening on the High Street side of the state house about 3000 individuals gathered to attend a previously announced Republican mass meeting. Standing on the steps of the capitol were the featured speakers. A newcomer to Republican circles, Judge Robert Bruce Warden was made temporary chairman. Formerly a Democrat who had voted for Buchanan, Warden deserted the party after the Dred Scott decision. A man of many words, Warden warmed up the crowd before introducing the featured speaker, Governor Salmon P. Chase.

With the massive building at his back and the faces of the crowd before him illumined by flickering torches, Chase's voice, the slight lisp under rigid control, rang out confident and clear on that warm evening. What he had to say he had said many times before, but the reception he received earlier at the Republican Convention seemed to have lent a special timbre to his voice, to have made his gestures more spontaneous.[36] Yet even as he spoke with such vigor, he knew that he had a taxing campaign ahead with a better prospect of defeat than victory, a defeat that would in all likelihood finish off his promising political career. There was a compensating factor, however: the Democrats had picked a weak candidate in Henry B. Payne to oppose him.[37] A Cleveland lawyer and a businessman, Payne was a Buchanan Democrat whom Ben Wade had easily defeated in the legislature when he ran for the United States Senate in 1851.[38] If Kansas, the Dred Scott decision, and the unpopular activities of federal marshals acting under the Fugitive Slave Law were issues, then Payne was highly vulnerable. And Chase meant to make them issues.

But the Breslin scandal was a formidable obstacle. And the Republican-dominated legislature, a political mixture where former Whigs and Whig Know Nothings predominated, had passed divisive pro-banking and soft-money laws. The Democrats would surely object to them as class issues, a hardship on farmers and workers alike. Chase himself, a hard-money man, opposed these laws but publicly he would be forced to defend them.

As Chase began his campaign tour, he learned that the state central committee had been far more interested in electing congressmen and members of the legislature than in supporting the gubernatorial candidate. It had directed the congressional candidates to campaign exclusively in their own particular districts. At the outset Chase found that he had to bear almost the entire burden of the campaign. Only Ben Wade for his own reasons and the new convert Robert Warden spoke out publicly in Chase's behalf.[39] Never one to accept meekly any opposition Chase belabored the old Whig and the American factions in his diary.[40]

Chase remained in Columbus for five days after his nomination. On August 17, accompanied by Adjutant General Carrington, who was to make all the local arrangements, he set forth for Morrow, his first stop, a town that was 83 miles southwest of Columbus.[41] From there he went to Washington in Fayette County then back to Columbus where he addressed meetings on the

18th and the 19th before taking the train to Cincinnati. He made a major speech at the city's Sixth Street Market, explaining that the previous Democratic administration was responsible for the Breslin affair, but not excusing Gibson's conduct. His remarks, which lasted several hours, spanned the gamut of national and state issues.[42] This address and the 46 stump speeches he made over 36 days in 42 counties carried similar themes that he adapted to the special interests of each locality.[43] As he wrote Sumner, "traveling night and day, sometimes in railroad cars and sometimes over imperfect roads in carriages over 3700 miles, God in his goodness gave me health."[44] He made light of the fact that several times during this arduous trek he suffered digestive upsets; when he finally returned home to Columbus on election day he was exhausted.[45]

The campaign had been a bruising one for Chase and only a sense of desperation, personal pride, and a firm belief in the antislavery cause kept him energetic and forceful to the end. In the midst of his canvass, the panic that ushered in a widespread depression swept through the economy of the northern states. The major Ohio banks managed to stay solvent, but money was in short supply and for a time credit was virtually unobtainable.

The Democrats, of course, made the most of this situation, but were hampered by the fact that their party was in power at Washington.[46] They also sought to tie Chase to Gibson's cover-up but again could not explain how it was that Breslin, the actual absconder, was one of their leading spirits. Openly supportive of the Dred Scott decision and Buchanan's policy in Kansas, they accused the Republicans and especially Chase of favoring social and political equality for blacks.[47] The chief Democratic paper, Medary's *Ohio Statesman*, in a series of intemperate editorials which were reprinted in whole or in part by the party press throughout the state made much of this racist theme. Excerpts from speeches of Giddings, Chase, and Wade were published under the rubric of "the Congo Creed."[48] The Republican press responded by referring to their opponents as Congos, which became a slang term for slaveholders.[49] A more serious threat to Chase than racial slurs was the emergence of a third party in the race. Diehard Whig Americans ran a candidate with the unlikely name of Philadelph Van Trump, who accused Chase of being soft on immigration and especially supportive of Roman Catholics.[50]

Chase was pessimistic about the outcome of the election. On election day, October 14, he was in his office at the capitol before eight o'clock when the returns began coming in.[51] The vote from solid free-soil counties in the northeast of the state was disappointing, well below what Fremont had received the year before. In Columbus and its environs in Franklin County, Chase trailed Payne from 500 to 600 votes.[52] Defeat seemed certain, until Greene County—formerly a Democratic stronghold—surprisingly turned up with a 1200 majority for Chase.[53] On Friday morning, October 16, the results were in from all counties except Monroe in the southeastern corner of the state, adjoining Virginia. Chase had little hope for that vote, traditionally Democratic and proslavery. Its last reported vote gave Payne a heavy majority.[54] On looking over the totals thus far, Chase said, "This seems almost decisive against us." But on October 17, corrected tallies from other counties reduced the Democratic vote significantly. Chase now concluded that he had won the election by the narrowest of margins.[55] The rest of the ticket ran well ahead of him.[56] The Republicans lost the legislature because, according to Chase, of "remissness and some divisions."[57] Divisions were the more likely reason. The American party drew off enough votes in an extremely close race to elect a majority of Democrats. Van Trump received over 9000 votes, while Chase's plurality over Payne was a mere 1500 votes.[58]

It had been a near thing for Chase and he was particularly irritated at the lack of support he had received.[59] Toward the end of the bitter campaign, when defeat seemed likely, he had telegraphed Caleb Smith to join him on the stump. Smith found some reason to reject his plea.[60] Though Ashtabula County in the Western Reserve home territory of the Wades gave Chase enough votes to win, the majority was far below his expectations.[61] His sense of having been betrayed spilled over to Edward Wade, whom he rebuked for not taking an active part in the campaign. Wade replied rather lamely, pointing out that he had contributed funds to both state and county committees but had not been asked to campaign for Chase or the ticket.[62] His brother Ben, who had helped out, must have understood Chase's far from charitable mood. With his own ambitions for the presidential nomination in 1860 carefully concealed, he departed from his accustomed blunt prose to apologize fulsomely for the poor results in the Western Reserve.[63]

Assured that he would be residing in Columbus for the next two years Chase decided to seek permanent accommodations.[64] Kate and Nettie were now living with him and both were attending schools in Columbus. Kate was seventeen, just finishing her formal education. She was an accomplished young lady, a tribute in a way to her father's more or less constant emphasis on study, orderly habits, manners, and appearance. What social graces he inculcated had been reinforced by her years at Miss Haines's fashionable school in New York.[65] At her father's insistence she had studied French as well as Latin and Greek, and when home she joined the family in daily French lessons with an expatriate instructor, Adolphus Mot.

Accustomed as Chase was from an early age to associate with learned individuals and something of a savant himself, he was anxious, perhaps overly anxious to have both of his daughters brought up to as high a standard in social and intellectual graces as he and others he admired in public life thought essential. Kate was no bluestocking along the lines of Margaret Fuller or even Chase's older sister Hannah. She seemed dutiful and responsive to her father's often tactless lectures and his endless moralizing, but she had a rebellious streak that welled up on occasion. More painful to Chase was a certain willfulness that he found difficult to control, a tendency to deception and extravagance that he found upsetting. Kate was very attractive, with fine auburn hair, a small delicate face, and lovely hazel eyes. A retroussé nose kept her from being considered a beauty in the fashion of the day, but lent a pert, mischievous air to her otherwise regular features.

Ten-year-old Nettie does not seem to have been subjected to the constant stream of advice and criticism that Chase doled out to her older sister.[66] But she too was lectured about her penmanship, the style of her letters, and other characteristics Chase felt necessary for the training of a young woman. When Chase found a suitable house in Columbus, he planned to have Kate act as hostess. This too would be a training period for the young lady, who would play the same role he hoped on the broader stage of the White House.

What Chase did not understand fully was that both children, Kate especially, had lonely, insecure childhoods. Kate had been placed in a boarding school when she was only seven years old. And when she was fifteen he had her moved to another boarding school also in New York City.[67] It was not until she was seventeen that she was brought to Columbus and was able to participate in, if not enjoy family life. As a small child, she could barely remember her invalid mother, who died when she was five years old.[68] Chase wrote faithfully to Katie, as she was called by the family, but when he wasn't advising her to wear loose clothing and be careful about her health he was admonishing her to improve her handwriting, to plan her days more carefully, to be more observant of people, to read her Bible daily, and the like.[69]

Through his Adjutant General Henry B. Carrington, he learned that the imposing Gothic revival home of Dr. Francis Carter, located in a fashionable area of town, was for sale. The house at Sixth and State streets was convenient to the horse-car line and the Trinity Church where Chase worshiped. It was secluded enough to protect his and his family's privacy, which now included besides his two daughters a widowed niece, her two daughters, and his sister Alice.[70]

When Chase brought the family together at Columbus, he continually sought to impose discipline and his conception of daily habits, a regimen that occasioned explosive results. He was especially concerned with Kate's interest in young men and on more than one occasion upbraided her for taking unchaperoned walks, or waltzing too closely with her partner at evening socials.[71] "Trouble at dinner," he noted. "More trouble after about Nevins walking with Kate. . . ." A week later after another lecture on propriety he exclaimed, "Katie asked how she had offended." He replied abruptly, "False conduct." After dinner she was "anxious to know what." Chase said he "could not then explain." But after her French lesson with Monsieur Mot, Chase had "a long conversation with Kate—she was sincerely sorry apparently. And in the morning seems sincerely penitential."

Small wonder that Kate liked to travel. Chase usually bowed to her pleas at least during the summer months when the weather was oppressive in Cincinnati and Columbus and when the political season was relatively dormant. But a barrage of letters from an anxious father invariably followed her. Typical was a letter in July 1856 when Kate was traveling with her Aunt Charlotte. "You are at the time of life," Chase wrote, "when all your acts will be observed. Think above all that God sees your most secret thoughts."[72] Chase's sister Alice, who was acting as the governor's housekeeper, provided understanding and comfort to the young woman whose famous and imposing father, was himself frequently absent from home. Even when in residence, Chase was usually deskbound or holding long conversations with visiting politicians and newspaper editors.[73]

Nettie also endured a difficult childhood. There had been many moves from one rented house or hotel to another. But early on Chase had sent her to her cousin Mrs. William Collins, who lived in Hillsboro, a pleasant town only 62 miles south of Columbus, and to one of her many Ludlow relatives at Clifton.[74]

After Chase finally established a permanent residence in Columbus, he brought the two half-sisters together. They were almost strangers except for summer vacations. Kate never established a very warm relationship with Nettie. And while Chase loved both his daughters he lavished more attention on Kate, probably because her growing maturity matched his maturing political career. Kate had become a striking young woman, poised and with a well-trained intelligence, qualities which made her a most useful if not indispensable adjunct to Chase's career plans.[75]

Yet all was not politics and family prayers and daily injunctions from a strict and overly protective parent. There were many visits, teas, and picnics when weather permitted. The Chases, Ludlows, and Smiths formed a large extended family that encouraged all those pleasant affairs. Whenever his tightly scheduled days permitted, Chase also enjoyed these simple diversions.

But there was little scheduled entertainment adapted to young people's needs unless one considers church services as amusement. Chase found the theater a waste of time, and balls and formal soirées where the two sexes got together provocative and dangerous. His taste and hence that of his family ran to lyceum lectures and to meetings of the literary societies in either Cincinnati or Columbus, particularly those where historical or scientific or philosophical topics were presented and discussed.[76] A high point during 1857 was Gustavus Seyffarth's lectures on Egyptian antiquities. Seyffarth, a German theologian and archaeologist, combined modern religion with ancient divine practices much to Chase's taste.[77] Chase also attended Emerson's lectures and met the Transcendentalist philosopher, but other than a passing mention he made no comment about either the man or his philosophy, which was not surprising since Emerson's rejection of traditional Protestant beliefs he would have found distasteful.[78]

Politics had become his consuming passion and much of his social life in Cincinnati and Columbus revolved around political discussions and planning. Family breakfasts, dinners, and teas were often politically motivated. And Kate was brought into the discussions, willingly, one supposes, to preside where her dazzling appearance and obvious intelligence complemented her father's image. Carl Schurz, a leading figure among his fellow Germans throughout the Northwest, never forgot the impression Kate made upon him during a breakfast meeting at the Chase home in 1859. "Her little nose, somewhat audaciously tipped up, her face with its large languid, but at the same time vivacious hazel eyes . . . the fine forehead was framed in waving gold brown hair . . . something imperial in the pose of the head, and all her movements possessed an exquisite natural charm. . . ."[79]

There was another reason why Chase relied on his beautiful daughter to act as his hostess apart from the impression she made on his political visitors. An ambitious politician in the public eye, Chase found it difficult, as a widower, to deal with the accepted social standards of the day which insisted on a spousal relationship. After the deaths of his three wives Chase could not bring himself to seek another marriage. Judge Robert Warden, who later wrote a very detailed, if poorly organized and opinionated biography of Chase and who knew him personally as well as any of his associates at this time of his life, wrote that "everybody well acquainted with him supposed the sexual feeling to be very strong with him."[80]

While there is no evidence that he did seek liaisons, he was certainly a handsome fifty-year-old man in reasonably good health. He would have had normal sexual drives which he must have sublimated to his single-minded drive for power.[81] Certainly there was no dearth of eligible ladies of his own age or younger who coveted the attractive governor. Nor was there any lack of women friends and female relatives who sought to be matchmakers. Prominent among them was Margaret Bailey, Gamaliel Bailey's wife, a vivacious, supremely well-organized woman who cared for a sick, overworked husband and managed a family of six children. She held her own in the lively discussions that went on far into the night at the Saturday evening parties she arranged at her home near the capitol. Susan Walker, sister of one of Chase's early law partners, and an attractive, educated woman, had long been a close friend of Chase.[82] Something of a mathematical genius with a logical mind that appealed to Chase's sense of order, she had a humanitarian bent, hated slavery, and was close to Sumner. In almost every respect except Chase's traditional religiosity (Walker was a Unitarian) they were a well-matched pair and at least at one point they were close to a marriage that Margaret Bailey tried so hard to arrange.[83] Mrs. Bailey asked Walker directly why she had never married Chase. She replied laughing, "Because we know each other too well."[84]

Chase maintained a long-standing romantic, but apparently nonsexual relationship with Charlotte Eastman, comely widow of Ben Eastman, a congressman from Wisconsin whom he knew while he was serving his first term as a senator.[85] Mrs. Eastman tried hard over the years to make their relationship more than platonic but seems not to have succeeded.[86]

Another woman who Chase saw much of in later years was Adele Cutts Douglas, the widow of his erstwhile political enemy Stephen A. Douglas. Prying eyes noted the many times that Chase's carriage was parked before the widow Douglas's door. And rumors flew about Washington that a marriage was impending. They turned out to be groundless.[87] Chase was fond of the thirty-year-old Adele and he must have been physically attracted to her abundant charms. But like all the women in Chase's life after the death of his third wife, he probably recognized the potential danger to his position if he engaged in any illicit affairs. As for marriage, he would be frequently tempted, but no doubt there was opposition from his doting daughter, Kate, and concern over other social complications. Chase was especially sensitive to the fact that the behavior of politicians, particularly those in the public eye, was constantly watched by friends and foes alike.

Yet Chase reveled in the enjoyment of domestic life no doubt in reaction to the discomfort he endured on his constant travels. When he bought Dr. Carter's mansion in Columbus and established Kate as his hostess, he also entrusted her with the purchase of new furniture, carpets, draperies, and linens. At the same time he gave her minute written instructions, underscoring economy and practicality over elegance.[88] Kate's shopping trips to New York and Philadelphia evidently were satisfactory.

The Carter mansion was large and included a greenhouse. Chase lived in the style he felt essential to his position as governor of the third most populous state in the Union. Invitations to his Thanksgiving dinners, which then were celebrated only by New Englanders, were much sought after in Columbus, especially by the press corps, whom Chase always cultivated. One such reporter, young William Dean Howells, came away with a highly favorable impression of Chase. "A large handsome man, of very senatorial presence," said Howells of Governor Chase, "and now in the full possession of his uncommon powers; a man of wealth and breeding, educated perhaps beyond any of the other Presidential aspirants except Seward . . . he gave more dignity to his office privately and publicly, than it had yet known among us."[89]

The Chase household consisted of half a dozen servants, including a black butler, an Irish coachman, a cook, and maids.[90] There were usually relatives about as well as Chase's sister Alice and her two daughters. Chase seems to have slipped easily into this rather sumptuous lifestyle. He wrote Pierce how much he enjoyed what he called "domestic felicity, comfortable easy chairs, nice morning gowns, facile slippers so prettily worked by such fair hands, good books, well printed in good type on fair paper and well bound. . . ."[91]

The most successful member of a large family, Chase had always looked after his less fortunate siblings and their children. He built a cottage for his niece Jane Auld and her family in Clifton. He supported his nephew Ralston Skinner until he passed his bar examination and then took him into his law office. Scarcely a month went by when there was not some plea for monetary assistance from close relatives. Considering Chase's lifestyle, his loans and gifts, it is no wonder that he worried about his financial condition.[92] His salary as governor was but $1800 a year.[93] His income from his law partnership had been drastically reduced since his election to the Senate in 1849. His property and other investments in Cincinnati were not yielding as much as they had since the advent of the depression, which struck the booming cities of Ohio with particular severity.[94]

Since many of Chase's assets were tied up in Cincinnati real estate and property values in the city had declined significantly, he was reluctant to raise cash through sales.[95] Instead he sought to call in notes on money he had lent to his law partner Flamen Ball and to force a settlement from Ball and his nephew Ralston Skinner on what he deemed to be his just share of the business.[96]

Chase's pressing of Ball came when his former partner was in most straitened circumstances and had fallen prey to alcoholism. Besides withholding further extensions on Ball's notes, Chase demanded a sizable share of the funds the partnership earned over the past six years. Ball hotly contested Chase's claims. The dispute continued for well over two years and drew in Ralston Skinner, who likewise complained of Chase's exactions. Eventually Chase backed down, a compromise was effected, and both Skinner and Ball resumed their former relationship with him.[97] That Chase went to such lengths with his closest business associates reveals not just his financial difficulties but his anxieties about his faltering fortunes in his drive for the Republican nomination of 1860.

chapter 16

Defeat at the Summit

The year 1859 began inauspiciously for Chase. It was scarcely three weeks old when he learned that his friend Bailey was supporting Seward. Bailey, unusually candid with Chase, said that Seward was an older and more discerning political leader, an accurate assessment but nonetheless hurtful to Chase's self-esteem. Bailey added that the New Yorker had a much better chance than Chase of carrying Pennsylvania and New Jersey, both of which were indispensable for a Republican victory.[1] On all sides came word that Chase's acknowledged free-trade stand was hurting his chances for the nomination as much as his alleged radicalism on the slavery issue.[2]

Now that Douglas had broken with the Buchanan administration on its support for the proslavery Lecompton Constitution of Kansas, an impending split in the Democratic party seemed likely. Yet the prospect of being nominated and elected to the presidency should have appeared slight if such a close friend as Bailey had such doubts. But for the time being Chase dismissed his somber analysis.

As he pondered his course of action on the chill Wednesday evening of February 16, a few weeks after receiving Bailey's discouraging letter, Kate interrupted him to declare that she heard someone "groaning" outside. "I hastened to the door," said Chase, "and found my dear sister. I got her into the house without delay and sent for medical aid. Her suffering from headaches was dreadful for some time . . . about 2 o'clock this morning she began to sink and continued to fail. . . ." At 1:30 on the afternoon of February 20, Alice Chase died. Seemingly in good health, she had gone to a church lecture and suffered a stroke on her return just as she reached the door." Chase had been closer to Alice than to any of his siblings. Her sudden death literally at his doorstep had shaken his usual composure. The death of "my only sister older than myself," he wrote Pierce, "the only survivor of six older brothers and sisters," left him feeling empty and disconsolate.[3]

The pressure of work and various events, however, soon proved an anodyne. As if to compensate for mounting evidence of Seward's strength accumulating in his correspondence, Chase worked even harder to convince important political leaders that he best represented the objectives of the party. All important to his plans for success was his reelection to the Senate seat held by the Democrat George E. Pugh, who had succeeded him in 1855. And this meant that the Republicans had to carry the state in the October election, not just the state ticket but the legislature as well. The ever-loyal Ashley, Stone, John A. Gurley, former member of Congress and former Cincinnati editor, and Richard C. Parsons of Cleveland, an enthusiastic newcomer to party politics, formed the core of Chase's political advisors. John Sherman, an influential member of Congress, Joshua Giddings, and Ben and Edward Wade were uncertain quantities. Chase was particularly wary of the Wades, as he had good reason to be, but he needed all the support he could muster for the state campaign.[4] An unforeseen event threatened briefly to upset all of Chase's plans.

A particularly disturbing slave kidnapping case that had been maturing since early spring took a dramatic turn that captured widespread attention. In April 1859 a slave catcher along with a federal marshall seized John Price as an alleged fugitive slave. This event took place in the heart of abolitionist country at the village of Wellington, a few miles from Oberlin College. Price may have been a slave, but he was surely no fugitive. A passerby who observed his seizure quickly alerted the community. Price was confined in the village tavern until he could be placed on the train for Columbus and points south. Many of the students and faculty of Oberlin together with some angry townfolk surrounded the tavern and forced the marshall and the slave catcher to give way. They freed Price and sent him on his way to Canada. The federal district attorney on complaint of the marshall issued an arrest warrant for some thirty citizens who led the rescue, among them several members of the Oberlin College faculty. They were taken to Cleveland where they were jailed awaiting indictment for obstructing justice and breaking the Fugitive Slave Law.

Federal authorities, embarrassed by the number and prominence of their prisoners, agreed to drop the charges. The prisoners promptly rejected the offer. Preparations to organize a mass protest meeting before the Cleveland

jail began with Joshua Giddings, the moving spirit for the meeting.[5] Ever since
the passage of the Fugitive Slave law in 1850, the seizure of blacks, whether
fugitive or not, and their transport south for either return or sale had become a
serious problem in the free states of Illinois, Indiana, and Ohio, where the
Ohio River separated them from the slave states of Kentucky and Virginia.
Kidnappers roamed about the northern river towns and cities, ready to seize
any blacks and hustle them south. Owners and alleged owners would pay $500
or more to the kidnappers for able-bodied adult blacks.[6] It was a business
more profitable and less dangerous than horse stealing, according to a contemporary observer.

The uncertain status of slaves in free states and in transit not only increased this nefarious trade, but brought collisions between state and federal
authorities that led to extensive litigation.[7] Most of the court actions appear to
have been decided in favor of federal authority. The Dred Scott decision, if
anything, improved the legal status of would-be kidnappers.

As soon as he read that decision, Chase had acted to have legislation to
protect blacks within what he perceived to be the limits of state power. Among
the laws the 1856 legislature passed were those that closed Ohio jails to the
confinement of fugitives and prescribed heavy penalties for any one who
would "forcibly or fraudulently carry off or decoy out of the state any free
black or mulatto person, or attempt to do so." A final law prohibited anyone
from bringing a slave voluntarily into the state and holding that person for any
period of time.[8]

The 1858 legislature, dominated by Democrats responsive to Dred Scott
case and to McLean's opinion in the Rosetta case, repealed these laws.[9] It
failed, however, to overturn the 1856 Ohio supreme court's ruling that declared that any slave other than a fugitive who came into Ohio automatically
became a free person.[10]

Price had lived for some time in a friendly antislavery Western Reserve
community. The Reserve had gained the reputation of providing a safe haven
for blacks. Its proximity to Lake Erie and access for escape to Canada had
attracted blacks from all over the state. The black population in Lorain
County, the site of Oberlin College and Cuyahoga, where Cleveland was the
county seat, increased over 100 percent between 1850 and 1860. Yet the
Reserve had been largely immune to kidnapping incidents that had plagued
the southern counties.[11]

Chase followed the Wellington affair closely, but he decided that he
should keep clear of any collision between federal and state power. As a law-
abiding citizen and the governor of a law-abiding albeit antislavery state, he
believed that he and all citizens of Ohio must obey the federal law so long as it
was adjudged constitutional and remained on the statute books. Needless to
say, he did not want to take any stand that might jeopardize his chances for

election to the Senate and nomination for the presidency. Precipitous action might alienate the great body of conservative and moderate public opinion. When Luther Griswold, a Cleveland abolitionist, invited Chase to attend Giddings's protest meeting, he declined, pointing out that his power as governor was limited by the state constitution and his appearance might be misconstrued.[12]

Whatever his scruples they were swept aside when he entered his office in the capitol on the morning of May 24, the day set for the mass meeting. There awaiting him was an urgent telegram from Cleveland stating that the authorities feared trouble. His presence was deemed essential. Chase was just able to catch the early train and reached Cleveland between two and three in the afternoon while the meeting was in progress. As he made his way to the temporary platform he could see a crowd of over 2000 persons in a highly excited state.[13] Though he sympathized with the prisoners whom he felt had been unjustly accused and imprisoned, it was Governor Chase not Salmon Chase who counseled moderation when his turn came to speak. With his accustomed deliberate delivery he reminded the crowd that the case was in the courts and that nothing should or could be done until a decision had been rendered. "I was most coldly received," said Chase, recalling the incident after seven years had elapsed, "than I ever had been or have been since by a Western Reserve audience."[14]

Chase may have lost some credibility but as a responsible public servant he had defused what could have become an ugly situation.[15] The *New York Times,* supporting Seward for the presidential nomination, called Chase's position "sensible" while censuring his remarks for not commending the prisoners who had been jailed for following "the dictates of their conscience."[16]

The Cleveland meeting had come at an inopportune time for Chase. With the state election drawing near he sought to repair any damage. He exerted all of his influence to have William Dennison, a successful Columbus lawyer and businessman, nominated for governor.[17] A former Whig and a supporter of the Fremont candidacy in 1856, Dennison's nomination, Chase hoped, would blunt some of the hostility to him personally that still lingered in the Whig component.

Chase succeeded in pushing through Dennison's nomination at the Republican convention, but it failed to take his advice regarding the platform resolution on residence requirement for suffrage.[18] Clearly the Oberlin-Wellington affair and its aftermath had affected the temper of the convention. Rufus Spalding had managed on a writ of habeas corpus to bring the case of the prisoners before Ohio's supreme court.[19] The court by a margin of one refused to rule against a federal law. Judge Swan, who had been so triumphantly elected to the bench on a fusion anti-Nebraska ticket almost five years before, had cast the deciding vote with great reluctance. He was soundly defeated for renomination. Radicals in the party had been outraged and were largely responsible for his repudiation.[20]

These events shook Chase's optimism in his campaign for the Senate. The Republicans seemed even more divided than their opponents.[21] Chase feared that the Americans in the Republican coalition would take offense at the suffrage plank and either oppose the ticket in local elections or not vote at all.[22] He and his supporters held the Americans within the party coalition, but Whig leaders Corwin and Ewing—both of whom took an active part in the convention—undercut Chase with conservative delegates.[23]

Chase had shared a platform with Corwin at a Columbus rally in September 1858, where the latter's popularity and rousing speech must have alarmed him. At least one of Wade's henchmen, John W. Jones, who was present, thought so and added in a letter to Wade that Chase "is always afraid somebody will get ahead of him." Whatever his reaction to Corwin's reappearance on the political stage, Chase was pleased by the strength he was bringing to the party in southern Ohio where he was persuading former Whigs and Americans to join the coalition.[24]

Chase had sought to modify his radical image for the past several years. In July 1857, he had been a featured speaker at the railroad celebration in Baltimore, a distinctive American party affair.[25] And he had followed the Lincoln-Douglas debates with great care. In the main he agreed with Lincoln's insistence that slavery was a moral issue. Clearly here was a man who could be of assistance to him in the forthcoming Republican presidential convention and campaign. That Lincoln was no radical, but came from an antislavery Whig background, Chase took to mean that his views were politically appealing in the Northwest.[26] Lincoln had taken exception to the language in the Ohio party platform that attacked the Fugitive Slave Law. "I enter upon no argument one way or the other," he wrote, "but I assure you the cause of Republicanism is hopeless in Illinois if it be in any way made responsible for that plank."[27]

Chase was quick to reply that he, too, believed it sound policy to avoid extremes. At the same time he defended the propriety of attacking the Fugitive Slave Law, which he felt was an unnecessarily harsh subversion of individual human rights. "Our friends in Illinois," he said, "will if not already prepared to take the same ground soon be educated up to it."[28]

Believing as he did, he had nevertheless campaigned for Lincoln in his unsuccessful bid for Douglas's Senate seat. He was one of the few distinguished out-of-state party leaders to speak for Lincoln and as such gained his gratitude.[29] Lincoln reciprocated by speaking for the Republican state ticket in Columbus, Dayton, and Cincinnati. Douglas also campaigned in Ohio, boosting popular sovereignty if honestly arrived at, which meant opposition to Buchanan's pro-Lecompton policy. A majority of the Democrats in Ohio favored Douglas's position on Kansas, but a sizable minority stood with the President for a variety of reasons including patronage, racist feelings in the counties bordering Virginia and Kentucky, and the usual fear of the slave states boycotting the river trade.[30]

Never a laggard when his career was at stake, Chase made stump speeches throughout Ohio.[31] He was not in the best of health during that summer of strenuous activity. Besides sick headaches, he began to have trouble with his eyes, especially his right eye, the lid of which would not close perfectly. Chase in all likelihood had suffered a slight stroke from which he recovered. But the seizure left a legacy of paralysis in the nerves that controlled the movement of his right eyelid, which henceforth imparted a sinister look to his otherwise handsome features.[32]

His efforts and those of other notable Republican speakers building upon significant newspaper support and a maturing organization throughout the state resulted in a solid but narrow victory at the polls.[33] Dennison had a 13,000-vote majority and the legislature a Republican majority.[34] Chase felt assured of his election to the Senate until John Brown's raid on Harper's Ferry cast another shadow upon his candidacy.

The Democrats made much of radical Republican support for Brown. They managed to unearth Chase's modest contribution to the fanatical abolitionist in 1856. Publication of this information which Chase quickly placed in its proper context absolved him of any complicity.[35] But the raid did frighten some conservative Republicans, prompting a fear that they would bolt the party and bring pressure to bear upon enough members of the legislature to fuse with the Democrats and defeat Chase.[36]

Yet Chase would not defer to conservative opinion when it came to principle, even if it weakened his candidacy. In his 1860 annual message to the legislature, his last as governor, he recommended that the acts "repealed by the last general assembly, prohibiting slaveholding and kidnapping in Ohio," be reenacted. With no little irony, he challenged the law that prohibited suffrage to anyone who appeared "to have a distinct and visible admixture of African blood." That was a matter for the courts to decide, not the legislature. Finally he alluded to "a spirit of distrust and alienation" that had developed in the country. "The people," he said, "desire union and concord; not discord and disunion." Speaking for Ohio he said firmly, "She will neither dissolve the Union herself nor consent to its dissolution by others." The message made good copy for the radical press such as Henry D. Cooke's *State Journal* and William C. Howells's *Ashtabula Sentinel*. Conservative journals such as the Cincinnati *Times* or the *Gazette* found its sentiments difficult to controvert.[37]

Privately he expressed his concern to a firm supporter in Cincinnati, the prosperous wholesale grocer Robert Hosea.[38] A number of newly elected members of the legislature were pledged to vote for Chase in advance, but conservatives of Whig persuasion held out against his nomination in caucus. As Chase explained the situation to Sumner, "They are few, but it has been feared that if excited to factious action they might be able, with the aid of the Democrats to defeat an election."[39] A number of Chase supporters thought it best to postpone the election until February so that the malcontents would have no pretext to delay action.[40] Even so the Republican caucus when it met on February 2 by the narrow margin of two votes opposed postponing the election and then went on to nominate Chase.[41] When the legislature voted the next day it elected Chase with a majority of 23 votes over George Pugh, the Democratic contender. Corwin received but eight votes.[42]

Chase was relieved, but by now he was too perceptive a politician not to note that a division was possible in the delegation that the party would send to Chicago. If this should occur, Chase knew that his nomination was virtually hopeless. For months now information had accumulated in Columbus of Seward's gains. Under the sure hand of Thurlow Weed a well-financed national organization had developed rapidly.[43] Chase had neither the funds nor the strategic position Seward commanded in Washington and New York. Alfred Stone, Ohio's member of the Republican national committee, Spooner, and Ashley, who acted as a proxy member of the committee for Cassius Clay, had been outmaneuvered on the site for the convention.[44]

Though scarcely a radical antislavery man, Spooner had been unable to persuade his colleagues that Chase would support a swing to the right on the platform. Ashley, an outspoken radical, in articulating the radical cause lent credence to the belief that Chase was not to be trusted on the slavery issue. Despite the fact that both men were protectionists, they could not convince their colleagues that Chase had altered his free-trade views.[45]

Well before the New York meeting of the national committee, two additional candidates had gained prominence, Edward Bates of Missouri and Abraham Lincoln. The sixty-six-year-old Bates was a prominent St. Louis attorney. Formerly a Whig regular with Know Nothing sympathies, he was a dedicated antislavery man from an important border slave state. He had written a long impressive letter to the New York Whig Committee in February, 1859, that attracted a widespread favorable response. And then in March, 1860, he sent to a Missouri Republican committee a far more comprehensive letter which covered all of the burning issues of the day. These communications so pleased Horace Greeley that he ignored Bates's inherent conservative stand and his Know Nothing background and brought all of the very real influence of the *Tribune* behind his candidacy.[46] The Blairs followed the lead of the *Tribune* in endorsing Bates. Lincoln had local support, but as far as

Chase could see, was not the serious threat Seward and now Bates posed as a compromise conservative candidate.[47]

Outside of the state, Ashley, Hiram Barney, and James A. Briggs furnished the nucleus of the Chase organization. Joseph Medill, formerly editor of the Cleveland Ohio *Leader* and now editor and publisher of the Chicago *Tribune,* was his most important backer among out-of-state editors.[48] The impetuous, overbearing Ashley tended to alienate the more phlegmatic of Chase supporters.[49] But clearly he was the ablest of the impromptu team. "He is," said Chase, "ardent and true and efficient but I fear expects too much from friends. . . ."[50]

Chase unfortunately did not take Ashley's advice on crucial matters. The willful but skillful congressman from Toledo had recommended a plan of action which involved a meeting of young Republicans right after Chase's election to the Senate and would include notable Chase-haters such as Corwin, Columbus Delano, and Benjamin Stanton, in Ashley's words, "so as to commit them either by letter or their presence then and there to be marked out by your friends."[51] Fearful of adding to his enemy's indictment of him as "a tricky politician," Chase would not take the risk.[52]

Ashley had worked hard for Chase at the Republican convention in the new state of Minnesota, as did Medill.[53] But on making the rounds, Ashley had an accident that crippled him badly for a time and which reduced his efficiency as a Chase promoter.[54] Briggs, a New York lawyer, was Ohio's financial agent in the metropolis. On his shoulders rested the heavy burden of convincing political leaders from the manufacturing areas of New York and New Jersey that Chase was not a free trader. At the same time Briggs was forced to argue Chase's flexibility on the issue with those consummate free traders, the powerful shipbuilding and commercial interests of the port of New York. Briggs was never able to rally such divergent interests behind his candidate.[55]

Carl Schurz, the charismatic refugee from Prussian militarism, was a special object of Chase's interest. A forceful speaker and publicist of democratic and antislavery ideas among his fellow Germans, Schurz had become an important political power not just in the emigrant communities of his home state, Wisconsin, but throughout the Northwest.

Chase enlisted an old friend, Dr. William H. Brisbane, who had moved from Ohio to Wisconsin to sound out Schurz on his behalf. Brisbane was one of those unique figures in the antislavery movement. A native of South Carolina and formerly an editor of a religious paper in Charleston and a planter on the Sea Islands off the South Carolina coast, Brisbane had clashed with public opinion on the issue of slavery. In 1835 he sold his slaves and moved to Cincinnati, where he became a member of Birney's abolitionist circle and editor of the *Christian Politician,* an abolitionist Baptist weekly.[56] Returning to his native state he bought back 27 of his former slaves, brought them north, freed them, and made provision for their welfare. In 1855 he moved to Wisconsin where he soon became a close friend of Schurz.

Brisbane contacted Schurz in Chase's behalf, but was unable to get a clear endorsement for his friend.[57] His report prompted Chase to renewed efforts. When Schurz went on a lecture tour during the fall and winter of 1859, Chase made it possible for him to speak in Columbus. While in the city he was a guest at Chase's home.[58] He arrived early at the governor's mansion and was captivated by Kate at the breakfast table.

After a final cup of coffee, Chase took his guest to his book-lined study and came right to the point. No doubt Schurz would be a delegate to the Republican convention. What did he think of Chase's candidacy? Schurz was taken aback by Chase's frankness but decided on the spot to be as candid as his host. He could not estimate the number of delegates who would be for Chase, but "If the Republican convention at Chicago have courage enough to nominate an advanced antislavery man, they will nominate Seward, if not, they will not nominate you." Chase was silent for a moment, but he could not conceal his disappointment. He did not understand why he should be held in a subordinate position to Seward, "a point," said Schurz, "which I could not undertake to argue."[59] That evening Schurz gave what Chase described as "a capital lecture." Afterward he wrote his friend Robert Hosea accurately reporting the conversation with Schurz, but still hopeful that he could swing Schurz around to his support. "This is important," he told Hosea. "Mr. S.[Schurz] will reach Cincinnati by 2:40 PM. If one of our friends could meet him at the depot and take him home, it would do well. I think Hassaurek knows him."[60]

In the midst of all these activities, Chase undertook to raise money for his friend Bailey's trip to Europe. Bailey had become seriously ill with tuberculosis and his doctors had prescribed the trip for his health. The strain of this additional burden was apparent in a letter Chase wrote Donn Piatt, the free-lance Cincinnati political writer. "If this thing takes up such time and gives as much annoyance hereafter as it has done thus far," he said, "I shall hold you pretty seriously responsible for getting me into the business."[61] A month later came the news that Bailey had died aboard ship.[62]

Chase experienced a sense of deep sorrow at the loss of Bailey. Despite his highly individualist style and sometimes irritating ways he had been Chase's closest friend for years. More than that the movement had lost its most powerful propagandist at the helm of the *Era*. Chase would have the double burden of trying to find a suitable successor who could take over the *Era* and also to provide for the support of Bailey's widow and her children.[63]

In the face of all these vexations, Chase made his usual summer trip to the East. He visited Hamilton Fish, the rich former New York Whig leader; he participated with Governor Banks in the Harvard commencement and went on to the Dartmouth commencement; then he traveled to Washington by way of Philadelphia and Harrisburg, where he was a guest at the estate of Simon Cameron, formerly Democratic, now Republican political sachem of Pennsylvania.

But Chase made a major mistake in the fall of 1859 when he refused the invitation tendered to him by William Cullen Bryant and other leading New Yorkers to give an address in the city.[64] Had he done so he might have upstaged Lincoln before the city's Republican elite. There is no doubt that Lincoln gained much momentum for the address he gave at Cooper Union some months later.[65] Chase was now paying more attention to Lincoln though he and his supporters still thought Bates the major threat.[66] But when Chase read the accounts of Lincoln's Cooper Union address he must have realized that the Illinoisian would prove a serious competitor. His chief campaign workers in the city, Briggs and Barney, entertained Lincoln and wrote Chase glowing accounts of his visit.[67]

Chase was buoyed up at the result of the party's state convention in Columbus which elected four delegates-at-large and by an overwhelming vote of 375 to 73 declared him its first choice for nomination at Chicago.[68] But Chase's optimism was a bit premature. At least one of the four delegates-at-large, David K. Carrter, a former Democratic congressman, was not firmly committed. Described as "a fierce partisan, an inbred vulgarian and a truculent conformist," expediency rather than principle had marked his career as an antislavery man.[69] District conventions would elect the balance of the delegates who were not bound by the state convention's action.

Chase already had a forewarning of conservative strength from the results of the Hamilton County district convention which elected only two delegates that could be considered Chase men. The rest indicated a preference for Bates.[70] Meanwhile Ben Wade was running a covert campaign in part to block Chase for whom he had formed a distinct personal dislike and in part because he thought his credentials were as good if not better than any other western man for the nomination.[71] If Chase recognized this threat he did not move to counteract it.[72] His correspondence for the period makes no mention of Wade or of McLean, who, though too old to be an effective candidate, still could have helped Chase in conservative Whig quarters.

But seeming ignorance of Wade's intentions and failure to patch up his former friendship with McLean were not the least of Chase's strange indifference to establishing an effective organization within Ohio and especially outside of the state. Even such a committed worker as Briggs in New York was in touch with Wade and expressed doubts about Chase's availability.[73]

As the date for the national convention drew near, the Bates candidacy went into a rapid decline. Thurlow Weed's organizational genius and his access to campaign funds now began to have a decided effect. Amos Tuck, the handsome New Hampshire lawyer who had been friendly with Chase when both were in Congress, sent depressing news after a trip through the West. Surprised at Seward's strength, the fruits of Weed's activities in Minnesota, Wisconsin, and Michigan, Tuck found little concrete support for Chase.[74] In addition he chided Chase for not building up an organization in New Hampshire, whose delegation he said was in Weed's pocket.[75]

Chase also learned that the Massachusetts convention gave Seward the edge. His protégé Pierce, who would be a delegate to Chicago, was leaning toward the New Yorker.[76] Despite all these negatives Chase would not give up. He asked Hosea to stir up the Cincinnati newspapers for his candidacy.[77] And he came to a decision which made sense, given his lack of organization and funds. He would concentrate his efforts on knowledgeable and popular congressmen in Washington.[78]

Chase had used whatever influence he could command in a vain effort to elect the youthful John Sherman Speaker of the House.[79] Failing in that endeavor he persuaded two of his close associates, Henry D. Cooke, now editor of the *Ohio State Journal,* and Richard Parsons to visit the national Capitol and help Ashley lobby his congressional colleagues for Chase. Neither individual had much experience in this line of work. Nor were either well acquainted with congressmen and politicians outside of Ohio.[80]

Chase followed up his initial instructions to Parsons with some additional advice. "Pike of the *Tribune,"* he wrote, "is at Mrs. Bailey's. You must see him. He is a man with a solid head—and has a wife who doubles him with her nobility of nature. . . ." He closed his letter with a cheerful note at variance with the despair he must have felt. "I have lost patience with what I hear of hunting after friends. It will do for paleontologists not for Republicans."[81] At the urging of Governor Dennison, of Ashley, and of Parsons, Chase agreed to make a personal visit to Washington.[82]

Accompanied by Kate and Dennison, he left on April 24. Typical of the poor communication and faulty arrangements of Chase's bungling campaign efforts he had neglected to telegraph ahead.[83] When Chase registered at Willard's, he found that Cooke and Parsons had left the city. All that he accomplished for the discomfort and sleeplessness of the overnight train from Columbus was information that Wade was attempting to divide the Ohio delegation and that Seward was much stronger than he had thought. "If Albany is to be transferred to Washington the party cannot survive," he lamented.[84]

As he bounced about on his return trip over the poorly ballasted line between Washington and Wheeling, Chase made one last, desperate attempt to have a coordinator at Chicago who would rally out-of-state delegates behind his candidacy. He penciled an urgent note to Briggs begging him to go to

Chicago and act as his spokesman. When he reached Columbus he followed up his note with another pleading letter. But to no avail: Briggs found that he had pressing business that would preclude the trip.

On May 10, in response to an inquiry from Benjamin Eggleston, a delegate from Cincinnati and no friend, who asked if there was any arrangement between him and Seward, Chase denied any such understanding. "I shall have nobody to speak or act for me at Chicago," he said, an unfortunate lofty tone creeping into his reply, "except the Ohio delegates who will I doubt not faithfully represent the Republicans of the state."[85]

The fact that he had not designated any one of a number of capable politicians who were loyal to him and were attending the convention, Ashley, Stone, or Parsons, for example, meant either that he had resigned himself to defeat or, more likely, that he expected Ohio to act as a unit behind his candidacy.[86] What is evident is that Chase mismanaged his own campaign from the start. His judgment of himself and his availability as a western man, the only twice-elected governor on the Republican ticket, just reelected a U.S. Senator from the third most populous state in the Union, may have nourished his ego but was faulty in the extreme.[87] A scattering of delegates from other states might support him if he survived the first ballot, but essential momentum depended on a united Ohio vote on the first ballot. Opposition there was bound to be fatal.[88]

Chase recognized the importance of unanimity in the Ohio vote. He urged Giddings to insist on a unit rule for the first ballot and subsequent ballots until it became apparent that another candidate seemed headed for a majority.[89] Erastus Hopkins, a delegate from Massachusetts, wrote that there was "lots of good feeling afloat here for you, but there is no set of men earnest for you."[90]

When Hopkins wrote that letter, the city of Chicago was in a state of exuberant pandemonium. As each special train bearing delegates reached the railroad depot on May 14 after a hot, dusty trip over the prairie, they were greeted by a horde of enthusiastic Chicagoans. Rockets streaked across the clear night sky, a pair of nine-pounder brass cannon roared out a salute, and on hand was a detachment of "Wide Awakes" armed with kerosene torches to escort the delegates to their hotel. The "Wide Awakes," a Connecticut invention, were companies of young Republican stalwarts who wore glazed cloth capes and matching caps. Their torches mounted on stout oak staffs provided illumination as well as clubs to protect party marchers from being assailed by idlers along the route whom the Democratic central committees hired to break up Republican rallies.[91]

The warm reception simply added a further note of good cheer to delegates, reporters, and political hangers-on who had imbibed freely of alcoholic refreshments to ease the tedium and the dust of the overcrowded cars. Most of the delegates were housed in the Tremont House, Chicago's largest and most elegant hotel.

Despite these spacious and imposing quarters, there were not enough public and private rooms to accommodate the crush. An estimated 2000 persons got what breakfast they could on the first day of the convention. And the jam at the various bars seemed impenetrable to one reporter at the scene.

The Seward contingent was the largest of all, noteworthy for the amount of ardent spirits consumed and bawdy songs sung when the occasion warranted. They had brought their own band and each delegate had a silk badge with Seward's bold features emblazoned in it. They made quite a show when they marched behind their band from their headquarters, the Richmond House, to the so-called "Wigwam," the site for the convention's proceedings. This great, barn-like structure on the corner of Lake and Market streets was Chicago's impromptu imitation of New York's Crystal Palace. It had been constructed of unplaned pine boards and rafters, its interior decorated with a profusion of pine boughs, wreaths, flags, buntings, and woodcuts portraying patriotic themes.

On the afternoon of May 16, before the convention was organized, the three doors, each some twenty feet wide, were opened to the public. The rush for seats astonished even the veteran observer Murat Halstead. Within five minutes he calculated that standing room alone held 4500 persons. The galleries restricted to men accompanied by women were quickly occupied by almost 3000 more.

After the preliminaries had been concluded, the sharp-featured, brilliant New York lawyer William M. Evarts gained the podium and nominated Seward as the party's candidate for President. His short speech was greeted with resounding applause. Next, Norman Judd, a suave politician who projected an earnest and honest demeanor, placed Abraham Lincoln in nomination.

As soon as Judd completed his brief remarks, a Lincoln claque responded with an incredible roaring shriek of approval. David Davis, who was managing Lincoln's campaign, had managed to salt the galleries and the standees at the rear of the Wigwam with Lincoln supporters. And when Caleb Smith seconded Judd's nomination, it was the signal for another cacophony of sound that Halstead described as "absolutely terrific." But Seward men were not to be outdone. Their chance came after Austin Blair, principal organizer of the party in Michigan, seconded Seward's nomination. "The effect was startling," said Halstead. "Hundreds of persons stopped their ears in pain. The shouting was absolutely frantic, shrill and wild. No Comanches, no panthers ever struck a higher note or gave screams with more internal intensity." But when Columbus Delano on behalf of a part of the Ohio delegation seconded Lincoln, "the uproar was beyond description." David Carrter, one of Ohio's delegates-at-large, managed to make himself heard through the uproar and nominated Chase. Tom Corwin named McLean.

At this point most delegates and reporters assumed that Seward would be the nominee. His political alter-ego, Thurlow Weed, had spared no expense on important delegations. But the little New Yorker had serious weaknesses mainly among the former Democrats in the Republican coalition and even among some ex-Whigs, who distrusted his financial policies and his presumed radicalism on the slavery issue. Gideon Welles, chairman of the Connecticut delegation, and Chauncey Cleveland, former governor of the state and a delegate-at-large, had been busy seeking to undermine Seward's strength in the New England contingent. Both men were for Chase but their prime motivation was to defeat Seward. Welles and Cleveland made the rounds of the New England delegations and drummed up support for Chase if Ohio should cast a unanimous vote for him on the first ballot. Even among the New York delegates there were at least two members, William Curtis Noyes and John T. Hogeboom, who were opposed to Seward and open to conversion.

Chase's brother Edward was unofficially representing him. But Edward was not skilled in political persuasion and seemed bewildered by the crush of individuals in the corridors and in the caucus rooms, which reeked of tobacco smoke and the permeating odor of liquor, the carpets bespattered by tobacco juice.[92]

At one of the parlors in the Tremont House, the Ohio delegation had taken note of Seward's apparent strength and sought to devise a strategy that would satisfy the pro-Chase resolution of the party's convention, yet not appear to be backing a loser. It was a situation that fit in well with a concerted plan for using Chase's own insistence on the unit rule to swing Ohio delegates behind Ben Wade at the appropriate time.[93] Several Ohio delegates had arrived in Chicago well ahead of most of their colleagues on Thursday, May 10.[94] Their object was to identify those delegates from other states who were opposed to Seward. When this was accomplished, they let it be known that Chase's name would be dropped after two ballots and that Wade would be presented as the unanimous choice of Ohio.[95]

The remainder of the Ohio delegation came in on Sunday morning, and as soon as they settled themselves at the Tremont House they were told that Chase could not be nominated. If the delegation persisted in supporting him, they ran the risk of nominating Seward. A caucus was arranged for Monday morning. Columbus Delano, a long-time Chase opponent, led off with a resolution that the delegation support Chase unanimously for two ballots and on the third back an Ohio man who had the most votes from other states on the second ballot.[96] Before a vote could be taken, the caucus adjourned for the day.

As the delegates left the room, members of other state delegations immediately accosted them. "How many of you O[hio] men are going for Wade?"
was the most frequent question. The entire Delaware delegation surrounded
a Chase supporter "and importuned [him] to go for Wade."[97] Over the next
three days a heated debate went on between Chase delegates, those backing
Wade and a handful of delegates headed by Tom Corwin who were for
McLean.[98]

The Delano resolution was finally carried, but as neither side would
agree, it could not be binding. David Carrter, one of the delegates-at-large,
presumably for Chase, was actually for Wade. Yet he managed to assume
unofficial chairmanship of the delegation.[99] On the first ballot Chase received
49 votes, just behind Simon Cameron, who gained $50^{1}/_{2}$ votes. Wade with
three votes had the least of all contenders. But destroying any chance Chase
may have had for the nomination should Lincoln and Seward deadlock was
the fact that Lincoln had eight votes and McLean four votes from Ohio. On
the second ballot Lincoln got six more votes from Ohio and with 73 additional
votes from other states he was within three and a half votes of Seward, who
still led with $184^{1}/_{2}$ votes, 233 being necessary for the nomination.

With Wade and Chase presumably out of contention Delano—true to his
Whig instincts and conservative leanings—had led a sizable number of Ohio
delegates into the Lincoln camp. Even then, the Chase supporters, fearful that
Wade or Seward would emerge as the nominee, kept Chase's name before the
convention until it became obvious that Lincoln was only two and a half votes
from the nomination. At this point, and hopeful of gaining something for the
state, Carrter persuaded four Chase delegates to swing over to Lincoln and
thus the majority. Carrter immediately climbed on a chair and gained a moment of relative silence in the chamber. A big man whose uncombed stiff hair
shot out in all directions and whose large eyes were sunk in a face deeply pitted
by smallpox, he had a further blemish of a speech impediment. Murat Halstead, the gifted reporter for the *Cincinnati Commercial*, described him at that
moment. Carrter said, "I rise (eh) Mr. Chairman (eh), to announce the change
of four votes of Ohio from Mr. Chase to Mr. Lincoln." A roar of affirmation
swelled though the Wigwam. Lincoln was the party's nominee.[100]

Chase's brother Edward confirmed that outside support for him came
mainly from New York and Massachusetts. It lasted only as long as Seward
seemed likely to prevail.[101] After the first ballot, David Dudley Field, a leading
figure of the New York bar; George Opdyke, the wealthy New York merchant;
John A. Andrew, the portly Massachusetts lawyer and reform politician; and
Gideon Welles, Connecticut's member of the National Committee, all favored
Chase at first to thwart Seward.[102]

Had the Ohio delegation come in unanimously for Chase on the first
ballot, it is possible that his candidacy might have achieved enough strength to

deadlock the convention. To Chase men, the risk was too great. Governor Chauncey Cleveland wrote to Chase that "when I got to Chicago I soon found there was a disposition to nominate either Lincoln or Wade of your state. My object then was to prevent the nomination of Wade." Cleveland added that "Whig and American delegates voted for Lincoln—Welles and myself [were] the only Democrats in the [Connecticut] delegation [who] voted for you."[103] They may have in another delegate's words "effectually killed, as the boys say it, 'died in the shell' the Wade movement." But the result of the contest between the two contenders was that "our state," as Giddings remarked contemptuously, "exerted no more power . . . than did Delaware."[104]

Chase felt betrayal, indignation, and hurt at being defeated for what he knew could be the presidency. Since the breakup of the Democratic party at Charleston, just a few weeks before, he was certain that the Republicans would win the election in November.[105] Governor Cleveland summed up in a few words what Chase must have sensed most deeply. "As usual," he wrote, "the man who has done the least for the party and the cause is at the head of the ticket. I am disgusted with this ingratitude."

Yet Chase was a seasoned politician. He wrote Lincoln a warm letter pledging his support, took the stump for him and his running mate Hannibal Hamlin, and marched at the head of the now traditional "Wide Awake" escorts in Ohio, in northern Kentucky towns, and in New York State.[106]

chapter 17

Visit to Springfield

January 4, 1861, was a clear, chilly winter day in Springfield.[1] A tall, imposing man left the depot of the Great Western Railroad and booked a room at the Chenery House. He was recognized as Salmon P. Chase, senator-elect from Ohio and one of three losing candidates for the Republican presidential nomination seven months before.

Since the election in November the little Illinois city had experienced an unprecedented influx of visitors, some of national renown like Chase, more of little or no distinction from all over the state, the Northwest and the East. Springfield's successful lawyer and upwardly mobile politician Abraham Lincoln was the cause of all this interest since his selection as the first candidate of the new Republican party to be elected President. Unlike most of the visitors Chase had come in response to Lincoln's invitation.[2] And it was to be supposed that the President-elect had eagerly awaited his arrival.

Springfield, though the capital of the state, was small enough for news of arrivals and departures of important folk to be circulated rapidly. Lincoln learned of Chase's appearance in town and his destination not long after he had reached his hotel. Travel-stained and weary after two days on the cramped, stuffy cars of the four different railroads he took from Columbus, Chase had scarcely settled himself in his room when he learned that Lincoln himself was in the lobby inquiring for him. Chase had sent his card to Lincoln's home with the brief message that he would call when convenient, but the President-elect had discarded all formality and came directly to the Chenery House, a distinct favor to the senator, but one that Chase, who concerned himself with matters of punctilio, found rather unusual.[3]

Curiously he had never met Lincoln. They had of course corresponded, and Chase was well aware of Lincoln's political background, his antislavery stand, and his social and economic positions. Except for his opposition to the extension of slavery, Chase thought of Lincoln as an "old Whig" whose views on current issues more approximated those of such political enemies in Ohio as Ewing or Corwin. Chase did not doubt, however, that this relatively obscure national figure was a strong moralist who expressed himself lucidly, and whose logical presentations were delivered with that kind of imposing rhetoric that Chase so admired.

He was familiar with Lincoln's debates, with his eloquent speech at Cooper Union which William Cullen Byant had praised as having "a certain mastery of clear and impressive statement."[4] Two years before when Lincoln was battling Douglas for the Senate, Chase had made a number of speeches in Illinois in support of his candidacy. Lincoln had appreciated Chase's support.

As soon as they shook hands Lincoln began their conversation by again expressing his thanks rather fulsomely for Chase's participation in that bitterly contested campaign.[5] While voicing appropriate amenities, Chase had an opportunity to observe Lincoln closely. The man who stood before him in his hotel room was just as he imagined him to be. He epitomized the self-made western lawyer and politician with his easygoing, open manner, his high-pitched voice with its inimitable western accent. Even the sallow, seamed face, deepset eyes, strongly marked features, lean, loose-jointed body, and ill-fitting, rumpled clothes all bespoke a small-town westerner who made his way in the narrow world of prairie towns and villages of Illinois and neighboring states.

Chase, after all, had spent much of his adult life in the new and raw frontier West. He had known and worked with many similar lawyers and politicians in Cincinnati, Columbus, Xenia, Dayton, and Defiance. But somehow Lincoln appeared a different person than the Corwins and the Ewings and the Wades. As Lincoln sought to put his distinguished visitor at ease, Chase found him attractive in a homely sort of way. Shrewd he certainly semed to be from his questions and comments, yet open and candid in manner. No one could doubt his careful appraisal of men and events, his practical assessment of political realities and possibilities.[6]

Accustomed to masking his motives Chase was taken aback when Lincoln closed the conversation by coming to the point of the interview. "I have done with you," he said, "what I would not perhaps had ventured to do with any other man in the country—sent for you to ask whether you will accept the appointment of Secretary of the Treasury, without however, being exactly prepared to offer it to you."[7]

Chase must have been startled as much by Lincoln's candor as by his own disappointment at not being asked to serve as Secretary of State, the first position in the Cabinet, and then by the fact that Lincoln could not even offer him the Treasury post. For months now he had brooded over his lack of recognition from the party he believed, and with considerable justification, for which he had done so much. Lincoln's forthright comment rubbed a raw wound.[8] Chase managed to control his feelings, but his reply was constrained. He had not come to Springfield with his cap in his hand for an appointment. He denied that he sought any position in the Cabinet and he implied that he would not accept a subordinate place. If Lincoln concerned himself about Chase's arch response, he gave no heed. At a subsequent interview he explained that he planned to offer Seward the State Department because he was the acknowledged leader of the party. Should Seward decline, he would offer Chase the post.[9]

Despite his initial disappointment and the blow to an already bruised ego, Chase was not about to foreclose what would be, after all, a distinguished and patronage-rich position. He agreed with Lincoln that Seward enjoyed a certain prominence in the party. By virtue of his long and impressive public service and his undoubted antislavery views, he also deserved a senior post. Beyond that he would not commit himself. In fact he was quick to say that he was unprepared to take the Treasury post if offered. He reminded Lincoln that he had six years in the Senate ahead of him. He could support the administration and be of assistance to the nation in that position as well if not better than in the Cabinet.[10]

Both men had taken the measure of each other and had skirted areas of potential tension. Lincoln had fared better than he had any reason to expect considering Chase's vanity and his well-known antipathy toward Seward. But Lincoln's problem with the Treasury appointment was not as yet fully resolved. It had originated with an ill-considered promise of the post that Lincoln's managers at the Chicago convention had given to Simon Cameron, now the leading Republican in Pennsylvania. His men had controlled the Pennsylvania delegation. Probably they exacted the pledge from Lincoln's managers in return for swinging the Pennsylvania delegates to Lincoln.[11]

A sharp-faced, hard-dealing businessman and politician of Scottish forebears, Cameron had made a fortune in banking and iron manufacturing. Politics, not careful management, had been the basis of his wealth, and every dollar that went into his sumptuous estate near Harrisburg, Pennsylvania, was in one way or another derived from his political connections and activities.

Lincoln was aware of Cameron's newspaper nickname, "The Great

Winnebago Chieftain," derived from his unsavory speculations while acting as the government's special commissioner to dispose of Winnebago Indian lands.[12] Yet Cameron's political acumen and apparent support from many quarters had impressed Lincoln when the crafty Pennsylvanian visited him in Springfield just five days earlier.[13] Acting impulsively he had handed Cameron a letter that he soon regretted in which he said that he would nominate him to be Secretary of the Treasury or Secretary of War "which of the two I have not yet definitely decided."[14]

When Cameron reached his home, he made public that he had been offered the Treasury Department. There was an instant uproar and Lincoln backtracked. The day before Chase's arrival Lincoln took the unusual step of writing Cameron a brusque letter saying that "since seeing you things have developed which make it impossible for me to take you into the Cabinet." He suggested that Cameron write him declining any Cabinet appointment. At the same time he telegraphed Cameron that a letter was on its way.[15]

Before Chase reached Springfield he had become aware of the rumor that Cameron had been offered and accepted the Treasury post. Lincoln's odd declaration clarified the Pennsylvania problem he alluded to. It was public knowledge that Edward Bates would become Attorney General in the new administration, an appointment that Chase found distasteful considering the Missourian's "old Whig" and American background. With Seward in the State Department and the possibility of Cameron whom he suspected of being under Weed-Seward influence in the Cabinet, it was not surprising that Chase would have doubts about Lincoln's political judgment and his own participation in the new administration.

The next day, Chase and Amos Tuck, who had just arrived, spent several hours with Lincoln. The conversation ranged over other Cabinet possibilities, upper-level patronage jobs, and the constitutional crisis. South Carolina had already seceded from the Union. News from the Deep South indicated that the states throughout the entire region would soon follow. The grave situation, of course, gave a special and demanding turn to the talks. Chase certainly felt the tension, and for the time being at least put aside his personal feelings in a desire to rally around this gaunt figure with such awesome responsibilities ahead of him.[16]

There was no pretense about Lincoln regarding the state of the Union or his own abilities to cope with the crisis. His willingness to accept advice on patronage and on the political currents that were roiling in the various states outside of Illinois and of which he claimed ignorance was most reassuring. He was so obliging, so self-deprecating, so warm and cordial that he thawed rather completely Chase's chilly reserve. Because of train connections, Chase stayed over the weekend.[17] He attended church with the Lincolns on Sunday. When he bade goodbye on Monday morning he carried with him Lincoln's parting request that he consult with close friends and associates about the Treasury post which he still was unable to offer.[18]

Lincoln was equally impressed with Chase, with what he took to be his sure grasp of the political and economic issues besetting the Union. Chase's self-confidence, his majestic port, which many of his contemporaries found distasteful, Lincoln seems to have equated with the kind of strength he needed for his administration. Although Chase in the Treasury Department would rouse the ire of Pennsylvania protectionists and Cameron's legion of friends, he would prove a counterbalance to Seward. As Lincoln expressed it to Lyman Turnbull, "he alone can reconcile Mr. Bryant and his class, to the appointment of Gov. S(eward) to the state department. . . ."[19]

When Lincoln saw Chase off on the train, he had made up his mind that it was "not only highly proper, but a *necessity,* that Gov. Chase shall take that place [the Treasury]."[20] As for Chase he may have been noncommittal with Lincoln about accepting the Treasury post, but his actions belied his words. While his railroad car moved along between Springfield and Lafayette, Indiana, he scribbled letters to Opdyke and to Barney which a fellow passenger who was getting off at Toledo agreed to mail. In his anxiety to make sure that immediate action was taken and fearful that Opdyke might be out of town, he authorized Barney in that event "to open Opdyke's letter and read it." What he wanted was to have his New York friends visit Springfield and impress his availability on Lincoln. "What is done must be done quickly and done judiciously," he wrote, "with the concurrence of our best men and by a deputation to Springfield." Characteristically he then gave his customary disclaimer. "If our New York friends," he continued, "think it unimportant to them, however to do anything I shall be perfectly content. I want nothing for myself."[21]

Chase had known for sometime that his supporters in New York were planning to bring pressure on Lincoln to thwart Seward's influence in the new administration. Well before election day the previous November, Chase had begun laying plans to advance himself as a shaper of public policy in the aftermath of what he believed would be a Republican triumph. Supremely confident of his position—containment of slavery to areas where local law and customs supported it—he brushed aside any criticism that his policy was sectional and disruptive. Yet he did make an effort to move away from what many fellow Republicans including Lincoln considered a radical stand.

On November 1, he had gone across the Ohio River to Covington, Kentucky, where he would give his first political speech on slave soil. He was prepared for a hostile audience when he appeared at the Odd Fellows Hall, but except for a few rowdies at the door, he made his way through the packed hall to the podium without incident.[22] Chase assured his audience that the Republicans, if they won the election, would "let slavery very severely alone in all the states." He emphasized that his party was determined to give free labor a proper chance in the territories. And he added after a territory became a state "if its citizens" chose to engraft slavery in their institutions there is no power in the federal government which can prevent them from so doing. While he condemned secession roundly, except "as a right of revolution," he maintained that he had no fears "of a dissolution of the Union."[23] Chase's speech was well received, though only a small fraction of the audience admitted to being Republican.

What a difference there was in public opinion, however, compared with what it had been when he expressed similar sentiments in Ohio, a free state, in 1841. Even such an avowed abolitionist as John Greenleaf Whittier, to whom he sent a copy of his Covington speech, complimented his free-soil propositions, a stand the Quaker poet would have condemned as morally bankrupt twenty years earlier.[24]

Virtually certain of a Republican victory in the electoral college, the telegraph simply confirmed Chase's belief on November 7. Almost as a portent of the times, the Neil House, Columbus's largest and finest hotel which occupied an entire block opposite the capitol, caught fire just when the final returns were coming in from the East. The blaze was spectacular. Chase, one of the onlookers, remarked that while "it was grand to see the fire gradually prevail over the enormous pile, it was sickening to feel human impotence to avert the devastation."[25] Had Chase been a sensitive literary man he might have seen in the destruction of the Neil House a metaphor for the collapsing Union. He was not however given to such poetic musings on such somber subjects.

He was more concerned with the condition of the party that had just won the national election. What he called the conservative and the progressive wings must be reconciled to each other. "Those who would convert the organization into "old Whiggism or the purpose of old Whiggism," he wrote, "those who insist on the development from Republicanism of a living Democracy, such as issued from the Republicanism of Jefferson must be conciliated if possible." Chase was just the person to make this adjustment, just the sort of political leader to rescue the party from the clutches of inveterate Whigs who bore a close resemblance to that hawk-nosed little manipulator from New York, William H. Seward, and his political fixer Thurlow Weed.

He was not alone in his concerns. On election day, the New York *Tribune* office was casting about for public men of the anti-Seward stripe who would mold the new administration. Lincoln for all his good points was considered by these self-anointed sophisticates easily moldable. Charles A. Dana, Greeley's right hand in editorial affairs, dashed off a note to Chase urging him to accept the Treasury post which he assumed would be offered.[26] Masking his motives Chase told Dana that he preferred to serve in the Senate, "as it was more pleasant on many accounts. Still I do not say that I would refuse the post you refer to. Indeed it would be superfluous to decline what has not been offered."[27]

George G. Fogg, the busy secretary of the Republican National Committee and soon to become one of the two official channels of information on Cabinet matters—Hannibal Hamlin, the Vice President-elect, being the other—found Chase decidedly negative to a Cabinet post.[28] Chase's supposed ambivalence was meant for Lincoln's consumption as he knew that Fogg was about to visit Springfield. At the time, Barney, Chase's man in New York, was actively promoting him for the State Department. Meanwhile Thurlow Weed learned that Hamlin was enroute to Chicago where he would meet Lincoln. Weed intercepted Hamlin and told him that New York and Seward deserved the State Department, but that the New Yorker would decline such an invitation.[29] Naturally the Barney group was tracking Weed's activities and knew of a prior attempt to have Lincoln consult with Seward at his home in Auburn, New York, a suggestion that Lincoln rejected.[30] Nor was Weed's assertion that Seward would decline the State Department post accepted with any degree of certainty in Springfield though it caused problems in the selection process.[31]

Reacting to these moves, Barney held a strategy meeting at his home on Saturday evening, November 24. In attendance was a roster of the city's most distinguished former free-soil Whigs and Democrats headed by William Cullen Bryant, his son-in-law Parke Godwin, David Dudley Field, the irrepressible senior member of that large irrepressible family, Charles A. Dana, Opdyke and William Curtis Noyes, legal scholar and prominent trial lawyer.

After a lengthy discussion before the meeting broke up at near midnight, it was decided to back Chase for Secretary of State subject to the views of Lyman Trumbull, who was expected to be in the city on the morrow. After consulting with Trumbull, who was believed to enjoy Lincoln's confidence, the group which soon included Schuyler Colfax, the amiable congressman from Indiana, met again, this time at Noyes's house.[32] Everyone present supported Chase for Secretary of State. It was also agreed that a deputation representing these views be sent to Springfield. Another meeting, this time made up exclusively of free-soil Democrats, was held in Albany on December 6 where Chase was again endorsed for the State Department.[33] The visit to Springfield was delayed for the time being.[34]

Joshua Giddings, however, made a personal plea for Chase when he visited Lincoln on December 3. He came away from the meeting with the impression that Chase would be offered State. He was mistaken because five days later Lincoln offered the post to Seward, though he enclosed his invitation in a letter to Hamlin whom he asked to discuss it with Trumbull and, if he had no objections, to give it to Seward "at once."[35] Lincoln made this decision after hearing from Trumbull about his consultation with the anti-Seward group at Noyes's home.

Accordingly Hamlin sought out Seward. After a general conversation during which the New Yorker said several times how weary he was of public life and how he would decline a Cabinet post, Hamlin handed him Lincoln's letter. Seward read it and again expressing reluctance said he was "willing to labor for his country," but would have to consult with his friends before replying.[36] He said as much in his reply to Lincoln and did not formally accept the post until December 28.

Thus when Chase spoke with Lincoln on January 4 and 5, Seward and Bates had been offered and accepted positions in the Cabinet, confirming Chase's suspicions that "old Whigs" would control the new administration unless he and other free-soil Democrats were in a position to check their influence. Cameron, though an ex-Democrat and Chase's foremost competitor, was seen as a tool of Seward and Weed, and there was considerable evidence of this.[37]

Chase had been home for only two days when he decided that he must try to keep another Whig out of the Cabinet. An accumulation of letters and rumors in the papers pointed to Caleb Smith as a likely prospect. Chase had no use for Smith, a practicing lawyer in Cincinnati and a Taylor-Whig congressman from Indiana.

He knew that this oval-faced, smooth-featured politician was a part of the Wade move to deprive him of the nomination in Chicago. It is also possible that Chase was acting on behalf of fellow former Democrat Norman Judd, who was angling for a berth in the Cabinet. And of course he knew that Smith not only had been chairman of the Indiana delegation that gave Lincoln all its 26 votes on every ballot, but that he had brought his oratorical skills to the fore in nominating Lincoln. Yet Chase decided, as he said, "with good deal of reluctance" to warn Lincoln about Smith. "But it is due you to say," wrote Chase, "that his reputation has been seriously effected by his railroad and other transactions that his appointment to a place in your cabinet would impair the credit and endanger the success of your administration."[38]

Hence the urgency of his letters to Opdyke and Barney that a deputation of like-minded New Yorkers travel to Springfield immediately. Enroute to Springfield, Opdyke, Barney, and Judge John T. Hogeboom, formerly a Van Buren Barnburner, saw Chase in Columbus where he indicated that he might accept Treasury if offered. On January 16, they reached Springfield, where they pressed Chase's case while arguing strenuously against Cameron on the basis of fitness and character.[39] Lincoln was impressed with the facts they presented, but under heavy pressure from Cameron's supporters withheld any positive assurance.[40]

Chase's concerns about Seward, his efforts to keep Smith out of the

Cabinet, his fears of a renewed Whig ascendency that would sap Lincoln's independence and move the new administration away from a free trade, free labor policy went back several months to information he received from George Fogg that Wade was among those in Washington who were working to keep him out of the Cabinet.[41] He had concrete evidence of Smith's close relationship with Wade's backers at the Chicago convention. The time was ripe to settle affairs with the senator from Ashtabula.

Chase decided he would make a direct approach in which he cloaked a warning. Seizing upon a speech Wade made in the Senate as a pretext, he praised it as an eloquent and correct statement of principles. But then he charged Wade with doing him "some harm" and the "wrong to me was a greater wrong to the Republican Party of Ohio."[42] More than a month passed before Wade replied, denying flatly that he had ever injured Chase or the party: "All this is [so] new and strange to me that I do not know what to make of it." In blunt language he accused Chase of laboring under a delusion.[43]

Chase had ample time to consider Wade's acerbic letter and to balance a six-year term in the Senate with a rough, politically devious colleague against an important patronage heavy position in the new administration where he could influence policy on the highest level. Despite anticipated problems with Wade there were attractions to being a senator, especially during these days of crisis. As he explained to his friend John Jay in a series of rhetorical questions:

Would you be willing to take charge of a broken down department, as a member of a cabinet with which you could not be sure of six months agreement and enslave yourself to the most toilsome drudging almost without respite for four years, exchanging a position from which you could speak freely to the country during half the year and during the other half retire to books, travel and friends for one you could not speak at all except through report and where no leisure is expected? Answer that.

Still, should Lincoln offer him the Treasury, "if really satisfied that I ought to take the post I shall."[44]

Meanwhile the deteriorating condition of the Union had claimed Chase's attention as it claimed that of most articulate Americans, northerners and southerners alike. On December 30 reports reached Columbus that General Scott, the venerable, Virginia-born commander of the United States Army, was about to resign his commission. Chase dashed off a letter to Scott imploring him to stand by the Union. Condemning unsparingly the action of South Carolina, he wrote, "Rebellion is treason until successful which God forbid! For successful rebellion must needs be followed by swift steps, by civil and servile war."[45]

The departure of four additional states in the Deep South from the Union during the next two weeks and the certain secession of two more did not shake Chase's uncompromising stand. No doubt he had voiced his opposition to Buchanan's appeasement policies in his talks with Lincoln. He may not have been surprised therefore when he received a letter from Springfield in mid-January that seemed to confirm the Cabinet position and at the same time demonstrate how his views had already made a significant impact on the President-elect. Norman Judd, chair of the Illinois Republican Committee and Illinois's member of the National Committee, wrote Chase from Springfield, obviously at Lincoln's direction. The Illinois legislature then in session was considering a series of resolutions that among other compromise measures called for a constitutional convention to work out an adjustment with the slave states.

"Some of our men," Judd wrote, "are alarmed at the aspect of public affairs and desire to do something but do not know what they want, and we have trouble holding them steady." He enclosed a copy of two resolutions, one calling for a constitutional convention, the other sustaining the federal Constitution and laws. Judd asked for Chase's opinion. The matter was so urgent in Lincoln's and Judd's estimation that Chase was asked to telegraph his approval or disapproval ahead of his letter.[46]

Chase was appalled as much by Lincoln's seeming inability to condemn the resolutions out of hand as his presumed failure to stiffen his own party members in his own hometown against what seemed to be outrageous demands from secessionists. Yet he was happy to have been asked for an opinion and vain enough to delight in the opportunity of showing the President-elect the proper course.[47]

In his rather lengthy reply, Chase condemned the calling of any constitutional convention which he was sure if held would simply confirm the action already taken or about to be taken by the states of the Deep South. Nor did he favor any constitutional amendments that made concessions. Let Lincoln be inaugurated and then if concessions were warranted let amendments be framed by the new Republican administration provided they were not inconsistent with the Republican platform.[48] His suggestion may have led to Lincoln and Governor Yates's opposition to the Peace Convention proposed by the Virginia legislature. But the Illinois legislature overrode their objections and recommended attendance at the convention, which among other things would propose to Congress any necessary amendments that would preserve the Union.[49]

Shortly after Chase rejected any concession in his reply to Judd, more alarming news came from Washington. Chase's old friend Edwin M. Stanton, Buchanan's newly appointed Attorney General, wrote that Washington would be seized and made the capital of "a Southern Confederacy." "The President," said Stanton, "does not believe and cannot be made to believe the existence of this danger. . . ."[50] And another friend from his distant past,

Thomas Swann, former mayor of Baltimore, while deprecating the sectional spirit of the times, spoke of heavy pressure on Governor Hicks to call a secession convention.[51]

Efforts at compromise in Washington, the Crittenden resolutions in the Senate that sought to extend the Missouri Compromise line to the California border, and Charles Francis Adams's House proposal that would, in effect, establish popular sovereignty in the vast New Mexico territory had met with no favor from Chase. Other plans, like that proposed by Thurlow Weed which advocated a compromise settlement, Chase quickly condemned as truckling to the slaveholding oligarchy in the South and a repudiation of basic Republican party doctrine.[52]

chapter 18

Loaves and Fishes

As he had in his letter to Judd on the Illinois resolutions Chase gave Lincoln the benefit of his information from Washington and his advice. He thought that the defense of the capital was totally inadequate. Buchanan was said to be "incredulous and apathetic." He took a direct shot at the Crittenden and Adams resolutions: a greater danger "and more imminent . . . is the disruption of the Republican party through Congressional attempts at compromises." Then he summarized what he believed policy should be in one of those striking phrases which quickly became a slogan for the Republican party. "Let the word pass from the head of the column before the Republicans move. . . . the simple watchword—Inauguration first—adjustment afterwards."[1]

On record as opposing all conciliation until the new administration was in place, Chase was embarrassed when Governor Dennison appointed him to be one of Ohio's delegates to the last-ditch Peace Convention of notables that the Virginia legislature proposed. Ex-President John Tyler had come out of obscurity to push for the conference and was to act as its presiding officer when it would begin deliberations in Washington on February 4. Chase was even more embarrassed after he learned who were to be his fellow delegates. All except the token Democrat William S. Groesbeck were Republicans heavily weighted to the conservative side. The appointment of Chase's bitter political opponent Thomas Ewing was especially galling.[2] Despite his uneasiness about being associated with so many conservatives and with a mission that if it was not doomed to failure might propose arrangements he could not support, Chase reluctantly accepted the appointment. As he explained to Giddings, his presence might do some good.[3]

Another factor prompted his decision. The "Peace Convention" would provide a timely pretext for him to be in Washington where he could judge for himself the situation at its focal point, to see and be seen by Lincoln when he arrived without seeming to be importunate about a Cabinet position. He knew that Seward and his adherents were aiming to exclude him from the Cabinet and the fact that he had not heard from Springfield meant his appointment was still in doubt. He would be on hand to marshall his forces and defend his interests. A final consideration must be the convention itself—a pulpit for expressing his own views without being charged a political opportunist or a rabid sectionalist.

Chase reached Washington on March 1. He rented temporary quarters at the Rugby, a large, unpretentious residential hotel on the corner of 14th and K streets. Nettie was with him and Kate was expected to join the family within a week.[4] His first few days in Washington were a sobering experience. After listening to opinions of all shades, he concluded that the situation was far more dangerous than he had thought. On March 3 he wrote Henry B. Carrington, now adjutant general of Ohio, urging that the bill then pending in the legislature to strengthen the militia be passed immediately and that a recruiting campaign be launched to enroll volunteers for the new regiments.[5]

A mood of deep apprehension that seemed to have infected the very atmosphere of official Washington softened Chase's insistence that there be no temporizing with the seceded states. Although he found kindred spirits in other delegates, men such as David Dudley Field, William Curtis Noyes, the dour William Pitt Fessenden from Maine, and Amos Tuck, Chase was uncomfortable with his minority status on his own delegation. His Ohio colleagues were insisting on compromises which would at least hold the wavering border states in the Union.[6] As much as he deprecated the convention and the conservatism of his colleagues, he did not allow his opinions to ignore conventional amenities.

On the opening day of the convention in the ballroom of Willard's Hotel, Chase as senior member of the Ohio delegation escorted his aged and nearly blind colleague John C. Wright to the platform. Wright, who had been elected chairman, opened the proceedings with a short, emotional speech.[7] Thereafter Chase took an active part in the convention, which foundered on the rocks of slavery, sectionalism, and political ideology as had the two previous compromise proposals.[8] Early on what might be termed the radical or progressive elements in the northern delegations separated from their more conservative brethren. Among the delegates from the slave states the moderates and those who demanded complete acceptance of the expansion of slavery in the territories were likewise divided on an acceptable compromise formula.

Chase saw an opportunity to consolidate the more radical delegates under his leadership. He was astute enough to realize that he and the party had nothing to lose by recommending to Congress the calling of a national constitutional convention. When Congress got around to considering such a measure, if indeed it ever did, his well-publicized goal of inauguration first, adjustment later would have been realized. And after that if it passed the congressional hurdle, it would have to contend with the states. Years could be involved.

Midway in the deliberations Chase's aged colleague Wright died. This time Governor Dennison hearkened to the pleas of the radicals and appointed former the attorney general of Ohio Christopher Wolcott. Although both men were still outvoted on the Ohio delegation, Chase did not feel quite so isolated. Not that he acted in an unfriendly fashion to delegates whose views were poles apart from his. The consistently uncompromising delegate from Virginia, James A. Seddon, wraithlike in appearance and husky of voice but given to logical discourse, exacted an admiring tribute from Chase.[9]

In fact Chase and his radical group generally voted with southern extremists that seldom supported compromise measures. Neither extreme prevailed, however, when the delegates, a majority of those from Ohio included, voted to accept a plan that James Guthrie proposed. Amos Tuck and other radicals offered amendments that their caucus had approved, but these were voted down despite Chase's best efforts.[10] Nor were southern extremists able to tack their proslavery amendments to the majority report.[11]

Early in the proceedings Chase gave his one major address. His only departure from accepted and well-known Republican doctrine was a suggestion that the federal government compensate slave owners for fugitives.[12] In decided contrast to the aged Tyler, a picturesque ruin who sat at the table beside him, Chase made an imposing figure.[13] Speaking extemporaneously he again and again reiterated that the Republicans would not, could not interfere with slavery where it existed in the states, but were fixed in their opposition to extend it into the territories.[14] Restriction not war on the institution was the aim of the party and, as far as he knew, would be the policy of the new administration.[15] He did not think there was need for "any new constitutional guarantees," but then, looking directly at Seddon, he said, "if you think otherwise, we are ready to join you in recommending a national Convention to propose amendments to the Constitution in the regular and legitimate way."[16] Chase closed his remarks by alluding to the oath the new President would take to protect and defend the Constitution of the United States and execute its laws. If he enforces the laws, and "secession or revolution resists what then?

War! Civil War!" Chase paused for dramatic emphasis and concluded with the phrase "Let us not rush headlong into that unfathomable gulf!"[17]

Chase's remarks caught the attention and raised the emotions of many border-state moderates. That evening, delegates from Tennessee, Kentucky, and North Carolina visited him at the Rugby to see if he had proposals to make that would establish a basis for an acceptable compromise. He refused to offer anything specific. The delegation soon discovered that there was more expediency than conciliation in his propositions. "I really sympathize with them," he mused, "but see no reason why we should sacrifice permanently a *large* power to help them, for the purpose of gaining temporarily a *little one*."[18]

The Ohio delegation, however, by a majority of six to two accepted every section of a proposed Thirteenth Amendment that protected slavery.[19] Radicals in other states were hopelessly outvoted. In other respects Chase's attendance could not have injured his image as a potent communicator of progressive Republican party doctrine to the President-elect, to his associates on other delegations, and especially to southern moderates.[20]

Chase and the Republicans were not seen as the awesome threat to southern institutions that had been trumpeted in the secessionist press.[21] By common consent, Chase acted as the leader of the convention delegates when they met with Lincoln at his quarters in Willard's Hotel. Standing next to Lincoln, Chase introduced each member with an appropriate phrase.[22] His nomination for the Treasury was still in doubt.[23]

The Washington press and the gossip-mongers who thronged the lobby of Willard's had kept a close eye on the movements of the President-elect. They noticed that Seward was much in Lincoln's company. There were dinners at Seward's home and church services with Seward at St. John's, where Chase probably saw them together because he also attended this most fashionable of the capital's six Episcopal churches.[24] He definitely observed Seward's close attendance on Lincoln at the Senate and the House and at a dinner given for Lincoln by E. G. Spaulding, a New York congressman, which he attended along with Vice President-elect Hannibal Hamlin, Charles Francis Adams, Bates, Seward, and Gideon Welles. He noticed how Seward monopolized Lincoln's attention.[25] Unquestionably he was privy to the onslaught on Lincoln that the jovial spoilsman Simeon Draper and his group of Seward enthusiasts were making.

Former Whigs all, conservative merchants, bankers, and lawyers from New York City, they were determined if possible to exclude from the administration Chase and all former Democrats suspected of radical tendencies regarding slavery or opposition to compromise with the South and in their eyes the heresies of free trade and hard money. Personalities entered into the final battle over supposed control of Lincoln. Horace Greeley, no reticent person when it came to political infighting, badgered Lincoln on his Cabinet appointments. *Tribune* editorials demanded that Chase receive the Treasury. William Cullen Byant backed him up in the *Post*. Greeley's curious mental mixture of Whiggish political economy, Jacksonian individualism, and radical antislavery impulses were combined with his personal animus toward Seward and Weed.

On March 1, responding to the Greeley-Bryant campaign for Chase, Seward in a conversation with Lincoln said that he could not serve in a Cabinet that had Chase as a member. He also opposed vehemently Gideon Welles and Montgomery Blair, both former Democrats, both seen as radicals on the slavery issue, and both regarded as probable appointees. Welles was already in Washington and Blair was seen entering Lincoln's suite at Willard's.

A nettled Lincoln restrained himself and asked Seward to reconsider. But Lincoln reacted strenuously to the insistent pressure of the Draper group, which reached its highest point on March 2.[26] In presenting a hypothetical proposition Lincoln asked, "How would it do, for Mr. Chase to take the Treasury and to offer the State Department to Mr. William Dayton?"—a New Jersey politician and Republican vice presidential candidate in 1856. Lincoln then said he would be happy to nominate Seward as Minister to Great Britain. When Draper relayed this information to Seward he promptly wrote Lincoln a note withdrawing his acceptance of the State Department.[27]

It became apparent that Lincoln wanted a coalition Cabinet in which previous party affiliations, competing ideologies, and representatives of the distinct sections of the Union were balanced. He had tried to include a representative from the uncommitted border state of North Carolina but had been unsuccessful. If necessary, it appears that he would have made good his threat to Draper, but by Sunday, March 3, he was virtually certain that Seward would retract his stand. Yet tension remained high among would-be officeholders who jammed the corridors of Willard's and made it unpleasant for the leading candidates. "I can't step into the halls which are crowded, or the streets," Gideon Welles complained, "that I do not find myself stared at and criticized all of which is to me, you know annoying. . . ."[28]

In any event, except for the Treasury and the State departments, all Cabinet posts had been filled as Lincoln wanted. That evening he entertained his appointees at dinner in his Willard's apartment.[29] Chase and Seward were present. Doubtless it was awkward for both men. On inauguration day Lincoln wrote a note to Seward asking him to "countermand the withdrawal" on personal grounds and urgent reasons of state. He asked for a reply not later than 9 a.m. on the fifth. Seward responded by visiting Lincoln, who persuaded him to drop his personal and political opposition to Chase, Welles, and Blair in the interest of the Union.[30]

If Seward had been temperamental and cost Lincoln some sleepless hours, Chase, too, had been difficult though for a shorter period of time.

Distracted by the solicitude of friends and the pretensions of Cabinet-makers, Lincoln had not had a private interview with Chase. Assuming that he would accept the Treasury he sent Chase's name into the Senate on March 5 along with the entire slate, which was confirmed unanimously.

Chase was absent from the Senate floor at the time. On his return he found that he had been nominated and confirmed when colleagues rushed up to congratulate him. Chase, ever conscious of his own importance and overly sensitive to matters of protocol with not a little assertiveness in his character, immediately visited the President and in effect read a lecture to him. He concluded by declining the office. Since he had already been confirmed, his withdrawal at this point would have been acutely embarrassing to Lincoln and would have sapped confidence in his administration before it had fairly commenced. Conversely Chase would have been injured too in a political as well as a public sense. He knew this and so did Lincoln, who, while being extremely deferential in his reply, called Chase's bluff. The stately but discomforted Chase had to back down, which one imagines he did with some grace.

The Cabinet was now set, and though it would be a contentious one, the new administration reflected faithfully the regional interests of the Union and the coalition nature of the Republican party. It was by and large made up of distinguished men who were seasoned politicians. Chase and Seward were outstanding individuals with national reputations, far better known to the general public than Lincoln. Welles, Blair, and Bates were all industrious and able administrators.

In ordinary times Cameron and Smith would have functioned satisfactorily though neither had really broad-gauged, decisive leadership qualities. Unfortunately all of the Cabinet members were decided partisans who carried their differences into Cabinet deliberations or informally with the President.

The competition for the Cabinet was as nothing compared with the struggle for subordinate offices. It had begun well before Lincoln's election, but as soon as the returns announced a Republican victory it took on a frantic quality. After the inauguration pressure increased almost exponentially. The majority Whig-American component had not tasted the benefits of office for eight years and it was an exceedingly voracious—indeed, insatiable—political beast.[31]

Before Chase could arrange his preferences for patronage, he had to consider what his resignation of the senatorship would do to his own goals. He knew that it would place a strain on the party and raise to a higher level the strife between conservatives, moderates, radicals, former Democrats, Whigs and Americans within the Republican coalition.[32] As soon as Chase sent in his resignation to Columbus five aspirants to his seat emerged.

To Chase's regret all were former Whigs, and four of the five tended to be on the conservative side. Governor Dennison, the only moderate on the slavery and secession questions, was Chase's choice, though not with any particular relish. Dennison's initial selection of conservatives such as Corwin who packed the Peace Convention delegation could not have pleased Chase. Yet considering all the candidates Dennison was closer to Chase's political philosophy than any of the others. Dennison, after all, had lent significant support to Chase in his recent election to the Senate.

Among the leading candidates Robert C. Schenck, the heavy-featured, blunt-speaking lawyer, was no friend. Nor was the conservative ex-congressman Valentine Horton, whose major attribute seemed to be his military gait and ramrod-stiff back; nor were the old spellbinders Corwin and Ewing. After many ballots in the legislature, John Sherman, of the chiseled features and trim beard, secured the prize.[33]

As he had during his pallid campaign for the presidential nomination, Chase had not made any concerted efforts to build up support for a candidate whom he would hand-pick to succeed him. More than six weeks had elapsed since his conversation with Lincoln in Springfield, a timespan during which he could have made some preparations for the succession among his Ohio supporters. He did nothing, while Wade and other Chase enemies were active in seeking support for their choices. In the end he was more fortunate than he should have been in the selection of Sherman despite his Whiggish background. As he wrote to a friend on March 23, "Sherman's election satisfies me; though as between him and the gov. I could take no part."[34]

Chase's first forays into the executive patronage struggle were more successful than his inept handling of the senatorial succession. More by luck than by careful planning he was able to place several of his own men in key Treasury positions. The most important and lucrative political post in the nation came within the Treasury Department patronage, the collectorship of the custom house in New York. The office was worth from $25,000 to $30,000 a year in salary and fees, more compensation than the salary of the President. The custom house controlled hundreds of employees whose salaries had been customarily assessed some 2 percent a year for party purposes.[35] Its management in New York and in other port cities was in many respects independent of the collector. Each custom house had ten subordinate officers whose positions roughly approximated the division of responsibilities involved in the collection of duties. The most important of these were the surveyor, naval officer, appraiser, and naval agent. For more than a month after the inauguration, the collectorships and other custom officers were the objects of intense competition among party leaders, congressmen, and Cabinet members.

Control of the custom house in New York City was a major objective of Seward and Weed, for they considered it—and with good reason—indispensable to their dominance in the party politics of the state. Chase also recognized its strategic importance and was just as determined to have his own men installed in the marble edifice that overlooked the busy harbor.

His choice for collector was Hiram Barney, a long-time friend from Columbus who had served him well as Ohio's school commissioner during his first gubernatorial term.[36] Barney had moved to New York City four years earlier and had established himself as a successful lawyer in partnership with Benjamin F. Butler's son William Allen Butler. Barney had worked hard to secure Chase's nomination for the presidency in 1856 and again in 1860.

At this time he was closely associated with the radical Bryant-Greeley-Opdyke clique in New York and was thus anathema to Seward and Weed. Personally Barney was a handsome man with iron-gray hair swept back from a broad forehead and a square, pugnacious jaw. His appearance radiated strength and a sense of purpose. Lincoln had known Barney too for a number of years and had, like Chase, been impressed with what he took to be his sincerity, honesty, and grasp of political realities. Moreover, Lincoln sought balance in these important appointments and Barney would be a makeweight against the party conservatives under Weed and Seward's thumb in the Empire State.

Yet behind Barney's imposing presence lurked a hesitant, insecure individual who would prove no match for Thurlow Weed. "Don't appoint Barney Collector," warned Charles A. Dana, speaking for himself and Greeley. "He is an excellent person but has no popular strength and no strength among the merchants. Nor does his political service give him title to such an important position."[37]

Dana wanted Opdyke in the post. This wealthy, self-assured merchant would have defended the radical cause much more vigorously than Barney.[38] But Lincoln had taken the measure of the New York City factions. Opdyke was simply too combative for such a sensitive post. As he expressed it in a memorandum, "Greeley, Opdycke [sic], Field and Wadsworth in favor of having the two big puddings on the same side of the board." But in the end Lincoln did just this. He appointed Chase's man, Barney, collector and, on Greeley's recommendation, Rufus F. Andrews, surveyor.[39]

Despite an apparent setback, Seward and his partner Weed would make off with five of the ten senior custom-house posts and a majority of the federal appointments in New York.[40] Chase had the collectorship in the Barney appointment and three of the subordinate offices.[41] In political influence and prestige he and the radicals came off quite well despite the fact that most of New York's Republican congressional delegation were partial to Weed and Seward.[42] Unfortunately, Barney's weakness would soon become apparent and he would in due course prove a liability to both Chase and the President.

Collectorships for other ports were just as difficult to fill, as Lincoln, Chase, Seward, other Cabinet members, and members of Congress spent endless hours in conferences trying to placate political rivalries yet at the same time satisfy administrative needs and personal preferences.

In this free-for-all, Chase had to settle for less than he had hoped, though he did succeed in placing his men as collectors in Philadelphia and Baltimore.[43] He lamented the fact that he was only "partially" responsible for appointments in his own department. David Dudley Field expressed the discomfort of the New York radicals when he wrote Chase that if Cabinet members were given plenary authority for patronage in their respective states, his group "will be very restive under it." Field wanted a rule that would give each head of department exclusive patronage in the selection or dismissal of his subordinates "except in the case of those higher offices, whom the President may prefer to designate himself." Chase agreed, but it was never to be during his tenure as Secretary.[44]

The Boston collectorship eluded his grasp, though Amos Tuck, who was friendly to Chase, secured the naval officer post.[45] The assistant treasurers in New York, Boston, and Philadelphia were important and well-paid men who acted as the Secretary's direct agents in the money centers of the nation, and all were placed by Chase. To the most important post—the assistant treasurer in New York City—Chase's appointment was not made on political grounds or even on that of personal preference, but on the experience and ability of the incumbent, John J. Cisco, a Democrat who had held that office since 1853.[46] As he did with other New York appointments, Seward sought to put his own man in the assistant treasurer's office. An alarmed Chase took the unusual step of writing directly to Lincoln on the matter. "Mr. Seward," he said, "*ought not* to ask you to overrule my deliberative judgment as to what is best for the department and your administration."[47]

Lincoln gave Chase, as he did all of his Cabinet members, free reign in staffing his own department in Washington. He continued the tenure of George Harrington, who had served as chief clerk and assistant secretary under both Whig and Democratic administrations.[48] A work-driven administrator, Harrington had become a proven and able specialist in helping to make and execute financial as well as fiscal policy. Like Cisco, Harrington filled an administrative rather than a political need.[49] With the exception of these officers and the comptroller of the currency, also a veteran Treasury employee, Chase saw to it that all the other subordinate offices and most of the clerks in Washington not only were political appointments but in some way would support his ambitions.[50]

Chase came out second best to Seward in appointments outside of the Treasury sphere. To his mortification, his choice for postmaster in Cincinnati was not heeded. The Cleveland post office went to a Wade adherent.[51] In the much-sought-after diplomatic posts, Chase soon found that his influence was practically nil. Of course these appointments came within Seward's department, but Chase felt that the wily Secretary was deliberately slighting him and Ohio. In a written communication to Lincoln he complained that Ohio was being overlooked in its fair share of the diplomatic patronage.[52] When Chase's close friend and political associate Richard C. Parsons was passed over for the consulate in London, despite his strong recommendation, he did not disguise his irritation in a note to Seward. "I want now to say that I think Ohio fairly entitled," he wrote, "both as a state and as a Republican state to a fair share of diplomatic appointments." In a postscript he said that "the whole number of Diplomatic appointments is 269, of which Ohio's proportion would be 33. My list with Corwin (appointed minister to Mexico) makes only 13." Chase warned that he might be forced to appeal to Lincoln if Parsons was not given a decent consular post.[53] He was made Consul General at Rio de Janiero.

Still smarting from his rebuffs in many of the positions he had sought for adherents, Chase became incensed when Seward substituted another candidate's name rather than that of Chase's brother Edward as a United States marshal for the northern district of New York. He appealed to Lincoln and he prevailed, but this incidence of Seward's arrogance and insensitivity in such a minor but personal matter rankled.[54] All of these contests, disputes, fulminations, hurt feelings, and constant harassment of Lincoln and the Cabinet officers must have taken their toll on Chase, the New York patronage being the most vexing. Yet the decisions had to be made, and time was allotted for hearing and settlements as if the secession crisis then at a crucial stage did not exist.[55] Those who saw Chase during those days invariably noticed how calm and dignified he seemed without any outward manifestation of his inward frustration.[56]

It was known that the Lincolns were entertaining at their first State dinner on March 28, 1861. Carriages and cabs filled the circular drive in front of the entrance to the mansion, a reminder of the almost perpetual crush of office-seekers that still plagued the new administration. Even if they could not gain access to the building they were on the wait for Cabinet members and other influentials whom they hoped to buttonhole on their arrival.[1] The new Secretary of the Treasury, escorting his lovely young daughter Kate, managed to push through the throng as they hastened to the entrance and moved through the main hall to the Blue Room, where some thirty guests were gathered. Mrs. Lincoln was already present to receive her guests when the Chases arrived. A plump, self-conscious little woman, her dress described as "gorgeous and highly colored," made a vivid contrast to the men, some in black evening dress, others simply in everyday frock-coats and trousers.

Kate Chase, who made a point to survey the guests, would have noticed that it was predominantly a male affair. All of the Cabinet members were present, most accompanied either by wives or daughters. Seward and the President's young secretary, John G. Nicolay, busied themselves introducing those guests who were strangers to the President and Mrs. Lincoln. Seward had brought with him William Howard Russell, the noted Crimean War correspondent for the London *Times*. He had a few words with each Cabinet member, whom he later described in his dispatches to London.

Simon Cameron, the War Secretary, with his "grey hair, and deep-set keen eyes and a thin mouth," struck Russell as a shrewd and forceful man. Welles of the Navy, bespectacled and slight, he dismissed as a typical place-seeker of little originality or ability. He decided that Smith of Interior was a nonentity. Montgomery Blair, Postmaster-General, reminded him of a practical Scot whose broad temples seemed "an anvil for ideas to be hammered on." But he also noticed his small, deep-set eyes that gave a "rat-like expression to his face." Blair was careful about what he said to Russell in a brief conversation, "as though he weighed every word." Bates he thought quite commonplace, a most ordinary individual. Elderly, thick-set, his hair and mustache black in contrast to his white beard, he projected a certain loquacious rusticity.[2] Chase impressed Russell as the most intelligent and distinguished person in the assembly, "tall, of good presence, with a well formed head, fine forehead, and a face indicating energy and power." The drooping lid of his right eye was a bit jarring and at first glance it gave a rather sinister look to his face. Kate Chase struck Russell as "very attractive, agreeable and sprightly." No doubt Mrs. Lincoln, who was unsure of herself in her new station, found Kate's poise and her popularity among the men disturbing. As for Lincoln himself the keen-eyed Russell had seen greatness in his homely face, his long, lank figure and awkward, shambling gait.[3]

Like Russell Chase had made assessments of his colleagues. Welles and Blair he counted as sympathetic to his views. Smith he ruled out as a cypher and Bates he considered a time-serving politician and a humdrum lawyer of conservative Whig propensities. For Seward he reserved a deep-seated antipathy mixed with the envy of a jealous rival whose political dexterity was matched only by his arrogance and his meddlesome duplicity. He too was much more of a conservative Whig than an earnest, idealistic Republican. As far as his feelings about the President, Chase was of two minds. Lincoln's attempts at fairness over the heated exchanges that went on over patronage, his natural bonhomie, his modesty, and his ability to pursue a logical train of thought to an appropriate conclusion soon raised him in Chase's estimate. Yet he still considered himself superior in both administrative and executive ability not just to Lincoln but to all of his colleagues in the Cabinet.

The Lincolns had delayed dinner in deference to General Scott, who had not as yet appeared. At length word was received that Scott had been taken ill and put to bed on the second floor. With Nicolay acting as protocol chief, the marine band struck up a martial tune and the Lincolns moved into the dining room.

Nicolay had also arranged the table setting. He seated the President in the middle of the long table with Mrs. Lincoln opposite him. It was seemingly a relaxed scene. Conversation was lively, but when Lincoln spoke, which was frequent, all attention was focused on him. He kept flowing a lively stream of amusing anecdotes and relevant witticisms which eased the formality and the stiffness of the occasion.

Tension was unmistakable, however, even though the President, Mrs. Lincoln, and their guests avoided such distracting topics of the day as the Provisional Confederacy, secession sentiment in the border states, and the situation at Union-held forts Sumter and Pickens.[4] After dinner the guests that now included some politicians who had gained entrance assembled in the Red Room, the women in an adjoining drawing room. Then Lincoln had Nicolay whisper in the ears of the Cabinet members that he wanted them to meet privately with him in a separate room.

When all were present Lincoln told them in strained accents that General Scott had advised him "it would be necessary to evacuate Fort Pickens and Fort Sumter." For a moment or so silence followed the President's remarks. Then a look of astonishment, of disbelief on most of the faces registered their emotions. Only Seward and his satellite Caleb Smith seemed unperturbed. With the exception of Montgomery Blair, the Cabinet members including Chase had been prepared to accept the evacuation of Fort Sumter as a military necessity. But Fort Pickens, which commanded the coast of Florida opposite the bay of Pensacola, was thought to be well manned, well provisioned, and completely secure. If the national flag must be flown for symbolic reasons in the Confederacy Pickens was an appropriate place.

Chase and his colleagues had been shocked to learn that Major Anderson, in command at Fort Sumter, had fewer than a hundred men to defend the fort and that his provisions were so scant that he would be starved out in less than thirty days. The Cabinet had been told that Confederate military authorities in Charleston had ringed the fort with heavy guns since the Buchanan administration's failed effort to reinforce it on January 8. Anderson himself and General Scott had estimated that a force of 20,000 soldiers with naval support was needed to break through the Charleston defenses and land adequate men and provisions at Sumter.

At these prior conferences, the naval officers consulted thought they could reinforce the fort with fast tugs under the cover of darkness, but they eventually accepted the army view as expressed by Scott.[5] And in fact so did the entire Cabinet after Lincoln's explanation, except Montgomery Blair.[6] A perplexed Lincoln, well aware of the political uproar that would result from the evacuation of Sumter, was at the same time deeply concerned about the uncommitted border states if a relief expedition provoked hostilities.[7] He respected Scott's military advice, but he resolved to have written opinions from his Cabinet.[8]

In response Chase wrote: "If the attempt will so inflame civil war as to involve an immediate necessity for the enlistment of armies I cannot advise it. . . ."[9] Chase had been retreating from his uncompromising stand on the crisis since his arrival in Washington for the Peace Convention. After he became better acquainted with the weakness of military and naval forces at the disposal of the government, the condition of the Treasury, and the perilous situation in the border states, his doubts about starting a war over Sumter increased. Since the Provisional Confederacy, made up of seven states, already existed, he thought that the best policy was to accept their independence as an accomplished fact, but maintain the authority of the Union everywhere else and consider any further secession as treason. The Provisional Confederacy then would be treated as a temporary situation, an experiment, which he was certain would not last. After this trial separation Chase believed the Union would return to its original state, a casual assumption which disregarded deeply held convictions on both sides.[10]

Like everyone in official Washington, Chase was aware of the presence of the Confederate commissioners in Washington and their efforts to secure recognition of their government. He also knew that a relief expedition was being readied for the relief of Forts Sumter and Pickens.

He surely did not know any of the details of Seward's indirect dealings with the commissioners, as he was too involved with patronage matters and familiarizing himself with the procedures of the Treasury department. He resented, as did his colleagues, Seward's meddlesome temperament, his arrogance, and his assumption of the premier's role. But Chase was not ready to test Seward's function in the ongoing crisis, especially since he too had reluctantly come to the conclusion that compromise and conciliation were the best policies.

When Lincoln announced that Scott had advised the evacuation of both Sumter and Pickens after the State dinner on March 28, he was as shocked as Montgomery Blair, though not outwardly as explosive in his comments. Chase knew enough about Seward's close association with Scott to believe that the aged General's advice on Pickens was more a part of the New Yorker's policy of conciliation than of any real military necessity. As Blair explained later, "Mr. Seward had overshot the mark this time".[11]

Lincoln lost no time in polling his advisors on the policy to be pursued on both Sumter and Pickens. He called the Cabinet into session at noon the next day after undergoing an agony of indecision that led to a sleepless night. There in the Cabinet room with the smell of tobacco left over from Buchanan's cigars in the heavy drapes and now more pungent with Seward's nervous puffing, it was obvious that a majority of the Cabinet favored maintaining both forts with force if necessary. Seward raised objections but they were not expressed with his usual persuasiveness. His only supporter was

Caleb Smith, and even he would give up the forts only on the grounds of military necessity. But no clear-cut decision was forthcoming until Edward Bates became impatient with the unstructured discussion. Looking directly at Lincoln, he . . . "proposed that the President should state his questions, and require our opinions" in writing. All agreed.[12]

Chase was now ready to accept war if it followed provisioning of Sumter. And as far as he could see the maintenance of Fort Pickens was as much a cause for hostilities as the relief of Fort Sumter.[13] Chase, Welles, and Blair were the most emphatic about maintaining both posts even if war was the result. Cameron's opinion is not recorded.[14] Smith had not changed his mind on the evacuation of Sumter, but he would defend Pickens. Seward's position was similar.[15]

Meanwhile, Lincoln had responded favorably to Montgomery Blair's Jacksonian approach to the Sumter crisis, which involved a plan his brother-in-law, Gustavas Vasa Fox, proposed. A former naval officer, Fox would reinforce Sumter at night with shallow-draft tugs or iron whaleboats supported by the guns of the fort and several heavily armed naval vessels.[16] Lincoln had approved of Fox's plan and after the Cabinet meeting authorized him to go ahead with his relief expedition.[17]

A desperate Seward, fearful of the loss of the border states, continued to seek means for effecting the evacuation of Sumter, even if this meant sabotaging the Fox expedition. He succeeded to a limited extent by depriving Fox of his one heavy warship, the *Powhatan*, which he managed to divert to Fort Pickens.[18]

Chase had been kept informed of the developments in the Sumter-Pickens situation along with the rest of the Cabinet at the frequent meetings, discussions, and reports of special agents. All of these reports stated emphatically that Unionist sympathies were virtually nonexistent in Charleston and that the Confederate government was determined to maintain itself as an independent state.[19] Chase was on cordial terms with Blair and Welles, and no doubt he learned something of the specifics about Seward's role in seeking to defuse the crisis. In fact at the behest of several Cabinet members he had acted as spokesman in suggesting to Lincoln that regular Cabinet meetings be held at least twice a week, instead of the on ad hoc basis that Seward had instituted on his own authority. Lincoln had readily agreed and chose twelve noon on Tuesdays and Fridays.[20]

Finally, on April 6, Lincoln drafted a note to Governor Pickens of South Carolina stating that provisions only would be sent to Fort Sumter. It was signed by Cameron and was entrusted to Robert S. Chew, a State Department clerk. Chew delivered the note to Pickens on April 8. On that day, the *Harriet Lane*, a Treasury Department revenue cutter, the advance element of Fox's expedition, left New York for Charleston.[21] The next day Fox himself set sail aboard an armed transport along with two light-draft tugs. On the 10th the naval support ship the *Pocahontas* followed.[22]

Chase and his colleagues, even the indubitable Seward, expected hostilities. They were not surprised when they learned of the bombardment of Sumter and Anderson's surrender of the fort on Saturday, April 13.[23] The next day a messenger who had observed the scene in Charleston harbor reached Washington. He described the defense of the fort and the evacuation of Anderson. Chase did not see Lincoln that morning. The President attended the nearby Presbyterian church while Chase and his daughters worshipped at St. John's Episcopal church across from the White House.

After church Chase received a summons for an urgent Cabinet meeting in the afternoon, a session that lasted almost all night. Lincoln's draft of the call for troops was approved without change. The critical situation in Virginia and Maryland, the weak defense of Washington and the possibility of its capture or blockade, measures to be taken for the security of government property in the border slave states in case they should secede from the Union—these and many other details essential for the maintenance of the Union occupied the more or less flexible agenda that the tense ministers and the virtually exhausted President discussed in the Cabinet room.[24]

Of major importance to Chase himself, as well as to the service secretaries, was the decision not to call Congress into session immediately. July 4 was set for a special session. Though Congress had sole authority to approve expenditures, increase taxes, approve loans, and expand military and naval forces, Lincoln thought it best for the administration to have a free hand in coping with the emergency. He made it evident that department heads would be largely independent in their various spheres. Indeed there was no other alternative considering the emergency and the enormity of the problems that lay ahead, with no precedents for guidance.[25]

Governors of northern states were prompt in telegraphing acceptance of Lincoln's call and began mustering militia regiments. Virginia rejected the call for troops and on Wednesday, April 17, adopted an ordinance of secession. North Carolina, Tennessee, and Arkansas soon followed. It was some comfort in Washington that in all of these border slave states there was significant opposition to secession. But telegraph reports of pro-Confederate mobs in Missouri and Kentucky countered any early optimism about a solid Unionist majority in these crucial areas.

As confusing and difficult as these problems were for the new administration, the situation in Maryland was so dangerous as immediately to imperil Washington. Secessionist mobs seized control of the streets in Baltimore. The two principal rail routes that connected Washington with the free states, the Baltimore and Ohio Railroad and the Pennsylvania lines, were cut off not more than 24 hours after the receipt of the President's call for militia. Governor Hicks of Maryland and Mayor Brown of Baltimore seemed to have lost control of the state and the city. With Virginia hostile territory and now Maryland apparently moving in that direction, Washington was effectively blockaded. Fear swept the city of an imminent attack from Confederate forces. General Scott was doing what he could to protect the capital. Loyal militia companies were hastily recruited, but trained manpower, munitions, and armament were painfully short.

Chase got a vivid picture of just how isolated Washington was from H. W. Hoffman, the new custom collector of Baltimore. Hoffman, who lived in far western Maryland, had started by train for Baltimore to take up his post on April 22. At Harper's Ferry a prosecessionist mob howling "Black Republican" and "Maryland traitor" very nearly pulled him off the train. Again at Frederick Junction a mob surrounded his car and threatened him with lynching. When he finally reached Baltimore he was warned that if he took charge of the custom house he would be removed forcibly. Feeling that his life was in danger Hoffman informed Chase that he would not take possession and would "await developments."[26]

A much greater worry to Chase was the safety of his daughters Kate and Nettie, who were visiting in New York City when hostilities began. Barney urged them to remain there until it was deemed safe to take the trains to Washington. But Kate, caught up in the excitement of the hour, insisted on being with her father. They managed to get through Baltimore and reached Washington just before the railroad tracks between that city and Washington were torn up.[27]

Relieved that his daughters had arrived home safely, Chase was nevertheless as deeply concerned about the breakdown in communications as he was about the security of Washington. Without any word from New York he feared that the city administration under the pro-southern mayor Fernando Wood would promote an insurrection against the authority of the Washington government. Ready for any emergency, he gave Barney extraordinary powers to execute policy without reference to Washington. He suggested in his official letter of instructions that it would be well for Barney to consult with John A. Dix, veteran Democratic politician and former Secretary of the Treasury.[28]

An ugly situation persisted in Baltimore, where a prosecession mob seemed about to control the streets. The skirmish between the Sixth Massachusetts Regiment enroute to Washington and the Baltimore mob had raised anxiety levels. Like other members of the Washington establishment, Chase had little faith in the local militia that had been called up and the few units of raw Pennsylvania militia that arrived for the defense of the capital.[29]

The abandonment of Harper's Ferry by its small garrison, followed by the loss of the Norfolk Navy Yard, added to everyone's concern. At the White

House Chase complained bitterly to Lincoln about the disorganized state of affairs. "All these failures," he said, "are for want of a strong young head. . . . General Scott gives an order. Mr. Cameron gives another. Half of both are executed, neutralizing each other."[30] By April 25, the Seventh Massachusetts Regiment arrived and joined its companion regiment encamped on Capitol Hill. Though the two regiments brought significant strength to the city's defense, and a way had been cleared through Annapolis for more northern troops to reach Washington, Chase gave vent to his feelings in a panicky yet at the same time scolding note to Lincoln. "Let me beg you," he wrote, "to remember that the disunionists have anticipated us in everything; and that as yet we have accomplished nothing but destruction of our property." He wanted Scott to send whatever forces he could spare to secure Baltimore before Confederate forces under the pretext of a secession ordinance that he was certain the Maryland legislature would enact took possession of the state.[31]

The next day, however, northern troops began pouring into the city, removing any prospect of sudden invasion from Virginia. Among them was the Rhode Island First, commanded by the balding ex-West Pointer Ambrose Burnside and accompanied by Rhode Island's Governor William Sprague, decked out a general's uniform. Sprague, "a small insignificant youth who bought his place," in John Hay's sour description, was one of the heirs to the largest textile fortune in New England.[32]

Much as he wanted to involve himself in the military buildup, Chase had to devote long hours to the financial and fiscal affairs of the Union. First he had to take stock of the Treasury and the current legislation governing its policy. Second, he had to educate himself in the unfamiliar field of government finance, now made incredibly difficult with the tremendous outflow of funds to support the expanding army and navy.

Chase was not completely untutored in financial affairs. As a lawyer and formerly a director of various banks, he was as well trained as any of his predecessors and probably better than most. Above all, he was well read in prevailing economic theories. He had a good, logical mind, a habit of intense industry and supreme confidence in himself. His one failing—and this he shared with virtually all of his contemporaries who subscribed to Jacksonian Democratic dogma—was his financial philosophy. He was a convinced hard-money man, not a promising attribute when one considers the immense and unprecedented expenditures the war was already demanding.

When Chase took possession of his spacious office in the imposing white-pillared Treasury building, the government had to its credit a mere $3 million balance as against a total debt of almost $65 million. More than a third of this sum was in unfunded Treasury notes paying high interest for short term and like specie payable for customs duties. The Depression of 1857 and the political crisis of 1860-61 had so impaired the government's credit that even the highly liquid Treasury notes could be sold only at ruinous discounts. About half of the $10 million authorized in such notes issued in December of 1860 were finally taken by the bankers at a 12 percent discount in specie.[33]

Under various acts of Congress, Chase had authority to issue Treasury notes and government bonds up to $40 million. Despite the crisis, he acted cautiously. He hoped to sell the 6 percent long-term bonds at par but set a limit at 94, six points below par. Many wary bankers would not purchase at this price and as a result only half of the loan was taken.

Now that war had begun and news was received in Washington of the great patriotic upsurge in the north Chase decided to market $9 million in bonds. The emergency was so acute that he relaxed his rule on the sale price and thus was able to dispose of more than $7 million between $85 and $93 a hundred and another sale of $9 million of notes and bonds at about the same rate. These sales together with what funds had accrued in the Treasury Chase thought sufficient to carry on the government until the special session of Congress.[34]

Chase was counting on the states to assist in expenses for recruiting, uniforming, arming, transporting, and initial victualing of the troops. In many cases, however, state bond and city issues such as those in Pennsylvania competed with the Washington government's offerings. Jay Cooke noted to his brother that the Philadelphia banks did not subscribe as readily as he had hoped, "because they had already a load of state and city stock."[35]

In a scant four months' time Chase had learned very quickly that he had to do more than just offer bond and note issues and count on the patriotic and political beliefs of the banking communities in the money centers of the Union. But his experience thus far with the hard-bitten money men had revealed that he could count on few major bankers, most of whom did not share his financial views.

In the post-Sumter outburst of support for Lincoln and the Union, all of the bankers rallied behind the Treasury. Yet Chase acted cautiously until Congress met, when he hoped to gain authority for increased taxation and a vastly expanded loan program should these policies become necessary.

Neither he nor any senior member of the Lincoln administration including Lincoln himself expected a long-drawn-out conflict. Their expectations seemed justified when order was restored in Baltimore and Maryland secured for the Union. The Pennsylvania railroad and the Northern Central railroad with their connections to the North and West were now open. Thousands of northern troops were billeted in Baltimore and at other trouble spots. Untrained, as most were, their very numbers and presence were nevertheless quite sufficient to overawe secessionist elements. Under the control of Ben Butler, the droop-eyed former Democratic politician and lawyer from the Bay

State who had emerged as the military strongman of the hour, the troops seized strategic positions in the city and established what was in effect martial law.

But the situation in other border slave states was not all that promising. Missouri was in a state of anarchy similar to that which had transpired in Maryland. Kentucky had a wavering secessionist governor and a predominantly Unionist legislature. Mountainous eastern Tennessee, under the leadership of its pro-Union Senator Andrew Johnson, seemed about to become a battleground when the far more populous western portion of the state declared for the Confederacy. Into this confusing mix of divided loyalties both the Confederate and the Union governments launched policies that sought to bring the entire western border region under the control of one or other side.

Lincoln was particularly concerned about Kentucky, the state where he and his wife had been born, where one of his heroes, Henry Clay, had made his lifelong residence, and where along its entire length lay Unionist western Virginia and the loyal free states of Ohio and Indiana. The Ohio River, along with the Mississippi the northwest's major commercial artery, constituted its northern border. A well-settled, rich, agricultural state, Kentucky was the prime source of horses in the nation, a major means of transport for civilian and military use. Nor should its moral influence as the oldest of the western states be discounted. Possession of Kentucky by either side could be crucial to the war. Missouri, Kentucky, and western Virginia—through which ran the vitally important Baltimore and Ohio railroad—claimed immediate attention.

Kentucky sought the well-nigh impossible task of proclaiming its neutrality, but this move gave pause to both belligerents. During the summer of 1861 as Confederate and Union forces began a preliminary jousting in Virginia and Missouri, Lincoln was especially careful to respect Kentucky's neutral posture. His cautious policy did not mean that he neglected the masses of loyal citizens in the state.

Information from various sources was contradictory. Some argued for vigorous action, even invasion of Kentucky; other reports warned that any hostile moves by Union forces could push the state into the Confederacy. As a long-time resident of Cincinnati, just across the Ohio River from Kentucky, and the Cabinet member most familiar with public opinion in that state, Chase naturally was sought by Lincoln for counsel on policies to be pursued. Chase himself was delighted to be of assistance, and in fact began to assert himself as the expert not just on Kentucky but on eastern Tennessee and western Virginia. He was in the process of creating a web of Treasury appointees to control the river traffic on the Ohio, the upper Mississippi, and other navigable streams that could be and had been used to supply munitions and other supplies for the Confederate forces further south.

Chase would have included Missouri in his sphere of activities, but this troubled state was the province of the Blairs. In these early months their surrogate, Fremont, whom Lincoln appointed a major general, commanded a newly created military district, the Western Department, with headquarters in St. Louis.[36]

In the main, Chase agreed with Lincoln's policy of respecting Kentucky's neutrality, but he pressed on the President the covert arming of loyalist elements. And he was instrumental in bringing two Kentuckians to Lincoln's attention whom he felt would begin the process of moving Kentucky away from neutrality and into the Union. His choices, one from the military and the other a civilian, would supervise arms shipments and the recruiting of volunteers ostensibly to protect loyal citizens from prosecessionists or possible attack from Tennessee. His military man was actually a naval officer, William Nelson, a huge, voluble person who was on detached duty in Washington at the time.[37] Chase had been impressed with Nelson's avowed loyalty, his intimate knowledge of the Kentucky locale, and above all his apparent leadership qualities which seemed in short supply at Washington.

If Chase knew of Nelson's drinking habits and his bad temper, he gave no sign. Acting through Cameron he got Nelson assigned as the principal military agent. He was empowered to recruit men drawn from east and west Tennessee and Kentucky and organize troops to be known as Union home guards in Kentucky.[38] For the equally important task of cultivating Union opinion and working with the loyalists in the Kentucky legislature, Chase's main reliance was Garrett Davis. One of the chief opponents of secession in Kentucky, Davis was as temperamental as Nelson. It seems almost foreordained that these two self assured individuals whom Chase expected to work as a team would instead engage in furious displays of rage against each other. With two such players it is a wonder that the loyalist cause in Kentucky succeeded.[39]

Both men met with Lincoln and Chase in May, and after a thorough briefing went west, Nelson to Cincinnati to await orders, Davis to Kentucky. It is surprising that neither Lincoln nor Chase appear to have consulted Joseph Holt, former Secretary of War and of Interior in the Buchanan administration, and a leading Kentucky Unionist. Nor did either man, and with good reason, bring Cassius Clay, blustering antislavery editor and Kentucky politician, into the discussions. Clay had appeared in Washington and had several interviews with Lincoln. Dressed up in a uniform of his own devise and armed with three revolvers along with a huge, vicious-looking knife, Clay was described as "certainly the most wonderful ass of the age."[40] He was surely not the man for the delicate job Chase and Lincoln had in mind.

While deploring the lack of system in Washington, and consistently underestimating Lincoln, Chase was not slow in moving into what he perceived to be a power vacuum in the War Department. It was apparent that Cameron was unequal to the vast responsibilities now thrust upon him. Chase not only sensed Cameron's incompetence but also saw that Lincoln was beginning to have similar doubts. Chase's first step was to wean Cameron away from Seward's influence and make him dependent on himself for both advice and support.[41]

Seward quickly detected these moves. The war was scarcely a month old when he complained about the activities of "the two C.'s." "It is the President," he wrote Weed, "General Scott and I against the two C.'s." Seward erred as far as Lincoln was concerned. The President continued to be impressed with Chase's expertise in financial matters, and welcomed his judgment in military affairs, especially in major army appointments. As he came to rely less and less on an increasingly befuddled Cameron, he came to accept more and more of Chase's advice.[42]

Chase was eager to push Ohioans for high military command, and among these Irwin McDowell claimed his early attention. McDowell, assistant adjutant general of the army, was on duty in Washington at the time and had earned General Scott's good opinion. Besides his Ohio birth and citizenship, McDowell appealed to Chase because of his scholarly interests, his lack of pretense, and his apolitical stance at a time when Washington was being flooded with politicians hungry for senior commissions. McDowell's very real faults seemed virtues to Chase. He was openly critical of many of his colleagues, and contemptuous of military arrangements made thus far. In particular he berated Scott despite all he owed to the aged general. A disciplinarian, brusque in manner with his subordinates, he may have abstained from alcohol and tobacco, but he was a glutton for food.[43]

Of compelling interest to Chase was that McDowell provided him with a plan of operations in northern Virginia which stressed a land movement from Alexandria to Manassas Junction, an important road and railroad head in northern Virginia. McDowell's plan would screen Washington while at the same time it would move the Union forces step by step toward Richmond, now the capital of the Confederacy.[44] Either unaware or ignorant of the fact that McDowell had spent most of his regular army career as a staff officer whose sole field experience had been as a company commander in the Mexican-American War thirteen years before, Chase succeeded through Cameron in having McDowell made a brigadier general and given command of a new military department, that of northeastern Virginia.

For the western command, Chase eagerly supported the young, trim commander—again of Ohio troops—George B. McClellan and also his subordinate, the native Ohioan William S. Rosecrans. McClellan had been an engineering and cavalry officer in the regular army, had served with distinction in the Mexican-American War, and had been an American army observer in the Crimean War.

Though considered one of the ablest of the younger officers in the army and marked for early promotion, he had resigned his commission four years earlier to become a top railroad executive in Illinois and Ohio. Soon after the Sumter bombardment, Governor Dennison of Ohio appointed McClellan to command that state's volunteer regiments. And during the first confusing months of the war, McClellan justified the governor's trust in him when he had the raw Ohio troops ready for an invasion of western Virginia within a brief period.

His eye always on Ohio affairs, and with the cordial support of General Scott, Chase again acting through Cameron had Lincoln appoint McClellan a major general in the regular army.[45] Together with Rosecrans, McClellan won a series of little, but important victories that pretty well saved western Virginia for the Union and secured an extensive segment of the vital Baltimore and Ohio Railroad.

As the hectic month of June slipped into July Cameron came under attack, especially from some of the ardent Republican papers in Ohio. Chase moved to defend him. He wrote stern letters to M. D. Potter, proprietor of the most outspoken anti-Cameron paper, the Cincinnati *Commercial*.[46] In their short professional acquaintance Chase had developed a close personal relationship with Cameron that was not unmixed with practical benefits.

It was flattering to have Cameron lean upon him for advice, yet at the same time the Secretary's administrative weaknesses aroused all of Chase's controlling instincts. Even more to the point, the President seemed to accept his influence over his bumbling war minister. Politically, Cameron had become an important element in Chase's plans for the future. The Pennsylvanian may have been a disaster in dealing with organizational matters, but he was a shrewd politician and a power in the second most populous state of the Union.

Despite crushing responsibilities in his own department as well as his increasing involvement in military planning, Chase also had to spare a few moments from each crowded day for personal matters. High on the list was the consideration of acquiring a permanent home for himself and his family. Daughter Kate was of estimable value to him in lessening this burden. She scoured the neighborhoods within a reasonable distance from the White House, the Capitol, and the Treasury Department for affordable rentals that would be of sufficient size and appearance befitting a senior Cabinet minister whose duties included official entertaining. Together father and daughter agreed on a three-story brick townhouse at the corner of Sixth and E streets. Chase leased the dwelling from J. B. Varnum, a New York attorney who had kept a Washington residence.

Once Chase had accepted the rental terms of $100 a month and two dollars a week extra in wages for Catherine "Cassie" Vaudry, Varnum's black housekeeper, Kate was given responsibility for whatever renovations she deemed necessary. She purchased furniture, Brussels carpets, and drapes, most of which she obtained in New York and Philadelphia.[47] By early July Chase and his daughters were comfortably settled in their new home.

Expenses had been high and Chase was forced to negotiate a personal loan through Barney and John Jay in New York when he found that he could not dispose of property he owned in Columbus and Cincinnati at prices he thought reasonable.[48] To all of those distractions and levies upon his time, there were in addition as the summer advanced reviews, demonstrations, and flag presentations for three-month militia regiments and the three-year volunteer regiments now encamped in and around Washington.[49] He had to be present at select drills and reviews of the Ohio regiments, and he felt compelled to join the many official parties that visited the regiments of other states.

The patronage hunters were less demanding now, but military commission seekers, contract seekers, contract brokers, and influence peddlers quickly replaced them. Important congressmen and politicians were conspicuous among the grasping horde. Most of them Chase was able to fob off on subordinates or direct to other departments. But enough got through into Chase's office as to be a nuisance.[50]

An imperative duty which could not be neglected nor postponed was his report for the special session of Congress to convene on July 4. Like other department heads, Chase had requested that members of the powerful House Ways and Means Committee and the Senate Committee on Finance meet with him in late June to consider his plans for financing the war during the next fiscal year.

From information supplied by his principal subordinates he worked out estimates and prepared calculations to support a series of bills that granted to the Treasury taxation and borrowing authority. These figures were made available to the members as a basis for their own opinions. Chase knew that the committeemen were among the more diligent and knowledgeable, and one must say the more articulate and caustic members of the Thirty-seventh Congress.

Thaddeus Stevens, soon to be a dominant figure on Ways and Means, was on hand. Old, almost seventy, testy, sardonic, he had a knack for analyzing figures and tearing out soft data.[51] Stevens had been a successful businessman in his own right and his easy money views and loose credit policies were in sharp distinction to Chase's hard-money precepts. It would not do to alienate Stevens. Nor would it be politic to underestimate Samuel Hooper, the wealthy and cultivated merchant and manufacturer from Boston, just elected to Congress but reputed to have decided views on currency and banking. Elbridge Gerry Spaulding, another member, certainly did not share the same political views of his illustrious namesake. Formerly a mainline Whig from upstate New York, he shared the easy money, easy credit ideas of his political lineage.

His business career as a banker and his tenure as treasurer of New York State had sharpened his understanding of the fiscal and financial aspects of public policy. He also knew politics and the ways of politicians, having served in a variety of local offices culminating in a term as mayor of Buffalo.[52]

Chase could count on the support of John Sherman and William Pitt Fessenden, both members of the Senate Finance Committee. They were friendly to Chase and though they had been Whigs, neither shared the doctrinaire philosophy of a Spaulding or a Stevens. Yet Sherman was given to fits of temperament, and the sharp-faced Fessenden, a chronic dyspeptic, could indulge in cantankerous hairsplitting over details. These men were the principals with whom Chase must work amiably if possible, but if it came to what he thought essential and they opposed him, he would match his sense of personal worth and his understanding of the issues against their contentions. Usually he prevailed in a relationship where they were happy to forgo any direct responsibility.

When these serious, even grim-visaged men met with the equally serious, dignified secretary in his office in late June, Chase had copies of the draft of his report available along with bills that he had prepared for submission to Congress. There may have been some grumbling about the taxation he proposed, an increase in excises on such items as tea, coffee, sugar, beer, and distilled spirits, a direct tax to be apportioned among the states on the basis of population as the Constitution provided.[53] These burdens seemed modest indeed and the $50 million to be raised by such means a rather trifling amount considering the enormous rise in anticipated military and naval expenditures even if the war proved a short one.

Chase's estimates of military and naval expenditures for the fiscal year 1861–62 of $318 million was more than six times what had been appropriated the previous year. He proposed to raise $240 million through loans, the remainder from increased imposts, excises, and the direct tax on the states. He urged authority to open a national loan of $100 million in Treasury notes bearing annual interest of 7.3 percent and redeemable at par any time after three years.[54]

To secure the widest possible market, Chase asked that these notes range in denomination from $50 to $5000. He also requested authority to issue, if necessary, $50 million additional in Treasury notes payable after one year at 3.65 percent and exchangeable for 7.3 percent three-year notes. And he asked for discretion in deciding whether these notes should be payable on demand for coin or issued without interest. Aware of the inflationary implications he assured the committee members that the "greatest care" would be taken to prevent these notes from becoming "irredeemable paper currency." In the face of Chase's imposing presence and his trenchant defense of his position, the members offered no opposition nor did they make substantive changes in the bills before them. The reports they made to the special session of Congress supported Chase's bills which passed the Senate and the House without extended debate.[55]

Chase's official responsibility did not end with his financial arrangements, but included the supervision of trade flowing through the custom houses. When Lincoln proclaimed a blockade of the Confederate states, Chase shared with Navy Secretary Gideon Welles the duty to inhibit suspected coastal trade with southern ports. In a series of Treasury circulars, Chase empowered collectors to halt all coast and river traffic south which by its very nature was deemed to be of aid and comfort to the enemy. He directed these officers to be especially vigilant about trade along the Ohio River, where articles broadly specified as contraband might be shipped through loyal states to the Confederacy.[56] A number of Treasury agents that the special session of Congress authorized assisted the collectors and the federal district attorneys in enforcing this internal blockade.[57]

Chase, however, was responsive to complaints from the river ports, especially Louisville, Cincinnati, and St. Louis. During the tense period when Kentucky was seeking to maintain its neutrality and the administration was being careful not to upset the delicate balance between loyalist and secessionist elements, Chase eased restrictions on commerce even of goods that seemed destined for the Confederacy.[58]

He instructed collectors to bear in mind that Kentucky was thus far a loyal state and only obvious contraband such as munitions being shipped into the state must be held back. He was also lenient about shipments into western Virginia. Supplies could go forward if the custom collector at Cincinnati was satisfied that this was their ultimate destination.[59] But Chase was quite explicit when he insisted that commerce must follow the flag. In far too optimistic a vein he declared on May 29 that apparent military successes in the west open "Missouri, Kentucky and Western Virginia to trade and will extend southward as rapidly and as far as the authority of the Federal Government can be restored."[60]

chapter 20

No Other Recourse

Thirteen-year-old Nettie Chase woke earlier than usual on July 22, 1861. It had been raining steadily for some hours and the air was hot and humid. But it was not the sound of the pelting rain that disturbed her sleep, it was the steady rumbling of heavy wagons moving along on Sixth Street, the cries of the drivers, the staccato sound of hundreds of nervous voices. Nettie moved to the window and saw what seemed to her an endless procession of "gloomy-looking vehicles" moving along the muddy, unpaved street. She remembered seeing these same "black curtained, curiously shaped carriages" along with supply wagons and gun batteries passing over the Long Bridge several days earlier. She had been told that they were ambulances. Everyone knew that a great battle was being fought in Virginia, but everyone was confident of victory. Could they be wrong? Nettie wondered. Were the ambulances "not empty now? I felt within a thrill of horror, as I remembered the big army hospital somewhat further down the street."[1]

Nettie was observing the end of the panic-stricken rout of McDowell's army after the Battle of Bull Run. Pouring into the city all day was a completely disorganized horde. Frightened civilians who had gone out with the army to watch the spectacle crowded the streets along with mud-spattered soldiers and officers who had lost touch with their commands and were hurrying they knew not where; they only knew that this is where they had come from.

"Soldiers were straggling into the city in all sorts of shapes," said Benjamin B. French, the busy Washington bureaucrat and diarist, "some without guns—some with two. Some barefooted, some bareheaded, and all with a hateful story of defeat."[2]

Before he left for army headquarters and the telegraph room, Chase had his household staff prepare buckets of hot coffee which were served to the stragglers from the basement door of the kitchen that opened on the street. Later on his return Chase made his home available as a temporary hospital. Eight or ten wounded were accommodated. The Episcopal bishop of Ohio, Charles McIlvaine, was a house guest at the time. Tall, slender, and with chiseled features, the bishop was a commanding presence as he assisted Chase and Kate in comforting the wounded. Nettie recalled one young soldier shocking the bishop with his extravagant vocabulary of curses. "Just let me swear a bit, it helps me stand the hurting," he said. But the bishop could not bring himself to let circumstances, however grave, interfere with a lifetime of religious conviction. "Learn to pray instead," he urged the young man. "God can help you much more than the devil can."[3]

Chase had to bear considerable responsibility for the debacle as he had made McDowell's appointment to command the Union army a matter almost of personal privilege. He had also, along with the President and the Cabinet, responded to public pressure in ordering the general to move out and engage the Confederates with an ill-trained army made up mainly of three-month volunteers. McDowell and Scott had sought delay, pointing out that most of the officers and men were raw troops who would be unreliable under combat conditions. Lincoln countered their argument by saying: "You are green it is true, but they are green also, you are all green alike."[4] It would appear that McDowell's army was greener than Beauregard's Confederates.

McDowell's plan had been a good one, but it required far more coordination than was possible with raw troops, given inadequate staffs and poorly mapped terrain.[5] Nevertheless he became a scapegoat for the disaster.[6] Chase did not dissent when Lincoln telegraphed McClellan on April 22 ordering him to Washington and bestowing upon him the command of what was now designated the Army of the Potomac.[7] Chase had been and still was a strong backer of McClellan, who, like McDowell, was one of Chase's Ohio appointments.

Not one week after Sumter Chase had written two letters to the general. In both, he inquired if Governor Dennison was interfering with McClellan's control of his troops. In a lengthy letter McClellan praised Dennison's efforts and gave Chase a brief synopsis of his plans to invade western Virginia.[8] Chase followed up with another letter in which he said that he was responsible for the change of his commission from Ohio to the commission of a major-general in the regular Union army and his assignment to the command of the Depart-

Salmon P. Chase, aspiring lawyer. (Courtesy of The Cincinnati Historical Society)

Philander Chase, the awesome uncle. (Courtesy of The Library of Congress)

William Wirt, Chase's law teacher and role model. (Courtesy of The Library of Congress)

James G. Birney, editor, abolitionist, frequent Liberty Party candidate for President. (Courtesy of The Cincinnati Historical Society)

Flamen Ball, Chase's longtime law partner. (Courtesy of The Cincinnati Historical Society)

James M. Ashley, flamboyant congressman, sometime Chase supporter. (Courtesy of The Cincinnati Historical Society)

George Hoadly Jr., one of Chase's fervent backers in Ohio. (Courtesy of The Library of Congress)

Gerrit Smith, former New York abolitionist, staunch supporter of Chase's presidential ambitions. (Courtesy of The Library of Congress)

Thomas Spooner, Cincinnati
neighbor, prominent Know
Nothing. (Courtesy of The
Cincinnati Historical Society)

Frederick Hassaurek, influential
editor of the *Ohio Staatszeitung.*
(Courtesy of The Cincinnati
Historical Society)

Murat Halstead, editor of the
Cincinnati *Commercial*. He
covered the 1860 Republican
convention. (Courtesy of The
Cincinnati Historical Society)

Whitelaw Reid, famed Washington correspondent of the
Cincinnati *Gazette*. (Courtesy
of The Cincinnati Historical
Society)

Charles P. McIlvaine, Episcopal Bishop of Ohio, Chase confidant. (Courtesy of The Cincinnati Historical Society)

U.S. Senator Salmon P. Chase, with his third wife Sarah Bella Dunlop Ludlow Chase. (Courtesy of The Cincinnati Historical Society)

Thomas Ewing, Ohio Whig leader and Chase hater. (Courtesy of The Cincinnati Historical Society)

Thomas Corwin, esteemed orator, Chase opponent on the Whig and later on the Republican side. (Courtesy of the United States Senate Historical Office)

aniel Webster as he appeared when Chase was st elected to the U.S. Senate. (Courtesy of The brary of Congress)

Gideon Welles, Secretary of the Navy. He thought Chase to be "clumsy, but strong." (Courtesy of The Library of Congress)

Rare photograph of Lincoln's first Inauguration, March 4, 1861. Note the unfinished Capitol. (Courtesy of the French Collection, The Library of Congress.)

Salmon P. Chase, the dignified Secretary of the Treasury. (Courtesy of The Library of Congress)

Edwin M. Stanton, Secretary of War, asthmatic, strong man in Lincoln's Cabinet. (Courtesy of The Library of Congress)

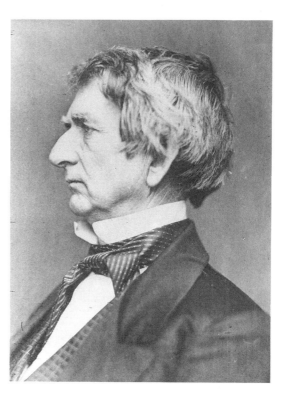

William H. Seward, Secretary of State. Chase's competitor in the Cabinet. (Courtesy of The Library of Congress)

Thurlow Weed, Seward's alter ego and New York political boss. (Courtesy of The Library of Congress)

Chase and his daughters, Nettie to his left, Kate to his right. (Courtesy of The Library of Congress)

William Sprague at the time of his marriage to Kate Chase. (Courtesy of The Library of Congress)

Major General Henry W.
Halleck in a pensive mood.
(Courtesy of The Library of
Congress)

The Carpenter portrait of Lincoln and his Cabinet discussing the Emancipation Proclamation. Left to right: Edwin M. Stanton, Salmon P. Chase, President Lincoln, Gideon
Welles, Caleb Smith, William H. Seward, Montgomery Blair, Edward Bates. (Courtesy
of The Library of Congress)

Benjamin F. Butler, Massachusetts political general as
military chief in New Orleans.
(Courtesy of The Library of
Congress)

James A. Garfield, a Chase in-
formant in Rosecrans's Army
of the Cumberland. (Courtesy
of The Library of Congress)

Charles Sumner, radical Republican senator from Massachusetts, erstwhile friend of Chase. (Courtesy of The Library of Congress)

The Supreme Court. From left to right: Daniel Middleton, clerk; in judicial robes, David Davis; Noah Swayne; Robert C. Grier; James M. Wayne; Salmon P. Chase, Chief Justice; Samuel Nelson; Nathan Clifford; Samuel F. Miller; Stephen J. Field. (Courtesy of The Cincinnati Historical Society)

William P. Fessenden, dyspeptic Maine senator, briefly Chase's successor in the Treasury. (Courtesy of The Library of Congress)

Chase as he appeared shortly before his death. (Courtesy of The Library of Congress)

ment of the Ohio. "I drew with my own hand the order extending it into Virginia," he said.

Chase went on to advance his own concept of military strategy, and acquaint McClellen with all he had done in organizing forces in Kentucky, western Virginia, and eastern Tennessee. Chase had wanted McClellan to remain in command on the Mississippi as well as points east but had been overruled. Lincoln had bowed to pressure from the Blairs and had given Fremont military responsibility for that region and west to the Rocky Mountains.

But Chase was optimistic about McClellan's future as soon as he with his Ohio and Indiana men had cleared western Virginia. Chase would now have the general "march down through the mountain region, deliver the whole of it, including the mountain district of North Carolina, Georgia and Alabama from the insurrection, and then reach the Gulf at Mobile and New Orleans, thus cutting the rebellion in two."[9] McClellan heartily approved of Chase's grand strategy, regarding it "as the most important that can be undertaken."[10]

The Bull Run fiasco did not injure perceptibly Chase's standing with Lincoln as his chief though unofficial advisor on military affairs. Chase certainly concurred if he did not advise bringing McClellan to Washington on General Scott's recommendation when it was anticipated that his experience in administration and organization would bring order out of the chaos that reigned in the capital.[11]

If Chase escaped responsibility for the McDowell appointment, he was not for the time being able to ease the impact of Bull Run on the money marts of the eastern cities. Chase had been as unsuccessful as his predecessor, John A. Dix, in disposing of long-term bonds to the cautious bankers. Rather foolishly, considering the crisis times of early April, Chase sought to sell the remainder of the 6 percent bond issue at par but was willing to reduce the price if necessary to six points below par. Only able to market about half of the issue, he was forced to make up the difference with short-term Treasury notes.

At first even this expedient which he was most reluctant to use seemed a failure. Confidence in the Lincoln administration was at a low in financial circles. Though aware of the pessimism among northern businessmen, Chase had a deeply ingrained suspicion of the motives of Wall Street speculators and of all bankers. He also suspected that Weed's henchmen were among the city financiers. "Was there a concerted effort of the Wall Street men to prevent the taking of treasury notes?" he asked Barney. "If there was who took part in it? Did Mr. Blatchford?"[12] Chase was being too edgy; the notes were taken up and the New York City, Philadelphia, and Boston banks that had formed themselves into associations subscribed to the remainder of the bonds. The wave of patriotism that swept through the North after Sumter had had its effect. But how long would this last?

One banker who had been most helpful during these trying days was an Ohioan named Jay Cooke. He did not know Chase personally, but his brother Henry D. Cooke as editor of the *Ohio State Journal* was one of the circle of journalists whom Chase cultivated in Columbus.[13] Cooke's father, Eleutherius, a prominent lawyer, formerly a congressman, and a long-time antislavery man from the Western Reserve, was of course well known to Chase.

Jay Cooke was then but thirty-one years old, and newly established as a Philadelphia banker. He saw much more accurately than his colleagues in New York and Boston the fortunes that could be made in government equities provided one had faith in the ultimate triumph of the Union cause and gained the confidence of the secretary.

Young Cooke, with his close-set bright blue eyes, his bearded chin and side whiskers, looked more like a country parson than a banker.[14] But he certainly could tease out a deal with the best of them and, more than that, he had an instinctive sense for publicity combined with a varied, largely success-ful business background in Ohio, Missouri, and Pennsylvania. Visionary, speculative in his approach to investments, Cooke had one of those open, amiable personalities whose strong religious convictions made him attractive to the stiff, self-conscious Chase. Cooke had gained a reputation of being one of the more imaginative and energetic bankers in the entire northeast, when he successfully floated Pennsylvania's first war loan bond issue at par after his Philadelphia colleagues had advised Governor Curtin and the legislature that they must expect a discount of from 20 to 25 percent for the issue.[15]

In the sale of the Pennsylvania bonds, Cooke had tried out his theory of selling bonds directly to the public aided by extravagant advertising in both the urban and the rural press. While most of the subscribers invested over $1000 each, a substantial number of citizens responded to Cooke's campaign by investing smaller sums, from $50 to $200.[16]

Of all the bankers, Cooke had been the most alert and supportive in helping to underwrite the 7.3 percent Treasury notes after the Bull Run defeat. Sales through John J. Cisco's assistant treasurer's office in New York had been very slow, and the news of Bull Run brought them to an abrupt halt. But by appealing to the patriotic instincts of the public Cooke managed to market about 34 percent of the entire issue in Philadelphia alone.[17]

It took a little more than three weeks after Bull Run for Chase with his manifold duties and interests to work out his policies for fulfilling the financial targets he estimated for the next year. He had the authority to float $250 million in long-term bonds, $50 million in short-term (one- to three-year) Treasury notes bearing interest, and $50 million in non-interest-bearing demand notes. All such notes were convertible to specie, but wide latitude was granted to the Secretary for their issue and redemption.[18]

The success of Jay Cooke's marketing techniques had impressed Chase. Henry Cooke, who had established himself in Washington, because of his prior friendship with the secretary was able to gain access to the department. Under careful instructions from his brother in Philadelphia, the younger Cooke advised the secretary "not to try too much to save the pennies but to keep on the right side of those capitalists who are disposed to dabble in the loans etc., of the government, and if they do make sometimes a handsome margin it is no more than they are entitled to in such times as these."[19] Since he penned these thoughtful lines Jay Cooke himself visited Washington several times and began to cultivate a warm relationship with Chase, which would benefit each from a personal and a policy viewpoint.

Chase had offered Cooke the assistant treasurer's post in Philadelphia as a measure of his esteem and his confidence in Cooke's ability. But the wily banker was not about to be fobbed off with a government post that paid $2000 a year and restricted his investment opportunities. Through his brother he suggested that he could not for business reasons accept the honor, but he would be happy to become "a secret agent of the Treasury Department" with nominal duties and salary.[20]

Chase shied away from that suggestion, but was happy to learn that Cooke in cooperation with Anthony J. Drexel, a well-connected Philadelphia banker, would establish "a banking establishment in Washington." Cooke's brother Henry would be associated with him and with Drexel in managing the bank.[21] Chase did, however, appoint Cooke along with others as a subscription agent for the sale of government bonds and notes.[22]

Chase's financial experience as counsel for the Cincinnati branch of Bank of the United States and director of several Ohio banks had convinced him that bankers generally placed their own interests before anything else, even appeals to patriotism. This seemed especially the case with the New Yorkers, many of whom had been closely tied in with the southern market and had opposed the war. Cisco himself had been an ardent peace Democrat, as well as a firm believer in his party's hard-currency stand. Chase, of course, leaned in that monetary direction too. He was anxious to secure for government needs as much specie as possible. Even after Bull Run, he still thought that the war would not last longer than a year.

Despite disruption of traditional commercial activities, the eastern banks were just now bulging with specie after devastating European crop failures were followed by extraordinarily high imports of American commodities, including heavy stockpiling of cotton in European warehouses. At the same time, the domestic and foreign loan market had contracted significantly. Uncertainties about the future in a war economy acted to pile up specie in the banks. The prospects of floating loans in Europe at high interest rates were bleak, as foreign bankers viewed the situation in America to be extremely hazardous for investment.[23]

Well aware of all these factors Chase in consultation with Cooke worked out an approach to the associated bankers, most of whom were strangers to him. Several months earlier Hiram Barney had suggested that Chase come to New York where he could meet the city's business leaders "and have some understanding with them about the loans of the government." Barney would make available "the private rooms in the Custom House" for his discussions.[24] On August 11 came word of the bitter engagement and defeat of Union General Nathaniel Lyon at Wilson's Creek, which brought at least half of Missouri under Confederate control. Chase was in New York when the news of the reverse reached Wall Street.

Accompanied by his young secretary, Homer Plantz, he had stopped over in Philadelphia, where he conferred with Cooke, who he took along with him to New York.[25] Chase had conceived of a plan that derived in part from Cooke's experience in marketing Treasury notes direct to the public. In his message to the special session of Congress on July 4 he suggested "the expediency" of opening subscription for a "National Loan" of 7.3 percent three-year notes to be offered directly to the public. Congress on July 17 had responded favorably and authorized Chase to implement such a plan.[26]

Having bitter memories of eastern banking policies during the panics and depressions of 1837 and 1857, Chase was not disposed to give the bankers a free hand in financing the war effort. Nor was he about to give up even a modicum of his personal leadership. But he needed cooperation from the banks which after all held on deposit much of the nation's specie. The banks of New York, Boston, and Philadelphia had long acted as members of a clearing-house for each other's notes, checks, and commercial paper. The New York Chamber of Commerce was the coordinating body for these clearing-house banks, or, as they came to be known, the Associated Banks.

Thus a form of association was in existence when Chase met with the representatives of the various banks in the ornate private meeting room at the custom house.[27] Radiating confidence and projecting a force and a dignity which had become second nature, Chase presented his program for raising $150 million in specie. The bankers, more responsive to their own fortunes and those of their share holders than they were to Unionist appeals, were completely unaccustomed to the size and the urgency of Chase's demands. The sums he was quoting seemed stupendous to these conservative men, and the government's financial program anything but secure, based as it was on loans rather than taxation.

James Gallatin, president of the National Bank of New York, was Chase's most vocal critic. Like his father James Gallatin, Sr., Jefferson's great Treasury secretary, the younger Gallatin always went to the root of the matter.[28] A hard-money man and a Democrat, he spoke for the most conservative of the city's financial institutions. Chase would have preferred to have the banks subscribe to the twenty-year, 7 percent long-term bonds Congress had approved. But as he suspected the interest on them was too low when compared with the three-year short-term Treasury notes. He was not surprised when they refused. If they subscribed in the amounts he requested, they declared, it would tie up their reserves for too long a term and result in a severe curtailment of their note issue.

Prepared for just such a position, Chase fell back on his authority to issue $150 million in 7.3 percent one- to three-year Treasury notes. To make them more acceptable to the bankers, he enlarged on his plan to call for a national loan made directly to the people. It was estimated that the public held about half of the specie in the nation.[29] In return for purchasing the notes with specie, the banks would presumably restore their hard-money reserves in coin from the public sale and from the government's disbursement for military expenditures. Gallatin criticized this proposal when he questioned whether the government could maintain a constant return of specie to the banks.[30] If a serious military reverse or some menace from abroad created a crisis of confidence, the whole arrangement might well collapse. In Gallatin's orderly mind, Chase's program was a makeshift one which shied away from the hard realities of prompt and adequate taxation.

But like so many self-confident individuals when confronted with a cogent attack on their basic premises, Chase brushed aside these objections. He refused to admit that his policy was a precarious one. He did agree, however, that the banks advance specie in relatively modest installments that he thought would keep pace with the return of specie from the national loan and military disbursements. Chase was determined to hold the specie collected in the subtreasuries rather than in special accounts in the clearing-houses as the bankers demanded. But he did not make his intentions on this point clear to them.

Had he, as the bankers thought, permitted the flow of specie directly to them, his program may have been more flexible, but it also would have been more profitable and safer for the banks. In any event, the banks held only $63 million in specie and they were being asked to purchase for cash a total of $150 million in Treasury notes, while at the same time keep up with their regular commercial loans. When they balked at this drain upon their solid assets, Chase threatened them with drastic action. One of the bankers present remarked that if the government delayed in returning specie to them, they should issue an ultimatum that they would not continue to honor the Treasury's warrants. In chilling accents, a vexed Chase said: "No! it is not the business of the Secretary of the Treasury to receive an ultimatum, but to declare one if necessary." He would issue demand notes "for circulation; for it is certain that the war must go on until the rebellion is put down, if we have to put out paper until it takes a thousand dollars to buy a breakfast."[31]

After all, the bankers had to comply with the secretary's policy, however blunt his language. Chase could not have made many close friends at this meeting. His harsh attitude after several days of bickering speaks more to an overbearing sense of rectitude than to any persuasive qualities. Chances are that he would have gotten his way without adopting such a menacing posture and insisting on a plan that called forth so many objections.

But so determined was he to save the government a point or two on its assumed debt, so suspicious was he of banks in general and the Wall Street community in particular, so assured was he of the righteousness of his cause, and so conscious was he of his own power in financial matters that he proved inflexible to any compromise. There is no doubt that the banks had to help with the Union war effort. But Chase and Lincoln, for political reasons, would not bring all of the people behind the government by seeking a much greater source of revenue than the newly enacted Morrill tariff, the direct tax on the states, and modest income and excise taxes. Nor was Chase's insistence that the coin the banks paid for the 7.3 percent notes accumulate in the subtreasuries rather than in direct deposits to the clearing-house banks helpful for rapid and flexible exchange.

Equally disturbing to the bankers was Chase's authority to issue $50 million in non-interest-bearing notes despite the fact that they were redeemable in coin and could be accepted for excise taxes and impost duties.[32] True, Chase had said in his report to Congress that he would not issue these notes except in dire emergencies. But in portentous tones he outlined the critical situation of the Union as he saw it, and his banker audience must have had second thoughts about that contingency. For if implemented it would amount to an issue of government paper currency. They worried about its inflationary impact and its impact on their own notes, which might be driven out of circulation.

Whatever their foreboding, the banks were in no position to reject Chase's demands. And when their representatives after a week of hard bargaining found that they could not make a dent in his chilly resolve, they agreed to underwrite the $150 million loan in three major installments with coin paid into the Treasury as the national loan and military and naval disbursements returned coin to their vaults.[33]

A few days later, John A. Stevens, heading a committee of the Associated Banks, went to Washington at Chase's request to work out the details of the loan. Cooke again was present at the meetings and again the bankers were skeptical. When the negotiations were finally completed, Chase gave a dinner at Willard's, where Stevens made some sobering remarks: "Mr. Chase, you have now received from the Associated Banks the vast sum of fifty millions of dollars. We all earnestly hope that this sum will be sufficient to end the war, should it not prove to be enough, we wish to notify you that you cannot depend upon further aid. . . . We owe a duty to our stockholders and dare not encroach further upon their rights. . . ."[34]

A week or so later, Chase complied with his part of the bargain by drafting and publishing the "Appeal on Behalf of the National Loan." Expressed in exuberant language, Chase aimed the loan at the widest possible market by offering the notes on an installment basis over a four-month period. He estimated that the general public had a surplus for investment "of more than four hundred millions of dollars," a portion of which he urged to be invested on good terms in these government securities. The economy, he said, was sound, an optimistic assertion that did not square with the facts. But he was on reasonably accurate grounds when he said, "the crops of the year are ample, granaries and barns are everywhere full."[35]

The bond agents throughout the North vigorously promoted the "Appeal" and none more so than Jay Cooke, who advertised in some 20 Pennsylvania newspapers with spectacular results. In addition he saw to it that editorials boosting the Treasury note issue were published in the three largest Philadelphia papers and in many of the state's dailies and weeklies. By the first week in September, he was receiving subscriptions close to $100,000 a day.[36]

Chase also took time out of his busy days to write newspaper editors and publishers for favorable publicity in their columns.[37] But faster than the funds collected were the disbursements in coin for military expenses. The Army paymaster general, for instance, requested the Treasury to supply almost $6.5 million for one week.[38] Chase alerted the bankers that they must pay in 30 percent of the first $50 million loan to meet these expenditures by September 11, 1861.[39] Alarmed at what seemed to be a geometric escalation of military and naval costs and unable despite constant reminders to secure reasonable estimates from the War and Navy departments, Chase felt that he had to resort to the non-interest-bearing demand notes which Congress had authorized.[40]

These notes were convertible to coin, but were looked upon at first with suspicion as simply rag currency. To Chase's irritation and not a little embarrassment, the public at first refused to accept them in exchange for goods and services.[41] As for the bankers, the demand notes implied that the Secretary had broken his word and that it was a Treasury dodge to drive their notes out of existence.[42] The bankers appealed in vain to Chase for the Treasury to stop issuing demand notes. But he, who even then was thinking about a national banking system and a United States government-backed uniform currency, refused to change his policy. Referring to state-authorized private bank notes, Chase reminded Joseph Medill, the editor of the Chicago *Tribune*, that no interest was being paid on them. They should be taxed and thus "should at least contribute something to the national burden." He had recommended to Congress such a levy, but bank interests prevailed and voted the tax down.[43]

Despite the constraints the Treasury was imposing on their capital structure, the banks began to regain their specie reserve. Government disbursements had achieved a certain regularity which returned coin to the banks faster than it was paid out for Treasury notes. Treasury and bank sales of the 7.3 percent notes were bringing in additional coin from the public.[44] Chase was vastly relieved. He had been keeping a careful watch on monetary trends and was quite certain that his policy of acting through the subtreasuries was working. He decided to take advantage of this favorable climate and call for a second installment of $50 million.

In late September, he convened another meeting of the Associated Banks in New York. In the meantime the banks had appointed a Treasury note committee which had submitted a series of questions for Chase and invited him to meet with them.[45] Chase was happy to accept and more than happy to set straight his policies in response to their questions. He knew that the bankers were unhappy with the demand notes, that they would try to pin him down on future costs for the military, that they were concerned about accumulations of specie in the subtreasuries and would seek to have him deal directly on bond and note sales with the banks.

He was not surprised when James Gallatin argued again for modification of the subtreasury clause and a halt on the issue of demand notes.[46] But when other members voiced their support for Gallatin's proposals, Chase was nettled by what he regarded as continued opposition for selfish ends. He said coldly that he had drawn that section of the loan act and that his interpretation of policy was that "the monies deposited must continue to be deposited in coin and that payments must also be made in coin," not in bank drafts which he thought was "bad system, bad for the country."[47] Regardless of the fact that disbursements in coin were now lagging behind payments, he felt that this problem would be straightened out when the Secretaries of War and Navy became more familiar with the paperwork involved and disbursing officers better acquainted with their responsibilities. But he warned the bankers he could not foretell what future expenditures would be and he would continue to issue demand notes as the occasion warranted.

The bankers, all successful businessmen, were not now about to be overawed by the secretary. The ugly phrase "suspension of specie payments" was voiced. Yet Chase would not back down. He would conform his policies "to the interests of the banks as nearly as he could," but if they did not subscribe to this second loan in coin, the government would suspend specie payments and place the nation on an inconvertible paper money system, a frightening prospect at this time to the bankers.[48] If he did not browbeat the bankers with his tough talk, he at least played enough on their fears for the future and their patriotism that they agreed to subscribe under his terms to the second loan installment.[49]

Chase returned to Washington well satisfied with himself and with his hard-money policy. By now he knew that the possibilities of a foreign loan were virtually nonexistent. He had asked August Belmont, the New York agent of the Rothschilds who was about to leave for Europe, to negotiate loans from French and British bankers. Belmont replied on October 31 that there was absolutely no chance even at impossibly high yields.[50] And Chase had not been home more than three weeks when the first of a series of military and diplomatic events laid bare the flimsy structure of his hard-money policy.

The military reverse to Union arms at Ball's Bluff on the south bank of the Potomac 45 miles west of Washington had a personal impact on Chase as well as on public confidence in the Lincoln administration. In a badly bungled reconnaissance, Union troops were caught beneath a bluff overlooking the river with inadequate means of escape. They were butchered by deadly Confederate fire, drowned in the river, or forced to surrender. Over half of the troops were killed, wounded, or taken prisoner. Lincoln's close friend Edward D. Baker, a former senator from Oregon who led the expedition, was killed and a young second lieutenant from Massachusetts, Oliver Wendell Holmes, Jr., was among those severely wounded. Convalescing from his wounds Holmes had been unable to find lodgings in any of Washington hotels. Chase learned of his plight and brought him home, where. Kate was unquestionably attracted to this handsome young man whose poet-physician father was a national celebrity.[51]

Balls Bluff shook the faith of many in the capability of McClellan. Few denied his organizing talents. The Army of the Potomac, now 100,000 strong, was not the loosely disciplined horde of three-month men that followed McDowell into defeat and disgrace. The camps that surrounded Washington had proper sanitary arrangements; the troops were well equipped, well disciplined and well drilled in the many dress reviews McClellan gloried in. Officers in the volunteer regiments were better versed in infantry, artillery, and calvary tactics than their military predecessors.

Politicians in residence and the reporters who flocked to Washington not only were impressed with the transformation, but jumped to conclusions that this splendid army should move at once against the Confederates. Reacting to the Balls Bluff fiasco, the pugnacious Ben Wade, Zachariah Chandler, and Lyman Trumbull headed a group that demanded action. They pestered the President and McClellan, neither of whom gave them any satisfaction. But public opinion was becoming increasingly restless, and the metropolitan press was acting as a goad.

Aware of these crosscurrents, Chase's initial enthusiasm for McClellan was being tempered to some extent, yet he and other Cabinet members pushed a reluctant Lincoln to replace General Scott with McClellan. As soon as the President signed the order Chase wrote a note immediately to Colonel T. M. Key, the army's judge advocate, that was obviously meant for the general's consumption. "McClellan is commander-in-chief, let us thank God and take courage," he said.[52] Besides his involvement through Cameron in military affairs and especially his compelling interest in the command and staff structure of the armies both east and west, Chase saw the appointment of McClellan to overall command as bolstering public confidence in his financial policies, easing, if not erasing the uncertainties that Wilson's Creek, Bull Run, and Balls Bluff had raised.

Not two weeks later came news of an important Union victory: the capture of Port Royal and Beaufort, South Carolina, by a joint army-navy expedition. Heavily fortified Port Royal and the inland port of Beaufort gave the Union forces a secure foothold in South Carolina and control of the sounds southwest of Charleston, thus making the blockade of the southern coast much more effective. The Union army would now control the adjacent Sea Islands with their rich long-staple cotton plantations. For the now cotton-short North this was no small premium.[53]

Chase took advantage of these successes to visit New York and step up pressure on the Treasury note committee for the third and last installment of the $150 million loan.[54] But just when the public mood was swinging positively came word that Captain Charles Wilkes, commanding the USS *San Jacinto*, had stopped the British mail steamer *Trent* and removed James M. Mason and John Slidell, Confederate envoys to Great Britain and France.[55] Sensitive to any event that might effect United States standing in Europe and subsequent impact on the American money market, Chase feared serious consequences from this overt act. But he put the best face on it that he could with the New York bankers. After his meeting he wrote John A. Stevens that he had just received press dispatches from England. "The aspect," he said, "is squally, but the clouds will disperse."[56]

Although Chase's temporary measures to finance the war effort primarily by loans from the banks and the public had worked quite well, he realized that the government's expenditures were so large and increasing so rapidly that over the long term there had to be a sounder policy. Complete reliance on the banks for specie on a demand basis and appeals to the public for national loans were too uncertain and put the national credit at greater risk than was warranted. Yet he shied away from the imposition of heavy and burdensome taxation which he felt was both politically and economically unjustifiable.

He was uncomfortable with the government's issue of paper currency not redeemable in equivalent specie. Reluctantly he had been forced to resort to demand notes, a move that came under severe criticism.[57] What was he to do?

He was well aware that there was not enough specie to sustain the enormous expenditures escalating each day. As he had stated publicly, much of the currency of the nation circulating in private bank notes chartered under state authority constituted several hundred million dollars in interest-free loans from the public to the banks.

Chase had imbued enough Jeffersonian concepts to regard this state of affairs as undemocratic, unpatriotic, and self-serving. For most of his adult life, he along with everyone else had been inconvenienced and occasionally fleeced by the changing values and bewildering issues of state bank notes. These inconsistences in the circulating medium had always repelled his orderly, systematic mind. It was time, he felt, to improve upon Jeffersonian theory and have the national government assume the interest-free loan for war expenses, which would at the same time accomplish two important goals. First, the public would have a paper currency constant in value and, he hoped, secure. Second, when state bank notes were taxed out of existence, a system of national banks would be established to replace state-chartered banks. In order to provide a circulating medium these national banks would be compelled to purchase government bonds, and thus a stable bond market would be provided. He noted that New York had adopted a similar system in 1838 and that it had worked well over the years.[58]

Chase did not propose such a new system in his annual report, made public on December 10. But he gave it sufficient space to foreshadow imminent government action, an indication that set in motion the hoarding of specie by the public and by dealers in foreign exchange. Hard-pressed banks experienced a sudden and serious drain not just on their profits but on their reserves which, if Chase's plan were enacted, would substitute government bonds for much of the specie in their vaults. Equally shocking to the business and mercantile communities was Chase's estimate that government expenditures had almost doubled in the five months since his report to the Special Session.[59] Yet he did not propose a commensurate increase in taxation. In fact, he recommended about the same level of taxes as he had requested in his report to the Special Session.[60]

If this was not disconcerting enough, the escalation of the "Trent Affair" which threatened war with Great Britain and possibly France occurring as it did shortly after Chase's report became public began to unravel public confidence in the stability of the Union. Chase rushed off to New York again and after conferring with the Treasury note committee learned that the banks were now so short of coin that suspension of specie payments was likely.[61]

Needless to say this news appalled him and on his return to Washington he did what he could to support Seward in the Cabinet discussion of the government's position in the "Trent Affair." The Cabinet with Sumner, chairman of the Senate Foreign Relations Committee, present met on December 25 at ten in the morning, and at two in the afternoon finally reached a consensus on Seward's reply to Lord Lyons, the British Minister. It was a tense group that sat around the cabinet table that Christmas day.

The Cabinet members and the President himself knew that Wilkes's rash act of seizing the *Trent*'s Confederate passengers had elicited overwhelming public support. Publicly, Chase and others had to be careful about how to defuse the crisis yet at the same time make it appear that the administration was not knuckling under to what all felt was an overbearing British demand for a mere technical violation of international law. Seward's response to the British artfully accomplished these two seemingly opposite goals. Wilkes had acted without instructions, Mason and Slidell would be released. But, as Seward contended, only because Wilkes had made the mistake of not seizing the *Trent* on the grounds that she was carrying contraband—the Confederate commissioners and their papers—and bringing her to port for judgment by an admiralty court in accordance with international law. Left unspoken was the fact that the United States had always insisted on neutral rights and in 1812 had opposed impressment. Seward's balancing act addressed whether individuals could be considered contraband and whether the Confederacy was a neutral power.

"The surrender of the two men and a disavowal of [Wilkes's] act" was, as Chase put it, "gall and wormwood to me. But we cannot afford delays while the matter hangs in uncertainty, the public mind will remain disquieted, our commerce will suffer serious harm, our action against the rebels must be greatly hindered."[62] A reluctant Cabinet and President accepted Chase's lengthy argument and Seward's carefully contrived note when they met the next day.[63] Mason and Slidell were released to British custody, and the indirect apology in the note satisfied the British. The crisis was over, but another one was in the making and burst upon the public on an unseasonably warm New Year's Day, 1862.[64]

Chase, Kate, Nettie, and Susan Walker, a house guest, made their way through the throng that crowded the entrance and the corridors of the White House. It was eleven in the morning and they were there to pay their respects to the President and Mrs. Lincoln as custom decreed. This accomplished, they hurried home where Chase held an open house and greeted visitors. Susan Walker assisted Kate in receiving guests, which included most of the diplomatic corps in full uniform, and many high army and navy officers. An imperturbable Chase greeted Lord Lyons, the British minister, with a brief Latin phrase on peace as a result of the settlement of the "Trent Affair" to which his lordship responded in kind.[65]

Seemingly a monument of dignity and of formal cordiality, Chase gave an impression of composure which he did not feel. The day before, the banks of New York had suspended specie payments and were followed by those in

Boston and Philadelphia. Chase had feared this would happen, but when it did come, he was taken by surprise and for once his confidence in his financial policies was shaken.[66] He had no recourse but to have the government follow suit on the morrow and also suspend specie payment.[67] A severe blow would be dealt the national credit.

Chase had been slow to recognize that his temporary loan policies were conditional at any given time on the broader context of the Union cause. The inadequacy of his taxation program, combined with his hard-money posture, simply could not withstand a sustained breach of public confidence. Suspension would have come sooner or later, but Chase's national bank scheme and "The Trent Affair" hastened the process.[68]

Suspension was not the only problem that was disturbing the secretary on that New Year's afternoon. General McClellan was seriously ill and incommunicado. No one knew of any plans for offensive action against the Confederate army in the Virginia region.[69] Secretary Cameron was about to be replaced. Action on all fronts was at a standstill. Command over the widespread armies seemed in a state of suspended animation. But where a power vacuum existed, there was always a self-confident person like Chase to fill it. Worried though he may have been, he was certain that if given the opportunity, he would straighten out the mess the awkward, joke-telling rustic from Illinois had brought upon himself through his lax and bungling moves in the conduct of the war. The New Year might not be as unpromising for Secretary Chase as the past year had been.

chapter 21

Military Moves and Missions

On the evening of January 6, an unusual meeting took place in the Cabinet room at the White House. A tense Lincoln and equally tense members of his Cabinet listened to a heated denunciation of General McClellan from members of the newly created Congressional Joint Committee on the Conduct of the War. The most outspoken were Ben Wade, chairman of the committee and Zachariah Chandler, the bibulous coarse-grained senator from Michigan. Much discussion ensued with Cabinet members and the committee participating. Seward supported McClellan with brief remarks. But Wade pressed on. He turned his deep-set eyes under shaggy brows on Lincoln. "What were McClellan's plans?" he demanded.[1] When the President did not answer Chase spoke up. He made a spirited defense of the general, which in a way was a rejoinder to Wade, who he now judged a serious rival.

Chase admitted that McClellan should consult more freely with his commanders, but that he was still "the best man for the place he held," and had he not been seriously ill, he would "have satisfied everybody in the country of his efficiency and capacity." Characteristically, Chase left an opening for himself should the situation change. McClellan, he maintained, had overtaxed himself, had taken on too many responsibilities. No one person could handle the "special duties of Commander of the Army of the Potomac and the general duties of Commanding General of the Armies of the United States." Mc-

Clellan in trying to direct both "had undertaken what he could not perform."
After these remarks Lincoln concluded the meeting and taking Chase's point
said that he would talk to McClellan on dividing his responsibilities.[2]

Previously, at Lincoln's request McClellan visited Chase and outlined
his plan to flank the Confederate army at Manassas by transporting his troops
down the Potomac and Chesapeake Bay to Urbana, a village on the south bank
of the Rappahannock River. His forces would then be poised between the
Confederate army and Richmond, about 40 miles away. The navy would
protect his supply lines as he marched on the Confederate capital. McClellan
thought the entire operation could be concluded before February 1, 1862.[3]

Considering the circumstances there is no doubt that Chase apprised
Lincoln of this plan. In light of later events, it is likely that the President
distrusted this combined operation because of the pressure he was already
feeling from impatient politicians and press lords for an onward movement.
But, more important, while McClellan and the bulk of the Union army were
many miles away, establishing a base in Urbana, it was possible that General
Joseph Johnston and the main Confederate army at Manassas, only 35 miles
from Washington, would move on the city.[4]

After the stormy session with the Committee on the Conduct of the War,
the President had to wait several days before McClellan was well enough even
to be contacted. There was some desultory discussion of the military stalemate
when the Cabinet met at noon on January 10. A disgusted Bates summed up
the meeting as a disclosure of "great negligence, ignorance and lack of preparation and forethought. Nothing is *ready*. McClellan is still sick, and nobody
knew his plans, if he have any."[5] Later in the afternoon a distressed Lincoln
conferred with Montgomery Meigs, the quartermaster general of the Army,
whose abilities had impressed him. Meigs suggested a meeting of high-
ranking officers and Cabinet members to familiarize the administration with
the plans and theater of operations. His suggestion prompted Lincoln to call
an emergency Cabinet meeting where some semblance of war planning might
take shape.

In response to the President's request, Chase left a meeting he was
chairing with members of the Associated Banks and hurried to the White
House.[6] There he found Lincoln, Assistant Secretary of War Thomas A.
Scott, Seward, and Generals McDowell and William B. Franklin. Franklin
had been invited because he was one of McClellan's close associates and was
supposed to know something about his chief's plans.

Lincoln opened the meeting by alluding to the deplorable state of the
nation's finances and then ran the gamut of political, diplomatic, and military
problems facing the administration. He had visited McClellan but could not
gain an interview. "If something was not soon done," he said with a sense of
desperation coloring his voice, "the bottom would be out of the whole affair."

He added in a more jocular vein, "If General McClellan did not want to use the army, he would like to *borrow* it, provided he could see how it could be made to do something." Then he asked McDowell for his opinion.[7]

The general proposed a simple frontal advance along the same lines he had taken in the Bull Run campaign. Franklin disagreed with his colleague. He thought a combined army-navy operation toward Richmond from the head of the York River was what McClellan had in mind. Chase listened carefully to these comments and heard the President lament the fact that his two commanding generals in the west, Henry W. Halleck, Fremont's successor in Missouri, and Don Carlos Buell, with headquarters in Cincinnati, were not cooperating with each other. Since even the two generals present were relatively ignorant about the condition of the army, Lincoln adjourned the meeting, but in doing so asked McDowell and Franklin to consult with each other, gather further information, and return for a second meeting at 8 p.m. the next day. Chase left with the two officers. On the way he suggested they meet for their work session at the Treasury building in a room near his office. They accepted the invitation.

The next morning as they discussed the various problems involved, Franklin suggested that McDowell ask Chase about the Burnside expedition, another combined operation that was aimed at further sealing the blockade by capturing Roanoke Island and the adjacent river port of New Bern, North Carolina. Seizure of these points would give the Union forces command of the northern and southern reaches of Pamlico Sound. The navy would then control most of the strategic waterway from the Virginia capes to Georgia.[8] But the Burnside expedition had tied up considerable shipping, naval support, and army manpower.

Chase was able to supply McDowell and Franklin with the information. Franklin wondered whether McClellan should be informed. Neither McDowell nor Chase thought so as the direction came from the President. Both officers then collected the data Lincoln requested and prepared papers for presentation. When they reached the White House on the evening of January 11, they found Blair had been added to the group. As far as a date for an advance was concerned, a point that Lincoln had emphasized, both officers were in agreement that arranging the logistics for the water route would take much more time and planning than a direct overland thrust from current bases.[9]

Blair, a West Point graduate whose opinion carried much weight with the President, objected. A direct assault toward Manassas would simply be a repetition of the Bull Run disaster.[10] Chase had been briefed thoroughly on the two plans and promptly engaged Blair in debate. He argued that what was needed was "the moral power of a victory over the enemy in his present position. It would be just as great as one elsewhere . . . and the danger lay in the probability that we should find, after losing time and millions, that we should have as many difficulties to overcome below as we now have above."[11] Chase had changed his mind since his briefing on the Urbana plan six weeks earlier. He knew that the President opposed it, and the critical financial problems he faced as well as the pressure from politicians and the press called for an immediate move.

After listening to Chase's responses to Blair's argument, Lincoln asked to have Meigs brought into the discussion on water transportation and again asked Franklin and McDowell to meet with him the following afternoon at 3 p.m. When all were assembled the next day, discussion was inconclusive because it had just been learned that McClellan was well enough to resume control of the armies. Meigs did report, however, that it would take at least six weeks to assemble the troops, transport, munitions, and supplies if a water route were chosen.[12] He also aligned himself with McDowell in supporting a direct frontal attack.

Chase had been appalled to learn that at least 400 vessels would be required, while the munitions, artillery, wagons, rations, ambulances, and pontoons needed to ford the many rivers and creeks between the York River and Richmond for an army in excess of 100,000 men ran into millions of items. Chase had been unable to keep up with expenditures for the expanding military and naval forces for some months. He was resorting to demand notes and would soon have to depend on legal tender backed only by the government's promise to pay. How could the Treasury stand such an additional burden?

From an economic and political viewpoint the water route seemed out of the question. Chase had also been in touch with many of the nervous, irascible members of Congress. All of his connections with home and in other states portended an ugly popular mood if inactivity were to continue for any protracted length of time.

Chase had been an early convert to McDowell's plan. And in fact that general had been with Chase almost constantly in his spacious office with the gray velvet carpets and the black walnut desk and chairs.[13] McDowell may not have been much of a commander, but he was an excellent staff man and he supplied the secretary not only with argument, but with specific topographical and communication intelligence regarding the two routes. The overwhelming evidence of course supported the direct assault.[14]

At one of these meetings Colonel Key, Chase's man at Army headquarters, was present. He was about to meet with McClellan and asked Chase, probably at his chief's request, what he would recommend. Chase had three suggestions. First, McClellan should purge his staff of nepotism and favoritism. Second, he must show respect for the President and his office and keep him regularly informed so Lincoln would not have to "wait on him." Third, he should consult with his senior officers and appoint McDowell a major general at once. The first and especially third of Chase's recommendations—the appointment of McDowell, a Chase protégé—must have irked McClellan and made him suspicious of the secretary's motives.[15] After these briefings and his understanding of the President's desires, his soundings among members of the Committee on the Conduct of the War—always excepting Wade—and his desperation over finances, he reversed himself on McClellan.

While Chase was attending war planning sessions at the White House and at the Treasury Department, he was also meeting with a committee of the Associated Banks and with members of the House Ways and Means and Senate Finance committees. The Treasury and the banks had suspended specie payment, and the government was also running out of demand notes even though the banks until now would not receive them.[16] All issues of government bonds including the 7.3 percent Treasury notes were being traded far below par value.[17]

After these exhausting conferences, by the sheer force of his personality Chase managed to convince the congressmen to increase his borrowing power. He also managed to bring the dubious bankers behind his financial policies. After they left his office Spaulding of Ways and Means was ushered in. He impressed upon Chase the necessity that the government issue United States notes (later to be called greenbacks). Reluctantly Chase said that he would meet with Ways and Means chairman Thaddeus Stevens to iron out the details.[18]

Two days earlier, with the discussions on finance reaching a critical point, Chase attended the last of Lincoln's war planning meetings. There, in the President's office, the air murky from Seward's puffing on his ubiquitous cigar, a pallid General McClellan finally made his formal appearance. He had talked several times with the President but no decisions had been made. He was now brought before a larger audience consisting of three of his junior officers, one of whom—McDowell—he disliked and suspected of intrigues against him. Chase had accompanied McDowell to the meeting, an event not lost on the suspicious commander.[19] It was common knowledge that Cameron had just resigned as Secretary of War and that Edwin M. Stanton, Chase's friend from bygone days and friendly also to McClellan, had been appointed in his place. But Stanton did not attend the meeting. Assistant Secretary Thomas Scott again represented the War Department.

When all were settled, Lincoln pointed to a large map of Virginia and asked McDowell to explain his plan of operations. Not given to succinct generalization the portly McDowell went into excruciating detail to back up his plan for a direct assault. Probably backed by Chase, he stressed the time factor, which he estimated at three weeks for preparation alone. But he also apologized in a way to his superior by saying that he had acted "entirely in the dark" and that his plan represented his own opinion.

McClellan, who had remained silent during McDowell's presentation but had not bothered to conceal his hostile feelings, said curtly: "You are entitled to have any opinion you please."[20] There followed a rambling discussion which Lincoln finally cut off by asking McClellan when anything could be done. McClellan replied again somewhat coldly that he had been deprived of troops for the Burnside expedition and for Butler, who was scheduled to capture Ship Island off the New Orleans delta as a first move against that city. Chase had grown impatient and uncomfortable at McClellan's apparent refusal to answer specifically Lincoln's request for a date when a forward move of the main Army of the Potomac could be made. He fixed his eyes on the general and just as coldly asked "what he intended doing with his army, and when he intended doing it?" There was a long silence as the two men stared at each other until finally McClellan spoke of a move he had under way in Kentucky. As to Chase's peremptory question, however, he said in an implied a rebuke that he had a plan which he would disclose to the President in a few days, but unless ordered would not speak of it now, "always believing that in military matters the fewer persons who were knowing of them the better." Again Lincoln asked if McClellan had "any particular time" in mind, and when McClellan said that he had, Lincoln adjourned the meeting.

Chase had been as abrupt in his questions as McClellan was in his answers. Tense about the financial and political situation, Chase was worried about his two daughters, both of whom had become ill while visiting the Cookes in Philadelphia.[21] No doubt these factors had an influence on his manner and his subsequent behavior, as he left for more grueling meetings with the bankers and the congressmen at the Treasury building. Chase now decided that McClellan had become hostile to him and that he was unfit for his responsibilities. Likewise he was determined to derail any extensive joint operation toward Richmond that he was certain McClellan was planning.[22]

Meanwhile McClellan and the looming financial disaster were not the only vexing problems that awaited action. During the last trying months of 1861 Chase had been caught up in the Fremont imbroglio that finally resulted in that feckless general's removal from command in the West.

Plagued by guerilla activity in Missouri, Fremont, a staunch antislavery man, on August 30 had proclaimed the emancipation of all slaves in Missouri whose masters were secessionists. Further, he ordered the confiscation of all property of Confederate sympathizers, and the court-martial and summary execution of guerillas and those who were convicted of destroying public property. The proclamation was a rash act that intruded into the political sphere and came at a most unfortunate time, when Kentucky would decide whether to remain in the Union or join the Confederacy. Lincoln promptly disavowed Fremont's action, a decision that helped retain Kentucky as a loyal state.

These series of events, however, placed Chase in a most uncomfortable position. Antislavery men in Ohio's Western Reserve especially, but also in other areas of the Union, applauded the proclamation. Republican party-oriented dailies with their pervasive influence, such as the New York *Evening Post*, Greeley's *Tribune*, and Joseph Medill's Chicago *Tribune*, endorsed Fremont's act. Chase's old abolitionist and free-soil associates joined in with high praise. Chase had made his opposition to slavery the thrust of his political career, but he was also a politician. As much as he approved of this first step toward a cherished goal, he had too much invested in Kentucky to jeopardize his own and possibly also the Union's future by openly espousing what he knew in practical terms would be a premature stand for emancipation.

For months now Chase had been the administration's point man not just in Kentucky but in western Virginia and eastern Tennessee. He had mediated as best he could between the administration's two advance men in Kentucky, the blustering Nelson and his civilian counterpart the combative Garrett Davis.[23] He had sent his trusted sixth auditor, ex-Judge Green Adams, to report on the situation. He was relieved when Adams said that while Nelson might be too voluble and caustic in his denunciations he was a firm and determined leader. "He drinks a little too much," said Adams, "and does not make himself popular with the troops . . . but Kentucky Unionists stand by him."[24] At the time of Fremont's proclamation Nelson, through Chase and Lincoln's efforts, had recruited, armed, and equipped several thousand men. Garrett Davis had been largely responsible in distributing covertly arms and ammunition to loyalists throughout the state.[25]

It had been an extremely difficult and delicate task. Chase worked continually through Cameron's befogged War Department for guns, munitions, and supplies to be sent to Nelson, only to have his requests go astray or some other theater commander requisition the materiel for his own purposes. How many times had he heard from an irate Nelson that there was not a cartridge in the camp.[26]

Though Missouri was not included in his sphere of military activity, Chase was pressed to keep up with payments for requisitions from Fremont's command in St. Louis. Word kept seeping through to Washington that mismanagement and corruption were flagrant at Fremont's headquarters. By the late summer of 1861, the current operations in Kentucky at least had taken on a much more open and professional look. First Robert Anderson of Sumter fame, now a brigadier general, had been assigned to the newly created Department of Ohio with special instructions to take charge of Nelson's activities. Anderson suffered a mental breakdown, however, and was replaced, largely at Chase's insistence, by Brigadier General William T. Sherman. As Kentucky edged closer to the Union, Fremont's bombshell threatened to blow apart the thin web that bound the state to the Union.

Joshua Speed, Lincoln's close friend, wrote from Kentucky predicting dire consequences unless the proclamation was modified. "Frankly I say to you," he wrote Chase, "that it will ruin us. . . . the practical working of this will produce insurrection."[27] Fremont's act, despite Lincoln's modification of it, influenced Confederate commanders to move into the state, though strategic objectives were the prime cause. This invasion swung the Kentucky legislature over to the Union.[28]

As evidences of Fremont's maladministration mounted, more vexing to the President and to Chase was his apparent inaction. Fremont had not been supplied adequately with munitions and transport. His subordinate commanders were a jealous, barely competent group, and Fremont had needlessly provoked the Blairs, who were determined to remove him.

There was no doubt that the situation in Missouri had gotten out of hand. In early October, Lincoln sent Cameron and Lorenzo Thomas, the Army's adjutant general, to St. Louis for investigation and report. Chase dashed off a note to Cameron urging action. "For Heaven's sake bear in mind," he wrote, "that we must have vigor, capacity and honesty. If F[remont] has these qualities sustain him. If not let nothing prevent you from taking the bull by the horns. We have had enough dilly dallying, temporizing and disgraces."[29]

Cameron bore with him an order to remove Fremont and appoint one of his subordinates, David Hunter, in his place, should he deem it necessary. But Cameron did not see fit to make the change and on his return argued in Cabinet council that Fremont be given a chance to make the advance he planned against Confederate forces in southwestern Missouri. Chase lined up with Seward and Cameron in support of Fremont, to the disgust of the conservative Missourian Edward Bates and Montgomery Blair, whose brother Frank was locked in a command struggle with Fremont.[30]

Chase had to balance his antislavery standing against plain evidence of wasteful, if not corrupt practices in St. Louis and what seemed to be Fremont's inactivity. Lorenzo Thomas's detailed and in some places inaccurate report had been damaging. But also disturbing to Chase was the shocking account of malfeasance and corruption that E. B. Washburne, chairman of a Congressional subcommittee on contracts, uncovered in St. Louis.[31] Washburne relied heavily on hearsay, but he presented enough direct evidence to shake further Chase's confidence in Fremont.[32] "I did not favor the appt. of gen. F[remont]," he wrote on October 23, "because I feared the financial mismanagement which has actually occurred—I have however supported him to the extent of the powers of the treasury, having provided for payments in his department not less than $10 million." In prophetic words Chase said: "I fear that as a military commander he will not equal my expectations which were high."[33] Lincoln warned Fremont and finally on October 24 he reached the end of his patience and relieved him of his command. He appointed General Hunter in his place.[34] When Hunter instead of giving battle began a long retreat, Lincoln replaced him with Henry W. Halleck, a scholarly West Pointer who had left the army for a legal career in California. At McClellan's request Lincoln placed another professional officer, Don Carlos Buell, to replace Sherman in Kentucky. Chase probably was consulted, but his was not the decisive voice.[35]

At the very time that these arrangements were being made, Simon Cameron was about to leave a War Department that was far too demanding for his minimal administrative and executive skills. Chase had long since taken Cameron's measure and had quite happily acted for him in matters of military personnel, command and strategy.

Cameron was a shrewd practical politician, a power in Pennsylvania, and an engaging individual Chase genuinely liked. He shared Chase's views on slavery and on enlisting blacks in the armed forces. Not that Chase could be so forbearing of Cameron when it came to his careless and frequently heedless administration of War Department accounts. When he was preparing his report for the special session Chase became so exasperated at Cameron's sloppy estimates of expenditures that he chided him warmly in an official letter.[36] And on receiving Cameron's estimates for fiscal 1862, Chase again censured the secretary. He returned Cameron's report of expenditures for clarification. "I beg you to bear in mind," he wrote, "that I have repeatedly and earnestly condemned the loose and unsystematic manner in which authority has been given irresponsible individuals all over the country, to raise troops, expend money and involve the government in debt."[37]

Cameron himself was aware of his own shortcomings and as early as September he had indicated to Chase his willingness to resign if a suitable foreign mission could be arranged.[38] He knew that the President had lost confidence in him. Bewildered by the demands made upon the War Department, he was hurt by incessant newspaper attacks that Chase had tried unsuccessfully to soften.[39]

Feeling as he did Cameron threw caution to the winds and openly espoused the enlistment and the arming of refugee slaves who had entered Union army lines. At a Cabinet meeting on November 15 when he broached the subject he encountered vehement opposition from Bates and Blair. Chase remained silent, as did Lincoln, though everyone present knew that he opposed enlisting blacks at this time.

Four days later Cameron attended an all-male party given by John W. Forney, the new Secretary of the Senate. Forney, formerly a Buchanan Democrat and newspaper editor, was a hard-drinking, hard-working, loquacious individual with a taste for political intrigue.[40] The entire Cabinet had been invited to Forney's rooms at New Jersey Avenue and what was then B Street—now Constitution Avenue—to meet George D. Prentice, combative editor of the *Louisville Journal.* Only Cameron and Smith accepted Forney's invitation. As much as Chase cultivated the press, he was too busy to waste his time in what was sure to be an alcoholic evening.[41] And it is well that he did not attend because Cameron, who had imbibed freely, got into a heated argument with Smith over enlisting black troops in the South. Someone present leaked the argument to the *New York Times,* which ran the story on November 20, 22, and December 2.

Already discomforted with Cameron's administration of the War Department and displeased with his previous comments on the delicate political subject of black troops, Lincoln was very upset by the public airing of these controversial views. For some months now Cameron had been associating rather closely with fellow Democrat Edwin M. Stanton, perhaps the most successful trial lawyer in the nation. Briefly Attorney General of the United States during the closing months of the Buchanan administration, Stanton had gained a favorable reputation in Republican party circles for his staunch Unionism.

Energetic, highly emotional, abrasive, deferential to those he regarded as helpful either in business or politics, Stanton could be brusque and blustering to the point of insulting to those he considered his inferiors or competitors. He was nevertheless a highly intelligent individual with well-recognized abilities in organizing and shaping masses of complex data. Cameron had employed Stanton as a special counsel for the War Department. The bearded lawyer was present at the Forney party. He had observed the whiskey-scented debate through his thick-lensed glasses but had said nothing. Later, at another affair, this time given by Cameron, Stanton was again present when his host disclosed that he would recommend black troops in his annual report. Again there was much heated debate and warnings that any such statement would result in serious consequences not just for Cameron but for the administration itself.[42]

Cameron was not about to change his mind, but he asked Stanton to read over the draft of his report. When Stanton did he made significant changes that put a more radical gloss on the document.[43] Yet even with Stanton's revision, the controversial passages were couched in speculative terms. Gideon Welles, hardly a radical on the slavery issue, studied the report and came to the conclusion that it was far less controversial than Fremont's proclamation. Since the navy was already employing blacks on shipboard and Welles had defended this policy in explicit terms in his own report, he believed Cameron was simply fishing for political support.

All Cabinet members had furnished the President with abstracts of their reports. Welles had not heard from Lincoln about his statement. He assumed that Lincoln found nothing objectionable about the navy's policy toward fugitive slaves. But when he took his place at the Cabinet table, he was startled at Lincoln's opening remarks. Pacing about as he frequently did during Cabinet meetings Lincoln said that his own report was unfinished and declared that the War Department's policy as stated by Cameron contradicted the administration's position on fugitive slaves. Peremptorily he demanded that Cameron delete his references before his report was accepted. Cameron, who had had a stormy conference with the President earlier, still argued the point. He said that the army's policy was no different from the navy's, an assertion that was true enough. As Welles prepared to defend his position, the President brushed over Cameron's comments and insisted that his report be edited. Cameron then said that when he had received no word from the President regarding the abstract of his report he had ordered his report mailed.[44]

Unquestionably Lincoln was at fault here. No doubt the "Trent Affair," which was reaching a threatening stage, and the continuous demands on his time from military, political, and financial concerns all had combined to keep him from reading Cameron's abstract, which contained a precis of the offending passage. Whatever the reasons, Lincoln angrily ordered Montgomery Blair to telegraph post offices all over the nation and have the postmasters hold up any distribution until a revised report was in their hands.

Chase, who had not spoken out on the question, now felt that he had to defend Cameron's position on arming fugitive slaves as a matter of principle and as a war measure. But Lincoln remained unmoved. He closed the discussion on that particular point by asking for Welles's full report, which the secretary promptly made available. Cameron was silenced, mortified, and all present regarded this turn of events as tantamount to his departure from the Cabinet.[45]

It now remained for the President to arrange for Cameron's resignation without giving further offense. He would provide a less sensitive, less demanding position (a senior diplomatic appointment, perhaps) and at the same time not seem to be directly involved in the negotiations. Fortunately a major diplomatic post was about to become available. Cassius Clay was anxious to vacate the Russian mission. Cameron could take his place.[46]

Lincoln had several candidates for the War Department under serious consideration. All were former Democrats, according to his formula for a coalition Cabinet: Montgomery Blair, who had a West Point education; Joseph Holt, former Cabinet minister in the Buchanan administration and a strong Unionist from Kentucky; and Edwin M. Stanton. It appears that Lincoln favored Holt, but was agreeably surprised when his two senior ministers, Chase and Seward—usually at odds over patronage and policy—and Cameron himself supported Stanton warmly.

Lincoln detailed Seward to make preliminary arrangements with Cameron and asked Chase to handle the final negotiations. In this way Chase, inordinately sensitive about his position, would not be excluded. Neither Seward nor Chase was aware of the other's direct role in easing out Cameron and easing in Stanton.

Sunday evening, January 12, 1862, Chase's servant announced Cameron. The Pennsylvanian came right to the point. Clay had vacated the Russian mission, and he would be willing to accept it. He urged Chase to see Lincoln with this information and also say that he endorsed Stanton as his successor. For once, Chase thought that it would be best to sound out Seward on both appointments before going to the President. He ordered his carriage, dropped Cameron off at Willard's Hotel, and from there went to Seward's home near the White House. When Chase explained his mission, Seward feigned surprise but then asked whom he would suggest to replace Cameron.[47] Chase replied either Holt or Stanton but he "feared Holt might embarrass us on the slavery question." As for Stanton he was "a good lawyer and full of energy," but he could not judge his executive ability. Seward had seen much of Stanton during the closing months of the Buchanan administration and was in a better position to assess this quality. Seward gave Stanton a strong endorsement, and it was agreed that both of them would see Lincoln the next morning.[48] Edward Bates for one and apparently other Cabinet members had not been advised of the change. Bates was astonished when he heard that Cameron had resigned and would become Minister to Russia. Stanton would be his successor in the War Department.

Chase looked forward to a cordial relationship with the new War Secretary.[49] And at first this seemed a reasonable assumption. A tempest of directed energy, within a few weeks he brought order and efficiency into the office, especially in the all important areas of contract administration, procurement, and the seemingly neverending quest for regular army commissions. Chase arranged for Stanton to meet the key figures on those congressional committees that dealt with financial matters. Fessenden was impressed with the new secretary. After a long interview he said, "If he acts up to his promise, he will be just the man for Secretary of War."[50]

For the first month of his tenure, Stanton labored impossible hours and underwent great strain as he tried to reorganize the War Department. On February 10, he suffered a slight stroke in his office, but was soon back at his desk, his energy and capacity for work undiminished.[51] On the all-important question of McClellan, he bided his time, however.

Chase was not directly involved in Lincoln's efforts to galvanize McClellan to action. Nor is there evidence that he was consulted on McClellan's plan for a joint army-navy operation toward Richmond by way of the peninsula between the York and the James rivers. He had a good idea what McClellan's strategy would be from General Franklin's presentation some weeks earlier, and he was opposed to it.

McClellan had broached his plan to Stanton, with whom he was then on cordial terms. Stanton advised him to bring it before the President. When he did so Lincoln disapproved of it for much the same reason Chase had opposed the plan Franklin had outlined. Lincoln wanted a direct overland assault on the Confederate army before Manassas. But he was willing to give in if McClellan could satisfy him on the specifics of his strategy. McClellan responded with a fairly detailed plan that was backed up with plausible argument and which dovetailed well with movements of the western armies. Reluctantly the President accepted it, though he remained concerned about the security of Washington.

Stanton's accession seemed also the harbinger of good tidings for other Union armies. While McClellan was assembling his expedition with characteristic thoroughness, word was received in Washington that Buell had won a victory at Mill Springs, Kentucky, and had broken the Confederate defense line in that state. Not three weeks later, on February 6, Fort Henry on the Cumberland River in central Tennessee fell to a combined army-navy assault, and two days after that Burnside defeated the Confederate forces holding Roanoke Island. These victories were followed closely by the surrender of Fort Donelson together with 12,000 troops to Brigadier General U. S. Grant under Halleck's command. Most of Kentucky and much of west Tennessee was now under Union control.[52] The only setback—and this a serious one—was when the Confederate army at Manassas shifted base and moved southward behind the Rappahannock River to the northern margins of the Peninsula, a body of land between the York and the James rivers, where it could screen Richmond from what was assumed to be an attack from the York River.

McClellan's Urbana plan had been posited on having his army planted between the main Confederate force at Manassas and Richmond. Now he had to revise his plans, and more time was required. He did move his army out and took over the important road and railroad junction at Manassas. But newspaper correspondents who followed the army filed stories that they found no enemy and instead saw a quantity of logs made to look like heavy artillery. Radical politicians and particularly the Committee on the Conduct of the War railed against McClellan's pretensions and his inactivity.

A further complication for McClellan's planning was the appearance of the Confederate ironclad vessel the *Merrimac* in Hampton Roads. On March 9 she steamed into the anchorage of the Union fleet near Fort Monroe and destroyed two of the navy's wooden warships before she retired unscathed up the James River. When word of the disaster reached the White House, Stanton staged what could only be described as an emotional breakdown.[53]

Before the President and other members of the Cabinet, the secretary upbraided his colleague Navy Secretary Welles as he marched from one window to another in the Cabinet room, now peering at the bend in the Potomac below Washington, now demanding that the river be blocked up to prevent the *Merrimac* from reaching Washington and bombarding the city. His alarm impressed Lincoln, who queried Welles about the danger and the blockading fleet of Norfolk.[54]

Welles stood his ground, calmly pointing out the absurdity of Stanton's histrionics. He said that the Union navy's new ironclad, the *Monitor,* was reported at Hampton Roads and would be more than a match for the lumbering *Merrimac.* Late that afternoon Assistant Secretary of the Navy Gustavus Fox, who was at Fort Monroe, telegraphed Washington that the *Monitor* had engaged the *Merrimac* in the world's first battle between ironclad vessels and had driven the Confederate ship back to her berth on the James.[55]

McClellan had been just as concerned as the President about the *Merrimac,* but Fox allayed the general's fears.[56] He had altered his strategy from the Urbana base to Fort Monroe for a movement up the Peninsula toward Richmond. Lincoln, Chase, and Stanton reluctantly approved of the revised plan. Lincoln, however, was insistent that McClellan provide an adequate screen for Washington. On March 17, the general began to move his large army to the Peninsula, and by April 5, he began a siege of Yorktown, at the mouth of the York River some twenty miles from his new base.

Two days later came word of the fierce battle at Shiloh on the western bank of the Tennessee, followed by Major General John Pope's capture of Island Number Ten, the principal Confederate stronghold remaining on that river. Shiloh was bloody but inconclusive, and Pope's victory, important as it was, lacked the glamour of McClellan's vast expedition. But then the northern public was cheered by the fall of New Orleans to a combined army-navy assault.[57]

Before McClellan could begin pounding Yorktown with his heavy siege guns, the Confederate defenders evacuated the town and fell back on Williamsburg, about fifteen miles to the northwest. This move uncovered Norfolk and the Navy Yard, where the *Merrimac* was berthed. The painstaking and expensive move up the Peninsula prompted the usual strident demands for action from radical congressmen and influential editors.

A disturbed President fell in with Stanton's suggestion that he see for himself the general's operations and decide whether his seemingly endless requests for more reinforcements were justified. Stanton also advised that Chase accompany them and that the revenue cutter *Miami* then at the navy yard be used for the trip.[58] Chase was delighted to accept the invitation but when he asked Stanton whether he could invite Denning Duer, an important New York banker he was trying to impress, and, for propriety's sake, Seward, he experienced for the first time the lash of Stanton's ill-temper in his emphatic negative.[59]

The *Miami* shoved off for Fort Monroe at dusk on May 5. Fifteen miles below Washington, a drizzling rain so reduced visibility that the captain and pilot could not make out the channel markings. The *Miami* was anchored. The weather cleared up sufficiently by 3 a.m., and at about noon the ship entered a rough Chesapeake Bay.[60]

Everyone sat down to lunch but after a bite or two at the careening table Lincoln lost his appetite and turned pale. He said he was too uncomfortable to eat and stretched himself at length on the locker. Stanton also gave up and lay down. Chase finished lunch with a hearty appetite and went on deck before returning to the cabin and his seasick companions.[61] Between eight and nine in the evening the *Miami* reached Fort Monroe. By now Stanton had gotten his sea legs; he sent a message announcing the presence of the party to General Wool, who commanded the fort. Wool and his staff soon appeared, and though it was almost 10 p.m. a revived Lincoln wanted to visit Commodore Goldsborough, who commanded the federal fleet in Hampton Roads, which now included the USS *Monitor*. Although late at night, there was nothing to do but obey the President's urgent request. The group boarded a tug and headed for Goldsborough's command ship, the USS *Minnesota*. She was a heavy wooden steam frigate, her steep sides thirty feet above the water line. After hailing the ship they were directed to a rope ladder on the port side. Lincoln scrambled up the swaying ladder and Chase was next, emphasizing his rank above that of Stanton, a small point that meant much to him.[62]

After the conference, where the principal subject discussed was the *Merrimac,* the little group with the tall form of the President in the lead descended the rope ladder and returned to the *Miami*. The next day Chase and Stanton acted as amateur tacticians—though they got in each other's way—as they sought the attention and the approval of the President.

Indulging his taste for action, Lincoln ordered the shore batteries and the fleet to bombard the Confederate fortifications guarding Norfolk at Sewall's Point. Stanton and Chase left Lincoln and boarded a tug to have closer and better observation of the bombardment's effects. Having satisfied their curiosity they returned to the *Miami*. Just as they came aboard, to the delight of three very important spectators, the *Merrimac* belching a plume of black smoke from her stack rounded Sewall's Point and came into view. The wooden warships that had been participating in the bombardment turned back, but the *Monitor* and the little USS *Stevens* ironclad battery (a self-propelled gun) advanced to meet her. One must imagine the disappointment of Lincoln and his colleagues when the *Merrimac* lumbered around and steamed slowly back to her berth behind Sewall's Point.[63]

That evening, Chase, Stanton, and Lincoln, with charts and maps before them, played at being military commanders for an assault on Norfolk. With General Wool offering professional advice they evolved three plans of operation, but as everyone realized none would work if the *Merrimac* guarded the approaches to the Elizabeth River, the Navy Yard, and the city itself. Chase volunteered to search out other landing places that the *Merrimac* could not reach with her heavy guns so that Wool's garrison could make a secure landing. He found what he thought was an appropriate place. When he returned to the *Miami,* however, Lincoln and Stanton, who had been studying charts of the Norfolk approaches, found what they believed to be a better landing place.[64]

Off again to survey the beaches, the President and Stanton were now in a tug, Chase in the *Miami.* Lincoln took charge but Stanton gave the orders, directing a part of Wool's garrison along with two brigades of troops and a cavalry detachment to advance on what had been described as a fortified camp. All expected action but none materialized. The Confederate defenders had abandoned their trenches well before the advance. When the Union troops reached a point two miles from Norfolk, they were met by a delegation of citizens bearing a white flag. The President accepted from them the surrender of the city. Carriages were provided for a tour. At sundown the presidential party returned to the *Miami.*[65]

Elated by his successful military exploit, Lincoln decided to leave for Washington early the next morning. Before they left Goldsborough brought the welcome news that the "rebels had set fire to the *Merrimac* and had blown her up."[66] It had been a lark for Chase, though he did not see it that way.

Characteristically, he exaggerated the military importance of the action, and while he heaped praise on the President and Stanton for "a brilliant week's campaign," he was piqued at Stanton's growing influence and his habit of issuing peremptory orders. Yet this brief expedition and the close quarters he maintained with Lincoln raised his opinion of the President.[67]

He had not changed his views about Lincoln's casual approach to administration, nor was he pleased with the way his advice on future military moves was disregarded. But the trip had provided needful relief from the drudgery and the heavy responsibilities in so many critical areas that awaited him in Washington.

chapter 22

High Stakes

The presidential party returned to Washington on May 12, 1862. Chase found his desk at the Treasury piled with documents requiring his immediate attention. More individuals than usual were crowded into the anterooms. Congress was in session. The financial committees of both Houses were considering comprehensive legislation to deal with what seemed to be the neverending fiscal crisis. Despite these demands on his time and energy, Chase continued to involve himself with Stanton and Lincoln in military affairs.

When Stonewall Jackson struck at the divided Union armies in the Shenandoah Valley, defeating Banks and moving on Harpers Ferry, whose fall could well open up Washington to attack, Lincoln halted the move of McDowell's corps to reinforce McClellan and ordered him to support the beleaguered Banks. Buoyed up by the Norfolk adventure the President had decided to coordinate the Union armies in the Valley by telegraphing specific orders to their commanders. His objective was to cut off Jackson and force his surrender. Chase participated in these strategic and tactical discussions. He was just as enthusiastic as Lincoln on a plan of action, which looked good on the maps and charts and estimates of troop strength that were available at the War Department.

The fact that their ideas about concentrating forces against Jackson did not take into account such problems as moving armies over difficult terrain or the competence of the generals involved, three of whom were not professional officers, did not deter their enthusiasm.[1] It was all to no avail. Jackson made the correct assumptions and retreated far more rapidly than the opposing forces could concentrate and cut him off.[2]

For some time Chase had been skeptical about McClellan's capabilities, but as Lincoln was unwilling to replace the general, he urged that additional troops be sent to him. At the same time, it seemed not only logical but eminently practical to Chase that McDowell's corps, enlarged by the forces that missed bagging Jackson, should proceed overland from the Valley to menace Richmond and relieve the pressure on McClellan. Lincoln thought otherwise.[3] McClellan was now within five miles of the Confederate capital, his army divided by the Chickahominy River.

Before McDowell could bring his corps to the Peninsula, the Confederate commander Joseph E. Johnston launched a massive offensive. McClellan managed to unite his army and to contain the attack. But the casualties were heavy on both sides. Johnston was badly wounded and Robert E. Lee replaced him. The action known variously as Fair Oaks or Seven Pines was so severe that it shook McClellan's faith in himself. It also impressed Washington. Unfortunately Union forces were so scattered in the Shenandoah Valley and in North and South Carolina that even with the best intentions Washington could not have sent the reinforcements McClellan was demanding.

Lee's first attack on McClellan's divided army was unsuccessful. But for the next week, he hurled his entire force—almost as large as McClellan's—in a series of vicious, costly attacks that drove the Union army back to the James River, where the navy kept open its supply lines.[4] In the last engagement, Malvern Hill, Lee was checked. Had McClellan counterattacked he might have forced the surrender of the Confederate Army and even captured Richmond. McClellan's spirit, however, was temporarily broken and he did not pursue his advantage.[5] Lincoln now accepted Chase's suggestion that the armies in the Valley be consolidated, though not under McDowell. John Pope, the western general who had taken Island Number Ten, was his choice for command of the new force.[6] Chase was not consulted, but he was quick to establish close and cordial relations with Pope.[7]

Until this turn of events Chase had been very much in the picture regarding decisions on high military personnel and movements. And he meant to keep at this way. Soon after Pope's arrival, he and Chase were at the War Department with Lincoln. Maps of eastern Virginia were spread out on a long table. As they examined the locale of McClellan's operations, Chase renewed his complaint about the Peninsula strategy. "What would you do?" asked Lincoln. McClellan's army should be recalled and Washington "made the basis of operations for an overland march. "Order McClellan to return and start right," said Chase. He traced the course he would take with his finger on the map. Obviously influenced by Pope, who had seen much of Chase, the plan would move the new Army of Northern Virginia from Manassas south to the Rappahannock River, where, reinforced by McClellan and by Burnside, the combined force would either crush Lee or capture Richmond, only fifty miles away. Pope remarked that "if Halleck were here, you would have, Mr. President, a competent adviser, who would put this matter right."[8]

Since McClellan's reverses on the Peninsula and McDowell's failure in the Valley, Lincoln, with Stanton a close coadjutor, was beginning to act without first consulting Chase on military decisions. Lincoln took Pope's advice about Halleck seriously, and without mentioning the matter to the Cabinet, he made his one and only trip north during the war to consult with General Scott, who seconded Pope's recommendation. On July 23, Halleck arrived in Washington with the understanding that he would act as overall commander of the armies and as Lincoln's professional counsel on strategy.

Chase learned from the newspapers and from gossip that Halleck had been asked to come to Washington. He thought little of the western commander who had been moving his large army at a glacial pace toward the Confederate stronghold of Corinth, Mississippi. Halleck's campaign reminded Chase of McClellan's massively expensive crawl up the Peninsula. Through his extensive sources of information within the western armies, he was inclined to discount Halleck's claims of credit for the victories of his subordinates. "The war is at a standstill," he wrote Kate, "Halleck is, I am told, invited here. I fear we are to have a repetition of McClellan."[9]

On a warm humid morning of July 22, Chase called on the President and with that masterful bearing he invariably adopted when he was deadly serious about any important question argued that McClellan be sacked. The evening before he had dined with Pope, who after the cloth was removed launched into a diatribe against McClellan. Pope had gained Chase's respect as an aggressive leader. When the expansive general charged that "McClellan's incompetency and indisposition to active movements were so great that if, in his [Pope's] operations, he should need assistance he could not expect it from him."[10]

Lincoln remained silent while Chase spoke against McClellan. Nor did he respond when Chase shifted to his alternate argument that McClellan's inactivity was exacerbating the already acute financial distress. Chase predicted that a change in command of the Army of the Potomac would "insure that, within ten days the bonds of the United States except the five-twenties would be so far above par that conversion into the better stock would take place rapidly." A final plea, almost a threat, came when Chase said that there were already $10 million of unpaid requests and this debt was increasing rapidly.

Obviously, Pope had influenced Chase on the immediate need for change in the top command structure. It seems likely that the general was hoping for command of all the eastern armies if McClellan were relieved. Lincoln no doubt saw through this attempt and was certainly not ready to risk giving a boastful western general of scant strategic and tactical experience command of the Army of the Potomac. Lincoln was aware that McClellan had cultivated a sense of personal loyalty among most of his subordinate commanders, that he was especially trusted by the rank and file. It would not do to make any drastic changes, at least not before he had the professional counsel of Halleck.[11] Lincoln heard Chase out, but to his chagrin made no commitment.

The very next day Halleck arrived in Washington and after conferring with Lincoln left for McClellan's headquarters at Harrison's Landing on the James. On his return to Washington Halleck ordered McClellan to abandon his position and move the Army of the Potomac to Alexandria, just across the Potomac River from the capital.

Chase had several interviews with Halleck, but was unable to penetrate the bland façade that the general customarily employed when he did not want to answer specific questions. Chase was impressed with Halleck's other qualities. His fluency in French, which Chase shared, and his understanding of military history, especially the strategy and tactics of the Napoleonic era, commanded his respect. His sobriquet of "Old Brains," which so many used for derogatory purposes, actually appealed to Chase's intellectual pretensions. But something about the man reinforced his earlier fears that Halleck was simply another McClellan.

Chase warned Halleck that the Treasury was almost $36 million behind its payments to the armed forces and contractors. It was without further resources except Treasury notes, and of these only $50 million remained. Unless there was a forward movement on all fronts, he foresaw great embarrassment in the money markets. He raised the dread possibility of either crushing inflation from successive printing of legal tender currency or even national bankruptcy. Halleck listened to his litany of possible disasters without comment or change of expression, leaving Chase understandably bewildered.[12] There was of course considerable pique on Chase's part because of his increasing exclusion from military planning and decision. "Since Halleck came to Washington," he remarked, "I have known no more of the progress of the war than any outsider. I mean so far as influencing it goes. My recommendations had been before he came in generally disregarded and since have been seldom ventured."[13]

Chase's irritation was evident at the Cabinet meeting held on Sunday, August 3. The subject was emancipation, a question that Lincoln had broached almost a month before. In some exasperation at the inconclusive drift of discussion Chase said that it was his "conviction for the tenth or twentieth time that the time for the suppression of the rebellion without interference with slavery had long passed. . . ."[14]

In the course of his heated comments he unwittingly diverted the attention of the President and his colleagues from the slavery issue to military moves on the Mississippi River.[15] Chase outlined a strategy that would involve the freed black population of the lower South in the military effort. His lecture on strategy meandered into another favorite topic, "the merits of generals," and now his rather acid remarks took on a partisan tinge that was in reality aimed at McClellan and indirectly at Lincoln himself. "I objected pretty strongly," he recalled, "to the policy of selecting nearly all the highest officers from among men hostile to the administration and continuing them in office after they had proved themselves incompetent. . . ."[16]

Nettled by Chase's indictment Seward demanded sharply in his husky voice, what would you do? Chase answered promptly that he would remove McClellan and Buell, another slow mover.[17] Considering the circumstances he would not specify whom he would put in their place. Lincoln had remained silent during the give and take between Seward and Chase. He ended the theorizing by sending for Halleck. When the new general-in-chief came into the Cabinet room, he must have appeared almost a caricature of the professional soldier turned lawyer that he was. But he impressed all, even the doubting Chase, with his calm and knowledgeable account of army manpower and distribution.

On being questioned further he made succinct recommendations on raising troops that included a military draft. He suggested that a selection board be organized to evaluate objectively all subsequent appointments of high military officers. Chase was dismayed at Halleck's recommendation that it was expedient to retain McClellan and Buell in their respective commands. What really upset him, though, was Halleck's response to Lincoln's query about the military potential of black population along the southern reaches of the Mississippi. "I confess," replied Halleck, pursing his mouth and rubbing his elbows, a nervous habit, "I do not think much of the negro."[18]

Given his political and moral precepts, sense of order, personal ambition, and confidence in himself it was not surprising that Chase should have deplored the military situation as Halleck saw it. He gave vent to his feelings in a letter to James Hamilton. "What I think ought to be done is so generally left undone," he said, "and what I think ought not to be done so generally done that I am led to doubt the value of my views on any subject."[19]

The next two weeks seemed to confirm Chase's cynical analysis. McClellan's slow evacuation and his regrouping of his army, and his apparent tardiness in reinforcing Pope as that impetuous and confused commander sought to grapple with Lee's host on the old Bull Run battlefield drove Chase to near distraction.[20] In concert with an equally distraught Stanton on Saturday afternoon, August 31, after receiving the news that Pope's army had been defeated and was falling back on the Washington defenses, both men were shocked to the depths of their very being. With some evidence that the day might have been saved if McClellan's army had come to Pope's rescue in time, they decided that the Cabinet had to force Lincoln's hand. At Chase's prodding Stanton drafted a document for Lincoln that rehearsed briefly McClellan's defects and called for his immediate dismissal. After both signed it Chase agreed to secure signatures from other Cabinet members.[21]

Late that afternoon he appeared at the Navy Department as Welles was about to leave for home. He handed the paper to the waspish secretary, who read it carefully. Peering at Chase through his reading glasses Welles said he was not prepared to sign the document, that he preferred a different method of meeting the question." Welles remarked that if the President should ask him what should be done with McClellan he would recommend his removal from command. Chase disputed the point. He said that "the cabinet must act with energy and promptitude for either the government or McClellan must go down." Welles asked if Bates and Blair had seen the document or been consulted. "Not yet," said Chase, "their turn had not come."[22] Neither Welles nor Chase alluded to Seward, who was out of town at the time.[23]

The next day, when the full dimensions of Pope's defeat became obvious, Chase again sought out Welles and presented him with another draft of the protest, this one written by Attorney General Bates. Chase had signed it and so had Stanton, Smith, and Bates. Spaces had been included for Welles and Blair but not Seward.

Welles found this draft "an improvement and less exceptionable."[24] But he again refused to sign it, citing that it was disrespectful to the President, an attempt to control him or bring down the administration at a time when it was most vulnerable. Chase denied that this was the case. He was less obtrusive than he had been the day before and in fact agreed with some of Welles's comments. He added, however: "Conversations amounted . . . to but little with the President on subjects of this importance. Argument was useless. It was like throwing water on a duck's back. A more decisive expression must be made and that in writing."[25]

Chase could not conceal his disappointment. He would not ask Blair until the others had been consulted. He made no mention of Seward.[26] The regular Cabinet meeting that met at noon the next day was a tense affair not just because of the Bull Run disaster but because Lincoln informed those present that he with Halleck's agreement had placed McClellan in command of Pope's shattered army. "McClellan knew this whole ground well," said

Lincoln,"his specialty is to defend; he is a good engineer, all admit; there is no better organizer; he can be trusted to act on the defensive; but he is troubled with the slows. . . ."

In their attempt to force Lincoln's hand and cashier McClellan, Chase and Stanton had been placed in a most awkward, if not humiliating position with their colleagues and, as they thought, with Lincoln, when word leaked out about their intrigue as they were certain it would. Actually no evidence exists that Smith, Chase, Bates, or Welles ever went to the President with this damning information. If any of them did, Lincoln took no notice of it.

Apart from the two schemers, every member of the Cabinet—even Blair—was cast down by the rush of events. Blair was especially hard on Pope, whom he had known "intimately" for years and whom he said "was a braggart and a liar, with some courage perhaps but not much capacity." All felt that McClellan and his coterie of generals had not sustained the hapless Pope with his large and experienced army. Chase spoke up, "earnestly and emphatically," that McClellan's reinstatement would prove a "national calamity."[27] Later, on September 4, Pope himself appeared before the President and Cabinet and read his report which was more of an indictment of McClellan and his generals than an account of the Bull Run engagements.

After the general left the room, everyone decided that the report must be suppressed. Publication would surely cause, in Welles's words, "war among the generals, who are now more ready to fight each other than the enemy."[28] More important, it would have a most unfortunate effect on the public, particularly now that McClellan was again in charge of the eastern army. McDowell, to Chase's dismay, was also relieved of command because of his failure to handle his force properly.

The Bull Run disaster, the heavy losses with no appreciable gain, excited extremely sharp criticism from the press and from the politicians. The Democratic papers of New York City, while applauding McClellan, mounted scathing attacks on the administration and especially upon Pope, McDowell, and Stanton. McDowell was a Chase protégé and in addition Chase felt a keen responsibility for his role in bringing Stanton into the Cabinet. For these reasons Chase wrote a series of letters to influential New Yorkers defending both individuals. He insisted that McDowell was "a loyal, brave, truthful, capable officer who never drinks, or smokes or chews or indulges in any kind of licence." Chase admitted that McDowell was "too indifferent in manner," but this personality problem, he concluded, should not detract from his military capabilities.[29]

As for Stanton, the victim of a storm of abuse, Chase wrote Horace Greeley a letter whose substance he obviously hoped would be the subject of an editorial. "He has faults like other men, but his energy has been all important," he said. "Mr. Stanton's voice has ever been on the side of the most vigorous and active employment of *all* our resources, moral and political as well as physical." In an explanation of the military reverses, Chase saw the hand of Providence because of "our complicity in crime against his poor" (the slaves and blacks everywhere).[30]

Chase had found it a distasteful necessity to utilize whatever influence he possessed to support an administration under severe attack from many quarters. He had for some time believed the President to be a failure as a chief executive whose lack of firm control violated most of his deeply held instincts for proper management and specific consultation with his Cabinet. More recently he censured his lack of judgment in the selection of military commanders. Yet with all his perceived shortcomings, Lincoln must be sustained at least until the military and the financial horizons had cleared sufficiently to see eventual if not speedy success.

Chase had involved himself in military affairs at least in part because of the financial impact of military demands and the defeatist psychology which he knew gripped the business communities reacting to battlefield reverses. But it took much more than a public relations effort to meet the constantly escalating costs of the war. Chase and his supporters in Congress had been through a bruising interlude as they grappled for the means of supporting the war economy. The creaky deposit and remittance system that depended on hard money and the banking institutions had collapsed with the suspension of specie payments. Chase had no recourse but to follow the bankers' lead and prohibit coin payments except on the interest of outstanding bonds. Now the only funds available for the government to meet military obligations were the rapidly dwindling Treasury notes and insignificant cash reserves received from customs duties, income taxes, and excise receipts.

Chase had foreseen some of these problems and made recommendations in his first annual report to Congress. He had sketched the formation of a national banking system, but suspension necessitated additional emergency measures. Still unwilling for political reasons to recommend a sharp increase in taxation, as the New York bankers wanted, Chase came very reluctantly to the favorite expedient of governments faced with overwhelming financial deficits: the circulation of fiat currency known variously as legal tender notes or greenbacks. Elbridge Spaulding of Ways and Means, the Buffalo banker and a strong advocate of such currency to meet immediate demands, acted as a powerful influence on softening Chase's hard-money beliefs.

"It is true," wrote Chase on February 3, 1862, "that I came with reluctance to the conclusion that legal tender . . . is a necessity, but I came to it decidedly, and I support it earnestly."[31] In order to give the legal tenders more substance and provide a market for the new 5–20 bonds (redeemable after 5 years, maturing at 20) whose interest at 6 percent was paid in coin, the bill made them convertible at par. Strong opposition to the proposed legislation, especially from hard-money Democrats, appeared at once. Some but not all powerful bankers saw the issues inflationary, and combined with Chase's proposal for a National Banking Act, a potential destroyer of their profitable note issues under state law. And finally there were those strict constructionists who saw in the measure a menace to individual economic freedom.[32]

Once Chase had made up his mind, he acted vigorously to expedite the legal tender clause written into the overall financial bill that he, Harrington, and others at the Treasury had drafted.[33] On February 6, he wrote Ohio congressman John A. Bingham that the $150 million issue of greenbacks was "a matter not merely of expediency but of vital necessity." It would take a least a week if the bill became law before the bills could be engraved, printed, and put into circulation. The troops were already several months behind in pay and many contractors had sold their certificates of indebtedness at 2 to 3 percent discounts.[34]

Where Chase was willing to let expediency rule, many members of Congress were not despite the Treasury's efforts to make open-market purchases of certificates of indebtedness a deflationary move.[35] The House Ways and Means Committee, which had charge of the proposed legislation, was deadlocked. Eventually one member was brought over to favor the bill, which was then reported to the House. There, a full-scale debate raged for several weeks. Opponents argued that the bill was an unconstitutional exercise of power not specifically enumerated; that the economy would be ruined and the people, especially the soldiers and sailors, defrauded as had been the case during the American and French revolutions; and that convertibility to 5–20 bonds gave an advantage to speculators and moneylenders that was not available to the poorer classes and especially the military.

Deeply involved as he was in military matters and in the delicate negotiations for replacement of Cameron at the War Department, Chase still played an important role in supporting Elbridge G. Spaulding, Samuel Hooper, and Thaddeus Stevens in the House and William P. Fessenden and John Sherman in the Senate. Besides personal lobbying at his home, Chase made the bill an administration measure, a move that gained support of many doubters not just in Congress but in the editorial chairs of the major metropolitan dailies.[36] Chase also had to contend with the banking communities in New York, Boston, and Philadelphia. A group of these opponents headed by Gallatin rushed to Washington, where they presented a plan of their own that they felt would obviate the need for legal tender. The plan featured much heavier taxation and another large issue and sale of bonds at market not par value with receipts going directly to the banks not through the subtreasuries.

Chase arranged for a meeting of the concerned bankers with members of the House and Senate finance committees, though, as he said at a later date, "I fear he [Gallatin] looks to me as an incorrigible financial sinner."[37] Spaulding took the lead in declaring that the legal tender clause was an absolute necessity and that the bankers' plan was simply, as he put it, a means of placing the government's credit at the mercy of Wall Street, "to 'shin' through the shaving shops of New York, Boston and Philadelphia."[38] Chase agreed with the plain-speaking Buffalo banker and lent his impressive weight to the argument. The government was behind in payments to the military and contractors, a floating debt that was estimated at anywhere between $80 to $180 million.[39] It did not occur to him at the time, but this floating debt actually profited the government since it acted as a non-interest-bearing, non-redeemable forced loan.[40]

Meanwhile, Spaulding had separated the legal tender clause from the finance bill and in this form it passed both House and Senate and was signed into law on February 25, 1862. The act provided for the issue of $150 million of greenbacks in notes of $5 or more. Of this sum, $60 million would be used to retire the demand notes that Chase had used as a temporary means of discharging the government's obligations. The Congress also approved the issuance of up to $500 million in 5–20 bonds that paid interest of 6 percent in coin redeemable in not less than five years or more than twenty years from issuance.[41]

By June, McClellan's frightfully expensive Peninsula campaign as well as increased military activity in the west had drained the first issue of greenbacks. The floating debt was again registering an ominously rapid rise. Complaints from military commanders about arrears in pay were pouring into Congress and the Treasury Department.[42] Chase responded rather testily to the House Resolution on the lag in military pay. He accused Congress of not promptly passing legislation he had recommended in his annual report. "No one can feel a deeper regret than the Secretary," he wrote the Speaker of the House, "that a single American soldier lacks a single dollar of his pay but means for funding the war adequately had not as yet been provided by law."[43]

This time Chase took the leadership in pushing for a second Legal Tender Act.[44] Experience over the past six months had shown that the issuance of greenbacks had not dramatically driven up prices on commodities. Convertibility which Chase and other conservative monetarists had thought would sop up greenbacks as monied interests would exchange them for 5–20 bonds at par had not worked at all. Financiers preferred to purchase other securities or gold in the open market with their greenbacks instead of government bonds while the fate of the Union was yet undecided.[45]

Chase continued to back convertibility, but not as law, rather as administration policy. "Convertibility," he wrote Cooke, "is good and necessary, but it should be administered not legislated." Since greenbacks were receivable for all loans made by the government as well as all taxes except customs duty, Chase saw no need for an explicit convertibility clause that tied greenbacks to a fixed position in terms of gold. In fact such a clause, he argued, would depress the market price of government bonds.[46] Congress, however, would not agree.[47]

But greenbacks at the same time had placed the Treasury in a reasonably good position with all audited claims paid and a favorable balance of about $13 million.[48] In the Congress, too, predictions about the dire consequences of greenbacks had not materialized. There was less heated debate over Chase's request for another $150 million issue of legal tender currency. Of this sum Chase requested the authority to issue $35 million in currency subject to the five- dollar-note limit. Since the suspension of specie payments, metallic coins had virtually disappeared. In order to make change there had been a run on postage stamps. Chase proposed that this inconvenience be met by the issuance of fractional currency in small denominations.[49] The second Legal Tender Act became law on July 11. Six days later at Chase's behest, fractional currency for payment of 50, 25, and 10 cents was authorized.[50] Congress had been reasonably amenable to Chase's financial policies thus far. He and his lieutenants in the House and Senate had put up a good fight. Much rhetoric had been expended, but the financing bills the Treasury proposed had been approved with substantial majorities and not on partisan or regional lines.

The one important piece of legislation that Chase regarded as the keystone to his financial program had not fared so well. This was a national banking system, or Associated Banks, as Chase had dubbed it. The bill had been reported from the House Ways and Means Committee, but encountered heavy opposition.[51] State banking lobbyists managed to kill the proposed legislation. They had been unable to thwart a 1 to 2 percent tax the Congress levied at Chase's request on their notes, however, which made it harder for their issues to compete against greenbacks or fractional currency or Treasury notes that were circulating.[52]

Meanwhile, the collapse of the Peninsula campaign, Pope's bloody defeat at the Bull Run battlefield, and the even more bloody battle of Antietam had so shaken the financial markets that greenbacks had fallen in terms of gold more than 30 percent with a corresponding increase in the dread specter of inflation.[53] The Treasury was again piling up an even more troublesome deficit, and payments to the military and to contractors were again lagging far behind.[54]

Chase had been unable to market the new 5–20 bond issue in any sufficient quantities to furnish his immediate needs. He was preparing three significant measures. One was the oft-proposed national bank system which he hoped would force the banking community to accept government bonds as security for their circulations. Second, he was seeking authority to sell bonds at the market without the par restriction. Third, he was drafting a Treasury order that would empower Jay Cooke as the Treasury's sole general agent to sell bonds not just to banks and other business enterprises but to the people in another national campaign.[55]

Several reasons explain the decline in greenback value. One was the seemingly constant demand for more troops. The drawn battle of Antietam, so costly in human lives, was inconclusive. State drafts were seen as inevitable and looked upon as the harbinger of a federal draft. The preliminary Emancipation Proclamation issued on September 22 caused many to believe that the war would be prolonged, an argument advanced by the Democratic press just as election campaigns in several important states were getting under way. These factors all combined to create a scare psychology which impacted on the skittish money market.

chapter 23

Emancipation with Exceptions

Though Chase would never admit it, emancipation was not that popular among the northern masses or conservative business communities. However he might discount the factor of racism, however he might scorn the fulminations of the New York *World* as partisan propaganda, he could not entirely dismiss the apparent upsurge of the Democratic party. Leading Democrats and their presses had seized upon emancipation as foreclosing any peaceful settlement of the conflict. And they used the implications of eventual equality among the races as a promising topic to drum up racist fears and a latent anti-abolitionist bias.

Chase's blindness to the connection between the failure to merchandize bonds and the Emancipation Proclamation was to be expected. Moral issues and economic problems were usually kept distinct from each other in his way of thinking. He did believe however that a temporary rally in the price of government bonds during October had resulted from the proclamation. This judgment turned out to be faulty.[1] Emancipation had been on his mind during much of his public career. He had seen it as an aspect of moral suasion to be carried out through state action that harmonized human freedom with Jeffersonian states' rights. Nevertheless he applauded Lincoln's action in the matter. Indeed, he had long considered the President to be a laggard in what he believed to be a matter of fundamental human concern.

Emancipation, compensated or otherwise, had been considered in Congress since the final weeks of the Buchanan administration. But the subject really came to the fore during the debates over the Confiscation Act during the second session of the Thirty-seventh Congress. The President had led off on March 6, 1862, when he recommended to Congress gradual emancipation with compensation. Chase was pleased at the action the Congress and the President took a few weeks later emancipating the slaves in the District of Columbia.[2] Efforts to make emancipation a part of the second Confiscation Act were repeatedly brought up in Congress and, with the exception of slaves liberated from rebel masters, repeatedly rejected.[3] The act delegated powers of enforcement to the President, who had been most concerned about the clause that liberated slaves. Still fearful of its impact on the border slave states, Lincoln's course on that particular issue was so tentative as to make some of its provisions virtually dead letters. In the bill of particulars Chase was building up against what he considered conservative influences surrounding the President, his policy on emancipation through confiscation claimed an important place.[4]

Earlier, Chase had been troubled when Lincoln revoked General David Hunter's proclamation freeing slaves under his control in the coastal areas of South Carolina, Georgia, and Florida. Chase had a special interest in that morose and querulous general, whose abolition views he found compatible with his own and whose new Department of the South controlled the Sea Islands where Chase's experiment of education, training, and land ownership for the blacks was just getting under way.[5]

Undeterred, Chase hoped that a course similar to Hunter's would prevail in the parishes under Union army control in Louisiana.[6] Yet whenever the subject was brought up at subsequent Cabinet meetings Lincoln had been in Gideon Welles's words "prompt and emphatic in denouncing any interference by the general government" in emancipation, which he and in fact all of the Cabinet, even Chase, believed to be a matter for the states.[7] Finally on July 13, despite bad news from the Peninsula as McClellan completed his withdrawal, Lincoln broached the subject of emancipation to Seward and Welles. The fact that Lincoln took Welles and Seward into his confidence on such a momentous decision and not Chase or Stanton, whom he knew were flirting with radical elements in Congress, or Blair, Bates, and Smith, arch-conservatives on the issue, was not lost on the two Cabinet members as events unfolded during the next fortnight.[8]

On Monday, July 21, a messenger appeared at Chase's home with a note from the White House calling a Cabinet meeting at ten o'clock. Since this was a Monday, not the formal Cabinet day, it struck Chase as unusual and he hastened to keep the appointment.[9] As soon as all had appeared, Lincoln said that he had prepared several executive orders, which he then read. They were four in number and all dealt in one way or another with provisions of the second Confiscation Act, though Lincoln had added compensation for slaves to be freed and colonization, both long-held personal convictions.

Chase objected to the order on confiscation of rebel property and the employment of freed blacks—on the grounds of expediency in keeping proper accounts—and also to the colonization order. At this point Stanton read letters from General David Hunter, who wanted to enlist, train, and arm blacks. He had backed up his request on the grounds that he had been stripped of troops to reinforce McClellan and his command was thus left in a perilous position unless he could recruit black manpower. Lincoln cut off any discussion of this subject, but he did say emphatically that he was opposed to arming blacks.[10]

The next day the Cabinet met at its scheduled time and at once began further discussion of the executive orders. Everyone including the President agreed to cancel the colonization order. Otherwise with minor changes the orders were approved. When Hunter's request came up for discussion Chase favored arming liberated slaves as a military necessity. Lincoln listened patiently to the passionate utterance of his otherwise imperturbable secretary, but calmly rejected his argument. Adjusting his glasses, Lincoln then read from papers he had before him. He proposed to issue a proclamation based on the Confiscation Act that called for the insurrectionary states to return to the Union, warning them that "the provisions of the act would have full force at the expiration of sixty days." Along with this provision he included his recommendation of gradual compensation for the abolition of slavery. Until now there had been nothing startling in these draft orders, but then Lincoln's reading came to an arresting conclusion—emancipation "of all slaves within states remaining in insurrection on the first of January 1863."[11]

Even Seward and Welles, who knew that the President was planning some sort of emancipation, were amazed at the scope of this draft. Chase was the first to recover his composure and warmly seconded Lincoln's proposal. As usual he had suggestions. He wanted to couple emancipation with enlisting and arming the freedmen. Military command could accomplish both objectives, he said, "more quietly . . . (thus avoiding depredation and massacre on the one hand and support to the insurrection on the other.)" Stanton, who had expected that the President would clarify the orders he had read the previous day, was as astonished as any. "The measure goes beyond anything I have recommended," he jotted down on a piece of note paper as he waited for his turn to speak. When it came he urged that all the orders be promulgated immediately. Bates, the inveterate conservative in the Cabinet, surprised everyone by agreeing with Stanton. Then Seward spoke up. As Stanton recorded the Secretary of State's remarks: he "argues that foreign nations will intervene to prevent abolition of slavery for the sake of cotton—argues in a long speech against its immediate promulgation—wants to wait for troops. Wants Halleck here. Wants drum and fife and public spirit. We break up our relations with foreign nations and the production of cotton for sixty years."[12]

Stanton's notes were surely biased, because Seward's comments had substance. Public opinion in general, despite radical fulminations in the Congress, was not as yet prepared for such a dramatic change while the military situation was still in the balance. Even Chase's suggestion of giving the generals the power to proclaim emancipation over areas they controlled recognized at least in part this potent factor.[13] After a talk with Thurlow Weed that evening, no doubt at Seward's behest, the President decided to pigeonhole his draft orders and await the logic of events.[14]

Chase, Seward, and Weed were correct in opposing immediate emancipation by proclamation from Washington at this time. As Seward maintained, emancipation without a significant military victory would be looked upon as a sign of weakness. Faced with a concrete measure that would accomplish something more than the rhetoric of a lifetime, Chase flinched. He thought the emancipation Lincoln contemplated to be "a measure of great danger and would lead to universal emancipation," which would have possibly a devastating effect on the government's fiscal policy.[15]

For the moment Chase clung to his idea of piecemeal emancipation and of an army of black troops under military discipline that would rationalize over the long term the principle of freedom for all and advance the idea of equality of the races. It would assist in reducing the looming shortage of military manpower, and thus hold off an impending federal draft that would be unpopular. Seward's position of delay, which it was soon learned stayed the President's hand, was seen by Chase as just another example of the little secretary's baneful influence. Yet as a pragmatist and a logical thinker Chase had to agree that the military position had to be stronger than it was to issue any kind of emancipation proclamation. As a politician he must hedge his bets on a possible McClellan victory. He had not long to wait.

Chase could not have been surprised from preliminary information that McClellan had finally met Lee at Antietam in Maryland and, inured to the losses on the Peninsula, fought a terrible battle with extremely heavy casualties. He was also prepared to expect that while McClellan claimed a victory, he did not follow it up with an attack the following day. Lee's invasion failed and he had been forced from the field but he had not been defeated.[16] On Monday, September 22, a State Department messenger handed Chase a note informing him of a special Cabinet meeting at noon.

All Cabinet members were present at the White House and all, concerned that the meeting was an urgent one, were in a serious mood. Lincoln, in an effort to cheer up his colleagues, opened the session by reading to them a humorous chapter from one of Artemas Ward's books entitled "A High

Handed Outrage in Uticky." When he finished he laughed heartily, as did all present, except Stanton.

Then the President adopted a graver tone when he said that he was about to proclaim emancipation of the slaves in the rebel states. "I think the time has come now," he said. "I wish it were a better time. I wish that we were in a better condition. The action of the army against the rebels has not been quite what I would have best liked. But they have been driven out of Maryland and Pennsylvania is no longer in danger of invasion." He would accept changes in the style of the document he held in his hand, but nothing of substance. The act and the consequences were his, he alone was responsible, he said, before reading the document to his solemn group of advisors. As he came to what he considered a key phrase, he paused and commented on it, an elaboration that indicated to all that he had thoroughly canvassed the subject. The Proclamation owed much of its content to the Confiscation Act, which he in fact quoted, to his oft-repeated idea of compensation, and much more to the draft that he had read to the Cabinet in July.

Based on military necessity as expressed in the Second Confiscation Act and on his position as Commander-in-Chief of the Union's armed forces, emancipation would take place on January 1, 1863, in those states and parts of states still in rebellion. Lincoln made no mention of the Proclamation applying to loyal slave states and those areas where the Union army was in control. When he finished his reading he invited opinion.

Seward had one or two suggestions on colonization, to which everyone agreed. Chase remarked that the President's course was not just as he would recommend, but without going into particulars said that he was ready to accept the document as written, "and to stand by it with all my heart." Blair said that the question having been decided, he would make no objection. But he feared that it would have an adverse impact on the border states and on the army. Bates had similar comments.[17]

The Preliminary Emancipation was published the next day. There was some carping in the press and from radical members of Congress, but the reaction among Republicans of every shade ranged from supportive to enthusiastic. Horace Greeley, who had bitterly attacked Lincoln's previous hesitations on emancipation, did not accuse him of hypocrisy. But Greeley did quibble in subsequent editorials about emancipation of slaves where they could not be freed and keeping them in bondage where they could be freed.[18]

On the day the Proclamation was published, throngs of citizens and military alike with an impromptu band serenaded the President and then moved on to Chase's home. John Hay joined them. After listening to remarks from Chase and Cassius Clay, he joined what he called "a few old fogies" who were served wine. In conversation with Hay, Chase made some very pregnant comments. "This," he said, "was a most wonderful history of an insanity of a class that the world had ever seen. If the slave holders had stayed in the Union they might have kept the life in their institution for many years to come."[19]

The eight weeks that followed Antietam confirmed Chase's low estimate of McClellan, who seemed to be following his usual policy of demanding more troops and remaining on the defensive. Feeling as he did, Chase was attracted to one of McClellan's corps commanders, Joseph Hooker, a Massachusetts-born West Pointer who like Halleck had emigrated to California where he had proven to be an excellent farm manager and businessman.

Hooker had distinguished himself as a courageous and dynamic commander in McClellan's Peninsula campaign and in Pope's disastrous defeat at Bull Run. But Chase was really impressed with Hooker's conduct at Antietam, where he earned the sobriquet "Fighting Joe Hooker." In the thick of that murderous engagement on the right of McClellan's line Hooker had received a slight flesh wound which hospitalized him in Washington. He seemed to Chase just the kind of general officer he sought to replace McClellan. A handsome, florid-faced man, Hooker, though approaching middle age, had just been commissioned a brigadier general. Chase ignored or overlooked rumors of Hooker's casual lifestyle and his fondness for liquor. It was his aggressive spirit and his following among the men of his command that Chase found compelling.

He hastened to pay a visit to Hooker, who was convalescing at an insane asylum that had been converted into a military hospital. He took Katie and the young, stalwart Ohio colonel and congressman-elect James A. Garfield, a house guest, with him. Kate had put together a basket of grapes, peaches, and other delicacies for the general. They found Hooker lying on a couch but in no pain. His physician assured Chase that he would be ready for active duty within a few days.

Though Chase gave him several leads, Hooker was cautious and would not openly indict McClellan. Disappointed at Hooker's reticence, Chase found "somewhat less breadth of intellect than I had expected. . . ."[20] After two more visits from Chase and Garfield, Hooker became freer in his comments. He now criticized McClellan roundly and at the same time boosted his own competence. Accordingly Chase's estimate of Hooker rose appreciably and when he came away from his third visit, he was ready to push the voluble general as McClellan's successor.[21]

Chase was also impressed with Garfield, whom he had known as an antislavery member of the Ohio legislature during his governorship. He learned much more about the big, handsome colonel's background—his harsh struggle against poverty, his educational and intellectual attainments, and especially his strong religious faith—during many conversations in the morning after early breakfasts and in the evenings when both busy men relaxed at home.[22] Chase thought Garfield marked for great things. He made every effort to encourage the younger man and to assure him that he would always be his friend at court. In return, though this was unspoken, Chase had an able, rising politician and military man who would provide him with yet another communication link to whatever army command he joined.

Chase's visits to Hooker were made in anticipation of McClellan's eventual removal. He would be ready when that time came to propose his replacement. Not fifteen days after Antietam, he again climbed the stairs to Gideon Welles's office in the Navy Department. He confronted the navy secretary with a long complaint which masked rather superficially another attempt to force the President's hand by a concerted move of the Cabinet. Chase said that he had "unpaid requisitions on his table at this time of $45 million" for the War Department alone. He added that Stanton was ready to resign, which Welles doubted. "If Stanton went," said Chase with magisterial solemnity, "[he] would go." "Things were serious," Chase remarked with much feeling, "that [he] could not stand it, that the army was crushing [him] and would crush the country." Chase blamed the situation on the fact that the President would consult only with army officers, "though the treasury, and navy ought to be informed." Welles agreed with Chase on that point but kept his own counsel.[23]

As the clear, dry Indian summer faded away with no forward move from McClellan, the pressure increased on Lincoln from almost all Republican factions in Congress and much of the metropolitan press, including even the *New York Times,* a staunch defender of the administration. On November 5, Chase learned that Lincoln had removed McClellan and appointed Ambrose Burnside to the chief command. Lincoln's move was taken without consulting either Stanton or Chase. The choice had narrowed down to Hooker or Burnside.

The senior man Burnside was less controversial in the army than Hooker, whose antipathy toward McClellan was now well known. Chase, however, saw in the Burnside appointment another example of an inferior, less aggressive officer supplanting a better commander. He had been consulted on the removal of the western commander Buell and his replacement by Rosecrans, another of his military protégés. But the Burnside appointment, coming as it did when all signs pointed to Republican defeat in the fall elections, was a further irritant to Chase's abundant amour propre.

He was now spending more of his precious time in complaints to congressional friends about the conduct of the war. He was careful, however, in his criticisms. Typically he balanced his damning with faint praise. He enlarged on the burdens of his office yet at the same time implied Lincoln to be a slow, irresolute executive whose Cabinet, when consulted—which was infrequent—was not a harmonious unit on policy matters.

Chase singled out Seward as largely responsible for this state of affairs.

The President meant to do well, but Seward muffled his good intentions with his compromising conservatism. Some of Chase's soft impeachments which he spread among his radical friends in Congress were close to the mark. The Cabinet did not act as a council of state on all matters. It was a coalition group to begin with. The trials and toils the war brought on had emphasized its latent differences rather than its fragile unity. Divided on politics, divided on the causes of the war, divided on Reconstruction after the war, which was now coming to the fore, and deeply suspicious of each other, Cabinet members were such an uncongenial group it is no wonder that Lincoln avoided meeting with them collectively except at the more or less pro-forma Tuesday and Saturday sessions.

The Cabinet officers courted their own special interest groups in Congress. And of these Chase was the most conspicuous in his lobbying for financial measures and in his dislike and distrust of Seward. He was building himself up in a subtle fashion to achieve a position of control in the Cabinet and with that the control of a "weak" President.[24]

The onward rush of events seemed to confirm Chase's plans and deepen, if that were possible, his suspicion of Seward. Pope's defeat, the timely absence of Seward from Washington in its aftermath, and the reinstatement of McClellan seemed to Chase and Stanton more evidence of Seward's complicity. The evidence was circumstantial but the coincidences were sufficiently marked for them to incite a near rebellion in the Cabinet which would have sorely weakened the war effort and the Union cause.

Lincoln must have known about the deep divisions among his closest councilors. He could have eased the situation if he had been more frank with men such as Chase and Blair and Stanton in his perception of their respective importance to his administration and their personal feelings. But Lincoln was a politician, too. He was presiding over a coalition government. He expected, if he did not condone, rivalries within his Cabinet. And he appreciated hearing about their divergent views on the conduct of the war, the problems of peace, of emancipation, of Reconstruction, as essential elements in developing his own careful policy.

Like any human being Lincoln had his personal likes and dislikes. Seward appealed to him personally. He enjoyed Seward's breezy anecdotes, his easy camaraderie, and his penchant for small talk, and he understood the underlying strength of the little New Yorker in his conduct of foreign policy. Moreover he felt he could count on Seward's loyalty, something he doubted in other members except Welles and probably Blair. That Seward spoke for many though not all moderate and conservative Republican members of Congress was also an important factor in their close relationship.

The President was so overworked, so riveted to the military situation and its political impact that he was not able to give much of his attention to Cabinet intriguers, even if he had wanted to. As for Seward, he was a likely target for mistrust and jealousy. He had an arrogant, egotistical, and selfish side to his personality. He was given to grandiose pronouncements, many of which hurt his public image. Secretive and expansive by turns, he fancied himself the arbiter of the administration.

His pretensions, presumptions, and taste for intrigue, going back thirty years when he shared with Van Buren and Silas Wright dominance on the political stage in New York, the most populous and wealthiest state in the Union, had gained him a host of enemies. His close connection with that supreme fixer Thurlow Weed made him and his ways personally reprehensible to many. Even those who granted him high marks for his ability to unravel complex political, diplomatic, and administrative problems were distrustful of his political gamesmanship.

With these crosscurrents operating, the Burnside appointment came as another dubious enterprise to the Cabinet and especially Chase, weighted down as he was with the immense burdens of directing the finances of the nation safely through uncharted ways. When Burnside's disastrous defeat at Fredericksburg occurred in December 1862, its repercussions were felt throughout the North. Radicals in Congress, already deeply suspicious of Seward, demanded not just an accounting from the Secretary of State but his removal.

Republican senators after several caucuses raised a committee of nine under the chairmanship of the venerable Jacob Collamer, who was approaching his seventy-second birthday. Primarily friends of Chase, the committee had a radical tinge.[25] All except Wade had heard Chase's grumbling about the conduct of the war and his indictment of Seward, whom he declared to be "a backstairs influence which often controlled the apparent conclusions of the cabinet itself." The most severe arraignment at the caucuses, though, was not of Seward but of the President himself and it came from one of Chase's strongest supporters in the Senate, John Sherman.[26] Collamer had drawn up a series of resolutions calling for a partial reconstruction of the Cabinet, which the committee approved. Then he requested an interview for the committee with the President. Lincoln had learned about the caucuses. He agreed to see the committee at seven in the evening of December 19.[27] Fearing a possible collapse of the government and the want of confidence in him, Lincoln was more upset than he had been during the Sumter crisis.[28] But no one on the committee could have known his inner tensions when they met him at the appointed hour. He was cordial and seemed relaxed when Collamer presented him with the resolutions. After reading them he invited each senator in turn to comment.[29]

For three hours the meeting went on, as each member complained about the direction of the war effort. Seward was singled out for a special indictment. Lincoln did more listening than speaking though he did offer some specifics on the administration's reinstatement of McClellan. He did not react to the charges against Seward.[30] When the senators left, though emotionally drained Lincoln quickly formed his strategy. He sent out word for a special Cabinet meeting at half past ten the next morning.

All were present except Seward, who had been informed of the caucus and committee proceedings and had sent in his resignation to the President. There were no humorous stories, no jokes this time. Lincoln outlined what had transpired and hoped that there would be, in Welles's words, "no combined movement on the part of other members of the cabinet to resist this assault, whatever might be the termination." After some brief remarks from Bates, Blair, and Stanton, Lincoln asked that the Cabinet meet with him and the committee that evening. Chase, who had been silent up to this point, rather lamely tried to excuse himself from the conference. But since all of his colleagues supported the President he perforce had to go along. It was clear to all that Chase was embarrassed by a possible confrontation.

Without mentioning that the Cabinet would be there, Lincoln sent word to Collamer that he would like another meeting at the White House at 7:30 in the evening. When the senators arrived they were surprised to see Cabinet members in the anteroom. Lincoln himself ushered the committee into his office and asked if there was any objection to having the Cabinet, with the exception of Seward, attend the meeting.[31] There being none, Cabinet members filed in and took seats at the long table.

Lincoln opened the conference with an admission that there had not been regular meetings with all of the Cabinet present because "the necessities of the times had prevented frequent and long sessions." But, he insisted, the Cabinet had always acted as a unit in supporting each and every important policy measure. Welles, a not unbiased witness, said that Lincoln "managed his own case, speaking frankly, and showed great tact, shrewdness and ability."[32] Despite his able presentation, Lincoln was unable to convince four of the senators.[33] They clung to their position that Seward's resignation be accepted.

Lincoln asked each Cabinet member beginning with Chase, as protocol demanded, whether the Cabinet was divided on policy as the committee charged. Lincoln's tactics put Chase at a grave disadvantage and he knew it. With the eyes of all upon him, he said that if he had known "that he was to be arraigned before the committee, he would not have attended." But since he was there he had to admit that "there had been no want of unity in the cabinet, but a general acquiescence on public measures." As best he could he sought to improve his position by complaining that consultations with the Cabinet as a whole were infrequent. After his condemnation of the administration so many times before in unsparing words to the senators who sat before him, they were all flabbergasted and none more so than Chase's friends Fessenden and Collamer.[34] It was not only an uncomfortable but a humiliating experience for one who was not used to being called to account in front of supporters whom he had in effect deceived. Later, when Orville Browning asked Collamer how Chase could have made such statements before the meeting, Collamer replied tartly: "He lied."[35]

The next day, Welles hurried to the White House and urged Lincoln to resist what he considered an unwarranted and unconstitutional invasion of the executive power. He offered to visit Seward and urge him to retract his resignation, an offer Lincoln gratefully accepted.

Welles found Seward mortified and deeply distressed but after explaining the President's position succeeded in his mission. When he returned to the White House, he found Stanton and Chase in the President's office. Lincoln himself appeared a few minutes later. He asked Welles if he "had seen the man." Welles replied he had and that he had "assented to my views."

The President turned to Chase and said, "I sent for you, for this matter is giving me great trouble." Chase explained that he had been "painfully affected by the meeting last evening, which was a total surprise to him." He was prepared to offer his resignation and indeed had written it out and had it with him. "Where is it?" asked Lincoln. Chase took the sealed letter out of his pocket. "Let me have it," said Lincoln abruptly. He snatched the envelope from Chase's hand, tore it open, and scanned its contents. Turning toward Welles, with a laugh of satisfaction he said, "This cuts the Gordian knot. I can dispose of this subject now without difficulty. I see my way clear[;] the trouble is ended." Stanton offered his resignation on the spot. But Lincoln said, "I don't want yours."[36] Chase was obviously disturbed when he left the White House with Welles. At his office he found Lincoln's senior secretary, John G. Nicolay, with a letter from Lincoln addressed to both him and Seward requesting them to take back their resignations and "resume the duties of your Departments respectively."[37]

Realizing that he had lost whatever initiative he had gained over the past three months of covert agitation and receiving a note from Seward that he had rescinded his resignation, Chase still temporized. "I will sleep on it," he replied to Seward. Later in the day a shaken and somewhat repentant Chase sought in another letter to Lincoln to mend his fences and retain his self-confidence but still clung to his shopworn belief that Cabinet disunity was hindering the conduct of the war.

As he had two years before he foolishly kept the President in suspense over the weekend. On Monday, December 22, in a lengthy, self-justifying letter he agreed grudgingly to remain in office. The confrontation which he had so clumsily precipitated seriously damaged Chase's prestige. His radical friends in Congress were now unsure of his probity, while still regarding him as indispensable in the Treasury Department. Had the extravagant praise and the harsh blame Bishop Chase meted out years before brought on his nephew's desperate attempt to achieve great purposes? Could Philander Chase's prophecy about his nephew been pertinent, that "His genius [is] extraordinarily good. If he finds some one to govern and direct him aright"?[38] Or was it the acute frustration of an essentially tidy administrative mind that caused him to forsake loyalty to a chief whom at times he was forced to admire? Ambivalence in such positions of great stress can be fatal in politics and in war. From this time forward Chase's political decline began.

chapter 24

Mixed Results

On an evening in late January 1863 Chase departed from his customary routine of relaxing with a book in his library. Instead he was writing letters at his table and he was in a grim mood, which matched the disagreeable weather outside the window. It had been a month since that ugly interlude in the White House when Lincoln exploded so adroitly the case Chase had been building up against the administration. He still felt acutely the humiliation he had suffered on that occasion. And he was still seeking to justify a stand he believed was correct. If he did not himself write, he certainly encouraged a memorial urging a reconstruction of the Cabinet that had been circulating among radical groups in New York for the past two weeks.[1]

On this particular evening Chase was especially upset. He had just learned that Burnside had relinquished command of the Army of the Potomac and that Hooker had replaced him. Chase had been pushing Hooker for command but when his selection took place, he had not been consulted.[2] Lincoln made the appointment, though not without much soul-searching, on his own responsibility and informed only Halleck and Stanton of his decision.

In Chase's sensitive state, he read more into the omission than was warranted. A sense of exclusion and deep frustration guided his pen as he wrote Bishop McIlvaine. "It is impossible for me to express my anxiety concerning the state of the country," he said, "but my ignorance of the real condition except so far as my own department is concerned is almost as great as my anxiety. Our administration under the President's system, if system it be, is departmental."

Especially goading to Chase were those areas dear to his heart and to his ambition that Lincoln reserved to himself—slavery, military affairs, and patronage. The change in command of the Army of the Potomac without his knowledge was not just a slight deeply felt but to him a prime example of all that was wrong with the administration. "I receive what is thought fit to impart," he complained, "and am left in ignorance of what is thought fit to withhold."[3]

Lincoln and Chase had been testing each other in Louisiana where much of the state's population and wealth which included the city of New Orleans was in Union hands. The President and his ambitious secretary considered the state to be ideal for an experiment in Reconstruction. Upstate well over half of Louisiana's population consisted of small farmers who owned few or no slaves. Before the war the city of New Orleans had been one of the nation's major sea ports. Bound in part by economic ties to the Northwest, it was known to harbor strong Unionist sentiments. Its free black population enjoyed privileges not accorded free blacks throughout the South. Strategically Louisiana as a Union state would, it was thought in Washington, influence the other gulf states of Texas, Alabama, Mississippi, and Florida to loosen their ties to the Confederacy.

Lincoln and Chase were at one on the objective of bringing Louisiana as rapidly as possible into what they regarded as its normal relation with the Union. Where they differed was that Chase wanted a broader construction of the Emancipation Proclamation than the President. In particular he pressed the President whenever he had a chance—and with Chase this was frequent— that the same formula being applied to Virginia be employed in Louisiana.

In the Virginia instance Lincoln construed that those citizens loyal to the Union made up the state and as such had approved the partition which created the new state of West Virginia. Thus their representatives sitting in Alexandria formed the government of Virginia, though it controlled only a modest amount of territory. In response to Lincoln's request on whether the partition of Virginia was constitutional, Chase had said it was. "In every case of insurrection," he wrote the President, "involving the persons exercising the powers of state government, when a large body of people remain faithful, that body, so far as the Union is concerned, must be taken to constitute the state."[4] This dictum would form the cornerstone of Chase's Reconstruction views and he thought it particularly applicable to Louisiana.

If Chase could persuade Lincoln to extend the same political condition to Louisiana, it would be a first step toward convoking a loyalist convention that would revise or rewrite the state's constitution. That constitution, he hoped, would extend the franchise not just to loyal whites, but also to blacks, those who were already free and those who were free under the Proclamation. Citing Attorney General Bates's decision on the status of a free black skipper of a coastwise vessel, U.S. citizenship was bestowed on all persons born or naturalized in the United States irrespective of color or previous condition of servitude.[5]

After the fall of New Orleans and its hinterland to a joint army-navy operation, Chase moved quickly to ensure Treasury Department influence in the affairs of the city and the adjacent countryside. Employees of the New Orleans custom house had fled when Union troops were advancing on the city. Under recent legislation, Chase had the authority to appoint an acting collector and other temporary officers as well as special Treasury agents to enforce the blockade and internal revenue officers to collect the various income and excise taxes Congress had imposed.[6]

A week or so after the news that New Orleans was in Union hands Chase appointed his cousin George Denison acting collector of customs in the city. After Chase listened to Denison's interesting account of his life in Texas and his travels through the Confederacy on the outbreak of the war, he considered him to be ideal for the job of organizing and directing Treasury operations in Louisiana. A graduate of the University of Vermont, Denison, though only in his late twenties, had lived and prospered in San Antonio, where he practiced law and managed his deceased wife's estate that at one time included 70 slaves. After Texas seceded, Denison made his way north and was in Washington when New Orleans fell.[7] Chase directed Denison to confer with Barney and others in New York regarding the reestablishment and staffing Treasury operations in New Orleans.[8] Barney selected from his own staff William C. Gray, brother-in-law of Parke Godwin of the New York *Evening Post,* to act as Denison's deputy collector.[9] By early June Denison was in New Orleans, where he busied himself establishing relations with the political general from Massachusetts Benjamin F. Butler, who commanded the new Department of the Gulf.

One of the tasks Chase imposed on his new appointee was the identification of local Unionist leaders. Denison did a thorough job of research and supplied Chase with profiles of four such citizens. Heading the list was Benjamin F. Flanders, whom Denison recommended for the surveyor's post in the custom house. By October, he had staffed the custom house with employees drawn primarily from New York. Under Denison's direction the staff promoted Chase's political presence in Louisiana as well as performed its regular functions for the Treasury department.[10]

Chase's involvement in the Reconstruction of Louisiana reflected both aspects of his character. He was concerned about the safety and well-being of the blacks and appreciated their loyalty and their essential humanity. At the same time, he looked to their eventual support for the advancement of the Republican coalition and their assistance in his displacement of Lincoln as leader of that coalition.

Convention delegates were to be gleaned not just from Louisiana but from other southern states as the Confederacy crumbled away. Nor was he unaware of the manpower potential the new citizens would provide for the Union army at a time when white manpower from the North had so dwindled that a national draft with all the political and social negatives it implied was being forced on the Lincoln administration. A final consideration and to Chase the most important of all was the growing popularity of Reconstruction, which would be based on enfranchising the blacks in the South and thus securing the fruits of victory for a democratic Union, a victory that would forever banish the threat of secession, the existence of slavery, and the power of what he believed to be the old planter oligarchy. Chase meant to seize the initiative on these issues and Louisiana was to be the opening display of his intent.

It did not start out as well as Chase had hoped. General Butler began his rule of New Orleans with harsh measures which did not go down well in Washington. He violated the diplomatic immunity of the French, Dutch, and British consuls in the city, whom he suspected of acting for the Confederate government. Under the martial law he proclaimed, Butler made a mockery of civil rights.

Butler's military moves showed a feeble grasp of strategy and tactics which he covered up with much bluster. Word of speculation in cotton and corruption involving Butler's brother and the general himself reached Washington and was widely publicized in the northern press. Denison kept Chase informed of the Butler family's connections with illicit trading.[11] In his dealing with free blacks and slaves, Butler acted at first with so much restraint that he seemed to court conservative racist opinions in the North, much to Chase's apprehension. But then Butler caught a change of public opinion in the North that was beginning to favor emancipation and the enlistment of black troops. He moved rapidly over to a more radical stand.[12] Encouraged, Chase wrote Butler that the military must "contribute the whole moral and physical power of the government" to release from slavery nearly four million loyal people. A month later he appealed to Butler's political sense when he predicted that military emancipation "in the Gulf states will settle, or largely contribute to settle the negro question in the Free States." "Let the south be opened to negro emigration by emancipation along the Gulf, and it seems pretty certain that the blacks of the North will go southward . . ."

If the planters in Louisiana were required to pay wages, the blacks would be grateful and would constitute a loyal following to the Republican party. White labor would approve also in that it would no longer be threatened by cheap slave labor. Though Chase hastened to describe Lincoln as "sound in head as he is excellent in heart," he still left the implication which could not have been lost on Butler that the President was woefully behind public opinion and the progressive spirit of the age.[13]

Lincoln had found Butler a liability and at the urging of Seward sent the Democratic senator from Maryland, Reverdy Johnson, to investigate. Johnson's report, which was not free of personal and partisan bias, seemed to confirm many of the allegations against the general. Seward managed to convince Lincoln that Butler be recalled. But since he was an influential War Democrat from an influential state, Lincoln appointed that other political general from Massachusetts who had been a prominent Democrat, Nathaniel P. Banks, as his successor. Banks's military record was somewhat better than Butler's and he was known to be more conciliatory on Reconstruction measures and more willing to follow the administration line. Lincoln was moving cautiously in Louisiana, still concerned about border-state opinion on slavery, yet at the same time seeking to conciliate or at least dampen vocal radical opinion in the Congress and in important metropolitan dailies such as the New York *Tribune.*

The nexus of the problem for Chase and for Lincoln was in identifying those few Unionist leaders in New Orleans who would promote their respective ideas on policy. Politics in New Orleans had always been tumultuous and baffling to the outsiders. Chase had a head start on the President because he had a trusted and competent advisor. Without attracting too much attention or engaging in overt displays Chase's alter ego used the power and prestige of the custom house to benefit his patron in Washington. Other appointments Chase made in this early period strengthened Denison's hand. Benjamin R. Plumley, an abolitionist friend of Chase's from Philadelphia, became a special Treasury agent.[14] Dr. Max Bonzano, formerly a New Orleans resident, was given a sinecure post at the New Orleans mint.[15]

From afar, however, it was difficult to sort out the appropriate local leaders as to their positions on Reconstruction. In mid-August, Chase interrupted his work on a labor of love—the selection of collectors and assessors for appointment under the new Internal Revenue Act—to dine with Dr. Thomas E. H. Cottman, Judge Christian Roselius, and Cuthbert Bullitt, New Orleans residents and though Unionist in sympathy hardly agreeing with Chase on the place of the blacks in Louisiana's political life or on other radical measures of Reconstruction. Again two days later he presided at a dinner with these same gentlemen as they all listened to Reverdy Johnson indict Butler for corrupt and arbitrary management of affairs in New Orleans.[16] The background of Chase's dinner guests from New Orleans would not bear careful scrutiny as to their previous sympathies.[17] This factor of political life soon became apparent as two groups, conservative and radical, jockeyed for position.

Lincoln instructed General Shepley, whom Butler had appointed military governor, to hold elections in the two congressional districts under Union control. Chase and his Treasury agents backed Benjamin F. Flanders, who Denison described as "an abolitionist but not of the blood-thirsty type." He was elected handily over Lincoln's candidate John E. Bouligny.[18] Michael Hahn, formerly a Douglas Democrat who had not been associated with the organized Unionist movement, defeated Edward H. Durrell, the more radical candidate.[19]

Lincoln had already decided to replace Butler with Banks. For political purposes his intentions were known only to Seward, Stanton, and Halleck within his official family. But as in the case of most important military and policy measures, word leaked out. Chase learned of the change through Washington gossip.[20] As for Butler, he resented the recall which he attributed to Seward's influence. By the time Butler reached New York on his return, Lincoln had disposed of the Chase-Seward affair, but still remained concerned, as he should have been, about radical repercussions and Chase's stand. The Banks appointment was made in part to blunt any radical incursion into Louisiana politics.

Through his allies Chase kept up a steady pressure on the President to reinstate Butler, and the President wavered. After several stormy interviews that the self-assured Butler had in Washington Lincoln finally bowed to radical pressure and directed Stanton to order Butler back to New Orleans and even offer him command over the contemplated advance on Port Hudson, which together with Vicksburg was the last important Confederate position on the Mississippi.[21] But the order was never sent and Butler never returned to New Orleans.[22] Lincoln's eventual refusal to send this political adventurer back was definitely a rebuff not just to Butler and the radicals but to Chase's plans for Louisiana.[23]

A more serious reversal had come on the very day Banks assumed command at New Orleans. Lincoln replaced George Denison with Cuthbert Bullitt. The son-in-law of one of the richest sugar planters in Louisiana and brother-in-law of Dr. Hugh Kennedy, editor of New Orleans *True Delta*, a conservative sheet, Bullitt would surely cast his political weight behind the moderate regime of Banks.[24] Whether Chase knew of Bullitt's background or not, the removal of his trusted relative from a post which he regarded of crucial importance proved a body blow. Chase protested but in vain. Bullitt was made a special agent with the title and position of acting collector.[25]

Denison was very disturbed. A rich source of bribes that he and his deputy Gray had been receiving was in jeopardy. Unaware of Denison's abuse of his position for personal gain, Chase arranged a solace by making him acting surveyor, a lucrative but far less powerful position politically. At first Denison welcomed Bullitt, but soon his letters to Chase were highly critical of the man, whom he charged with cheerful impunity of speculation.[26]

What was most troubling to Denison and to Chase though for different reasons was the discharge of custom-house employees, presumably loyal to Chase and the radicals.[27] Bullitt had done this despite Chase's warning not to displace Denison's appointments which had been made with his approval.[28] After digesting Denison's complaining letters and taking the pulse of the Washington scene, Chase thought it prudent to rise above the rapidly changing politics and policies in New Orleans. In a long, carefully considered letter to Bullitt, which he meant for Banks's eyes, Chase decried the idea that there was a Banks policy and a Butler policy. "I am a friend of both generals and only prefer one to the other where a choice is to be made on public grounds," he explained.

Yet at the same time he applauded the move, long contemplated, that Banks should invade Texas and if possible detach that important state from the Confederacy. Chase made this suggestion plain to Bullitt, neglecting to mention, however, that such an expedition would remove the general from involvement in New Orleans politics and the subsequent Reconstruction of Louisiana.[29]

While seeking to influence moderates through Bullitt and Banks, Chase was encouraging radicals through Benjamin F. Flanders. Ten days after his straddling letter to Bullitt, Chase wrote Flanders by far the most straightforward statement he had yet made on Reconstruction. Referring to the Virginia precedent that the loyal population of a part of a state could constitute a state, he suggested that a convention be called to reestablish the state government under a constitution adapted to "new exigencies." This new organic act would outlaw, he said, "the heresy of secession," establish freedom for the entire population without exception or delay, and provide for universal suffrage or, if limitation be considered necessary, "light property qualifications."

Chase's views as expressed to Flanders were much the same views he would advance throughout the remainder of the war and into the postwar period. To Chase, universal suffrage was the ultimate solution that would protect the blacks' civil rights and economic privileges yet at the same time preserve states' rights. Never far from his thoughts was the expectation that broader, interracial suffrage would extend the Republican coalition in the South.[30] As he saw it a first step was to have Lincoln rescind the exceptions in the Emancipation Proclamation.

Chase had been agitating for such a move since the Proclamation took effect on January 1, 1863. His more or less constant campaign must have been annoying to the President especially since it jibed with similar pressure from congressional radicals and from the radical-oriented press. Conservative and many moderate Republicans, and all the Democrats were pushing in the opposite direction. Lincoln continued to be extremely shy of broadening emancipation because of probable political repercussion from loyal slave states.[31] He also doubted his constitutional power to do so.

The appointment of a nationwide web of collectors under the new internal revenue legislation, which Chase at first regarded as a patronage bonanza, simply increased the tension between the President and his Treasury secretary. Chase regarded these appointments as exclusively Treasury concerns. As usual his argument was based on fitness, not political considerations, though loyalty to the administration as a whole was always a test.

With Chase, however, fitness and loyalty also meant support for his ideas on government and Reconstruction, which had come to mean his campaign for the presidency. Lincoln's motives, like those of Chase, reflected his own ideas on Reconstruction and his own campaign for reelection. Equally important to him and to a lesser extent Chase was the establishment of harmony between factions within the rebellious states as they were recovered for the Union. In such a contest with the President, Seward, and his partner Weed Chase held a losing hand which had not been improved by his role in the Cabinet crisis the past December.

Rebuffed by the Bullitt appointment, Chase was defeated again when Lincoln refused to back the confirmation of the radical-leaning Mark Howard for an internal revenue collectorship in Connecticut. An intense, capable, insurance magnate, Howard was also an ambitious politician who had been instrumental in establishing local Union League associations.

The President had appointed Howard in accordance with Chase's wishes. But Connecticut Senator James Dixon, a conservative Republican, blocked the nomination. Without consulting Chase, Lincoln withdrew Howard's appointment. In a written protest Chase argued that congressmen should not interfere with executive appointments when they were not responsible for the actions of the appointees.[32] It was all to no avail: James G. Bolles, a friend of Welles and presumably not then identified with either faction, became collector for the Hartford District. All of the other Connecticut appointments went to Dixon's men. Not one of them could be converted to a Chase candidacy in the forthcoming presidential contest.[33]

Chase learned of the Howard withdrawal when he returned to Washington after heated discussions with Philadelphia, New York, and Boston bankers.[34]

Weary after his trip, not in the best of health, concerned about what appeared to be Weed's growing influence in the New York custom house and the uncovering of extensive frauds by custom-house clerks that had gone back to the Buchanan administration, Chase found to his chagrin that the President had made an additional decision on Treasury Department patronage.[35]

It involved a comparatively obscure resident of Westchester County, Abram Hyatt, and Chauncey Depew, a young, popular lawyer free of Weed's influence and thus favored by the New York radicals yet not unacceptable to the conservatives. Probably on Seward's advice Lincoln appointed Hyatt in the face of Chase's warning that it would stir up trouble.[36] There were no political repercussions except to Chase's increasing sensitivity. Many of his patronage problems he now traced exclusively to the work of Weed and his associates in New York.

Irritated by the Howard and Hyatt reverses, Chase was roused to anger against the President over a personal grievance which had little to do with his political fortunes but much to do with a further erosion of his standing in the administration. The trouble began when Lincoln directed Chase to look into the affairs of Victor Smith, a long-time friend of Chase's, who was serving as the collector of the Puget Sound district with his headquarters at Port Angeles, Washington Territory.

Chase was familiar with the charges that had been made against Smith. He had talked with Dr. Anson G. Henry, the surveyor general of the territory, who had urged that Smith be removed. Henry told Chase that Smith had long acted in an arbitrary fashion that made for bad political feeling on the West Coast and in addition had been lax in his duties. Henry did not accuse Smith of corrupt practices but of bad judgment and frivolous behavior. The doctor was a close friend of Lincoln's. His advice could not be taken lightly. Yet Chase chose to ignore it.[37] He put the matter in the hands of his assistant secretary, Harrington.[38] But before Harrington could complete his investigation, Chase learned that Lincoln had removed Smith and appointed his successor. Chase had not yet complied with Lincoln's order when another note came from the President explaining that his appointee was dead and requesting a commission for another person.[39] At this point Chase's temper flared. He wrote a caustic note to Lincoln complaining bitterly that he had not been consulted in a matter affecting his department and offering his resignation.[40]

Lincoln wrote on Chase's letter—not quite accurately—"His first offer of resignation."[41] He would not accept Chase's offer, and he did seek to mollify his angry secretary by appointing his nominee for collector in Smith's place. This comedy of errors reflects on the judgment of both principals. Neither Chase nor especially Lincoln was thinking clearly. Caught up as they were in the fearful aftermath of Hooker's defeat at Chancellorsville. It was, not just the awful casualties and Hooker's inept performance but its baneful impact on the northern public, on the army, and indeed on the very outcome of the war. In that light their impulsive actions become understandable.

For Chase, the Smith affair, as other patronage cases, added to his air of injured rectitude, as it whetted his ambition to displace this blundering person who seemed now determined to undermine his political strength. What Lincoln felt can be summed up by two comments John Hay made in his diary. Remarked Hay: "[Senator] Wade says 'Chase is a good man but his theology is unsound. He thinks there is a fourth person in the Trinity.'" In the other comment Hay described pungently Lincoln's annoyance with Chase's presidential aspirations. In a half-humorous, half-sardonic metaphor, Lincoln compared Chase "to a horsefly on the neck of a plow horse—which kept him lively about his work."[42]

Even Chase's pet project of free labor for free blacks, the experiment then taking place at Port Royal and the Sea Islands off the South Carolina coast, seemed in jeopardy.[43] Chase had promised his surrogate at Port Royal, Edward L. Pierce, appointment as military governor of the Beaufort-Port Royal area. He explained to Pierce that the military rank would carry with it "the authority of course, far greater than anything from the treasury department."[44] After Chase made the offer, Stanton appointed General Rufus Saxton to take charge at Beaufort-Port Royal.[45] An obviously upset Pierce resigned.[46] Chase was as distressed at what he chose to believe was yet another rebuff as he was at the loss of a valued subordinate.

Despite his concerns over the Pierce resignation the experiment seemed to be working out even though clashes continued between the civilian workers, mainly teachers and ministers from New England, and the military. For a voluntary, largely philanthropic operation, the Port Royal experiment spoke much for the zeal of its participants and the effort that was being made to show an indifferent even hostile public that plantation blacks could compete in a white free-market economy. But these lofty objectives were never quite realized.

Not long after the navy had captured Port Royal harbor and the army occupied the Sea Islands, the Treasury Department began to implement its responsibility to manage the plantations abandoned by their owners. The Islands were major producers of valuable long-staple cotton, and the initial objective for Chase was the collection and shipment of this staple to the cotton-starved North. On the receiving end were cotton manufacturers primarily in New England who were eager to exploit this newly opened source through their connections with the government. Alert to these opportunities was William Sprague, whose family controlled a textile empire in Rhode Island and Connecticut and who had formed a friendship with Chase and his lovely daughter Kate. On Sprague's recommendation, Chase appointed one of his associates in the cotton business, former Rhode Island militia officer William Reynolds, to act as the Treasury's agent in collecting and shipping north the cotton already harvested.

Having solved as he thought the business side of the experiment he had in mind, Chase turned to the labor side. He needed a trusted person who was sympathetic to his goal of converting former slaves to free workers and eventually free holders of the land they were cultivating. The task he had in mind was the direct supervision of the field hands in producing not just cotton for profit but food crops that would enable the black population to be self-sustaining. Edward L. Pierce, former law student and friend, a protégé of Sumner, and a practicing attorney in Massachusetts, seemed just the right person for the job. He was an energetic, well-educated young man whose views on slavery approximated Chase's. Leading antislavery persons in Massachusetts thought well of him, an important qualification. In making the appointment Chase overlooked Pierce's arrogance, his acute sensitivity, and his tactlessness in dealing with those who might disagree with him.[47] In conference with Pierce, Chase emphasized the recruitment of individuals from the North who would begin the necessary education and training of what were then called "contrabands." Dovetailing with his Louisiana program, the Sea Islands' initiative was both an experiment and another effort to wrest Reconstruction planning from the White House.

Pierce went off to Beaufort, examined the situation, and came up with a plan that would divide some 200 abandoned plantations and organize them under a network of superintendents who would be responsible for the cultivation of the land and for the education and care of the workers.[48] Chase was delighted with the breadth, depth, and authoritative nature of Pierce's proposal, which he outlined in a special report.[49]

Pierce noted that some of the living habits of the "contrabands" were not up to middle-class standards in the North. He attributed these defects to their condition of slavery, with all the social ills it implied. But a positive note dominated the report. The native intelligence and skills of the blacks, their ardent desire for education of themselves as well as their children, and their interest in religion all were underscored in his survey. With proper inducements and especially protection from whites until they had achieved a higher level of literacy and gained an understanding of the duties and the rewards of the work ethic it would then be possible for them to make their own way in a free society. Chase had the report copied and sent out to the liberal metropolitan press which editorialized it in generally favorable terms.[50]

Apart from on-the-spot military assistance—a mixed blessing—no federal funds were available, not even for food relief. Clearly something had to be done if the soil was to be prepared and new crops, including cotton, planted and harvested. Despite all the high-flying rhetoric that the abolitionists had charged against the iniquity of slavery over the years, despite all of the arguments, excluding the constitutional, that the free soilers had advanced on the stump, in the state legislatures, and on the floors of Congress, almost no one had considered what would happen to the former slaves once emancipation had taken place. Nor had any concrete plans been proposed to ease the transition to freedom for the largely illiterate, largely unskilled agricultural laborer trained for a generation under a gang system to perform the routine, repetitive tasks of cotton culture and accustomed to receive food, clothing, and shelter from the planter. Nor for that matter had much thought been given to the consequences of such a rapid and complete disruption of the economic and social system of the South for black and white alike, let alone the destruction the war itself imposed.

The military had first confronted this perplexity at the outset of the war when fleeing blacks crowded into Union army lines and were fed, clothed, and sheltered after a fashion. At best an ad hoc approach to a grave social problem, the army could not be expected to develop what was clearly a political and social policy of the highest order, if not the priority. While radicals and many moderates in Congress and the country at large increased their agitation for total emancipation, many seemed to think that if there were a problem, it would solve itself.[51] After all, almost everyone in the North had started life as a farm worker. There was no reason why the freedmen could not support themselves and their families by tilling the soil like millions of whites both north and south had done and were doing.

Chase's ideas on economic theory were more advanced than those of his fellow countrymen. Unlike the majority he was thoroughly familiar with the theoretical justifications of laissez-faire economics that European thinkers had offered over the past century. As his thinking was in advance of his party on the consequences of emancipation, he was in the forefront of those who recognized that something more than moral persuasion was essential if the former slaves were to take their place as free farmers. With Chase, his political ambitions always came first, however. And it was his hope for his personal future that gave impetus to the Port Royal experiment.

The Lincoln administration was under intense pressure to renew the cotton supply for northern and European factories. All classes in the North for various special reasons were united in keeping the blacks in the South where they had always been. While cotton manufacturers were anxious to maintain a reliable supply of cheap labor, black or white, that would produce cotton in quantity at the lowest possible cost, workingmen in the cities and factory towns feared a drastic cheapening of the labor market if millions of blacks moved north. Even in rural areas tenant farmers and itinerant white farm laborers could understand how a mass immigration of blacks could threaten or even destroy what little security they had.[52]

Chase responded, as best he could, to satisfy all these constituencies. His blend of the moral with the practical was aimed at making the postwar South hospitable for the emancipated blacks and the emancipated blacks hospitable to the South, all in the name of freedom. Pierce was given a free hand in raising money and recruiting personnel in the Boston area. For New York Chase appointed an old friend, the Methodist minister Mansfield French. Backed by the Tappans and other New York abolitionists French arrived in Port Royal a week after Pierce. His sense of the situation corresponded with that of Pierce. On Mansfield's return north he canvassed New York for funds and recruits. As a result of their dual labors, Pierce and French enlisted 74 individuals, of whom 19 were women.[53]

Chase assigned Barney the tasks of administering the oath of allegiance and providing for transport south. The collector was also made responsible for selling the cotton at auction. It was hoped that the experiment would produce enough net funds to show the northern public that Port Royal was not just self-sustaining but would show a profit. Free black labor would demonstrate to a skeptical public that it was more profitable than slave labor had ever been.[54] In the early stages these expectations were not realized.[55]

Colonel Reynolds turned out to be a bad choice. He was exclusively interested in immediate profits and in future exploitation of land and labor for himself and his associates, among whom were William Sprague. Indifferent to the welfare of the blacks or to the success of the overall experiment, Reynolds soon clashed with Pierce and French.[56] Chase heard repeatedly from both sides and finally, in response to a specific series of charges from Pierce that Reynolds and his agents were defrauding their black workers, directed that an investigation be made. When one of Reynold's agents assaulted Pierce, Chase decided to dispense with the colonel and his group of speculators. On the same day that Pierce sent in his resignation, Chase dismissed Reynolds.[57]

By then the 1861 crop had been harvested, baled, and sent to New York for ginning and sale. Reynolds, who was short in his accounts, had to forgo his 10 percent commission worth about $50,000.[58] His agents, however, collected their 5 percent fees. After Reynolds's departure, Pierce's group of preachers, missionaries, and young professionals who stayed on and who were completely inexperienced in cotton culture struggled to plant and harvest the 1862 crop. It failed.

Congressional opponents, certain that something was awry at Port Royal, demanded an accounting. Chase concealed a loss of approximately $75,000 by combining the income from 1861 with that of 1862 in his report to Congress.[59] By now the Army had taken over Treasury's responsibility for abandoned plantations and the civilians at Port Royal were completely under military control. Private organizations in New York and Boston, however, continued to pay their salaries. Fortunately the Army commander directly responsible, General Saxton, was most sympathetic to the activities of the civilians, many of whom his officers and men contemptuously dubbed "Gideonites."

Slowly and painfully the civilian superintendents began achieving results in the production of cotton and in the education and training of their charges. General David Hunter, the overall commander of the Department of the South, was replaced by Chase's friend from Cincinnati days, the West Point-trained astronomer Orsmby Mitchell, whose brief tenure was marked with a conservative policy on race relations, though he, like his predecessor, was anxious to form black regiments.[60] Mitchell died of yellow fever after less than two months at Port Royal. Hunter resumed command until mid-June, 1863, when Quincy A. Gillmore, an artillery specialist, replaced him.[61] Gillmore cooperated with Saxton and the experiment went forward with considerable gains and much publicity (favorable and otherwise) in the northern press.

Meanwhile Pierce had gone back to his law practice in Boston. "I thought you had seen enough of things to know that the government has never taken much account, if any, of this social experiment", Chase wrote Pierce. "What has been done I did without suggestion or sympathy. . . ."[62] And later in a more positive vein he said to William Curtis Noyes, the radical-minded New York lawyer, that the experiment must be a model for Reconstruction in other rebellious states as the army brought them under Union control. "The forgotten people," he said, "who we must conciliate are black Americans, who till the soil or load the boats and cars or pursue the handicrafts. . . ."[63]

Congress had alleviated some of Chase's stress when it restored to the Treasury control of abandoned property and enlarged the powers of supervisory special agents. These actions were accomplished after some lobbying from the Treasury Department itself, more likely from the web of agents throughout the land who were deeply interested in profits to be made if they gained supervision over the disposal of abandoned property. Whatever the pressures applied, Lincoln signed the bill which gave the Secretary of the Treasury power to establish a fourth district that included South Carolina, Georgia, and Florida.[64]

Chase now saw an opportunity to mollify Pierce, to ingratiate himself with the Massachusetts radicals, and at the same time have a creative, energetic, and experienced person take charge not just of the Port Royal experiment, but of furthering his Reconstruction ideas in Florida, which was seen to be lightly held by the Confederates. Pierce accepted the new post and established himself at Port Royal in early August 1863. Instructions were sent out to other supervising agents detailing just how they could use their expanded powers over trade and abandoned property.[65]

Serious problems had developed at Port Royal, where Chase felt the need of Pierce's expertise and his objective judgment. Chief among these was the horde of speculators in and about the area who were seeking to purchase at bargain prices choice plantations or to secure favorable leases to the lands. Many of the resident freedmen were being treated merely as present or potential manpower to be hired at subsistence wages, much of which was siphoned off by inflated prices they were paying for provisions. As early as January 1863, French wrote Chase that "plans for stock companies are already before the public, and speculators are privately contriving to secure these plantations." Existing legislation held that abandoned property must be sold for unpaid federal taxes.[66] Said French, "[we have] the aged, infirm and sick, including many women and children whose husband or fathers are yet in bond or in the army and we have very many such would find no favor at the hands of mercenary land-holders."[67]

Chase had already received a letter from Governor John A. Andrew of Massachusetts, who argued along the same lines. He urged Chase to have the government delay any tax sales for a year "until proper legislation is passed to protect the interest of the blacks."[68] Chase was sympathetic and acted promptly.[69] He asked Congress to pay "special attention to the importance of proper legislation to secure the laborers in their district, homes and homesteads on the lands they have cultivated." He also requested permission for collector Barney to release the funds he held from the sale of Port Royal cotton so that the Sea Island blacks could purchase their lands at tax sales.[70]

Before any of this proposed legislation made its way through Congress, Lincoln was beginning to recognize the political and social importance of Port Royal. He appointed a commission, most of whose members were favorable to the local blacks. When a tax auction took place on March 9, 1863, the government retained over 85 percent of the land up for sale, much to the relief of French and other like-minded civilians. Resident blacks pooling their small sums managed to purchase 2000 acres of land, but over 16,000 acres of prime cotton-producing land went to speculative interests.

At Chase's behest, Lincoln approved the sale of 60,000 acres of government-owned land in the Sea Islands that had been delayed for a year.[71] Chase hoped that the freedmen including black veterans would be able to purchase small plots, from 20 to 40 acres, for $1.25 an acre. He inserted a provision specifically setting forth this policy, but only about 26 percent of the plantations were reserved for the freedmen.[72] Many if not most of the freedmen could not supply the required payment. Saxton and French sought to circumvent the instructions by advising them to build a cabin or make some improvements on the land they tilled so that they might claim preemption rights even though these were not included in the instructions. Several thousand freedmen and some grasping civilians doing missionary or educational work in the Port Royal area availed themselves of preemption.

A bitter division almost immediately developed between the tax commissioners and Saxton and French. Both sides bombarded Chase, the one claiming its legal responsibilities under the Internal Revenue Act, the other emphasizing the social and economic and moral worth of private land ownership for the freedmen.[73]

In response Chase altered the instructions for Lincoln's signature. These now specifically included preemption rights as well as graduated payments.[74] Unlike Chase's previous state papers, his new instructions were loosely worded. Political and economic woes had so piled up on him that he had been unwilling or, more likely, unable in distant Washington to prepare the document with his usual thoroughness.[75] Moreover he did not have the facts at hand that Pierce would have supplied. He had resigned his post after only two months on the job to accept the appointment of internal revenue commissioner for the Boston District.[76] So many arguments and counterarguments had reached Chase's desk over the preemption proviso that he was forced to prepare new instructions that voided preemption.

The Port Royal experiment had achieved significant positive results, primarily in the education and the training of the former slaves. Free labor was demonstrated to be the equal in productivity of slave labor, not simply in the routine, highly specialized tasks of cotton culture, but in the more demanding individual skills required for diversified farming and animal husbandry. Unfortunately the hope of visionaries like Saxton and French and of Chase himself that most of the former slaves quickly would become freeholders was largely dashed under the weight of prevailing notions about property rights and laissez-faire economics.[77] Caught between the material interests of some of the northern missionaries and the idealistic motives of French and Saxton, Chase finally capitulated to what he saw as the political imperatives of private enterprise.[78]

In South Carolina and Louisiana, Chase's plans for Reconstruction reflected both sides of his character. They must be judged to be mixed in their social and economic consequences. Politically his efforts were scarcely useful, in fact harmful to his ambitions because they placed him more directly in opposition to the administration of which he was a leading member. And it ranged him openly in a contest against far shrewder politicians than he. The first effects of a weakening position came from Missouri in late September, 1863, when the radical so-called "Charcoals" arrayed themselves against the conservatives, dubbed the "Clay Banks," whose leading spirit was the popular political general Frank Blair, brother of Chase's Cabinet colleague Montgomery.[79]

chapter 25

Old Greenbacks

It had been a year of vexing trials and of limited triumphs for Chase and the administration as a whole. In the ongoing patronage contest, Chase had generally gotten his way, but not before the President had slowly and inexorably reduced his scope for independent choice on important patronage positions. However, in minor posts that could be useful politically, Congress had passed legislation broadening Chase's power to appoint Treasury agents and increasing their numbers. Jay Cooke, whom Chase had made general agent for marketing the 5–20 bonds, had performed magnificently. Utilizing innovative organizing and sales techniques that tapped the currency reserves of the general public, Cooke had sold more than $320 million of these securities.[1]

Over Chase's objections to certain aspects of the bill, Congress approved and Lincoln signed the Third Legal Tender Act which added another $150 million worth of greenbacks and another $50 million in fractional currency to the circulating medium. Chase was also given authority to borrow $900 million dollars in bonds carrying 6 percent interest. At his discretion, $400 million of this sum could be issued as Treasury notes that bore no more than 6 percent interest payable in "lawful money," or as legal tender, excluding interest payments. The law recognized that Chase should have the authority to set prices in accordance with fluctuating market values.[2] With strong support from the President, who made the National Banking Bill an administration measure, Chase's cherished project—a system of federally chartered banks whose currency was based largely on their holdings of United States bonds— became law early in the new year. With the legal tender acts, the National Banking Act, a substantial increase in excise duties, and increased rates on basic items in the Morrill Tariff Act, Chase's financial policy was now relatively complete. The Treasury was meeting most of the government's obligations to contractors; there was no imminent problem of insolvency. But military and naval expenses continued to soar in the wake of the Chancellorsville defeat and the bloody but slender victory of Union arms at Gettysburg. Grant's costly but successful capture of the Mississippi river port of Vicksburg and Bank's of Port Hudson were balanced against Rosecrans's defeat at Chickamauga.

Public confidence in government stocks was not strong. Inflation took its toll with each successive greenback issue and each increase in bonded indebtedness. Cooke's success with the 5-20s had pretty well soaked up most available specie in the Union. But bumper crops the previous year and heavy exports of commodities eased the shortage of coin. European creditors, however, continued to be skeptical about the fate of the Union. In any event Chase felt secure enough about the government's credit to ease off on his efforts to secure a European loan.

With the national bank system in place Chase had high hopes that the federally chartered banks would be forced to purchase the new issue of 6 percent 10–40 bonds and interest-bearing Treasury notes in order to maintain or increase their note issue.

As far as the Treasury accounts were concerned, enough money was available during the year to satisfy all needs. Chase mentioned proudly to Attorney General Bates in the spring that "there is not an unpaid requisition in my Department."[3] But the money was slow in reaching the armed forces who were of course paid not in coin, but in discounted greenbacks without a commensurate pay increase.[4]

More serious problems lay ahead. Chase had counted on widespread chartering of national banks to provide an expanding market for the new bonds. But up to December, 1863, despite lavish promotion by Jay Cooke and his agents, only about $10 million of capital had been invested in the new associations.[5] Chase found that financial interests in the northern cities and towns were skeptical of the new system. This unease contributed to the failure of the new 10–40 loan. An overconfident Chase had assumed the sale would provide the cash to meet the government's immediate obligations. It did not. Another factor, and a most important one, was that the Cooke agency been forced under heavy political pressure to give up its exclusive marketing of the bonds. There is also reason to believe that the surplus purchasing power of the investing public had been reduced sharply.

In reaction to these negative aspects, Chase finally concluded that heavier taxes had to be imposed on a wider variety of consumer products and through adjusted income tax schedules. If Congress passed the necessary legislation, Chase estimated that the new taxes would yield an additional $150 million, a sum that would preclude a further issue of greenbacks.[6] But Congress did not see fit to follow Chase's recommendations. He worried about inflation without comprehending that the sharp rise in living costs as well as prices for luxuries like carriages was in effect a direct though regressive tax on all consumers. Nor did his estimates take into account the dramatic rise in the gross national product. Of course, all of these factors were not and could not be measured by the government of that day, but they like the arrears in military pay were nevertheless important segments of the Union economy during a period of unprecedented deficit financing.

Chase's financial policy seemed to be working while Union military successes were on the rise. He took full advantage of the trend. In his 1863 report, he cast himself as the careful, but creative and confident master of an economy that was reaching over $1 billion a year as compared with prewar annual outlays that averaged from $50 to $60 million. To drive this point home to the average citizen and thus advance his political prospects he had his portrait engraved on lesser denomination greenbacks. Lincoln's face appeared on the larger notes. When asked why his picture appeared on notes most commonly used, he replied, "I had put the President's head on the higher priced notes, my own, as was becoming on the smaller ones."[7]

Chase, and in fact all of the Cabinet, supported the administration's conscription bill which was signed into law on March 3, 1863. The draft seemed to be proceeding, if slowly, through the spring and summer without undue opposition. Chase was not overly concerned. Rather his attention was riveted on Lee's invasion of Pennsylvania during late June and July. The terrible carnage at Gettysburg proved shocking enough, but more deeply felt was the failure of General Meade, the new commander of the Army of the Potomac, to attack and finish off Lee's defeated army. Lincoln was especially distraught. In one of his rare appearances at the Treasury Department, the President seemed in Chase's words "more grieved and indignant than I have ever seen him." For once Chase unbent and sought to console him. Chase mentioned the rather trite phrase "that daylight always came after darkness and that all we had to do was to gather a new force and pursue. . . ."[8]

If some of the new force that Chase spoke of was to come from the draft then in progress, his statement must have been more rhetorical than realistic. He already had at hand an alarming telegram from Cisco that New York City was in the hands of rioters who were resisting the draft. "The police [are] powerless," wrote Cisco, "and we have no military." Expecting an attack on the subtreasury building, Cisco was taking whatever steps he could to defend it.[9]

As the riot worsened, Lincoln and Stanton assured Chase that an adequate force was on its way to New York.[10] Beyond that Chase could not get any specifics out of the War Department. "When in my anxiety," he said, "I venture some suggestions, I find after that they have been anticipated, and am never quite sure whether anticipated or not, they are very welcome."[11] The riots were eventually brought under control, only to have another crisis develop and this one of equally serious proportions, the fate of Rosecrans's Army of the Cumberland.

This time Chase was fully informed of the disaster at Chickamauga. Both Rosecrans and Garfield, his chief of staff, were Ohio men and officers whose careers Chase had fostered. On the morning of September 20 while breakfasting Chase read ominous telegrams from the West in the Washington papers.[12] Concerned, he had his carriage drive him to the War Department first instead of to his office in the Treasury building. There he found Stanton in a highly excited state. He handed Chase two telegrams, one from Rosecrans and the other from Charles A. Dana, a New York *Tribune* editor, now on a special mission for the War Department at Grant's headquarters. Both telegrams reported a very serious defeat at Chickamauga where the Confederate army under Braxton Bragg, reinforced with Longstreet's corps from Lee's army, broke the Union army and drove it into the small city of Chattanooga, Tennessee. More telegrams poured into the War Department that afternoon, bringing a bit of good news that a portion of Rosecrans's army under George Thomas had made a stand that held Bragg back long enough for a safe withdrawal to the city's fortifications. But the next day, as a fuller picture began to unfold, the condition looked perilous.

A deeply concerned Lincoln at the regular Cabinet meeting on Tuesday, the 22nd, took what comfort he could from the fact that the army though badly beaten was still intact.[13] Of personal concern to Chase was the news that his brother-in-law, Lieutenant Israel Ludlow, was wounded and a prisoner.[14] He spent most of the next day with Stanton at the War Department, but finally, very tired, very concerned, he left for home and went to bed. Around midnight a messenger awakened him with an urgent message from Stanton to come to the War Department immediately. "The summons really alarmed me," said Chase. He feared the worst: "More bad news?" "No," replied Stanton, "what there is, is favorable." He handed Chase a telegram from Garfield which said that Rosecrans "could hold out at least ten days where he was," but had to have reinforcements and resupply.[15]

Thousands of horses had already died either in battle or from lack of forage; the army was on half-rations; and ammunition was in short supply.

Halleck, who was there with Stanton said nothing, but his watery eyes and his bulging, ill-fitting uniform did nothing to instill confidence.[16] Stanton had already sent for Seward and for the President, who was at the Soldier's Home. Lincoln arrived with his usual plaid shawl draped around his narrow shoulders.[17] The weather had been unseasonably cold and the open fireplace lent a cheerful glow to the map-strewn table just opposite. He sat in the chair of Major T. T. Eckert, the chief telegrapher, and, leaning back, tipped his feet on the desk.[18]

Stanton opened the conference by reading the latest telegrams from Dana, Garfield, and Rosecrans. He noted that reinforcements from Sherman and Grant could not arrive in time to reinforce Rosecrans. The same problem applied to Bank's force, which was already stretched too thinly from Port Hudson to New Orleans. Lincoln knew that Burnside's troops at Knoxville were the closest to Chattanooga, but despite peremptory orders from Washington over the past few days he could not be made to move and was in danger of being flanked by Longstreet's corps, which had been sent to reinforce Bragg weeks earlier.[19]

Stanton asked Halleck how many men could Burnside spare for Rosecran's relief and how long would it take for them to be in Chattanooga? Halleck said that Burnside could move 20,000 men in ten days, "if uninterrupted." "How many in eight days?" asked Stanton, "Twelve thousand." Lincoln interjected, "After Burnside begins to arrive the pinch will be over." But Stanton rejoined, "Unless the enemy, anticipating reinforcements, attacks promptly. When will Sherman's [army] reach Rosecrans?" Stanton asked Halleck. "In about ten days," was the reply, "if . . . every available man ordered forward, say from twenty to twenty-five thousand."[20]

Stanton then followed up his estimate of available forces in the West with the startling recommendation that 30,000 men from the Army of the Potomac be sent to Rosecrans's rescue. This meant transport with full baggage, rations, and equipment over some 1200 miles from eastern Virginia to southern Tennessee via the rickety, many-gauged, independently managed railroads. Lincoln exclaimed, "I will bet that if the order is given tonight, the troops could not be got to Washington in five days." Stanton replied that he was certain 30,000 bales of cotton "could be sent in that time." By taking control of the railroads and excluding all other business, he could not see "why 30,000 men cannot be sent as well. But if 30,000 can not be sent, let 20,000 go."

Lincoln and Halleck demurred. Both worried about weakening Meade's army on an improbable excursion. Discussion frequently rose to the level of heated debate until Chase and Seward backed up Stanton, arguing effectively that Meade's army could easily spare such a force and still be strong enough to engage Lee as well as protect Washington.[21] The meeting broke up around 2:30 a.m., leaving Lincoln, Stanton, Eckert, and the telegraphers to summon the officers of the B & O, the Philadelphia, Wilmington and Baltimore, and the Pennsylvania Railroad to Washington.[22] Stanton got marvelous cooperation from the half-dozen or so railroads, each under separate management and each coordinated from Washington by telegraph. The first contingent of federal troops reached Chattanooga seven days after leaving Washington. "It is a great achievement," Stanton wired Tom Scott of the Pennsylvania Railroad.[23]

Chase had been out of town. When he returned to the capital three days after the meeting and learned that the risky operation was running smoothly, he could not resist a dig at Lincoln's skeptical comment.[24] "Thus in five days," Chase confided to his diary, "the men who as the President was ready to bet, could not be got to Washington, would already be past that point on their way to Rosecrans, while their advance had reached the Ohio River."[25] Within two weeks' time from the date the decision was made to send Hooker's corps west, the entire force of more than 23,000 men complete with equipment, artillery, horses, rations, and ammunition were at the federal fortifications around Chattanooga.[26]

With that front stabilized, Chase found time to entertain a delegation of radicals, or "Charcoals," from Missouri. Their strident demands for the removal of General John M. Schofield, the theater commander, had stirred up the ire of conservatives, or "Clay Banks," such as Edward Bates and the Blairs. The issue was joined when Montgomery Blair departed from the customary silence of Cabinet officers in public on controversial political topics. At Rockville, Maryland, on October 3, the lean, ascerbic Postmaster General roundly attacked the radicals and singled out Sumner as a specific example. He did not mention Chase by name but the inference was clear, particularly when taken in conjunction with his brother Frank's anti-Chase diatribe in St. Louis a week or so before.[27]

Politics spiced the crisp autumn air in Washington. Election campaigns were under way in two important states, Pennsylvania and Ohio. War aims and war fatigue were prime topics for electioneering. Peace Democrats and even some disaffected War Democrats and conservative Republicans were attacking the administration vigorously and vociferously on its conduct of the war, its violation of civil rights through suspension of habeas corpus, the Emancipation Proclamation, inflation, and host of other issues. A focal point in the contest was Clement Vallandigham, the outspoken ex-congressman and extremist opponent of the war who had been tried by a military court in Ohio and found guilty of seditious remarks.

His arrest and conviction had been a source of acute embarrassment to the Lincoln administration. Without setting aside the verdict or commenting on the impropriety, if not illegality, of courts-martial trying civilians in loyal states where the courts were open, Lincoln had Vallandigham banished to

Confederate lines. Every Cabinet member approved of his decision.[28] The Confederate government, equally embarrassed by the presence of their uninvited guest, provided him with passage to the West Indies and from there he went to Canada. Democrats of all persuasions condemned the Vallandigham arrest and trial. The party in Ohio nominated him for governor.

Needless to say, Lincoln was worried about the Ohio campaign. Far more attuned to Ohio politics, Chase saw an opportunity to display his patriotism and put himself and his policies on display. He decided to intervene personally in the contest when it neared its critical phase.

He made careful arrangements for a trip to Ohio. As a pretext for the venture, Chase decided that he was, as he put it, "going home to vote." But ever prudent, he consulted Edward Jordan, the Treasury department solicitor, on whether he could vote in a state where he had not resided for more than two years. Jordan assured him that he could claim Ohio his permanent residence.[29]

Chase then wrote a confidential note to William Prescott Smith, operations manager of the B & O, informing him of his plans and requesting special transportation west. Smith was not only happy to comply but informed Chase that he would clear the tracks on the B & O and on connecting trains to Columbus. Smith placed his private car at Chase's disposal, and agreed to accompany him so that he could take charge of all rail connections.[30] Whitelaw Reid, who had been acting as Chase's unofficial Washington correspondent, accepted Chase's invitation to go along; he would file dispatches on the trip to his paper the Cincinnati *Gazette* as well as to the western branch of the newly created Associated Press.[31]

Chase, Smith, and Reid arranged to leave Washington on the early evening of Friday the ninth.[32] There remained only the mention of his absence to Lincoln. The President thought Chase's trip would do some good, though he was well aware that it would incidentally help Chase's presidential aspirations. On his return to the Treasury Department from the White House Chase directed that leave be given all Ohio personnel who wanted to return home and vote.[33]

Despite frequent stops for fuel and water, despite the frequent jolting when the car was uncoupled and coupled, Chase slept soundly through the night.[34] If he himself did not notify the Ohio people in advance, Reid probably did, because when his train arrived several hours late at the Columbus depot of the Ohio Central railroad, hundreds of citizens and a brass band awaited him even though it was 2 a.m.

Supporters had worked the crowd and as Chase stepped down to the platform he was greeted with cheers. What must have pleased him most and confirmed his political judgment was the repeated chant of "How are you old Greenbacks!" It was not until 3:30 a.m. that Chase finally got to his hotel.[35]

He rested over Sunday, but early on Monday morning he made an unscheduled speech at the Loyal League's meeting hall. It was an impressive performance. Chase was at his best replying vigorously to the Blairs, excoriating their conservative position on emancipation and praising the radicals in Missouri and Maryland.

Governor Dennison, once a strong adherent, now a secret opponent, was of course present and was forced to make complimentary remarks. He said that at first he had opposed Chase's financial policies but admitted that he had been wrong and that "neither William Pitt nor any financier of whom history makes mention, could boast of such achievements."[36]

This statement from the politically circumspect governor was as unusual as it was gratifying to Chase. Another brief speech at the depot and then off to Cincinnati, with impromptu remarks from the platform of his car at Xenia, Monroe, and to the soldiers at Camp Dennison. In a repetition of his arrival at Columbus a large and enthusiastic reception awaited him at the Cincinnati depot. A driving rainstorm canceled the outdoor evening meeting, but the local committee was equal to the task of rearranging plans.[37]

They secured Mozart Hall, the largest in the city, and when Chase moved to the stage a mighty roar of approval came from the densely packed floor and balconies. Inspired by his reception, Chase delivered a lengthy, eloquent, and telling speech that set forth in comprehensive terms the causes, the impact, and the objectives of the conflict.

For the thinking man and woman, he made clear that slavery was the root of the nation's troubles. His voice raised, his massive features flushed, Chase flailed what he called a landed aristocracy in the South that would protect its slave institution at any cost. He warned that without complete victory, free labor would be at risk and democracy would give way to oligarchy. The southern rich not only controlled but debased the southern poor. As a result this ruling class endangered free institutions everywhere. "Is this country worth a war?" he asked his audience and then answered his own question. "Look through the history of the world," he said, "and tell me where you will find a people struggling for a nobler object." From then on he rehearsed all the proposals he had urged upon the administration—removal of the exceptions to the Emancipation Proclamation—"the loyal citizens of a state constitute the state." Slavery must be abolished everywhere by state action or by constitutional amendment. "We make war against the rebellion," he said, pausing for dramatic effect, his features highlighted by the flickering gas lights, "and against slavery because it is the life of the rebellion, and we don't leave slavery untouched, because we don't want to preserve the seminal principle of the rebellion under the forms of restored national supremacy." Throughout his remarks, Chase emphasized the free-labor theme and not just as a moral imperative. "Free laborers will bring more for themselves than masters will buy for slaves," he declared. And he linked this argument to his financial policies, where he indulged in that rhetorical modesty that was favored by audiences of the day. "It seemed to me that if labor was henceforth to have fair wages, it was highly desirable to have for a medium of payment, a substantial, permanent and uniform medium so that labor should not be cheated of its rewards," he said. "So I set my poor wits to work to devise a uniform currency for the whole country. . . ." But, as he concluded, "unless we are to have one Republic it is not worthwhile to have one currency."[38]

Levi P. Morton, the energetic Republican governor of Indiana, had come over from Indianapolis to hear Chase. He was so impressed that he begged the secretary to visit Indiana for at least one speech. Chase was happy to oblige. In fact he did more than that. As his car traveled west, he spoke at three Indiana towns before his major speech at Indianapolis. It was here that Chase, reveling in his newfound popularity, spent much of his time on the podium explaining and glorifying his financial policies as vital to the eventual success of the Union armies and navies. "I went to work," he said in one of his colloquial asides, "and made 'greenbacks' and a good many of them. I had some handsome pictures put on them; and as I like to be among the people . . . and as the engravers thought me rather good looking I told them they might put me on the end of the one-dollar bills."[39]

Chase did pause in what had become less a thrust at Vallandigham than an electioneering jaunt for himself to telegraph Lincoln that the Republican-Union ticket had achieved a landslide in Ohio.[40] On his return, he made another brief speech at Columbus, where he spent the night, but he was up at 4 a.m. to begin his return trip to Washington. The crowds, the processions, the brass bands, the decorated halls, the fulsome praise from politicians such as Dennison and Morton, and the enthusiastic response in the Republican press all were exhilarating.[41]

His speeches and remarks, unlike those of the Blairs, did not castigate his personal and political opponents by name nor criticize their conservative approach to Reconstruction and Emancipation. But inferences there were aplenty and those who read between the lines could see a thinly disguised attack on the administration's policies, especially its lack of any specific plan to reconstruct the South after the war was won.[42] For one brief period Chase had stolen a march on Lincoln. One could surely agree with the lead editorial in the Cincinnati *Enquirer* on the Sunday after the election that the Republican-Union victory in Ohio was a "Chase triumph."[43]

On one more occasion he could exhibit himself and this one close to his adopted home. Though he had claimed frequently that as a Cabinet member he would not involve himself in Maryland politics, he reversed himself and accepted an invitation from Baltimore custom collector Henry Hoffman to address a mass meeting of the "Unconditional Unionists" in Monument

Square on the 29th.[44] His speech, shorter and more general than his remarks in the Midwest, in openly identifying himself with Henry Winter Davis was challenging Montgomery Blair on his home ground. Blair and Davis were as bitter political enemies as those in that sphere of power and personality could possibly be.[45]

Edward Bates, cynical observer of Chase's maneuvers, had read the Ohio and Indiana addresses with interest if not approval. "That visit west," he confided to his diary, "is generally understood as Mr. Ch[a]se's opening campaign for the Presidency." Bates correctly understood that "war is openly begun between Mr. C[hase] and the Blairs." Bates was more disturbed than he would acknowledge by Chase's warm relationship with the "Charcoal" faction in Missouri.[46]

Lincoln had written a long and carefully framed letter to the Missouri radicals refusing to replace General Schofield and reiterating various points he had raised in his now famous letter to Horace Greeley, which put saving the Union first among war aims. This time Lincoln recognized all shades of opinion on emancipation as pertinent and disparaged the savage guerilla warfare then ravaging Missouri.[47] Clearly he was trying to mediate between contending factions. Lincoln's letter disappointed Chase, though as he explained to Charles Drake, one of the Missouri radical leaders, he "did not expect one more satisfactory than it is."[48]

Lincoln finally decided that he must explain again and more explicitly why he included exceptions in the Emancipation Proclamation not only to Chase but to all his associates. On the morning of September 17, 1863 he read Chase a letter on the subject which he had not yet completed to his own satisfaction. After making the case for the military necessity of emancipation, Lincoln posed a series of rhetorical questions. If he abandoned the military necessity argument would he "not thus give up all footing on the constitution or law? . . . Could it fail to be perceived that without further stretch; I might do the same in Delaware, Maryland, Kentucky, Tennessee and Missouri, and even change any law in any state?"

Chase became increasingly uncomfortable as he listened to the measured phrases, the argument which he had to admit was "strongly put." Yet he sought to debate the issue until Lincoln cut him off with the remark that "any revocation, at all events was not expedient at present, and should be deferred until after the Fall elections."[49]

The elections Lincoln spoke of came and went, but the President had not rescinded the exceptions. Chase took further notice of this failure among other complaints he had about Lincoln's policies or, as he felt, lack of policy. "Oh! that the President could be induced to take the positive responsibility of prompt action," Chase remonstrated, "as readily as he takes the passive responsibility of delay and letting bad enough alone!"[50]

Lincoln had begun to downgrade Chase's campaign, but the secretary's speeches in the Midwest and the angry, indeed rancorous attitude of the Missouri radicals remained disturbing. In an conversation with his young secretary, John Hay, Lincoln said, "Whenever he [Chase] sees that an important matter is troubling me, if I am compelled to decide it in a way to give offense to a man of some influence, he always ranges himself in opposition to me and persuades the victim that he has been hardly dealt by and that he would have arranged it very differently."[51]

In good spirits after the affirmative reaction to his first public speeches in three years, Chase looked forward to his daughter Kate's wedding. This event, like much of Chase's activities that fall, was not without its political implications. The twenty-three-year-old Kate had acted as Chase's hostess in the townhouse at Sixth and E streets. She had also become the toast of Washington to the young army and navy officers, high-placed government clerks and visiting lobbyists of some importance, and to the older generation as well.

Kate had made life pleasant for the overworked, sometimes overwrought secretary. Along with her charming manners, her lovely appearance, and obvious intelligence was her managerial ability. She ran Chase's busy household with a sure hand, relieving her father of burdensome chores.[52] Chase entertained a good deal, quite apart from his expected formal dinners and receptions. Scarcely a day went by when he breakfasted alone or with his immediate family. Congressmen, military officers, ministers, bankers, and other businessmen enjoyed the bountiful meals he provided. A teetotaler and nonsmoker himself, wine, liquor and cigars were always available.

Of all the Cabinet officers and including the President, Chase was the most active in making political points out of his socializing. Thus when Kate became engaged to William Sprague, former governor, now senator from Rhode Island, Chase went about converting the forthcoming marriage into a political as well as a personal event.[53] As early as June, Chase was actively promoting the wedding. A revenue cutter was to be launched in one of the New York shipyards. Chase instructed Barney to have the vessel named for "one of the small streams in Rhode Island on which one of Sprague's factories are." He added that he wanted Kate to christen the vessel.[54]

Of course the wedding would be a Washington affair and confined to the small circle of important people who lived and worked in the capital. But a favorable impression made on this select and powerful group added to the secretary's already imposing status and stature. That the bridegroom-to-be was one of the richest men in the nation was an attraction to the material-minded Washington community and a factor of some awe to Chase, who while moderately well-off still had to watch his expenses.

Politically Sprague seemed well connected, though rumors persisted that he had bought his nomination and election as governor of Rhode Island and U.S. senatator.[55] Gossip impugned the young senator's private life that could not if true accord with Chase's standards of morality.[56] But he overlooked any presumed faults in Sprague's character. Like any doting parent it was painful to lose a daughter and such an accomplished one at that, but he saw the match as a good and proper one.

Yet he was worried about the couple's future, more concerned about Kate's temperament than he was about Sprague's, whose wealth and political importance seemed to have blinded him to the younger man's personal reputation.[57] Chase "feared some inequalities of temper in Kate's personality, some too great love of the world either of its possessions [or] . . . something I hardly know what." He was also concerned about her apparent obsession with his career. "She must not be so," he wrote Sprague. "There is nothing so uncertain as the political future of any man."[58]

Chase confessed how dear she was to him, how much he would miss her, how "more thoughtful, more affectionate, more loving" she was. "She has known almost nothing of a mother's care," he said, as he urged Sprague not to imperil their relationship over the larger concerns, the tragedies which would surely arise, but to be on guard for those small everyday problems, those trivial disagreements, the ones that would corrode and could eventually destroy mutual love and respect.[59]

Sprague at this early stage in the courtship was equally deferential. Chase must have appeared to the small, slight senator not simply a power in the land but a physically imposing power as well. He respected Chase's council and in a moment of candor said that he did not "expect that all will, at all times run smoothly. . . ."[60] In perhaps the only time in his life, he sought to bare his soul to another person. He said in a rather confusing letter that he recognized "the delicate link which has so long united father and daughter." He would do his best to maintain this link. As for himself he confessed, "I have taken little or no care for myself during my past life. It has been my luck to have others interested in my welfare. From my earliest youth, I have neglected both mind and body . . . I have not had a father's care for 20 years, Katie has missed a mother." Sprague wanted a father's guidance, council, and affection. Chase was delighted to play the foster parent.[61]

Once he had approved of the match, Chase managed the affair, apparently without opposition from either Kate or Sprague. He set the wedding date for early September, then he extended it because the fall weather would be just right for the ceremony and the honeymoon.[62] Nor was Sprague spared advice, particularly on living arrangements after the wedding.[63] Most of the year Chase's duties kept him close to the White House and Capitol Hill.

Sprague as a senator spent at least six months each year in Washington. It made sense that the married couple establish their permanent residence in the capital.

When the matter was first broached Chase thought that they should occupy separate houses.[64] This time Kate overruled her father. It was agreed that the house on 6th Street be purchased and renovated in such a way that the two families could occupy it. They would share the servants, the large downstairs parlors for receptions, and would dine together. A sense of privacy would be maintained with Chase retaining the bedroom he now occupied and the library he used as a study. Chase would bear the costs of servant's wages; Sprague, the table expenses; and they would divide the stabling costs. Chase already owned two carriages and did not think it necessary for Sprague to purchase additional ones. As he explained, "nobody makes much use of them but Katie. You and I will hardly require either. . . . Better give the money it would cost to the hospitals."[65] Again Chase soon learned what it was to deal with a millionaire in league with a spendthrift daughter.[66] Sprague went ahead and purchased the carriages.[67] He also bought the house at 6th and E and the adjoining lot. To Chase's consternation, Kate began an costly expansion and remodeling program.[68]

When it came to the guest list for the wedding and reception, however, Chase was the principal arbiter. He saw to it that those of political importance to him received invitations. He selected the fifty or so persons who would witness the ceremony: the President and Mrs. Lincoln, of course, all the Cabinet members including Montgomery Blair, senior army and navy officers who happened to be in Washington, a select group of congressmen and other local notables, and family members on both sides. The guests from Rhode Island were housed at Chase's expense at Willard's. Just before the appointed time for the ceremony, President Lincoln arrived and joined the group. Mrs. Lincoln did not attend, ostensibly still in mourning for her son Willie, but more probably because she disliked Kate.

Promptly at 8:30 in the evening, the double doors that separated the two parlors were thrown open. The bride followed by her bridesmaids, among whom were her sister Nettie, her cousin Alice S. Skinner, and Ida Nichols, Sprague's niece, descended the stairs from the second floor. Kate was a striking sight, dressed in a white velvet gown that displayed her lissome figure. A tiara of matched pearls and diamonds, her wedding gift from Sprague, encircled her bridal veil. Chase stood at the bottom of the stairs, ready to accompany his daughter to the center of the room where the Episcopal bishop of Rhode Island, Thomas March Clark, in full vestments, was waiting. As the group advanced, the marine band played a wedding march that the composer of popular tunes Frederick Kroell had written for the occasion.

The contrast was startling between the slim but statuesque figure and the beautiful features of the bride and the small, pale bridegroom, whose droopy mustache accentuated rather than enhanced his nondescript features. The thirty-three-year-old Sprague could scarcely be taken as a man of the world. Even dressed as he was in formal attire, he seemed more like a clerk in one of his family's textile mills. The bishop joined the two in marriage, the bride and the wealthy bridegroom. Chase kissed his daughter, congratulated his new son-in-law, and the marine band struck up again the Kate Chase wedding march. Street doors were opened to the crowd, who had come to indulge in the lavish refreshments that had been provided on the second floor. The rear parlor had been kept clear for dancing and Kate led off with Richard Parsons, internal revenue collector for the Cleveland area. Parsons was one of Chase's chief political organizers.[69]

It had been a gaudy affair. Wedding gifts on display were worth more than $60,000. Kate's tiara alone was said to have cost $50,000. The jewels, the silver and gold plate, and other gifts exceeded Chase's net worth. But the ambitious secretary, whose strict morality at times was overcome by his devotion to the main chance, failed to see an extravagance which he had so often warned his daughters against. After all the President stayed for two hours and seemed to enjoy himself. Even old Francis Preston Blair was present and in good humor despite the well-known antipathy of his two sons for Chase. Perhaps Blair's presence was a favorable omen.[70]

Chase was in a buoyant mood for a change, though as usual he concealed any outward manifestations of personal satisfaction. He could and did take credit that public finances were no worse than they had ever been despite mounting costs for the war. Indications were now evident that the national banking system was gaining credibility from the banks and the public.

The military situation was neither good nor bad. Grant and Sherman relieved Rosecrans and lifted the siege of Chattanooga. They had gone on to defeat Bragg's army in a series of brilliant engagements that drove it into northwestern Georgia. Burnside's battered army still held Knoxville in eastern Tennessee astride Bragg's supply line from Virginia, but the Confederate army of the Tennessee was still very much intact. Meade's Army of the Potomac was stalemated in eastern Virginia. Fort Sumter remained in Confederate hands despite its pounding by thousands of artillery rounds and mortar shells. Charleston, the objective of the Union army on the coast of South Carolina, seemed impregnable.

Chase's good spirits may have stemmed from his belief that a combination of war weariness and the conservative policies of the Lincoln administration, such as its hesitancy about total abolition, was working in his favor. He took comfort in the fact that he had laid out the specifications of his program in his Ohio and Indiana speeches and that they had met with a favorable reaction from the trend-setting Republican dailies. He had what he thought was the support of the congressional radicals. He believed that he had put behind him his ill-fated attempt to drive Seward from the Cabinet. Henry Winter Davis, the able, and contentious critic of Lincoln and the Blairs, was friendly, as were John Sherman, Kansas senator Samuel Pomeroy, Iowa senator James Grimes, a political associate of long standing, and Governor Morton of Indiana.[71] Chase had been cultivating apparently with favorable results the new senator from California, John Conness.[72] Sumner, of course, could be counted on, and Andrew Johnson, politically potent among the Union Democrats, remembered Chase's early support of his stand in east Tennessee.[73]

But Chase's position with the radicals was uncertain. Here it was mainly a matter of trust. Thaddeus Stevens, the caustic yet powerful chairman of the House Ways and Means Committee who had worked closely with Chase, had little use for the secretary's basic financial policies, distrusted his politics, and disliked his pompous demeanor. Ben Wade, a commanding figure on the Committee for the Conduct of the War, long an enemy in Ohio and in national politics, thought Chase was the prince of hypocrites, an entirely undeserved, but nevertheless harmful characterization.

However, Chase had more to fear from the conservatives and moderates in the party. Seward and Weed were no mean antagonists, and the Blairs— especially Frank—were dangerous enemies, made more so by Chase's courting of Henry Winter Davis. In the west Chase's lieutenants were attacking Frank in the columns of the *Missouri Democrat*.[74]

Making few public statements and fewer private ones except to his secretaries, the President was watching the political imbroglio with a practiced eye, always listening to personal jibes about Chase and his moves, but rarely commenting on them.[75] When driven by the radicals, as in the Missouri case, he would respond verbally and in a careful, thoughtful letter.[76] When driven by Chase's constant refrain that he eliminate the exceptions in the Emancipation Proclamation, he answered with a carefully conceived statement of policy which even Chase had to praise. When the Democrats were stirred up about the Vallandigham arrest and military trial and much conservative and moderate opinion was disturbed by the suspension of the writ of habeas corpus in draft and enlistment cases, Lincoln wrote a masterful defense of his actions.[77]

But Chase's campaign worried Lincoln. His mood was evident in his response to John Hay's suggestion that Chase would seek political advantage from the sacking of Rosecrans after his defeat at Chickamauga. Lincoln laughed but then mused, "I suppose he will, like the bluebottle fly lays his eggs in every rotten spot he can find."[78]

Gideon Welles, whose views about Chase were sometimes admiring but more often harshly critical, observed that he was "clumsy but strong."[79] In a political sense Chase during that fall of 1863 was far too clumsy and too obvious to improve his chances, considering the forces and the political talent arrayed against him. Comforted by his nationwide web of agents that he had in place after the passage of the Internal Revenue Act,[80] he naively thought this patronage machine would drive his campaign.[81]

Thurlow Weed, acting on his own but believing that Lincoln would be renominated and reelected, was slowly gaining control of custom house patronage through Barney's personal secretary, Albert Palmer. Chase's friends in New York, Mayor Opdyke and David Dudley Field, had broken with Barney, a fact that further shook Chase's faith in the collector.[82] He dispatched one of his confidential clerks, John F. Bailey, to investigate the political temper of the custom house and if possible harmonize the divergent elements there. After a long talk with Barney, Bailey wrote Chase that whatever may have been the better course two months ago, "it seems certain that the only way now is to make the best of him and to influence him as far as possible the control of the means at his command." Bailey implied that Barney would help the Chase candidacy but reluctantly.[83] Chase also called on William Orton, the internal revenue collector in the city, and Rufus Andrews, the surveyor in the custom house, for support against Weed, who was mounting a major assault on the New York radicals and was winning the battle.[84]

Complicating Chase's problem was recurring evidence of corruption and mismanagement in the custom house.[85] Yet Chase remained sublimely confident, belittling the political problems that were thickening around him. He was receiving strong newspaper backing from Greeley's *Tribune*. George Wilkes's popular *Spirit of the Times* was also a Chase boomer.

Unresolved difficulties could hurt Chase severely. Though his network of agents may have given him nationwide support, many of them could not resist taking advantage of their power and position to enrich themselves. His prestige as a successful director of the nation's finances during an enormously costly conflict was high, but inflation and currency speculation detracted from his very real achievements. And equally important among these negatives was that Chase was losing his political power base in Ohio, a loss that he did not at first comprehend.

chapter 26

Bad Company

The year 1864 was scarcely two months old when the House of Representatives resolved itself into a committee of the whole for debate. Francis Preston Blair, Jr., or Frank, as he was generally known, had the floor. Everyone present expected an attack on Chase and they were not disappointed. Blair was a handsome, dynamic figure, slightly under six feet tall, lean but well muscled, his reddish-brown hair and full beard showing little sign of graying despite his forty-three years. His piercing gray eyes and high cheekbones, which complementing his wide brow and full chin, gave him a youthful appearance. Unhappily his nature was impulsive, even reckless as a military commander and as a politician. He was a heavy drinker and an equally heavy smoker of strong cigars, weaknesses that were already undermining his strong frame.

Blair had been elected to a second term in Congress from the St. Louis district of Missouri. While serving as a corps commander in General Sherman's Army of the Tennessee, he had given a good account of himself in the battles around Chattanooga. Blair enjoyed army life and was in a quandary over whether he should resign his commission or take his seat in Congress. He asked his brother, Montgomery, to explain his dilemma to Lincoln and say that he would be guided by the President's wishes. After thinking over the matter for a few days Lincoln wrote Montgomery that it would be best for Frank to place his commission in his hands, "take his seat, go into caucus with our friends, abide the nominations, help elect the nominee, and thus aid to organize a House of Representatives which will really support the government in the war."

After that he could remain in Congress or reclaim his commission and return to the army.[1] Frank Blair acted belatedly on the President's advice. He arrived in Washington on January 10, 1864, after the House organized.[2] He placed his commission in Lincoln's hands, though he did not formerly resign.[3]

A senior officer whose courage was as well known as his turbulent political career, Blair commanded the attention of his audience when he began to speak. As he warmed to his topic he referred to the radicals in Missouri and Maryland as "Jacobins" who were bent on destroying the Union coalition, attempting to defeat the President's policies and his reelection for purely selfish reasons.[4]

But the major thrust of his speech was a full-scale attack on Chase and his Treasury appointees. He stood by his desk, his voice at times shrill, his eyes flashing, and charged that "a more profligate administration of the Treasury Department never existed under any government; that the whole Mississippi valley is rank and fetid with the fraud and corruptions practiced there by his [Chase's] agents. These dependents of the secretary, these agents and missionaries . . . have been secretly forming an organization in his favor all over the country. . . ." There was some truth to Blair's overblown charges, much more of speculation that bordered on falsehood.[5]

The intensity of Blair's two-hour speech took the Chase men by surprise. He had only one interruption of little consequence. Speaker Colfax, hitherto friendly to Blair, now an opponent, saw to it that his demand for an investigation of the Treasury Department be referred to the radical-dominated Committee on the Conduct of the War. Many of its members were skeptical of the Chase candidacy, but they were sure to block any meaningful investigation of the Treasury.[6]

Meanwhile, a radical fellow congressman had accused Blair of corrupt practices and wrong-doing. He bided his time. After a special investigation committee cleared him completely, he learned that his principal accuser, a Treasury agent, had forged the incriminating document. Again Blair went on the offensive. The galleries and the floor of the House were treated to a spectacle of unrelenting invective against Chase, whose "Treasury Empire" and ideas on Reconstruction—"a pretentious title"—meant destruction of the states. Chase supporters interrupted Blair repeatedly. Speaker Colfax declared him out of order. But so many congressmen either for or against Blair enjoyed the histrionics that Colfax lost control of the debate. Blair continued with what he termed evidence of "flagitious" corruption. Many of the letters and communications he read into the record were anonymous. Some of the names he cited were would-be dealers in contraband for cotton. Others were political enemies of Chase who were interested in driving him out of the party. Not a few were opposed to his views on emancipation and civil rights for the blacks but equated these stands with corrupt practices to finance them. Chase's relationship with Jay Cooke in marketing government securities did not escape notice and censure. Nor were the cotton dealings of Chase's son-in-law William Sprague ignored. It was a vicious assault on Chase's character, a strenuous effort to mark him as the supreme Judas of the administration who would stoop to flagrant abuse of power and trust to further his ambitions.[7]

Blair had reason for his resentment of Chase and his agents and there was considerable truth to his allegations, but he had very little firm evidence. He had been ill with rheumatism and severe headaches since his arrival in Washington. Probably he had imbibed freely before his diatribe, whose language bore signs of overheated rhetoric.

Lincoln may have appreciated Blair's defense of his policies, but the excessive hyperbole was embarrassing. Montgomery, who was in the President's confidence at the time, said that "Lincoln sent for him from the army to defend him and to assault Chase on the floor of the House of Representatives."[8] Yet Lincoln was annoyed at the depth and breadth of the accusations against Chase, who was after all still a senior member of his administration and could possibly become a formidable enemy. The radicals, if they did not altogether trust Chase's motives, certainly agreed with his objectives on emancipation and Reconstruction. Their program, still in its formative stages and not yet supported by a majority of congressmen or public opinion, represented a sizable segment of the Union coalition.

Blair was fighting for his political life in Missouri, where Chase and his adherents were anxious to destroy the machine he had built up over the past twelve years.[9] Opposing views on Reconstruction and emancipation had drawn the lines more sharply. They had led to recriminations that radiated outward and distinctly impaired the efficiency of the government in Washington, threatening the fragile cohesion of the Republican-Union coalition. Bemoaning the severity of Frank Blair's attacks on Chase, Gideon Welles remarked: "It is unfortunate that these assaults should be made on political friends, or those who should be friends."[10]

A disturbed Lincoln sent for Blair late in the evening after his philippic. He was undecided just how to handle the situation. "Within three hours," he remarked, "I heard that this speech had been made. When I knew that another beehive was kicked over, my first thought was to have cancelled the orders restoring him to the army and assigning him command. Perhaps this would have been best." But Lincoln finally concluded "to let them stand. If I was wrong in this, the injury to the service can be set right."[11] These comments as Congressman Albert G. Riddle remembered them were not exactly accurate. It seems likely that Lincoln was troubled by the extent of Blair's vilification and deeply concerned about its impact not just on Chase but on the party.[12] He must also have been disturbed at what could be charged as an arbitrary and unconstitutional act. The Constitution stipulated that no person could hold two positions of public trust at the same time. If Blair had resigned his commission to take his seat in Congress, the President was bound to recommend and seek Senate confirmation for his reappointment as a major general. He had not done so.

Lincoln cherished the Blairs as friends, loyal supporters, and leaders of conservative opinion within the party. Had he followed the prescribed line and resubmitted Blair's name to the Senate, he risked certain delay, even possible refusal, which would have injured the administration and opened further the growing schism between the various wings of the party, not to mention the political capital the Democratic minority would have made out of the affair. Military necessity also weighed on the President's mind. After a long discussion with the errant congressman-major general that lasted until the early hours of the morning of April 24, Lincoln returned Blair's commission to him. When he reached home and asked his sister Elizabeth to awaken him within the next few hours, she concluded from their brief conversation that his meeting with Lincoln "was not a disagreeable one."[13]

As anticipated there was a furor in the Congress and demands for Lincoln's impeachment but the partisan-inspired heat quickly died down. Not so with Chase, whose reaction was one of sustained fury. He had managed to control himself despite the provocation of Blair's previous attacks. He had offered his resignation when the activities of his campaign committee became public in the ill-fated Pomery circular, which attacked the President and praised Chase. Lincoln had refused to accept it, though their relationship was further strained.

But now, smarting over the collapse of his presidential campaign, he was in no mood to accept what he regarded as a vicious attack on his character. In this state of mind, he decided to attend the Sanitary Commission Fair in Baltimore.[14] At the last minute he invited ex-congressman Riddle, a firm political supporter, to join the party. When Riddle reached the station, he found Kate standing on the platform. She said that her father wanted to see him privately in the car John W. Garrett, president of the B & O, had put at his disposal. "He was alone," recalled Riddle, "and in a frightful rage." Riddle was amazed. He had known Chase for years and had admired his ability to control himself under the harshest of provocations. After Riddle told him that Frank Blair had visited Lincoln and had his commission as a major general restored, Chase in a hoarse, trembling voice jumped to the conclusion that Lincoln had engineered the entire episode to humiliate him before the country and drive him out of politics. Chase said that he would cancel his trip, remain in the city, and immediately resign his post.

Riddle reasoned with the angry man. He advised him to wait until all the facts in the matter could be ascertained. Chase finally pulled himself together. Still believing that the President had played him false, he grudgingly accepted Riddle's point that even if "the President had acquiesced silently, it was purely a matter between him [Mr. Chase] and Mr. Blair." Chase's friends would find it difficult to accept his resignation after merely a personal attack from a political enemy. With pardonable exaggeration, Riddle said that Chase's position was "more important than the command of the armies in the field." His resignation would jeopardize the finances of the nation. It would injure the party on the eve of a presidential election in the midst of a difficult and bloody conflict.[15]

Riddle felt that he had managed to head off any precipitous action. As soon as he saw the Chase party off, he boarded the first train back to Washington, where he hoped to get the facts from Lincoln himself. On his arrival he sought out his successor in Congress, Rufus Spalding, another of Chase's long-term political associates, and together they went to the White House. There they explained their mission to the President's senior secretary, John G. Nicolay, who got them an interview with Lincoln the following Monday.

Nicolay had briefed Lincoln, who must have suspected that they were emissaries from Chase. No doubt sensitive about his decision to restore Blair's commission, he received them "politely but with no pretense of cordiality." He moved away from the two gentlemen and sat down on the opposite side of the long, wide table in his office.

After explaining that he was a personal and political friend of Chase's, Riddle laid out the case of what he termed the "alert, jealous and somewhat exacting abolitionists." Citing the immediate departure of Frank Blair after his vituperative speech with his major general's commission in his pocket yet still presumably a member of Congress, he said plainly that these "abolitionists" believe Blair "must have had at least your countenance in this wretched business and they demand the instant resignation of Mr. Chase."

Riddle then went on to say that such a course would be a catastrophe that could break down the coalition and "might be the destruction of our cause." He explained that he was not speaking for the "abolitionists" and that he had not come "to demand terms." But he would be happy to carry back a message that Lincoln was not "a party to or responsible for a word uttered by Mr. Blair." When Riddle finished his remarks, Lincoln's mood changed abruptly. He arose from his chair, picked up some papers, and came around to Riddle and Spalding. Projecting an air of warmth and cordiality he took them both by the hands and said, "Gentlemen, I am glad to meet you, glad for your mission and especially for your way of executing it. Have you seen my letter to Mr. Chase of February 29th in reply to his of the 22nd, concerning his candidacy and offering his resignation?" "I have," said Spalding. "I have not," said

Riddle. Lincoln read his letter refusing Chase's resignation on account of the Pomeroy circular. He was referring to a pamphlet that Chase's campaign committee had circulated accusing Lincoln of incompetence in his conduct of the war and nominating Chase as the party's candidate for President.

He then gave his version of the events leading up to Blair's first attack in Congress on Chase, which he found both "mortifying and annoying." The second most recent onslaught, he claimed, was made without his knowledge. But he accepted full responsibility for the decision to restore Blair's commission. The interview lasted more than an hour, during which Lincoln spoke of the political problems in Missouri and Maryland. Said Riddle: "He was plain, sincere and most impressive." Both men met with Chase when he returned to Washington and after giving him a full account of the meeting were able to convince him that he must remain in the Cabinet. Chase remained skeptical of Lincoln's innocence in the affair, which further damaged his relationship with the President.[16] Chase's acute sensitivity to the Blair assault and his belief that Lincoln was implicated in it is not wholly explained by his embarrassment over the reaction to the Pomeroy circular.

The past year had been one of considerable trial to him. What had been a source of some anxiety was whether he could count on the honesty and the efficiency of his Treasury Department officials. The area of greatest concern to Chase was also the area of greatest political friction, the New York custom house, the theater wherein opposing forces within the Republican coalition vied for control of its patronage. Chase's friend Barney was the collector, and another associate, Henry B. Stanton, was one of the many deputy collectors. The collector had broad powers over procedures, less over direct political patronage. Seward-Weed men controlled a majority of the subordinate officers, who were to some extent independent of the collector.

Chase cherished his reputation as an experienced and honest administrator. At the same time he firmly believed that his political base anchored upon patronage gave him the means that made him a capable public servant. Understandably then he was ever ready to expand his hold on patronage and to defend it whenever menaced. He was especially sensitive about custom-house appointments, not just in New York but in Boston, Philadelphia, Baltimore, and far-off San Francisco.[17]

In late October, 1863, just as Chase's presidential campaign was beginning to show some signs of strength, George Denison, the naval officer, who owed his job to Lincoln, telegraphed Washington about irregularities in Stanton's office. Chase reacted quickly.[18] He sent his solicitor Edward Jordan to New York, who then telegraphed that regretfully he had found evidence that Stanton and his son were guilty of mishandling the bonds of many importers.

Chase had been kept informed about the increasing traffic in what was suspected to be contraband material traveling to and from New York, the

British West Indies, and Matamoros, a Mexican port city on the Rio Grande just opposite Brownsville, Texas.[19] Among Stanton's responsibilities was the taking of bonds from importers covering their manifests. If their cargo was found to be contraband, the importer would forfeit his bond. Before the vessel could be cleared, a bond signed by Stanton had to be attached. Jordan found that many of the bonds were not on the clearance papers and others had signatures forged or otherwise altered.[20]

The politically sensitive investigation of a senior custom-house officer was sure to be leaked to the press. Four days after Jordan completed his preliminary investigation the *New York Times* and the New York *World* carried stories of extensive frauds in the custom house and named Stanton as the culprit. From there the New York press kept the story alive by reporting conversations with talkative custom-house employees. The harassed deputy pleaded with Chase for assistance, claiming innocence and trial by the press. Chase's answer to Stanton was that the public interest demanded a complete investigation and that he either ought to resign or ask for a temporary leave of absence while Congress looked into the allegations.[21]

Stanton was undoubtedly guilty of malfeasance, if not direct graft. His son Neil was the principal culprit, however. Under pressure from Barney and Chase, Stanton resigned a month or so later after implying in the press that he was a victim of the Seward-Weed influence.[22] As much as Chase deplored Stanton's guilt and its damage to his own reputation, he was far more concerned that his share of the custom-house patronage was weakening under a direct attack from Weed, who was presumably acting in Lincoln's interest.[23] Weeks before the Stanton investigation Chase's banker friend John A. Stevens had told him that "Weed men" were in the custom house, unknown to Barney.[24] An alarmed Chase had Jordan talk to Barney about his presidential preferences.[25]

Jordan's report was not that satisfactory. He said that Barney told him he would support a Chase candidacy but he was sure Lincoln would be the nominee.[26] Chase continued to back Barney even after he learned that the collector's private secretary, Albert Palmer, his chief patronage dispenser and political organizer, was secretly acting for Weed and was directly responsible for the defeat of the radical ticket in the New York city mayoralty contest.[27] Caught in the crossfire between the Seward-Weed group and the New York radicals, Barney was becoming a political liability to Lincoln and to Chase.[28] As Lincoln said, ". . . I am convinced that he has ceased to be master of his position."[29]

Beset by custom-house problems Chase never probed a scandal involving the department that had worked its way into the highest of Washington circles. It was all the more difficult because it cast a shadow over Chase's connections with the Cookes, inviting yet a further congressional investigation. Jay Cooke had become indispensable to Chase's policies in marketing government bonds. He and Chase's new son-in-law Sprague were the principal sources of funds for Chase's presidential campaign. And Cooke's nationwide program for marketing government equities entailed running clever newspaper advertisements which featured Chase as the essential person in sustaining the war effort.[30]

Quite apart from Cooke's political and financial roles, Chase had formed a close personal relationship with the Cookes, the amiable Henry D. in Washington and Jay in Philadelphia. Kate, Nettie, and Chase himself frequently stopped over at Jay Cooke's mansion, "The Cedars," in the Chelten Hills, northwest of Philadelphia. Cooke could be counted on for short-term loans and acted as Chase's broker, investing for him small sums in stocks and bonds. Their relationship at times worried Chase. More than once he cautioned Jay not to mix private matters with public in his letters.[31] And Chase was careful—in Cooke's eyes, parsimonious—in his allowance of an eighth of 1 percent commission at par value on the sale of government bonds, out of which the banker had to bear the costs for advertising and other expenses due to delayed payment and fluctuating values of checks, commercial and agricultural paper, and other financial instruments Cooke received in payment.[32] If Chase drove a hard bargain with the Cookes they in turn were able to profit immensely on the advance information they gleaned from their close association with Treasury funding. At his strategic desk in the Washington branch, Henry Cooke was particularly useful to the Philadelphia bank. More a journalist and lobbyist than a banker, he was a jovial person whose reportorial instincts were unusually sharp when it came to offhand remarks about Treasury personnel, clerks in other departments, high-ranking military and naval officers, Cabinet members, and congressmen.

Unlike his brother Jay, he was not as careful about his own personal investments, some of which revealed his contacts with Chase on forthcoming Treasury moves. He used this inside information to engage in a particularly flagrant speculation in army quartermaster supplies. His associates were an army captain stationed in Cincinnati and an editor of the *Ohio State Journal*. Cooke's role was exposed just as Chase's campaign for the Republican presidential nomination began to gain momentum in December of 1863 and January 1864. War Secretary Stanton saw to it that the affair was covered up.[33]

Chase never learned of Henry Cooke's dealings, which also involved some of his trusted Treasury agents in Cincinnati and Columbus.[34] Enough suspicion of favoritism and large profits gained had emerged as a result of the Cookes' relationship with the Treasury to bolster attacks in the press. Congress passed a resolution early in January requesting Chase to supply pertinent information about the Cookes' role.[35] Chase was able to refute all charges of exorbitant profits to the Cooke firm and his congressional friends made an able defense of the Treasury's policies in marketing the 5–20s.[36] But political pressure and public criticism was too manifest for Chase to ignore. He dissolved Cooke's exclusive agency.

Despite the enthusiastic reception Chase received on his well-publicized Ohio trip, his Treasury agents and internal revenue collectors in the Mississippi valley had earned an unsavory reputation. Chase's close friend and chief political organizer in Ohio, William Mellen, had been in close touch with the corrupt army quartermaster in Cincinnati.[37] Chase brushed aside information he had received that the internal revenue collector in Columbus was a member of an illegal cotton ring.[38] Nor was he concerned about the activities of Treasury people in setting up "trade stores" in areas under Union military control or about profits gained by trafficking in leases and sales of "abandoned plantations."[39]

As far as Chase was concerned these were legitimate practices so long as they met the scrutiny and approval of the supervising special agents whom Chase trusted. He never insisted on a specific accounting from them. Nor did he question their power in the Mississippi Valley which engendered jealousy among a host of aspiring claimants.[40]

Chase did act promptly to deny any special license to trade for cotton, even when one of his closest political friends—Richard C. Parsons, internal revenue collector at Cleveland—asked for one as a personal favor. "Of course if I could grant special favors to anybody while administering a public trust," he wrote Parsons, "you would be a little more apt to be the recipient of them than any other person. But it would be wrong to do."[41] Lofty sentiments these and Chase believed in them, ignoring harsh realities and the damage they were doing to his reputation for probity and efficiency. It was not until Frank Blair's attacks on Chase's network that he took steps to have the Treasury regulations awarding permits to the agents tightened.[42]

chapter 27

"It Is a Big Fish"

If Chase was responsible for the actions of his agents in the Mississippi Valley and thus vulnerable to political attack, he was also guilty of that cardinal political sin of not looking after his home base. With the exception of his brief barnstorming tour of Ohio and Indiana in October 1863 Chase had counted on his handful of trusted associates—the Cookes, his son-in-law Sprague, a half-dozen or so newspapers, some tottering like the *Ohio State Journal* (whose management was part of the corrupt army quartermaster ring), and the gifted Whitelaw Reid, nominally Washington correspondent of the Cincinnati *Gazette*—to support his candidacy.[1]

A decision he made the year before—not to be a candidate against Wade for election to the U.S. Senate—had been unwise. No doubt had he actively worked for the Senate nomination, which had become deadlocked in the Republican legislative caucus, he would have been elected[2] and would have disposed of a dangerous rival. At the same time Chase would have removed himself from a President in whom he had little confidence and who had just blocked his attempt to remove Seward from the Cabinet.[3] But deeply concerned about the fate of his National Banking Bill, pushing hard for Hooker to receive command of the Army of the Potomac in place of the discredited Burnside and with a myriad of other interests and concerns, financial and otherwise, he let his chances lapse without making the requisite moves.[4]

One other consideration affected Chase's decision. He could not afford to offend or split the radicals in Ohio and elsewhere by opposing Wade if he wanted their support for his presidential candidacy. Again his judgment was in error. He was overestimating Wade's strength and underestimating his willingness to back a Chase candidacy despite his well-known antipathy for Lincoln and Seward.[5]

There had been a coalition movement in Ohio as in other states to bring the War Democrats into alliance with the Republicans in a new Union organization.[6] Essentially unstable, the Union party was cohesive enough and commanded enough popular support to nominate and elect David Tod, a leading Douglas Democrat, governor the year before. Chase had not opposed Tod but he remained skeptical of his views and those of the Union Democrats generally on emancipation.

Chase had one more chance to secure the senatorial nomination and to control the party in Ohio. When the Republican and Union Democrats met in January 1863 for the caucus nomination, opposition to Wade brought about another deadlock. A member of the Ohio legislature telegraphed Chase that "we are in much difficulty here. Union Democrats will not support Wade. Would you be willing to stand as a compromise candidate?"[7] But Chase thought he had a deal with Wade in the forthcoming presidential canvass. Nor would he bid for Union support at the expense of his basic principles. Again he disregarded the realities of politics in his home state. He refused to intervene and after a series of moderate to conservative candidates withdrew, Wade was finally reelected.[8]

A further incidence of mishandling Ohio affairs came when the Union party held its state convention in mid-June. Governor Tod was a candidate for reelection. He had acquitted himself well during his tenure as a strong Union man, acting energetically and decisively to counter John Hunt Morgan's cavalry foray that frightened the citizens in southern Ohio. A conservative to moderate in his political philosophy, he was a firm backer of the Lincoln administration's policy on emancipation. Chase made clear his displeasure with Tod in an important Treasury appointment, and if not directly connected with the newly organized Union League in Ohio, he certainly sympathized with its radical goals. Largely through the League's efforts and through such Chase men as Ashley, Richard Parsons, and Rufus Spalding, Tod was denied renomination.[9]

When the Union party convention went ahead and nominated another War Democrat, the hard-drinking, tough-talking John Brough, Tod felt humiliated and was deeply chagrinned. Chase made haste to say that he had not personally opposed him, but the rejected candidate and his group of cooperating Democrats viewed the denial with skepticism, a mood that would have some bearing on the Chase candidacy.[10]

Heartened by the victory in Ohio, which he attributed in large part to his own electioneering efforts, Chase pushed harder his not-so-covert campaign. With funds supplied by Sprague and Jay Cooke, newspapers throughout the Union began carrying editorials and public letters that extolled Chase's Treasury policies. These were not direct campaign efforts, but took their cue from Chase's Treasury Report which one admirer considered "the ablest state paper [he had] seen for years."[11] Such a burst of engineered enthusiasm naturally focused blame as well as support and not just partisan attacks from the Democrats.[12] But Chase warned his people not to malign Lincoln. Richard Parsons, writing from Cleveland, agreed with Chase that Lincoln's "integrity and apparent unselfishness entitle him to every courtesy."[13]

The White House inner circle was alarmed. Seward and Weed were convinced that Chase men were infiltrating the Union or Loyal leagues. Wayne MacVeagh, fervent Lincoln supporter and chairman of the Pennsylvania Republican Central Committee, while having a morning drink with John Hay said that Chase was "at work night and day laying pipe." The affable Ohio Democrat Samuel S. Cox echoed MacVeagh but with the more alarming statement that Chase had "gotten nearly the whole strength of the New England states."[14]

If these and other comments made directly to Lincoln or relayed to him by Hay and Nicolay were not distressing enough to the embattled President, he received word through Hay on December 13 that the venal Kansas senator Samuel Pomeroy was heading a covert Chase campaign yet at the same time openly pledging loyalty to Lincoln. Hay on his own account sought to bring pressure on Whitelaw Reid, threatening to have him removed from his position as "Washington correspondent of the Western Associated Press."[15] What Hay heard about Pomeroy and his Chase movement was true, not just gossip. The Kansas senator was indeed heading a Chase for President movement.

He had seen in Chase an opportunity to further his own political and railroad schemes. The Treasury department held substantial funds to be expended at the secretary's discretion for the construction of the Kansas-Pacific Railroad, a branch of the Union Pacific in which Pomeroy had an interest. Chase was a prime target for the Kansas politician and speculator. Pomeroy's round face, amiable smile, balding head, and side whiskers projected an air of pompous piety not unlike in appearance the proverbial small-town New England deacon. He combined smoothly an abolitionist morality with a highly developed materialist sense.[16]

He began organizing a Chase committee that eventually would be composed of B. Gratz Brown, the radical senator from Missouri; Ohio senator John Sherman; Chase's New Orleans Treasury agents; and James A. Garfield. Sprague and the Cookes were major contributors of funds to the committee. The Cookes were particularly active agents in public relations directly and through their editorial contacts. A fulsome piece praising Chase's character and explaining in flattering terms his life and his financial policies was written in December 1863. Henry Cooke put up the money for its publication in a monthly magazine of dubious repute, the *American Exchange and Review*. Most of the substance came from material Chase had supplied to potential authors of campaign biographies in the fifties.[17]

While the article in the *Exchange and Review* was being typeset in Philadelphia, Chase sent the first of 27 letters to John T. Trowbridge, a Boston writer of light fiction who specialized in books and articles for young people. Chase had met Trowbridge on one of his annual summer jaunts to New England before the war and had been favorably impressed with his ability and his avowed antislavery sentiments. Under an informal arrangement, Chase would supply material on his early life, his career, and always his importance to the national war effort. He wrote his last letter to Trowbridge in May 1864 when he still had hopes of supplanting Lincoln.

The first fruits of the Trowbridge relationship appeared in the April edition of the *Atlantic* monthly, which published a chapter from Trowbridge's manuscript biography. Jay Cooke paid a Boston bookseller $2000 to place this article.[18] But it was the *Exchange* article that prompted the most attention and grated on the nerves of critics and defenders. One of Chase's fervent supporters in New York City, William Orton, the Treasury's internal revenue commissioner for Manhattan, criticized it roundly.

Chase had relied on Orton as a trusted agent to sort out and advise him on the political climate that surrounded Barney and the custom house. In addition Orton was well acquainted with the periodical field through practical experience as a printer, publisher, and book dealer.[19] On January 4, Orton received an unsigned letter from the internal revenue bureau in Washington that enclosed a copy of the January issue of the *Exchange Review* with Chase's face engraved on its flyleaf and the lead article praising him. Two days later one of the magazine editors was in town soliciting contributions from Chase's friends and declaring to all that his supporters in Philadelphia and Washington had advanced funds. Jay Cooke was on the list for $5000. Such a blatant performance disturbed Orton and others in the city who were solicited.

But Orton was aghast when he finally read the letter from the bureau and the article in the *Exchange Review*. The extravagant language was bad enough but its appearance in what Orton regarded as a cheap periodical widely known to pander to anyone who would pay for its services was in very bad taste. Orton promptly wrote a letter to Chase asking that "immediate steps" be taken to check and suppress the movement and the article. "The very best investment he [Cooke] can make will be to buy up the edition of this before unheard of magazine, rub out Sartain's mezzotint counterfeit of your person and convert the whole concern to the flames." Orton condemned the *Exchange Review* as the "work of some 'seedy' clap trap publishers of yellow covered literature which stamps it as a flimsy political trick."[20]

This indictment from an upright man and loyal backer should have concerned Chase. But he took no action in the matter; nor is there any evidence that he replied to Orton. He did reply, however, to a note from Lincoln, who had seen a prepublication copy of the article and had been told that Jay Cooke had paid for it. Lincoln's note must have conveyed displeasure because Chase's reply was a defensive exercise. "If anyone wants my autograph," he said, "and I have time, I give it, if anybody wants to take my daguerreotype or photograph, and I have time, I sit for it, if anybody wants to *take my life* in the way of a biographical sketch, *I let him take it*, and if I have time, give such information as is wanted. . . . ." Henry, he added, not Jay Cooke was responsible for the "unfortunate biography," but what he did was done "without prompting from me or from his brother."[21] Seemingly unaware of how it must have applied to himself, Chase said to John Hay at this very time: "It is singularly instructive to meet so often as we do in life and in history, instances of vaulting ambition, meanness and treachery failing after enormous exertions and integrity and honesty march straight in triumph to its purpose."[22]

Chase had in hand the Orton letter and was aware of the campaign committee that was forming under the aegis of Pomeroy and James M. Winchell. Winchell was the New York agent of the Union Pacific and the Kansas Pacific railroads.[23] After listening to Chase's pious comment on ambition Hay confided to his diary, "a noble sentiment, Mr. Secretary."[24]

Three weeks before this evening homily Edward Bates, John P. Usher, the new Secretary of Interior, and an earnest young man, Edmund Clarence Stedman, well seasoned in Washington politics, sat facing Chase in his Treasury Department office. Chase knew of Stedman's reputation as a poet, whose recent volume of verse had attracted considerable attention in literary circles. As Attorney General Bates's former pardon clerk Stedman had access to higher levels of government and was a prominent figure in Washington's social life.[25] He was a close friend of Jacob Schuckers, Chase's private secretary. Through Schuckers Chase had been made aware of Stedman's career after he left Washington to become a stockbroker on Wall Street. Stedman had the right mix of the practical with the poetic that Chase so admired. And he could not fail to be impressed that this fashionable person with the stylish muttonchop whiskers was the nephew of the New York merchant prince William E. Dodge.

Stedman had just returned from Kansas where he inspected the forty miles of track laid down on the prairie by his Wall Street partner, Samuel Hallett, who owned a controlling interest in the Kansas-Pacific Railroad. Hallett had charged Stedman with the mission to convince Chase that he should release to the road $640,000 which it was due for construction under the Railroad Act of 1862. No doubt Stedman failed to mention that Hallett's forty miles of track had been laid without the benefit of a competent engineer and that there was no road bed to speakof.[26]

Stedman felt that the meeting had gone so favorably that he telegraphed Winchell to come to Washington and help clinch the deal. As soon as he arrived, the two men had another conference with Chase. Though feeling feverish and with a heavy cold, Stedman had a final talk with Chase on December 22, when the secretary agreed to sign off the funds for the Treasury.[27] It would be surprising if politics were not also discussed. For Chase was already deeply involved with the Pomeroy committee and had agreed to be a formal candidate against Lincoln. Three weeks later Stedman was again in Washington, where he spent a good many hours consulting with the Pacific Railroad men who now formed the core of the Chase for President committee.

Pomeroy and Winchell were the prime movers but the Pacific Railroad group was the principal source of money to finance the campaign. Stedman agreed to establish an office, or, as he put it, a "Bureau of Action" in New York. For his services he was paid a salary so handsome that he could take four months' leave from his partnership with Hallett. He received an additional $1000 for expenses.[28]

Stedman was not comfortable working with his new political associates in New York—Greeley, Opdyke, and David Dudley Field—whom he considered "impracticable men." Early on he decided not to "come out ostensibly for Chase, but to unite the radical elements and the friends of all other candidates." He rented rooms for the "Central Committee" on the corner of 13th Street and Broadway, and then turned his attention to the custom house. He was dismayed at what he found. "Mr. Chase," he said, "has shockingly mismanaged all his patronage. The custom house, etc., in the hands of his enemies and of many disloyalists."[29]

But Stedman achieved some political benefits. He succeeded in organizing for Chase an "unconditional Union Central Committee." During the remaining days of January and on into February Winchell and Stedman worked hard for Chase, who was informed through his "long letters" to Schuckers.[30] On February 16, Stedman was back in Washington, where he found the Pomeroy committee deadlocked on how to proceed.

Either Winchell or Stedman had written and published a slim pamphlet entitled "The Next Presidential Election," a slashing attack on Lincoln. Anonymously written, it did not mention Chase by name. Lincoln was accused of jailing innocent citizens on the one hand and on the other described as an indecisive, inept executive. The pamphlet argued in strident tones that Lincoln must be replaced in 1864. One paragraph coupled Lincoln with Jefferson Davis and implied that Davis, with trifling human and material resources compared with those that Lincoln commanded, was turning in a much better performance. Senator John Sherman and other congressmen associated with the Chase committee franked hundreds of copies of this diatribe to newspaper editors and other molders of public opinion.[31] Chase may not have seen the pamphlet before publication. It restated though in far harsher terms than he would have used all of his complaints about the administration. Certainly it did not treat the President with the "courtesy" and "integrity" that he had laid out as a guideline for his campaign.[32]

The pamphlet was not as well received as its authors had hoped. Yet it did attract editorial support for Chase from Theodore Tilton's New York *Independent,* the popular religious daily, the New York *Tribune,* and George Wilkes's *Spirit of the Times,* which enjoyed a large audience in northern metropolitan areas.[33] Chase was now prey to the very indecisiveness he had so frequently found in Lincoln. Winchell said that he was "vacillating to a painful degree," not because of any lessening of his ambition or of his firm belief that he was a better man than Lincoln, but because he feared failure. The committee, however, finally convinced him that he must take the plunge, and, using the pamphlet as a basic text, members wrote a circular that nominated Chase for the Republican Union nomination. Pomeroy signed it as chairman of the "Republican Executive Committee."[34] Marked confidential, the circular was sent out to over a hundred political movers and shakers and soon found itself in print.[35] This time the reaction was far more critical of Chase. Lincoln's supporters in several states were inspired to renewed action. Four state legislatures that happened to be in session, including that of Chase's home state, Ohio, beat back a Chase effort and went on record in Lincoln's support.[36]

The Chase committee had failed to coordinate action on the state and local level. William Dennison, now firmly behind Lincoln along with Ben Wade and his Ohio circle, had long suspected a Chase boom and had taken steps to counter it.[37] Lincoln's close friends in the Cabinet—Gideon Welles, Montgomery Blair, Edward Bates, and Seward—all hastened to dampen the arguments set forth in the circular by actively contacting their associates in New Hampshire, Connecticut, Maryland, Missouri, and New York. In Louisiana, General Banks saw to it that the Chase men were isolated.[38] Chase himself felt an explanation was due Lincoln. He wrote a placatory letter on February 22 in which he denied he had anything to do with the circular, but admitted that he had allowed the use of his name to the Pomeroy committee. Chase's letter concluded with an offer to resign should he not merit the President's confidence.[39] Lincoln replied that he would answer "a little more fully when I can find time."[40]

Lincoln would not disclose his hand until he heard the decision of the Ohio Republican-Union Convention. Six days later, when the convention in Ohio and also the party's convention in Indiana both overwhelmingly supported his renomination, Lincoln wrote a graceful letter to Chase. The President was still wary of Chase and his radical supporters, but he acknowledged Chase's right to be a candidate and he refused to consider his resignation. Moreover, he retained his high regard for Chase's financial prowess and for reasons of state wanted him to remain in the Treasury.[41] His relationship with Chase, however, which had been wearing thin over the past year now became far more formal.

As for Chase he already knew that his personal efforts to reconstruct Louisiana and Florida so that they would achieve his antislavery objectives and provide him with delegates to the Republican Union convention had failed.[42] The Ohio and Indiana rejections and, even more humiliating, a Rhode Island vote for Lincoln despite Sprague's influence and money, prompted Chase to withdraw and do so publicly.[43] Military affairs were still grim even though Grant had just taken over command of all the Union armies and Sherman had been made chief of the western armies. The draft had produced few additional recruits, but an infusion of black troops from Louisiana and other Union-controlled areas in the South was easing the manpower strain. The financial situation had again worsened; gold was rising rapidly in terms of greenbacks value. Grave financial distress and military stalemate could again make Chase a formidable candidate.

The President had been well aware of these trends. His sources had kept him abreast of the Pomeroy committee's activities. Despite political successes he was gaining in Louisiana, Florida, and many northern states, he realized that the groundswell could become a mere ripple or subside completely. On February 13, Edward Bates, old in years and conservative in his ways, passed half an hour in conversation with Lincoln. The President was not his usual jocular self. He was angry and defensive, yet hopeful by turns. Chase and his group, he said, were not only "almost fiendish" but "hypocrites" in their efforts to weaken him. But, said Bates, "the machinations of the Radicals will fail and that in the matter of the nomination, his [Lincoln's] friends will be able to counteract them effectually."[44]

For the past month Lincoln had had his eye on the New York custom house where embarrassing scandals had been uncovered and where Chase had finally brought collector Barney back to his camp.[45] Probably adding to Lincoln's irritation and rare displays of anger in his talk with Bates was that he had finally decided Barney must go. That he had drifted into the radical orbit bolstered Lincoln's decision.

Until now Chase had worn down the President with arguments that supported Barney. But Joshua Bailey, a Treasury agent who had been investigating the custom house and was in reality acting to root out the Seward-Weed influence, raised the President's ire. Bailey made so bold as to inform the chairman of the congressional committee investigating the custom house in advance of hearings that he might as well stop the investigation, because "whatever might be developed the President would take no action." An angry Lincoln exploded in his letter to Chase: "The public interest," said the President, "can not fail to suffer in the hands of this irresponsible and unscrupulous man."[46] In the face of Lincoln's obvious desire to have Bailey discharged, Chase balked.[47]

At Chase's insistence Lincoln saw Bailey on June 6, but he was unable to convince him of his truthfulness. In the afternoon after his interview with Bailey, Lincoln himself paid Chase a visit. The President opened the conversation on the persistent custom-house problem. After he gave his opinion, an unfavorable one about Bailey, he went on to speak of Barney's replacement. Chase as usual was well prepared and his tone of voice as usual was self-assured. He denied that Bailey had been so indiscreet to say what he was alleged to have said and he backed this statement up with a detailed account of Bailey's activities.

Then he launched into a defense of Barney, admitting that he had at times doubted his efficiency. But if the collector should be replaced, Chase recommended several New York lawyers and businessmen whom he knew were opposed to the Weed group. Lincoln suggested Preston King, an old Jacksonian Democrat, now a conservative Republican and an able politician. Chase's response was that he was "doubtless a man of integrity, but entirely unfamiliar with the duties of the post and would not have the confidence of the New York mercantile community," a tenuous argument indeed.

King was an experienced politician, affable, shrewd, honest, and a veteran free-soiler.[48] As for Bailey, who Chase so stoutly defended and retained as a special agent, he turned out to be an embezzler of government funds. When his frauds were uncovered he left the country before facing prosecution.[49] The Bailey-Barney affair was just one more flagrant instance of Chase's inability to judge correctly the character of his subordinates and his political coterie. Easily flattered, he turned a blind eye to the activities of those who stroked his self-assurance, provided they artfully concealed their true purpose. He tolerated such corrupt officers as Denison and Gray in New Orleans, Alfred Stone in Columbus, and Lyman Stickney in Florida, and seemed oblivious to the designs of the railroad lobbyists who surrounded him from December 1863 through February 1864.

But once again Chase prevailed and once again Lincoln held back despite the commotion the Pomeroy circular raised. He decided, however, to have Nicolay go to New York and consult in as much secrecy as possible that redoubtable conservative and political boss Thurlow Weed. Weed told Nicolay that Lincoln should "remove Barney and his four deputies as well who were intriguing against you." Chase and Fremont, who were being talked of as presidential candidates, "might yet form and lead dangerous factions."

Weed recommended that the Cabinet, "notoriously weak and inharmonious," be changed: "no cabinet at all." Chase would have agreed with Weed but for opposite reasons.[50] With Chase's formal withdrawal from the contest, the Pomeroy group of malcontents quickly deserted him and began moving toward Fremont, who was seen as supporting their radical views and who had long been associated with Hallett and others in the Kansas-Pacific scheme.[51]

Protected by Chase, Barney continued to hold his post at the custom house, much to Lincoln's annoyance and constant pressure from the Weed-Seward group, until suddenly an unforeseen event broke the impasse. John J. Cisco, Chase's trusted assistant treasurer in New York, resigned. Chase tried hard to keep him in place, but Cisco was ill and weary beyond any devotion to duty and would not reconsider. Unless replaced by a loyal, knowledgeable person, his departure removed a key figure in Chase's New York patronage machine. More important, it left a vacancy that had to be replaced by someone who understood the intricacies of the New York money mart, yet at the same time supported Chase's financial policies.

Should the post fall into alien hands, Chase believed that it would bring down in ruins what remained of his painfully maintained, seriously weakened structure. There was also the matter of pride, of the impression that any weakness on his part would have a damaging effect on the department itself, on his web of agents, and on the confidence of the financial community. Chase's standing with this powerful, vociferous enclave, always brittle, had been badly strained by the failed experiment of selling government gold in a vain effort to raise the value of greenbacks.[52]

The Union convention at Baltimore renominated Lincoln. Chase had reluctantly and temporarily bowed to that result, while he watched the Fremont movement that was seeking to replace Lincoln. He was ready as usual should circumstances warrant to accept a draft from the party. The political direction of the New York custom house was crucial to any plans he might make for 1868 whether or not Lincoln was a candidate in November. As soon as Cisco's resignation was known there was a scramble of potential aspirants. Weed, of course, began pushing hard and enlisted former governor, now Senator E. D. Morgan to challenge any appointment Chase and the radicals might make.

At first it seemed that all would be well. Morgan, stout, self-assured, rich in personal wealth and political experience, was ushered into Chase's office at the Treasury Department. After some initial sparring both men agreed to offer the appointment to Denning Duer, a New York banker who was acceptable to the commercial and banking fraternity in New York and who was not directly connected with Weed.[53] Should Duer decline, Chase was to offer the post to another banker, John A. Stewart of the U.S. Trust Company, whom he deemed capable and neutral regarding the two leading Union factions in the city. Duer declined and so did Stewart.[54] Chase turned to Maunsell B. Field, Assistant Secretary of the Treasury and a confidant, who agreed to serve. Chase made a morning visit to Morgan and proposed Field for the post. The suave Morgan did not personally object but promptly offered alternatives to Field. He produced a list of officers and clerks in the custom house that he said were Democrats and should be replaced. He recommended that either R. M. Blatchford, Dudley Gregory, or Thomas Hill be named.

All were close associates of Weed and Seward. None had any extensive banking or financial experience.[55] Chase was taken aback and argued that the qualifications for such an important post should be determined not by politics but by merit and should coincide with support for Chase's financial policies. Morgan maintained his noncommittal pose, and Chase on leaving said that he would try to "gratify his wishes." That evening Chase's definition of meeting Morgan's wishes was the dispatch of Field's blank commission to the President.

On arriving in his office the following morning he found a letter from Lincoln on top of his pile of mail. To his surprise and infinite displeasure, Lincoln disapproved of the Field nomination. Frankly, he said, he could not make the appointment "without much embarrassment." Morgan was too firmly opposed. The senator had met with Lincoln and made the recommendations he had offered to Chase. Lincoln suggested that Chase select one of these gentlemen, "or any other man senators Morgan and Ira Harris will be satisfied with."

Chase requested an interview, but, dreading another debate, the President declined with a letter that explained his position on the factions in New York and the "great burden" Barney's retention placed upon him.[56] Chase immediately telegraphed Cisco in New York, urging him to withdraw his resignation "for at least one quarter more."[57] Cisco bowed to Chase's imperative. He telegraphed the withdrawal of his resignation to the President and to Chase. Without thinking through the consequences, Chase acted impulsively. He wrote Lincoln a note in which he declared that the difficulty was now resolved, but he did not stop there. Acknowledging that their official relations were not of the best, that his position was not "altogether agreeable to you," he proffered his resignation.[58]

In the stack of papers and letters Lincoln's secretaries placed before him, the Cisco telegram first caught his eye. Happy that the difficulty had been resolved, he put the Treasury papers in his pocket and busied himself with other urgent matters. The next day as he was about to write a congratulatory letter to Chase, he read with amazement then with mounting anger Chase's letter and his formal resignation.[59] As he saw it Chase was trying to usurp his patronage prerogatives. The whole annoying business of the secretary's constant badgering on emancipation may have brought him to the edge.[60] No doubt he remembered what Thurlow Weed had told Nicolay about his dysfunctional Cabinet several months earlier.

Lincoln was under even greater strain than before Sumter or after the bloody defeats of Burnside and Hooker. Figures of Grant's and Sherman's casualties were crowding the newspaper columns. Peace seemed as illusive as ever. Lincoln took a sheet of executive office stationary and wrote a few lines accepting Chase's resignation. It was an impulsive act from a person not given to rash moves. But Lincoln's long patience had finally come to an end. Shrewd and careful politician that he was, in this instance he threw caution away and damned the financial and political consequences. He sent for Hay and asked, "When does the Senate meet today?" "Eleven o'clock," said Hay. "I wish you to be there when they meet," he said. "It is a big fish. Mr. Chase has resigned and I have accepted his resignation. I thought I could not stand it any longer."[61]

Chase was unprepared for the acceptance of his resignation. Later he regretted his act but when he thought about the correspondence that had gone between them he gave vent to bitterness and self-justification. He wrote in his diary on June 30 that he "had found a good deal of embarrassment from him [Lincoln] but what he had found from me I could not imagine, unless it has been created by my unwillingness to have offices distributed as spoils or benefits to the claims of divisions, factions, cliques and individuals, than to fitness of selection."[62]

chapter 28

"So Help Me God"

If the acceptance of his resignation caught Chase by surprise, it was met with consternation in the Congress and particularly among members of the finance committees. Government accounts were as usual in bad shape. Gold had continued to rise. Business and banking interests blamed speculators for the precipitous decline in the value of the currency. In response Congress had hastened to pass a law giving the secretary wide latitude in selling government gold reserves on the open market, the reason being that this action, it was thought, would curb speculation and increase the monetary value of the paper currency.[1]

Chase believed the problem lay elsewhere and was averse to tinkering in this way with the gold market, but, responding to pressure from important business interests and members of Congress, and after trying various expedients that did not work in mid-April he went to New York and personally supervised the sale of about $11 million in surplus gold held in the treasury over a period of five days.[2] The sale caused a panic in the stock market that ruined many traders, and did force the price of gold down significantly in greenback value, which inflicted severe losses on Wall Street and on the financial districts of other major cities.[3] As Chase suspected, the gain was only temporary. He wrote a carping banker in New York, "I see that gold is again going up. This is not unexpected. Military success is indispensable to its permanent decline or, in the absence of military success, taxation. . . ."

This ill-fated experiment and others including closing the futures market in gold for which Chase had to bear the responsibility, though he was in no way the major culprit, was compounded by the Treasury's failure to market sufficient quantities of the new 10–40 bonds.[4] To a degree Chase was culpable. He had bowed to complaints, some justified, of undue favoritism to the Cooke firm.[5] Reluctantly he dispensed with Cooke's services and sought to market the bonds directly through the subtreasuries and through the new national bank system. Without Cooke's organization and his promotion abilities, most of the new bond issue remained unsold.

The deficit was ballooning again. Expenditure exceeded Chase's estimates for the fiscal year by over $200 million.[6] Nor had the military situation improved. Sherman had been repulsed at Kennesaw Mountain with heavy losses. Bank's invasion of Texas and Gillmore's of Florida had both been checked with serious casualties. Grant was piling up dreadful carnage in the Virginia wilderness yet had been unable to destroy Lee's army. And Congress still refused to raise taxes sufficiently to ease the strain on the Treasury.[7]

The timing of Chase's resignation could not have been worse. Lincoln's nomination of David Tod, the relatively unknown and recently repudiated ex-governor of Ohio, showed clearly that he had not thought the matter through. The Senate Finance Committee, to whom Tod's nomination had been referred, came in a body to the White House, most of its members in great distress.[8] And Lucius Chittenden, register of the Treasury, warned the harried President that "there was a movement for a general resignation in the Department." Harrington, who was now acting secretary, seemed frightened by the responsibility if only temporary of his new role. A little man, prey to illness and to fears, real and imaginary, he was described as in "a constant twitter," opening "his eyes like saucers, pursing his lips and speaking in a *basso profundo*."[9] The person most upset by the news was Samuel Hooper, the able, immensely rich Boston congressman. He had been Chase's right arm on the House Ways and Means Committee. When Tod declined the appointment, Hooper told the President bluntly that "this imbroglio will slough off from the Union party a large and disastrous slice."[10]

Excitement in Congress and in the financial community calmed down considerably when Lincoln nominated William P. Fessenden in Tod's place. It took considerable pressure from the President before this respected, though chronically captious senator and senior member of the Finance Committee agreed to accept.[11]

Over the weekend, following his resignation, Chase spent most of his time at home, meeting anxious politicians and Treasury officeholders and conferring with Fessenden. On Monday, July 4, the first session of the Thirty-eighth Congress adjourned. In its closing hour, Lincoln pocket-vetoed the Wade-Davis bill, which would have imposed much harsher terms for Reconstruction than his own plan that was already under way in Louisiana and Arkansas. On receiving the news, Chase deprecated Lincoln's action. He accused Lincoln and his advisors—by which he meant the Blairs—of a Reconstruction plan that would leave slavery in place. That night he entertained at dinner Sumner, Hooper, and Governor John A. Andrew of Massachusetts. The conversation at the table centered on the pocket veto which Sumner said created "intense indignation" though it was obvious that he was speaking for the more extreme men in Congress.[12] After dinner, Fessenden called and gave an account of his conversation with Lincoln. He reported that the President hoped he "would not without real necessity remove any friends of Governor Chase." Later Chase said, "Had the President in reply to my note tendering my resignation expressed himself as he did now to Mr. Fessenden, I should have cheerfully withdrawn it." He had not, mused Chase, because "I am too earnest, too anti slavery and say, too radical to make him willing to have me connected with the Administration."

There was nothing of the self-criticism about his conduct or his motives that, so often in the past, he vented in his diaries. His stand was simply a matter of the politics of principle, his position one of high morality, the equality of all men. In his mind Lincoln was not "earnest enough; not anti-slavery enough; not radical enough—but goes naturally with those hostile to me. . . ."[13] In this frame of mind he made plans to leave the capital for a lengthy trip through New England, where he would refresh his spirit among friends and relatives in his cherished native heath.

But Chase could not resist political temptation. He thought he was right on Reconstruction, which he judged was the coming issue. The journey in the Northeast would provide him with a sounding board for his opinions. Gideon Welles made a succinct and on the whole accurate analysis of Chase's character at this time. He said that Chase had "a good deal of intellect, knows the path where duty points, and in his calmer moments, resolves to pursue it." But then Welles described him as having "inordinate ambition, intense selfishness for official distinction and power to do for the country, and considerable vanity." Welles touched on another trait amply borne out by Chase's political past, a trait concealed behind a façade of the calm, unruffled, dignified person who knew how to act decisively at critical moments. Welles found Chase "irresolute and wavering, his instinctive sagacity prompting him rightly, but his selfish and vain ambition turning him to error. . . ."[14]

For the next week, Chase busied himself in briefing Fessenden on the workings of the department, conferring with politicians who were still in Washington, and closing up temporarily his Washington home. Tension was on the rise again in the city, which was expecting an invasion from Jubal

Early's force, rampaging through nearby Maryland. By July 13, however, the danger was past. Early's troops were retreating toward Leesburg to the west. On that day Chase said goodbye to Stanton, who was "warm and cordial as ever." Rather hurt that none of his other Cabinet colleagues called to see him off, he left for Philadelphia, where Jay Cooke met him at the station and hurried him off to "The Cedars" for the night, and then he was on to New York. Kate and Nettie were waiting for him at the Astor House. On the 17th they were all at Newport.

During July, August, and the first half of September Chase traveled extensively throughout New England. The reception he received from old friends and associates such as Pierce, William Curtis Noyes, who maintained a summer home in Litchfield, Connecticut, Sumner, and John Murray Forbes restored much of his injured ego. It did more than that: it kept him abreast of the moves being made by the New York and Boston radicals to shelve Lincoln and propose a new Union-Republican nominee.[15]

For once Chase would not commit himself to support any independent action. Noyes, his close friend and host for several weeks, attended a conference of anti-Lincoln party men on August 30 where it was decided to hold a nominating convention in Cincinnati on September 28.[16] Chase would have been more forgiving than a Christian martyr if he did not blame the Blairs, Seward, Weed, and other conservatives for their influence with Lincoln. But Chase was a politician, too, even if sometimes an inept one. Given Lincoln's popularity and his political following in the Northeast, it is unlikely that he abused the President as roundly as his radical friends.[17]

Apart from politics, Chase enjoyed the fishing trips, picnics, clam bakes, and visits to various picturesque or historical sites. He paid decorous attention to his warm friend and correspondent Charlotte Eastman, who lived in the Boston suburb of Beverly. Chase was delighted with his son-in-law Sprague's summer home. Simply a large, rambling farmhouse, it was beautifully situated west of Newport on Narragansett Bay. He prepared to enjoy himself, far from the cares of politics and patronage and currency problems. After a dusty ride from the Providence depot with Sprague, who had met him there, he found the house "full—a merry game of croquet . . . dinner at seven." On walks with Nettie he was enchanted with "the grand roll of the ocean, dash of waves magnificent."[18]

He had not been at Narragansett long when he noticed that all was not well between Kate and William. From chance remarks, he concluded that Kate was bored with life in Rhode Island and was disappointed that Sprague had not taken her to Europe. She had just become pregnant, which may have contributed to her short temper. Sprague himself had resumed his drinking though still moderately. Chase was concerned at a heated argument between husband and wife a week after his arrival, and the next day he had a long talk with Kate, no doubt urging her to be a dutiful wife.[19]

Chase did not neglect the intellectual and cultural savants of the Boston area. He dined with Emerson and his circle on August 18, declining a second invitation because of a prior commitment.[20] He spent the last ten days of his New England sojourn with the Spragues and Nettie at Narragansett.[21]

As could be expected, given his temperament and the abrupt closure of a public life he had enjoyed for the past fifteen years, Chase found adjustment to the much slower pace of private pursuits difficult. If most individuals of his age and position found retirement irksome, it was near torture for Chase. He could not help but remind Fessenden of Lincoln's pledge on patronage and to offer advice that at times carried an admonishing tone. When Fessenden did not answer one of his letters promptly, he rebuked his successor. "My temper, I fear, is a little proud and jealous," he wrote, "very grateful for kindness and appreciation—but easily repelled when kindness and appreciation are unre-turned."

Overwhelmed as he was with his new position, and always of uncertain temper, Fessenden responded in a surprisingly meek assurance of his dependence on Chase's recommendations and of his warm friendship.[22] Like Chase before him, Fessenden found himself embroiled in arguments with powerful New York bankers, many of whom were opposing the new national bank system. He needed Chase's prestige and his council as much as Chase needed Fessenden's reliance on him. On August 18, Fessenden met Chase for breakfast in Boston, where they discussed the problems facing the Treasury.

Fessenden bore also an indirect offer from Lincoln of a major European mission.[23] Chase may have been tempted, having just suffered another humiliating political defeat which he could have avoided had he not taken such an equivocal position. Several of Chase's friends in Ohio, chief among whom was Mellen, had without his knowledge put him up for nomination as the Union candidate for Congress from Cincinnati's first district. Chase received word that his nomination would be opposed but that it could be overcome "by active exertion." He telegraphed that only if the district convention made the nomination "unanimous would he accept."[24] His friends disregarded Chase's refusal as an excess of modesty. But even with "active exertion" Chase was defeated. He was dismayed at the result and instead of considering that his popularity in his home district may have been on the wane, he saw the hand of his tormentors the Blairs in the defeat.[25]

Chase learned that Nicolay had again visited New York and that Barney had resigned to be replaced by Weed's whimsical bagman Simeon Draper.[26] He wrote Fessenden about this. Fessenden's reply simply confirmed in Chase's mind that Lincoln was determined to weaken him politically and to undermine radical strength in the city. His suspicions seemed substantiated when Fessenden indicated that he had not been consulted either in Barney's resignation or in Draper's appointment.[27]

Chase was in New Hampshire when he heard the details of the Democratic convention in Chicago, its nomination of McClellan, and his repudiation of the extreme peace plank in the party's platform. Whatever thoughts he may have had about a Democratic victory in 1864 if Lincoln remained at the head of the Union ticket were pretty well scotched when he came down to Boston on September 3. The newspaper boys along State Street were crying that Sherman had taken Atlanta. This victory on top of Farragut's successful capture of the Confederacy's last major—port, Mobile, Alabama—not a month earlier made it virtually certain that the war was nearing an end and that Lincoln would be reelected. Chase's neutral attitude began to change. He wrote Jay Cooke from upstate New York on September 8 that "however much cause I have to dislike some acts of Mr. Lincoln, I cannot but feel that my duty [is] to sustain the government."[28]

After writing Cooke Chase went directly to Rhode Island and left for Washington on the twelfth. Following a grueling trip on the storm-tossed overnight boat between Providence and New York, he arrived in no good humor at his home in Washington on September 14. His disposition was not improved to find the house being painted inside and out with workmen everywhere remodeling the dwelling under orders from Kate. His first visit was the Treasury Department, where he had long conversations with Harrington, Fessenden, and Hugh McCulloch, the Indianapolis banker, now comptroller of the currency. McCulloch and Fessenden urged him to take part in the presidential campaign.[29]

Well before Chase had made a pitch for the Union nomination a year earlier he had mentioned to Lincoln and to Joshua Leavitt his interest in a judicial post to cap his career.[30] Quite frequently when his political plans went awry or he wearied of the constant turmoil of the political scene, he yearned for what he supposed was the relative peace and quiet of the Supreme Court. That the post could be a useful base for his presidential ambitions was certainly a factor in his planning.

Chase's Cincinnati neighbor and in-law John McLean had set a precedent when he sought the presidency from his seat as an Associate Justice. McLean had failed in his quest. But he had been an important contender and Chase felt that if he were in a similar position, he could profit from McLean's mistakes. Balanced against these secular yearnings was the brighter side of Chase's character which saw the opportunity of a lifetime to have his moral and idealistic views on the equality of man enshrined in the supreme law of the land. But for the moment these wishful assumptions must take second place.

Rebuffed for the presidential nomination, refused a nomination and election to Congress from his home district, no longer endowed with the power and the status of the Treasury, Chase really had no other option than to seek a Supreme Court appointment if he wished to remain in public life. There was, of course, a senior diplomatic position. But acceptance of such a post would remove him from the political scene. Compelling reasons of personal mission which Chase always associated with his ambition demanded that he take part in the unfolding drama of peace, reconciliation, and finally equal rights for the long-suffering blacks.

A vacancy on the Court was imminent. Eighty-six-year-old Chief Justice Taney was fatally ill. Chase was determined to succeed him and was ready to pull out all the stops for the nomination. These would be many, for several politically important rivals could not be overlooked—his former colleagues Edwin M. Stanton and Montgomery Blair, Associate Justice Noah Swayne of Ohio, and William M. Evarts, the brilliant lawyer from New York and a close friend of Chase's nemesis Seward.[31]

In his conversation with Fessenden and McCulloch the secretary had mentioned that the President would like him to call. Chase wasted no time in hurrying to the White House. He had hoped for a private interview, but when he was admitted to Lincoln's office, he found several others present. The President was cordial but very circumspect about what he said and how he said it. Chase found his manner reserved, "not at all demonstrative either in speech or manner." Nor was Lincoln any more direct when Chase visited him a second time at the Soldier's Home. Again there were others present which the anxious ex-secretary found disconcerting.[32]

Nevertheless, Chase resolved to place the President under obligation by taking the stump for his election in the doubtful states of Ohio, Michigan, Kentucky, Missouri, and Pennsylvania. Crisscrossing Ohio and Pennsylvania, he made over twenty speeches to large crowds. All of his remarks were well reported in the press and no doubt did add to Lincoln's majority.

In Cincinnati, Chase learned that Montgomery Blair had resigned from the Cabinet and a day later that Fremont, a third-party radical candidate, had withdrawn from the race. It was clear now that he had made the right move in openly and vigorously backing Lincoln. As a radical who could now be considered a loyal one, his credentials for Taney's post had improved.

Chief Justice Taney died on the very day Chase addressed a large crowd at Covington, Kentucky, reminding his audience that he had spoken there four years before and in support of the same candidate. The campaign in the Midwest and in the border states had reached a fever pitch. En route to Toledo Chase was recognized and several McClellan Democrats tried to force him off the train. He held his ground and reached his destination safely. The impending election made matters worse in Kentucky and Missouri, where guerillas managed to halt the train to Lexington on which Montgomery

Blair was riding. A gang of ruffians tried to kidnap him but he managed to elude them. Chase took the same train the next day, though nothing untoward happened.[33]

Meanwhile in Washington, the pressure on Lincoln from Chase supporters was intense.[34] The President refused to be drawn out, commenting as usual that he would make no nominations until after the November elections. He had on several occasions hinted that Chase would be his choice. And in fact he appears to have settled on Chase before Taney died. In an evening conversation with his old friend Ward Hill Lamon he confided that he would appoint Chase. After insisting that Lamon keep their talk confidential, he said, "I looked over the ground. I was satisfied that the appointment of Governor Chase would satisfy the country (what there was bet[ween] him and myself was not to be taken into account). . . . His appointment will satisfy the Radicals. . . . The Radical party and Mr. Chase's friends would not with reasonable countenance interpose a reasonable objection."[35]

Lincoln here in Lamon's account puts the Chase appointment purely on political grounds. But he had other compelling reasons for deciding on Chase. He had a great deal of respect for Chase's ability as a lawyer and a constitutional scholar in addition to his proven financial capabilities. Chase's ideas on Reconstruction were already on record and though he was ahead of public opinion on granting suffrage to the former slaves, he would achieve it through State action. Chase did not subscribe publicly to the more extreme views of "state suicide" or "conquered province" theories on Reconstruction that Charles Sumner and Thaddeus Stevens were espousing.

Lincoln said later to Augustus Frank, a congressman from New York, that there was no question of Chase's ability "and of his soundness on the general issues of the war. . . . I should despise myself if I allowed personal differences to affect my judgment of his fitness for the office of Chief Justice." Lincoln was concerned that Chase's inordinate ambition would interfere with his rulings, that he would be a politician first and a judge second. Connecticut senator Lafayette Foster recalled that Lincoln told him: "Mr. Chase will make an excellent judge if he devotes himself exclusively to the duties of his office and don't meddle with politics. But if he keeps on with the notion that he is destined to be President of the United States, and which in my judgment he will never be, he will never acquire that fame and usefulness as Chief Justice which he would otherwise certainly attain."[36]

In an agony of anxiety Chase remained in Ohio until the very last minute lest he be accused of being personally too eager for the nomination. When the date for the convening of the second session of the Thirty-eighth Congress drew near, he resolved his qualms and returned to Washington. On December 6, he learned that Lincoln had nominated him and that the Senate unanimously confirmed the appointment. Before retiring for the night Chase wrote

Lincoln a warm note of thanks. He assured the President that he "prized [his] confidence and goodwill more than nomination of office."[37] Lincoln made no comment about Chase's gratitude. Nicolay perhaps best sums up what those close to the President felt: "Probably no other man than Lincoln would have had, in this age of the world, the degree of magnanimity to thus forgive and exalt a rival who had so deeply and so unjustifiably intrigued against him."[38]

Chase had to wait another nine days before he was actually sworn in. It was one of those little complications, in part political and in part procedural, that caused the delay. Attorney General Edward Bates had resigned on November 24. Lincoln nominated James Speed of Kentucky to succeed him. A little-known Louisville lawyer, Speed was the brother of one of Lincoln's closest friends.[39] Considered a lightweight by leading members of the Kentucky bar, Bates referred to Speed as "my poor imbecile successor," an opinion that the perceptive Associate Justice Samuel Miller shared.[40]

Procedurally the Attorney General had to certify the nomination and the confirmation before any Supreme Court Justice could be sworn in. Speed's fitness for the office was questioned in the Senate and as a result his confirmation was held up for over two weeks during which there was no acting Attorney General. By the 15th he had been confirmed and certified Chase's papers.

On that day the small Supreme Court chamber was crowded with dignitaries who came to witness the first Chief Justice installed since 1836. In the audience were the Spragues, the pregnant Kate beautifully coiffed and dressed in a fashionable gown by the Parisian couturier Charles Frederick Worth. Her eighteen-year-old sister Nettie sat beside her. Several of Chase's political enemies were present, among them Ewing and Wade. Sumner, who had labored so intensively and persistently for his friend, struck a theatrical pose as he leaned casually against one of the green marble columns that supported the rotunda.[41]

At the appointed hour one of the ushers announced, "The Honorable Justices of the Supreme Court of the United States." From the left entrance behind the bench came Chase and the senior Associate Justice, James M. Wayne, seventy-four years old and in precarious health.[42] The other eight justices followed, most of them big, corpulent men who filled out their black robes with substantial dignity. Bowing to each other left to right they all took their seats in order of their tenure. Chase and Wayne rose and came forward. Wayne handed him the paper on which the oath was written. Chase read the short document aloud, slowly and distinctly. When he finished he laid down the paper and, looking straight up at the rotunda, his voice clouded with emotion yet emphatic enough to be heard throughout the chamber, he proclaimed, "So help me God." Chase resumed his seat. The clerk read his certificate of office, concluding the brief ceremony. Noah Brooks, the Washington reporter for the *Sacramento Union* who was covering the proceedings for his paper, met Wade on leaving the chamber. Said that profane senator who could be wickedly witty at times like these, "Lord, now lettest thou thy servant depart in peace, for my eyes have seen thy salvation."[43]

The judicial term had only fourteen more weeks to go when Chase joined in the Court's deliberations. Its business was primarily concerned with appeals involving admiralty cases stemming from the blockade. Chase was better informed about the facts of these actions than his colleagues. As secretary of the Treasury he had shared with the service secretaries the responsibility for maintaining the blockade of the Confederacy. Even so he found the routine of his new office unfamiliar and tedious, "the painful monotony of hearing, reading, thinking and writing on the same class of subjects and in the same way, all the time—morning, noon, evening and night."[44] Accustomed to deference for years he quickly found that he could not impose his will upon his colleagues.

Though supremely industrious, Chase had little liking for reading and digesting hundreds of pages of briefs, depositions, and lower court testimony, where one had to be scrupulously careful about trivial points of language. Matters of statute law and common law precedent that involved contracts, real property, trusts, estates, and the whole range of civil proceedings had been made far more complex because of the war. Beyond these unique aspects, Chase found himself almost a beginner again in tort law, which he had not studied for over ten years. He was working as hard as he had ever worked, but not for great issues or worthy causes. "At court as usual," he said, "—no event worth mentioning—I try to do a little good by writing nearly every day to somebody to stir him up to support universal suffrage in reconstituted states so as to protect the blacks from wrongs & the country from future dangers."[45]

Feeling as he did, he was reluctant at first to betray any ignorance of fine points of law in the face of his colleagues' expertise. On one of these cases, he noted that "Clifford read sharp dissent from Swayne. I of the same opinion as C. [lifford] but declined to dissent thinking that except in very important cases dissent inexpedient."[46] Yet if his public standing and national prestige were not respected by his colleagues as he had assumed he felt he must distinguish himself in discussion and opinion so that he could lead the court, rather than simply act the part of first among equals. He assigned himself the writing of the majority opinion in the *Circassian* case, which he considered raised important points in international law. The ship *Circassian*, bound for New Orleans, was seized as a blockade runner even though the Union military was then in the process of capturing New Orleans. Thus the *Circassian* was not technically bound for a hostile city. Chase made a distinction between the city of New Orleans and the port, which he asserted was not in Union hands. He upheld the lower court decision that the ship and its cargo be confiscated.[47] Chase worked diligently on this and other admiralty cases through the evening hours and whenever he could spare some time.[48]

Chase's colleagues were polite and careful of each others' feelings even if they disagreed at their conferences.[49] The atmosphere tended to be clubbable and rather closed in that they socialized with each other. Clifford, who loved good food and drink and whose girth testified to this interest, gave small, many-coursed dinner parties. He was friendlier to Chase than the other Justices perhaps because they shared a New England heritage. James M. Wayne was frequently absent because of ill health, but still retained his critical faculties. A southerner, he had also been a staunch unionist, and remained on the court after his native state, Georgia, seceded in 1861. Wayne was uniformly kind though differing widely from Chase in politics and in matters of racial equality.[50] Seventy-eight-year-old John Catron was likewise so seriously ill that he did not serve on the 1864–65 term.[51] He died on May 30, 1865. For the time being he was not replaced. Crusty Robert Grier and, as he put it, "weak in the legs," was not impressed with Chase.[52] Though a Pennsylvanian he harbored a dislike for all "Yankees." Edward Bates, no Yankee and no radical, considered Grier "a natural born vulgarian, and by long habit coarse and harsh."[53]

Samuel Nelson was a querulous jurist yet timid when asked to venture along an uncharted way. An arch-conservative, he could not be expected to adopt progressive views on either social or economic problems. Nelson had no use for Chase's natural right theory on slavery or his positive law doctrine. He was indifferent or downright hostile to Chase's position on the issues of the day, universal male suffrage and a color-blind Reconstruction of the former Confederate states. Along with Catron, Grier, and Wayne, he had concurred with Taney in the Dred Scott case. Noah Swayne, Samuel Miller, and David Davis were the only Justices of Republican background.[54]

Davis, Swayne, Miller, and Stephen J. Field were all Lincoln appointees, and all were better versed than Chase in the finer points of civil law. Davis shared Chase's abiding interest in politics and political issues. A close friend of Lincoln's, the immensely fat Davis had served as an Illinois circuit court judge for many years. During this period, Lincoln appeared before him as a trial lawyer. In the 1860 presidential campaign, Davis acted as Lincoln's manager. He proved to be as shrewd a politician in engineering Lincoln's nomination as he was an experienced judge. Davis was born on a plantation in the eastern shore of Maryland. His background was every bit as distinguished as Chase's. A graduate of Kenyon College, like his cousin Henry Winter Davis, he was a literate, industrious individual. He lacked his cousin's flair for political in fighting, and was far more conservative in his politics. But Davis was temperamental, insecure, and quick to anger over real or fancied slights. When Chase inadvertently failed to consult him before giving notice to counsel in a California land grant case Davis upbraided him. Other personality differences injured their relationship, though Chase tried at least once to bring about a reconciliation.[55]

Chase was far more compatible in the beginning with Justice Field, whose political and social views more nearly approximated his own. Chase entertained the bearded, saturnine Field at private dinners and enjoyed his anecdotes of life in rough-and-ready California.[56] Chase soon discovered that the big, forthright Samuel Miller was a man to respect. Though they were never close, Chase said of him "that [he was] beyond question, the dominant personality [then] upon the bench, whose mental force and individuality [were] felt by the court more than any other."[57] Noah Swayne, a formidable, round-faced individual with hooded eyes, would never be close to Chase. Formerly a Jacksonian Democrat, and a leading lawyer at the Columbus, Ohio, bar, Swayne was now a progressive Republican in politics. He had become as fiercely opposed to slavery as Chase and indeed was something of a rival in Ohio politics for leadership of the free soil movement. When Chase joined the Court, Swayne was considered its best lawyer, with a firm grasp of civil as well as criminal law and the ardent defender of civil right.[58] At first, Chase found Nathan Clifford, a native of Maine and a Democrat in politics, much too conservative on matters affecting society as a whole. Humorless, plodding, and eminently prolix in his opinions, he became in time, however, a dependable supporter of Chase's views. As a result the Chief Justice appreciated his devotion and came to rely on his advice.

Chase was not in the best frame of mind for dealing with a new environment and with a close-knit group of veteran lawyers, none of whom he knew well and most of whom seemed far removed from the real world where he had played a major role. He had not been on the Court two weeks when he learned that his younger sister Helen had died. Chase had acted as Helen's guardian for some years before her marriage and had always taken a paternal interest in her welfare.[59] If this was not unsettling enough, the mounting friction between Kate and Sprague was a cause of constant worry. Kate was sick a good bit of the time and in a captious mood.[60] On one occasion she lashed out so bitterly at her sister that Nettie came crying to her father. Chase sought to soothe her injured feelings but must have taken Kate's side, who was now six months pregnant. He confided to his diary that Nettie was "but a thoughtless child and as sensitive as she is thoughtless."[61]

If family matters were depressing Chase was cheered at the rare coming together of moderate, conservative, and radical groups in Congress to pass the proposed Thirteenth Amendment, prohibiting slavery in the United States. He took this action as a sign that the states would approve also. There was now no problem in Chase's mind about the exceptions in the Emancipation Proclamation which he had so long and so persistently urged the President to remove.

At noon on March 4, 1865, after the Senate adjourned, Chase led the Justices to their appointed seats in the Senate chamber on the right of the rostrum opposite the Cabinet and the President for the inauguration ceremonies that would usher in Lincoln's second term. The hall was crowded with bedraggled onlookers who had braved a rain shower to witness the inauguration of Andrew Johnson, the new Vice President, before the dignitaries moved to the portico for the main event.

Custom decreed that the outgoing Vice President's valedictory be brief. Ward Lamon, in overall charge of the program, had allotted just seven minutes each to the outgoing Vice President Hannibal Hamlin and to Johnson. Hamlin's remarks were perfunctory. Then Johnson moved to the rostrum. He had not spoken a few sentences, his voice thick and slurred, before Chase and others realized that he was either ill or drunk. Repetitious phrases and incoherent statements followed in loud, hoarse tones as he rambled on. Lincoln bowed his head in embarrassment, as Johnson over and over proclaimed the power of the people. When his speech finally came to an abrupt halt, his eyes moved over the Cabinet members, each of whom he addressed, though he had to be reminded what position they held and their proper names.

Chase was not excluded from the list. Johnson turned a bleary eye upon him and said: "You too got your power from the people, whose creature you are!" Turning to the audience and mumbling for five minutes or so on the nature of the oath he was about to take, Hamlin seized the opportunity of a pause to administer the oath. Lamon helped him to his seat. On the way out to the east portico, Lincoln whispered to one of the marshalls, "Do not let Johnson speak outside!"[62]

When President Lincoln with Chase by his side walked to the edge of the portico, suddenly the sun, which had been hidden by rain clouds all day, broke through. Reading from a single sheet of paper, Lincoln delivered in his penetrating voice one of the shortest inaugural addresses ever given. But it contained memorable phrases as he pleaded for reconciliation with what every one present knew would be the soon-defeated South. When he came to his memorable conclusion, Chase stepped forward. He raised his right hand and beckoned to the clerk of the Supreme Court, who handed him an open Bible, which he placed on a stand in front of the President. Lincoln, with his right hand on the Bible, repeated the oath after Chase, and then as customary after being sworn in bent over and kissed the book. Booming of cannon signaled the end of the brief ceremony. The crowd cheered lustily and Lincoln bowed repeatedly in acknowledgment before he left the portico on his way to the basement entrance, where his carriage awaited him.[63]

What thoughts must have gone through Chase's mind as the person he had so often belittled became the first President since Jackson to be entering a second term of office. Unfortunately Chase did not record his impressions in his diary or in his correspondence except to note what he termed Johnson's unfortunate performance.[64] He marked the passages that Lincoln kissed in the Bible, the 27th and 28th verses of the fifth chapter of Isaiah, warlike phrases that the clerk had chosen randomly and which contravened Lincoln's message of peace and good will.[65]

For the remainder of the month Chase busied himself with Court business, and after the session adjourned, he spent several days in late March and early April in Baltimore where he sat as circuit judge for appeals. At the Eutaw House, where he was staying,[66] he learned of Lee's surrender and took that occasion of general rejoicing at the near end of the war to write Lincoln on Reconstruction.[67] His letter concentrated specifically on the Reconstruction of three former Confederate states, Virginia, Louisiana, and Arkansas. He recommended that the Pierpont regime in Virginia be sustained. For Louisiana he could not resist a backhanded criticism of Lincoln's policy there. He noted, however, that the new constitution of Louisiana authorized legislation to expand the privilege of suffrage. "The national authority," he urged, "be the means for extending it to colored citizens, on equal terms with white citizens. . . ." As a general rule, suffrage should be widened through state action, but with the "encouragement" of Washington universal manhood suffrage was the key to Reconstruction and the only way the former slaves and free blacks could protect themselves from reprisals and improve their lot socially and economically.[68]

The next day as he was having breakfast he read in the Baltimore *American* Lincoln's speech from the White House to a crowd of well-wishers and celebrants over peace at last. He was gratified that the President praised the new constitution of Louisiana, which removed the exceptions in the Emancipation Proclamation. All that was lacking, the President said, was the conferring of suffrage "on the very intelligent and on those who serve our cause as soldiers."[69] But he implied that this privilege would eventually be entrusted to them. Chase was disappointed that Lincoln had not gone far enough "for universal or at least equal suffrage." After the conclusion of his circuit court session Chase completed a much longer letter of advice to the President on Reconstruction. He mailed it on Thursday the 13th and returned to Washington on the evening train.[70] Chase again emphasized the importance of universal or equal suffrage. At one time he would have been satisfied with limited suffrage for blacks, he wrote, but now "sound policy and impartial justice demanded a universal suffrage."[71]

On Friday afternoon Chase called for his carriage. His purpose was to call upon Lincoln and press personally his views on suffrage. Nettie accompanied him and was to continue on for some errands after leaving her father at the White House. But Chase changed his mind. He thought for once that such a visit might annoy him, after all Chase had just written two letters to Lincoln on suffrage not to mention all the other times going back eighteen months in time when he had urged on the President full emancipation and equal rights.[72] He returned home a little after dark and went to bed at 10 p.m.

Chase was sound asleep when one of his servants woke him, saying that there was a gentlemen downstairs who wanted to see him. Chase asked that he be shown in. When he came in Chase recognized that he was a Treasury employee. "The President had been shot," he said. He gave a brief account of the tragedy at Ford's Theatre. Chase, still in his nightshirt and robe, hoped he was mistaken, but no sooner had the employee left than William P. Mellen, a supervising Treasury agent, Charles M. Walker, the fifth auditor of the Treasury Department, and Homer Plantz, formerly one of Chase's secretaries who happened to be in Washington, appeared and confirmed the news, adding that Seward also had been assassinated and that guards were being placed at the doors of all prominent officials.

Chase's first impulse was to dress and go immediately to the scene. But after thinking the matter over he decided he could not possibly be of any service. He decided to wait until morning for further news. Soon after, he heard the tramp of the guards in front of his house. Mellen stayed over but no one got much sleep. As Chase said, "it was a night of horrors."[73]

Mellen and Chase were up at dawn. They walked through a downpour until they came to Ford's Theatre and Petersen's little house opposite, where a crowd of soldiers and civilians were congregated. When they were told that the President was already dead, they continued on to Seward's house, where the guards, who recognized the tall, portly form of the Chief Justice, promptly admitted them. One of the physicians in attendance informed them that Seward and his son had both been attacked. The secretary had recovered his senses and would probably survive but his son Frederick was in critical condition from a head injury and would probably die. Everything seemed confused. Widespread plots were spoken of. Excitement was intense.[74]

Chase determined that his place was to be with the acting President, Andrew Johnson. He left Seward's home and made his way to the Kirkwood House, Johnson's Washington residence. There he found Johnson "calm apparently but very grave." Stanton had already informed him that Lincoln was dead.[75] Hugh McCulloch, who had succeeded Fessenden as Secretary of the Treasury, and Attorney General Speed came into the parlor where they joined Johnson, Chase, and Mellen. After a brief colloquy, it was determined to meet again in the same place at 10 a.m. when Chase would administer the oath of office. He and Speed then went to the Attorney General's office where both examined precedents in the cases of Vice Presidents Tyler and Fillmore.

They also looked into the Constitution and the laws pertaining to the succession. On the way back to the Kirkwood House, Speed recounted Lincoln's last Cabinet meeting. He had never seen him "in better spirits." The principal topic had been Reconstruction. Lincoln had shown Speed Chase's letter from Baltimore (probably the one he wrote on the 13th), which he complimented highly. Despite all their previous disagreements, Chase sincerely mourned "the country's great loss."[76]

When they reached the entrance of the Kirkwood House, they encountered the senior Blair and his son Montgomery. In a spirit of conciliation Chase greeted them warmly. "I had determined, I would bury resentments," he said. In the parlor Chase found a small group of about a dozen individuals, all saddened, some such as McCulloch, Speed, and Stanton tired as they had spent the entire night at the dying President's bedside.[77]

Chase administered the oath which Johnson, a sturdy figure in black, repeated after him. As soon as Johnson said, "so help me God," Chase replied, "May God guide, support and bless you in your arduous duties." Others came forward and offered their "sad congratulations." In an excess of humility, Johnson asked Chase in a low voice "if he ought to say anything to those present." Chase advised him not to say anything at the moment, but to make "a brief announcement in the public prints." "Would you prepare something?" he asked, no doubt to the irritation of the Blairs, who must have been certain that Chase would make the most of the occasion and align the new President formally and publicly with the radicals on Reconstruction.[78] Their concerns about Chase making policy for the new administration were shortlived. His paper was never printed. It got shelved among all the emergency measures being taken to deal with Lincoln's funeral and the impending surrender of Confederate General Joseph E. Johnston's army.[79]

But Chase could not be put off indefinitely. Despite the fact that he was not a Cabinet member and despite the confusion that reigned in Washington he gave Johnson little respite to consider long-range policy measures. Chase and his son-in-law, Sprague, called on the new President at the Kirkwood House on the 17th, but he gave only a hasty greeting before hurrying off to a Cabinet meeting.[80] On the 18th, however, Chase managed to have a long talk with the distracted President, who seemed to agree with him on Reconstruction. Chase saw Johnson at least twice on ensuing days. On the 22nd Sumner accompanied him and they talked of suffrage as the basis for Reconstruction. Either at this meeting or at one later on, he broached the subject of a trip south to evaluate conditions there and provide the President with facts on which to base his policies.

Chase had been considering such a trip along the southern coast for at least three weeks.[81] William Mellen, his close friend and supervising Treasury agent for the upper Mississippi Valley, had suggested a tour on April 4.[82]

Soon after, Chase made up his mind to confer with Lincoln about it, but was unable to see him because of his absence from Washington. On Lincoln's return from Grant's headquarters, Chase was holding circuit court in Baltimore. It was not until after the assassination that he was able to present his travel plans to Johnson, who heartily approved of them.[83]

Soon after the surrender of Johnston's army, near the end of the war, Chase wrote the President suggesting a conference before he embarked on his trip.[84] Johnson quickly responded with an invitation to discuss what he thought would be details of the trip. He was surprised when the Chief Justice appeared and read him an address he had prepared on Reconstruction. Chase wanted "a distinct recognition of the loyal colored men as citizens, entitled to the right of suffrage." At Johnson's request Chase read that portion several times. "I agree to all you say," said Johnson, "but I don't see how I can issue such a document now. I am new and untried and cannot venture what I please."

Always tenacious when he gave an opinion Chase proceeded in his precise logical way to convert the President to his point of view. Whatever Johnson may have felt, he was as stubborn as Chase and would not be brow-beaten. And he was too much of a politician to be drawn out on this complex subject. Chase recorded in his diary he "almost hoped the President's reluctance was conquered and that the new and crowning proclamation would be issued securing equal and universal suffrage in reorganization." He obviously misunderstood his man[85] when he took Johnson's comments to mean that he backed his proposal. Sumner also was misled in thinking that Johnson approved of Chase's position.[86]

In a letter to General Sherman Chase wrote that the President "would be gratified to have all loyal citizens participate in this work without reference to complexion, believing that by general suffrage the best, safest and most permanent reorganization would be secured." The President did agree with Chase that Reconstruction should come about through state action, but he was far less emphatic about what constituted action by "loyal citizens."[87]

chapter 29

A Trip South

Before Chase broached the idea of a trip south to Johnson, he had learned from Mellen that Secretary McCulloch had entrusted him with a special mission to New Orleans and that he would travel south in the revenue cutter *Wayanda*, then undergoing refit at New York. The *Wayanda* was an ocean-going, single-screw steamer and from all accounts could accommodate several passengers. McCulloch was delighted to make the vessel available to his former chief.

Chase decided to include Nettie, Whitelaw Reid, Dr. Richard Fuller, pastor of the Seventh Baptist Church in Baltimore, and Russell Lowell, a special Treasury agent who would act as an aide, performing whatever services the members of the party required. Mellen and his son made up the final passenger list. Chase had struck up a recent friendship with Fuller, who was a native of South Carolina and whose plantation at Port Royal had been taken over in 1862. At that time Fuller had sought advice from Chase regarding his property, including his slaves. Chase had told him that as a loyal man, he retained ownership in his property. His slaves, however, were free, a broad construction of the Confiscation Acts. Fuller grudgingly accepted Chase's explanation but quoted Machiavelli when he said "next to making freeman slaves, it is most difficult to makes [*sic*] slaves freemen." Since then Fuller had changed his mind and now believed in emancipation and a gradual bestowing of suffrage. Chase was eager to show Fuller what had transpired at Port Royal. He admired the pastor's intellectual precocity and was attracted to Fuller's expertise on the South and race relations.[1]

Armed with special letters from the President, Secretaries McCulloch, Stanton, and Welles, the group left Washington on a small dispatch vessel which would take them to Norfolk, where they would board the *Wayanda*.[2] The fact that Chase had brought along Whitelaw Reid and Dr. Fuller cast the trip as a political mission. Reid would supply his own paper, the Cincinnati *Gazette*, and the Associated Press with articles which would publicize widely Chase's views on Reconstruction. Fuller as the onetime resident, sometime expert on blacks would add weight to Chase's accounts. There was also a vacationing side to the venture. Chase and his guests were eager to see the scenes of recent battles, to visit such storied cities as Charleston, Wilmington—with its once defiant Fort Fisher—Mobile, New Orleans, and Port Royal, which had figured so importantly in the experiment with free black labor. A brief excursion to Cuba was more of a junket than anything else, though Chase could justify it by making the comparison of a region where slavery was in actual practice with the anticipated slave-free United States.

Uppermost in Chase's mind, however, was an opportunity to provide the President with his observations. During the brief stopover at Norfolk he began his first letter to Johnson, which he completed and sent off when the *Wayanda* reached Beaufort, North Carolina. After landing at Beaufort's rickety old wharf, Chase was met by a large, badly dressed individual with an air of command. He was ex-Senator Michael F. Arendell, a Unionist until the Sumter bombardment.[3] Accompanied by the county clerk, Arendell responded eagerly to Chase's questions, and had questions of his own. He wanted to know what terms Washington would impose on the defeated Confederacy. "What terms do you think would be right?" asked the Chief Justice. Arendell replied that former Governor Zebulon Vance should convene the legislature, "repeal the ordinance of secession and order a convention to amend the constitution." Reid interrupted, asking what would be done about the blacks? They would be free as wards of the state but subject to vagrancy laws, or "black codes," as they came to be known later in the North.

Chase asked about suffrage for them and their participation as citizens of the United States in Reconstruction. Arendell had no objection to their American citizenship but balked at suffrage and any significant role in Reconstruction.[4] Chase said he had no authority to speak for the federal government but his personal view was that if the blacks were free, were American citizens, and residents of a given state they should be part of the Reconstruction process.[5] Not nearly as outspoken in describing the Arendell interview to Johnson as his young friend Reid in his dispatch to the *Gazette*, Chase did insert a subtle reminder to Johnson that universal suffrage was the key to Reconstruction.[6]

From Beaufort Chase was escorted to Morehead City and thence to New Bern, North Carolina. He noted that the poor white refugees in the area seemed far more helpless than the blacks. The next day he received a note from General W. T. Sherman inviting him to visit aboard his ship the *Russia*, moored at the wharf in Morehead City.

Sherman began the conversation castigating Stanton's and Halleck's treatment of him because of the hasty, ill-considered surrender terms he gave Confederate General Johnston. Chase did what he could to calm the nervous, irascible general and brought him back to the *Wayanda*, where they had a long talk on topics, dearer to Chase's heart than Sherman's thoughtless surrender agreement. He went as far as he could in telling Sherman that the President believed "reorganization should proceed from the people," adding that the President "would be grateful to have *all* loyal citizens participate in this work without reference to complection. . . ."[7] He was disappointed at Sherman's reaction.

The general was not prepared to extend political rights to the blacks. He believed any such a move would have violent consequences in both the North and the South even to the extent of reviving "the war and spread[ing] its field of operations." Barring the extension of political rights to the blacks, he was confident that "the southern people were so thoroughly defeated and disarmed that there would be no trouble provided we deal with them with frankness and candor and not with doubt and hesitancy."[8] Sherman portrayed a very grim picture of the situation in the South. "All is pure anarchy," he said, "the area is too vast for the military power of the United States to reach most of the people." "We can control the local state capitals," he asserted, "and it may be slowly shape political thoughts, but we cannot combat existing ideas with force."[9]

Chase also spoke with General John M. Schofield, the thirty-four-year-old veteran of hard fighting in Missouri and Tennessee and Sherman's Atlanta campaign. A calm, thoughtful person, he listened to Chase and, more knowledgeable than Sherman in the way of politics, neither accepted nor denied the Chief Justice's argument for universal suffrage. Schofield's courteous and careful responses led Chase to believe that he was just the right person to provide protection for the blacks in North Carolina and to advance the cause of suffrage for whites and blacks alike. Chase was so impressed that he recommended to Johnson that Schofield be intrusted as a military governor, "either with that State or Department."[10] Privately, Schofield was as dubious as Sherman about Chase's plans for black suffrage. Like most of the army officers in the former Confederacy he was opposed to having the blacks participate on an equal basis with the whites in Reconstruction.[11]

Offshore gales kept the *Wayanda* in Beaufort harbor. Chase busied himself with talking to the inhabitants and visiting points of interest. On Sunday,

May 7, Dr. Fuller gave a vigorous antislavery sermon at the local Methodist church, urging the parishioners to have patience and charity toward their ex-slaves. Fuller made no mention of suffrage and in fact as Chase now knew he doubted it should be implemented rapidly.

On Monday the weather had improved sufficiently for the *Wayanda* to put to sea. But a strong head wind off the Carolina capes made the vessel roll and pitch dramatically. Everyone, including Chase, became ill. His seasickness did not dampen his desire to see the famed Fort Fisher, which commanded the entrance to Wilmington harbor and had stubbornly resisted all Union army and navy efforts to capture it until near the end of the war.[12] The *Wayanda* made its way up to Wilmington, where General Joseph R. Hawley met the party. Stocky, self-assured, a journalist and politician in civilian life, Hawley was a friend of Gideon Welles and his group of Hartford, Connecticut, Republicans, which included Chase's failed nominee, Mark Howard. But Hawley was moving away from Welles's conservatism and was most receptive to Chase's ideas on Reconstruction.[13] He made it possible for Chase to meet many different segments of Wilmington society, including blacks.

Reid's impression was that most of the residents—white and black— were destitute. The heavy loss of life among white males left few to till the fields, manage the plantations, or revitalize local industry. Demoralization and with it economic stagnation seemed everywhere present. The disorganization of the labor system and the destruction of railroad transport made much of the population dependent on either the Union army commissaries or hastily established outposts of the Freedman's Bureau. Reid thought that most of the whites were "thoroughly cowed by the crushing defeat" and that they would submit "to anything the government may require—negro suffrage, territorial pupilage—anything."[14]

Influenced by Sherman's appraisal, and certainly more mature in his judgments than his younger, brash colleague, Chase gave a more realistic appraisal in his third letter to Johnson. He divided the southern population into three classes. The first, or "old conservatives," as he referred to them were opposed to black suffrage and would like slavery reimposed. This group was the smallest. A second class of individuals also would prefer a return "to the old order of things," but yearned for a stable society and economy. Though they would dislike the imposition of black suffrage, they would accept it. A third element were what Chase called "the progressives": they saw a new social order, were happy that slavery had been abolished, and supported universal male suffrage. He truthfully noted that these men were "few, & few of the few have been heretofore conspicuous." "In the end," he ventured, "they will control."[15]

Like all northern visitors, Chase was curious about Fort Sumter, Fort Moultrie, and all the other points within and without Charleston that had been featured over four years in the press and in military dispatches that came to his attention. As the *Wayanda* made her way up the channel by Morris Island Chase was on deck watching intently the slowly passing coastline. He had been reading William Howard Russell's account of Charleston in April 1861 to refresh his memory about the events of those stirring times. "How like a dream the past seems," he mused, "Wigfall, Anderson, Pickens, Whiting, Beauregard, Sumter, the bombardment the surrender—the call for 75,000— for Congress—the War!"[16] Waiting for him at Charleston were two senior officers whom he knew were sympathetic to his ideas on Reconstruction, Generals Q. A. Gillmore and Rufus Saxton. They outdid themselves in arranging for Chase to see all to be seen and to hear all to be heard. Both bewiskered gentlemen were of New England heritage, Gillmore from the old abolition country of Ohio's Western Reserve, Saxton Massachusetts-born, the man most responsible for the success of the Port Royal experiment, as limited as it was.

Chase was surprised to see less damage to the buildings and houses of Charleston than he expected. But evidence of the war's backwash was obvious at every hand. Refugees from the country, black and white, moved through the streets seemingly in hopeless confusion. Most were on foot though an occasional wagon or broken-down carriage loaded with a family's possessions rode by.

On the last day of their visit General Saxton arranged a public meeting at the Zion church, the city's largest black hall. When Reid arrived, the square in front of the church was jammed with blacks and a few whites. A way was made for him through the dense throng and he was given a seat in a pew just below the pulpit from which General Saxton was delivering a speech. Near him were three black army officers in full dress uniform, two majors and a first lieutenant. When Saxton concluded his remarks, Major Martin L. Delaney, the senior black officer present, climbed to the pulpit and began a speech which was poorly delivered and gained little applause.[17] Suddenly he was interrupted by a tremendous burst of prolonged cheering. Reid turned his head and saw the massive figure of Chase advancing up the main aisle with General Gillmore.[18] The Chief Justice was already well known by word of mouth as a friend of the blacks. The presumed spokesman for the new administration in Washington, he was expected to bring good news.

Major Delaney quickly vacated the pulpit to Saxton, who introduced Chase. A willing subject when asked to address the multitude of blacks he saw before him, Chase spoke for about half an hour in what Reid described as "familiar and fatherly talk to helpless negroes."[19] Reflecting on what he had heard that the freedmen were ignorant and shiftless, Chase rejected that description, but at the same time urged his audience to make sure such criticism would not be leveled at them. He asked them to be industrious, economical with their wages, and above all sober, helpful members of the community. He stressed education, formal or self-taught, and the acquisition of useful skills. Lastly he hoped they would get the vote; but he was careful to say that this was a personal view and that he did not speak for the administration in Washington. Should the government "come to a conclusion different from mine, and delay to enroll you as citizens and voters," he said, "your best policy, in my judgment, is patience."

In due time they would receive the privilege of suffrage because it was a matter of justice. They must use it wisely, not merely to protect themselves and their families but to show potential naysayers that they were law-abiding, progressive members of the community.[20] Chase spoke in his usual style though at the end of his paternalistic talk, sensing the empathy of the audience, he raised his voice and gave an emotional conclusion which brought everyone present to his or her feet in a prolonged bout of cheering.[21]

Chase's speech was taken down by reporters present, Reid included, and found its way north, where depending on the policy of the newspaper was praised or attacked as just another example of Chase's electioneering. Actually his impromptu speech in Charleston and some remarks he made to largely black audiences at Dr. Fuller's old plantation were scarcely examples of radical propaganda.[22] His message of patience, education, sobriety, thrift, and industry were quite appropriate given the disordered conditions in the South and the rampant racism which existed there and in much of the North. He did not speak of such harsh economic measures as confiscation and distribution of the lands, even those abandoned or state-owned, which Thaddeus Stevens and others of his group in Congress were advocating.[23]

His emphasis on equal suffrage as the key to Reconstruction may have been naive, considering the actual state of the public mind in the South and the North, but his position was well known. It was a logical extension of his long-held belief in the natural rights of man, his linkage of the Declaration with the Constitution. That as Chief Justice he spoke out on such a divisive political issue that was legitimately in the province of the legislative and executive branches may have been ill-considered. Nor could his detractors—and they were many—ignore Chase's ambition and his taste for political intrigue, but on the whole the public speeches were scarcely that provocative.[24]

During the next ten days, Chase made extended visits to the Sea Islands, where he satisfied himself that the experiment in the labor of free blacks was working out. He saw evidence also of land ownership in small garden plots.[25] Elsewhere, however, it was clear that much more assistance, either public or private, was needed if Chase's vision of free black workers supporting themselves and improving their material conditions were to become a reality.[26]

In his fifth letter to Johnson Chase described his meeting at the Zion church and repeated his belief in the importance of universal manhood suffrage. He was careful to say that "the whole question of reorganization is in your hands." He added that when he visited Savannah he had been urged to make another address. He had refused, as he explained to Johnson, because he feared that he "might be taken for a politician or preacher rather than a Chief Justice."[27] Chase was responding to the Democratic press and to criticism in the New York *Herald*. From that time on, every move he made was seen by many as having sinister political implications. At Fernadina, Florida, where the *Wayanda* put in, Chase met an old friend from his Ohio days, Adolphus Mot, who had just been elected mayor of this insignificant little port. Mot, whose surname implied his vocation as a teacher of the French language, had tutored Chase and Kate. Chase was delighted to administer the oath of office to Mot, a simple gesture of good will on his part that the New York *World* quibbled was demeaning the stature of a Chief Justice of the United States.[28]

Back in Washington, conservatives and Chase-haters such as Montgomery Blair were certain that the Chief Justice was using the trip not simply for reporting on conditions of blacks and evaluating whether to revise or abolish wartime trade regulations but actually to prepare his former Treasury agents and tax commissioners to begin a Chase for President boom three years hence. Blair urged Johnson to squelch "those Chase vermin . . . summarily."[29]

There is no doubt that Chase had good things to say about his former agents, many of whom were old friends from his Liberty party, Free Soil days. And it is equally true that many, if not most of the agents were in some way using their posts to enrich themselves. Lyman D. Stickney, a speculating Vermonter and Chase's tax commissioner and special Treasury agent at Key West, later indicted for graft, is a prime example of the "vermin" of which Blair spoke.[30] Chase saw nothing wrong with Stickney's speculations in Florida real estate and authorized him to purchase Dungeness, a large plantation near Fernadina for his own account. Soon after Stickney was indicted for fraud and the deal never went through.[31]

In Chase's fifth and most important letter he included eight specific recommendations on Reconstruction. Entitled "Military Matters," they were similar to his ideas on emancipation that he had urged on Lincoln in 1862. Chase thought that the army should be in control of the process during its preliminary stages. Sherman's advice on the state of the South had made an impact. "As yet," he said, "the rebels are disarmed only; not reconciled; hardly acquiescent: and there are no state governments to prevent outbreaks." Chase recognized that the army would be the primary stabilizing influence in the southern states and in a unique position to control the direction locally of Reconstruction, whatever policy Washington might develop.[32]

Once a military commander established his authority over a state, he might enroll "loyal white or black citizens." The key word here was "citizens," in Chase's mind, of the United States. Once this process was completed, the loyal "citizens" would vote for delegates to a constitutional convention which would provide the fundamental law of the reorganized state based on universal manhood suffrage.[33] Some of Chase's suggestions on technical points seem to have made an impression on Johnson, but not his overall approach.

On May 29, while Chase was visiting Mobile, Alabama, near the end of his tour, he received word of the President's Proclamations of Amnesty and Reconstruction for North Carolina. The North Carolina Proclamation placed that state under a provisional governor who would take the initiative in having loyal citizens adopt measures for reinstating appropriate relations with the federal government. Loyal citizens were defined as those who had voted in the 1860 election and were not excluded by the Amnesty Proclamation. Except for this mention no provision was made for suffrage, which was implicitly recognized to be a state right. In all probability southern blacks would be denied enfranchisement.

Previously Johnson had extended the same mandate to the Pierpont regime as the legal government of Virginia and had omitted mention of black suffrage. Before he began his southern journey Chase had tried to convince the President that he should begin Reconstruction in Louisiana and in Florida. Both states had abolished slavery and seemed to be making progress toward black enfranchisement. Johnson had not commented on Chase's advice, and now it was obvious he had rejected it.[34]

Chase had not spent all of his time on serious matters. Since he had never ventured further south than Norfolk, Virginia, he found the tropical foliage charming, the exotic birds and animals he saw in Florida and Cuba interesting. The Cuban trip was especially gratifying because he was able to observe a radically different culture than that of his own country. For Chase, so workbound, so narrow in his experiences of other lands and faraway places except in his imagination, the visits to Havana and to other Cuban towns was an adventure. For brief moments the cares of his office, the concerns over Reconstruction, even his gnawing ambition gave way to sheer pleasure. He was of course treated with great deference. There were salutes and manning of the yards by United States naval vessels, grave courtesies from the Spanish authorities in Cuba, banquets, and always a plenitude of refreshing tropical fruit and juices as well as the best coffee he had ever drunk.[35]

Yet he had not let the novelty and the ease of his journey interfere with his reports to Johnson or his proselytizing of the military on universal suffrage. At Mobile, Alabama, he had a long talk with the Union army commander General Christopher Andrews. Andrews had said that the illiterate blacks would not know which candidate to support. Chase replied: "When I go to the polls to vote; it is true I can read the ticket, but it is seldom I know the man. I have to ask some friend whom I should vote for. The freedman will do the same." That evening Chase made another convert to equal suffrage.[36]

Chase wrote two more letters to the President, one before his trip to Cuba and a final one on his return to Key West. His last letter, posted on May 23, made an important suggestion on amnesty. He knew that former Confederate military men were being paroled with the proviso that they conform to the laws existing prior to secession. Chase said that this stipulation sanctioned slavery, though not "presumed as such."[37] And he remained sensitive to anything that connoted racial inferiority. At the start of his trip, he had written Stanton urging him to issue "an order forbidding the calling of freedmen 'contrabands.'" "Words," he went on, "implying degradation help to degrade."[38]

If anything the trip reinforced Chase's feelings about equality of the races. But as his tolerance on racial matters was strengthened and his hatred of slavery persisted, Chase's sympathy, even forbearance for the defeated foes, and his hopes for a speedy readjustment were moving him toward a more lenient Reconstruction tempered always with loyalty and acceptance of universal suffrage. A property-minded lawyer and a careful reader of the Declaration and the Constitution, where property was protected along with life and liberty, Chase was shocked at the destruction and the looting.

His companion and his publicist Reid, on the other hand, could not conceal his racist feelings which appear now and then with pejorative adjectives when describing blacks. Paradoxically Reid was much more contemptuous of the white southerners irrespective of their position in society than Chase. He was more radical than Chase on political and economic objectives in Reconstruction, far more willing to approve indiscriminate confiscation. Of course, as a journalist, he could afford to be more positive in his comments than Chase, a Justice and still a politician. Yet subtle differences between the two men provide a sort of microcosm of the complex and treachorous political currents that were swirling around Reconstruction.

When the Chase party reached New Orleans and made the rounds of the city as they had previously at Mobile, they were ready to part with the *Wayanda*.[39] Chase sought passage for himself and Nettie on one of the river steamboats that would carry them north to Cincinnati. None was available when Chase planned to leave. Without Chase's knowledge Mellen and Reid went to the military authorities, who promptly commandeered the *Fashion*, a privately owned vessel. When their arrangement came to Chase's attention he promptly vetoed it. He insisted that Mellen see the captain of the *Fashion*, apologize, and say that he would not interfere with her schedule. All he wanted was a state room and would change his plans rather than cause any inconvenience. The *Fashion* sailed without him, but Mellen and Reid persisted and again without Chase's knowledge had General E. R. S. Canby requisition the *W. R. Carter* of the Atlantic and Mississippi Steamship Company,[40] which would carry Chase and his party up the river along with other passengers.[41]

After making short excursions from New Orleans and having lengthy conversations, political and otherwise, with the military commanders and with New Orleans lawyer Thomas J. Durant, his cousin George S. Denison, former Unionist congressman Benjamin F. Flanders, his ex-brother-in-law Randall Hunt, and local judge Christian Roselius—a mix of New Orleans radicals and conservatives—Chase boarded the *Carter* for the final leg of the trip. On June 17, when he reached Memphis, he received welcome news that Kate had borne a son. Both mother and child were recovering nicely.[42] On June 22, the *Carter* reached Cincinnati and tied up at the Fifth Street pier. The trip upriver had been pleasant after the intense heat of southern Alabama and Louisiana. He was disappointed, however, at further evidence of Johnson's intransigence on the suffrage issue after reading his proclamation that set up a provisional government in Mississippi.[43]

Despite his concerns about affairs of state and his chagrin that his letters to the President seemed to have made no impression, Chase was happy to be on home ground after more than a year's absence. This time he was not pressed for speeches or rationed for time. He could afford a degree of relaxation. Chase booked rooms at the Burnet House, where friends and acquaintances soon came to greet him. That afternoon he was able to break away from the throng and was whisked off to Bishop McIlvaine's home at Clifton, where he was to spend the night. McIlvaine's lovely daughter and other young folk served a bountiful tea and engaged in relaxing small talk. Unfortunately the heat that Chase thought he had escaped came on with a torrid vengeance. It seemed hotter than New Orleans, just as humid and still, "not a leaf stirred no breeze to sweep away the mosquitoes and gnats." Yet the Bishop and Chase talked far into the evening, not retiring until 11 o'clock.[44]

Chase remained in Cincinnati for a week. He talked politics and Reconstruction with dozens of friends and foes. On June 29 he was off to Columbus for a brief stopover that included Cleveland, where among other visits he called on the ailing Governor John Brough and was squired about town by his friend George M. Parsons.[45] After a rather harrowing journey by train during which Chase did not undress in the sleeper car because he feared an accident, he and Nettie finally reached New York City. He put up at the St. Nicholas Hotel.

Although he must have been tired out after little or no sleep for two nights on the train, Chase was on the move for the brief time he spent in the city. He was happy to learn that all but seven banks in the metropolis had joined the national bank system. But as much as he enjoyed the excitement, the political and business talk of the New Yorkers, Chase was anxious to be off to Rhode Island to see Kate and his new grandson, who had been named William Sprague after his father. Chase had vetoed Kate's suggestion that the baby be named after him. One Salmon Portland was enough. He would not inflict it on anyone, much less an innocent baby.[46]

On July 5 he boarded the *Oceanus* for the overnight trip to Providence. From there he, Nettie, and one of his long-time investment counselors, Joshua Hanna, took horsecars to Kingston and the Sprague farm at Canonchet. He found the baby healthy and active. Kate had put on some weight during her pregnancy and Chase thought she looked better and prettier than she had for years. The Spragues seemed to have settled down. Both were devoted to the infant. Kate was happily engaged in managing the design and building of an enormous mansion in the latest exuberant blend of Gothic and Mansard styles. As usual she was being her extravagant self, spending Sprague's money liberally with no compunction nor apparently any objection from him.[47]

Chase enjoyed the beautiful landscape, bracing air, and cool nights of Narragansett Bay after the heat and humidity of the South and the Midwest. As always the politics of Washington and the opening phase of presidential Reconstruction claimed first attention. During his tour, he had been in touch with Sumner but Chase's letters simply confirmed in more graphic terms disappointment at Johnson's policies and unabated adhesion to equal suffrage for all before any blanket amnesty was conferred. Chase believed that Johnson had made "a great mistake in refusing to recognize the colored citizen as part of the people. . . . It is a moral, political and presidential mistake." Should Johnson continue in his present course, Chase scouted the possibility of another constitutional Amendment beyond the Thirteenth that outlawed slavery, then in its final stages of acceptance by the states.[48]

Neither individual had given up on the President. Sumner urged Chase to forgo his summer plans and return to Washington where he could rally resistance to Johnson's policy, which he said was dividing the party and giving the nation over to the "Peace" Democrats. Chase refused to alter his plans. Apart from his personal reasons, he was enough of a politician to wait until the situation in Washington had clarified. Even Sumner admitted that Johnson was experimenting until presumably he reached some kind of political consensus that would involve Congress in Reconstruction.[49]

Chase was disturbed, as he had been on his southern trip, that military commissions were acting as courts. The news of the trial by a military commission of the Lincoln conspirators he found unsettling since the act occurred in the District of Columbia, where the civilian courts were open and functioning. Denial of habeas corpus for the accused assassins he thought unjustified, though he hedged a bit when he said, "probably not unwarranted." Sprague was particularly vehement in condemning the action and vigorously opposed any infringement the military might impose on civil rights. Chase had long cherished the writ of habeas corpus as a bulwark protecting human freedom. He had never failed to argue this point in his defense of fugitive slaves. When Lincoln brought up the question of suspension in September 1863, Chase had insisted that it pertain strictly to military affairs and to those civilians then in custody for subversive activities. Suspension, he argued, must be based on the congressional act delegating such powers to the President. His views were given formal acceptance when Lincoln's Proclamation suspended the writ in specified instances.[50]

A little over a month after he voiced his misgivings about the military trial of the Lincoln conspirators, his concerns about criminal trials stemming from the war were put to the test. He received a telegram from the President asking for a conference on "the time, place, and manner of trial of Jefferson Davis."[51] Chase immediately wired his acceptance and was in Washington on August 17.[52]

He found the city as dirty and hot as ever. A rather prolonged dry spell had laid inches of dust on the streets. Carriages, buggies, and horsecars threw it up in clouds that enveloped all who ventured out, including the Chief Justice as he made his way to the White House. Johnson had been ill and looked gaunt as he greeted Chase less warmly than he had before the southern trip. He came straight to the point on a proposed trial of Davis. Chase heard him out and then proceeded to deliver a short lecture on the impropriety of the executive discussing such an important matter of state as a treason trial with the chief of the judicial branch.

Rather than risk further argument Johnson agreed with Chase. But when Chase sought to steer the conversation to Reconstruction, a political matter, the President blocked tactfully, but firmly any discussion. That evening Stanton called at Chase's home. Though steadfast in the views he shared with Chase on suffrage, he would not press that issue with the President.[53]

For the next month Chase braved the discomfort of Washington, gleaning information and seeking to convert important politicians, newspaper editors, and those members of Congress who were in the city. As he summarized Washington opinion on Johnson for Sumner he found a variety of views. "Some insist that the President is trying an experiment," Chase wrote, ". . . which is sure to fail and that he will either change the plan himself or will agree cheerfully to have it changed by Congress. . . ." But most of those he spoke with thought that Johnson did not believe the two races could coexist on terms of equality. Chase believed that Johnson was in a quandary and was uncertain what further steps he would take.[54] Chase had no such qualms about the trial of Jefferson Davis. Even at this early date he foresaw constitutional and legal problems of a formidable nature that would hamper if not foreclose a trial.

The Lincoln administration had treated the rebellion as war at home. After a brief attempt to try the officers and crew of a Confederate raider as pirates, the administration had to back down when the Davis regime declared it would hang prisoner for prisoner if the raiders were executed for the capital crime of piracy. Thereafter the thousands of Confederate soldiers captured were treated as prisoners of war rather than rebels who committed treasonable acts. Did not this policy apply to Confederate leaders, military men such as Lee and Longstreet and John B. Gordon, who had not been granted amnesty, but otherwise were free, or to Alexander Stephens, Vice President of the Confederacy, and other important dignitaries, some of whom had served brief prison sentences, but had been released under habeas corpus writs?

Should Davis be singled out as the only person responsible for the war? Many northern politicians thought that he should, but a substantial and grow- ing opinion both political and otherwise disagreed. Chase was well aware of this development. What of constitutional concerns? Sections 2 and 3 of Article III declared that trial for all crimes except impeachment had to be held in the state where the acts took place, and this included treason. Where had Davis's treasonable acts taken place, in Virginia? Montgomery, Alabama? Would a jury of Davis's peers in either state be impartial? Chase thought not.

Beyond the political and legal and constitutional concerns, Chase took the long view. It would be a needless act of vengeance to try, convict, and execute Davis. The hostility of the northern public toward a good third of the nation's population that had supported the Confederacy must eventually dis- appear if the nation was to fulfil its vaunted destiny. Davis could become a symbol of reunion as before he was the archetype of disunion. Nor should the romantic notion of compassion for a fallen but valiant foe be disregarded. Chase was as susceptible as the reading public to this idea, which popular novels and poetry had inculcated for years. If the Chief Justice could delay any proceedings against Davis until the passions of the hour subsided, he would do so. He had a powerful weapon at his disposal. So long as Virginia and Alabama were under military control, he and his colleagues could not preside over Davis's trial. After the initial venting of political fury began to subside, Congress and the Johnson administration saw a treason trial of Davis in much the same way as Chase.[55]

chapter 30

Universal Suffrage, Universal Amnesty

From mid-September to mid-November, 1866, Chase resumed his working vacation in New York City and New England, and took a leisurely fishing excursion with Jay Cooke at his summer home, "Gibraltar"[1] among the picturesque solitude of the Lake Erie islands. Everywhere he went, with every person of consequence he met—including Governor John A. Andrew, William P. Fessenden, Ralph Waldo Emerson, Samuel Hooper, Charles Sumner, of course, and George Bancroft—he pressed his ideas of universal suffrage as the key measure for Reconstruction.

By the end of Chase's travels, President Johnson had reconstructed all of the former Confederate states except Texas and had begun pardoning former Confederate officers, both military and civil, who had been excluded from his general amnesty proclamations. Like others of his close friends and associates, Chase feared that Johnson had entrusted the fate of over 4 million blacks to their former white masters. If they did not restore slavery, the plantation owners would in all likelihood establish a system of peonage or other forms of forced labor equivalent to slavery. Once the white elites had regained power Chase saw them allied with northern "Peace" Democrats to form a political combination that would undo the fruits of victory after four years of conflict and the expenditure of billions of dollars.

Chase's southern tour had confirmed his preconceptions that the blacks were loyal to the Union and he believed could be relied on if given the power to check any such reactionary moves. He concluded that they would exercise the elective franchise as well as, if not better than the white masses of the northern cities. Though radical by contemporary standards, Chase's approach to the complex and vexing problems of Reconstruction was more realistic than the explosive fulminations and caustic rhetoric of his friend Sumner.

As he had years before when he sensed the makings of a prime public issue in the antislavery movement, Chase could see another great reform in the offing—equal rights, both political and economic, for a race that had been enslaved and exploited. Social justice for the underprivileged he believed to be the prime objective of an enlightened people. He shared with Sumner a devotion to natural rights for all. But as his long experience in the forefront of the antislavery ranks had taught him, the process of public enlightenment was slow and fraught with temporary setbacks. No longer the youthful lawyer who had little to lose by exposing a cause so far in advance of public opinion, he was now a statesman whose reputation he would not put at risk. He was also a mature politician who thought in terms of consensus and a Chief Justice, the head of the Supreme Court and presumably the defender—symbolically, at least—of a coordinate branch of the government.

If Chase disliked the labor and the tedium of the bench, he was aware of its potential power in shaping the direction of Reconstruction. He recognized the perils involved in judgments over essentially political matters. Chase had to pick his way carefully in what he discerned as an emerging contest over Reconstruction between the Congress and the President. Would the Court adopt the passive mode of mediator or would it define new spheres of judgment as the nation made its way out of the travail of war into an uncertain peace? Or would it be caught up in the contest in such a way that its prestige would suffer?

Given Chase's temperament, consuming ambition, and devotion to moral causes, the situation seemed ideal. If he could advance himself through the medium of the Court, yet incidentally satisfy his conscience that he was advancing the cause of human freedom and enhancing the scope of the judicial function, he was prepared to play an activist posture and persuade his colleagues to do likewise. Even if he differed from a majority of the Justices on significant points of interpretation, he would shape his dissenting or concurring opinions in such a way as to cultivate powerful interests as he perceived them.

At the same time he was aware that the expedient motive which so often worked for the politician could be dangerous for a judge. What others took to be irresolute or contriving in Chase was his recognition of the pitfalls in his path. Charged, as he had been frequently in the past, of using ignoble means, Chase would ignore the imputation and proclaim his noble ends. Nor did he deem this hypocrisy on his part. Basically there was a bedrock of moral substance in Chase's character. He really cared for the unfortunate whether they be poor, friendless blacks, beggars in the streets, or family members experiencing hard times. Yet he was curiously blind to the lifestyle of the rich and the extravagances of his daughter Kate. He surrounded himself with servants. He enjoyed the privileges of a private railroad car. But when duty called he would take the train or ride the public horsecars and share his food with unknown fellow passengers.[2]

Enough of an idealist to cherish the personal rights and privileges embedded in the Constitution, Chase was enough of a realist to accept under certain conditions their temporary abrogation in times of civil strife.[3] Well versed in history and political theory, he was a firm believer in federalism as expounded in the Constitution and in the separation and distribution of powers. Whenever possible and practical, he would call upon states' rights as the basic concept of American government, but he always conditioned this Jeffersonian credo with the overarching power of the central state to protect the individual from local or regional excesses. His colleague on the Court Samuel F. Miller came as close as any to understanding this complex character. "Religious by training and conviction and outward discipline," he wrote, "endowed by nature with a warm heart and a vigorous intellect, but all these warped, perverted, shriveled by the selfishness generated by ambition. . . . But he was a great man and a better man than public life generally leaves one after forty years of service."[4]

Miller may have overemphasized Chase's unrelenting ambition, but if it flawed his nature, his other attributes brought a strong presence to the Supreme Court at a critical time in its history. Paradoxically, it was this driving ambition which made Chase the appropriate person to represent the Court to the public and to the other branches of government. His commanding figure, his imperious nature, his political connections and interests may have been a trial for his colleagues on the bench, but they were of great importance to the image of a Court that the Dred Scott case had sullied. Chase had to be taken seriously. For he was too well known as a distinguished administrator, litigator, and financier. His stature as an eminent public man carried over to the Court. His confident even aggressive personality meant that the Court would be heard on public policy decisions that would shape the future of the still distracted nation.

Chase reached his home in Washington in mid-November. He spent the remainder of the month and the first week in December conferring informally with his fellow Justices and arriving members of Congress. The Thirty-ninth

Congress that reassembled on December 3 was immediately faced with the problem of whether to admit senators and representatives from the former Confederate states elected under the provisions Johnson had set forth for their Reconstruction. Among them were high officials of the Confederacy, men such as the recently released state prisoner and ex-Vice President of the Confederacy Alexander H. Stevens. Schuyler Colfax over a sumptuous break-fast with Chase said that Congress would not seat the southern senators and representatives "except possibly those elected from Tennessee." He expected to be elected Speaker and to Chase's dismay said that Congress was "un-prepared for universal suffrage." He himself was "rather against it." Later that day Senator Henry Wilson of Massachusetts called. Upon his request Chase agreed to draft an act that would enfranchise all qualified males in the District of Columbia irrespective of race.[5]

Later Chase read Johnson's Annual Message to Congress with great care. It was an impressive document, well written well organized, that calmly and dispassionately outlined the President's case for his Reconstruction pol-icy. In many respects it resembled Chase's writings with its reliance on histori-cal development and careful enunciation of the Constitution and constitu-tional precedent. So unlike Johnson's occasional addresses, Chase must have wondered whether the President had written it.[6]

But the hub of the problem was still there as Chase saw it. Johnson had assigned the issue of suffrage to the states. Unless one accepted the fact that the southern states had forfeited or suspended their corporate status Johnson had a valid argument that extending suffrage to the blacks through executive fiat would also require the same extension to the northern and western states. "Such an act," he said, "would have created a new class of voters and would have been an assumption of power by the President which nothing in the Constitution or laws of the United States would have warranted."[7]

Johnson was relying on a strict constructionist view of the Constitution. But Chase had used a similar argument in justifying free soil, arguing that slavery was a state matter. Where he differed from Johnson was that he would have the President make equal suffrage a condition imposed on the former Confederate states through their constitutional conventions before they were accepted as states of the Union. All blacks were free and now held American citizenship, if not citizenship of the state where they resided. In due course, he expected northern and northwestern states which denied or limited suffrage for blacks to remove these impediments.

Logic and federal complexities aside, 4 million blacks resided in the South, not even a small fraction of that number in the North and West. The South had been an enemy and was defeated in war. The freedmen in the South must now be counted fully in apportioning representatives and electors for President and Vice President, yet southern blacks were not permitted to vote by state law. The erstwhile enemy would have increased representation in Congress by counting all of the blacks, not just three-fifths as formerly. Such a political reality as distinguished from any considerations of morality or social justice was in part recognized when Congress refused to seat the representatives of the states reconstructed under presidential proclamation.

The so-called "black codes," or vagrancy statutes that the provisional governments had quickly imposed on the southern blacks, seemed to confirm the fears of many northerners that they were a means of reinstating slavery under another form. The radical inclined northern press, in particular, the New York *Tribune* and the *Evening Post,* condemned this legislation unsparingly. Yet the Union Republican majority in Congress was still willing to compromise with the President, if he would initiate a policy that would protect the freedmen from errant discrimination. Moderate and even radical members conceded that suffrage was a state right. But the power and prestige of the President's office should compel the former Confederate states to extend at least limited suffrage to the blacks.[8]

Congress established the Joint Committee on Reconstruction soon after the President's annual message. Senator Lyman Trumbull of Illinois, a moderate Republican of Democratic antecedents, began drafting bills for the committee that would protect the civil rights of blacks and enlarge and extend the powers granted in the Freedman's Bureau Act, which Lincoln had approved in the closing months of the war. The bureau was designed to assist former slaves and to provide some help for education and famine relief for blacks and whites alike. Military commanders were authorized to administer the aid. Trumbull's bills, however, would go considerably further than simply providing education and material assistance. Aimed at protecting the civil rights of the freedmen, they gave additional powers of enforcement to the military in cases of racial discrimination and they invalidated the black codes.[9]

While these developments were occurring in Congress, Chase was shocked to learn that his friend, the thoroughgoing radical Henry Winter Davis, had died suddenly in Baltimore. Chase was a pallbearer, as was Secretary Stanton. After the funeral Chase and Stanton had a long talk about Reconstruction as they returned to Washington. Chase was happy to learn that Stanton favored universal suffrage in the District of Columbia and in the southern states "without qualification of property or education," despite the President's opposition. Where he differed from Chase was in the relative weight of political rights as opposed to economic assistance. Stanton thought the vote was less important to the freedmen than government-sponsored economic assistance that would grant them lands for farming. Departing from his practical ideas on Reconstruction, Chase relegated the economic aspect to secondary importance, revealing a strain of conservatism that would eventually separate him from his radical friends. He maintained stoutly that it was "easier to reach farms through suffrage than suffrage through farms."[10]

Congress adjourned over the holidays, and Kate—then in Washington along with Nettie—gave a series of receptions to which Washington's society turned out en masse.[11] Chase always mixed business with pleasure at breakfasts, small "family dinners," and dinner parties.[12] The more formal affairs gave Chase an opportunity to ease personal frictions among his colleagues, disputes that inevitably arose in the closed circle of intense lawyers who made up the Court. Stephen J. Field, an emotional individual, frequently got on his colleagues' nerves. Samuel Miller, a big bear of a man in a Court noted for its height and girth, was a powerful personality who was often at odds with Field and resented Chase's pretensions.[13]

Chase hastened to speak with Miller after Field told him that the Iowan was dissatisfied with his "assignment of cases." Miller blandly replied that he had been misunderstood, but then went on to explain that Field's "excitability" was due to his drinking habits. An astonished Chase resolved to speak to Field "like a brother; for he is one of our best men and dear to me."[14] It is not recorded whether Chase spoke with Field, and if so what his reaction had been. We may conjecture that the Justice used to the rough and tumble of frontier California and Nevada was not amused. Apart from seeking to bring his colleagues closer together at social affairs where his daughters were pressed into service, Chase used these occasions to drum up support for his by now monotonous reiteration that universal suffrage was the key to Reconstruction.

One subject the Justices did not discuss publicly was the trial of civilians by military commissions in areas where the courts were open.[15] The Lincoln conspirators had been tried by just such a commission. Only through attenuated reasoning was the new Attorney General Speed able to justify military jurisdiction in those cases. Washington, he had claimed, was within battle lines when Lincoln was assassinated, though Lee had surrendered and the capital was scarcely a war zone. Chase was a staunch defender of habeas corpus and all of his colleagues in one way or another opposed courts-martial of civilians in states or territories where no threat of insurrection or grave social disturbances existed. He and his colleagues were now faced directly with a case on appeal of a military trial and death sentences for three alleged organizers of rebellion in Indiana. All three men were prominent Democrats who had opposed the war and who were convicted of planning to free Confederate prisoners in the Midwest. The best known of the condemned men was Lambdin Milligan.

Respited by Lincoln, Johnson ordered the sentences to be carried out on May 19, 1865. A hearing for a writ of habeas corpus on behalf of the three prisoners was held before Justice David Davis and the district court judge for the region. Though they did not rule on the writ, Davis sent a long letter to Johnson urging that a delay be granted so that a hearing could be held before the Supreme Court to test the constitutionality of the proceedings which had convicted them. Davis's letter along with a plea of clemency from Governor Morton of Indiana prompted Johnson to delay the execution of Milligan and one of his associates. Two weeks later, he commuted all the sentences to life imprisonment.

The Milligan case would have been a relatively minor question for the Court to decide had not the contest between the President and Congress over Reconstruction assumed alarming proportions. Johnson's veto of the Freedman's Bureau Bill and his ill-tempered, ill-considered harangue to a crowd that gathered in front of the White House on Washington's birthday raised congressional tempers. Most of the more influential Union-Republican press and a majority of the moderates joined the radicals in Congress to condemn Johnson's remarks as libelous, vulgar, and irresponsible.[16]

Chase was less critical than his friends. "It is very much regretted I think," he wrote, "that Mr. Stevens and Mr. Sumner have excited the president's anger against the whole class of earnest men by remarks which he construed as personal assaults." He hoped that Johnson would sign the Civil Rights Bill, an action that would do much toward restoring cordial relations with Congress.[17] Like the revised and broadened Freedman's Bureau Bill, the Civil Rights Bill was Congress's response to the "black codes" that imposed virtual peonage on the former slaves. Drafted by Lyman Trumball, an outspoken defender of personal liberty, the bill sought to protect blacks and unionist whites from discrimination. But Johnson vetoed the measure. This action drove many wavering moderates into radical ranks. Now Congress promptly overrode his veto of the Civil Rights Bill and passed again a Freedman's Bureau Bill which again Johnson vetoed and again the Congress passed over his veto.

Meanwhile the Joint Committee on Reconstruction had drawn up and reported a bill that would enact a Fourteenth Amendment to the Constitution. The committee's purpose was to protect the freedmen's civil rights in the South from white-dominated provisional governments. It would graft on the Constitution the more important features of the Civil Rights Act.[18]

In this atmosphere of contest and confusion the Milligan case was argued before the Supreme Court. As Chase and his associates looked down at the array of legal counsel on both sides, they were well aware of the intense political pressures that were building up over Reconstruction. Joseph E. McDonald, a distinguished Indiana lawyer, opened for the petitioners. James A. Garfield followed.[19] Thirty-five years old, an ambitious Republican congressman, he seemed to be in strange company with other members of the defense, Democrats all and far more distinguished as lawyers. Garfield was making his first appearance before the Supreme Court.

Like Chase Garfield had a strong moral and religious background, and as a former army general he understood well how the military mind could endanger civil rights. Nor was he unaware of the prestige he might gain in legal circles. The Milligan case, Garfield noted later, "gave me immediately a standing before the Supreme Court of the United States and began to bring me cases."[20] Garfield acquitted himself well with a learned argument that delved deeply into European precedents.[21]

His contentions merely served as counterpoint to the surges of melodramatic eloquence from the chief counsel for the petitioners, veteran lawyer, Democratic politician, and former Attorney General of the United States Jeremiah Sullivan Black. A large man whose bald head was crowned with a wig of gray, flowing locks, seamed of face, his piercing dark eyes and beetling brows gave him a somber appearance and lent a severity of expression to his courtroom dramatics. Seldom without a wad of tobacco in his cheek, Black spoke extemporaneously for the better part of two days. As was his style he called up references he knew by heart from the Bible, Shakespeare, Suetonius, Tacitus, British and even French precedents and especially the opinions of learned judges in the past on the protection the Constitution extended to individual rights. He was particularly vehement in his interpretation of the due process clause of the Fifth Amendment. These rights, he thundered, were "unchangeable and irrepealable."[22] At one point in his argument, he advanced on Attorney General Speed, who was appearing for the government. Black accused Speed of supporting a "despotic and lawless" policy that ranged him with the "oppressors of mankind." Orville H. Browning, who attended all six days of the proceedings, thought Black's summation the "most magnificent speech to which I ever listened."

Browning was a conservative Republican and strenuously opposed to military trials of civilians. His comment was not altogether free of prejudice. But Black's presentation was tremendously effective, even, one imagines, on the carefully controlled and composed Chief Justice.[23] Whatever impression Black made upon the Court, his argument revolved around a single point that the military commission in this case had acted without jurisdiction under the Habeas Corpus Act of March 1863, the Judiciary Act of 1789, and the federal Constitution itself.

After Black's impassioned presentation Benjamin Butler opened for the government. In his typical self-confident way he claimed that in wartime, the executive power was supreme. The President was the sole judge in determining when individual rights threatened the nation, the Constitution to the contrary notwithstanding. As far as the Habeas Corpus Act of 1863 Butler said that it applied only to "state or political" offenses, a category of crimes he did not define. It did not apply to prisoners of war, and Milligan was just as much a prisoner of war as an armed rebel.[24] Browning was aghast at his impudence and wondered how the Attorney General could have permitted such an argument. Said Browning of Butler, "His manner pompous, and his matter paltry, he is a weak man—a humbug."[25] Henry Stanbery, who followed, was precise in speech and argument. He made Butler's points more palatable as he concentrated on the matter of jurisdiction which he claimed broadly for the military in times of extraordinary danger to the government. A paragon of the peerless advocate celebrated in some of Dickens's novels, Stanbery made the best of a poor case.[26]

Attorney General Speed closed for the government. Speed was a handsome person, full-bearded and mellow of eye. He seemed everybody's friend. Unfortunately his abilities as a lawyer did not match his appearance. And he came to the Court with the stigma of upholding as Attorney General the, military trial of the Lincoln conspirators. He was not as agile in argument as Butler or as meticulous in presentation as Stanbery, and he made a tortuous, rambling statement that earned the scorn of Browning and of at least one Justice, Miller.[27] He said of Speed: "certainly one of the feeblest men who has addressed the Court this term."[28]

The stately, gray-eyed David Dudley Field closed for the petitioners. A leader of the New York bar, Field's legal expertise had been honed by years of practice before municipal, state and federal courts to expand or diminish fine points of law and of fact as they supported his argument. His lawyerlike presentation—dry, precise, and logical—brought him to the conclusion that the executive branch had transcended its powers in ordering or permitting courts-martial of civilians outside of actual war zones.[29] Field surely made an impression on Chase and on his younger brother Stephen, who sat at the extreme right of the bench next to the massive, seemingly indomitable Miller.

When the Court went into conference during the latter part of March, it was agreed that it would hand down a unanimous decision for the petitioners, though there were differences of opinion on the justification for the ruling. Chase assigned the writing of the majority opinion to Davis, who in the circuit court had divided in opinion with the Indiana district court judge McDonald to provide the means for appeal to the Supreme Court. On April 3, 1866, Chase announced the decision of the Court. Habeas corpus would issue for Milligan and his associates. They must be discharged from prison; the military commission that tried and condemned them acted without jurisdiction.[30] Opinions would be announced at the next term of the court.

Meanwhile the Court had heard arguments for two test oath cases that were more of a political nature and therefore riskier to hand down in the highly charged partisan atmosphere.[31] The first case involved an act of Congress that imposed an "iron clad" oath on lawyers who wished to practice before federal courts. Anyone who had borne arms against the United States, served in any official capacity in the former Confederate government, or had been a federal official before the war and then served the Confederacy was ineligible to take the oath and therefore barred from practice.[32] Augustus Garland, an Arkansas lawyer who had been a Confederate senator, sought restoration of his right to practice without taking the oath prescribed. The President had pardoned him and he petitioned the courts to resume his practice on the grounds that he could not be punished after receiving executive clemency that wiped out the alleged offense.[33]

At the same time the Court had before it on appeal a state case involving even further sweeping provisions on test oaths. Under a recently enacted Missouri law, several specific classifications of professional persons were deprived of employment unless they took the oath. Father John A. Cummings, a Roman Catholic priest, was barred from preaching under this legislation. He brought suit in Missouri charging that the oath abridged religious freedom guaranteed in the Missouri and the federal Constitution. In addition he claimed that the law was a bill of attainder because it abolished his civil rights without any judicial process and ex post facto since his alleged disloyal act had taken place before there was a law making it a crime. Construing state police powers broadly, the Missouri courts decided against Cummings's petition, which was thereupon appealed to the Supreme Court.[34]

Before hearing the cases, Stephen Field on circuit duty in California wrote a stinging attack on the test oaths as a violation of individual freedom.[35] The Cummings case had wider political consequences than the Garland case. A very heated Missouri political campaign was then under way. The oath was a major issue for conservative Republicans allied with the Democrats against the radical Republicans. Like the Milligan case, these test oath issues bore directly upon Reconstruction and the problem of civil rights in the former rebellious states, or, as Chase always preferred, the rebellious people in those states.[36] If the oaths were struck down the Supreme Court would have taken a step that was rarely taken, indeed tried only twice before in the history of the nation—the judgment that an act of Congress was null and void.

Field made the most telling argument against test oaths in both cases. Since the laws that framed both oaths were being applied in both instances retroactively, he supported Cummings's argument that the constitutional provision specifically prohibiting ex post facto laws and bills of attainders applied. Field remarked tartly that test oaths such as these "might compel one to affirm, under oath, that he had never violated the ten commandments, nor exercised his political rights except in conformity with the views of the existing majority."[37]

By a majority of one in conference, the Court agreed to postpone the matter until the next term. It seems likely, given Chase's predilection to avoid antagonizing either the President or the Congress at this time, that he and possibly Miller managed to convince Grier, who would have made up a majority for striking down the oaths, to postpone any decision. But to the outrage of Field and the embarrassment of Chase, Justice Nelson leaked this information to Reverdy Johnson, a counsel for Cummings. Johnson, a Democrat who was anxious to assist his party in Missouri, made public the postponement and the apparent position of the Justices on the test oath cases.[38] Chase kept no record of the Court's action and had to rely on his memory. He was not certain whether his colleagues were acting without his knowledge and behind his back. Ever the politician, he raised this point in a letter to Miller.[39] Actually it was Reverdy Johnson's disclosure in a hotly contested political campaign rather than any indiscretion of the Justices. Field himself, Grier, and Nelson all had confided to Browning the details of the postponement. By a majority of one, the Court held the test oaths in both cases to be unconstitutional. Miller wrote the dissenting opinions in which Chase concurred.

But Chase was deeply concerned about all these cases. His political antennae were vibrating as he judged the temper of Congress and the activities of Johnson. His sense of the issue was to preserve the independence of the Court and if possible enhance it and his own prestige. His overall approach was the promotion of harmony between Congress and the President. In this effort he aligned himself with the moderates among the Republicans in the Congress. That he would vote against treasured concepts embedded in the Constitution such as religious freedom and other First Amendment rights shows a wavering of principle in the interest of expediency.[40] This stand and the decision in the Milligan case clearly brings out his motive of steering clear of any collision with the legislative branch. Davis drafted the majority opinion of the Court. In a ringing statement he wrote that "martial law cannot arise from a threatened invasion. The necessity must be actual and present, the invasion real . . ." for any suspension of habeas corpus. Milligan had been deprived of his rights under Articles III and IV and the Fifth Amendment of the Constitution, which he said provided "a law for rulers and people, equally in war and in peace, and covers with the shield of its protection all classes of men, at all times and under all circumstances."[41] Chase wrote a concurring opinion in which he was joined by three of his colleagues. Rather than place doubt on the constitutionality of the Freedman's Bureau and Civil Rights acts, Chase held that regarding military trials of civilians, where "peace exists, the laws of peace must prevail." He had borrowed this idea from David Dudley Field's reference to an ancient British precedent laid down during the reign of Edward III. Since Milligan was a citizen of Indiana, a loyal state where the courts were functioning, he was entitled to due process. In his interpretation of the habeas corpus Act of 1863, Chase said that "the act seems to have been

framed on purpose to secure the trial of all offenses of citizens by civil tribunals in states where these tribunals were not interrupted in the regular exercise of their functions."[42] By implication that condition could not be said to
apply to the former Confederate states which were then under provisional
governments. By so doing Chase gave a liberal interpretation to the act and in
a political sense was appealing to the moderates in Congress, particularly
those such as Lyman Trumbull who were passionate defenders of civil rights.

Before the details of the Milligan decision became public in December
1866,[43] a series of events had strengthened the radical mood in Congress. In
July, a fearful race riot erupted in New Orleans when a group of blacks sought
to hold a political convention. The city police, in an effort to break up the
convention, killed 37 blacks and two white supporters and wounded 117
blacks and 17 whites. Northern public opinion was horrified at the carnage.
Many who thought that the freedmen in the South could protect themselves
now found the continuance of a strong military presence essential. Nor was
the temper of the northern public improved by the sight of former Confederate dignitaries appearing arm and arm with administration supporters at a
hastily contrived National Union Convention in Philadelphia. Publicity about
these events galvanized Republican party leaders to organize a Southern Loyalist Convention in the same city a month later. By then the Union label had
been discarded.[44]

Chase took part in the convention, which was as much dedicated to airing
the grievances of southern loyalists both black and white as it was to provide an
anti-administration platform on Reconstruction. Chase witnessed the proceedings and consulted freely with the delegates during the three days of the
meeting. Well pleased with the attendance and the activities of the Convention, he was certain that "the rebel states are not to be restored to more than
their old political power in the government just as their oligarchy pleases."[45]

As the convention was breaking up President Johnson began a public
campaign to secure acceptance of his Reconstruction policies and to win
public support for a coalition of conservative Republicans and moderate
Democrats in a reorganized Union party. Accompanying Johnson in what was
termed "a swing around the circle" were prominent Cabinet members, General Grant, and Admiral Farragut. Republican leaders either avoided the
President or placed hecklers in the crowds he addressed to play upon his
explosive temperament and goad him into making embarrassing outbursts.
Johnson responded in kind, providing newspaper copy that simply confirmed
in the minds of many northerners that he was unfit to be President.[46]

The Fourteenth Amendment had received the requisite majority in Congress and was before the states. Chase supported the Amendment but feared
that it went too far. He had urged members of the Joint Committee on
Reconstruction to confine the Amendment to two points: (1) no underwriting

of the Confederate debt and no payment for emancipated slaves, and (2) no representation beyond the constituent basis, or, in other words, representation in Congress for the reconstructed states to be reduced by the numbers of male citizens excluded from suffrage. Chase fretted about the disqualification of former Confederate officials or those who had held office under the United States government and then had supported the Confederacy. Only Congress could remove the disability. True to his states' rights background Chase was concerned about infringement of state power.[47] But as public opinion developed in the North favoring the much broader amendment Congress had approved Chase became more enthusiastic.[48]

The November elections were a triumph for the Republican party and a repudiation of Johnson's policies. They destroyed his hopes for a Union-Republican coalition and sealed Chase's support for the amendment. Before the election, Johnson sounded out Chase on Reconstruction. When the two men met for the first interview, Chase advised him to recommend that the states ratify the amendment. Without contradicting him, Johnson simply repeated his well-known stand in which he would offer no advice on the amendment and no conditions beyond loyalty to the Union. The Senate and the House, he said, would decide on whether they would seat representatives that the southern states elected.

After the election Chase had two more interviews with the President at his request. Chase again "strenuously" recommended that if he could not advise ratification, he could at least suggest that he favored "universal suffrage with universal amnesty." No doubt annoyed at Chase's "strenuous" argument, Johnson simply reiterated the same position he had voiced at their first interview.[49] It is significant that the trial of Jefferson Davis did not come up in their conversation despite the fact that Johnson had put the burden of delaying the trial on Chase during his "swing around the circle" speeches.[50] Chase had consistently refused to hold circuit court in Virginia, where Davis would have to be tried when martial law was lifted. As he explained to Schuckers after he read Johnson's proclamation of peace, he thought that "it might be fairly construed as restoring the writ of habeas corpus, but subsequent orders from the War Department have put a different construction on it." He would not hold "any courts in the lately rebel states until all possibility of claim that the judicial is subordinate to the military power [and] is removed by express declaration of the President."[51]

Chase's position on the Davis case, like Johnson's, was in part at least motivated by political as well as practical considerations. Even though the President had pardoned almost all high dignitaries of the late Confederacy, he hesitated to include Davis, who of course was the premier symbol of the rebellion. Stanton and many of the congressional Republicans were averse to a pardon for Davis and still wanted him tried for treason. A federal grand jury actually indicted Davis, and the federal district court in Virginia was prepared to arraign him. Chase made no comment when Horace Greeley, Cornelius Vanderbilt, and Gerrit Smith offered to put up bail since Davis was still a military prisoner. Bail was denied.[52]

In early May of 1866, Chase drafted and sent to the President a proclamation declaring that habeas corpus was restored in the former Confederate states under such restrictions as would avoid clashes between judicial and military authority. He got no response from the White House, but in August Johnson did issue a proclamation that seemed to reinstate habeas corpus throughout the nation. It was not specific enough to satisfy Chase, and it was of course at variance with the Freedman's Bureau and the Civil Rights acts.[53] There the matter rested until it was caught up in an Act of Congress reducing the Justices of the Supreme Court from nine to seven, but neglecting to allot revised circuits to the Justices. An oversight that would be rectified, it relieved Chase for the time being of joining the Virginia district court judge, John C. Underwood, in any trial of Davis. After that, Chase's obligations to the Supreme Court in Washington precluded his appearance. Eventually the indictment was quashed and no trial was ever held.[54]

Throughout these tedious and technical and political proceedings, Chase was involved with members of the judiciary committees of both Houses on reforms that concerned the federal courts. A Senate bill favored by all the Justices except Clifford would create an appellate court for each circuit. Appeals were so circumscribed that the Supreme Court would be spared hearing routine cases that would be handled at the circuit level. Since the Supreme Court's docket was three years behind, the reform would afford considerable relief. A House bill reducing the number of Justices to seven and fixing allotments for the new circuits was likewise reported for debate.

Before either bill was acted upon, Chase had prepared an amendment to the Senate bill that would reduce the number of Justices to seven and apply the savings in salaries to increase the compensation of the Justices. It was certainly a fair proposal as the Justice's salaries had not been increased for years and were less than that of the highest army and navy officers. Since the House bill with its allotment provisions would have diminished significantly the work of the Court, a reduction in the number of Justices seemed warranted. Another section would make the marshal a Court-appointed office and give the Chief Justice the power of appointment. Chase wanted the place for his close friend and political associate, Richard C. Parsons the Cleveland attorney and sometime spoilsman.

He conferred with his colleagues about these bills and on the amendments he would propose to the judiciary committees. None were opposed to his suggested reforms in principle, though they probably saw through his patronage ploy. Miller's chief concern was that Chase's amendment to the

House bill would delay, possibly kill the passage of what he considered the more essential Senate bill. His fears proved groundless. Congress passed both bills with certain changes and the President signed them. Chase did not get his marshall patronage at this time; the court was reduced to seven; appellate features were retained. But no new allotments were made to adjust for the reduction, nor were the salaries of the Justices increased.[55] It would not be until March of 1867 that an amendment to the revised Judiciary Law included Chase's marshall post and adjusted the allotments.[56]

The second session of the Thirty-ninth Congress was but two weeks old when Chase's hot-tempered, erratic friend James Ashley of Ohio introduced a resolution looking toward the impeachment of Johnson. At this time the ten southern states operating under provisional governments had either refused to accept the Fourteenth Amendment or were in the process of doing so. Johnson had made it plain that he opposed the Amendment and in some instances advised the provisional governors to have their Legislatures reject it. General Wager Swayne, son of Chase's colleague on the Court and head of the Freedman's Bureau in Alabama, told the Chief Justice how Governor Lewis E. Parsons of that state had received a telegram from Johnson urging him to use his influence to defeat the amendment, which until then had a fair chance of passage.[57]

Before the vote in the legislature Chase had talked with Johnson, whom he described as "courteous and kind." Chase suggested a compromise: Congress was to remove the clause disqualifying certain classes of former Confederate officials from holding federal office. This action, he thought, would make it more palatable to the South. In return the President would support the revised amendment. Although Johnson was adamant in his opposition, upon reflection and consultation with leading southerners who held moderate opinions, he floated a version of Chase's compromise plan that removed the disqualifying clause and accepted impartial suffrage with property and literary requirements.[58]

The provisional legislatures rejected this plan and signified that they would not accept the amendment on any terms. Chase was dismayed, and even more deeply concerned by reports of a growing number of murders and instances of mob action and harassment of white loyalists and blacks, all of which lent credence to the heated rhetoric of the radicals in Congress.

After much debate Congress passed a series of measures aimed at developing its own policy on Reconstruction and curtailing the President's power to interfere and his use of the patronage to thwart its will. The so-called Command of the Army Act, secretly suggested by Stanton but drawn up by George Boutwell, a Massachusetts congressman of radical persuasion, was slipped into a military appropriation bill. Under its provisions the President was stripped of the power to move army headquarters away from Washington and was compelled to issue all military orders through Grant, the general of the armies. Johnson was outraged by this proposed legislation and was prepared to veto it, but most of his Cabinet members argued that it would be prudent not to do so at this point and he signed the act under protest.

But Congress determined to curtail the President's power over patronage passed the Tenure of Office Bill, which insisted that the Senate consent to any removals from office. It included also a provision that applied to Cabinet officers appointed during a presidential term. The entire Cabinet including Stanton felt that this bill was patently unconstitutional. In fact Stanton had a hand along with Seward in drafting Johnson's veto message. Congress promptly overturned the President's veto. Thereupon it passed the first of the Reconstruction Acts which provided for a military government in the southern states and demanded ratification of the Fourteenth Amendment and impartial suffrage in the various state constitutions before any former Confederate state could be readmitted to the Union.[59] Congress overturned Johnson's veto and the bill became law.[60] Almost at once inconsistencies in language and the lack of precise definitions of the power of the military chiefs to execute the law became evident.

Additional legislation was necessary before the military could carry out the will of Congress. Senator Henry Wilson visited Chase and after presenting the problems involved asked him if he would draft a supplementary bill that would clarify Congress's intent. Chase was delighted to oblige. He grafted what were essentially moderate features onto the bill as he laid out procedures for the registration of voters and subsequent election of delegates to new constitutional conventions. Obviously Chase was seeking to mitigate possible collisions between the military and the civilian authorities. Congress, however, deleted these clauses when it adopted Chase's draft.

If anything Chase's provision that the governors could act for the military gave some of the sharp-eyed lawyers of a radical bent in Congress an inkling of where the Chief Justice was veering in his thinking on Reconstruction, possibly to his detriment and to the detriment of the Court. But Chase hailed the result. "Our political sky seems to be clearing," he wrote in March 1867. "It seems probable that under the Military Act and the supplemental and Restoration bills all the southern states will be back with full representation within a year. I do not think this will hurt but rather help us."[61]

The decisions in the Milligan and the test oath cases (Garland and Cummings) did not improve Chase's standing with radical-minded congressmen. But most of their ire was vented on Justice Davis for his majority opinion in Milligan. Neither Chase nor his colleagues escaped censure for their concurring opinion that Congress had specifically excluded military trials for civilians in areas where the courts were open. In the test oath cases Miller wrote the dissenting opinions in which Chase and two other justices joined him. Miller's opinion in Garland and Cummings seems to have been dictated more by expediency than by any even tentative gesture towards civil rights. In accepting the will of Congress to exact ironclad oaths he relied primarily on technical arguments. He maintained that anyone engaging in the practice of law was doing so as a privilege not a right, that the Congressional Act demanding an oath for lawyers was discretionary in nature and not specifically aimed at individuals. Nor did the oath inflict punishment, according to Miller. *Ex post facto* laws and bills of attainder applied only to criminal acts, not civil offenses. No criminal indictments and no trials were involved.

If these quibbles were not enough, Miller went ahead in the Cummings case with an extremely narrow interpretation of the First Amendment to the Constitution. The federal government, he claimed, was forbidden to make laws prohibiting the "free exercise" of religion, but not the States. And again reiterating his argument in the Garland case, Miller declared that the oath required of a minister was simply a qualification of the terms for licensing him, not a punishment. That Chase went along with these justifications in Miller's dissenting opinion indicates that he would not at this point antagonize Congress. He, as well as Miller, assumed that test oaths would eventually, be abolished.

These dissents, however, gained little in the estimation of extremists.[62] Yet they took some of the sting out of their outrage over Milligan. Chase was largely responsible for helping to keep the Court clear of potentially embarrassing political matters.[63]

For the remainder of the first session of the Fortieth Congress, which assembled on March 4, 1867, the screws were tightened on the as yet unreconstructed South. There were additional Reconstruction Acts. Legislation was now in place that divided the South into five military districts, each of which was under the command of a general. Congressional Reconstruction was complete, though the President as Commander-in-Chief of the armed forces was directed to enforce these acts through the military, which gave him some latitude as to how he would instruct the military commanders.

On the advice of Attorney General Stanbery, Johnson issued orders that conformed to a very narrow interpretation of the laws. Johnson and Stanbery came under immediate and vociferous attacks in which it was claimed that they were deliberately frustrating the will of Congress and in effect breaking the law. John Russell Young, the young Irish-born journalist who was then acting as editor of the New York *Tribune*, gave Chase an opportunity to present his views on these charges. Chase exonerated the President but he disagreed with Stanbery's opinion and hence Johnson's policy. "I start," he wrote, "with the premises that Congress has full power to govern the rebel states until they accept terms of restoration which will ensure future loyalty; the fulfillment of national obligations, the repudiation of all rebellion & the obligations of rebellion the secur[ity] of [all rights] for all men." Stanbery, on the other hand, begins with the interpretation that the reconstruction "acts are punitive & must [be] enforced strictly." Chase was very clear that the existing provisional governments must not be set aside. "It would be," he said, "a very mischievous measure in its effects on private rights, and lead to much litigation."[64]

chapter 31

Impeachment

On February 26, 1868, the Supreme Court adjourned. After Richard Parsons, the new marshall, proclaimed this fact the Justices made their stately way along the east wall of the chamber to the robing room, where they doffed their judicial attire. Here, Daniel Middleton, the clerk of the court, whispered to Chase that Senators Jacob Howard of Michigan and George F. Edmunds of Vermont wished to see him. They were waiting in the Court's reception room.[1] Chase knew both of them well and since they were members of the Senate Select Committee to consider the House Resolution to impeach Andrew Johnson for high crimes and misdemeanors, he assumed that their mission was to consult him on procedures for the trial before the Senate.

Two days earlier the House had impeached Johnson. The Constitution provided that the Chief Justice would preside at the trial.[2] As they explained to Chase, their committee had been charged to provide rules for the trial. Did the Chief Justice have any suggestions? Chase said that he had "nothing but impressions on the subject for [he] had not considered it, but supposed that he would be a member of the court and as such have a right to vote. . . ." He added that he thought his role would be like that of the Vice President and might be limited to a vote in case of a tie. The operative words here were "right to vote" and "member of the court." They were not lost on Edmunds, who everybody conceded was a sharp lawyer. From what the senators said,

Chase understood that some members of the committee had raised that point and doubted or denied the Chief Justice's right to a vote.[3]

Chase knew that the extremists on Reconstruction in the Senate and House suspected him of harboring conservative opinions. That he was not with them in their punitive measures was true, but he had not abandoned his life-long belief in equal rights. He supported wholeheartedly the Fourteenth Amendment and deplored the obstructionist attitude of the southern states and President Johnson on that issue. Yet many heated partisans dismissed his well-publicized positions and others that Chase considered essential for the adequate protection of southern blacks and loyalists as merely a cover for his ambition.[4] Wade was busy distorting Chase's views among his colleagues in the Senate who were dubious about his role in impeachment. In Wade's words, "His movement with respect to impeachment was in the interest of the Democrats. He never deceived me for a moment."[5]

Chase had watched carefully the duel between the President and the congressional majority in the new Fortieth Congress. Some of the additional Reconstruction legislation he approved. But he disapproved of the Command of the Army Act, designed to limit the scope of Johnson's instructions to the military commanders. In his opinion it was a serious encroachment of executive power.[6] Likewise, he considered privately that the Tenure Office Act was unconstitutional. This legislation was a congressional move to restrict the President's patronage powers and to protect Stanton, who continued as Secretary of War despite his well-known antipathy to administration policy on Reconstruction.

The state of Georgia had attempted to enjoin Stanton and certain military officers from executing the Reconstruction Acts, deemed to be unconstitutional. Mississippi launched a similar suit against President Johnson. Even though the administration disapproved of these laws, Attorney General Stanbery argued before the Court that there could be no hindrance to the executive in having the laws faithfully carried out. Chase delivered the opinion of a unanimous court accepting Stanbery's argument in dismissing the plea of counsel for the provisional government of Mississippi. Nelson wrote the opinion of the Court dismissing the Georgia case for want of jurisdiction.[7] Chase and the Court got little or no acclaim for resisting these attempts to defeat Reconstruction from radicals in Congress, from their spokesmen in the press, and from conservative Democrats.[8] These pressure groups had now turned their attention to another case before the Court involving again the competency of a military court to decide cases against civilians. The Court had accepted jurisdiction of just such a case, the trial of William McCardle.

McCardle, an ex-Confederate colonel and a combative journalist, had been editor of the *Vicksburg Times*. He had used his editorial post to make outrageously abrasive attacks on the generals assigned to the military districts.

His object was to solidify white opposition to congressional Reconstruction, his weapon the press. The military authorities in Mississippi arrested McCardle and held him for trial. His counsel sought a writ of habeas corpus under the provisions of the Judiciary Act of 1789 as amended on February 5, 1867. This statute gave the federal judiciary power to grant writs in circumstances under which McCardle presumably qualified. It also provided for direct appeal to the Supreme Court.[9] At issue was not McCardle's editorials as such, which were clearly libelous, nor did his counsel appeal for First Amendment rights. But, as in the Milligan case, the basic issue was the arrest and trial of civilians by military authorities. The district court ruled against McCardle's petition, which was then appealed to the Supreme Court.

If the Court sustained the petitioner, the Reconstruction Acts insofar as they granted authority over civilians could be in jeopardy, ironically a jeopardy created by Congress itself to extend judicial protection to the blacks. Chase gave notice on January 3, 1868, that a majority of the Court had decided to advance McCardle's case, and set arguments on the appeal for March 2. After a hearing that lasted four days, the Court decided to postpone any decision, with only two dissenters.[10] Chase had impressed a majority of his colleagues with the political importance of the case, taking note that Congress was then seeking to remove direct appellate jurisdiction in certain habeas corpus cases. His argument was that it would not become the Supreme Court to hasten its decision on an appeal for the purpose of getting ahead of Congress. "The Constitution," he continued, "gives the Supreme Court jurisdiction on appeals only with such exceptions and under such regulations as the Congress shall make." At first a majority would not support him, but it soon came around to his viewpoint though he was absent from conference presiding over the Johnson impeachment trial when the second vote was taken.[11]

Congressional opinion was mixed on Chase's views of Reconstruction. The predominate feeling was that he was opposed to military trials of civilians but would continue to support the Reconstruction Acts, though it was unclear how these acts could be executed without a strong military presence.[12] Chase along with the rest of the still fragmented nation followed carefully the increasingly bitter contest between the President and Congress.

He knew that Stanton was opposed to the administration's policy on Reconstruction and wondered along with many others in Washington why Johnson had not removed his irascible, duplicitous Secretary. Perhaps he suspected that Johnson was merely biding his time until Congress adjourned for the summer. If such were his speculations they were only partially correct. Johnson had formulated a plan that would frustrate Congress's intention, yet still remain within the letter of the law. After Generals Sheridan and Sickles, two of the five military commanders in the South, openly defied the President—the one by summarily removing local and state officials including the provisional governors of Louisiana and of Texas, the other by suspending all judicial processes in his military district—Johnson decided to replace them with generals more amenable to his policies. He was also prepared to ask for Stanton's resignation.

But the President would not move until he could enlist General Grant's support. Accordingly he had a long meeting with Grant, who at first objected strenuously to Sheridan's removal on the grounds of his proven ability and his popularity but who eventually came round to Johnson's point of view, even to the extent of agreeing to act temporarily as Secretary of War if and when the office became vacant.

Word of Johnson's intentions to remove Sickles, Stanton, and Sheridan reached Chase. As he explained in a letter to Garfield some months earlier, he had already had an interview with Johnson in which he "remonstrated most earnestly against interference with either Sheridan or Stanton." He had nothing to say about General Sickles, who had raised Chase's ire when he summarily suspended all judicial processes and judgments, criminal as well as civil, in both state and federal courts in his district, which included Chase's circuit of the Carolinas.[13] "Had I been in the District when the process of the Court was interfered with by the military," said Chase, "the judicial authority would have been maintained. I hardly think that Gen. Sickles would have arrested me. . . . Certainly no fear of the consequences would have deterred me from the performance of my duty."[14] But the President, Chase said, "does not realize at all the feeling against him in the country; but if he does not it is not my fault. I dealt faithfully and honestly by him." Chase the politician was speaking here, not Chase the judge. And in the same letter to Garfield he brought up his possible candidacy for the presidency on the Republican ticket.

Ignoring Chase's warning of adverse public opinion Johnson went ahead and removed the two generals, replacing them with officers he felt he could count on to carry out his interpretation of the Reconstruction Acts. When the obstinate Secretary of War, assured of congressional support, refused, Johnson suspended him as required by the Tenure of Office Act during a recess of the Congress. Although Johnson doubted the constitutionality of the act, he was careful at this point not to violate the law. He appointed Grant Secretary of War ad interim to serve until the first session of the Fortieth Congress reconvened on November 21.

Impeachment efforts had failed until Stanton's temporary removal seemed to point the way for a renewed attempt. The Senate early in 1868 refused to confirm Johnson's action and Grant relinquished his office to Stanton. Apparently breaking an agreement with Johnson, Grant did not deliver up the office to him. The angry President thereupon decided deliberately to challenge the Tenure of Office Act and provoke an action for the courts to determine. After several possible candidates refused to assume the post, he found a willing nominee in the garrulous, bibulous Lorenzo Thomas, adjutant general of the Army. The President then removed Stanton, but when Thomas appeared at the War Department with his orders, Stanton overawed the general and refused to obey the President's directive. Barricading himself in the War Department Stanton waited for congressional support, which was immediately forthcoming. With clear evidence that the President had deliberately violated the Tenure of Office Act, ignoring any court action to test its constitutionality, a majority in the House voted impeachment of Johnson for high crimes and misdemeanors.

Chase's confidence in the political process was shaken by these sensational events, some of which took on the aspect of high comedy, such as Thomas's confrontation of Stanton. The Senate did have a theoretical case to approve removals as an incident to its power to confirm. But abundant precedents existed where Presidents from Jackson to Lincoln had removed federal officers on political grounds or for reasons of state. Moreover Stanton was a Lincoln appointee and a clear argument could be made that he was not covered by the terms of the act. Chase was convinced that the act was unconstitutional for these and other reasons, and as a good lawyer he also believed that a scrupulous reading of the legislation demonstrated that Johnson had not broken the law. He deplored the impeachment process, and while he was opposed to Johnson's policies on Reconstruction, he looked to the long-term impact of the trial on the structure of the national government.

The House had finally approved eleven articles of impeachment, which ranged from contempt of Congress to misappropriation of funds to giving direct orders to General Emory, who commanded the troops in the Washington area. But the nub of the indictment as Chase and other careful observers concluded was the violation of the Tenure of Office Act, whether constitutional or not. These charges were lumped together in the eleventh article. It soon became obvious that this article would be the test in the forthcoming trial.[15]

All of these specifics aside, Chase was aware in a broad sense that the trial was more than a partisan adventure, that Johnson had been made to symbolize an obstruction to what many believed to be a just peace. Prewar political combinations of northern and southern Democrats, which leading Republicans assumed were largely responsible for the war and the attempted perpetuation of slavery, were put on warning that any such alliance for these ends was not to be permitted. Yet it was all a matter of degree. Above all Chase wanted a reunified nation and he put his faith in the Fourteenth Amendment as a surety that the emancipated bondsmen would never be returned to slavery or to peonage and that the nation would never again be split asunder.

It is no wonder with such conflicting information about Chase that Senators Howard and Edmunds were dubious about how he would interpret his role as presiding officer over the impeachment trial. Their brief conversation confirmed suspicions that the Chief Justice might prove an obstacle in the drive for conviction.

After his interview with them Chase looked up the constitutional provision that named the Chief Justice as presiding officer in impeachment trials of Presidents. It was brief, a mere fourteen words, and did not define the verb "preside." He examined what few precedents existed for impeachment trials, and none of course applied to a President. Nevertheless as he pondered what his course should be, he decided to raise the point of whether the Senate should act in its legislative capacity or as a court of law in the trial. He wrote a brief note to Howard raising this question and added that he did not think it applicable as in other impeachment cases, the president of the Senate—in this instance his political enemy Ben Wade—should preside.[16]

During the few days that remained before the impeachment trial would begin, Chase discussed the rules of procedure with members of the Senate committee.[17] No doubt after some heated discussion, Chase persuaded the committee to adopt rules recognizing that the Senate be organized in some particulars as a court. His argument was a simple but convincing one: the Constitution designated the Chief Justice as the presiding officer. He reiterated his position in a letter to the Senate and in a further note to Senator Pomeroy, who had questioned his role.[18]

Chase held the trump card and the committee knew it. If it rejected his claim, he could refuse to preside. There was no way the Senate could compel him to serve. In short unless the Senate chose to make a direct violation of the Constitution and proceed without the Chief Justice presiding, no trial could be held. Chase did not broach this topic with the committee and was willing to compromise, although he insisted he should rule on the competency of witnesses and on the evidence, in the latter instance subject to the vote of the Senate. He also insisted that the presiding officer have a vote in breaking a tie. The committee accepted Chase's stipulations, which were embodied in the fourth, fifth, and seventh rules. Other than these major exceptions the Senate's regular legislative rules governed; but Chase maintained they were for general guidance and to be utilized only "as far as they are practicable."[19]

On March 5, at precisely one p.m., Chase entered the Senate chamber along with the senior Associate Justice Samuel Nelson, and accompanied by Senators Pomeroy, Wilson, and Buckalew. In a quavering voice the frail seventy-six-year-old Nelson administered the oath to Chase. Then Chase turned to Forney, the Senate secretary, and asked him to call the roll. He did so in alphabetical order, each senator advancing to the secretary's chair where he took the same oath, some no doubt with a touch of irony.

When Forney called Wade's name and he walked the few paces to the chair, a challenge rang out from Democratic Senator Thomas A. Hendricks.

He asserted that as president pro tempore of the Senate Wade would become President if Johnson was convicted and therefore could not be an impartial juror because he had a direct interest in the outcome of the trial. Debate over Wade's status went on for the better part of two days before Hendricks withdrew his challenge and Wade took the oath. In the wrangle over Wade Chase was able to win an important detail. The Senate sustained him on deciding points of order.[20]

After the Senate approved the rules of procedure the committee presented the seven impeachment managers from the House, who were admitted and escorted to their chairs. As Chase observed the managers, he found them to be political friends of the past but now scarcely on speaking terms with him. Chairman John A. Bingham was an Ohio man, a moderate, and the only member who might be considered as holding relatively impartial views. Chase had once cultivated the truculent Ben Butler, another manager, but any cordiality between the two men had long since disappeared. Nor could Chase expect any kindnesses from George S. Boutwell or grim Thaddeus Stevens. Boutwell had served as Chase's Commissioner of Internal Revenue, but had resigned in disgust over Chase's financial policies. A narrow-minded, intense partisan always on the make, Boutwell was a political paragon of the gilded age.

Chase experienced a sense of isolation from the party he had once helped form. He was not unmindful of the election results in Ohio the past year. The Republican state ticket had won by a thin margin in a race where the legislature had gone Democratic. His old enemy Wade would be replaced in the Forty-first Congress.[21] Countering any satisfaction he may have felt at the Democratic resurgence not just in Ohio but in New York, Connecticut, and Pennsylvania was the defeat of black male suffrage in Ohio and other states.[22]

From the beginning Chase detected personal rejection. "I feel and am felt," he said, "as a sort of foreign element. The Senate, like all other bodies, has a good deal of *esprit du Corps.* "[23] Yet he was determined to utilize what limited powers the rules allowed him. He concluded that only one of the eleven articles of impeachment, the last, had the best chance of passage. This article maintained that Johnson had not executed the Reconstruction Acts in good faith and accused him of violating the Tenure of Office Act when he removed Stanton from the office of Secretary of War.[24]

Chase had profound misgivings about the trial. He considered the articles more of partisan rhetoric than substantive evidence for a conviction. As he explained his position to Gerrit Smith, "the whole business seems wrong, and if I had any opinion, under the Constitution, I would not take part in it . . . nothing is clearer to my mind than that acts of congress, not warranted by the constitution, are not laws."[25]

Chase had managed to give some substance to his role of presiding officer in the shaping of procedural rules five and seven. He regarded his position as presiding officer an "important duty to be sure, but not the source of power."[26] When he made this comment on rule seven as originally accepted by the Senate he had gained some power to conduct the trial impartially because the rule required "one-fifth of the members present" to demand a roll call that might overturn his ruling on "all questions of evidence and incidental questions." Six days later on March 31 when Chase made a ruling on the competency of a particular witness, a motion was made to remove the one-fifth provision.[27]

At that point Senators Summer and Drake sought to strip Chase of power to make any ruling on evidence or on procedure. Sumner's amendment was particularly insulting to Chase and to his position as presiding officer. It would also weaken seriously Chase's requirement that the impeachment proceedings be conducted as a trial and not as a legislative matter. Sumner held that since the Chief Justice was not a member of the Senate, "and has no authority under the constitution, to vote on any question during the trial, he can pronounce decision only as the organ of the Senate, with its assent." Sumner's and Drake's amendments to the rules were narrowly defeated, but Sumner's amendment deeply troubled Chase. Had it prevailed he told Schuckers that he would have ended his participation in the trial, thereby precipitating a constitutional crisis.

The Senate did remove the one-fifth provision. Now any senator could call for the yeas and nays on Chase's rulings but any such action would delay the trial and place the Chief Justice's opinion on a judicial matter in direct opposition to a single senator's. The majority for conviction was too thin and too variable for extended challenges.[28] This turn of events shook whatever remaining confidence Chase still had in his ability to conduct a relatively nonpartisan trial. Later, he was further distressed when the Senate refused to take evidence of Cabinet consultations on the constitutionality of the Tenure of Office Act even though it was known that Stanton not only had participated but had actually assisted in preparing Johnson's veto of that measure.[29] "The Senate in my opinion," he wrote, "made its greatest and most injurious mistake yesterday when it refused to receive the testimony of the heads of departments."[30]

Chase's forebodings about the trial had been enhanced as he listened to what he considered the reckless allegations of the impeachment managers. Butler was the most overbearing and extravagant in his examination of witnesses. To Chase and many others on the Senate floor and in the crowded galleries, he was acting not as counsel against the President of the United States, but more as a combination of inquisitor or prosecutor in a common criminal trial.[31]

The defense team turned in a far better performance. Although Benjamin R. Curtis, the President's lead counsel, read his statement, he made the most convincing case for the defense. He denied that the Tenure of Office Act applied to the Cabinet and he argued that the executive had not only a right but a duty to test the constitutionality of an Act of Congress in the courts. Evidence of Johnson's intention to do just that would be presented in direct testimony.[32] Attorney General Stanbery, William S. Groesbeck, a leading Cincinnati lawyer and formerly a War Democrat, Thomas A. R. Nelson, a Tennessee Unionist, an able lawyer, and close friend of Johnson's, and William M. Evarts, a conservative Republican and perhaps the finest litigator in the New York bar, appeared as counsel for the President. They all gave convincing performances. If the trial had been anything more than a highly charged partisan adventure, Johnson would have been acquitted by a large majority of the Senate. The burden of direct and cross examination of witnesses naturally fell to Evarts for the defense as it had to Butler for the prosecution. The sharp-featured Evarts, calm and deadly in his sparring with Butler, was easily the outstanding counsel for Johnson. Chase had trouble keeping up with the Niagara of volubility on both sides. "Too much speaking by half," he wrote, as the strain of always being on the ready to intervene on points of examination and testimony began to tell on him in the overcrowded, overheated chamber.[33]

Contributing to the tensions were newspaper reports that Chase was exercising undue influences for acquittal on several senators adjudged to be wavering. Sprague, Chase's son-in-law and fellow resident in the house at Sixth and E streets, was singled out, of course. Reporters kept Chase under close surveillance. He was seen having a conversation on the street with Peter G. Van Winkle, a West Virginia senator, considered to be one of the doubtful ones. The New York *Tribune* promptly accused Chase of seeking to influence Van Winkle's vote. Van Winkle denied that Chase had brought any pressure to bear on him.[34] Other presumed targets were Sprague's Rhode Island colleague Henry B. Anthony and John B. Henderson, a Missouri senator who had dined with Chase and was seen riding with him in his carriage.[35] Chase responded sharply to these innuendos from journalists he had regarded as friendly. He admitted that he had participated in discussions of the trial on social occasions, as had virtually everyone else in Washington.[36]

A desponding Chase wrote Barney, "We have surely fallen upon evil times. Think of legislatures, political conventions, even religious bodies, undertaking to instruct senators how to vote, guilty or not guilty." To Chase all of this was unpatriotic and unconstitutional. In a letter to Barney he held that the Constitution was explicit in the oath each senator took "to do impartial justice according to the constitution and the laws."[37]

As for Sprague, Chase denied emphatically that he had tried to influence his vote. Kate was not so diffident. She had attended every open session of the trial, generally escorted by a congressman, though once by General Grant. Dressed in the height of fashion, which complemented her figure, she attracted attention and was even compared to the Empress Eugenie of France as the social arbiter of the Washington court. Knowing how her father felt about the trial and fearing that conviction of Johnson would injure perhaps irreparably his political future (for she was as ambitious as he), Kate sought strenuously to move her husband into the not-guilty ranks. Sprague refused to be moved. The closest he came to any commitment was an ambiguous remark that was quoted in the press. He would vote to acquit if his vote was needed, but would not "sacrifice his political future unnecessarily."[38] Sprague may well have been concerned about evidence Secretary Stanton had that implicated him in treasonable traffic with Confederate officers in the exchange of weapons for cotton.[39]

Whatever Sprague's reasoning his mulishness infuriated Kate, who abruptly left town for Canonchet before the end of the trial. Her departure and the circumstances that provoked it upset the already weary and worried Chase. In one of his loving yet didactic letters he both pleaded and instructed her that "while you have sometimes forgotten that the happiness of a wife is most certainly secured by loving submission . . . you generally conquer by sweetness." Chase added that he had never seen Sprague "so much affected by the differences that occurred between you just before you went away. He was almost unmanned."[40]

While Chase was seeking to restore some measure of domestic harmony in his household, the impeachment trial was moving toward a conclusion. There had been another heated dispute between the Democrats and the Republicans on the wording of the Chief Justice's call upon each senator for his vote on guilt or innocence,[41] a sort of a final judgment on the political shape of the trial. The issue was finally resolved, and May 16 was set for a verdict.[42] There were signs that there were enough doubtful Republican senators who along with the Democrats would vote to acquit Johnson. And the President was willing to meet with them and give assurances on patronage and in his selection of military commanders in the South. Many moderate and even some radical-minded senators were disturbed about Wade's succession to the presidency if Johnson were convicted. His soft-money views, which were widely known, his radical social and economic opinions, and especially if he became President the obstacle this might pose for the nomination of Grant had an impact on many. But influential northern metropolitan newspapers such as the New York *Tribune* and the New York *Independent* kept up pressure on uncommitted senators to convict. The usual resolutions of public and private bodies continued to flood their desks. The pressure for conviction seemed so great that Chase decided that rules of evidence and of law that he had fought so hard to maintain would be ignored in the final result.

On that bright spring afternoon as Chase looked over the densely crowded floor and the galleries he had already concluded that Johnson would be convicted.[43] Accordingly he had prepared himself to preside over the last sorry chapter, the administration of the presidential oath to his hated enemy, Ben Wade. Again he researched what precedents existed and studied with care the law of March 1, 1792, that established the succession in case of resignation, death, disability, or removal of a President and Vice President. The law fixed the president pro tempore of the Senate as the successor and after him the Speaker of the House. But it specified that such a person would act as President only "for the time being until the disability was removed or a new Presidential election held and this should take place within 34 days before the first Wednesday in December." Other requirements seemed to permit the acting President to serve until the succeeding March 4, the regular date for a new administration to take office.[44] The statute was a poorly crafted document subject to varying interpretations. Chase doubted whether the president pro tempore of the Senate could "act as President," but assuming for the time being that the law was constitutional, he had no alternative but to administer the oath.[45] He drafted a brief one in which he included the verb "act" and had this paper in his pocket when he rose from his seat after order in the hall had finally prevailed. The roll-call vote was to be taken on the eleventh article, the omnibus article and the one most likely to convict Johnson.

"Call the role," said Chase to Forney. "Henry B. Anthony," he intoned. Anthony, whose vote was considered doubtful for conviction, rose from his desk. Chase looked at him directly and asked, "Mr. Senator Anthony, how say you? Is the Respondent, Andrew Johnson, President of the United States, guilty or not guilty of a 'high' misdemeanor, [not crime] as charged in this article?" Anthony responded, "Guilty."[46]

A vote of two-thirds of the Senate was required for a verdict of guilty. Twenty-four senators had voted guilty and fourteen not guilty when Chase called Sprague's name.[47] The nondescript senator from Rhode Island had spoken only three times during the trial, twice calling for the yeas and nays and once to declare that a senator was out of order. He stood and in a quiet voice said, "Guilty." Would Sprague's vote be sufficient to convict? The roll continued and five more senators voted not guilty, bringing the total to 35, just one vote short of the two-thirds mandated. Chase announced the vote and pronounced Johnson innocent of the charges in article eleven. Ten days later, the same result was recorded on articles two and three. The majority was now willing to give up and the Senate voted a final adjournment. Stanton vacated his office.[48]

It had been a terribly trying time for Chase. Old friends were ranged against him politically; personal relations which had been so close were now pretty much severed. Rancor had replaced amity. The seven Republican senators who had voted to acquit Johnson were not blamed more savagely than Chase for his conduct as presiding officer.[49] He had done his best to remove the stigma of a kangaroo court whipped on by partisan frenzy and to preserve what he felt was a bedrock principle embedded in the Constitution, the separation of powers. Never before in his political life had he acted so much on principle to his own immediate detriment. Yet in balancing the record could it not be said that he was taking a calculated risk, that in aiming for a lofty objective, he was mindful of long-term benefits to himself? Evidence exists that this might have been the case as it had been so often in his political career where he confused his means with the ends he had in mind.

Throughout the trial leading Democrats were importuning him to be the party's candidate for President. And he was a ready correspondent with these party fixers. Chase's stand on the impeachment trial may be considered a courageous one, his flirtation with the Democrats not one of high political standards. In his own mind, however, in his association with those who had opposed the war and its objectives, Chase could and did rationalize his apparent turnabout as an effort to utilize Jefferson's principles to clarify what he believed had become a political and a moral quandary.

Essentially he was seeking what he had hoped for in the 1850s, a movement that would purge the Democracy of slavery, make it truly independent of a great evil, and restore it to the natural rights that Jefferson wrote into the Declaration. Now he would try again to excise from the Democracy its denial of equal rights for all so that it could champion a new slogan he had created: "universal suffrage and universal amnesty."[50] If carried out Chase felt, naively to be sure, that military rule would be abolished and military chieftains such as Grant, whom he now knew would be the Republican nominee, could be defeated, the reunited country returned to its democratic civilian rule. He relied strongly on the Fourteenth Amendment, which, while not yet approved by three-fourths of the states, seemed most likely to be accepted as a condition for the admission of the former Confederate states to the Union.

Public opinion in the north, Chase decided, was turning against congressional Reconstruction with its military overtones. As self-serving as Chase's political agenda seemed during the impeachment trial, it bore a strain of righteous continuity in an institutional sense, which he hoped to protect. Only as the leader of a great but purified party could he preserve what was beneficial of the past and what was needed to settle the accounts the war had won. He had no use for third parties, as he explained to Murat Halstead. "To make and unmake parties is the work of the people," he said. "Politicians can't do it and their attempts to do it are always failures."[51]

His three years' tenure on an essentially conservative Court had tempered his political outlook, made him more objective in his understanding of the many complex issues that the war and the peace had left unsettled. The

Court, especially his circuit duties, had broadened his outlook. His years of political experience and his devotion to natural rights and individual standing before the law had likewise made an impression on his colleagues, leading them in many instances to avoid fruitless collisions with Congress and with public opinion.

Chase laid out his political philosophy in an unusually candid, carefully worded response to a letter from the New York financier and Democratic leader August Belmont just four days after the collapse of impeachment. On "questions of finance, commerce and administration generally," he wrote, "the old democratic principles afford the best guidance." For the past twenty-five years he claimed he had been separated from the party only on the slavery issue. He thought Johnson had acted correctly in regarding the former Confederate states (except Virginia and Tennessee) to be without any government the United States could recognize, but "wrong in limiting by his Reconstruction Proclamations the right of suffrage to whites and only such whites as had the qualification he required."

Yet he believed Congress's Reconstruction Acts were right in not limiting suffrage to whites, but wrong in excluding certain classes of "citizens" and those unable to take its prescribed retrospective oath and wrong also in the establishment of military government for the states and in authorizing military commissions for the trial of civilians in time of peace.

The pith of Chase's concern, however, was not in specific acts of Congress or executive obstructionism, but more broadly in what he feared was the danger to the separation of powers, "the aggression of Congress upon the Executive and Judicial departments." In his broad frame of reference he saw even "the subversion of the Senate by the House."[52] To be sure, Chase's letter was not free of presenting his availability to the powerful New York Democrats. And it is presumed that Belmont shared it with Samuel Jones Tilden, Horatio Seymour, and others of the Democratic leadership.

For some months Chase had corresponded with Alexander Long, next to Vallandigham the most outspoken former "Peace Democrat" in Ohio. Long, an unsavory politician and ex-congressman, had narrowly escaped expulsion from the House during the war. In fact his colleagues censured him for making seditious speeches in 1864.[53] As the impeachment trial moved on, Chase's hope to forge a coalition of progressive Democrats and disaffected Republicans had become a near obsession that blinded him to politicians like Long.

The Democratic party in Ohio had split often in the past on the money issue between those who followed George H. Pendleton, an early apostle of soft money and continued inflation in government financing, and those who cleaved to the old Jacksonian shibboleth of hard money and specie resumption. Pendleton's "Ohio Idea" which demanded payment of principal and interest on government bonds in greenbacks was popular among agricultural interests in the West but denounced vigorously by business interests there and in the banking centers of the East.

Chase had resorted to greenback currency as Secretary of the Treasury. It was well known that he had done so as a matter of necessity in a unique situation, and that he had always been a hard-money man. But a majority of the party in Ohio would not accept Chase's stand on equal rights for the blacks. His equal position of universal amnesty for southern whites and his opposition to military rule were not sufficient grounds to overcome racist antipathies. Nor had veteran Democratic leaders forgotten Chase's role in his election to the Senate in 1849. To such practical politicians for whom party discipline was an Eleventh Commandment, Chase was considered an opportunist of remorseless ambition.

These concerns were not taken so seriously in New York. Chase's major link with the Democratic party there was John Dash Van Buren, a distant relative of Martin Van Buren, the seventh President and a lawyer and financial writer who was close to Tilden.[54] Jacob Schuckers, Cisco, who had never abandoned his Democratic affiliation, Hiram Barney, and other former employees of the custom house began working for Chase in the city and were achieving results.[55] Yet reports kept coming in that the party and especially its southern wing remained opposed to Chase's universal suffrage idea. In a letter to Milton Sutliff, former Ohio supreme court justice, Chase wrote that "it has seemed to me well nigh impossible to get over the difficulty induced by the almost universal commitment of the party to hostility to the colored people." Such views were completely incompatible with his lifelong devotion to natural rights and equality of political rights without regard to race or color. "I have lost none of my faith in these ideas," he said.[56]

Despite his disclaimers Chase had become a major candidate for the Democratic nomination. He was seen as the only possible candidate who could rally enough conservative and moderate Republicans, which together with the Democratic organization would be strong enough to defeat Grant. Chase's well-known aversion to greenbacks gained support from many New York financiers including August Belmont.[57] In mid-June with only three weeks remaining before the Democratic convention in New York, William Cullen Bryant was confident that Chase would be nominated.[58] The *Herald* and the *World* were also out in his favor. A committee was being formed in Philadelphia to promote his candidacy.[59] Gerrit Smith got up a pro-Chase circular which he mailed out by the hundreds.[60] That shrewd, cautious, highly influential leader of the New York Democracy, Samuel Tilden, began to move behind Chase. And so did New York's wartime governor, and a power in the party, Horatio Seymour.[61]

All of this apparent pre-convention support, the most he had ever enjoyed during his three runs for a major party nomination, seemed to have drawn Chase down a perilous course where his principles of equal rights for all were being eroded. The bright side of his character, the oft-spoken belief in common humanity, was swinging slowly to the dark side of political expediency and even cynicism. As he unburdened himself to Judge Sutliff a month or so before the convention, he knew that neither the leadership nor the masses of the Democratic party had any use for his professions of racial equality. Ever the rationalizer, when his nomination seemed more likely, his ambition, his belief that once in the executive chair, he would use the power of the office and the Fourteenth Amendment to see that justice be done, wore down his scruples. His daughter Kate, ambitious for her beloved parent, encouraged this flight from faith.

Sprague temporarily disappeared after the impeachment and Kate moved to the Fifth Avenue Hotel in New York, where she took charge of Chase's campaign. The Sprague interest was not entirely absent. Amasa, Sprague's brother, had been instrumental in forming the "Committee of a Hundred" for Chase. Kate and her small group of political workers were well supplied with funds and advice.[62]

Had Chase been certain of the nomination he might have had a solid basis for a position that risked so much for his reputation not to say his probity. But he was well informed that his own state of Ohio was divided on his candidacy. Pendleton would not step aside, a grave obstacle to Chase's nomination. Van Buren, speaking for Tilden, warned that Pendleton's withdrawal before the convention was "essential."[63] Even more embarrassing to Chase was the support he was receiving from some of the former "Peace Democrats" headed by Vallandigham, a minority of the party in Ohio but vocal as usual.[64]

On the national level, the Blairs, who were now associated with the Democracy and who represented a significant body of opinion, were, of course, openly hostile.[65] Significant segments of political opinion in the Deep South and the border states were unfriendly to a Chase candidacy. His wartime trade policies in the Mississippi Valley, his encouragement of radical factions in states such as Louisiana, Florida, and Missouri, and his support of the Fourteenth Amendment and the Reconstruction Acts were considered examples of his unreliability.[66] Chase was a shrewd enough politician to assess accurately the forces arrayed against him. Yet having ventured thus far and with possible victory in his grasp he could not back down. He had already earned the scorn of his erstwhile political boosters Garfield, Pomeroy, and Sherman. Even Jay Cooke was amazed that he would break an allegiance of over ten years to join those whom he had so vigorously opposed.[67]

For all his pains, for all his misguided efforts that had generated so much opinion and publicity, Chase was now faced with watering down his position on suffrage to placate party leaders. On July 1 he wrote Alexander Long that suffrage must be governed under state mandate. That same day the press carried a platform that Chase and Van Buren devised. It echoed the positions Chase took in the letter to Long.[68] As such it posed a serious dilemma for Chase. His position on suffrage still did not square with political and social realities in the North and the South. Unless the Democrats pledged themselves to accept Reconstruction and acting through the states protect the civil rights of the blacks they could not support Chase.[69]

Van Buren sent Chase a copy of another draft platform that Tilden, Seymour, and others had agreed upon which had no explicit pledge on suffrage and Reconstruction. Chase replied that though this platform was not quite what he would like, it was acceptable.[70] Further pressure came from New York. Chase was asked to condemn the Reconstruction measures because military rule was imbedded in them. Chase handled badly this attempt to commit him. At first he agreed to these stipulations in a letter to Long provided that he clear his agreement with Van Buren; then, realizing his mistake, he retracted his approval. Chase finally drew the line and refused to make any more concessions. The platform he had in mind and which had been published in the press was not that far removed from the Republican platform, which was also evasive on universal suffrage. Nor would Chase accept beforehand a convention-drawn platform and its candidates for President and Vice President.[71] His waffling on these points damaged his credibility with party leaders. From that time forward his chances rapidly diminished.

Meanwhile Chase's managers in New York set up a headquarters at the Chanler House on 14th Street just opposite the new Tammany Hall building where the actual proceedings would take place.[72] It was clear from the outset of the convention which Governor Seymour as chairman called to order that two western candidates, Pendleton of Ohio and Senator Thomas A. Hendricks of Indiana, would command significant delegate strength. President Johnson and General Winfield Scott Hancock, the hero of Gettysburg, were also in contention. But Tilden would determine who would eventually succeed. He was the leader of the New York Democracy, the largest contingent of delegates, and he spoke for the hard money side of the party. He had been friendly to Chase and had probably spoken with him on his several visits to Washington and Baltimore.[73]

But cool, cautious, and noncommittal, Tilden moved through the steamy rooms of Tammany and the various hotels where delegations were staying, impeccably dressed, unfailingly courteous. Few, not even Seymour, could determine what his preference was. Whom he opposed was evident: Pendleton because of his soft-money views, President Johnson because of his political liability. He was interested in Hendricks, mainly as a counterfoil to Pendleton. Chase had supporters within the New York delegation and among some of the delegates from the New England states.[74] In order to satisfy Tilden he had to have a majority of the delegates from the West and this he did not have. Nor were Pennsylvania and New Jersey delegates comfortable with Chase's views on currency, tariffs, and wartime taxes.

It was a novelty to have a woman, and one as beautiful and intelligent as Kate Chase Sprague, actively working in the hurly-burly of a man's world where cigars and chewing tobacco, whiskey and coarse language were the raw mix of the convention. Kate did not venture to the convention floor or the galleries of Tammany, nor did she personally visit Chase's headquarters at the Chanler House. She directed Chase's lieutenants from her comfortable suite at the Fifth Avenue Hotel. She bore up well under the terrific July heat wave that fell upon the city and prostrated Chase's old friend Hamilton Smith, who had come to New York to give what help he could.[75]

Kate played the hand dealt her with skill, not seeming abrasive, not always available to importuning politicians, recognizing the importance of Tilden's role and thus keeping in close touch with Van Buren. She was informed and apparently approved of Tilden's strategy as she understood it from Van Buren, and that was to let Pendleton, Hendricks, and Hancock run their course while New York held back, casting vote after vote for Sanford Church, a highly respected, but scarcely magnetic jurist from western New York.[76] At the appropriate time when none of the candidates had achieved the two-thirds' vote required and the hot and weary delegates were ready for a break, Chase would be placed in nomination and a stampede would ensue. These, however, were only speculations. All the solid information Kate had was that the New Yorkers were partial to her father, though extremely careful, even tentative in coming to his support.[77]

Was Kate being gulled? Were the New Yorkers manipulating Chase? Were men like Tilden and Church seeking to benefit the party by exploiting Chase's reputation which a seasoned observer described as one of "official, political and moral influence, that should not be lightly thrown away" in order to broaden the Democratic appeal? Or were they even using Chase's name to confuse the electorate before casting him aside?[78] There is some evidence for such a cynical political maneuver.[79] The convention went ahead and adopted a platform that Chase could not support, one which savagely denounced Reconstruction and was tainted with negrophobia. It would seem that Chase was a victim of an intrigue in which Tilden, Church, and Van Buren had had a hand. Yet there was still hope at the Fifth Avenue Hotel, the Chanler House, and Sixth and E streets in Washington.

On the sixteenth ballot, a California delegate cast half a vote for Chase, which almost created the bandwagon, but other delegations maintained enough discipline to forestall any precipitous action until New York was heard from.[80] The balloting went on. One after another of the leading candidates went down to defeat; New York still clung to Church. Now Van Buren suddenly made himself scarce. What happened was that Tilden had opted for Seymour despite that gentlemen's frequent and vigorous rejection of any thought of nomination.[81] Some seasoned political observers had predicted this move when Chase first became a possible candidate but it seems to have taken Seymour by surprise.[82] When the convention roared its approval, he tried unsuccessfully to withdraw. In a surge of momentum the convention then nominated Frank Blair for Vice President.

Despite Kate's enthusiasm and her self-assurance, she realized before the balloting began that she and her cohort of convention strategists had been overmatched. She wrote her father on July 7 that there were "snares and pitfalls everywhere." Chase himself warned her that he feared she was acting too much the politician. "Have a care," he wrote. "Don't do or say anything which may not be proclaimed from the house tops."[83]

Chase was disappointed by the outcome of the convention, especially the platform which he could not endorse. He could never back the candidate for Vice President, Frank Blair, whom he personally detested and politically scorned. He had let the dark side of his character overwhelm his proper political instincts. In the end he found himself identified as a weak and contradictory person before the public. His reputation had suffered badly. Yet he felt even more responsible for the rebuke his beautiful daughter suffered in her effort to play the kingmaker. His first words after he learned of the result in New York were framed in a question. "Does Mrs. Sprague know and how does she bear it?"[84]

chapter 32

One Clear Call

After the tense moments of the impeachment trial, the brief excitement of his abortive candidacy for the Democratic nomination, and, it must be said, his rejection by his former friends and party associates who held him under that dread political ban of apostasy, the election of U. S. Grant to the presidency, Chase could find little time for contemplation and for reassessing his position as a Justice and a public man. He was not able to escape for more than a few weeks from the miasmic heat of a Washington August. He could gain no respite from the family problems at Canonchet nor the grueling routine, the careful judgments, and the decisions to be made on his circuit court rounds.

Mounting claims on the Supreme Court involving all sorts of war and Reconstruction matters were requiring additional sessions. Some of these decisions were of a political nature, more were increasingly complex business transactions as the economy expanded and diversified after the war. Chase himself decided a range of political, economic, and social cases while on circuit duty that brought legal stability to investment, to financial transactions, and to property ownership that existed before and during the war.[1] Though associated with the district court judges, most of the business that came before the circuit as the senior man he handled himself and in so doing established the framework for crucial aspects of Reconstruction.

During the less than four years that Chase presided over his circuit which extended from Delaware to North Carolina, he heard and wrote opinions on 47 cases.[2] Free from the distraction of debating with other critical minds and presiding over divisions of opinion on the Supreme Court, Chase found circuit court duties more to his taste. For there he was very much his own man and most of his decisions had immediate, direct impact. Chase's approach is best summarized in a letter he wrote John Dash Van Buren after two years of circuit court duty. "It is only as a Circuit Judge that the Chief Justice or any other Justice of the Supreme Court, has, individually, any considerable power."[3]

In Virginia, Chase came into conflict with the corrupt and vengeful district court judge, John C. Underwood. Under Section III of the Fourteenth Amendment and in the absence of any enforcing legislation Underwood sought to sweep away the legal structure of the state. Chase's decisions in Virginia and other states on his circuit influenced an entire range of civil and criminal law. Common sense underlay a keen appreciation of existing law and precedent. In Caesar Griffin's case, for example, Chase managed to persuade Underwood to reverse his orders and narrow the disqualification section of the Fourteenth Amendment so that it did not apply to the routine application and administration of the law. Had Underwood's dictum remained in place, Chase said:

No sentence, no judgment, no decree, no acknowledgment of a deed, no record of a deed, no sheriff's or commissioner's sale in short no official act—is of the least validity. It is impossible to measure the effects which such a construction would add to the calamities which have already fallen upon the people of the state.[4]

Unlike Sumner, Stevens, and other extremists in Congress who thought of Reconstruction in abstract terms, Chase's immersion in the practical implications of not just Reconstruction but eventual reunion brought with it a strain of realism that his critics failed to understand.

For the sixty-year-old Chief Justice, who had put on a lot of weight over the past three years, and who had always worked too hard and ate too much, the strain was building up and undermining his health. On the overcrowded docket the Court had accepted hearings of four cases of appeal in which Chase had a distinct interest. Three would be argued and decisions handed down in 1869 and in 1870.

Chase and others of his colleagues had smarted under the criticism, largely partisan, that was directed at them and at the Court as an institution. His opposition to military trials of civilians was well known.[5] Yet it has appeared to some critics that he led the way in backing off from a firm defense of civil rights if it meant a direct confrontation with Congress. Frequently cited was the court's postponement of a decision in the McCardle case so that

Congress could remove its appellate jurisdiction in certain habeas corpus proceedings. But in handing down the decision in *McCardle*, Chase reacted strenuously to any such understanding that the court had relinquished its appellate jurisdiction in other habeas corpus actions. Chase accepted the plain fact that the Constitution gave Congress the power to enact specific "exceptions and regulations," but he questioned whether it could, as he put it, "oust an appeal already taken and perfected."[6]

A year later Chase was presented with an opportunity to resolve his doubts about congressional reaction to the McCardle case. An unbalanced citizen of Jackson, Mississippi, Edward M. Yerger, murdered in cold blood a Union army major who had confiscated his piano for nonpayment of taxes. Yerger was promptly arrested and brought before a court-martial to be tried for murder under the Reconstruction Acts. His counsel sought a writ of habeas corpus to discharge Yerger from the military court on the grounds that the murder was an offense against Mississippi law not federal law. Associate Justice Swayne, whose circuit temporarily included Mississippi, denied the writ, but in his decision approved its referral to the Chief Justice.[7] Chase learned of Swayne's opinion while he was on circuit duty in Richmond, Virginia. He was not averse to hearing the application, but he was concerned that Yerger's crime was committed outside of his allotted circuit.

Yerger's counsel tracked down Chase in Richmond and presented him with the application for the writ supported by opinions of other counsel that the Judiciary Act of 1789 defining appellate jurisdiction did not restrict such appeals to circuits but was general in nature.[8] Before deciding on the application Chase asked advice of his colleagues Nelson and Clifford, both of whom supported the argument of Yerger's counsel.[9] Following a complicated appeal process, Chase delivered the opinion of the Court sustaining appellate jurisdiction. He declared that it extended "to all cases of commitment by the judicial authority of the United States, not within any exception made by Congress."[10] Predictably the decision was the source of partisan praise as well as indignation. Sumner and Drake of Missouri both sought legislation that would remove all appellate jurisdiction in habeas corpus cases from the federal courts. But neither of these attempts made any headway in Congress.

Congressional Reconstruction was nearing an end. Most of the southern states had accepted Reconstruction terms and had been accorded full representation in Congress. Not only had Chase made his point, but he affirmed individual rights and preserved the original intent of the framers that the United States would be a government of laws not of men.[11] In extenuation, however, it must be said that the period between 1868 and 1870 while the Chase Court boldly asserted its appellate jurisdiction and by implication condemned military trials of civilians, it did so when it was less risky than earlier when congressional Reconstruction was at full tide, and military control had been removed from many of the former Confederate states.

If Chase carried his Court with him in this assertion of judicial power, he also wrote an opinion that would, he hoped, solve the problem that had haunted the legal theorizers of Reconstruction. Had the Confederate states by their secession from the Union given up their former identity as Sumner and Stevens and other radical politicians argued? If they had, then it would logically follow that secession was a lawful act and the Union had existed only at the sufferance of the states, an argument Lincoln dismissed as an abstraction, but Johnson had clung to with Jacksonian fervor, as did many Democrats.

After the war the issue took on a meaning beyond that of political debate. What was the standing of contracts in which a former Confederate state was a party? In particular could bonds that the United States government issued in 1850 to settle Texas boundary claims be recovered with principal and accrued interest in gold? Many of these bonds were outstanding. A Texas commission house, White and Chiles, had held and disposed of a substantial number of these equities. As Secretary of the Treasury Chase had refused payment for any unendorsed Texas bonds or any such bonds in private hands that the Confederate government of Texas had endorsed.

Agents for the Reconstruction government of Texas sued for the recovery of these bonds and of others that were still outstanding and remained in private hands. Obviously their arguments had been and continued to be based on the supposition that Texas was a state. Otherwise their case would have no standing in the federal Courts.

Chase had wrestled with the theoretical problem of secession for many years.[12] On circuit duty in North Carolina a year before the Texas suit, he declared that secession had not affected the corporate status of a State.[13] He was as eager to crystalize his own thinking on the subject as he was to set forth an abiding settlement, not simply to validate Reconstruction but to settle all the business affairs that bound the North to the South before the war and which had been in jeopardy while the status of the ex-Confederate states remained undefined.

The major problem with *Texas v. White* from a constitutional viewpoint was whether the suit came within the Court's original jurisdiction as defined in Article III, Section 2 of the Constitution. But that problem itself satisfied the questions Chase wanted to solve. If Texas was a state, the answer would be affirmative; if not, the Court had no jurisdiction.

When the suit was commenced, Texas was under a provisional government. Yet that government and successive Reconstruction governments had initiated and maintained suits to reclaim the bonds that the Confederate regime had sold. As to whether these provisional government were competent to bring suit, Chase decided in the affirmative, or, as he would put it, "The acts of the executive and subsequently of the legislative branches of the federal government necessarily imply recognition of actually existing government. . . ." Texas could bring suit and the Supreme Court had original jurisdictions.

Apart from these considerations Chase was determined to achieve two objectives he deemed fundamental. First, he would rule, as he had earlier indicated, in public comments that the people and the war-time government of Texas had been enemies of the United States but not the State of Texas. It had always remained in the Union. Actions such as the sale of U.S. bonds by the Confederate government of Texas whether the buyer was aware or not of their prior ownership were null and void. That would dispose of the White and Chiles issue, yet at the same time settle the troublesome wartime problems of the political relationship of former Confederate states to the United States.

His reasoning up to this point brought him to his other major position: his insistence that the former bondsmen would enjoy suffrage and other civil rights that only a state could confer under the American federal system of government. He would bolster his position by calling up the precedents of the Emancipation Proclamation that everyone now conceded gave U.S. citizenship to blacks, the Fourteenth Amendment that forbade any state from abridging "the privileges or immunities of citizens of the United States" or "depriving any person of due process of law" and the impending Fifteenth Amendment that enjoined the states from discrimination in conferring suffrage.

Chase began his opinion with a careful analysis of how the Constitution defined a state. He found that in some instances it referred to a state as a geographical unit, in others a body of people; often the document combined terms, considering "people, territory and government as one."

He traced these definitions until he came to the conclusion that Texas had never ceased being a state even though its government and its citizens formed an alien group. Thus the United States in suppressing the rebellion was "reestablishing the broken relations of the state with the Union." In doing so, it was removing the temporary impediments that had existed in its external relations. Chase closed this argument with one of his rhetorical flourishes that the Constitution "in all its provisions looks to an indestructible Union composed of indestructible states." Texas recovered the bonds whose principal and interest were redeemable in gold, and Chase made his point on suffrage for the blacks as a consequence of state and federal citizenship.[14]

Chase did not comment directly on the Reconstruction Acts, for any such dictum was not relevant to the case before the Court. But in asserting that the Constitution directed Congress to guarantee a republican form of government for the states, he implied that Congressional Reconstruction was an appropriate political response to the changes that had occurred since the war began. Reconstruction was a political question, not one that judicial interpretation could determine. The decision not only followed Chase's thinking over the years but coincided with mainstream Republican views on Reconstruction. Three of Chase's colleagues dissented vigorously from the majority opinion, insisting that it was a legal fiction to describe Texas as a state.[15]

As they had in the Milligan, McCardle, and Yerger cases, Republican extremists denounced the decision as another example of Chase's treason to a cause he once espoused. Likewise from their viewpoint the Democrats, some of whom had recently championed Chase for President, found little comfort in his implied support for congressional Reconstruction.

While writing his lengthy opinion in the Texas case, and after some arduous circuit court duty in Virginia and West Virginia as well as a hurried trip to Rhode Island where he tried ineffectually to patch the failing marriage of Kate and Sprague, Chase experienced a heart attack in December, 1870. The symptoms were severe enough for him to consult his New York physician, Dr. John G. Perry, who prescribed medicine that seemed to alleviate his condition.[16]

Changes in the composition of the Court that had occurred during the previous year had been unsettling and doubtless contributed to his failing health. Congress approved the addition of another Justice which brought the Court again to nine. Grier, who had been ailing for some time, gave evidence of mental deterioration. Congress had recently approved a retirement plan for federal judges, and under some pressure from his colleagues, the seventy-five-year-old Justice was induced to retire.[17] As the new year approached, there were two new appointments to be made. President Grant nominated Edwin M. Stanton to one of the seats. Chase could not have been pleased at his choice. Stanton had once been a close friend and associate, but for some years he had severed all personal relations with Chase. It is safe to say that he did not mourn long and deeply when Stanton died soon after his confirmation.[18] After some difficulties in securing the confirmation of his nominees Grant appointed and the Senate confirmed William Strong and Joseph P. Bradley to the Court.[19]

No sooner had the new Justices taken their seats than it became apparent to Chase that a majority on the Court would go along with the new Attorney General Ebenezer R. Hoar's argument and hear a legal tender case that bore the same characteristics of *Hepburn v. Griswold,* which had just been decided. That case had caused more acrimony between the Justices than any previously contested decision. During the conference that would determine the outcome, the court split evenly four to four. After it was pointed out to the aged and forgetful Grier that his argument holding the Legal Tender Acts to be constitutional was the complete reverse of his opinion in a prior case, Grier changed his vote to concur with that of the Chief Justice, Clifford, Field, and Nelson, making it a five to three majority.

As Secretary of the Treasury Chase had supported the issue of greenbacks, deeming them a matter of necessity. But he had always opposed in principle any government's reliance on paper currency that had no specie basis. He regarded the greenbacks in circulation as the prime cause of inflation, detrimental in his opinion to all classes of the community. Chase was not unmindful that inflated currency was a boon to debtors and a bane to creditors. Had he been a seasoned economist he might have recognized that the money supply after the war even with greenbacks in circulation was not sufficient to underwrite the tremendous surge in investment, especially in railroads, that was then being undertaken.

Chase paid little heed to such conditions. Rather he based his argument that the Legal Tender Acts were unconstitutional on two major points. The first dealt with the provision in Article I, section 10, that forbade states "to emit bills of credit; make any thing but gold and silver coin a Tender in Payment of Debts," and the Fifth Amendment, which forbade the government from taking property without due process of law. Chase cited Marshall's doctrine of implied powers in the famous *McCulloch v. Maryland* as supporting his contention that even though Article I dealt with state power it could be legitimately implied to inhibit national power because fiat currency violated the spirit of the Constitution. There was some plausibility to his contentions. But, as Justice Miller acidly observed, his position "would authorize this court to enforce theoretical views of the genius of government, or vague notions of the spirit of the constitution and of abstract justice." The Hepburn case involved contracts prior to the war, but it could be used as a precedent for all contracts made after the first Legal Tender Act in 1862.[20]

Since the decision was so close and since the very day Chase announced the majority opinion, Strong and Bradley were appointed to the Court, the business community was not that disrupted. For it was widely recognized that the new appointees would in some way reverse the Hepburn decision. Bradley had acted as general counsel and lobbyist for the notorious Camden and Amboy railroad monopoly.[21] Strong, formerly a Justice of the Pennsylvania supreme court, was on record as supporting the constitutionality of the Legal Tender Acts.[22] The Grant administration had enough votes for Senate confirmation.

Chase, however, remained confident that the issue had been settled. He could not have been more credulous. Several other cases involving the constitutionality of the Legal Tender Acts were making their way through the courts.[23] Strong took the oath and was seated on March 14, and on March 24, 1870, Bradley was seated. Two days later in conference Chase was taken aback when the two new Justices joined with Swayne, Miller, and Davis to force the rehearing of the legal tender questions with "a fixed determination as I fear," said Chase, "to reverse the decision already made."[24]

In announcing the decision of the Court, Chase made a statement that infuriated Miller and other dissenters in the Hepburn case. He had anticipated the move and had arranged with counsel for one of the appellants to declare that the Hepburn case had settled the matter. In doing so he made no mention that any agreement to that effect had been concluded between counsel and members of the Court. After another division in conference where tempers were further frayed, it was agreed that the appeals would be taken before the Court on April 20.

Chase had been busy in the meantime and when the counsel for the appellants appeared, they asked the Court to dismiss the case. Attorney General Hoar objected vehemently and so did Miller and Bradley. Before any decision was made the Court went into conference where the two big men, Chase and Miller, squared off. Chase won this skirmish and the appellants were permitted to withdraw. An angry Miller accused Chase of having "resorted to all strategies of the lowest political trickery to prevent their being heard, and the fight has been bitter in the conference room."[25] Through counsel for one of the appellants Chase had advised that the claims could be settled through legislation, and this course was followed.[26]

After the encounter in conference, the vigorous, resilient Miller confessed that he was "nearly used up." So certain was Chase of his belief in a specie standard that he brought all of his formidable powers of logic, persuasion, and status as a premier public man to bear upon his colleagues. Exchanges between Miller and Chase were especially pungent.[27]

The acrimonious split in the court and the votes of the newly appointed Justices were very troubling to a man who was accustomed to prevail in what he considered to be important decisions that bore directly on the national economy. He was now quite certain that another attempt would be made to reverse *Hepburn* at the next session and that it would probably prevail.[28] For a person already suffering from heart disease and high blood pressure, threatened also by chronic malaria and diabetes, the contest surely weakened a precarious physical condition. That he had carried the Court with him in upholding Congress's power to tax state bank notes out of existence in favor of national bank notes was scant solace to one whose pride was impressive and whose self confidence could reach monumental proportions.[29] Almost two years later when he returned to the Court, his health shattered by a serious stroke, his humiliation would be complete. On January 15, 1872, Justice Strong, speaking for the majority in *Knox v. Lee* and *Parker v. Davis* sustained the Legal Tender Acts and reversed *Hepburn v. Griswold*.[30] "It is I think a sad day for the countrary [*sic*]," Chase confided to his diary, "& for the cause of constitutional government. The consequences of the sanction this day given to irredeemable paper currency may not soon manifest themselves but are sure to come."[31]

Shortly after the adjournment of the Court for its winter and spring session of 1870 and before he became immersed in his circuit court duties, the last of those onerous burdens he was to shoulder, Chase and his daughter Nettie spent a week at Jay Cooke's lavish hunting and fishing lodge "Gibraltar." For many years, Chase had enjoyed brief fishing excursions to the rushing streams and secluded ponds of rural Pennsylvania with Cooke. He found in them a much-needed respite from his work heavy days and the sultry summer heat of Washington.[32]

Chase had grown accustomed to the lavish lifestyle of his successful friends, immediate family, and many associates. He took for granted the comfort, the servants, even the gaudy splendor. He enjoyed the picnics, croquet games, excursions from Canonchet, his daughter's eighty-room mansion.[33] During summer and autumn vacations when circuit court duties were over and before the fall session of the Supreme Court Chase customarily visited New England, usually attending the Dartmouth commencement and then spending some time with Massachusetts friends.

In the summer of 1867 Chase came very near consummating an affair with the widow of Wisconsin congressman Ben Wood Eastman.[34] Charlotte, or "Lottie," as Chase and other close friends called her, had set her bonnet for Chase. He managed to avoid any commitment, though at times he yearned for the domestic and sexual satisfaction of marriage. Lottie, a New Englander like himself and something of a bluestocking—a quality he admired in the opposite sex—did her best to maneuver him into a permanent relationship.

His vacation took him to New Hampshire and Vermont and then to the Boston area. But the most enjoyable and restful time for Chase was the several days he spent under the hospitable roof of Mrs. Robert Rantoul, another comely widow. Lottie Eastman was also a guest. Mrs. Rantoul left Lottie and Chase alone in her house while she visited friends elsewhere. The night after she left, Lottie made some coy advances which must have aroused Chase. After both had retired, Chase ventured to her room and knocked on her door. Receiving no answer, he returned to his own room.[35] The next evening Lottie left the key to her room in a prominent place where Chase found it. And with this signal, armed of course with an excuse, if his attentions were rebuffed, the portly Chief Justice in his nightshirt and robe walked as softly as possible to Lottie's chambers. But when he tried to open the door he encountered some slight resistance. Assuming the door was barred, Chase beat a quick retreat. Later Lottie confessed to Chase that "she had wanted [him] and would have yielded, if [he] had come in." She showed him the bar that she had put across the door and tied with her garter, explaining that "it would have given way if pulled." In the aftermath of Lottie's confession, Chase may have regretted his lack of persistence but he seems to have been relieved that he had not committed the act and to have felt guilty that he had wanted to.[36]

Lottie Eastman made frequent visits to Washington and at some point acquired a cottage on a small plot of land overlooking the ocean near Gloucester. Chase visited there and was charmed by its coziness and comfort. If he indulged in other comforts with Lottie, he did not record them, but his letters to her were most affectionate.[37] The fact that they were often seen together in Massachusetts and Washington led to frequent speculations in the press that Chase would soon marry. He answered one query from a friend denying that he had any immediate intentions to do so. "It is possible," he said. "But at my time of life that is hardly to be hoped."[38]

Apart from his timid romantic adventures, his enjoyment of the luxuries of the nouveau riche, Chase could and frequently did act as any ordinary citizen in his daily affairs. His home for most of his Washington years was at 601 Sixth Street, which Kate had enlarged and embellished. At least half a dozen servants ministered to the family's needs. Chase rarely had his carriage wait for him when he had several errands. Horsecar lines now served most sections of the city, and were more convenient and cheaper than tying up a carriage with driver and footman for an extended time.[39]

When Kate was in Washington, the mansion at Sixth and E was the scene of much lavish entertaining. But for most of 1869 she was at Canonchet and social life for Chase returned to its more normal routine. The household now consisted of Sprague, who was frequently absent, Nettie, and Chase, though there were frequent visits and extended stays of family and friends.

Chase enjoyed the dinners President Grant gave and the many multi-course extravaganzas deemed so essential at the dinner parties and receptions that the wealthier congressmen and the diplomatic corps hosted. Chase, of course, reciprocated, despite the strain these affairs put on his budget. His income including his salary ranged between $12,000 and $13,000 a year. But he found that this was not sufficient to support his establishment and he was usually in debt to the Cookes, who handled his finances and were unusually tolerant of his overdrafts.[40]

Sprague contributed more than his share to the upkeep of the Washington house, a source of concern to Chase and a major reason for his lobbying to increase the salaries of the Justices. Chase had hoped that the Congress would increase salaries to at least $10,500 a year for the Chief Justice and $10,000 a year for the Associates. A bill including these advances passed the House but was defeated in the Senate by the one vote Chase's son-in-law William Sprague cast. The Senate did accept a smaller increase, from $6500 to $8500 a year for the Chief Justice and from $6000 to $8000 for the associate Justices.[41] This petty and in fact vicious act on Sprague's part reflected an ambivalent attitude toward Chase and his estrangement from Kate.

When Chase learned that his salary would not be increased, he and Nettie had moved to another home on I Street which for the time being he rented. But well before that Sprague's relationship with the Chases existed only for appearances. During the winter of 1868–69, Kate indulged in a constant round of entertainment at Canonchet. Sprague was in Washington most of that time, attending the third session of the Fortieth Congress, which convened on December 7, 1868. He was recorded as voting for the Fifteenth Amendment on February 9, and he answered another roll call on February 10, 1869.[42] A month or so later Nettie, who was with her sister at Canonchet, mentioned that Charles Leary, a New York bon vivant, had been staying with them for a few days. Chase viewed his presence at Canconchet with alarm. "Does she mean," Chase queried Kate, "that Mr. Leary is your guest? I hope not. You cannot be too careful, my child."[43]

Kate was two months' pregnant at the time, but no one, not even her sister, knew about her condition. Whether the child she was expecting was Sprague's or had been conceived with another is a subject of speculation. In any event Kate did not inform her father of her pregnancy until a month before her confinement. "It was wrong of you to leave me to be informed by others that you expect to be a mother again in October," he wrote.[44] But he was happy and relieved that Sprague and Kate had again become reconciled.[45]

Chase's hopeful assumption soon proved wrong. The couple settled their differences for only a brief period. Sprague went back to his heavy drinking and rumors of infidelity appeared. Just before Kate gave birth in late October to Chase's second grandchild, Ethel, he unburdened himself in a letter to his daughter. Admitting that Sprague had not answered his letters, he went on to say, "I wish I could find him loving me and trusting me. But his nature is reserved and he has been always in the habit, as I have been myself of acting on his own judgment and saying little of his matters to anybody." He might have said the same thing of Kate's independence and her willfulness. Instead he urged Kate as a wife "not to expect him to change his nature, not to complain if he is reticent".[46]

Chase had purchased Edgewood, a large rundown farm house with forty acres of land, on a gentle hill in the District near the Soldier's Home, about two miles from the Capitol. Captivated by the view of Washington, the Potomac beyond, and the hills in Virginia,[47] Chase paid $22,000 for the property. The outlay put a heavy strain on his financial resources. He was forced to put much of his Cincinnati property on the market.[48] In addition he had to borrow a substantial sum for extensive repairs and remodeling. He employed Edward Clark, architect of the Capitol, to design and supervise the renovations which included the construction of a "gas house" where coal gas for illumination was produced and then piped to the residence.[49]

The Edgewood house and its grounds were a primary interest of Chase for the remaining years of his life. From his distant past, he called upon an extensive knowledge of farming techniques, of fertilizers and contour plowing, of the planting and care of dozens of fruit trees he had planted on the estate, apparently with an eye to future marketing of the crops.[50]

Worried about his health since the mild heart attack he suffered the past year, Chase cleaned up his current duties and, accompanied by Nettie, traveled west to Minnesota where he spent some time resting at the mineral springs he visited.[51] Returning east by way of Niagara Falls, on August 24 Chase suffered a stroke on the train to New York. The paralysis increased gradually during the night and when he reached New York City his entire right side was affected. He could barely speak. But with Nettie's help he managed to climb the stairs to his room at the Hoffman House. Under medical care Chase remained at the hotel for a week. Kate and Sprague, who had again patched up their marital difficulties, hastened to his side.[52] A week later, on August 31, Chase's condition had improved sufficiently that the doctors decided he could be moved to Canonchet. There he continued to improve but much too slowly for an active person.

For several weeks Chase was not permitted to write or dictate. His secretary Eugene Didier, who had been called to Canonchet, after Chase's move there, was not able to take dictation until the last week in September.[53] But the physicians insisted he take exercise and so he limped about the grounds, his right leg dragging.[54] Conscientious as always when permitted to write, he practiced each day, though his script which in ordinary circumstances was barely legible was quite indecipherable.[55]

For the next two months Chase convalesced. At times he felt well enough to extend his activities until a visit to Senator Anthony's home nearby brought about a relapse. Foregoing a lifelong habit of abstinence from alcoholic beverages, he had topped off the hearty meal of fish, oysters, beef steak, mushrooms, corn on the cob, and baked apples with a glass of sherry and one of champagne. When he reached home Chase suffered a heart attack. For two months thereafter, his physicians placed him on a rigid diet which he followed scrupulously. His recovery was slow punctuated by bouts of insomnia and excessive urination that left him spiritless and dehydrated.[56]

Chase's condition and his diet brought on constipation that in common with his contemporaries was a source of constant apprehension. He was dosed with various strong laxatives which brought temporary relief but could not have been helpful to his overall condition. Yet by December Chase's health had improved to the extent that he was able to move to New York City where he would receive daily medical attention and where the winter weather was not quite so harsh as the gale-swept Narraganset peninsula. He rented quarters at 15 Fifth Avenue, just south of the Brevoort House. A commodious residence, the building could accommodate Chase, his black attendant, household staff,

Jacob Schuckers, who had replaced Didier as Chase's private secretary,[57] Nettie, Kate, and her children.[58]

Chase spent the month in New York where he took long walks, whatever the weather. The change of scene if not the ministrations of Dr. Perry hastened his convalescence. With his improving health he was anxious to return to Washington and to resume his court duties. He was interested in an income tax case that was before the court, *Collector v. Day*, one that again explored the boundaries between federal and state power. The case was similar in some respects to his opinion in *Lane County v. Oregon*, decided the previous year. Chase upheld the state of Oregon's law that taxes imposed locally must be paid in gold or silver coin, not in greenbacks. Drawing his major conclusion, as he had in the Hepburn case, from Marshall's opinion in *McCulloch v. Maryland* Chase had carried a majority of the court in sustaining a state's powers over its internal affairs provided its action was not in conflict with the federal Constitution. *Collector v. Day* touched on the Hepburn decision that was in danger of being reversed, and Chase's opinion in *Texas v. White*.

It involved the authority of the federal government to levy an income tax on the salary of a state judge. Chase was in his chair when Justice Nelson handed down the decision of the Court. He quoted extensively from Chase's opinion in the Lane County case that "in many of the articles of the Constitution, the necessary existence of the States, and within their proper spheres, the independent authority of the States are distinctly recognized."

With only the new Justice Bradley dissenting, Nelson relied also on Article X of the Constitution, which declared the states to have reserved powers in defined areas of responsibility. Thus they were as immune from federal power as the federal government was immune from state power, at least as far as taxation was concerned. The federal income tax on state officials was thus unconstitutional.[59]

Chase was well satisfied by this decision and happy to be settled again in Washington. But slowing down his recovery was the added emotional strain of parting with Nettie. His constant companion for many months, she would soon be leaving her father's side. While at the many social occasions in Canonchet and New York City, this unobtrusive young woman, though no match for her more glamorous sister, did not lack for beaux.

She and Sprague's cousin, William Hoyt, a New York banker, were attracted to each other. Before the family left New York, they had become engaged.[60] The wedding was set for late March. Not the conspicuous affair of Kate's wedding to Sprague eight years before, it put a further burden on Chase's slender means, requiring again a loan from the Cookes and another sale of Cincinnati property.[61] Chase was still hoping for an increase in salary and an allowance for a clerk, both of which items were inserted in a bill for the expenses of the State Department that had passed the House. Nothing came of the salary increase and allowance, however.[62] The government did provide funds for a personal messenger or attendant, whose duties included everything from acting as a valet to a secretary who could take shorthand. The pay was meager even for those times, $872.50 for seven months of duty each year.[63]

Chase continued his efforts to advance and protect civil rights for the blacks, in particular, suffrage, which many of the states both north and south were evading despite the Fourteenth Amendment. Before his illness, he had brought pressure on Ohio Democrats through the remnants of his organization to help carry the Fifteenth Amendment through the legislature.[64] The Fourteenth Amendment's first section that dealt with privileges and immunities of United States citizens had proven not specific enough to protect the vote of blacks. In an effort to rectify this oversight, Congress approved the Fifteenth Amendment that restricted state action to deny suffrage on account of "race, color, or previous condition of servitude." The requisite number of states ratified the amendment, which was proclaimed on March 30, 1870.

But Chase's primary attention upon his return to Washington was divided between his presiding over the Court and the care and maintenance of Edgewood. He was now well enough to walk from his new home to the Capitol and return.[65] It took him about an hour if the road was dry to make the journey one way.[66]

His colleagues on the Court as well as acquaintances in Washington were shocked at his appearance. The illness and the strict regimen his physicians laid out had almost halved his weight.[67] Always vain about his appearance, for a time he grew a beard that covered up the folds of flesh around his neck. His hollow cheeks and gaunt appearance marked him as a sick man.[68] It was obvious that his grasp of technical points or questions of counsel were not as penetrating as they had been.[69] His dissent in *Knox v. Lee* which overturned *Hepburn v. Griswold* lacked his customary felicity of style and tight construction. Nor did his lone dissent in *Tarble's Case* reflect his usual clarity of thought. This case arose on an appeal from the state supreme court of Wisconsin, which granted a habeas corpus writ discharging from federal custody one Edward Tarble, an army deserter. Chase maintained that the Wisconsin court had acted properly in protecting a citizen from arbitrary arrest or imprisonment. In delivering the court opinion Field said that "the United States are as much interested in protecting the citizen from illegal restraint under their authority as the several states. . . ." Tarble was remanded to military custody. On further reflection Chase was somewhat troubled by his opinion. He wrote a rather apologetic letter to the reporter of the Massachusetts supreme court. "My health did not permit me to give my views in that case as fully as I should have otherwise." He said that he had not participated in "the discussions in conference, of which indeed, there was little or none before the opinion was written."[70]

In the last important cases to come before the Court during Chase's life time, and the last of a series of actions taken in interpreting the Fourteenth Amendment, the Slaughter House Cases, Chase wrote no opinion. These cases arose from an act of the Louisiana legislature that gave a slaughter house in New Orleans the sole right of operations within the city of New Orleans. The monopoly grant was aimed at protecting the health of the city's citizens. Competing companies brought suit, challenging the act as a violation of their property rights without due process of law as specified in Section I of the Fourteenth Amendment. A majority of the Court which decided the case on appeal agreed with the Louisiana legislature's action and opted for state police power, in protecting the health and welfare of its citizens. Thus the Fourteenth Amendment was relative in application. Quite conceivably then the states might have the power to limit suffrage or legislate other forms of discrimination. Chase joined Field, Swayne, and Bradley in rejecting the argument that the constitutional privileges and immunities of a citizen were relative and not absolute. Weakened in body and mind Chase nevertheless saw in the argument of former Associate Justice John A. Campbell a means of strengthening the protection the Fourteenth Amendment afforded to the civil rights of blacks.[71]

After his apparent recovery, Chase pushed himself too hard and too soon regarding his judicial duties, his social life in Washington, his penchant for travel to the West and to New England, and his concern for Kate and her tempestuous marriage.[72] He was relieved and delighted at Nettie's safe delivery of a ten-pound girl on January 14, 1872.[73] Kate too was pregnant and about a month later gave birth to another daughter. Since Kate had decided to have her baby at the Sprague home in Washington, Chase visited her almost every day toward the end of her pregnancy.[74]

Despite his physical condition, Chase still flirted with a run for the presidency.[75] He supported the Liberal Republican movement, a fusion of progressive Republicans and mainline Democrats, which had achieved much of what Chase had sought to do in reshaping the Democrat party and moving it away from its traditional lines.[76]

The indefatigable Kate gave a lavish party in her father's honor at the Sixth Street home to show doubting politicians that Chase was fully recovered and the only person of experience, intelligence, ability, and political background to draw the progressive wings in both parties together. But those who observed Chase closely, as they sipped Kate's champagne and partook of the choice edibles on the buffet tables, saw a man whose hands trembled and whose enunciation was not clear. Doubters were confirmed in their judgments that he was not fit physically for the responsibility of the presidency.[77] Again he was passed over when the new coalition nominated Horace Greeley. Chase supported Greeley, who lost the election to Grant.[78] Shocked at Greeley's sudden death a few weeks after the election Chase went to New York, where he acted as one of the pallbearers.

On March 4, 1873, he administered the oath of office to Grant for the second time. A skeletal figure that even his black robe could not disguise, he was in decided contrast to the short, compact President. Chase remained in the background on the east portico as Grant read his inaugural address. It was the coldest day anyone could remember for an inauguration. A gale of wind was blowing from the southwest that brought the chill factor to below zero. After moving with the procession from the crowded, stuffy rotunda of the Capitol to the frigid outside, Chase remained bare-headed, his robes offering little protection to the wintry blast.[79] For a person as fragile as the Chief Justice, his presence at the inauguration was simply courting disaster.[80] And from then on his physical condition began to decline rapidly.

Though he took his place regularly at the bench, his attention wavered and at times he bent his head down on his hands for lengthy intervals. He wrote the opinion of the Court that sustained state police power in a taxing case, but when it was time to hand down the decision, he found it took all of his strength simply to read it.[81] On the last day of the 1872–73 session, he felt too weak to preside and turned over his duties to Justice Clifford.[82] Chase continued to preside at the usual Saturday conferences and attended Court faithfully during the winter of 1873.

His relationship with Sumner and other radical Republicans, which had fallen to a low ebb during the impeachment trial, was now much improved. He saw them frequently on formal and informal occasions. He even made overtures to the Blairs, Montgomery, and old F. P. Blair, which they reciprocated. When Charles Francis Adams in his laudatory address on Seward implied that he, not Lincoln, had governed the country during the war, Chase compared notes with Montgomery Blair and Gideon Welles for a joint refutation of Adams's piece.[83] Ever-conscious of his involvement in the political and social events of the past thirty-five years and recognizing the drastic changes that had occurred since he began his law practice in the West, Chase commissioned his old associate and occasional friend Robert B. Warden to write his biography.[84]

Always methodical, particularly so when it concerned his personal affairs, Chase had kept and filed thousands of letters, documents, journals, commonplace books, memoranda, and newspaper clippings, which dated as far back as the 1820s. It was the practice for nineteenth-century politicians and lawyers to retain their correspondence for reference needs but Chase early in his career had an eventual biography or memoir in mind.

His papers in Warden's hands, the 1872–73 session of the Supreme Court finally adjourned, Chase looked forward to seeing his family in New

York—the Hoyts and their daughter, at their home on West 33rd Street—and Kate and her three who were staying at the Clarendon Hotel. He left Washington on the morning train on Saturday, May 3, planning to stay in New York for a few days and then travel to Boston, where he would visit his niece Alice Skinner Stebbins. She had suggested that he consult a noted Boston physician and he agreed, though he did not expect any treatment would alleviate his condition.[85] A depressed Chase wrote Parsons that he was "too much of an invalid to be more than a cipher. Sometimes I feel as if I were dead . . . the lapse of 65 years is hard to cure." Yet he planned to go west after his Boston visit as far as Colorado.[86] He would never make it.

About 9:30 p.m., May 5, he felt tired, excused himself, and, attended by his black valet of many years, William Joice, made ready for bed. After Joice left the room, Chase wrote two notes, one to Parsons and the other to his niece saying that he would be in Boston on the 14th or the 15th, and hoping that he would not be an inconvenience.[87] "Mind," he wrote, "I insist that you do not disturb yourselves in the least. If you have a spare room I will gladly occupy it—nothing more."[88]

On the morning of May 6, Joice entered Chase's room, drew the curtains and opened the windows. At first he thought that the Chief Justice was still asleep but, unable to awaken him, realized that something was wrong and called for help. The physicians diagnosed a critical, probably fatal stroke. He remained unconscious for the next twenty-four hours, his labored breathing slowly becoming fainter. Death came at 10 o'clock in the morning on May 7. At his side was Kate, then five months' pregnant with her last child; Nettie, her husband Will Hoyt, and his brother Edwin; Dr. Perry and Dr. Metcalf; Hiram Barney; and William Joice. Thus the last of that singular trio of Chase, Seward, and Stanton had passed away.

If he was not the greatest of Lincoln's advisors he was surely as capable as any of his colleagues in his area of responsibility, and more capable than most. His tenure as Secretary of the Treasury during the most wasteful of this the first of modern wars was fraught with the gravest difficulties. In the main he had found the funds to support almost a million well-equipped troops in the field and for a time a navy second only to that of Great Britain. He achieved this objective in a relatively unstructured economy without imposing a crushing burden of drastic inflation or government controls.

Chase was indeed an unusual person. Cold, dignified, handsome, some thought imperial in appearance and manner, he nevertheless craved human warmth and friendship which, except for that of a handful of devoted friends and his family, he was never able to attract. The old-fashioned idealism and republican virtue that William Wirt, his friend, teacher, and model inculcated always seemed to clash with the hard-driving, even ruthless precepts that his uncle the Bishop instilled at an early and formative stage in Chase's life.

It may have been a sixth sense that informed him that the antislavery movement would soon emerge as a popular political venture. But during the late 30s and early 40s this particular reform did not hold out promising career prospects in Cincinnati, only a mile or so from a slave state. Quite the reverse. The plight of the slaves stirred a reticent, even awkward young lawyer to the depths of his being. And from then to the end of his life he was in the forefront first of the antislavery movement and eventually of the drive for equal rights. He never wavered in this dedication. Balanced against such high-minded moral and social goals was an insidious ambition—that "maggot" in the brain, as Lincoln described it. Though he was realistic and generally accurate in assessing political goals, he was clumsy and faltering in the means he employed to attain them. Nor was he a good judge of individuals. Personally honest in administering the great powers entrusted to him as Secretary of the Treasury, he was blind to the subtle acts of corruption and abuse of power in his subordinates. A person of courage and self-confidence, developed over years of political life, always certain of his status, his education, and wide administrative experience, he viewed the unkempt, self-taught Lincoln with a mixture of condescension and exasperation at what seemed to be his casual approach to significant problems of state. Yet he could not fail to note at times Lincoln's finer qualities and came to understand his mastery of the political maneuver.[89]

Contemporary and modern economists have not been kind in assessing Chase's financial policies. He has been charged with being ignorant of the world of finance, of being guided in his dealings with the nation's money managers by outworn Jacksonian precepts of hard money when vast unprecedented sums were demanded to support the war.[90] Chase certainly did have a healthy suspicion of bankers and his early funding measures were inept. But he learned by experience and he quickly mastered the intricacies of public and private finance. More than that he directed the bankers, all men of wealth and self-importance by the sheer force of his personality. And he guided the finance committees of the Congress with a firm though not always a certain hand. He must be given the credit for establishing the national banking system, which for the times placed the nation on a sound currency basis while it acted as a market for the government debt. Reluctantly and as a matter of expediency Chase agreed to inflating the currency. And his reasoning on the Supreme Court that declared greenbacks unconstitutional did not square with the nation's needs. Generally a most practical person, his views in the Hepburn case must be viewed as an aberration which frequently afflicts strong minds.

Chase's tenure as Chief Justice has also been the subject of criticism. But he led the court through most perilous times, contributing his political knowledge and his standing with Congress to the tone as well as the decisions of his colleagues whether his opinions were in the majority or the dissenting minority. His insistence that the impeachment trial of Andrew Johnson conform in some important aspects to judicial rather than legislative procedures had a modifying influence on an essentially partisan body. Chase's well-grounded belief in the separation of powers between the legislative, executive, and judicial branches of the government was sound in theory and in practice. In this respect Chase knowingly cast himself outside of the pale of his party for what he felt strongly to be the greater good of the nation's political institutions.

In the end, however, Chase remains a tragic figure. He witnessed his beautiful and gifted daughter Kate on whom he had lavished such care and devotion married to an unworthy and dissolute man. When he sought to help in maintaining the union of these polar opposites, he failed and well before his death he recognized this fact.

The ambitions of his restless nature were never fully satisfied. He died a frustrated, lonely individual aware that even his much-loved daughter had been sacrificed to the tawdry materialism of the moment. As much as he enjoyed the opulence of Canonchet, of Jay Cooke's Ogontz, an enormous new palace of 52 rooms near his former home, and the marble mansions of rich New Yorkers such as A. T. Stewart, the merchant mogul, in the deeper recesses of his ever-nagging conscience he recognized them for what they were, transient episodes in ostentatious exhibitionism, merely a sounding brass or a tinkling cymbal.[91] In a note he wrote Parsons from New York City just before suffering his fatal stroke, he said wistfully, "It seems odd to be so entirely out of the world in the midst of this great Babylon."[92]

Abbreviations Used in Notes

CLU-S/C	Department of Special Collections, University Research Library, University of California, Los Angeles
CSmH	Huntington Library, San Marino, Calif.
CSmH-Barney	Hiram Barney Papers, Huntington Library
CSmH-Sherman	Isaac Sherman Papers, Huntington Library
CU-BANC	Bancroft Library, University of California, Berkeley
CU-BANC-Atkins	Atkins Family Papers
CU-BANC-Field	Stephen Johnson Field Papers
Chase Manhattan	Chase Manhattan Archives, New York, N.Y.
CtY	Yale University Library, New Haven, Conn.
CtY-Carrington	Carrington Family Papers
CtY-Webb	James Watson Webb Papers
DLC	Library of Congress, Washington, D.C.
DLC-Banks	Nathaniel P. Banks Papers
DLC-Belmont	August Belmont Papers (Miscellaneous)
DLC-Blair	Blair Family Papers
DLC-Butler	Benjamin F. Butler Papers
DLC-Cameron	Simon Cameron Papers
DLC-Chase	Salmon P. Chase Papers

DLC-Denison	George S. Denison Papers
DLC-E.B.Washburne	E. B. Washburne Papers
DLC-Fessenden	William Pitt Fessenden Papers
DLC-Garfield	James A. Garfield Papers
DLC-Giddings-Julian	Joshua R. Giddings and George W. Julian Papers
DLC-Johnson	Andrew Johnson Papers
DLC-Lincoln	Abraham Lincoln Papers
DLC-Marble	Manton M. Marble Papers
DLC-Marcy	William L. Marcy Papers
DLC-Nicolay	John G. Nicolay Papers
DLC-Reid	Reid Family Papers
DLC-Schuckers	Jacob W. Schuckers Papers
DLC-J.Sherman	John Sherman Papers
DLC-W.Sherman	William Tecumseh Sherman Papers
DLC-Stanton	Edwin M. Stanton Papers
DLC-T.Stevens	Thaddeus Stevens Papers
DLC-Taft	William Howard Taft Papers
DLC-Van Buren	Martin Van Buren Papers
DLC-Wade	Benjamin F. Wade Papers
DLC-Welles	Gideon Welles Papers
DNA	National Archives, Washington, D.C.
DNA-RG36	Records of the Bureau of Customs
DNA-RG46	Committee on Finance Papers, 37th Congress
DNA-RG53	Records of the Bureau of the Public Debt
DNA-RG53,LD,PC	Record of Secretary's Private Correspondence, April 11, 1861, to January 6, 1862
DNA-RG53,LDLS	Loan Division Letters Sent
DNA-RG56,A,LS	Letters Sent to the President (A Series)
DNA-RG56,AB,1st Aud.	Letters Received from Executive Officers (AB Series). Letters from the First Auditor
DNA-RG56,AB,Atty.Gen	Letters from the Attorney General
DNA-RG56,AB,Solicitor	Letters from the Solicitor of the Treasury
DNA-RG56,Bb,LS	Letters Sent to Heads of Bureaus (Bb Series)
DNA-RG56,Bc,LS	Letters Sent to the Cabinet (Bc Series)
DNA-RG56,BE,LS	Letters Sent Relating to Restricted Commercial Intercourse and Captured and Abandoned Property (BE Series)

DNA-RG56,Bc,LS	Letters Sent to the President of the Senate and the Speaker of the House of Representatives (C Series)
DNA-RG56,D,LS	Letters Sent to Committees of Congress (D Series)
DNA-RG56,H,LR	Letters Received from Collectors of Custom at New York (H Series)
DNA-RG56,H,LS	Letters Sent to Collectors of Custom at New York (H Series)
DNA-RG56,K,LS	Miscellaneous Letters Sent (K Series)
DNA-RG56,LRAT	Letters Received from Assistant Treasurers
DNA-RG56,LRHC,WM	Committee on Ways and Means
DNA-RG56,LRWD	Letters Received from the War Department, 1832–1910
DNA-RG56,T	Circular Letters Sent (T Series)
DNA-RG56,XA	Telegrams Sent, 1850–74 (XA Series)
DNA-RG59	Greenhow, Records of the Department of State
DNA-RG60	Attorney General's Papers. Letters Received from Treasury Department, 1860–64
DNA-RG94	Records of the Adjutant General's Office, 1780–1917
DNA-RG107	War Department Letters Received from the Secretary of War
DNA-RG206	Records of the Solicitor of the Treasury
DNA-RG206,LRST	Letters Received from the Secretary of the Treasury
DNA-RG267	Records of the Supreme Court
DNA-RG366	5th Special Agency, Port Royal
DNA-RG393	Records of the U.S. Army, Continental Commands
Dauphin Co.Hist.Soc.	Dauphin County Historical Society, Simon Cameron Papers, Harrisburg, Penn.
IaHA	State Historical Society, Des Moines, Iowa
IHi	Illinois State Historical Library, Springfield
IHi-Chase	Salmon P. Chase Papers
In-Julian	George W. Julian Papers, Indianapolis, Ind.
InU-Li	Lilly Library, Indiana University, Bloomington
InU-Li-Smith	Hamilton Smith Manuscripts

KHi	Kansas State Historical Society, Topeka
MH-H	Houghton Library, Harvard University, Cambridge, Mass., John T. Trowbridge Papers, John P. Bigelow Papers, Charles Sumner Papers
MHi	Massachusetts Historical Society, Boston
MHi-J.Schouler	James Schouler Papers
MHi-W.Schouler	William Schouler Papers
MHi-Washburn	Washburn Collection
MSaE	John G. Whittier Papers, Essex Institute, Essex, Mass.
MdHi	Maryland Historical Society, Baltimore, Md.
MdHi-Wirt	William Wirt Papers
MeB	Bowdoin College, Brunswick, Me.
MeB-Mellen	Clara H. Mellen Papers
MeHi	Maine Historical Society, Portland, Me.
MeHi-Clifford	Nathan Clifford Papers
MeU	University of Maine, Orono, Me.
MeU-Pike	James Shepherd Pike Papers
MeWC	Special Collections, Colby College, Waterville, Me.
MiU-C	William L. Clements Library, University of Michigan, Ann Arbor
MiU-C-Birney	James G. Birney Collection
MnHi	Minnesota Historical Society, St. Paul
MnHi-Ramsey	Alexander Ramsey Papers
MoSHi	Missouri Historical Society, St. Louis
MoSHi-Cisco	John J. Cisco Letters
MoSHi-Harrington	George R. Harrington Papers
NBuHi	Buffalo and Erie County Historical Society, Buffalo, N.Y.
NBuHi-Spaulding	Elbridge Gerry Spaulding Papers
NHi	New-York Historical Society, New York, N.Y.
NHi-O'Reilly	Henry O'Reilly Papers
NHi-Stevens	John Austin Stevens Papers
NHi-Chase	Salmon P. Chase Papers

NN	Rare Books and Manuscripts Division, New York Public Library, New York, N.Y., Astor, Lenox, and Tilden Foundations
NN-Bigelow	John Bigelow Papers
NN-Chase	Salmon P. Chase, Personal-Miscellaneous Collection
NN-Goddard—Roslyn	Goddard-Roslyn Collection
NN-Greeley	Horace Greeley Papers
NN-Tilden	Samuel Tilden Papers
NNC	Rare Book and Manuscript Library, Columbia University, New York, N.Y.
NNC-Dix	Dix Collection
NNC-Gay	Gay Collection
NNC-Jay	Jay Family Collection
NNPM	Pierpont Morgan Library, New York, N.Y.
NRU	University of Rochester Library, Rochester, N.Y.
NRU-Seward	William H. Seward Papers
NSyU-Smith	Gerrit Smith Collection, George Arents Research Library, Syracuse University, Syracuse, N.Y.
NcD	Manuscript Department, William R. Perkins Library, Durham, N.C.
NcD-Hilliard	Henry W. Hilliard Papers
NcD-Tucker	Tucker Family Papers
NhD	Special Collections, Dartmouth College Library, Hanover, N.H.
NhHi	New Hampshire Historical Society, Concord
NhHi-Chase	Salmon P. Chase Papers
NhHi-Hale	John Parker Hale Papers
NjP	Princeton University, Princeton, N.J.
NjP-Butler	Butler Family Papers, Benjamin Franklin Butler, 1795–1858
NSchU	Union College Special Collections, Schenectady, N.Y.
OCHP	Cincinnati Historical Society, Cincinnati, Ohio
OCHP-Chase	Salmon P. Chase Papers
OCHP-Follett	Oran Follett Papers
OCHP-Halstead	Murat Halstead Papers

OCHP-Long	Alexander Long Papers
OCHi	Ohio Historical Society, Columbus, Ohio
OCHi-Campbell	Lewis D. Campbell Papers
OCHi-Chase	Salmon P. Chase Papers
OCHi-Giddings	Joshua R. Giddings Papers
OCHi-Mansfield	Edward D. Mansfield Papers
OCIWHi	Western Reserve Historical Society, Cleveland, Ohio
OCIWHi-Norton	Norton Collection
OCIWHi-Riddle	Albert G. Riddle Papers
OFH-Chase	Salmon P. Chase Papers, Fremont, Ohio
OR	U.S. War Department, *The War of the Rebellion: A Compilation of the Official Records of the Union and Confederate Armies* (Washington, DC, 1880–1901)
PHi	Historical Society of Pennsylvania, Philadelphia
PHi-Chase	Salmon P. Chase Papers
PHi-Cooke	Jay Cooke Papers
PP	Carson Collection, Rare Book Department, Free Library of Philadelphia, Philadelphia, Penn.
PSC-Hi-Codding	Codding Collection, Swarthmore, Penn.
RPB-JH	John Hay Library of Rare Books and Special Collections, Brown University, Providence, R.I.
RPB-JH-Chase	Chase Manuscripts
ViHi	Virginia Historical Society, Richmond, Va.
ViU-Whittier	John Greenleaf Whittier Collection, Charlottesville, Va.
WHi	State Historical Society of Wisconsin, Madison
WHi-Brisbane	William H. Brisbane Papers
WHi-Chase	Salmon P. Chase Papers
WM-Mansfield	Jared Mansfield Collection, Local History and Marine Room, Milwaukee Public Library, Milwaukee, Wisc.
Wv-Ar	Boyd B. Stutler Collection, State Archives, West Virginia Department of Culture and History, Charleston

Notes

Chapter 1. Threshold

1. Cincinnati *Daily Gazette*, 10 March 1868; *Trial of Andrew Johnson, President of the United States Before the Senate of the United States on Impeachment by the House of Representatives for High Crimes and Misdemeanours*, 3 vols. (Washington, D.C., 1868), I: 11.

2. S. P. Chase to Gerrit Smith, 19 April 1868, DLC-Chase; Philander Chase to Baruch Chase, 30 July 1823. NhHi-Chase.

3. S. P. Chase to John T. Trowbridge, 27 Dec. 1863, PHi-Chase.

4. William H. Child, *History of the Town of Cornish, New Hampshire*, 2 vols. (Concord, N.H., 1910), 158, 162, 164.

5. S. P. Chase to Trowbridge, 19 Jan. 1863, PHi-Chase; J. W. Schuckers, *The Life and Public Services of Salmon Portland Chase* (New York 1874), 2, 3, 6; Robert B. Warden, *An Account of the Private Life and Public Services of Salmon Portland Chase*, 2 parts (Washington, D.C., 1872), I: 25.

6. Child, *Cornish*, I: 6–7.

7. Ibid., II: 62.

8. Ibid., 130–31; S. P. Chase to John T. Trowbridge, 27 Dec. 1863, PHi-Chase.

9. Helen Maria Walbridge to Chase, 6 Feb. 1864, DLC-Chase.

10. S. P. Chase to Trowbridge, 27 Dec. 1863, MH-H; S. G. Griffen, *A History of the Town of Keene, New Hampshire* (1904; rpt., 1980), 373, 567, 638; S. P. Chase to Trowbridge, 19 Jan. 1863, PHi-Chase.

11. S. P. Chase to Trowbridge, 19 Jan. 1863, PHi-Chase.

12. Warden, *Chase,* I, 56.

13. S. P. Chase to Trowbridge, 21 Jan. 1864, PHi-Chase.

14. Ibid.

15. Griffen, *Keene,* 373.

16. S. P. Chase to Trowbridge, 21, 23 Jan. 1864, PHi-Chase.

17. As he recalled humorously years later, "the Ohio, as the country was then called, was a great way off—it was very fertile—cucumbers growing on trees—there were wonderful springs whose [waters] were like New England rum—deer and wolves were plenty—people few"; S. P. Chase to Trowbridge, 23 Jan. 1864, PHi-Chase.

18. Ibid.

19. Walter Havighurst, *The Long Ships Passing* (New York, 1942), 121–23; S. P. Chase to Trowbridge, 23 Jan. 1864, PHi-Chase.

20. Chase to Trowbridge, 23 Jan. 1864, PHi-Chase; Havighurst, *Long Ships,* 79.

21. S. P. Chase to Trowbridge, 23 Jan. 1864, PHi-Chase.

22. Ibid.

23. Henry Howe, *Historical Collections of Ohio,* 2 vols. (Cincinnati, 1907), I: 989; S. P. Chase to Trowbridge, 25, 26 Jan. 1864, OCHP-Chase.

24. Chase to Trowbridge, 25, 26 Jan. 1864, OCHP-Chase.

25. Ibid., 29 Jan. 1864, PHi-Chase.

26. Ibid.

27. Ibid., 25 Jan. 1864, OCHP-Chase.

28. S. P. Chase to Worthington, 27 Jan. 1864, PHi-Chase.

29. Ibid.

30. S. P. Chase to Trowbridge, 29 Jan. 1864, PHi-Chase.

31. Ibid.

32. Ibid., 31 Jan. 1864, OCHP-Chase.

33. Ibid.

34. Ibid., 1 Feb. 1864, PHi-Chase.

35. Ibid., 2 Feb. 1864.

Chapter 2. Trials and Triumphs

1. S. P. Chase to Trowbridge, 29 Jan., 2 Feb., 1864, PHi-Chase.

2. S. P. Chase to Adeline Hitchcock, 29 April 1826, PHi-Chase.

3. S. P. Chase to John P. Bigelow, 23 Sept. 1854; S. P. Chase to Trowbridge, 7 Feb. 1864, PHi-Chase.

4. Chase to Trowbridge, 7 Feb. 1864, PHi-Chase.

5. Janette Chase to S. P. Chase, 14 Aug. 1824, PHi-Chase.

6. S. P. Chase to Trowbridge, 7 Feb. 1864, PHi-Chase.

7. Leon Burr Richardson, *History of Dartmouth College,* 2 vols. (Hanover, N.H., 1932), I: 373, 375.

8. S. P. Chase to Thomas Sparhawk, 29 Nov. 1825, OCHi-Chase; Charles Franklin Emerson, comp., *General Catalogue of Dartmouth College and the Associated Schools, 1769–1910* (Hanover, N.H., 1910–1911), 123, 139, 143, 150, 152, 154, 162, 166, 171, 173.

9. S. P. Chase to Trowbridge, 7 Feb. 1864, PHi-Chase; to Sparhawk, 29 Nov. 1825, OCHi-Chase.

10. S. P. Chase to Trowbridge, 8 Feb. 1864, PHi-Chase; to Thomas Sparhawk, 14 Dec. 1825, OCHI-Chase.

11. Janette Chase to S. P. Chase, Aug. 1825, PHi-Chase.

12. Ibid., 10 July 1825.

13. S. P. Chase to Trowbridge, 8 Feb. 1864, PHi-Chase.
14. Ibid., 7 Feb. 1864.
15. S. P. Chase to Sparhawk, 16 March 1826, OCHP-Chase.
16. Ibid.
17. Ibid., March 16, 1826; Nathaniel Folsom, member of the class of 1828, who became a professor of theology, said that Chase was deeply affected by the revival. B. P. Smith, *The History of Dartmouth College* (Boston, 1878), 134–39. Folsom's opinion is confirmed in a letter Chase wrote to his friend Adeline Hitchcock in April 1826. He had just finished reading Gibbon's *Decline and Fall of the Roman Empire* and had been so impressed by its stately prose, its impressive argument, and its anti-Christian theme that he confessed the work "would have made me an infidel had it not been that during the revival, which commenced here, it has pleased God of his infinite mercy to bring me as I would humbly hope to the foot of the cross thro' the blood of his son." S. P. Chase to Adeline Hitchcock, 29 April 1826, PHi-Chase.
18. S. P. Chase to Trowbridge, 8 Feb. 1864, PHi-Chase.
19. M. B. Chase to Chase, 15 Nov. 1826, OCHP-Chase.
20. S. P. Chase to Trowbridge, 8 Feb. 1864, PHi-Chase.
21. Ibid.
22. Ibid., 10 Feb. 1864.
23. S. P. Chase to Trowbridge, 10 Feb. 1864, PHi-Chase; *Daily National Intelligencer*, 23 Dec. 1826.
24. S. P. Chase to Trowbridge, 10 Feb. 1864, PHi-Chase.
25. Ibid.; Schuckers, *Chase*, 24.
26. S. P. Chase to Trowbridge, 13 Feb. 1864, PHi-Chase.
27. Ibid.
28. S. P. Chase, "Diary," 10 Jan. 1829, DLC-Chase; John B. Boles, ed., *A Guide to the Microfilm Edition of the William Wirt Papers* (Baltimore, 1971), 3–8; Warden, *Chase, part I*.
29. S. P. Chase to Sparhawk, 18 Sept. 1827, Sept. 1828, 20 April 1829, OCHi-Chase; Schuckers, *Chase*, 29.
30. S. P. Chase, "Diary," 1 Dec. 1829, DLC-Chase, Schuckers, *Chase* 30.
31. S. P. Chase to Sparhawk, 18 Sept. 1827, OCHP-Chase.
32. Schuckers, *Chase*, 24.
33. Philander Chase, *Reminiscences: An Autobiography*, 2 vols. (2nd ed., Boston, 1848), II: 588, 589, 592, 593.
34. S. P. Chase, "Diary," 28 Jan. 1829, DLC-Chase.
35. Ibid.
36. Alexander Brown, *The Cabells and Their Kin* (Boston, 1895), 257–58; Charles Lanmen, *Biographical Annals of the Civil Government of the United States* (Washington, D.C., 1876), 338.
37. S. P. Chase, "Diary," 17 Nov. 1829, DLC-Chase.
38. Ibid., 1 Jan. 1829.
39. Ibid., 9 Feb. 1829.
40. Ibid., 14 Feb. 1829.
41. Schuckers, *Chase*, 27, 28.
42. Ibid.; S. P. Chase, "Diary," 20 April, 9 Oct., 24 Dec. 1829, DLC-Chase.
43. S. P. Chase, "Diary," Feb. 1830, DLC-Chase.
44. Ibid., 7 Jan. 1830.
45. S. P. Chase to William Wirt, 28 Jan. 1830, PHi-Chase.

46. S. P. Chase, "Diary," 7, 9, 14 Dec. 1829; Personal Memoranda, 30 June 1853, DLC-Chase.

47. S. P. Chase, "Diary," 14 Dec. 1829, DLC-Chase.

48. Howe, *Historical Collections,* I: 817; S. P. Chase, "Diary," 22 Feb. 1830, DLC-Chase.

49. S. P. Chase, "Diary," 22 Feb., 1 March 1830. DLC-Chase.

50. S. P. Chase to Smith, 10 May 1829, InU-Li-Smith.

Chapter 3. The Young Professional

1. S. P. Chase, "Diary," 1 March 1830, DLC-Chase. Under the entry for 1 March Chase wrote a general narrative of his trip and his early days in Cincinnati. He neglected to set off by date his diary for the period.

2. Ibid.

3. Howe, Ohio, I: 155.

4. Ibid.

5. Frances M. Trollope, *Domestic Manners of the Americans* (rpt. London, 1927), 33, 34, 72, 73.

6. S. P. Chase, "Diary," 1 March 1830, DLC-Chase.

7. S. P. Chase to Thomas Sparhawk, 12 June 1830, OCHI-Chase; to Charles Cleveland, 21 Dec. 1831, DLC-Chase; S. P. Chase, "Our City," Cincinnati *American,* 3 Dec. 1831.

8. S. P. Chase, "Diary," 13 March 1830, DLC-Chase; Howe, *Ohio Collections,* I: 818.

9. William Wirt to Chase, 4 May 1829, MdHi-Wirt. "I spoke this day, in the moot court," he said, "upon a case in which I was counsel for the plaintiff and failed completely. . . . My self possession nearly destroyed by the presence of several of the faculty"; S. P. Chase, "Diary," 22 May 1830, DLC-Chase.

10. Warden, *Chase,* I: 192; S. P. Chase, "Diary," June 1830, DLC-Chase; to Sparhawk, 12 June 1830, OCHP-Chase.

11. S. P. Chase, "Diary," Aug. 1830, DLC-Chase.

12. Ibid., 1, 5, 30 Sept. 1830, DLC-Chase; S. P. Chase to Charles D. Cleveland, 2 June 1830, DLC-Chase. Chase continued to be pinched for funds during the winter and spring of 1830–31. S. P. Chase to Hamilton Smith, 4 April 1831, InU-Li-Smith.

13. S. P. Chase "Diary," 30 Sept. 1830, DLC-Chase.

14. S. P. Chase to Sparhawk, 12 June 1830, OCHi-Chase.

15. Warden, *Chase,* I: 198, 199.

16. Ibid., 201–4.

17. *Edinburgh Review* 33 (Jan. 1820): 109–31; 41 (Jan. 1825): 508–10; 42 (April 1828): 206–23, 241–55; 45 (Dec. 1828): 51; (July 1830): 583–84.

18. See especially S. P. Chase, "Life and Character of Henry Brougham," *North American Review* 33 (1 July 1831): 220–47; S. P. Chase, "Diary," 2 March 1831, DLC-Chase.

19. S. P. Chase, "Diary," 7 Dec. 1831, DLC-Chase.

20. Ibid., 29 April, and July 1831, DLC-Chase.

21. S. P. Chase to Charles D. Cleveland, 4 Jan. 1831, PHi-Chase; Prospectus in Cincinnati *American,* 28 Oct. 1831.

22. Thomas Swann to S. P. Chase, 23 April 1832; William Wirt to Chase, 16 May 1832; Alexander Everett to Chase, 9 May 1832, PHi-Chase. Chase to Webster, 10 May 1832, NNC; S. P. Chase to George Ralston, 17 Aug. 1832, PHi-Chase.

23. S. P. Chase to Joseph A. Denison, Jr., 15 Nov. 1831, DLC-Chase; to Hamilton Smith, 5 Aug., 10 Nov. 1831, InU-Li-Smith.

24. Abigail Colby to Chase, 2 Jan. 1831, 10, 21 April 1832, PHi-Chase.

25. Ibid., 10, 21 April 1832, PHi-Chase.

26. Ibid., 24 Oct. 1831, 8 Feb. 1832; William F. Chase to Chase, 3 June, 7 Aug. 1832, PHi-Chase.

27. Abigail Colby to Chase, 10, 21 April 1832, PHi-Chase. William F. Chase to Chase, 7 May 1832; S. P. Chase to E. Parker, 25 June 1832; "Diary," 22, 23 June 1832, DLC-Chase.

28. *Cincinnati City Directory* (Cincinnati, 1834), 38.

29. S. P. Chase, "Diary," 2 Aug. 1833, DLC-Chase.

30. E. W. Mitchell, "Cholera in Cincinnati," *Ohio State Archaeological and Historical Quarterly* (Oct.–Dec. 1942): 51.

31. S. P. Chase to Hamilton Smith, 14 Nov. 1832, InU-Li-Smith.

32. S. P. Chase "Diary," 21 Jan. 1833, DLC-Chase; S. P. Chase, "Diary," 18 Jan. 1833, DLC-Chase.

33. S. P. Chase, "Diary," July 1831.

34. Ibid.

35. Albert Bushnell Hart, *Salmon P. Chase* (rpt., New York, 1980), 46, 47.

36. Schuckers, *Chase*, 34.

37. S. P. Chase, "Diary," undated, 1835, 18 Dec. 1832; 21 Jan. 1833, DLC-Chase.

38. James Kent to Chase, 20 Dec. 1833; Joseph Story to Chase, 1 March 1834, PHi-Chase.

39. S. P. Chase to Smith, 9 May, 10 Nov. 1831, InU-Li-Smith.

Chapter 4. Upward Bound

1. King was a son of Rufus King, an influential delegate to the committee that framed the federal Constitution, formerly a senator from both Massachusetts and New York, and one of the framers of the Northwest Ordinance. Heather Pentland, "Sarah Worthington, King Peter and the Cincinnati Ladies Academy of Fine Arts," *Cincinnati Historical Bulletin* 39 (Spring 1981): 9; S. P. Chase, "Diary," 10 April 1832, DLC-Chase.

2. S. P. Chase, "Diary," 1 Nov. 1833, DLC-Chase.

3. Ibid., April 1830.

4. S. P. Chase to Hamilton Smith, 3 March 1828, InU-Li-Smith.

5. Ibid.

6. Frances M. Trollope, *Domestic Manners of the Americans* (rpt. London, 1927), 126, 127.

7. S. P. Chase, "Diary," 19 Oct. 1830, 1 March 1831, DLC-Chase.

8. Warden says "that everybody who knew him well supposed the sexual feeling to be very strong in him." Warden, *Chase*, I: 140.

9. S. P. Chase to Smith, 10 Nov. 1831, InU-Li-Smith.

10. S. P. Chase, "Diary," 30 Sept. 1830, 21 Jan., 5 May 1833, DLC-Chase.

11. Warden, *Chase*, I: 238–41.

12. Ibid., 238; S. P. Chase, "Diary," 3, 7, May 1833, DLC-Chase.

13. Warden, *Chase*, I: 240; S. P. Chase, "Diary," 8 Feb. 1834, DLC-Chase.

14. S. P. Chase, "Diary," undated, 1835, DLC-Chase.

15. "Chase Family Memoranda," DLC-Chase; Schuckers, *Chase*, 3; Warden, *Chase* I: 241.

16. S. P. Chase to Helen Chase, 24 April 1836, PHi-Chase.

17. S. P. Chase, "Diary," 15 Nov. 1835, DLC-Chase.

18. Ibid., 18, 19 Nov. 1835.

19. Ibid., 20, 21 Nov. 1835.

20. Ibid., 24, 26, Nov., 27 Nov.–1 Dec., 25 Dec. 1835.

21. Ibid. Chase reconstructed in great detail Kitty's condition and the treatments prescribed. But the editors of the Chase Papers have been unable to find the manuscript. Thus the account is rendered in Warden, *Chase*, I: 259–63.

22. Ibid.; S. P. Chase, "Diary," 26, 28, 29 Dec. 1835, DLC-Chase.

23. Ibid., 17, 18 Jan. 1836.

24. S. P. Chase to Helen Chase, 4 April 1836, PHi-Chase.

25. William F. Chase to S. P. Chase, 20 April 1836; S. P. Chase to Edward I. Chase, 25 March, 27 April 1835; to William F. Chase, 6, 15 June, 30 Sept. 1835, DLC-Chase.

26. S. P. Chase to William F. Chase, 12 Sept. 1836; Samuel Wiggins to S. P. Chase, 17 Oct. 1836; G. S. Hubbard to S. P. Chase, 30 Nov. 1836, DLC-Chase.

27. James Denison to Chase, 2, 27 April 1838, DLC-Chase.

28. S. P. Chase, "Diary" 9 Jan. 1836, DLC-Chase.

29. "McLean Circular," 10 Aug. 1835. Chase wrote Samuel Vinton, a prominent lawyer and an anti-Jackson congressman from southeastern Ohio, "I believe that Judge McLean is the choice of the reflecting men of our party in this quarter": S. P. Chase to Vinton, 8 Feb. 1835, DLC-Chase.

30. Hart, *Chase*, 49.

31. *Cincinnati Whig*, 21 Dec. 1835; Edward Mansfield et al. to S. P. Chase, 26 Nov. 1834, PHi-Chase; Cincinnati *Gazette*, 19 Dec. 1834, p. 49; Paul Finkelman, *An Imperfect Union, Slavery Federalism, and Comity* (Chapel Hill, N.C., 1981), 160.

32. *Cincinnati Whig*, 21 Dec. 1835; *Cincinnati Republican*, 16 June 1836.

33. William Birney, *James G. Birney and His Times* (New York, 1890), 213–17; *Cincinnati Republican*, 22 Jan. 1836; Cincinnati *Gazette*, 23 Jan. 1836.

34. Birney, *Birney*, 240.

35. Ibid., 241.

36. James G. Birney to Lewis Tappan in Dwight L. Dumond, ed., *Letters of James Gillespie Birney*, 2 vols. (Washington, D.C. 1938), I: 245.

37. *Cincinnati Whig*, 25 July 1836; Betty Fladeland, *James Gillespie Birney: Slaveholder to Abolitionist* (Ithaca, N.Y., 1955), 138, 139.

38. *The Philanthropist*, 26 July 1836; Fladeland, *Birney*, 136.

39. Cincinnati *Gazette*, 1 Aug. 1836; Birney, *Birney*, 243–47; S. P. Chase to My Dear Sir, 10 July 1853, DLC-Chase.

40. S. P. Chase to John P. Bigelow, 23 Sept. 1854, MHH-Bigelow; S. P. Chase, "Autobiographical Sketch," DLC-Chase.

41. S. P. Chase to C. D. Cleveland, 17 Feb. 1837, PHi-Chase; S. P. Chase, "Autobiographical Sketch," 10 July 1853, DLC-Chase; Cincinnati *Gazette*, 4 Aug. 1836.

42. Cincinnati *Gazette*, 4 Aug 1836.

43. Hart, *Chase*, 49; S. P. Chase, "Autobiographical Fragment," DLC-Chase; Fladeland, *Birney*, 138, 139.

44. Hart, *Chase*, 23.

45. Cincinnati *City Directory, 1836*, 37; Helen Chase to S. P. Chase, 20, 21 Dec. 1837, PHi-Chase.

46. S. P. Chase to Trowbridge, 16 March 1864, OCHP-Chase.

47. Ibid.

48. S. P. Chase to John P. Bigelow, 23 Sept. 1854, MHH-Bigelow.

49. Fladeland, *Birney*, 149–51.

50. Ibid.; James G. Birney to Lewis Tappan, 18 April 1837, DLC-Tappan; Birney, *Birney*, 261–63. Cincinnati *Philanthropist*, 17, 24, 31 March 1837.

51. S. P. Chase to Trowbridge, 16 March 1864, OCHP-Chase.

52. Chase, "Speech of Salmon P. Chase in the Case of the Colored Woman, Matilda" (Cincinnati, 1837), 2, 13, OCHP-Chase.

53. Ibid.

54. Finkelman, *Imperfect Union*, 112–14, has a succinct and lucid discussion of Shaw's opinion.

55. Chase, "Matilda," 2.

56. William Wiecek, Jr., "Somerset, Lord Mansfield and the Legitimacy of Slavery in the Anglo-American World," *Univ. of Chicago Law Review* 42 (Fall 1974): 86-125, 146; Wiecek, *The Sources of Anti-slavery Constitutionalism in America, 1760–1848* (Ithaca, N.Y., 1977), 191.

57. Cincinnati *Gazette*, 13 March 1836.

58. Chase, "Matilda," passim.

59. Wiecek, *Anti-slavery Constitutionalism*, 192, 193.

60. S. P. Chase, Memorandum on "Case of the Colored Woman, Matilda," DLC-Chase; see also Finkelman, *Imperfect Union*, 161.

61. Chase Memorandum, "Case of the Colored Woman Matilda."

62. Birney, *Birney*, 264.

Chapter 5. A Distant Shore

1. The Ohio Anti-slavery Society provided funds for this venture which the Quaker printer Achilles Pugh published. S. P. Chase, "Matilda."

2. Birney, *Birney*, 264; Blue, *Chase*, 32, 33.

3. S. P. Chase to John P. Bigelow, 23 Sept. 1854, MH-H-Bigelow.

4. See S. P. Chase, Memorandum on "Case of the Colored Woman, Matilda," DLC-Chase.

5. Birney, *Birney*, 265.

6. S. P. Chase, "James A. Birney v. the State of Ohio, Report,"in Charles Hammond, *Cases Decided in the Supreme Court of Ohio in Banc at December Terms, 1837, 1838, Ohio Reports* (Cincinnati, 1872), 8: 230–39; S. P. Chase, "Memorandum," DLC-Chase.

7. S. P. Chase to John T. Trowbridge, 10 March 1864, DLC-Chase; Hammond, *Ohio Reports*, 238, 239.

8. S. P. Chase to Bigelow, 23 Sept. 1859, MH-H-Bigelow.

9. S. P. Chase, "Diary," 24 Aug. 1837, DLC-Chase; Marcellus, "Review of the Committee on the Judiciary," Cincinnati *Gazette*, Feb. 1838; clipping, DLC-Chase.

10. Hart, *Chase*, 88.

11. S. P. Chase to Trowbridge, 18 March 1864, OCHi-Chase.

12. Ibid., 31 Jan. 1864.

13. Ibid., 27 Jan. 1864.

14. S. P. Chase, "Diary," 1 July 1840, DLC-Chase.

15. Cincinnati *Gazette*, 6, 8 April 1840; S. P. Chase to Charles D. Cleveland, 29 Aug. 1840, PHi-Chase.

16. See for example, S. P. Chase, "Diary," 1 July, 1840, DLC-Chase.

17. *History of the Cincinnati City Council 1802–1902* (Cincinnati, 1902), 17.

18. S. P. Chase, "Diary," 13 May 1840, DLC-Chase.

19. Ibid., 13 March 1841.

20. Cincinnati *Gazette,* 19 March, 7, 13 April 1841.

21. S. P. Chase, "Diary," 29 May 1840, DLC-Chase.

22. Ibid.

23. Ibid., 21 May 1840.

24. S. P. Chase, "Diary," 1 July 1840, DLC-Chase.

25. Stanley Harrold, *Gamaliel Bailey and Anti-slavery Union* (Kent, Ohio), 34, 35.

26. S. P. Chase, "Memorandum," DLC-Chase.

27. S. P. Chase to Harrison, 13 Feb. 1841, DLC-Chase.

28. Harrold, *Bailey,* 415.

29. Fladeland, *Birney,* 155, 161, 162.

30. *Philanthropist,* 4 Feb. 1840; Dumond, ed., *Birney Letters,* I: 524.

31. Blue, *Chase,* 44.

32. See, for instance his argument in the Matilda case, S. P. Chase, "Matilda," 17–21, DLC-Chase.

33. Warden, *Chase,* I: 329; Cincinnati *Gazette,* 21 May 1841.

34. *Philanthropist,* 16, 30 June 1841.

35. Cincinnati *Gazette,* 1 June 1841.

36. Ibid., 21 May 1841; *Philanthropist,* 20, 27 May, 16, 30 June 1841; Finkelman, *Imperfect Union,* 166–67.

37. S. P. Chase to Alvan Stewart, 22 May 1841, NHi-Chase. My italics.

38. *Philanthropist,* 16, 30 June 1841.

39. Harrold, *Bailey,* 42; Leonard L. Richards, *Gentleman of Property and Standing, Anti-Abolition Mobs in Jacksonian America* (New York, 1970), 41.

40. Flamen Ball to S. P. Chase, 4 Sept. 1841, DLC-Chase; Cincinnati *Philanthropist,* 8 Sept. 1841; Richards, *Gentlemen of Property and Standing,* 126–28; Harrold, *Bailey,* 42.

41. For a further account of the riot see Richards, *Gentlemen of Property and Standing,* 126–29. Ball wrote that many were killed or wounded but the fullest report in the Cincinnati *Enquirer,* 9 Sept. 1841, does not list any. Flamen Ball to S. P. Chase, 4 Sept. 1981, PHi-Chase; Harrold, *Bailey,* 42. For a brief summary of the Black Laws see Richard H. Sewell, *Ballots for Freedom* (New York, 1976), 180. Leon Litwack, *North of Slavery: The Negro in the Free States* (Chicago, 1961), 74.

42. Harrold, *Bailey,* 43.

43. S. P. Chase to Cleveland, 22 Oct. 1841, PHi-Chase.

44. *Philanthropist,* 16 Dec. 1841.

45. Ibid.

46. S. P. Chase to Cleveland, 22 Oct. 1841, PHi-Chase.

47. Earl Wittke, ed., *A History of the State of Ohio,* 6 vols. (rpt. Columbus, Ohio, 1968), vol. III: Francis P. Weisenburger, *The Passing of the Frontier 1825–50* (Columbus, Ohio, 1941), 77.

48. S. P. Chase to Cleveland, 22 Oct. 1841, PHi-Chase.

49. *Philanthropist,* 22 Dec. 1841. Chase wrote the call for the Columbus convention.

50. Weisenburger, *Passing of the Frontier,* 99, 110; *Philanthropist,* 5 Jan. 1842.

51. S. P. Chase to Joshua Giddings, 30 Dec. 1841, OCHi-Giddings.

52. *History of Trumbull and Mahoning Counties,* 2 vols. (Cleveland, Ohio, 1882), I: 309, 310.

53. *Philanthropist,* "Proceedings and Resolutions of the Ohio Liberty Convention," 29 Dec. 1841.

54. Ibid.

55. Ibid., 25 May 1842.

56. S. P. Chase to Lewis Tappan, 15 Sept. 1842; Cassius Clay to S. P. Chase, 21 Dec. 1842, DLC-Chase; S. P. Chase to Thaddeus Stevens, 8 April 1842, DLC-Stevens.

57. John Duffey to Chase, 20 July, 24 Aug. 1842, DLC-Chase.

58. Joshua Gidding to Chase, 4 Jan. 1842, PHi-Chase.

59. S. P. Chase to Lewis Tappan, 24 Sept. 1842, DLC-Chase. Chase's choices were William H. Seward or John Quincy Adams.

60. S. P. Chase to Stevens, 8 April 1842, DLC-Stevens; James A. Birney to S. P. Chase, 2 Feb. 1842, MiU-C-Birney.

61. S. P. Chase to Giddings, 15 Feb. 1842, DLC-Giddings-Julian; Joshua Giddings to Chase, 19 Feb. 1842, PHi-Chase.

62. S. P. Chase to Giddings, 15 Feb. 1842, PHi-Chase.

63. S. P. Chase to Smith, 15 May 1842, NSyU-Smith.

64. S. P. Chase to Tappan, 26 May 1842, DLC-Chase.

Chapter 6. To Recognize the Distinctions

1. Helen Chase to Chase, 20, 21 Dec. 1837; John P. Garniss to Chase, 7 July 1834, PHi-Chase.

2. Mary D. Leonard to Chase, 8 Feb. 1838, DLC-Chase.

3. Samuel Wiggins et al. to Chase, "Deed of Trust of E. C. Smith for Eliza Ann Smith," DLC-Chase; S. P. Chase to Charles P. Cleveland, 3 Feb. 1845, PHi-Chase.

4. John P. Garniss to S. P. Chase, 5 Sept. 1839, PHi-Chase.

5. S. P. Chase to Charles D. Cleveland, 7 Feb. 1840, DLC-Chase.

6. S. P. Chase to William Henry Harrison, 13 Feb. 1841, DLC-Chase.

7. S. P. Chase, "Diary," 1 Jan. 1841; Alexander R. Chase to S. P. Chase, 10 Sept. 1840, DLC-Chase.

8. S. P. Chase to William F. Chase, 12 Sept. 1836; G. S. Hubbard to S. P. Chase, 30 Nov. 1836, DLC-Chase.

9. Lewis F. Thomas to S. P. Chase, 17 Jan. 1840; Rev. William G. Elliot to S. P. Chase, 12 Feb. 1840, DLC-Chase.

10. S. P. Chase to William Chase, 11 April, 13 May 1849; "Diary," 10 Dec. 1852, 1, 23 March 1847, DLC-Chase.

11. Ibid., 26 July 1840.

12. Ibid., 12 Aug. 1840. "Second daughter of S. P. Chase and E. A. C. born August 13, 1840." Chase was referring to Dr. John Eberle, *Treatise on the Disease and Physical Education of Children* (Cincinnati, 1833).

13. S. P. Chase, "Diary," 23 May 1841; "Family Memoranda." No date. DLC-Chase.

14. Dumond, ed., *Birney Letters,* II: 690n; John Duffy to Chase, 20 July, 24 Aug. 1842, DLC-Chase.

15. Dumond, ed., *Birney Letters,* II: 690, 691n.

16. Charles Satterly to Chase, 18 May 1841, PHi-Chase.

17. Noah Worcester to Chase, 5 Sept. 1842, DLC-Chase.

18. S. P. Chase, "Diary," 16, 20, 22, 23, 25, 26 June 1843.

19. Ibid., 30 April, 3 July 1843, 25 April 1848.

20. Ibid., 2 July 1843.

21. S. P. Chase, "Family Memorandum," 24 July 1844; Eliza Ann Smith Chase to S. P. Chase, 22 June 1844; S. P. Chase to William P. Matlin, 2 July 1844, DLC-Chase.

22. Edward Curtis Smith to Chase, 31 Dec. 1844, DLC-Chase.

23. S. P. Chase to Cleveland, 3 Feb. 1845, PHi-Chase.

24. S. P. Chase to Flamen Ball, 14 July 1845, DLC-Chase; to Gerrit Smith, 31 July 1845, NSyU-Smith.

25. S. P. Chase to Cleveland, 10 Oct. 1845, DLC-Chase.

26. "Eliza Ann Smith, born Nov. 12, 1821; married S. P. Chase Sept. 26, 1839; died Mon. 2³/₄ p.m. Sept. 29, 1845; 23 y. 10 m. 17 d." S. P. Chase, "Family Memorandum," no date, DLC-Chase.

27. S. P. Chase, "Diary," 2 Nov. 1845, DLC-Chase.

28. S. P. Chase, "List of Parties to whom Van Zandt Argument Sent, 1847," DLC-Chase.

29. "Transcript," *Circuit Court of the United States for the District of Ohio, July Term, 1842,* Case files John Van Zandt, DNA-RG267AC.

30. Steven Middleton, "Ohio and the Anti-slavery Activity of Attorney Salmon Portland Chase, 1830–1849" (Ph.D. diss., Miami University, 1987), 127.

31. S. P. Chase to Trowbridge, 18 March 1864, DLC-Chase.

32. S. P. Chase, "An Argument for the Defendant Submitted to the Supreme Court of the United States at the December Term, 1846, in the Case of *Wharton Jones v. John Van Zandt*" (Cincinnati, 1847), 6, 7.

33. Probably, given his past activities, Van Zandt knew of the arrangement beforehand, but this was never proved.

34. "Circuit Court of the United States for the District of Ohio, Cincinnati, July term, 1843," in Timothy Walker, ed., *Western Law Journal* I, no. 1 (1844): 80.

35. The Warren County prosecutor indicted Hargrave and Hefferman for kidnapping but they were never brought to trial. Others who helped them were also indicted, tried, and acquitted. Paul A. Freund, ed., *History of the Supreme Court of the United States,* 11 vols. (New York, 1978), vol. V: *The Taney Period,* Carl B. Swisher, ed., (New York, 1974), 548, 549.

36. William E. Barringer, "The Politics of Abolition," *Cincinnati Historical Society Bulletin* 24 (Summer 1971): 93.

37. Schuckers, *Chase,* 52–54.

38. *Prigg v. Pennsylvania,* 16 Peters, 669.

39. Chase, "An Argument for the Defendant in the Case of *Jones v. Van Zandt,* " 4–9.

40. *Jones v. Van Zandt,* 13 Federal Case 1040, Case no. 7501 (1843).

41. S. P. Chase, "An Argument for the Defendant . . . ," 85.

42. Ibid., 64–68.

43. Ibid., 90.

44. Ibid., 84.

45. Ibid., 99.

46. Ibid., 84.

47. Ibid., 83.

48. Francis P. Weisenburger, *The Life of John McLean, a Politician on the Supreme Court* (Columbus, 1937), 226, 227.

49. Finkelmen, *Imperfect Union,* 246; Swisher, *Taney Period,* 548–52.

50. Stevens never answered Chase's query. S. P. Chase to Stevens, 8 April 1842, DLC-Stevens; William H. Seward to Chase, 22 Oct. 1843, PHi-Chase.

51. S. P. Chase to Joshua Giddings, 21 Jan. 1842, DLC-Giddings-Julian; to Lewis Tappan, 15, 24 Sept. 1842, DLC-Chase.

52. S. P. Chase to Lewis Tappan, 4 Feb. 1844, DLC-Chase.

53. "Every year," said Seward, "enables us to assume higher ground and ripens the

sentiments of moral justice and the opinions of national policy to be invoked." William H. Seward to Chase, 26 Dec. 1846, DLC-Chase.

54. Ibid., 10, 12 Jan. 1845.

55. Swisher, *Taney Period,* 52.

56. Ibid.

57. John McLean to S. P. Chase, 19 Oct. 1840, PHi-Chase.

58. Ibid. A day earlier, Washington Hunt had written Chase that Morehead would not agree to a continuance and that printed briefs must be submitted by February 1. He added that McLean wanted Chase to present an oral argument before the court. Washington Hunt to S. P. Chase, 18 Dec. 1846, DLC-Chase.

59. S. P. Chase, "An Argument for the Defendant . . . ," 93.

60. The text of Seward's argument may be found in the Albany *Evening Journal,* 6 March 1847.

61. William H. Seward to Chase, 28 May, 4 Aug. 1845, Jan. 22, 1846, DLC-Chase.

62. Washington Hunt to Chase, 18 March 1846; Cassius M. Clay to S. P. Chase, 28 Jan. 1845, 20 March 1846; Joshua Giddings to Chase, 3 Aug. 1846, PHi-Chase.

63. James Riley to Chase, 14 Feb. 1845, MHi-Washburn.

64. Leo Alilunas, "Fugitive Slave Cases in Ohio Prior to 1850," *Ohio Archaeological and Historical Quarterly* 49 (Jan.–March, 1940): 177–78.

65. Stanley Matthews to Chase, 11, 24 Jan. 1840, DLC-Chase.

66. Ibid.; Finkelman, *Imperfect Union,* 168.

67. Ibid., 168, 169.

68. Ibid., 109–72.

69. Ibid.

70. "Address and Reply on the Presentation of a Testimonial by the Colored People of Cincinnati to Salmon P. Chase" (Cincinnati, 1845).

71. Schuckers, *Chase,* 78, 79.

72. Dumond, ed., *Birney Letters,* I: 419, 419n.

73. When his new partner Flamen Ball at Tappan's request said that he would furnish the rich New Yorker with their estimate of the credit risk of Cincinnati businessmen, Chase angrily reprimanded him for what he considered unethical behaviour. He immediately wrote Tappan a diplomatic note that he had doubts "respecting the propriety of furnishing such information. We may be misled—and on the other hand we may be instrumental in doing great injustice. For it cannot be supposed that our estimates formed so rapidly and without that particular inquiry which we should make." Lewis Tappan to Chase and Ball, 3 March 1842; S. P. Chase to Tappan, 10 March 1842, DLC-Chase.

Chapter 7. Climbing the Slippery Pole

1. S. P. Chase, "Diary," 24, Nov. 1845, DLC-Chase.

2. Ibid.

3. S. P. Chase, "Diary," 24 Nov. 1845, DLC-Chase.

4. Ibid., 24 Nov., 1 March 1846.

5. S. P. Chase, "Diary," 24, 25, 26, Nov., 2, 6 Dec. 1845, DLC-Chase.

6. S. P. Chase to Giddings, 9 Feb. 1843, DLC-Giddings-Julian.

7. S. P. Chase, "Address of the Southern and Western Liberty Convention," 8; Charles D. Cleveland, ed., *Antislavery Addresses of 1844 and 1845* (Philadelphia, 1867), 102–4.

8. Ibid.; see also S. P. Chase to Dear Sir, 15 Aug. 1846, DLC-Chase; to Giddings, 20 Oct. 1846, DLC-Giddings-Julian.

9. S. P. Chase, "The Address of the Southern and Western Liberty Convention" (Cincinnati, 1845), 8; William Jay to Chase, 24 March 1845, PHi-Chase; S. P. Chase to Giddings, 15 Aug. 1846, DLC-Giddings-Julian.

10. Harrold, *Bailey*, 72, 73.

11. Joshua Leavitt to Birney, 14 Feb. 1842, in Dumond, ed., *Birney Letters*, II: 673.

12. Ibid., 713, 714.

13. Joshua Leavitt to Chase, 31 Dec. 1844, PHi-Chase.

14. In Cincinnati, the younger Birney complained: "We have Chase and others who belong to the temporizing, bargain and sale class of politicians and are frequently hazarding our cause by their recommendation of petty demagogical tricks to gain a largely increased floating vote." Dumond, ed., *Birney Letters*, II: 887.

15. Gerrit Smith, "Circular Letter," 7 May 1845, DLC-Chase.

16. Dumond, ed., *Birney Letters*, II: 645–59; S. P. Chase to Lewis Tappan, 3 April 1844, DLC-Chase; Kirk H. Porter and Donald B. Johnson, comps., *National Conventions and Platforms* (Urbana, Ill., 1956), "Election of 1844," 55.

17. Henry B. Stanton to Chase, 6 Feb. 1844; Chase agreed wholeheartedly with Russell Errett, the Pittsburgh editor, who wrote, "Disunionists like Abby Kelley Foster and her new husband, Steven," had done much harm especially in the Western Reserve where they "labored very assiduously." Errett warned that "unless you take some measure to win back those whom they have estranged, your new recruits will not make up for the old one's lost." He added that if "the men of the west . . . do not consent and combine their opposition, the eastern men in the National Convention will ride them down as they did in Buffalo in 1843"; Russell Errett to Chase, 9 May 1846, DLC-Chase.

18. S. P. Chase, "Biographical Memoranda 1823–1848" DLC-Chase; S. P. Chase, "Address of the Southern and Western Liberty Convention," 9.

19. William H. Seward to Chase, 4 Aug. 1845, PHi-Chase.

20. Woolsey Welles to Chase, 12 Nov. 1844, DLC-Chase.

21. John McLean to Chase, 10 Jan. 1845; Cassius Clay to Chase, 28 Jan. 1845, PHi-Chase; see also Millard Fillmore to Chase, 8 April 1844, DLC-Chase; S. P. Chase, Gamaliel Bailey, Samuel Lewis, et al. to Birney, 30 March 1844, MiU-C-Birney.

22. George W. Ells to Chase, 15 Feb. 1844, DLC-Chase.

23. S. P. Chase to Brinkerhoff, 26 Feb. 1845, PHi-Chase; John G. Whittier to Hale, 24 Jan. 1845, in John B. Pickard, ed., *The Letters of John Greenleaf Whittier*, 3 vols. (Cambridge, Mass. 1975), I: 654, 655.

24. Dumond, ed., *Birney Letters*, II: 1026; Cincinnati *Herald and Philanthropist*, 25 June 1845.

25. Richard H. Sewell, *Ballots for Freedom* (New York, 1976), 127–29.

26. S. P. Chase to Hale, 30 June 1846, NhHi-Hale.

27. Dumond, ed., *Birney Letters*, II: 1025, 1026.

28. Ibid.

29. Cassius M. Clay to Chase, 20 March 1846. PHi-Chase.

30. John G. Whittier to Joseph Sturge, 28 Nov. 1846; to John Quincy Adams, 19 Dec. 1846; to Gamaliel Bailey, Dec. 1846, in Pickard, *Letters of Whittier*, II: 44, 46, 47.

31. Lewis Tappan to Chase, 9 March 1846, PHi-Chase.

32. Harrold, *Bailey*, 81, 82.

33. Hugh Davis, *Joshua Leavitt, Evangelical Abolitionist* (Baton Rouge, 1990), 230, 237; Lewis Tappan to Chase, 23 June 1847, PHi-Chase.

34. See Cincinnati *Emancipator*, 26 March 1846; Joshua Leavitt to Chase, 24 Nov. 1846, PHi-Chase.

35. Harrold, *Bailey*, 80, 84.

36. Ibid., 85–88.

37. For a full discussion of the proviso see the venerable but still valuable biography of Wilmot by Charles B. Going, *David Wilmot Freesoiler* (rpt., Gloucester, Mass., 1966), 106–41. See also Howard K. Beale and Alan Brownsword, eds., *Gideon Welles Diary*, 3 vols. (New York, 1960), II: 386.

38. John Niven, *Martin Van Buren, The Romantic Age of American Politics* (New York, 1983), 573, 574.

39. S. P. Chase to Giddings, 15 Aug. 1846, DLC-Chase.

40. Ibid., 23 Sept. 1846, DLC-Chase.

41. Joshua Giddings to Chase, 20 Oct. 1846, DLC-Chase.

42. Flamen Ball to Chase, 19 July 1845, DLC-Chase.

43. Ithamar Chase Whipple to Chase, 9, 10 July 1845; to Chase, 10 July 1846, DLC-Chase.

44. S. P. Chase, "Diary," 1 March 1847, DLC-Chase.

45. Ibid., 23 March 1847.

46. Ibid., 30 March 1847.

47. Ibid., 4 April 1847.

48. Ibid., 23 April 1847.

49. Ibid., 7 April 1847.

50. Ibid., 2 Dec. 1845, 30 March 1847.

Chapter 8. "Free Soil, Free Labor and Free Men"

1. S. P. Chase, "Autobiographical Memoranda," 1823–48, DLC-Chase.

2. Cassius Clay to Chase, 20 June, 27 Dec. 1847, PHi-Chase; S. P. Chase to Gerrit Smith, 1 Sept. 1846, NSyU-Smith; Smith to Sumner, 26 Nov. 1846, MH-H-Sumner.

3. Dumond, ed., *Birney Letters*, I: 476, 522.

4. S. P. Chase to Smith, 1 Sept. 1846, NSyU-Smith; Geritt Smith to Sumner, 26 Nov. 1846, MH-H-Sumner.

5. S. P. Chase to Gerrit Smith, 1 Sept. 1846, NSyU-Smith.

6. S. P. Chase to Giddings, 20 Oct. 1846, DLC-Chase.

7. Ibid., 15 Aug. 1846, DLC-Chase; Joshua Giddings to Chase, 3 Aug. 1846, PHi-Chase.

8. See Charles Francis Adams to Chase, 4 March 1847, PHi-Chase; Charles Sumner to Chase, 12 March 1847; S. P. Chase to Tappan, 18 March 1847, DLC-Chase.

9. My parentheses; S. P. Chase to Sumner, 22 Sept. 1847, MH-H-Sumner.

10. S. P. Chase to Hunt, 15 Feb. 1847, PHi-Chase.

11. S. P. Chase to Sumner, 26 Nov. 1846, MH-H-Sumner; Charles Sumner to Chase, 12 Dec. 1846, DLC-Chase.

12. William H. Seward to Chase, 8 Sept. 1846, 24 March 1847, DLC-Chase. These included funds he collected or were pledged. Clay himself made a cash contribution. S. P. Chase, "Diary," 3 Jan. 1848, DLC-Chase.

13. Harrold, *Bailey*, 111, 146.

14. Washington Hunt to Weed, 26 Dec. 1847, NRU-Seward.

15. S. P. Chase to Joshua Leavitt, 16 June 1847, DLC-Chase.

16. S. P. Chase to Lewis Tappan, 16 Sept. 1847, CSmH-Barney.

17. S. P. Chase to Hale, 15 June 1848, NhHi-Hale.

18. Henry B. Stanton to Chase, 6 Aug. 1847, DLC-Chase; Stanton to Chase, 17 July 1847, PHi-Chase; *National Era*, 9 Sept. 1847.

19. S. P. Chase to Hale, 12 May 1847, NhHi-Hale.

20. S. P. Chase to Edward Wade, 23 June 1847, DLC-Chase.

21. Gamaliel Bailey to Chase, 14 Sept. 1847, PHi-Chase; Joshua Leavitt to Chase, 27 Sept. 1847, PHi-Chase.

22. S. P. Chase to Belle Chase, 15, 17 Oct. 1847, DLC-Chase.

23. Ibid.

24. S. P. Chase to Sumner, 2 Dec. 1847, MH-H-Sumner.

25. Gerrit Smith to Chase, 1 Nov. 1847, OCHi-Chase.

26. Doubtless he saw Preston King, one of the leading Barnburners with whom he had established contact earlier. S. P. Chase to King, 16 Aug. 1847, PHi-Chase.

27. Hart, *Chase*, 80.

28. S. P. Chase to Belle, 16 Nov. 1847, DLC-Chase.

29. Samuel Medary to Van Buren, 27 Dec. 1847, 25 May 1848, DLC-Van Buren.

30. S. P. Chase to Stanton, 9 Jan. 1848, DLC-Stanton; to Stanton, 16 Feb. 1848, PHi-Chase.

31. S. P. Chase to Belle, 7 Jan. 1848, DLC-Chase.

32. S. P. Chase to Belle, 23 Aug. 1847, DLC-Chase; Edwin M. Stanton to Chase, 2 Dec. 1847, PHi-Chase.

33. Clement L. Vallandigham to Stanton, 26 June 1848, DLC-Stanton.

34. S. P. Chase to Stanton, 9 Jan. 1848, DLC-Stanton.

35. Jacob Brinkerhoff to Chase, 11 Nov. 1847, PHi-Chase; but his commitment was a shaky one. See ibid., 2 Feb. 1848.

36. John McLean to Chase, 22 Dec. 1847, PHi-Chase.

37. S. P. Chase to Sumner, 19 Feb. 1848, MH-H-Sumner.

38. Ibid.

39. Charles Sumner to Chase, 7 Feb. 1848, DLC-Chase.

40. Benjamin Tappan to Chase, 7 April 1848, PHi-Chase.

41. S. P. Chase to Sumner, 25 March 1848, MH-H-Sumner.

42. Joshua Leavitt to Chase, 21 Feb. 1848, PHi-Chase; S. P. Chase to Giddings, 10, 14 March 1848, OCHi-Giddings.

43. E. S. Hamlin to Chase, 18 March 1848, PHi-Chase.

44. Call for an "Ohio Free Territory Convention," 23 March 1848, to be held in Columbus on June 17. Convention date was changed to the 21st. PHi-Chase.

45. See Leavitt's wariness about an antislavery convention irrespective of parties. Joshua Leavitt to Chase, 7 April 1848, PHi-Chase. "I am willing to do and to sacrifice anything if the result be certain and important," said Brinkerhoff, "but I am not willing to take part in a movement likely to effect nothing." Jacob Brinkerhoff to Chase, 28 March 1848, PHi-Chase; Joseph M. Root to Chase, 5 April 1848, DLC-Chase; Joshua Giddings to Chase, 7 April 1848. PHi-Chase.

46. Niven, *Martin Van Buren*, 580.

47. Ibid.

48. Benjamin Tappan to Chase, 29 May 1848, PHi-Chase; Henry B. Stanton to Chase, 6 June 1848, DLC-Chase.

49. John Van Buren to Chase, 9 June 1848, PHi-Chase.

50. Ibid., 14 June 1848.

51. S. P. Chase to Giddings, 10 March 1848, OCHi-Giddings; Giddings to S. P. Chase to John Van Buren, 19 June 1848, NN-Tilden.

52. See, for instance, S. P. Chase to Hale, 29 April, 15 June 1848, HhHi-Hale.

53. John P. Hale to Chase, 14 June 1848, PHi-Chase.

54. Joshua Leavitt to Chase, 7 July 1848, PHi-Chase.

55. Lewis Tappan to Chase, 14 June 1848, PHi-Chase.

56. The reaction of regular Democrats was best described in a cutting remark of William L. Marcy, New York's leading Hunker: "The Barnburners with little Ben [Butler], Randy John [Van Buren] and stolid C. C. [Churchill C. Cambreleng] at their head seem determined on mischief, they are a pretty set of pot knaves." William L. Marcy to Prosper Wetmore, 10 June 1848, DLC-Marcy.

57. William H. Seward to Weed, 10 June 1848, NRU-Seward.

58. Horace Greeley to Giddings, 20 June 1848, NN-Greeley.

59. S. P. Chase, "Diary," 5 July 1848, DLC-Chase.

60. S. P. Chase, "Scrapbook Clippings," 24 June 1848, DLC-Chase.

61. S. P. Chase to John Van Buren, 19 June 1848, DLC-Chase.

62. Samuel J. Tilden to Chase, July 1848, NN-Tilden; John McLean to Chase, Aug. 1848, PHi-Chase.

63. Article IV, section 3; *Daily National Intelligencer*, 23 Dec. 1847.

64. It is significant that Samuel Lewis was not with them. Lewis had made it plain to Chase that he could not support Van Buren. Joshua Leavitt to Hale, 22 Aug. 1848, NhHi-Hale.

65. S. P. Chase to McLean, 12 Aug. 1848, DLC-McLean.

66. Henry B. Stanton to Hale, 20 Aug. 1848; Joshua Leavitt to Hale, 22 Aug. 1848, NhHi-Hale; S. P. Chase to Trowbridge, 21 March 1864, PHi-Chase.

67. S. P. Chase to My Dear Sir, 1 Dec. 1848, NhD. A meeting of antislavery Whigs, Democrats, and Liberty men had already adopted the slogan except for "Free Men" early in July 1848. But Chase in all likelihood coined the slogan independently and of course added the final two words to it. John G. Whittier to Sumner, 10 July 1848, in Pickard, ed., *Letters of Whittier*, II: 109.

68. Charles Francis Adams, "Diary," 10 Aug. 1848, MHi-Adams.

69. Hugh Davis, *Joshua Leavitt*, 246; Richard Henry Davis, ed., *Richard Henry Davis, Jr.: Speeches in Stirring Times and Letters to a Son* (Boston, 1910), 158; S. P. Chase to James W. Taylor, 15 Aug. 1848, PHi-Chase.

70. Hart, *Chase*, 96–102. A concise but full account of the proceedings and Chase's role is related in a long letter he wrote from Lockport, New York, to one of his law partners, James W. Taylor. See Salmon P. Chase to Taylor, 15 Aug. 1848, PHi-Chase.

71. S. P. Chase to Dear Sir, 29 July 1851, NBuHi.

72. S. P. Chase to Belle, 26 July 1848, DLC-Chase.

73. Ibid., 25 Aug. 1848.

74. *History of Cuyahoga County*, 3 vols. (Columbus, 1929), I: 44.

75. S. P. Chase to Belle, 19, 25 Aug. 1848, DLC-Chase.

76. Ibid.

77. Ibid. 24 Aug. 1848.

78. S. P. Chase to Van Buren, 21 Aug. 1848, DLC-Van Buren; Joshua Leavitt to Chase, 21 Aug. 1848, PHi-Chase.

79. John Van Buren to Chase, 30 Aug. 1848, PHi-Chase.

80. S. P. Chase to Briggs, 12 Sept. 1848, DLC-Chase; S. P. Chase to Van Buren, 30 Sept. 1848, DLC-Van Buren; Amos Jewett to Chase, 9, 16 Oct. 1848; W. Farnwell to Chase, 16 Oct. 1848; Benjamin Welch, Jr., to Chase, 16 Oct. 1848, DLC-Chase.

81. Adams Jewett to Chase, 24 Oct. 1848, DLC-Chase.

82. Hart, *Chase*, 102.

83. S. P. Chase to Gerrit Smith, 1 Sept. 1846, NSyU-Smith; Donn Piatt to Chase, 27 July 1848, PHi-Chase.

Chapter 9. Among the Great

1. S. P. Chase to Belle, 14 Nov. 1848, DLC-Chase.

2. For a good discussion of money, banking, and politics see Weisenburger, *Passing of the Frontier*, chaps. 15 and 16.

3. Samuel Medary to Martin Van Buren, 5 May 1848, DLC-Van Buren.

4. Ibid.; Weisenburger, *Passing of the Frontier*, 184, 409, 424, 462, 465.

5. Edward S. Hamlin to Chase, 18 Jan. 1849, PHi-Chase.

6. Samuel Medary to Chase, 11 Nov. 1850, PHi-Chase.

7. S. P. Chase to Samuel Wood, 15 Feb. 1860, DLC-Chase; Hamlin to Chase, 18 Jan. 1849, PHi-Chase.

8. S. P. Chase to Belle, 24 July 1847, DLC-Chase; John McLean to Chase, 22 Dec. 1847, PHi-Chase.

9. James Brewer Stewart, *Joshua R. Giddings and Tactics of Radical Politics* (Cleveland, 1970), 5; William Dean Howells, *Years of My Youth* (New York, 1916), 120, 121.

10. Weisenburger, *Passing of the Frontier*, 250.

11. Cincinnati *Enquirer*, 26, 27 Oct. 1871.

12. Weisenburger, *Passing of the Frontier*, 204, 266, 470, 471.

13. Reginald C. McGrane, *William Allen, A Study in Western Democracy*, (Columbus, 1925), 130.

14. Ibid., 133, 134.

15. George Hoadly, Jr., to Schuckers, 16 Aug. 1873, DLC-Schuckers.

16. Columbus *Ohio Statesman*, 10–13 Jan. 1848.

17. The opposing candidates were George W. Runyan and Oliver Spencer (Whig) and George E. Pugh and Alexander Spencer (Democrat). Cincinnati *Globe*, 23 Nov. 1848. Albert G. Riddle, "Recollections of the Forty-seventh General Assembly of Ohio, 1847, 1848," in *Magazine of Western History* (Aug. 1887): 342.

18. George Hoadly, Jr., to Schuckers, 16 Aug. 1873, DLC-Schuckers.

19. Eli Nichols to Chase, 25 Oct. 1848; S. P. Chase, "Diary," 22 Nov. 1848, DLC-Chase; S. P. Chase to My Dear Sir, 1 Dec. 1848, Nhd.

20. S. P. Chase, "Diary," 25 Jan. 1849, DLC-Chase.

21. S. P. Chase to Hamlin, 19 Jan. 1849, DLC-Chase.

22. S. P. Chase, "Diary," 3 Jan., 5 July 1848, 25–27 1849; DLC-Chase; Edward S. Hamlin to Chase, 22 Oct. 1848, PHi-Chase; John C. Vaughan to Chase, 7 Dec. 1848, PHi-Chase.

23. E. S. Hamlin to Chase, 22 Nov. 1848, DLC-Chase. Hamlin was not considered a good businessman. Both McLean and Bailey warned Chase that he needed a competent manager for the new paper. John McLean to Chase, 3 Dec. 1848, PHi-Chase.

24. S. P. Chase to Gerrit Smith, 1 Sept. 1846, NSyU-Smith.

25. S. P. Chase, Diary, 22 Nov. 1848, DLC-Chase; Charles Grant Miller, *Donn Piatt, His Work and His Way* (Cincinnati, 1893), 56, 77.

26. E. S. Hamlin to Chase, 22 Nov. 1848, PHi-Chase.

27. Norton S. Townshend to Schuckers, 20 Sept. 1873, DLC-Schuckers.

28. John C. Vaughan to Chase, 7 Dec. 1848, PHi-Chase.

29. S. P. Chase, "Diary," 22 Nov. 1848, DLC-Chase.

30. Eli Nichols to Chase, 15 Dec. 1848, DLC-Chase.

31. Ibid.

32. S. P. Chase to Belle, 18 Dec. 1848, DLC-Chase.

33. Charles Beecher, ed., *Autobiography, Correspondence of Lyman Beecher, D. D.*, 2 vols. (New York, 1868), I: 524–28; S. P. Chase, "Diary," 1, 4 Jan. 1849, DLC-Chase.

34. Howe, *Historical Collections*, I: 616; S. P. Chase to Vaughan, 21 Dec. 1848, NhD.

35. S. P. Chase to Belle, 18, 20 Dec. 1848, DLC-Chase.

36. Ibid.

37. Eugene Roseboom, *The Civil War Era, 1850–1873* (Columbus, 1944), 6, 7.

38. Weisenburger, *Passing of the Frontier*, 46, 51; Roseboom, *Civil War Era*, 6, 7.

39. S. P. Chase to Riddle, 24 Feb. 1849, OCIWHi-Chase.

40. Frederick J. Blue, "The Free Soilers and Problems of Factionalism," *Ohio History* 76 (Winter/Spring 1967): 23.

41. S. P. Chase, "Diary," 2–5, 7 Jan. 1849, DLC-Chase.

42. Ibid., 2-4 Jan. 1849.

43. Ibid., 8 Jan. 1849.

44. Ibid., 10, 24, 25 Jan. 1849.

45. Hamlin warned, however, that Chase be prepared to write "an elaborate defense" for the two Free Soilers who would break the tie. E. S. Hamlin to Chase, 18 Jan. 1849, PHi-Chase.

46. Ibid., 20 Jan. 1849.

47. S. P. Chase to Hamlin, 17 Jan. 1849, DLC-Chase; ibid., 25 Jan. 1849.

48. S. P. Chase to Giddings, 20 Jan. 1849, PHi-Chase.

49. See S. P. Chase to Stanley Matthews, 13, 18, 24, 27, 29 Jan., 27 Feb. 1849, in Annie A. Nunns, ed., "Some Letters of Salmon P. Chase, 1848–1865," *American Historical Review* 34 (1929): 536–48; to Matthews, 19, 20, 23 Jan. 1849, DLC-Chase; A. G. Riddle to Chase, 28 Jan. 1849, PHi-Chase; E. S. Hamlin to Chase, 11 Jan. 1849, DLC-Chase; Chase to Matthews, 24 Jan. 1849, WHi; S. P. Chase to Hamlin, 20 Jan. 1849, DLC-Chase.

50. S. P. Chase to Hamlin, 1 Jan. 1849; *Diary*, 27 Jan. 1849; S. P. Chase to Matthews, 27 Feb. 1849, WHi.

51. S. P. Chase, "Diary," 27 Jan. 1849, DLC-Chase; to Riddle, 27 Jan. 1849, OCIWHi-Riddle.

52. A. G. Riddle to Chase, 28 Jan. 1849, PHi-Chase.

53. S. P. Chase to Matthews, 24 Jan. 1849, WHi-Chase; see also Chase's "notes" on election of U.S. senator, Feb. 1849, PHi-Chase.

54. S. P. Chase to Matthews, 2 Feb. 1849, WHi-Chase.

55. S. P. Chase to Belle, 3 Feb. 1849, DLC-Chase; Chase referred to the American as the "Capitol Hotel" since it was directly across High Street from the Capitol.

56. S. P. Chase to Belle, 3 Feb. 1948, DLC-Chase.

57. Ibid. 7, 11, 12, 13, 15, 19 Feb. 1849.

58. E. S. Hamlin, "Tally," 22 Feb. 1849, PHi-Chase.

59. S. P. Chase to Belle, 20 Feb. 1849, DLC-Chase; E. S. Hamlin to Chase, 23 Feb. 1849, PHi-Chase.

60. Hamlin reminded Chase of his promise that if he were elected and Hamlin continued to edit the paper, he would see to it that Hamlin was appointed president of the Board of Public Works, a post that paid $1500 a year. Chase made good on the appointment, but now that he had his Senate seat his interest in the *Standard* waned. There was an effort to have Giddings purchase an interest in the paper, but when his proposal was deemed too vague, Chase refused

to contribute any additional funds. See S. P. Chase to Hamlin, 27 Feb. 1849; Stanley Matthews to Chase, 1 March 1849, DLC-Chase.

61. S. P. Chase to Riddle, 24 Feb. 1849, OCIWHi-Riddle.

62. Chase took his niece, young Hannah Whipple, with him to Washington. They boarded the boat for Wheeling on the warm, sunny morning of March 1. But it suddenly clouded over and began to rain, which delayed departure. Held up again at Marysville, the boat was eight hours late in reaching Wheeling. S. P. Chase to Belle, 4 March 1849, DLC-Chase.

63. Ibid., 6 March 1849, DLC-Chase.

64. Ibid.,

65. S. P. Chase, "Diary," 6 March 1849; Chase, "Memo on Trip to Washington," 6 March 1849, DLC-Chase.

66. S. P. Chase to Belle, 15 March 1849, DLC-Chase.

67. Ibid.

68. S. P. Chase to Giddings, 6 March 1849, OCHi-Giddings; to Stanley Matthews, 12 March 1849, WHi.

69. See, for instance, S. P. Chase to My Dear Sir, 1 Dec. 1848, NhD; to Riddle, 24 Feb. 1849, OCIWHi-Riddle.

70. A. G. Riddle to Chase, 4 March 1849; Joshua Giddings to Chase, 14 March 1849, PHi-Chase.

71. See, for instance, Henry O'Reilly to Chase, 16 Jan. 1849; S. P. Chase to O'Reilly, 18 June 1849, NHi-Chase; to Belle, 27 June 1849, DLC-Chase.

72. S. P. Chase to Sumner, 14 May 1849, OCHi-Chase. In early July, Chase said that "near nine hundred died last week and the number of deaths this week will probably exceed a thousand." S. Bradburn, *Memorial of George Bradburn* (Boston, 1883), 174.

73. S. P. Chase, "Diary," 1 July 1849, DLC-Chase.

74. S. P. Chase to O'Reilly, 18, 20 June 1849, NHi-O'Reilly.

75. S. P. Chase, 27 June 1849, DLC-Chase.

76. Warden, *Chase,* I: 312.

77. S. P. Chase, "Diary," 13–16 July 1849, DLC-Chase.

78. Ibid.; S. P. Chase to Belle, 19 July 1849, DLC-Chase.

79. The O'Reilly case dragged on for several years, eventually resulting in a complete victory for Morse and his associates. S. P. Chase to Belle, 16 July 1849, DLC-Chase; S. P. Chase to Townshend, 17 July 1849, PHi-Chase; to O'Reilly, 23 July 1849, NHi-O'Reilly.

80. See Chase's comments on "the money power." S. P. Chase to Charles R. Miller, 20 Aug. 1849, Chase Manhattan.

81. Pickard, ed., *Letters of Whittier,* I: 323n, 324. Bradburn, *Bradburn,* 172–74.

82. S. P. Chase to Butler, 26 July 1849, NjP-Butler. See also the *National Era,* 2 Aug. 1849.

83. Benjamin F. Butler, presumably speaking for the Barnburners, reassured Chase about the constancy of the radical Democrats in the Empire State. But Chase remained wary. B. F. Butler to Chase, 30 July 1849, PHi-Chase; S. P. Chase to Giddings, 26 July 1849, OCHi-Chase.

84. S. P. Chase to Norton Townshend, 24 April 1849, PHi-Chase.

85. S. P. Chase to Hamlin, 6 Aug. 1849, DLC-Chase.

86. S. P. Chase to Norton Townshend, 24 April 1849; to Dear Friend, 2 May 1849, PHi-Chase; to Hamlin, 26 July 1849, DLC-Chase.

87. S. P. Chase to Belle, 11, 19 Aug. 1849, DLC-Chase.

88. S. P. Chase to Sumner, 2 Sept. 1849, MH-H-Sumner.

89. Charles Sumner to Chase, 18 Sept. 1849; Chase to Sumner, 14 Sept. 1849, MHi-Sumner; S. P. Chase to Belle, 30 Sept. 1849, DLC-Chase.

90. Edward Wade to Chase, 20 Nov. 1849, PHi-Chase; Stanley Matthews to Chase, 2 Dec. 1849; E. S. Hamlin to Chase, 8 Dec. 1849, PHi-Chase.

91. Charles Sumner to Chase, 25 Sept. 1849, DLC-Chase; S. P. Chase to Townshend, 15 Oct. 1849; Edward Wade to Chase, 20 Oct. 1849, PHi-Chase.

92. John Niven, *John C. Calhoun and the Price of Union* (Baton Rouge, 1988), 338.

93. Stephen E. Maizlish, *The Triumph of Sectionalism: The Transformation of Ohio Politics, 1844–1856* (Kent, Ohio, 1983), 153, 154; Stanley Matthews to Chase, 2, 3 Dec. 1849; E. S. Hamlin to Chase, 8, 20, 21 Dec. 1849, DLC-Chase.

Chapter 10. Mid-passage

1. S. P. Chase to Stanley Matthews, 27 Jan. 1849, in Nunns, ed. "Some Letters," 543, 544.

2. Quoted in Richard H. Sewell, *Ballots for Freedom* (New York, 1976), 208.

3. S. P. Chase, "Diary," 18 May 1850, DLC-Chase.

4. Blue, *Chase,* 74.

5. S. P. Chase to Belle, 5 Jan. 1850, DLC-Chase; Alice Hunt Sokoloff, *Kate Chase for the Defense* (New York, 1971), 28.

6. S. P. Chase to Hamlin, 21, 30 Dec. 1849, 2 Jan. 1850, DLC-Chase.

7. Robert W. Johannsen, *Stephen A. Douglas* (New York, 1973), 26.

8. James Ludlow to Chase, 2 Jan. 1850, DLC-Chase.

9. Ibid., 2 Jan. 1850, DLC-Chase.

10. S. P. Chase to Belle, 3 Jan. 1850, DLC-Chase.

11. Ibid., 4, 5, 7, 10 Jan. 1850, DLC-Chase.

12. John P. Garniss to Chase, 7 Jan. 1850, PHi-Chase.

13. S. P. Chase to Belle, 18 Jan. 1850, DLC-Chase.

14. *Cong. Globe,* 31st Cong., 1st sess., 10 Jan. 1850, pp. 135, 136.

15. Ibid., 329, 330.

16. S. P. Chase to Hamlin, 12 Jan. 1850, DLC-Chase.

17. Ibid.

18. S. P. Chase to Belle, 2 Jan., 9 Feb., 16 March 1850, DLC-Chase.

19. Ibid., 13 Feb. 1850.

20. S. P. Chase to James R. Skinner, 8 Jan., 27 Feb. 1850, DLC-Chase.

21. Chase's home and furniture in Cincinnati were sold in July 1850; Flamen Ball to Chase, 30 April, 16 July 1850, DLC-Chase.

22. S. P. Chase to Belle, 29 Jan. 1850, DLC-Chase.

23. Chaney and Co. to Chase, 28 Jan. 1850, DLC-Chase; S. P. Chase to Sumner, 28 Jan. 1850, MH-H-Sumner.

24. S. P. Chase to Belle, 4 March 1850; to My Dear Sir, 5 March 1850, DLC-Chase.

25. S. P. Chase to Belle, 31 March 1850, DLC-Chase.

26. S. P. Chase to Sumner, 7 March 1850, MH-H-Sumner; to Phllips, 26 Dec. 1852, MHH-Philips.

27. S. P. Chase to Hamlin, 2 Feb. 1850; 14 April 1850, DLC-Chase.

28. E. S. Hamlin to Chase, 19 Feb. 1850, PHi-Chase.

29. The *Republican* kept afloat until 1858. Stephen Gutgesell, ed., *Guide to Ohio*

Newspapers 1793–1973 (Columbus, 1974); John R. Miller to Chase, 15 Jan. 1850, DLC-Chase; E. S. Hamlin to Chase, 28 Jan. 1850, PHi-Chase.

30. S. P. Chase to Hamlin, 5 Dec. 1851, DLC-Chase.

31. Ibid., 22 Jan. 1850.

32. Ibid., 2 Feb. 1850; S. P. Chase to Sumner, 15 March 1850, MHH-Sumner.

33. George Hoadly, Jr., to Chase, 9 April 1850, DLC-Chase.

34. S. P. Chase to Sumner, 12 March 1850, MH-H-Sumner.

35. See, for instance, Charles Sumner to Chase, 11, 22, 24 March 1850, DLC-Chase.

36. *Cong. Globe,* 31st Cong., 1st sess., 468–78.

37. Ibid., 478. See also *Daily National Intelligencer,* 4 April 1850; *National Era,* 11 April 1850.

38. Benjamin F. Butler to Chase, 29 April 1850, DLC-Chase; New York *Tribune,* 12 Jan. 1850.

39. *Cong. Globe,* 31st Cong., 1st sess., 80, 81, 83, 329, 330, 323, 329, 331, 33, 713; S. P. Chase's amendment was rejected 20-25, DNA-RG46.

40. S. P. Chase to Hamlin, 27 May 1850, DLC-Chase.

41. S. P. Chase to Belle, 14 April 1850, DLC-Chase; to Lewis Tappan, 3 May 1850, CSmH-Barney.

42. S. P. Chase to Belle, 22 May 1850, DLC-Chase; to Sumner, 25 May 1850, MH-H-Sumner.

43. S. P. Chase to Belle, 8 June 1850, DLC-Chase.

44. Chase's euphemism for pregnancy; S. P. Chase to Belle, 20, 27 July 1850, DLC-Chase.

45. Ibid., 28 July 1850.

46. S. P. Chase to Hamlin, 14 Aug. 1850, DLC-Chase.

Chapter 11. Independent Democrat

1. S. P. Chase to Belle, 25 May, 25 Aug. 1850, DLC-Chase.

2. Grace Greenwood, "An American Salon," *Cosmopolitan,* 8 (1890): 440.

3. S. P. Chase to Belle, 30 June 1850, DLC-Chase.

4. Harrold, *Bailey,* 133, 134. Grace Greenwood recalled an impromptu jingle Chase composed in an epigram game when asked to respond to his hostess's name. Chase wrote down: "She sang 'Love in a Cottage' gayly; but later years brought graver cares, she now is prisoner of old Bailey." Greenwood, "An American Salon," 445.

5. S. P. Chase to Belle, 20 Dec. 1850, DLC-Chase.

6. S. P. Chase to My dearest little Kate, 13 Aug. 1850, PHi-Chase; to Belle, 26 Aug. 1850, DLC-Chase.

7. "I wish to see you as accomplished as a lady I saw in Philadelphia. A Miss Furness who understands French, Italian, German," he wrote Kate, "converses in all languages, writes beautifully and talks as well as she writes." S. P. Chase to My darling child, 4 Aug. 1853, PHi-Chase.

8. See, for example, S. P. Chase to My dear child, 10 Aug. 1852, PHi-Chase.

9. S. P. Chase to Belle, 26 Aug. 1850, DLC-Chase.

10. Charlotte Ludlow Jones to Chase, 9 March 1852, DLC-Chase.

11. S. P. Chase to Belle, 20 Aug. 1850, DLC-Chase.

12. Ibid., 8 Nov. 1850.

13. Ibid., 5 Jan. 1851, DLC-Chase; John P. Garniss to Chase, 7 Jan. 1850, PHi-Chase.

14. Weisenburger, *Passing of the Frontier,* 473, 474.

15. Roseboom, *Civil War Era,* 261, 262.

16. S. P. Chase to Giddings, 24 March 1851, OCHi-Giddings.

17. E. S. Hamlin to Chase, 4 March 1851, PHi-Chase; Stewart, *Giddings,* 198. See also Giddings to Chase, 6 Sept. 1851, PHi-Chase.

18. S. P. Chase to Hamlin, 24 Feb. 1851, DLC-Chase.

19. Frederick Douglass, to whom Chase submitted his voluntary emigration plan, replied with caustic vehemence. Chase must have smarted at Douglass's dismissal of his facile approach to such a complex problem as race relations. Douglass argued vehemently that blacks do just as well as whites in any climate and he provided examples. The question, he reminded Chase, was not a geographic one but a moral and social imperative. S. P. Chase to Douglass, 4 May 1850, PHi-Chase; Frederick Douglass to Chase, 30 May 1850, DLC-Chase.

20. S. P. Chase, "Diary," 10 Dec. 1851, DLC-Chase.

21. S. P. Chase to Hamlin, 1, 9 Jan. 1852, DLC-Chase; "Family Memoranda," 12 Jan. 1852, DLC-Chase.

22. S. P. Chase to Kate, 7 Jan. 1852, PHi-Chase; S. P. Chase to My dear sir, 9 March 1852, CU-BANC-Atkins.

23. J. H. Smith to Chase, 21 Feb. 1852, DLC-Chase.

24. Horace Greeley to Chase, 16 April 1852, PHi-Chase.

25. S. P. Chase to Cleveland, 10 March 1852; "Notes" for a speech at Sandusky, Ohio, 1852, PHi-Chase.

26. *Ohio State Journal,* 19 Jan., 22 July 1852.

27. Ibid., 12 Feb. 1852.

28. S. P. Chase to Hamlin, 28 June 1852, DLC-Chase.

29. Sewell, *Hale,* 146, 147; S. P. Chase to Hamlin, 19 July, 3 Aug. 1852, DLC-Chase; S. P. Chase to Hale, 5 Aug. 1852, NhHi-Hale.

30. S. P. Chase to Hamlin, 13 Aug. 1852, DLC-Chase; to B. F. Butler, 16 Aug. 1852, NjP-Butler.

31. S. P. Chase to Gerrit Smith, 15 Aug. 1852, DLC-Chase.

32. S. P. Chase to Townshend, 23 Sept. 1852, PHi-Chase.

33. *Ohio Statesman,* 2 Nov. 1852.

34. *Ohio State Journal,* 23 Nov. 1852.

35. Chase to John Bigelow, 2 Dec. 1852, NSchU.

36. S. P. Chase to Hamlin, 2 Dec. 1852, DLC-Chase. Wade's brother Edward, however, remained a friendly colleague in the House. Edward Wade to Chase, 17 Oct. 1853, PHi-Chase.

37. S. P. Chase to Hamlin, 3 Aug. 1852, DLC-Chase.

38. Ibid., 4, 8 Feb. 1853.

39. S. P. Chase to My dear sir, 7 May 1853, DLC-Chase.

40. He cast a covetous eye on the Cincinnati labor reform paper *The Nonpareil.* But before he could line up funds and interest a competent editor the paper ceased publication. S. P. Chase to Hamlin, 5 Dec. 1851, 25 Feb., 10 March 1852; 8 Feb. 1853, DLC-Chase.

41. S. P. Chase to Sumner, 13 Sept. 1853, MH-H-Sumner; to My dear friend, 12 Sept. 1853, PHi-Chase.

42. S. P. Chase to Hamlin, 6 June 1853; S. P. Chase to My dear sir, 10 July 1853, DLC-Chase. He also drafted a narrative of his life he did not complete, but it was obviously meant for newspapers or pamphlet publication should the state canvass result in the possibility of his reelection to the Senate. The narrative ends with the year 1837 (DLC-Chase).

43. *Ohio Statesman,* 14 Dec. 1853.

44. S. P. Chase to Hamilton Smith, 19 Oct. 1853, DLC-Chase.

45. S. P. Chase to My dear friend, 31 Oct. 1863, PHi-Chase.

46. S. P. Chase to Hamlin, 17 Oct. 1853, DLC-Chase.

47. S. P. Chase to Kate, 8 Nov. 1853; Ibid., 10, 20, Dec. 1853, PHi-Chase; to Sumner, 28 Nov. 1853, M-HH-Sumner.

48. S. P. Chase to Alfred P. Edgerton, 14 Dec. 1853, DLC-Chase.

49. S. P. Chase to Hamlin, 22 Jan. 1854, DLC-Chase.

50. *New York Times*, 18 Jan. 1854; *National Era*, 22 Jan. 1854; Johannsen, *Douglas,* 417–22, 424.

51. See William E. Gienapp, *The Origins of the Republican Party 1852–1856* (New York, 1987), 70, 71.

52. *Cong. Globe,* 33rd Cong., 1st sess., 239.

53. "Appeal of the Independent Democrats to the People of the United States," 19 Jan. 1854, DLC-Chase; Don E. Fehrenbacher, *The Dred Scott Case* (New York, 1978), 182, 183.

54. S. P. Chase to Hamlin, 10 Feb. 1854, MH-H-Chase.

55. See, for instance, S. P. Chase to Giddings, 15 Feb. 1847, DLC-Chase.

56. S. P. Chase to Edward L. Pierce, 12 March 1854, MH-H-Pierce; *Cong. Globe,* 33rd Cong., 1st sess., 3, 4 March 1854, pp. 281–87, 335–37.

57. *Cong. Globe,* 33rd Cong., 1st sess., 4 March 1854, pp. 283, 284.

58. For the "Appeal" itself see *Cong. Globe,* 33rd Cong., 1st sess., 30 Jan. 1854, pp. 281, 282; for the debate see *ibid.,* 275-82; *Cong. Globe,* 33rd Cong., 1st sess., 2, 3, March 1854, pp. 281–87, 332, 335–37.

59. S. P. Chase to Hamlin, 23 Jan. 1854; to Follett, 15 Feb. 1854, DLC-Chase.

60. S. P. Chase to Edward L. Pierce, 5 Aug. 1854, MH-H-Sumner.

61. Schuckers, *Chase,* 155, 156.

Chapter 12. An Uncertain Future

1. S. P. Chase, "Diary," 25 March 1855, DLC-Chase.

2. Allan Nevins, *Ordeal of the Union,* 2 vols. (New York, 1947), I: 312, 313; James A. Rawley, *Race and Politics* (New York, 1969), 86, 87.

3. Hart, *Chase,* 25; see also James Ford Rhodes, "Memoir of Edward L. Pierce," *Proc. Mass. Hist. Soc.* 2nd ser. 18 (9 June 1904): passim.

4. Rhodes, "Pierce Memoir," 363, 364; S. P. Chase to Pierce, 17 Jan. 1854, MH-H-Pierce.

5. Rhodes, "Pierce Memoir," 364; S. P. Chase to Pierce, 28 Nov. 1854, MH-H-Pierce.

6. S. P. Chase, "Diary," March 1854, DLC-Chase; see also S. P. Chase to Hamlin, 23 Jan. 1854; to Albert G. Riddle, 15 Feb. 1854, DLC-Chase.

7. Charles Robson, ed., *The Encyclopedia of Ohio* (Cincinnati, 1876), 310; Carl Gustav Reemelin, *Life of Charles Reemelin* (Cincinnati, 1892), 108, 109, 129; Henry John Groen, "A History of the German American Newspapers of Cincinnati before 1860" (Ph.D diss., Ohio State Univ. 1944), 78–82, 289, 290–95.

8. S. P. Chase to Pierce, 12 March 1854, MH-H-Pierce; see also S. P. Chase to Sidney Harold Gay, 14 March 1854, NNC-Gay.

9. S. P. Chase to Townshend, 9 March 1854, PHi-Chase.

10. S. P. Chase to William Allen, 8 April 1854, DLC-Allen.

11. Ibid.

12. *Ohio State Journal,* 3, 4 March 1854.

13. Roseboom, *Civil War Era,* 279.

14. S. P. Chase to Icabod Codding, 15 April 1854, PSC-Hi-Codding.
15. *Ohio State Journal,* 23, 24 March 1854.
16. *Cong. Globe,* 33rd Cong., 1st. sess, "Appendix," 557.
17. S. P. Chase to Hamlin, 25 April 1854, MH-H-Hamlin.
18. S. P. Chase to Grimes, 29 April 1854, PHi-Chase; Gienapp, *Republican Party,* 88, 89.
19. S. P. Chase to John Greiner, 10 May 1854, OCHP-Follet.
20. Roseboom, *Civil War Era,* 283.
21. Ibid., 284
22. See S. P. Chase ledger, "Vote by Counties, German Votes," 1848–51, DLC-Chase.
23. *Daily National Era,* 24, 28 March, 1 June 1854; *Ohio State Journal,* 25 Nov. 1854.
24. *Ohio Columbian,* 10 June, 1854; Cincinnati *Gazette,* 10 July 1854.
25. Cassius Clay as early as January wrote Chase that a new party was forming in several states that was styling itself Republican. Cassius Clay to Chase, 1 Jan. 1854, PHi-Chase.
26. Henry B. Carrington, "Early History of the Republican Party in Ohio," *Ohio Archaeological and Historical Quarterly* 2, no. 2 (Sept. 1888): 327–31.
27. S. P. Chase to E. L. Pierce, 20 Sept. 1854, MH-H-Pierce.
28. S. P. Chase to Hamlin, 21 Nov. 1854, DLC-Chase.
29. E. S. Hamlin to Chase, 10 Nov. 1854, PHi-Chase.
30. *Ohio State Journal,* 25 Nov. 1854.
31. Gienapp, *Republican Party,* 192.
32. S. P. Chase to Follett, 14 Feb. 1855; L. Belle Hamlin, ed., "Selections from the Follett Papers," Ohio Historical and Philosophical Society, *Quarterly Publication,* 13 (April–June 1918): 65.
33. Robert F. Horowitz, *The Great Impeacher: A Political Biography of James M. Ashley* (New York, 1979), 3–12, 15–18.
34. Nevins, *Ordeal,* I: 310; Rawley, *Race and Politics,* 28.
35. Nevins, *Ordeal,* I: 311, 312; Rawley, *Race and Politics,* 83, 84; William E. Parrish, *David Rice Atchison of Missouri, Border Politician* (Columbia, Mo., 1961), 161, 164.
36. S. P. Chase to My dear sir, 12 Jan. 1855, DLC-Chase.
37. S. P. Chase to Pierce, 20 Sept. 1854; MH-H-Pierce; to Hamlin, 2 Nov. 1854; to Hamlin, 10 Nov. 1854, PHi-Chase; to Oran Follett, 1 Jan. 1855, in Hamlin, ed., "Selections," 60, 61; S. P. Chase to Follett, 14 Feb. 1855, OCHP-Follett.
38. See, for example, Kinsley Bingham to Chase, 8 Jan. 1855, DLC-Chase; S. P. Chase to Grimes, 10 Jan. 1855, PHi-Chase.
39. S. P. Chase to Hamlin, 9 Feb. 1855, DLC-Chase.
40. S. P. Chase to Katie, 8, 15 Jan. 1855, PHi-Chase.
41. S. P. Chase to Hamlin, 12 Jan. 1855, DLC-Chase.
42. S. P. Chase to Julian, 20 Jan. 1855, DLC-Giddings-Julian.
43. S. P. Chase to Hamlin, 12 Jan. 1855, DLC-Chase.
44. Oran Follett to Thomas Ewing, 1 May 1854, in Hamlin, ed., "Selections," 52–54.
45. S. P. Chase to John Bigelow, 21 March 1855, NSchU; Joshua Leavitt to Chase, 13 March 1855, PHi-Chase; S. P. Chase to James F. Conner, 20 March 1855, OCHi-Chase.
46. He would position his strategy on class lines. Would the Know Nothing leadership accept mob-driven social disorder or the moral and lawful objectives of free soil? He had few doubts what their choice would be but it was a sensitive issue that must be approached discreetly. S. P. Chase to Schouler, 3 Sept. 1855, MHi-Schouler.
47. S. P. Chase to Kate, 22 April 1855, PHi-Chase.
48. Ibid.
49. William A. Baughin, "Bullets and Ballots: The Election Day Riots of 1855," *Bulletin of Historical and Philosophical Society of Ohio* 21 (Oct. 1963): 267–73.

50. Ibid., 267.

51. Joseph Medill to Follett, 18 April 1855, in Hamlin, ed., "Selections," 71, 72; see also Joshua Giddings to Chase, 8 April 1855, DLC-Chase.

52. Hamlin, ed., "Selections," 71, 72. Giddings and William C. Howells of the *Ashtabula Sentinel* were working with Medill.

53. Edward Wade to Chase, 14, 18 April 1855, PHi-Chase.

54. S. P. Chase to My dear sir, 13 April 1855, DLC-Chase.

Chapter 13. On the Campaign Trail

1. S. P. Chase to Pierce, 14 May 1855, MH-H.

2. Howard K. Beale and Allan Brownsword, eds., *Diary of Gideon Welles*, 3 vols. (New York, 1911), II: 386; Gienapp, *Republican Party*, 194.

3. S. P. Chase to Follett, 14, 27 Feb., 14, 23 March 1855, in Hamlin, ed., "Selections," 63–70.

4. Joseph Medill to Follett, 20 Dec. 1854, in Hamlin, ed., "Selections," 77, 78.

5. Oran Follett, "The Coalition of 1855," in Alfred E. Lee, *History of the City of Columbus*, 2 vols. (Columbus, 1892), I: 430, 431.

6. Ibid., 431.

7. Joseph Medill to Follett, 18 April 1855, in Hamlin, ed., "Selections," 71, 72.

8. Ibid.

9. Ibid., 74.

10. Follett, "Coalition," 432.

11. Ibid.

12. Oran Follett to Chase, 2 May 1855, DLC-Chase.

13. S. P. Chase to Follett, 4 May 1855; in Hamlin, ed., "Selections," 73, 74.

14. Jacob Brinkerhoff to Follett, 21 May 1855, in Hamlin, ed., "Selections," 74, 75.

15. Follett, "Coalition," 432.

16. Lewis D. Campbell to William Schouler, 26 June 1855, MH-H-Schouler; S. P. Chase to Lewis Campbell, 25, 29 May 1855, DLC-Chase; S. P. Chase to Campbell, 2 June 1855, OCHi-Campbell; to Chase, 28, 31, May, 15 June 1855, DLC-Chase.

17. Joseph Medill to Follett, 18 April 1855, in Hamlin, ed., "Selections," 71.

18. Horowitz, *Ashley*, 27, 29; James M. Ashley to Chase, 16 June 1855, DLC-Chase.

19. Ibid., James M. Ashley to Chase, 16 June 1855, DLC-Chase.

20. James M. Ashley to Chase, 2 May, 16 June 1855, DLC-Chase.

21. Ibid., 16 June 1855; Horowitz, *Ashley*, 26; S. P. Chase to Norton Townshend, 21 June 1855, PHi-Chase; to James Grimes, 27 June 1855, PHi-Chase.

22. Mathias Nichols to Chase, 3 June 1855, DLC-Chase.

23. S. P. Chase to Paul, 27 Dec. 1854, PHi-Chase.

24. James M. Ashley to Chase, 29 May 1855, DLC-Chase; S. P. Chase to James S. Pike, 20 June 1855, in Pike, *First Blows of the Civil War* (New York, 1879), 295, 246; to Grimes, 27 June 1855, PHi-Chase.

25. S. P. Chase to A. M. Ganguer, 15 Feb. 1855, MH-H-Hamlin.

26. S. P. Chase to Pierce, 20 June 1855, MH-H-Pierce.

27. S. P. Chase to Campbell, 23 June 1855. Many of the delegates, including a sizable number of Know Nothings, voted for Chase in fusion primary elections. Eugene Roseboom,

"Salmon P. Chase and the Know-Nothings," *Mississippi Valley Historical Review* 25 (Dec. 1938): 345.

28. S. P. Chase to Pike, 20 June 1855, in Pike, *First Blows*, 295, 296.

29. S. P. Chase to Kate Chase, 27 May 1855, PHi-Chase.

30. Blue, *Chase*, 100; *Ohio State Journal*, 13, 14 July 1855; *Daily National Era*, 19, 26 July 1855; Roseboom, "Chase and the Know-Nothings," 344; Follett, "Coalition," 433.

31. Follett, "Coalition," 432.

32. James Elliott to Chase, 1 Dec. 1858, DLC-Chase.

33. Ibid., 433.

34. Ibid.

35. *National Era*, 19, 26 July 1855.

36. Roseboom, "Chase and the Know-Nothings," 344.

37. Quoted in ibid., 346.

38. Ibid., 346, 347; Cincinnati *Gazette*, 20–23 July 1855; *Ohio State Journal*, 24 July 1855.

39. *National Era*, 26 July 1855.

40. Roseboom, *Civil War Era*, 307.

41. See the Cincinnati *Enquirer*, Aug.–Sept. 1855.

42. S. P. Chase to Pike, 7 July 1855, MeU-Pike.

43. S. P. Chase to Follett, 4 May 1855, OCHP-Follett; to Pike, 18 Oct. 1855, MeU-Pike; to Kinsley Bingham, 16 Oct. 1855, PHi-Chase.

44. S. P. Chase to My darling child, 30 Sept. 1855, PHi-Chase.

45. See, for instance, Lewis Campbell to Chase, 6 Aug. 1855, DLC-Chase; S. P. Chase to Schouler, 7 Aug. 1855, MHi; William Schouler to Hamlin, 27 Aug. 1855, DLC-Chase.

46. Oran Follett to Chase, 9 Sept. 1855, DLC-Chase; S. P. Chase to Pierce, 18 Oct. 1855, MeU-Pike.

47. S. P. Chase to Schouler, 3 Sept. 1855, MH-H-Schouler.

48. Dr. John Paul to Chase, 30 May 1855, PHi-Chase.

49. S. P. Chase to Kate, 30 Sept. 1855, PHi-Chase.

50. S. P. Chase to Pike, 18 Oct. 1855, MeU-Pike; to Sumner, 15 Oct. 1855, MH-H-Sumner.

51. Gienapp, *Republic Party*, 12 ff.

52. *Ohio State Journal*, 27 Nov. 1855.

53. Gamaliel Bailey to Chase, 27 Nov. 1855, PHi-Chase.

54. C. L. Pierce to Chase, 13 Oct. 1855, DLC-Chase.

55. Charles Sumner to Chase, 11 Oct. 1855, DLC-Chase.

Chapter 14. As Others See Us

1. S. P. Chase to Pike, 18 Oct. 1855, Meu-Pike.

2. S. P. Chase to Sumner, 14 Feb. 1856, MH-H-Sumner.

3. See S. P. Chase, "Inaugural Address of Salmon P. Chase Governor of the State of Ohio," 14 Jan. 1856, Columbus, 1–15 passim.

4. Howe, *Historical Collections*, I: 614.

5. W.P.A., *The Ohio Guide* (New York, 1940), 251–54; Howe, *Historical Collections*, I: 621.

6. S. P. Chase to Sumner, 3 May 1856, MH-H.

7. Samuel Galloway to Chase, 10 Jan. 1856, PHi-Chase.

8. S. P. Chase to Wade, 9 Jan. 1856; Samuel Galloway to Chase, 10 Jan. 1856, DLC-Chase; S. P. Chase to John P. Hale, 11 Jan. 1856, NhHi-Hale; for Chase's attitude toward Wade at this time see his letter to Hale, 10 Dec. 1856, NhHi-Hale.

9. *Ohio Statesman,* 28 Feb. 1856.

10. Gienapp, *Republican Party,* 250. Chase was now better known to eastern leaders than most aspiring candidates. For instance one of the principal financial backers of the party and its state chairman in New York, the merchant banker E. D. Morgan, did not know personally N. P. Banks, then one of the leading American-Republican candidates for the speakership. E. D. Morgan to Banks, 4 Feb. 1856, DLC-Banks.

11. E. D. Morgan to Banks, 4 Feb. 1856, DLC-Banks.

12. Gamaliel Bailey to Chase, 27 Nov. 1855; Henry Wilson to Chase, 17 Nov. 1855, PHi-Chase.

13. See F. P. Blair, Jr., to Chase, 1 June 1853, 30 June 1855, PHi-Chase.

14. S. P. Chase to S.O. Butler, 10 Oct. 1854, PHi-Chase.

15. John Bigelow to Welles, 27 Dec. 1855; Welles to Dear Sir [Bigelow], 28 Dec. 1855, DLC-Welles.

16. Welles to Dear Sir, 28 Dec. 1855, DLC-Welles.

17. Gamaliel Bailey to Chase, 18 April 1856, PHi-Chase.

18. Ibid.

19. Lewis Clephane, *Birth of the Republican Party* (Washington, D.C., 1889), 12; Gienapp, Republican Party, 252.

20. Preston King to Welles, 2, 3, 10 Jan. 1856, DLC-Welles.

21. Henry Wilson to Chase, 15 Jan. 1856, PHi-Chase; Gienapp, *Republican Party,* 242; Lewis Campbell to Chase, 11, 16 Oct., 5 Nov. 1855, DLC-Chase; S. P. Chase to Campbell, 8 Nov. 1855, OCHi-Campbell.

22. S. P. Chase to Henry Wilson, 9 Nov. 1857, PHi-Chase.

23. *Congr. Globe,* 34th Cong., 1st sess., 335, 336; S. P. Chase to Banks, 4 Feb. 1856, DLC-Banks.

24. James W. Taylor, *A Manual of the Ohio School System* (Cincinnati, 1857), 391, 392.

25. S. P. Chase to Barney, 15 Feb. 1856, CSmH-Barney.

26. James M. Lane to Chase, 21 Jan. 1856, DLC-Chase; Nevins, *Ordeal,* II: 391, 392.

27. Gamaliel Bailey to Charles Francis Adams, 14 Jan. 1856, MHi-Adams.

28. S. P. Chase to Cleveland, 21 March 1856, PHi-Chase.

29. Ibid.

30. Ibid., 26 Feb. 1856, OCHi-Chase.

31. *New York Times,* 22 Feb. 1856.

32. E. D. Morgan to Dear Sir, 28 Feb. 1856, DLC-Banks.

33. Thomas Bolton to Chase, 25 Feb. 1856, PHi-Chase; S. P. Chase to Barney, 28 Feb. 1856, CSmH-Barney.

34. "Gov. Chase is," Wade wrote, "as I have every reason to believe, a good friend of mine." B. F. Wade to David Chambers, 25 Feb. 1856; Frederick Wadsworth to Wade, 25 Feb. 1856, DLC-Wade.

35. New York *Evening Post,* 25 Feb. 1856.

36. B. F. Wade to Chase, 5 May 1856, PHi-Chase.

37. Gamaliel Bailey to Chase, 8 May 1856, PHi-Chase; S. P. Chase to Gerrit Smith, 15 Feb. 1856, DLC-Chase; Gerrit Smith to Chase, 20 April 1856, PHi-Chase.

38. S. P. Chase to Barney, 13 May 1856, CSmH-Barney.

39. Edward Hamilton to N. P. Banks, 20 May 1856, DLC-Banks.

40. S. P. Chase to Sumner, 23 May 1856, MH-H-Sumner; T. F. Hicks to Wade, 19 June 1856, DLC-Wade.

41. Joseph Cox to Chase, 15 May 1856, DLC-Chase.

42. See, for instance, Theodore Parker's condemnation in Henry S. Commager, *Theodore Parker, Yankee Crusader* (Boston, 1936), 258.

43. S. P. Chase to Trowbridge, 13 March 1864, DLC-Chase; Stanley W. Campbell, *The Slave Catchers* (Chapel Hill, 1970), 144–47; S. P. Chase to Charles S. Morehead, 4, 7 March 1856; to Joseph Cooper, 11 March 1856; to Timothy C. Day, 13 March 1856, DLC-Chase; Isaac F. Patterson, *The Constitution of Ohio* (Cleveland, 1912), 118, 126-28; Samuel Joseph May, *The Fugitive Slave Law and Its Victims* (New York, 1861), 52–55, 100–102; Julius Yanuck, "The Garner Fugitive Slave Case," *Mississippi Valley Historical Review*, 40 (June 1953): 47–66.

44. *Ex parte* Robinson, 20 *Federal Cases* 296 (1855): 175–77.

45. Weisenburger, *McLean*, 194, 195.

46. S. P. Chase to Barney, 21 May 1856, CSmH-Barney.

47. *Ohio State Journal*, 29, 30 May 1856; Charles M. Johnson, comp., *Proceedings of the First Three Republican National Conventions* (Minneapolis, 1893), 39.

48. S. P. Chase to Hamlin, 2 June 1856, DLC-Chase; see also S. P. Chase to Barney, 6 June 1856, CSmH-Barney.

49. D. McBride to Chase, 7 June 1856, DLC-Chase; Joshua Leavitt to Chase, 12 June 1856, PHi-Chase.

50. S. P. Chase to Hamlin, 12 June 1856, DLC-Chase.

51. James W. Stone to Banks, 14 June 1856, DLC-Banks; Weisenburger, *McLean*, 147.

52. Gamaliel Bailey to John G. Palfrey, 19 Oct. 1856, Palfrey Papers, MH-H; to Chase, 21 Feb. 1856, DLC-Chase; *National Era*, 12 June 1856; Joshua Giddings to Joseph Giddings, 1 July 1856, OHi-Giddings.

53. See Cassius Clay to Chase, 24 June 1856, PHi-Chase; Glynden Van Deusen, *William H. Seward* (New York, 1967), 175–77; Pike, *First Blows*, 344, 345; Harrold, *Bailey*, 181; Elizabeth Pike to Chase, 14 Sept. 1856, PHi-Chase. Elizabeth Pike attended the convention with her husband, New York *Tribune* reporter James Pike. She quoted Thurlow Weed as saying to her, "Madame we must have someone who breaks the ranks of the Hards"—the conservative Democrats in New York. Obviously Chase was far too radical on slavery to accomplish this feat.

54. Elizabeth Pike to Chase, 14 Sept. 1856, PHi-Chase.

55. Hiram Barney to Chase, 21 June 1856, PHi-Chase.

56. Ibid.

57. Thomas Bolton to Chase, 12 July 1858, PHi-Chase.

58. John McLean to John Teesdale, 3 Sept. 1859, Teesdale Papers, OCHi.

59. Though he expressed his bitterness almost a year after the convention, it seems plausible to ascribe these sentiments to Chase's immediate post-convention mood; S. P. Chase to Sumner, 1 May 1857, MH-H-Sumner.

60. S. P. Chase to Hamlin, 12 June 1856, DLC-Chase.

61. S. P. Chase to George Hoadly, Jr., 12 June 1854, DLC-Chase.

62. Thomas Ford to Chase, 4 Aug. 1857, DLC-Chase; see also Roseboom, "Chase and the Know-Nothings," 349, 250. Another bitter man whom Chase seems to have rather summarily discarded after his usefulness had run its course, and in fact had become a political liability in the new climate of R·publican ascendancy, was Lewis Campbell. "My Americanism was no great sin when I used it for the triumphs of 1854 and 1855," he wrote Chase. Campbell added

that Giddings had "insulted [me] at Philadelphia. Greeley and others had kicked [me] out of the convention." Lewis Campbell to Chase, 4 July 1856, DLC-Chase.

63. S. P. Chase to My dear cousin, 22 July 1856, PHi-Chase.

64. S. P. Chase to Hoadley, 12 June 1856; S. P. Chase, "Diary," DLC-Chase.

65. S. P. Chase to Fremont, 27 June 1856; S. P. Chase, "Diary," DLC-Chase.

66. S. P. Chase to John Sherman, 11 Aug. 1856, DLC-Sherman.

67. Thomas Ford to Chase, 4 Aug. 1857, DLC-Chase; see also Roseboom, "Chase and the Know-Nothings," 349, 350.

68. S. P. Chase to George W. Julian, 17 July 1856, DLC-Giddings-Julian.

69. From Chase's correspondence during that period, it appears that he did not visit Fremont. See S. P. Chase to John Sherman, 11 Aug. 1856; to Bigelow, 12 Aug. 1856; to Nettie, 22 Aug. 1856, DLC-Chase; to John F. Morse, 22 Aug. 1856, PHi-Chase; to Sumner, 22 Aug. 1856, MH-H-Sumner.

70. Henry B. Stanton to Greeley, 5 Aug. 1856, NN-Greeley.

71. John Bigelow to James L. Pettigru, 11 Oct. 1856, NN-Bigelow.

72. S. P. Chase to Hannibal Hamlin, 12 Sept. 1856, IaHA; S. P. Chase to James V. Grimes, 23 Aug. 1856, PHi-Chase.

73. See the exhaustive analysis in Gienapp, *Republican Party,* chap. 13.

74. S. P. Chase to Sumner, 1 May 1857, MH-H-Sumner.

75. S. P. Chase to Parker, 17 July 1856, in John Weiss, *Theodore Parker,* 2 vols. (New York, 1864), II: 519–20.

Chapter 15. For the Good of the Party

1. S. P. Chase to Grimes, 8 Nov. 1856, PHi-Chase.

2. S. P. Chase, "Message of the Governor of Ohio to the Fifty-Second General Assembly," 5 Jan. 1857 (Columbus, Ohio, 1857), 29.

3. T. H. Porterfield et al. to Chase, 14 Nov. 1856; S. P. Chase to John W. Geary, 3 Dec. 1856, DLC-Chase; John W. Geary to Chase, 6 Jan. 1857, OCHi-Chase.

4. Franklin B. Sanborn, ed., *Life and Letters of John Brown, Liberator of Kansas, Martyr of Virginia* (2nd ed., Boston, 1891), 363, 364.

5. See S. P. Chase, "Kansas History," 10–29 Aug. 1856, "Memorandum Book," PHi-Chase.

6. S. P. Chase, "Message of the Governor," 28–30.

7. Ibid., 23, 25, 26.

8. Ibid., 28–30.

9. *Ohio State Journal,* 7 Jan. 1857.

10. *New York Times,* 29 Aug. 1857.

11. S. P. Chase, "Diary," 3, 4 Jan. 1857, DLC-Chase.

12. C. S. Williams, comp., *Williams' Columbus Directory, City Guide and Business Mirror,* vol. I: 1856–57 (Columbus, 1857), 107.

13. S. P. Chase, "Diary," 5 Jan. 1857, DLC-Chase.

14. *Ohio State Journal,* 7 Jan. 1857.

15. Ibid.

16. S. P. Chase, "Diary," 6 Jan. 1857, DLC-Chase.

17. *Ohio State Journal,* 7 Jan. 1857; M. D. Handy, a close friend of Wade's, was much impressed with the celebration and with Chase's message, all of which he communicated to the senator; M. D. Handy to Wade, 9 Jan. 1857, DLC-Wade.

18. S. P. Chase to Pierce, 21 Dec. 1856, MH-H-Pierce; No sooner had members of the legislature settled themselves in their elaborate new chambers than many of the Republican contingent besought Chase to head the ticket again. A few close advisors, however, warned of possible defeat. See, for instance, S. P. Chase, "Diary," 12–15, Jan. 1857, NhHi-Chase.

19. S. P. Chase to Frederick Hassaurek, 7 April 1857, OCHi-Hassaurek; Frederick Hassaurek to Chase, 11 April 1857, PHi-Chase.

20. S. P. Chase, "Diary," 30 May, 2–6 June 1857, NhHi-Chase.

21. Schuckers, *Chase*, 185, 186; Roseboom, *Civil War Era*, 325, 326.

22. S. P. Chase, "Diary," 11, 12 June 1857, NhHi-Chase; Howe, *Historical Collections*, I: 653, 654.

23. William Dennison to Chase, 23 June 1857, OCHi-Chase.

24. S. P. Chase to Francis Wright, 22 June 1857, DLC-Chase.

25. S. P. Chase to Henry Reed, 25 June 1857, DLC-Chase; S. P. Chase, *Diary*, 11–12 June 1857, NhHi-Chase; Edwin Ludlow to Chase, 19 June 1857, PHi-Chase; *New York Times*, 29 Aug. 1857; *Ohio State Journal*, 25 Aug. 1857; Edwin Ludlow to Chase, 19, 22 June 1857, PHi-Chase; S. P. Chase, "Diary," 24, 27 June 1857, NhHi-Chase.

26. S. P. Chase, "Diary," 14, 15 July 1857, NhHi-Chase.

27. S. P. Chase to Cass, 27 July 1857, OCHi; *New York Times*, 29 Aug. 1857.

28. Kenneth M. Stampp, *America in 1857, a Nation on the Brink* (New York, 1990), 219–21.

29. Edwin Ludlow to Chase, 19 June 1857, PHi-Chase; S. P. Chase to Ludlow, 25 June 1857, DLC-Chase; Stampp, *America in 1857*, 219–21.

30. S. P. Chase to Pierce, 4 July 1857, MH-H-Pierce.

31. Rufus Spalding to Chase, 23 June 1857, PHi-Chase.

32. Charles Reemelin to Chase, 25 June 1857, PHi-Chase; S. P. Chase to Reemelin, 26 June 1857, DLC-Chase.

33. *Ohio State Journal*, 21 July, 13 Aug. 1857.

34. Ibid., 13 Aug. 1857.

35. *Ohio State Journal*, 13 Aug. 1857; Cincinnati *Gazette*, 14 Aug. 1857.

36. *Ohio State Journal*, 13 Aug. 1857.

37. S. P. Chase, "Diary," 6 Aug. 1857, NhHi-Chase.

38. Roseboom, *Civil War Era*, 261, 262, 328; Hans L. Trefousse, *Benjamin Franklin Wade, Radical Republican from Ohio* (New York, 1963), 65.

39. S. P. Chase to Sumner, 23 Nov. 1857, MH-H-Sumner; Joshua Giddings to Chase, 3 Nov. 1957, PHi-Chase. Chase was not entirely correct in his complaints about support. Giddings spent some time electioneering in Mahoning County.

40. S. P. Chase, "Diary, the Canvass of 1857," DLC-Chase.

41. Ibid.

42. Ibid.; *Ohio State Journal*, 25 Aug. 1857.

43. Chase, "Diary, the Canvass of 1857."

44. S. P. Chase to Sumner, 23 Nov. 1857, MH-H-Sumner.

45. Chase, "Diary, the Canvass of 1857," 12 Oct.; To my darling Nettie, 13 Oct. 1857, PHi-Chase.

46. Chase, "Diary, the Canvass of 1857."

47. *Ohio Statesman*, 6, 20 Sept. 1857.

48. Ibid., 22 Aug., 3, 18 Sept. 1857; Roseboom, *Civil War Era*, 328; Chase, "Diary, the Canvass of 1857."

49. Roseboom, *Civil War Era*, 328.

50. Ibid.

51. Chase, "Diary," 14 Oct. 1857, NhHi-Chase.

52. Ibid.

53. S. P. Chase to Pierce, 15 Oct. 1857, MH-H.

54. Ibid., 16 Oct. 1857.

55. Ibid., 17 Oct. 1857.

56. Except for Jacob Blickensderfer, who was a candidate for reelection as president of the Board of Public Works. He lost out to his Democratic opponent Abner Backus, because he was suspected of graft in connection with contracts for maintaining the canal system. Roseboom, *Civil War Era*, 329.

57. S. P. Chase to Sumner, 23 Nov. 1857, MH-H-Sumner.

58. *Ohio State Journal,* 11 Nov. 1857.

59. Chase, "Diary, the Canvass of 1857."

60. S. P. Chase to Charles D. Cleveland, 3 Nov. 1857, PHi-Chase; S. P. Chase to Smith, 5 Oct. 1857, DLC-Chase.

61. S. P. Chase to Giddings, 27 Nov. 1857, OCHi-Giddings.

62. Edward Wade to Chase, 3 Nov. 1857, PHi-Chase.

63. B. F. Wade to Chase, 3 Nov. 1857, PHi-Chase.

64. Williams, *Columbus Directory,* I: 43.

65. For an extended discussion of Miss Haines's School see Mary Merwin Phelps, *Kate Chase, Dominant Daughter* (New York, 1935), chap. 5.

66. S. P. Chase, "Diary," Feb. 8, 1857, NhHi-Chase; S. P. Chase to Kate Chase, 13 April 1855, PHi-Chase.

67. S. P. Chase to Kate Chase, 13 April 1855, PHi-Chase.

68. Warden, *Chase,* I: 301, 302.

69. S. P. Chase to Kate Chase, 1 Jan., 8 Feb., 23 March 1855, PHi-Chase.

70. See, for instance, S. P. Chase, "Diary," 10 Nov. 1857, DLC-Chase; to Kate Chase, 4 Dec. 1857, PHi-Chase; Ruth Young White, ed., *We Too Built Columbus* (Columbus, Ohio, 1936), 103–4.

71. "K. waltzed with Chambers—forbid," Chase wrote in his diary. S. P. Chase, "Diary," 15 Jan. 1857, NhHi-Chase. Lest one be too severe on Chase in this instance the partner in question was probably Francis T. Chambers, a Kentucky-born Cincinnati lawyer whom a contemporary described as a person "of such awful superciliousness and absolute arrogance sometimes not to be endured." Alfred G. W. Carter, *Old Court House* (Cincinnati, 1880), 342.

72. S. P. Chase to Kate Chase, 25 July 1856, PHi-Chase; S. P. Chase, "Diary," 28 Jan., 5, 6, Feb. 1857, NhHi-Chase.73. Charlotte Ludlow Jones to Chase, 23 Feb. 1859, DLC-Chase.

74. S. P. Chase to Kate Chase, 13 April 1855, PHi-Chase; Catherine Collins to Chase, 11 Dec. 1855, DLC-Chase; Howe, *Historical Collections,* I: 864. When Chase lived in Cincinnati, he owned a farm in Clifton.

75. Kate also was prone to colds and other illnesses. Overly sensitive to tuberculosis, which had killed two of his wives, Chase was always concerned about Kate's health. See, for instance, S. P. Chase, "Diary," 20 Oct. 1857, NhHi-Chase; to Kate Chase, 27 April 1855, PHi-Chase.

76. For instance he spent a good deal of what spare time he could extract from his crowded schedule to prepare a lecture on Galileo, which he gave before the local literary society in Columbus. S. P. Chase, "Diary," 9, 14 Feb. 1857, NhHi-Chase.

77. Ibid., 18 Jan., 8 Feb. 1857.

78. Ibid., 20, 31 Jan. 1857.

79. Carl Schurz, *The Reminiscences of Carl Schurz,* 3 vols. (New York, 1907), II: 169, 170.

80. Warden, *Chase*, I: 140.

81. Such an assumption is borne out in his intimate letters to his third wife, Belle Ludlow. See, for example, S. P. Chase to Belle, 28 July 1850, DLC-Chase.

82. Margaret Bailey to Chase, 11 Jan. 1857, DLC-Chase.

83. New York *Tribune*, 18 Dec. 1887.

84. Margaret Bailey to Chase, 11 Jan. 1857, DLC-Chase. Mrs. Bailey added in her letter, "I may as well tell you, as there seems to be no secrets between you."

85. S. P. Chase, "Diary Notes," DLC-Chase.

86. S. P. Chase, "Diary," 6 March 1857, NhHi-Chase, 26 July 1862, DLC-Chase.

87. Virginia Jeans Laas, ed., *War Time Washington: The Civil War Letters of Elizabeth Blair Lee* (Urbana-Chicago, 1991), 222.

88. S. P. Chase to Kate Chase, 13 Dec. 1857, PHi-Chase.

89. W. D. Howells, *Years of My Youth* (New York, 1916), 153, 154; S. P. Chase to Nettie, 4 May 1860, PHi-Chase.

90. S. P. Chase to Nettie, 4 May 1860, PHi-Chase.

91. S. P. Chase to Pierce, 29 April 1858, MH-H-Pierce.

92. See, for instance, letters from Gamaliel Bailey pleading for financial assistance to keep the *Era* from going under. Chase finally lent Bailey $6000 in a four-month promissory note dated 15 July 1857. Gamaliel Bailey to Chase, 13 Jan. 1857, 11 Jan., 13 Feb. 1858, PHi-Chase; S. P. Chase to Riggs and Co., 13 July 1857; see also Mary E. Chase to Chase, 17 Aug. 1857; Alexander Ramsey to Chase, 14 May 1858, DLC-Chase; S. P. Chase to My dear sir, 14 Aug. 1857, MnHi-Ramsey.

93. "Annual Report of the Secretary of State to the General Assembly and Governor of the State of Ohio for the Year 1856 (Columbus, Ohio, 1856).

94. He had also lost money on stocks he bought in the bankrupt Ohio Liberty and Trust Company; S. P. Chase to Ball, 10 July 1858, DLC-Chase.

95. S. P. Chase to Gerrit Smith, 22 Aug. 1859, DLC-Chase.

96. S. P. Chase to Ball, 22 April 1857; Flamen Ball to Chase, 7 April 1857; 10 April 1858; Ralston Skinner, 20 Nov. 1857, 4 Oct., 20 Nov. 1858, DLC-Chase; Flamen Ball to Chase, 7 March 1859, PHi-Chase.

97. Ralston Skinner to Chase, 15 April 1858, DLC-Chase.

Chapter 16. Defeat at the Summit

1. Gamaliel Bailey to Chase, 16 Jan. 1859; S. P. Chase to Bailey, 24 Jan. 1859, PHi-Chase.

2. Rowland Hazard to Chase, 15 Jan. 1859; Israel Green to Chase, 26 Jan. 1859, DLC-Chase.

3. S. P. Chase, "Diary," 17 Feb. 1859, DLC-Chase; to Charles Sumner, 19 Feb. 1859, MH-H-Sumner; to E. L. Pierce, 28 Feb. 1858, MH-H-Pierce.

4. S. P. Chase to Gurley, 20 June 1859; John A. Gurley to Chase, 22 June 1859; Richard C. Parsons to Chase, 10 July 1859, DLC-Chase.

5. William C. Cochran, "The Western Reserve and the Fugitive Slave Law: A Prelude to the Civil War," *Collections of the Western Reserve Historical Society*, no. 101 (Jan. 1920): 119, 120.

6. Ibid.

7. Ibid., 112, 113.

8. Ibid., 115–17.

9. Ibid., 118.

10. Arden V. Poindexter et al. eds., *Ohio Statutes* 622 (1856). See also Finkelman, *Imperfect Union*, 177, 178; Stephen Campbell, *The Slave Catchers* (Chapel Hill, 1968–70), 164–67.

11. Cochran, "Western Reserve," 115.

12. S. P. Chase to Griswold, 21 May 1859, PHi-Chase.

13. Another estimate gives 10,000 people attending the mass meeting, but the number seems excessive. Roseboom, *Civil War Era*, 349.

14. S. P. Chase to John Sherman, 3 March 1866, DLC-John Sherman.

15. S. P. Chase to Pierce, 24 May 1859, MH-H-Pierce.

16. The *Times* editorial is reprinted in the Cincinnati *Daily Gazette*, 3 June 1859; for a full account of the meeting see Cincinnati *Daily Gazette*, 26 May 1859. Eventually the federal district attorney dropped all charges when it was proven that Price was not the fugitive that was described in the original warrant. Cochran, "Western Reserve," 141–201, has a detailed account of the trials, protest meeting, and eventual release of the prisoners.

17. W. C. Earl to Chase, 3 Feb. 1859; S. P. Chase to Earl, 7 Feb. 1859; George Hoadly, Jr., to Chase, 15 Feb. 1859, DLC-Chase.

18. W. C. Earl to Chase, 3 Feb. 1859; S. P. Chase to Earl, 7 Feb. 1859, DLC-Chase.

19. Joseph Medill to Chase, 26 May 1859, PHi-Chase; S. P. Chase to Solon Foot, 26 May 1859, DLC-Chase; Julius Yanuch, "The Fugitive Slave Law and the Constitution" (Ph.D. diss., Columbia Univ., 1953), 179–86.

20. Roseboom, *Civil War Era*, 349, 350.

21. S. P. Chase to Sumner, 20 June 1859, MH-H-Sumner; Joseph H. Barrett to Chase, 22 Aug. 1859, DLC-Chase.

22. S. P. Chase to John A. Gurley, 20 June 1859; John A. Gurley to Chase, 22 June, 1 July 1859, DLC-Chase.

23. James Elliott to Chase, 7 May 1859, DLC-Chase; S. P. Chase to Pierce, 2 June 1859, MH-H-Pierce; *Ohio State Journal*, 2 Aug. 1859.

24. John W. Jones to Wade, 16 Sept. 1855, DLC-Wade.

25. Jean H. Baker, *Ambivalent Americans: The Know Nothing Party in Maryland* (Baltimore, 1986), 15, 49, 61–69; *Ohio State Journal*, 22 July 1857.

26. S. P. Chase to Lincoln, 14 April 1859, DLC-Lincoln.

27. Abraham Lincoln to Chase, 9 June 1859, DLC-Lincoln.

28. S. P. Chase to Lincoln, 13 June 1859, DLC-Lincoln.

29. Abraham Lincoln to Chase, 30 April 1859, DLC-Lincoln; S. P. Chase to Kate, 28 Oct. 1858, PHi-Chase.

30. Roseboom, *Civil War Era*, 359; *New York Times*, 28 Oct. 1859.

31. S. P. Chase to Pierce, 28 Aug. 1859, MH-H-Pierce; to Kate, 15 Sept. 1858, DLC-Chase; to Sumner, 10 Sept. 1859, MH-H-Sumner.

32. Dr. Elkanah Williams to Chase, 17 June 1859, DLC-Chase.

33. Roseboom, *Civil War Era*, 356.

34. *Ohio State Journal*, 4 Nov. 1859. In the Senate the Republicans had a majority of 15 and in the House a 22-vote majority; S. P. Chase to M. W. Delahay, 18 Oct. 1859, KHi.

35. S. P. Chase to Barrett, 29 Oct. 1859, Wv-AR.

36. Chase's concern was no doubt increased by a frantic letter from Joseph Medill, editor of the Chicago *Tribune*. See Joseph Medill to Chase, 30 Oct. 1859, PHi-Chase.

37. "Message of the Governor to the Fifty-fourth General Assembly," 2 Jan. 1860 (Columbus, Ohio, 1860), passim.

38. S. P. Chase to Hosea, 23 Jan. 1860, MH-H-Hosea.

39. S. P. Chase to Sumner, 20 Jan. 1860, MH-H-Sumner.

40. Ibid.

41. The vote: Chase 51 votes, Corwin 8, Columbus Delano 10, John Sherman 1, Valentine B. Horton 7. *Ohio Statesman,* 2 Feb. 1860.

42. Ibid. 4 Feb. 1860.

43. See, for instance, Gamaliel Bailey to Chase, 23 March 1859, PHi-Chase; J. R. Williams to Chase, 9 June 1859, DLC-Chase.

44. Thomas Spooner to Chase, 18 Dec. 1859, DLC-Chase.

45. Horowitz, *Great Impeacher,* 51, 52; James M. Ashley to Chase, 26 Aug. 1859, DLC-Chase.

46. Howard K. Beale, ed., *The Diary of Edward Bates 1859–1866,* (Washington, D.C. 1933), 1–9, 15, 111–14; New York *Tribune,* 27 March 1860; Marvin R. Cain, *Lincoln's Attorney General: Edward Bates of Missouri* (Columbus, MO, 1965), 100. As Greeley explained to Chase much later, he believed Bates was the best candidate to head off a disruption of the Union. "I knew he [Bates] was an old Fogy, but I thought for that reason just the man to maintain a powerful backing at the south." Horace Greeley to Chase, 29 Sept. 1863, PHi-Chase.

47. James M. Ashley to Chase, 26 Aug. 1859, DLC-Chase.

48. Joseph Medill to Chase, 26 April, 8 June, 27 July 1859, PHi-Chase; James M. Ashley to Chase, 29 July 1859, DLC-Chase.

49. S. P. Chase to Barney, 29 Jan. 1860, CSmH-Barney.

50. Ibid.

51. James M. Ashley to Chase, 19 Dec. 1859, DLC-Chase.

52. S. P. Chase to Pierce, 29 Jan. 1860, MH-H-Pierce.

53. James M. Ashley to Chase, 29 July 1859, DLC-Chase; Joseph Medill to Chase, 27 July 1859, PHi-Chase.

54. James M. Ashley to Chase, 14 Jan. 1860, DLC-Chase.

55. S. P. Chase to Israel Green, 16 March 1859, PHi-Chase; S. P. Chase to Briggs, 9 April 1859, PHi-Chase; James A. Briggs to Chase, 16 April, 19 Oct. 1859, DLC-Chase.

56. Willie Lee Rose, *Rehearsal for Reconstruction* (New York, 1964), 196, 202; Dumond, ed. *Birney Letters,* I: 520, 520n, 521, 521n.

57. William H. Brisbane to Schurz, 14 March 1859, OCHi-Chase; Carl Schurz to Chase, 3 Sept. 1859, PHi-Chase.

58. Carl Schurz to Chase, 5 Dec. 1859; S. P. Chase to Hosea, 14 Jan. 1860, MH-H.

59. Carl Schurz, *The Reminiscences of Carl Schurz,* II: 169–72.

60. S. P. Chase to Hosea, 18, 20, 27 Jan. 1860, MH-H-Hosea.

61. S. P. Chase to Donn Piatt, 26 May 1859, PHi-Chase.

62. S. P. Chase to Sumner, 20 June 1859, MH-H; *New York Times,* 23 June 1859.

63. Donn Piatt to Chase, 29 June 1859, DLC-Chase; S. P. Chase to Pierce, 2 July 1859, MH-H; Elizabeth Pike to Chase, 7 July 1859, DLC-Chase; S. P. Chase to Pike, 19 March, 2 April 1860, in Pike, *First Blows,* 502–6.

64. Chase also turned down E. D. Morgan's invitation to give a lecture in Albany. Edwin D. Morgan to Chase, 6 Jan. 1860, DLC-Chase.

65. S. P. Chase to Wilson Hunt et al., 1 Nov. 1859, DLC-Chase.

66. William H. Bissell to Chase, 4 Feb. 1860; George Hoadly, Jr., to Chase, 6 Feb. 1860, DLC-Chase.

67. James H. Briggs to Chase, 17 March 1860, DLC-Chase. Lincoln was on his return trip from New England. Earl S. Miers, ed., *Lincoln Day by Day,* 3 vols. (Washington, D.C., 1960), I: 275.

68. S. P. Chase to Pierce, 4 March 1860, MH-H-Pierce; Earl Wiley "'Governor' John

Griener and Chase's Bid for the Presidency in 1860," *Ohio State Archaeological and Historical Quarterly* 58 (1949): 259–73; *Ohio State Journal,* 2 March 1860.

69. Robert F. Paine to Wade, 22 March 1860, DLC-Wade; Beale, ed., *Bates Diary,* 310.

70. James Elliott to Chase, 23 Feb. 1860, DLC-Chase.

71. See, for instance, D. Cadwell to Wade, 14 Feb. 1860; S. P. Jones to Wade, 20 Feb. 1860, DLC-Wade.

72. There is evidence that he was ignorant of Wade's campaign. See S. P. Chase to Wade, 4 March 1860, DLC-Wade.

73. James A. Briggs to Wade, 27 Feb. 1860, DLC-Wade.

74. Amos Tuck to Chase, 14 March 1860, DLC-Chase.

75. Ibid. Joseph Barrett, one of the Ohio delegates-at-large, reported from Vermont that its delegation was uninstructed. He could find no one in the state who was working for Chase. Barrett thought that the only chance Chase had was if the convention deadlocked between Bates and Seward. Joseph H. Barrett to Chase, 9, 20, April 1860; James Stone to Chase, 23 March 1860. DLC-Chase. Governor Cleveland of Connecticut voiced the same complaint, lack of effective organization; S. P. Chase, 22 March 1860, DLC-Chase.

76. Edward L. Pierce to Chase, 12 March 1860, PHi-Chase.

77. S. P. Chase to Hosea, 4 April 1860, MH-H-Hosea.

78. Ashley had been urging such a course of action for some time. J. M. Ashley to Chase, 5 April 1860, DLC-Chase.

79. Henry D. Cooke to Chase, 28 Jan. 1860, PHi-Chase.

80. For Parsons, who would later play an important role in Chase's career, see Cleveland *Plain Dealer,* 19, 20 Feb. 1857. For Cooke, see W. D. Howells, *Years of My Youth,* 145, 146.

81. S. P. Chase to Parsons, 13 April 1860, PHi-Chase.

82. James M. Ashley to Chase, 5 April 1860, DLC-Chase; S. P. Chase to Parsons, 13 April 1860; Richard C. Parsons to Chase, 7 April 1860, PHi-Chase.

83. S. P. Chase to Pierce, 10 May 1860, MH-H-Pierce.

84. S. P. Chase to Pierce, 10 April 1860, MH-H-Pierce; John A. Bingham to Chase, 10 May 1860, DLC-Chase.

85. S. P. Chase to Briggs, 8 May 1860; to Eggleston, 10 May 1860, DLC-Chase.

86. Ibid.

87. Ibid.

88. Edward L. Pierce to Chase, 13 May 1860, PHi-Chase; Robert Hosea to Chase, 6 May 1860; Erastus Hopkins to Chase, 17 May 1860, DLC-Chase.

89. S. P. Chase to Giddings, 10 May 1860, DLC-Chase.

90. Erastus Hopkins to Chase, 17 May 1860, DLC-Chase.

91. John Niven, *Gideon Welles, Lincoln's Secretary of the Navy* (New York, 1973), 292–98; William B. Hesseltine, ed., *Three Against Lincoln: Murat Halstead Reports the Caucuses of 1860* (Baton Rouge, 1960), 141–49; Edward Chase to Chase, 21 May 1860, DLC-Chase. Hiram Griswold said he was satisfied that the Wade movement has been going on in secret for the past three months: "the presidency is no place for Wade." Hiram Griswold to Chase, 24 May 1860, DLC-Chase.

92. Hesseltine, ed., *Three Against Lincoln,* 141–49.

93. James Elliott to Chase, 21 May 1860, DLC-Chase.

94. The delegates who came early and worked for Wade were Benjamin Eggleston and Joseph Barrett, both of Cincinnati; ibid.

95. David Taylor to Chase, 22 May 1860, DLC-Chase; Joshua Giddings to Chase, 24 Aug. 1860, PHi-Chase.

96. David Taylor to Chase, 22 May 1860; Lyman W. Hall to Chase, 21 May 1860; F. M. Wright to Chase, 21 May 1860, DLC-Chase.

97. Wiley, "'Governor' John Griener," 261. See also John A. Bingham to Chase, 2 June 1860, DLC-Chase.

98. Johnson, comp., *Conventions*, 148, 149.

99. Giddings opposed this tactic as a convention ploy and urged that Chase's name be withdrawn, but he was overruled; Joshua Giddings to Chase, 24 May 1860, PHi-Chase.

100. Hesseltine, ed., *Three Against Lincoln*, 167–72.

101. Edward Chase to Chase, 21 May 1860, DLC-Chase.

102. James A. Briggs to Chase, 30 May 1860, DLC-Chase.

103. Chauncey F. Cleveland to Chase, 28 May 1860, DLC-Chase.

104. Joshua Giddings to Chase, 24 May 1860, PHi-Chase.

105. S. P. Chase to Samuel N. Wood, 24 May 1860, KHi; S. P. Chase to Parsons, 30 May 1860, PHi-Chase.

106. Chauncey F. Cleveland to Chase, 28 May 1860, DLC-Chase. S. P. Chase to Lincoln, 17 May 1860; Abraham Lincoln to Chase, 26 May 1860, DLC-Lincoln; *Ohio State Journal*, 18 June, 6 Nov. 1860.

Chapter 17. Visit to Springfield

1. Theodore C. Pease and James G. Randall, eds., *The Diary of Orville Hickman Browning*, 2 vols., Collections of the Illinois State History Library (Springfield, 1925), I: 447.

2. Roy P. Basler, ed., *The Collected Works of Abraham Lincoln*, 8 vols. (New Brunswick, 1953), IV: 168; S. P. Chase to Lincoln, 2 Jan. 1861, DLC-Lincoln; to George Fogg, 3 Jan. 1861, NhHi-Fogg.

3. Schuckers, *Chase*, 201.

4. Allan Nevins, *The Evening Post, A Century of Journalism* (New York, 1922), 261.

5. Basler, ed., *Works*, III: 378.

6. S. P. Chase to Pike, 10 Jan. 1861, MeU-Pike.

7. Schuckers, *Chase*, 201.

8. See Chase's sensitivity as expressed to Trumbull, 12 Nov. 1860, DLC-Trumbull.

9. S. P. Chase to Opdyke, 9 Jan. 1861, PHi-Chase; to Elihu Washburne, 14 Jan. 1861, DLC-E.B. Washburne.

10. Chase to Washburne, 14 Jan. 1861, DLC-E. B. Washburne.

11. Willard King, *Lincoln's Manager: David Davis* (Cambridge, 1960), 140, 141; Samuel Purviance to Cameron, 23 May 1860; Joseph Casey to Cameron, 24 May 1860, Cameron Papers, Dauphin County Historical Society, Harrisburg, Penn.

12. See Erwin S. Bradley's account of this transaction in *Simon Cameron, Lincoln's Secretary of War* (Philadelphia, 1966), 37, 58; but see also E. H. Bowen to Elihu Washburne, 19 May 1860, DLC-E. B. Washburne, and Reinhard H. Luthin, *First Lincoln Campaign* (Cambridge, 1944), 103.

13. Abraham Lincoln to Hannibal Hamlin, 27 Nov. 1860, DLC-Lincoln.

14. Basler, ed., *Works*, IV: 168, 174.

15. Ibid., 169–170.

16. New York *Tribune*, 7 Jan. 1861; *Illinois State Journal*, 7 Jan. 1861.

17. S. P. Chase to Banks, 7 Jan. 1861, CtY-Beinecke; S. P. Chase to Opdyke, 9 Jan. 1861, PHi-Chase.

18. Basler, ed., *Works*, IV: 171.

19. Ibid.; on Sunday morning, January 6, before meeting Chase for church, Lincoln had walked over to the hotel where Lieut. Governor Gustave Koerner was staying and woke him up

to discuss the Cameron dilemma. Koerner and Norman Judd, one of Lincoln's close associates, who was staying at the same hotel, were pressed into service. Both men warned Lincoln that he would be making a serious blunder if he made Cameron a member of his cabinet; Thomas J. McCormack, ed., *Memoirs of Gustave Koerner 1809–1896*, 2 vols. (Cedar Rapids, Iowa, 1909), II: 114.

20. Basler, ed., *Works*, IV: 171.

21. S. P. Chase to Barney, 8 Jan. 1861, DLC-Chase.

22. S. P. Chase to John G. Whittier, 4 Dec. 1860, VIU-Whittier.

23. Cincinnati *Daily Gazette*, 2 Nov. 1860.

24. S. P. Chase to Barney, 5 Nov. 1860, CSmH-Barney; S. P. Chase to Whittier, 4 Nov. 1860, ViU-Whittier; John G. Whittier to Chase, 9 Nov. 1860, DLC-Chase.

25. S. P. Chase to Pierce, 7 Nov. 1860, MH-H-Pierce.

26. Charles A. Dana to Chase, 7 Nov. 1860, PHi-Chase.

27. S. P. Chase to Dana, 10 Nov. 1860, DLC-Dana.

28. Beale and Brownsword, eds., *Welles Diary*, II: 389, 391; George G. Fogg to Barney, 15 Nov. 1860. CSmH-Barney.

29. Beale and Brownsword, eds., *Welles Diary*, II: 389.

30. Ibid., 388–92.

31. Beale, ed., *Bates Diary*, 166, 166n, 171.

32. William D. Bickham to Chase, 4 Dec. 1860, DLC-Chase.

33. Hiram Barney to Chase, 26 Nov. 1861, PHi-Chase; James A. Briggs to Chase, 27 Nov. 1860, DLC-Chase.

34. Henry B. Stanton to Chase, 7 Dec. 1860, DLC-Chase.

35. Abraham Lincoln to Seward, 8 Dec. 1860; Basler, ed., *Works*, IV: 148, 149.

36. Beale and Brownsword, eds. *Welles Diary*, II: 389.

37. Ibid.; see also William H. Seward to Lincoln, 13 Dec. 1861,NRU-Seward; to Lincoln, 15 Dec. 1861, DLC-Lincoln.

38. S. P. Chase to Lincoln, 10 Jan. 1861, DLC-Lincoln.

39. Harry Carman and Reinhard Luthin, *Lincoln and the Patronage*, (New York, 1943), 35, 36.

40. Earl S. Miers, *Lincoln Day by Day*, II: 5.

41. George G. Fogg to Chase, 12 Dec. 1860, DLC-Chase.

42. S. P. Chase to Wade, 21 Dec. 1860, DLC-Wade.

43. B. F. Wade to Chase, 29 Dec. 1860, PHi-Chase.

44. S. P. Chase to Jay, 16 Jan. 1861, NNC-Jay.

45. S. P. Chase to Scott, 29 Dec. 1860, in Warden, *Chase*, I: 367, 368.

46. N. B. Judd to Chase and enclosure, 16 Jan. 1861, DLC-Chase.

47. It is not known whether he telegraphed his reaction as requested. No telegram of that nature with the appropriate date is in the Lincoln Papers. In his endorsement of Judd's letter, Chase makes no mention of a telegram.

48. S. P. Chase to Judd, 20 Jan. 1861, DLC-Lincoln.

49. Arthur C. Cole, *The Era of the Civil War* (Springfield, 1919), 258; "Defeat of Compromise in 1861" (Washington, D.C., 1860), 1.

50. E. M. Stanton to Chase, 23 Jan. 1861, PHi-Chase.

51. Thomas Swann to Chase, 28 Jan. 1861, PHi-Chase.

52. S. P. Chase to Giddings, 31 Jan., 1 Feb. 1861, OCHi-Giddings; S. P. Chase to Whittier, 1 Feb. 1861, MSaE.

Chapter 18. Loaves and Fishes

1. S. P. Chase to Lincoln, 28 Jan. 1861, DLC-Lincoln. Chase had coined the slogan two days before in a letter to Sumner, 26 Jan. 1861, MH-H-Sumner.

2. Roseboom, *Civil War Era*, 376, 377.

3. S. P. Chase to Giddings, 3 Jan., 1 Feb. 1861, OCHi-Giddings.

4. Albert G. Riddle, *Recollections of War Time* (New York, 1895), 12.

5. S. P. Chase to Henry B. Carringon, 3 Feb. 1861, CtY-Carrington.

6. S. P. Chase to Richard Yates, 19 Feb. 1861, IHi-Yates.

7. Robert G. Gunderson, *Old Gentlemen's Convention: The Washington Peace Conference of 1861* (Madison, Wisc., 1961), 43.

8. Ibid., 82, 84.

9. Ibid., 65, 68.

10. Ibid., 86; Joseph E. Segar to Chase, 14 Nov. 1863, DLC-Chase.

11. "Defeat of Compromise", in 1861," 2–5.

12. Ibid., 8, 9.

13. Gunderson, *Convention*, 66.

14. "Defeat of Compromise," 6, 8.

15. Ibid., 6.

16. Ibid., 10.

17. Schuckers, *Chase*, 205.

18. Thurlow Weed Barnes, *Memoir of Thurlow Weed* (Boston, 1884), 329.

19. Gunderson, *Convention*, 90.

20. Ibid., 100–102.

21. Ibid.

22. Ibid., 84.

23. S. P. Chase to Dana, 1 March 1861, IHi-Chase.

24. William D. Haley, *Philp's Washington Described* (Washington, D.C., 1860), 208.

25. Beale, ed., *Bates Diary*, 175.

26. Allan Nevins, *Emergence of Lincoln*, 2 vol. (New York, 1950), II: 455.

27. William H. Seward to Lincoln, 2 March 1861, DLC-Lincoln.

28. Quoted in Niven, *Welles*, 322.

29. Miers, *Lincoln Day by Day*, II: 24.

30. Nevins, *Emergence of Lincoln*, II: 455; Beale and Brownsword, eds., *Welles Diary*, II: 391, 392; Basler, ed., *Works*, IV: 273, 373n.

31. S. P. Chase to William Dennison, 6 March 1861, PHi-Chase.

32. A. Haines to Chase, 25 Dec. 1860, DLC-Chase.

33. Jacob D. Cox to Chase, 5 March 1861, PHi-Chase.

34. S. P. Chase to My Dear Friend, 23 March 1861, DLC-Chase.

35. In 1864, the estimate was 1200 employees; Carman and Luthin, *Lincoln and the Patronage*, 60.

36. Howe, ed., *Ohio Historical Collections*, I: 169.

37. Charles A. Dana to Chase, 22 Feb. 1861, PHi-Chase; see also Victor Smith to Chase, 9 June 1861, DLC-Chase.

38. Basler, ed., *Works*, IV: 300, 325. Horace Greeley, George Opdyke, David Dudley Field, and James Wadsworth, the wealthy New York landowner.

39. Ibid., 325n.

40. Carman and Luthin, *Lincoln and the Patronage*, 61–63.

41. The naval officer, after the collector, drew the largest salary and emoluments. Lincoln

made this officer his own appointment despite Chase's opposition; Abraham Lincoln to Chase, 18 May 1861, in Basler, ed., *Works,* IV: 373.

42. Carman and Luthin, *Lincoln and the Patronage,* 63.

43. Ibid.

44. David Dudley Field to Chase, 29 March 1861, PHi-Chase.

45. Chase could not have been pleased when an Ohio friend wrote that the New York custom house had more patronage than the entire state of Ohio. David Taylor to Chase, 27 May 1861, PHi-Chase.

46. Maunsell B. Field, *Memories of Many Men and of Some Women* (New York, 1874), 160, 167; John J. Cisco to Chase, 28 March 1861, PHi-Chase.

47. S. P. Chase to Lincoln, 18 April 1861, DLC-Lincoln.

48. Ibid., 12 March 1861, CSmH-Barney.

49. Carman and Luthin, *Lincoln and the Patronage,* 57.

50. Ibid., 58, 59.

51. W. K. Upham to Chase, 13 March 1861, DLC-Chase; Cincinnati *Daily Gazette,* 12, 14 March, 1 April 1861; Albert G. Riddle, *Recollections of War Times: Reminiscences of Man and Events in Washington, 1860–1865* (New York, 1895), 20, 24.

52. S. P. Chase to Lincoln, 21 March 1861, DLC-Lincoln.

53. S. P. Chase to Seward, 20 March 1861, NRU-Seward; see also David Taylor to Chase, 27 May 1861, PHi-Chase.

54. S. P. Chase to Lincoln, 28 March 1861, DLC-Lincoln; William H. Seward to Chase, 28 March 1861, PHi-Chase; S. P. Chase to Seward, 27 March 1861, NRU-Seward; to John Sherman, 28 March 1861, DLC-J.Sherman.

55. Basler, ed., *Works,* IV: 296, 297.

56. S. P. Chase to John Bigelow, 11 March 1861, NSchU.

Chapter 19. War

1. William Seale, *The President's House,* 2 vols. (Washington and New York, 1986), I: 367.

2. Fletcher Pratt, ed., *William Howard Russell, My Diary North and South* (New York, 1954), 23–29.

3. Ibid.; Jay Cooke, "Memoirs", ms., "To My Children," Baker Library, Harvard University.

4. Pratt, ed., *Russell Diary,* 28, 29; Seale, *President's House,* I: 367, 368.

5. Beale, ed., *Bates Diary,* 177, 178; Montgomery Blair to Welles, 17 May 1873, DLC-Welles.

6. Beale and Brownsword, eds., *Welles Diary,* I: 13.

7. Ibid., 6.

8. Ibid., 13–15.

9. S. P. Chase to Lincoln, 16 March 1861, DLC-Lincoln.

10. S. P. Chase to Alfonso Taft, 28 April 1861, DLC-Taft. Influential citizens had noticed Chase's backsliding. See, for instance, J. H. Jordan to Chase, 8 May 1861, DLC-Chase.

11. Gideon Welles, *Lincoln and Seward* (New York, 1874), 65. Montgomery Blair to Welles, 17 May 1873, DLC-Welles.

12. Beale, ed., *Bates Diary,* 180.

13. S. P. Chase to Lincoln, 29 March 1861, DLC-Lincoln.

14. Burton J. Hendricks, *Lincoln's War Cabinet* (Boston, 1946), 172.

15. Allan Nevins, *The War for the Union* 4 vols. (New York, 1959), I: 56; Kenneth Stampp, *And the War Came* (Baton Rouge, 1950), 278; Richard Current, *Lincoln and the First Shot* (Philadelphia and New York, 1963), 80, 81; Niven, *Welles*, 326; see also John G. Nicolay and John Hay, *Abraham Lincoln, a History*, 10 vols. (New York, 1890), III: 194, 383, 384.

16. Nicolay and Hay, *Lincoln*, III: 194, 383, 384; R. M. Thompson and R. Wainwright, eds., *Confidential Correspondence of Gustavas Vass Fox*, 2 vols. (New York, 1920), I: 7–9.

17. Nevins, *War for the Union*, I: 58.

18. Ibid., 59, 60, 64, 65; Niven, *Welles*, 328–36.

19. Nevins, *War for the Union*, I: 53, 54; Thompson and Wainwright, *Fox Correspondence*, I: 12, Nicolay and Hay, *Lincoln*, III: 391, 392.

20. Welles, *Lincoln and Seward*, 53; Welles, *Diary*, vol. I; Niven, *Welles*, 329.

21. Yet Chase along with all his Cabinet colleagues found Lincoln irresolute, spending more time on the distribution of minor appointments than on affairs of state. See Basler, ed., *Works*, IV: 304–13, 325–26.

22. Thompson and Wainwright, *Fox Correspondence*, I: 31–35; Miers, *Lincoln Day by Day*, III: 35.

23. *Baltimore Sun*, 15 April 1861.

24. *New York Times*, 16 April 1861.

25. Frederick W. Seward, *Seward in Washington, 1846–1861* (New York, 1891), 544.

26. H. W. Hoffman to Chase, 23 April 1861, DLC-Chase.

27. Hiram Barney to Chase, 21 April 1861, PHi-Chase; Asa Howard to Chase, 21 April 1861, DLC-Chase; William P. Smith to Chase, 21 April 1861; S. P. Chase to Kate, 22 April 1861, PHi-Chase.

28. S. P. Chase to Barney, 24 April 1861, DNA-RG 56,BE,LS. Several weeks earlier John Jay had warned Chase that there was a danger of insurrection in New York if hostilities occurred. And Chase's letter to Barney was simply one of his taking elementary precautions; John Jay to Chase, 4 April 1861, DLC-Chase.

29. William H. Seward to Weed, 26 April 1861, in Thurlow Weed Barnes, *Thurlow Weed* (Boston, 1884), 332, 333.

30. Tyler Dennett, ed., *Lincoln and the Civil War in the Diaries and Letters of John Hay* (New York, 1939), 7.

31. S. P. Chase to Lincoln, 25 April 1861, DLC-Lincoln.

32. Dennett, ed., *Hay Diaries*, 12.

33. Nicolay and Hay, *Lincoln*, III: 238–42; the balance was finally disposed of at the very end of the Buchanan administration.

34. His assumptions were considerably above what he realized from the sale of the bonds, none of which was sold at par. Even the Treasury note issues he was forced to market at a heavy discount. S. P. Chase to Lincoln, 2 April 1861, DLC-Lincoln; to John Jay, 6 April 1861, NNC-Jay; George Opdyke to Chase, 26 April 1861, DLC-Chase.

35. Jay Cooke to Henry D. Cooke, 4 May 1831, PHi-Cooke. In Connecticut the same situation occurred. The state bore the outfitting, pay, and subsistence of the first five Connecticut regiments, which by May 1861 had cost $1,866,097. The legislature voted a $2,000,000 bond issue to meet this obligation. Unlike the Treasury Department loan the issue was readily marketed at an average premium of $1.570 above par; John Niven, *Connecticut for the Union* (New Haven, 1965), 407, 408.

36. Nevins, *War for the Union*, I: 307–9.

37. Nelson, according to William Howard Russell, weighed 260 pounds. Pratt, ed., *Russell Diary*, 30.

38. Nelson was given authority to raise and equip five regiments of infantry and one

regiment of cavalry. He was to receive 10,000 muskets, six pieces of field artillery, two mountain howitzers, and appropriate ammunition; Lorenzo Thomas to Nelson, 1 July 1861; William Nelson to Thomas, 16 July 1801; OR, ser. I, vol. I, pp. 251–53. Chase drafted the orders.

39. See Thomas E. Bramlette to Chase, 17 Aug. 1861, PHi-Chase.

40. Dennett, ed., *Hay Diaries*, 124.

41. See, for instance, Simon Cameron to Chase, 11 May 1861, PHi-Chase.

42. William H. Seward to Weed, 17 May 1861, in Barnes, *Weed Memoir*, 333, see also 330. Chase's role became public knowledge in Washington circles. See, for instance, Rose O'Neal Greenhow, the famous Confederate spy in the capital. Mrs. Greenhow wrote Chase, "But now I learn that you have charge of the reconstruction of the army and feel it is proper to address you." Rose Greenhow to Chase, 25 or 26 May 1861. DNA-RG59 - Greenhow.

43. Pratt, ed., *Russell Diary*, 192, 193; S. P. Chase to William C. Bryant, 4 Sept. 1862, NN-Goddard-Roslyn; to Parsons, 5 Sept. 1862, OCHP-Chase.

44. Irwin McDowell to Chase, 16 May 1861, PHi-Chase.

45. S. P. Chase to Henry B. Carrington, 5 May 1801, CtY-Carrington; Carrington to William Dennison, 15 May 1861, PHi-Chase.

46. New York's, *Evening Post* was also a persistent critic of Cameron. See William Cullen Byant to John Murray Forbes, 21 Aug. 1861, in Sarah Forbes Hughes, *Letters and Recollections of John Murray Forbes*, 2 vols. (Boston, 1900), I: 236, 237; S. P. Chase to Cameron, 8 July 1861; to Potter, 8 July 1864, DLC-Cameron; to Potter, 22 Aug. 1861, PHi-Chase.

47. J. B. Varnum to Chase, 31 July 1861, DLC-Chase.

48. John Jay, 11, 20 March 1861, NNC-Jay; S. P. Chase to Carrington, 27 March 1861, CtY-Carrington; Charles A. Heckscher to Chase, 29 June 1861, DLC-Chase; J. B. Varnum to Chase, 31 July 1861, DCL-Chase.

49. See, for instance, an occasion when Lincoln stopped by the Chase residence and insisted that he and his house guest Jay Cooke join him to attend a review. Jay Cooke, "Memoirs," 4.

50. Chase apologized to Senator James W. Grimes, who thought him rude. He excused his lack of courtesy by declaring that he "was oppressed by anxieties, perplexities and labors without number"; S. P. Chase to Grimes, 30 July 1861, PHi-Chase.

51. Stevens did not become a member until 8 July 1861. *House Journal*, 37th Cong., 1st sess., see "House Misc. Docs No. 5," 36th Cong., 1st sess.; "House Misc. Docs. No. 2," 37th Cong., 1st sess.

52. See De Alva Stanwood Alexander, *A Political History of the State of New York*, 3 vols. (New York, 1906–9), II: 188, 214, 350; III: 32.

53. Chase did not recommend an income tax, but Congress went ahead and levied a tax of 3 percent on annual incomes of over $800 as a part of its revenue bill; see U.S. *Statutes at Large*, vol. 12, 37th Cong., 1st sess., ch. 45, sec., 49, p. 309.

54. Ibid.

55. "Report of the Secretary of the Treasury"; "Senate Exec. Doc. No. 2," 37th Cong., 1st sess., passim.

56. J. H. Jordan to Chase, 18 April 1861, DLC-Chase; John Jay to Chase, 19 April 1861, DNA-RG60,LRT; S. P. Chase to Barney 1, 13 May 1861, DNA-RG56,BE,LS; S. P. Chase to William Nolan, 24 May 1861, DNA-RG56,XA.

57. William P. Mellen to Chase, 9 Aug. 1861, DNA-RG36; authority to appoint special agents was given in chap. 5, "An Act to Authorize a National Loan and for Other Purposes," *U.S. Statutes at Large*, 37th Cong., 1st sess.

58. George D. Prentice to Chase, 31 May 1861; S. P. Chase to Prentice, 28 Aug. 1861, PHi-Chase. George D. Prentice, the Connecticut-born editor of the *Louisville Journal*,

complained that stopping the transport of provisions going south on the Louisville and Nashville Railroad would have a disastrous effect on local merchants and injure the Unionist cause.

59. S. P. Chase to William Nolan, 29 May 1861; to Enoch Carson, 30 May 1861, DNA-RG56,XA.

60. S. P. Chase to William P. Mellen, 29 May 1861. MeB-Mellen.

Chapter 20. No Other Recourse

1. New York *Tribune*, 7 June 1891.

2. Donald B. Cole and John J. McDonough, eds., *Witness to the Young Republic, A Yankee's Journal* (Hanover, N.H., 1989), 300; for a graphic account of the aftermath of Bull Run, see Pratt, ed., *Russell Diary*, 232–34, 237–39.

3. New York *Tribune*, 7 June 1891. Howe, ed., *Historical Collections*, I: 989, 990; New York *Tribune*, 7 June 1891.

4. Quoted in T. Harry Williams, *Lincoln and His Generals* (New York, 1952), 21.

5. Pratt, ed., *Russell Diary*, 207–10; Niven, *Connecticut for the Union*, 130–34; see also Benjamin F. Butler, *Butler's Book* (Boston, 1892), 222, 223.

6. S. P. Chase to R. C. Parsons, 5 Sept. 1862, OCHP-Chase; Schuckers, *Chase*, 451.

7. OR, ser. I, vol. 2, p. 753; Stephen W. Sears ed., *The Civil War Papers of George B. McClellan* (New York, 1989), 66, 67.

8. Sears, ed., *McClellan Papers*, 36, 37.

9. Schuckers, *Chase*, 427, 428.

10. Sears, ed., *McClellan Papers*, 50.

11. S. P. Chase to Bryant, 4 Sept. 1862, NN-Goddard-Roslyn.

12. S. P. Chase to Barney, 16 April 1861, PHi-Chase. Richard M. Blatchford, a rich New York lawyer, was a close friend of Seward's. See Glyndon Van Deusen, *William H. Seward* (New York, 1867), 50, 53, 216.

13. Jay Cooke, "Memoirs," 39, 40.

14. E. P. Oberholtzer, *Jay Cooke, Financier of the Civil War*, 2 vols. (Philadelphia, 1907), I: 60ff.

15. Ibid., 38, 46, 50, 102–16. Cooke took only $10,000 worth of Pennsylvania bonds while other Philadelphia bankers and the Pennsylvania Railroad subscribed to sums ranging from $100,000 to $300,000.

16. Ibid.

17. Ibid., 148–49.

18. *U.S. Statutes at Large*, vol. 12, chap. 5, sec. 1, p. 259.

19. Jay Cooke to Henry D. Cooke, 8 April 1861, PHi-Cooke.

20. Ibid., 5 May 1861.

21. Ibid., 12 July 1861.

22. S. P. Chase to Cooke, 9 May 1861, PHi-Chase.

23. *Economist*, 24 Aug. 1861.

24. Hiram Barney to Chase, 9 May 1861, PHi-Chase.

25. S. P. Chase to Lincoln, 9 Aug. 1861, DLC-Lincoln.

26. S. P. Chase, "The National Loan Embracing the Appeal in Its Behalf" (Washington, 1861), 3.

27. Chase arrived in New York on August 11. The next day he gave a short, uplifting speech to the city's leading merchants at the rooms of the Chamber of Commerce. Introduced by Barney and Cisco, he shared the podium with Caleb Smith, who had come to New York

to sound the opinion of the city's leading figures on the war. *New York Times,* 13 Aug. 1861.

28. He had a plan of his own, which he had submitted to Chase. James Gallatin to Chase, 19 June 1861, PHi-Chase.

29. *New York Times,* 17, 19 Aug. 1861; James G. Blaine, *Twenty Years of Congress,* 2 vols. (Norwich, Conn., 1884), I: 410.

30. George S. Coe to E. G. Spaulding, 8 Oct. 1865, in E. G. Spaulding, *The Credit of the Government Made Immediately Available: History of the Legal Tender Paper Money* (2nd ed., Buffalo, 1875), appendix, 97–99.

31. S. P. Chase to Trowbridge, 21 March 1864, PHi-Chase.

32. *U.S. Statutes at Large,* vol. 12, chap. V, sec. 1, p. 259.

33. Jay Cooke, "Memoirs" (transcript), 75, 76.

34. The remarks are as near as Jay Cooke could remember them many years later. Ibid.

35. S. P. Chase, " The National Loan Appeal," 8–10.

36. Jay Cooke to Chase, 4, 6 Sept. 1861, PHi-Cooke.

37. See for instance James Gordon Bennett to Chase, 9 Sept. 1861, DLC-Chase.

38. S. P. Chase to Franklin Haven, Boston, John A. Stevens, New York, and C. H. Rogers, Philadelphia, Sept. 1861; to Henry F. Vail, 10 Sept. 1861, DNA-RG53,PC.

39. Ibid.

40. Ibid.; S. P. Chase to Henry F. Vail, 13 Sept. 1861, DNA-RG53LD, 5.

41. S. P. Chase to Cooke, 17 Sept. 1861, PHi-Cooke; to Samuel M. Felton, 13 Oct. 1861; to S. M. Hubley, 14 Oct. 1861, DNA-RG-53PC.

42. Wesley C. Mitchell, *A History of the Greenbacks* (Chicago, 1903), 26, 27; S. P. Chase to Trowbridge, 21 March 1864, PHi-Chase.

43. S. P. Chase to Medill, 16 Oct. 1861, PHi-Chase.

44. John A. Stevens to Chase, 14 Sept. 1861, PHi-Chase.

45. "Minutes of the Meeting with the Treasury Note Committee," 28 Sept. 1861, NHi-Stevens; Jacob Schuckers, "Shorthand Notes of Meeting with Treasury Note Committee," 28 Sept. 1861, NHi-Stevens.

46. Schuckers, "Shorthand Notes."

47. Ibid.

48. Ibid.

49. Ibid.

50. S. P. Chase to Belmont, 10 Aug. 1861, NNC; August Belmont to Chase, 31 Oct. 1861, PHi-Chase.

51. S. P. Chase to My darling Kate, 28 July 1865, DLC-Chase. Chase confused Ball's Bluff with Bull Run. Holmes does not mention his stay at the Chase's in his account of his first wound. Mark DeWolfe Howe, *Justice Oliver Wendell Holmes, the Shaping Years,* vol. I: 1841–70 (Cambridge, Mass., 1957), 108.

52. S. P. Chase to Key, 1 Nov. 1861, DLC-McClellan. Key had been a Cincinnati lawyer, judge, and politician. He was one of Chase's sources within McClellen's intimate circle.

53. See Edward Bates's estimate of the value of the cotton and rice plantations in the immediate vicinity of Port Royal. Beale, ed., *Bates Diary,* 195.

54. Bates noted that "'Sec.' Chase hasten[e]d to N.Y. to take the tide at the flood and telegraphs back that prospects are very good—credit rising"; *ibid.,* 201.

55. Ibid.

56. S. P. Chase to Stevens, 15 Dec. 1861, NHi-Stevens.

57. James G. Blaine, *Twenty Years of Congress: From Lincoln to Garfield,* 2 vols. (New York, 1884–86), I: 407.

58. S. P. Chase, "Report of the Secretary of the Treasury," *House Exec. Doc.*, 37th Cong., 2nd sess., 1861, passim.

59. Ibid., 11, 12.

60. Ibid., 15; "Federal Finances Examined," *Hunt's Merchant's Magazine* (Dec. 1861): 476, 507; Blaine, *Twenty Years*, 407.

61. John J. Cisco to Chase, 9 Dec. 1861, DLC-Chase; 10 Dec. 1861, DNA-RG56,LRAT.

62. S. P. Chase, "Diary," 25 Dec. 1861, DLC-Chase.

63. For a fine, but brief account of the Cabinet discussion, see Nevins, *War for the Union*, I: 388–94; see also Van Deusen, *Seward*, 308–16.

64. Beale, ed., *Bates Diary*, 221; Madeline Vinton Dahlgren, *Memoir of John A. Dahlgren* (New York, 1891), 354.

65. S. P. Chase, "Diary," 1 June 1862, DLC-Chase.

66. Jay Cooke to Chase, 27 Dec. 1861, PHi-Chase; John J. Cisco to Chase, 9 Dec. 1861, DLC-Chase; to Chase, 16 Dec. 1861, DLC-Cisco; John C. Hamilton to Chase, 17 Dec. 1861, PHi-Chase; S. P. Chase to Harrington, 19 Dec. 1861, MoSHi-Harrington; Henry Vail to Chase, 27 Dec. 1861; S. P. Chase to Cisco, 29 Dec. 1861, DNA-RG56,LRAT; S. P. Chase to Harrington, 29 Dec. 1861, CSmH-Barney; Hiram Barney to Chase, 30 Dec. 1861, PHi-Chase.

67. S. P. Chase to Ezra Lincoln, 10 Jan. 1862, DNA-RG53.

68. When Chase's report on December 10 became public the metropolitan banks held sufficient specie reserves to meet government demands and satisfy their private customers, but country banks had been drawing on them for coin and contractors were hoarding their specie. Thus the banks were depleting their reserves at a rapid rate, an outflow which reached very serious proportions when war with Great Britain seemed imminent. See "House Exec. Doc. No. 25," 37th Cong., 3rd sess., 125–42. *Hunt's Merchant's Magazine* (Dec. 1861): 476, 507.

69. Beale, ed., *Bates Diary*, 218–20.

Chapter 21. Military Moves and Missions

1. Hans L. Trefousse, *Benjamin Franklin Wade* (New York, 1963), 159, 160.

2. S. P. Chase, "Diary," 6 Jan. 1862, DLC-Chase. Beale, ed., *Bates Diary*, 218, 219. Bates held similar views. Not a month earlier, Chase had been most solicitous of McClellan. He asked the general "if you could give me a few minutes, and not desiring to waste any in fruitless endeavors to see you." S. P. Chase to McClellan, 11 Dec. 1861, PHi-Chase.

3. S. P. Chase, "Notes on the Union of the Armies of the Potomac and the Army of Virginia," 2 Sept. 1862, PHi-Chase.

4. Williams, *Lincoln and His Generals*, 51–53; George B. McClellan, *McClellan's Own Story* (New York, 1887), 202–3.

5. Beale, ed., *Bates Diary*, 223.

6. S. P. Chase, "Diary," 8–12 Jan. 1862, DLC-Chase.

7. Irwin McDowell, "Minutes," in William Swinton, *Campaigns of the Army of the Potomac* (New York, 1866), 80. McDowell wrote down his recollections, which are detailed. Later he asked Lincoln to read them and vouch for their authenticity. According to McDowell, the President did so and objected to only one phrase, where he referred to the radicals as "Jacobins."

8. Ibid., 82.

9. Ibid.

10. Ibid., 83.

11. Ibid.

12. Ibid., 84.

13. David Herbert Donald, ed., *Inside Lincoln's Cabinet: The Civil War Diaries of Salmon P. Chase* (New York, 1954), 27.

14. S. P. Chase, "Diary," 9, 11 Jan. 1862, DLC-Chase; S. P. Chase to My dear Katie, 12 Jan. 1862, PHi-Chase.

15. S. P. Chase, "Diary," 11 Jan. 1862, DLC-Chase.

16. Chase managed to get the banks to accept the demand notes; S. P. Chase, "Diary," 15 Jan. 1862, DLC-Chase.

17. Ibid., 8–15 Jan. 1862.

18. Ibid., 15 Jan. 1862.

19. Swinton, *Campaigns of the Army of the Potomac*, 84.

20. Ibid.

21. Ibid., 85. Shortly after the last meeting Chase received word from Cooke that both Kate and Nettie were convalescing; S. P. Chase to My darling Kate, 10 Jan. 1862; Henry D. Cooke to Chase, 17 Jan. 1862; Jay Cooke to Chase, 31 Jan. 1862, PHi-Chase.

22. Swinton, *Campaigns*, 85.

23. S. P. Chase to Garrett Davis, 24 Aug. 1801, PHi-Chase.

24. Green Adams to Chase, 9 Sept., 24 Aug. 1861, PHi-Chase.

25. William Nelson to Chase, 5, 12, 18, 24, 26 Aug. 1861, 12 Sept. 1861, PHi-Chase; E. M. Coulter, *The Civil War and The Adjustment in Kentucky* (Chapel Hill, 1926), 101–3; Green Adams to Chase, 14 Oct. 1861, PHi-Chase.

26. William Nelson to Chase, 15 Nov. 1861; S. P. Chase to Nelson, 19 Nov. 1861, PHi-Chase; W. T. Sherman to Chase, 9, 10 Oct. 1861, DNA-RG56PC; to Chase, 14 Sept. 1861, DLC-Lincoln.

27. Joshua Speed to Chase, 6 Sept. 1861, PHi-Chase; see also William Nelson to Chase, 4 Sept. 1861, PHi-Chase; R. R. Williams to Chase, 2 Sept. 1861; Elias F. Drake to Chase, 29 Aug. 1861, DLC-Chase.

28. On November 18, 1861, a convention of dissenters passed an Ordinance of Secession, and on December 10, 1861, Kentucky was admitted to the Confederacy, but for most of the war the state remained loyal, and was represented in Congress.

29. S. P. Chase to Cameron, 7 Oct. 1861, DLC-Cameron.

30. Beale, ed., *Bates Diary*, 198, 199.

31. Pease and Randall, eds., *Browning Diary* I: 507.

32. E. B. Washburne to Chase, 31 Oct. 1861, DLC-Chase.

33. S. P. Chase to Joseph Cable, 23 Oct. 1861, PHi-Chase.

34. The order was not to be delivered if Fremont had fought a battle and gained a victory or was about to be engaged. Basler, ed., *Works*, IV: 562.

35. McClellan, *McClellan's Own Story*, 207-10.

36. S. P. Chase to Cameron, 28 June 1861, DNA-RG56,Bc,LS.

37. Ibid., 27 Nov. 1861, DNA-RG107.

38. S. P. Chase to William Gray, 18 Sept. 1861, PHi-Chase.

39. See, for instance, S. P. Chase to Murat Halstead, 25 Dec. 1861, PHi-Chase. Had Cameron known precisely what Lincoln thought of him, he would have resigned on the spot. In a conversation with Nicolay, Lincoln said among other disparaging remarks that Cameron was "selfish and openly discourteous . . . obnoxious to the country—incapable of either organizing details or conceiving and advising general plans." Quoted in Helen Nicolay, *Lincoln's Secretary, a Biography of John G. Nicolay* (New York, 1949), 125.

40. Dennett, ed., *Hay Diaries*, 119.

41. S. P. Chase to John W. Forney, 19 Nov. 1861, DLC-Forney; *New York Times*, 20, 22 Nov., 2 Dec. 1861; Beale, ed., *Bates Diary*, 203.

42. John W. Forney, *Anecdotes of Public Men* (New York, 1877), 76.

43. Benjamin P. Thomas and Harold M. Hyman, *Stanton, the Life and Times of Lincoln's Secretary of War* (New York, 1962), 134.

44. Niven, *Welles*, 393–96.

45. A. Howard Meneeley, ed., "Three Manuscripts of Gideon Welles," *American Historical Review* 31 (1926): 486, 487, 491; *New York Times*, 6 Dec. 1861; New York *Tribune*, 4 Dec. 1861; Nicolay and Hay, *Lincoln*, V: 125–28.

46. Basler, ed., *Works*, V: 96.

47. S. P. Chase to Katie, 12 Jan. 1862, PHi-Chase.

48. S. P. Chase, "Diary," 12, 13 Jan. 1861, DLC-Chase; Beale, ed., *Bates Diary*, 226; Beale and Brownsword, eds., *Welles Diary*, I: 57–59; Meneeley, ed., "Three Manuscripts," 488; Basler, ed., *Works*, V: 96, 97.

49. S. P. Chase to My Dear Child [Kate], 14 Jan. 1862, PHi-Chase.

50. S. P. Chase to Fessenden, 15 Jan. 1862; Fessenden's endorsement, 15 Jan. 1862, MeB-Fessenden.

51. Stewart Van Vliet to Barlow, 10 Feb. 1862, CSmHBarlow.

52. These actions lifted the immediate fear of foreign intervention; S. P. Chase to Bishop Charles P. McIlvaine, 17 Feb. 1862, NNPM.

53. See Niven, *Welles*, 404–6, for a full account of Stanton's reaction.

54. Ibid.

55. Ibid.; Dennett, ed., *Hay Diaries*, 36, 37.

56. George B. McClellan to Gustavus V. Fox in Stephen W. Sears, ed., *McClellan*, 206, 209; G. V. Fox to McClellan, 13 March 1862, O.R. Ser. I, IX, p. 27.

57. Beale, ed., *Bates Diary*, 247–49.

58. *Daily National Intelligencer*, 21 April 1861; S. P. Chase to Horace Greeley, 12 Sept. 1862, DLC-Chase.

59. "I shall invite no one," he said in a brusque tone of voice, "nor do I see why Mr. Duer should go, but of that you will do as you please and also in respect to Mr. Seward." E. M. Stanton to Chase, 5 May 1861. PHi-Chase; Frank A. Flower, *Edwin McMasters Stanton* (New York, 1905), 153.

60. S. P. Chase to My darling Nettie, 7 May 1862, DLC-Chase.

61. Ibid.

62. OR, ser. II, Vol. I, p. 148.

63. S. P. Chase to My darling Nettie, 8 May 1862, DLC-Chase.

64. Ibid., 11 May 1862.

65. Ibid.

66. Ibid.

67. S. P. Chase to Horace Greeley, 12 Sept. 1862, DLC-Chase.

Chapter 22. High Stakes

1. Since McDowell was deemed to be key to the movement, and was close to Chase, Lincoln had him make a personal visit to McDowell's corps. S. P. Chase to Lincoln, 25 May

1862; Basler, ed., *Works,* V: 234, 235; Chase to Stanton, 25 May 1862, DLC-Stanton; "Narrative of Operations," 26 June 1862, DLC-Chase.

2. Williams, *Lincoln and His Generals,* 100, 101.

3. S. P. Chase, "Narrative," 26 June 1862, DLC-Chase.

4. Basler, ed., *Works,* V: 298, 298n.

5. Williams, *Lincoln and His Generals,* 124–27.

6. Ibid., 122, 123.

7. S. P. Chase, "Narrative," 26 June 1862, DLC-Chase.

8. Beale and Brownsword, eds., *Welles Diary,* I: 108.

9. See, for instance, Ormsby M. Mitchell to Chase, 3 Aug. 1862, PHi-Chase; S. P. Chase to My darling Katie, 11 July 1862, PHi-Chase.

10. S. P. Chase, "Diary," 21 July 1862, DLC-Chase.

11. Ibid., 22 July 1862.

12. S. P. Chase to B. F. Butler, 23 Sept. 1862, DLC-Butler.

13. S. P. Chase to William M. Dickson, 29 Aug. 1862, PHi-Chase.

14. S. P. Chase, "Diary," 3 Aug. 1862, DLC-Chase.

15. Ibid.

16. Ibid.

17. Ibid.

18. Ibid., Stephen E. Ambrose, *Halleck, Lincoln's Chief of Staff* (Baton Rouge, 1962), 9, 10.

19. S. P. Chase to Hamilton, 15 Aug. 1862, OCHP-Chase.

20. Beale and Brownsword, eds., *Welles Diary,* I: 102.

21. S. P. Chase, "Diary," 29, 30 Aug. 1862, DLC-Chase; Beale and Brownsword, eds., *Welles Diary,* I: 94.

22. Beale and Brownsword, eds., *Welles Diary,* 95. Chase had spoken to Bates about McClellan and secured his verbal agreement. But Bates had not seen the document which was being drafted at the War Department; S. P. Chase, "Diary," 30 Aug. 1862, DLC-Chase.

23. Beale and Brownsword, eds. *Welles Diary,* I: 100, 101.

24. Ibid.; S. P. Chase, "Diary," 31 Aug. 1862, DLC-Chase.

25. Beale and Brownsword, eds., *Welles Diary,* I: 101, 102.

26. Ibid., 103.

27. Ibid., 104, 105.

28. Ibid., 110, 111.

29. S. P. Chase to W. C. Bryant, 4 Sept. 1862, NN-Goddard-Roslyn.

30. S. P. Chase to Horace Greeley, 12 Sept. 1862, DLC-Chase.

31. John Sherman, *Recollections of Forty Years,* 2 vols. (New York, 1895), I: 273; S. P. Chase to Spaulding, 3 Feb. 1862, in Spaulding, *Legal Tender,* 59–60. See also W. C. Bryant to Chase, 2 Feb. 1862, PHi-Chase.

32. See the *Daily National Intelligencer,* 25 Jan. 1862, and the New York *Evening Post* for editorials during late January and early February 1862. See also Henry Douglas Bacon to Barlow, 8 Feb. 1863, CSmH-Barlow; E. G. Spaulding to Isaac Sherman, 8 Jan. 1862, CSmH-Sherman.

33. S. P. Chase to Spaulding, 22 Jan. 1862, DNA-RG56,D,LS; to Fessenden, 8 Feb. 1862, DNA-RG56,D,LS.

34. Montgomery Meigs to Chase, 4 Feb. 1862; S. P. Chase to John A. Bingham, 6 Feb. 1862, DNA-RG56,D,LS.

35. S. P. Chase to Cisco, 22 March 1862, DNA-RG53,LDLS; Oberholtzer, *Jay Cooke,* I: 194, 195.

36. S. P. Chase to Thaddeus Stevens, "Congressional Globe," 37th Cong., 2nd sess., 618.

37. S. P. Chase to George Coe, 24 Oct. 1862, PHi-Chase.

38. Spaulding, *Legal Tender,* 21.

39. Spaulding, Vail, Hunt & Co., to Chase, 25 Jan. 1862, DNA-RG56,LRWD; Mitchell, *Greenbacks,* 86, 87.

40. Though it depressed government bond prices, it would be difficult if not impossible to fix the amount with the data available.

41. *U.S. Statutes at Large,* 1862, vol. 12, sec. II.

42. *Cong. Globe,* 37th Cong., 3rd sess., 344; W. S. Rosecrans to Chase, 23 Nov. 1862, DNA-RG56,XA, is an example.

43. S. P. Chase to Galushu Grow, 18 Dec. 1862, PHi-Chase.

44. S. P. Chase to Thaddeus Stevens, 23 Dec. 1862, DNA-RG56,D,LS; Thaddeus Stevens to Chase, 19 Dec. 1862, DNA-RG56LRHC,WM.

45. S. P. Chase, "Report of the Secretary of the Treasury," 4 Dec. 1862 (Washington, D.C., 1862), 13, 14, 25, 3; Mitchell, *Greenbacks,* 89, 90.

46. John J. Cisco to Chase, 10 Oct. 1862, PHi-Chase; S. P. Chase to Fessenden, 28, 30 June 1862, DLC-John Sherman.

47. According to Chase a majority of its members still clung to the belief that the end of the war was in sight and convertibility would have a positive effect, "though still, not so well as receivability"; S. P. Chase to John Bigelow, 7 Oct. 1862, NSchU.

48. S. P. Chase, "Report" (1862), 3.

49. S. P. Chase to Fessenden, 8 July 1862, DLC-Sherman; to Cisco, 10 July 1862, DNA-RG56K,LS; "Report" (1862), 28.

50. *Cong. Globe,* 37th Cong., 2nd sess., 592.

51. S. P. Chase to W. P. Fessenden, 28 Jan. 1862, DNA-RG56,D,LS; S. P. Chase to Bigelow, 7 Oct. 1862, NSchU.

52. S. P. Chase, "Report" (1862), 15, 16.

53. Edward Haight to Chase, 23 July 1862, PHi-Chase; William Aspinwall to Chase, 15 Sept. 1862, PHi-Chase. Chase was not sure why there was a sudden rise in gold. "Is not a bond of the United States drawing 6 percent [gold] payable semi-annually intrinsically worth more than gold in equal amount?" he asked George S. Coe, a New York banker. "I think so—indeed I know so. . . . The solution I suppose is in the doubt cast on the credit by our military inaction and ill success." S. P. Chase to Coe, 24 Oct. 1862, PHi-Chase.

54. On October 21, Chase wrote James Watson Webb that "In spite of all embarrassments, I yet raise a million a day! but warrants exceed that by half a million and have for more than three months. The unpaid requisitions have therefore now reached the frightful sum of fifty six million. Misplaced confidence in the President and inertia if not worse in one general [McClellan] have brought us into bad straits." S. P. Chase to Webb, 21 Oct. 1862, Cty-Webb.

55. S. P. Chase to Cooke, 23 Oct. 1862, DLC-Chase; William G. Moorehead to Cooke, 28 Oct. 1862, PHi-Cooke.

Chapter 23. Emancipation with Exceptions

1. S. P. Chase to Morris Ketchum, 13 Oct. 1862, PHi-Chase.
2. S. P. Chase, "Diary," 6 March 1862; Basler, ed., *Works,* V: 144–46.

3. Phillip Paludan, *The Presidency of Abraham Lincoln* (Lawrence, Kans., 1994), 143–146.

4. S. P. Chase, "Diary," 22 July, 11, Sept. 1862, DLC-Chase.

5. Edward McPherson, *The Political History of the United States During the Great Rebellion* (Washington, D.C., and New York, 1864), 250, 251; S. P. Chase to Lincoln, 16 May 1862, DLC-Lincoln; to B. F. Butler, 24 June 1862, PHi-Chase.

6. Chase to Butler, 24 June 1862, PHi-Chase.

7. Beale and Brownsword eds., *Welles Diary*, Vol. I, 71.

8. Niven, *Welles*, 448.

9. S. P. Chase, "Diary," 21 July 1862, DLC-Chase.

10. Ibid.; Thomas and Hyman, *Stanton*, 238. Thomas and Hyman have made a case on circumstantial evidence that Hunter had already enlisted black troops, but other evidence seems to indicate that he was merely making preparations to do so. If he actually was enlisting such troops he was acting in open defiance of the President and Chase and Stanton were in on the coverup. Ibid., 234–38.

11. S. P. Chase, "Diary," 21 July 1862, DLC-Chase.

12. Quoted in Niven, *Welles*, 419, 420.

13. S. P. Chase, "Diary," 22 July 1862, DLC-Chase.

14. Ibid., 22 July 1862; Niven, *Welles*, 418–20.

15. Quoted in Thomas and Hyman, *Stanton*, 239.

16. S. P. Chase to John Cochran, 18 Oct. 1862, PHi-Chase.

17. S. P. Chase, "Diary," 22 Sept. 1862, DLC-Chase; Basler, ed., *Works*, V: 336–38, 338n, 433–36, 434n; Niven, *Welles*, 420–22; Dennett, ed., *Hay Diaries*, 50.

18. *New York Tribune*, 23–26 Sept. 1862; Nevins, *War for the Union*, II: 235.

19. Denett, ed., *Hay Diaries*, 50.

20. S. P. Chase, "Diary," 23 Sept. 1862, DLC-Chase.

21. Ibid., 24, 25 Sept. 1862, DLC-Chase.

22. Ibid.

23. Beale and Brownsword, eds., *Welles Diary*, I: 160, 161.

24. See his conversation with James A. Hamilton as an example of Chase's careful, calculating campaign. S. P. Chase, "Diary," 10 Sept. 1862, DLC-Chase. My quotation marks.

25. Pease and Randall, eds., *Browning Diary*, I: 599.

26. Francis Fessenden, *Life and Public Services of William Pitt Fessenden*, 2 vols. (New York, 1907), I: 234, 237; Pease and Randall, eds., *Browning Diary*, I: 596–99.

27. Nicolay and Hay, *Lincoln*, VI: 264; Pease and Randall, eds., *Browning Diary*, 601; Beale and Brownsword, eds., *Welles Diary*, I: 194.

28. Pease and Randall, eds., *Browning Diary*, I: 601.

29. Ibid., 265; Nicolay and Hay, *Lincoln*, VI: 262–65.

30. Fessenden, *Fessenden*, 242.

31. Beale and Brownsword, eds., *Welles Diary*, I: 194, 195.

32. Ibid., 196–98.

33. Nicolay and Hay, *Lincoln*, VI: 266.

34. Fessenden, *Fessenden*, I: 244–46.

35. Nicolay and Hay, *Lincoln*, VI: 266; Pease and Randall, eds., *Browning Diary*, I: 603.

36. Beale and Brownsword, eds., *Welles Diary*, I: 201–2.

37. Nicolay and Hay, *Lincoln*, VI: 268–70; Basler, ed., *Works*, VI: 12, 13.

38. S. P. Chase to Seward, 21 Dec. 1862, NRU-Seward; to Lincoln, 20, 22 Dec. 1862, DLC-Lincoln; Philander Chase to Baruch Chase, 30 July 1823, NhHi-Chase.

Chapter 24. Mixed Results

1. W. C. Bryant to Fessenden, 12 Jan. 1863, DLC-Fessenden.

2. Joseph Hooker to Chase, 16 Jan. 1863; S. P. Chase to Hooker, 26 Jan. 1863, PHi-Chase.

3. S. P. Chase to McIlvaine, 25 Jan. 1863, PHi-Chase.

4. S. P. Chase to Lincoln, 29 Dec. 1862, DLC-Lincoln.

5. Edward Jordan to Chase, 4 Sept. 1862, DNA-RG56,AB,Atty.Gen; S. P. Chase to Bates, 24 Sept. 1862, DNA-RG60; Edward Bates to Chase,29 Nov. 1862, DNA-RG56,AB,Att.Gen.

6. *U.S. Statutes at Large,* 37th Cong., 1st sess., vol. 12, chap. III, p. 256.

7. George S. Denison to Chase, 15 May 1862, DLC-Chase.

8. Ibid., May 1862.

9. Ibid., 4 Feb. 1863, 28 June, 19 July, 10 Oct. 1862, DLC-Chase.

10. There has been considerable speculation about Chase's activities in Louisiana. Fred Harrington, in his biography of Banks, argues that the Treasury personnel in Louisiana exercised their influence to promote Chase's Reconstruction ideas and his bid for the Republican nomination in 1864. His evidence is drawn largely from newspaper accounts, Banks's and Chase's correspondence, John Hay's diary, and the *Official Records of the Union and Confederate Armies;* Fred Harrington, *Fighting Politician, Major General N. P. Banks* (Philadelphia 1948), 61, 101–2. An opposing view is taken by Peyton McCrary in his *Abraham Lincoln and Reconstruction* (Princeton, N.J., 1978). He disputes Harrington's findings and maintains that there is little evidence of Treasury personnel working with the radical factions in New Orleans in Chase's behalf; see 169–71.

11. George H. Denison to Chase, 20 Aug., Nov., 14, 10 Dec. 1862, DLC-Chase; Hans Trefousse, *Ben Butler, the South Called Him Beast* (New York, 1957), 122–30.

12. Dr. Max Bonzano to Chase, 14 June, 6 Sept. 1862; George H. Denison to Chase, 9 Sept., 10, 16 Oct., 14 Nov. 1862; 12 Feb. 1863, DLC-Chase.

13. S. P. Chase to Butler, 24 June 1862, PHi-Chase; 31 July 1862, DLC-Butler; Schuckers, *Chase,* 375–78.

14. McCrary, *Lincoln and Reconstruction,* 145.

15. Ibid., 96, 97.

16. S. P. Chase, "Diary," 16, 18 Aug. 1862, DLC-Chase.

17. George Denison to Chase, 29 Nov. 1862, DLC-Chase; Harrington, Banks, 100; Jessie A. Marshall, comp., *Private and Official Correspondence of General Benjamin F. Butler,* 5 vols. (Norwood, Mass., 1917), II: 447.

18. George H. Denison to Chase, 14, 29 Nov. 1862, DLC-Chase.

19. Ibid., 29 Nov., 4 Dec. 1862, DLC-Chase.

20. S. P. Chase to Bullitt, 14 April 1863, PHi-Chase.

21. Ibid., 24 Feb. 1863, DLC-Butler.

22. Basler, ed., *Works,* VI: 73, 74, 76, 77, 77n, 100, 100n.

23. S. P. Chase to Butler, 10 April 1863, DLC-Butler.

24. Basler, ed., *Works,* V: 344, 346; George Denison to Chase, 9 May 1863, DLC-Chase.

25. Basler, ed., *Works,* IV: 16, 16n. V: 16, 16n. Ludwell H. Johnson, *Red River Campaign, Politics and Cotton in the Civil War* (rpt.) Kent, Ohio 1993), 53.

26. George Denison to Chase, 8 Jan., 8 Feb., 7, 14, 31 March, 13, 30 April, 9 May 1863, DLC-Chase. In deference to Chase's wishes regarding Denison, Lincoln refused to name Bouligny acting surveyor; John E. Bouligny to Lincoln, 23 April 1863, DLC-Lincoln; Basler, ed., *Works,* VI: 172.

27. George Denison to Chase, 30 April, 9 May, 13 June 1863, DLC-Chase.

28. S. P. Chase to Bullitt, 26 Feb. 1863, DLC-Chase.

29. Ibid., 14 April 1863, PHi-Chase.

30. S. P. Chase to Flanders, 24 May 1863, NhD-Flanders; see also S. P. Chase to Stanton, 12 Jan. 1863, PHi-Chase.

31. Basler, ed., *Works*, VI: 428, 429.

32. S. P. Chase, "Diary," 15 Aug. 1862, DLC-Chase; Chase to Lincoln, 27 Feb., 2 March 1863, DLC-Lincoln; to James Dixon, 28 Feb. 1863, PHi-Chase.

33. Beale and Brownsword, eds., *Welles Diary*, I: 78, 81, 235, 239, 246; Carman and Luthin, *Patronage*, 236, 237; Mark Howard to Chase, 19 Dec. 1862, DLC-Chase.

34. S. P. Chase to Lincoln, 22 April 1863. DLC-Lincoln.

35. S. P. Chase to Edward Jordan, 17 Dec. 1862, DNA-RG206; Edward Jordan to Chase, 25 Jan. 1863, DNA-RG56,AB,Solicitor; S. P. Chase to Fessenden, 4 Feb. 1863, DNA-RG46; Hiram Barney to Chase, 8 Jan. 1863, PHi-Chase.

36. S. P. Chase to Edward Haight, 20, 23 May 1863; Hiram Barney to Chase, 20 May 1863, PHi-Chase; John Jay to Chase, 21 May 1863, DLC-Chase; Basler, ed., *Works*, VI: 224; John Jay to Chase, 21 May 1863; William A. Hall to Chase, 22 May 1863, DLC-Chase. 37. S. P. Chase to Harrington, 23 March 1863, MoSHi-Harrington; A. G. Henry to Lincoln, 13 April 1863, DLC-Lincoln; Thomas Heaton to Chase, 23 May 1863, DLC-Chase.

38. S. P. Chase to Harrington, 23 March 1863, MoSHi-Harrington.

39. S. P. Chase to Lincoln, 11 May 1863, DLC-Lincoln; Basler, ed., *Works*, VI: 209.

40. S. P. Chase to Lincoln, 11 May 1863, DLC-Lincoln.

41. Ibid.; Basler, ed., *Works*, VI: 210, 213.

42. Dennett, ed., *Hay Diaries*, 53, 54.

43. S. P. Chase to Pierce, 20 Dec. 1861, DLC-Chase.

44. Ibid., 11 April 1862.

45. Ibid., 23, 26 April 1862.

46. E. L. Pierce to Chase, 7 May 1862, DNA-RG366.

47. Warden, *Chase*, I: 395, 396, 396n; E. L. Pierce to Chase, 26 Oct. 1863, PHi-Chase; S. P. Chase to Pierce, 20 Dec. 1861, DLC-Chase; E. L. Pierce to Chase, 29 Dec. 1861, PHi-Chase; S. P. Chase to Reynolds, 4 Jan. 1862, OCHP-Chase; New York *Tribune*, 9 Jan. 1862.

48. Boston *Daily Advertiser*, 24 Feb. 1862.

49. E. L. Pierce to Chase, 3 Feb. 1862, in Frank Moore, ed., *The Rebellion Record*, 12 vols. (New York, 1861–63), Supplement I: 314.

50. S. P. Chase to Pierce, 2 Aug. 1862, MH-H; see, for instance, Boston *Daily Advertiser*, 24 Feb. 1862.

51. See Gen. Ormsby M. Mitchell to Chase, 22 Sept. 1862, PHi-Chase.

52. See, for instance, Niven, *Connecticut for the Union*, 283, 284.

53. New York *Tribune*, 17 June 1862.

54. S. P. Chase to Reynolds, 30 Dec. 1861, OCHP; S. P. Chase to Barney, 31 Dec. 1861, 4 Jan. 1862, DNA-RG56,H,LS.

55. Rose, *Rehearsal for Reconstruction*, 61.

56. Ibid., 67; W. H. Reynolds to Chase, 2 April 1862, PHi-Chase; E. L. Pierce to Chase, 16 Feb. 1862, DNA-RG60.

57. Gen. Henry W. Benham to Chase, 9 May 1862, PHi-Chase; S. P. Chase to Rufus Saxton, 16 May 1862, DNA-RG366; to Pierce, 18 June 1862, MH-H.

58. Rose, *Rehearsal*, 204, 205.

59. Ibid.; House Exec. Docs., no. 72, 37th Cong., 3rd sess.

60. Ormsby M. Mitchell to Chase, 19, 22 Sept. 1862, PHi-Chase; Frances Dana George

to Chase, 30 Oct. 1862; Mansfield French to Chase, 23 Oct. 1862; Dwight Bannister to Chase, 8 Sept. 1863, DLC-Chase.

61. E. L. Pierce to Chase, 2 April 1863, PHi-Chase.

62. S. P. Chase to Pierce, 2 Aug. 1862, MH-H-Pierce.

63. S. P. Chase to Noyes, 7 April 1863, PHi-Chase.

64. Senate Exec. Doc., no. 3, 37th Cong., 1st. sess. The act itself is dated 12 March 1863.

65. S. P. Chase to Pierce, 1 May 1863, DNA-RG366 S. P. Chase to Pierce, 11 Aug. 1863, DLC-Chase.

66. See the Taxation Act of 7 June 1862, *U.S. Statutes at Large*, vol. XII, pp. 422–26.

67. Mansfield French to Chase, 2, 6 Jan. 1863, DLC-Chase.

68. John A. Andrew to Chase, 3 Jan. 1863, Phi-Chase.

69. Senate Exec. Docs., no. 26, 37th Cong., 2nd sess.

70. S. P. Chase to Hannibal Hamlin, 26 Jan. 1863, DNA-RG56,BC,LS; About half of this acreage was purchased by one of Pierce's superintendents, Edward Philbrick, at the ridiculously low price of one dollar an acre on behalf of himself and a Boston syndicate. Philbrick himself eventually cleared over $81,000 on the 1863 crop alone. He did not escape criticism from his coworkers, however; Rose, *Rehearsal*, 214, 215, 222, 223, appendix, 434.

71. Basler, ed., *Works*, VI: 453–59.

72. Rose, *Rehearsal*, 275, 275n.

73. Mansfield French to Chase, 7 Feb. 1863, DLC-Chase.

74. S. P. Chase to Brisbane et al., 30 Dec. 1863, MeWC; Basler, ed., *Works*, VII: 98, 99.

75. Basler, ed., *Works*, VII: 98 99.

76. Rose, *Rehearsal*, 291; Edward L. Pierce to Chase, 21 Sept. 1863, PHi-Chase.

77. E. L. Pierce to Chase, 2 April 1863, PHi-Chase; Mansfield French to Chase, 22 Aug. 1863, DLC-Chase.

78. Willie Lee Rose has made a careful analysis of the activities of the northern abolitionists in and around Port Royal. Her conclusions were that there was no massive onslaught of would be entrepreneurs, but "enough to stiffen action." Rose, *Rehearsal*, 288.

79. Missouri *Daily Democrat*, 23 Sept. 1863.

Chapter 25. Old Greenbacks

1. "Report of the Secretary of the Treasury for the Year Ending, June 30, 1863," 38th Cong., 1st sess., 1863, pp. 14–16.

2. For debates on the Third Legal Tender Act, see *Congr. Globe*, 37th Cong., 3rd sess., 383, 455, 522; *U.S. Statutes at Large*, 37th Cong., 3rd sess., vol. 12, p. 709

3. Beale, ed., *Bates Diary*, 292.

4. S. P. Chase, "Report on the Finances, 1863," 2; Beale and Brownsword, eds., *Welles Diary*, I: 160.

5. S. P. Chase, "Report on the Finances, 1863," 20.

6. Ibid., 17, 18.

7. Nicolay and Hay, *Lincoln*, IX, 395, 396.

8. S. P. Chase to Sprague, 15 July 1863, PHi-Chase.

9. John J. Cisco to Chase, 13 July 1863, DNA-RG56,LRAT.

10. Ibid., 14 July 1863; S. P. Chase to Cisco, 15 July 1863. DNA-RG56,XA; for an interesting account of Cisco's activities during the riot, see John J. Cisco to Chase, 23 July 1863, DNA-RG56,LRAT; see also Hiram Barney to Chase, 15 July 1863, PHi-Chase.

11. S. P. Chase to David Dudley Field, 16 July 1863, PHi-Chase.

12. S. P. Chase, "Diary," 20 Sept. 1863, DLC-Chase.

13. Beale and Brownsword, eds., *Welles Diary*, I: 438–41; S. P. Chase, "Diary," 21, 22 Sept. 1863, DLC-Chase.

14. S. P. Chase, "Diary," 21, 22 Sept. 1863, DLC-Chase.

15. Ibid., 24 Sept. 1863.

16. Bates described Halleck as being "something bloated and with watery eyes. . . . But whether from brandy or opium I cannot tell." Beale, ed., *Bates Diary*, 311.

17. George S. Boutwell, *Reminiscence of Sixty Years in Public Affairs*, 2 vols. (rpt., New York 1968), I: 311.

18. David Homer Bates, *Lincoln in the Telegraph Office* (New York, 1907), 146n.

19. Basler, ed., *Works*, VI: 469, 470, 481.

20. S. P. Chase, "Diary," 24 Sept. 1863, DLC-Chase.

21. Ibid.

22. Ibid., 25 Sept. 1863; Flower, *Stanton*, 286, 287; Bates, *Lincoln in the Telegraph Office*, 173–75.

23. Quoted in Thomas and Hyman, *Stanton*, 289.

24. S. P. Chase, "Diary," 26–28 Sept. 1863, DLC-Chase.

25. Ibid.

26. Allan Nevins, *The War for the Union, the Organized War, 1863–1864* (New York, 1971), 202.

27. Beale and Brownsword, eds., *Welles Diary*, I: 467; William E. Smith, *The Francis Preston Blair Family in Politics*, 2 vols. (New York, 1933), II: 237–40; Chase, 8 Oct. 1863, PHi-Chase.

28. Beale and Brownsword, eds., *Welles Diary*, I: 306, 321, 344.

29. Ibid., 469, 470; S. P. Chase to Jordan, 8 Oct. 1863, DNA-RGAB56; Edward Jordan to Chase, 9 Oct. 1863, DLC-Chase.

30. William Prescott Smith to Chase, 9 Oct. 1863, PHi-Chase.

31. Dennett, ed., *Hay Diaries*, 138.

32. William Prescott Smith to Chase, 9 Oct. 1863, PHi-Chase.

33. Beale and Brownsword, eds., *Welles Diary*, I: 469. Later on the urgent plea of Thaddeus Stevens Chase gave leave to Treasury personnel from Pennsylvania; Thaddeus Stevens to Chase, 21 Sept. 1863, PHi-Chase; Dennett, ed., *Hay Diaries*, 99; S. P. Chase to Benjamin F. Butler, 9 Oct. 1863, DLC-Butler; to Edward D. Mansfield, 18 Oct. 1863, PHi-Chase.

34. S. P. Chase to Simon Cameron, 19 Oct. 1863; Dauphin County Hist. Soc. *Ohio State Journal*, 12, 13 Oct. 1863; Cincinnati *Gazette*, 12, 13 Oct. 1863.

35. S. P. Chase, "Going Home to Vote," Oct. 1863, pp. 3–5, DLC-Chase; *Ohio State Journal*, 12, 14 Oct. 1863; Cincinnati *Gazette*, 20 Oct. 1863.

36. Beale and Brownsword, eds., *Welles Diary*, I: 469; S. P. Chase, "Going Home to Vote," 7.

37. Ibid., 8.

38. Ibid., 9, 10, 13, 14, 18, 20.

39. Ibid., 20–31; Beale, ed., *Bates Diary*, 311.

40. S. P. Chase to Lincoln, 13 Oct. 1863, DLC-Lincoln.

41. S. P. Chase to Elihu Washburne, 17 Oct. 1863, PHi-Chase; S. P. Chase, "Going Home to Vote," 32–36.

42. Chase himself so interpreted his remarks. S. P. Chase to William D. Bickham, 18 Oct. 1863, PHi-Chase.

43. Cincinnati *Enquirer*, 18 Oct. 1863; Flamen Ball to Chase, 21 Oct. 1863, DLC-Chase.

44. Henry Hoffman to Chase, 19 Oct. 1863, DLC-Chase.

45. S. P. Chase, "Going Home to Vote," 31, 35, 36.
46. Beale, ed., *Bates Diary,* 311, 308.
47. Basler, ed., *Works,* VI: 499–504.
48. S. P. Chase to Drake, 26 Oct. 1863, PHi-Chase. As befit his conservative stance, Gideon Welles thought Lincoln's response showed "tact, shrewdness and good sense"; Beale and Brownsword, eds., *Welles Diary,* I: 471.
49. Basler, ed., *Works,* VI: 428, 429; S. P. Chase, "Diary,"17 Sept. 1863, DLC-Chase.
50. S. P. Chase to William D. Bickham, 18 Oct. 1863, PHi-Chase.
51. Dennett, ed., *Hay Diaries,* 100, 101.
52. William Sprague to Chase, 31 May 1863, DLC-Chase; S. P. Chase to Kate, 22 June 1863, PHi-Chase.
53. The couple became engaged in May. Hiram Barney to Chase, 26 May 1863, PHi-Chase; Beale and Brownsword, eds., *Welles Diary,* I: 306.
54. S. P. Chase to Barney, 29 June 1863, PHi-Chase.
55. R. G. Hazard to Chase, 10 April 1863, DLC-Chase.
56. Phelps, *Kate Chase,* 127.
57. S. P. Chase to Sprague, 16 July 1863, PHi-Chase.
58. Ibid., 26 Nov. 1863.
59. Ibid., 31 Oct. 1863.
60. William Sprague to Chase, 8 June 1863, DLC-Chase.
61. Ibid., 4 Dec. 1863.
62. S. P. Chase to Sprague, 6 June, 21 July 1863, PHi-Chase.
63. S. P. Chase to My darling Katie, 21 Sept. 1863, PHi-Chase.
64. S. P. Chase to Sprague, 6 June, 14 July 1863, PHi-Chase.
65. Ibid., 14 July 1863.
66. For Kate's expensive tastes see, for instance, John J. Cisco to Chase, 13 June 1863; S. P. Chase to Kate, 19 Aug. 1863, PHi-Chase; J. Prentice Tucker to Chase, 10 Oct. 1863; Francis B. Antz to Chase, 16 Sept. 1863; A. P. Pillot to Chase, 26 Sept. 1863, DLC-Chase.
67. William Sprague to Chase, 18 July 1863, DLC-Chase; S. P. Chase to Kate, 17 Sept. 1863, PHi-Chase.
68. S. P. Chase to Kate, 9 Sept. 1863, PHi-Chase.
69. *New York Times,* Washington *Daily National Intelligencer,* 13 Nov. 1863.
70. Virginia Jeans Laas, ed., *The Civil War Letters of Elizabeth Blair Lee* (Urbana and Chicago, 1991), 314.
71. William P. Mellen to Chase, 5 Nov. 1863, PHi-Chase; R. L. B. Clarke to Chase, 21 Oct. 1863, DLC-Chase.
72. S. P. Chase to Conness, 8 Aug., 18 Oct. 1863; to George Wilkes, 2 Sept. 1863; to Conness, 31 Oct. 1863, PHi-Chase.
73. S. P. Chase to Andrew Johnson, 19 Oct. 1863, DLC-Johnson.
74. S. P. Chase to Thomas Swann, 6 June 1863; to Henry Winter Davis, 8 June 1863; Hugh L. Bond to Chase, 18 Aug. 1863; S. P. Chase to Henry Wilson, 24 Aug. 1863, PHi-Chase.
75. Dennett, ed., *Hay Diaries,* 99, 100.
76. Ibid., 97.
77. Abraham Lincoln to Erastus Corning and others, 12 June 1863, DLC-Lincoln; see, for instance, Richard C. Parsons to Chase, 15 June 1863, PHi-Chase; Basler, ed., *Works,* VI: 260–69.
78. Dennett, ed., *Hay Diaries,* 110.
79. Beale and Brownsword, eds., *Welles Diary,* I: 139.

80. William P. Mellen to Chase, 6 Nov. 1863, PHi-Chase. The triumph of the radical Republicans in Missouri heartened Chase. He took the result to mean vindication of his views as opposed to those of Frank Blair and indirectly the President's; S. P. Chase to Barney, 21 Oct. 1863, DLC-Chase; to Barney, 7 Nov. 1863, PHi-Chase.

81. William Prescott Smith to Chase, 10 Oct. 1863, PHi-Chase; Beale, ed., *Bates Diary*, 310; William P. Mellen to Chase, 29 Oct. 1863, PHi-Chase.

82. Hiram Barney to Chase, undated, 1863, DLC-Chase.

83. John F. Bailey to Chase, 13, 26 Dec. 1863, DLC-Chase.

84. John A. Stevens to Chase, 15 Sept. 1863, PHi-Chase; Rufus F. Andrews to Chase, 15 Dec. 1863, DLC-Chase.

85. S. P. Chase to Edward Jordan, 7 Dec. 1863; Edward Jordan to Chase, 25 Jan. 1863, DNA-RG56AB; Horace Greeley to Chase, 3 Nov. 1862, PHi-Chase.

Chapter 26. Bad Company

1. Basler, ed., *Works*, VI: 554, 555.

2. Laas, ed., *Blair Lee Letters*, 335.

3. C. B. Rollins, "Some Impressions of Frank Blair," *Missouri Hist. Rev.* 24, no. 3 (April 1930): 352; Smith, *Blair Family*, II: 116, 117; Elbert B. Smith, *Francis Preston Blair* (New York, 1980), 334, 335.

4. *Cong. Globe*, 38th Cong., 1st sess., "Appendix," 47, 48.

5. Ibid., 50, 51.

6. Smith, *Blair Family*, II: 258, 259.

7. For the debate see *Cong. Globe*, 38th Cong., 1st sess., part 2, 1827–32.

8. John Bigelow, ed., *Letters and Literary Memorials of Samuel J. Tilden*, 2 vols. (rpt., New York, 1971), I: 233.

9. William P. Mellen to Chase, 6 Nov. 1863, PHi-Chase.

10. Beale and Brownsword, eds., *Welles Diary*, I: 533.

11. Albert G. Riddle, *Recollections of War Times: Reminiscences of Men and Events in Washington* (New York, 1895), 275.

12. As well he might be. For example, see Henry B. Moore to Jay Cooke, 10 April 1864, PHi-Chase.

13. Lincoln later declared to a complaining Sumner: "Now Mr. S[umner] the B.[lair]s are brave people & never whine—but are ready always to fight their enemies and very generally whip them." Laas, ed., *Blair Lee Letters*, 371.

14. Riddle, *Recollections*, 266.

15. Ibid., 266–69, 267n.

16. Riddle in a note to his account of the interview says that two to three weeks after it took place, Chase requested a verbatim account, which he made, and though he was not entirely satisfied with his draft, he implied that it was reasonably accurate. He added that after the account was made he offered to send it to the President. Through Nicolay Lincoln said that he would trust to the accuracy of Riddle's report and he was at perfect liberty to send it to Chase. Riddle, *Recollections*, 270, 271n, 274–77. The editors of the Chase Papers have been unable to find Riddle's report or any mention of it in Chase's correspondence.

17. Hiram Barney to Chase, 17 April 1862, PHi-Chase.

18. S. P. Chase to Jordan, 17 Nov. 1863, DNA-RG206.

19. Hiram Barney to Chase, 8 Jan. 1863, PHi-Chase.

20. Edward Jordan to Chase, 25 Jan. 1863, DNA-RG56AB. Jordan suggested grand jury

indictments be handed down in New York City on three custom-house employees. Chase approved but no evidence has appeared of either indictments or trials. Edward Jordan to Chase, 29 Jan. 1863; S. P. Chase to Jordan, 2 Feb. 1863, DNA-RG206,LRST. William J. Hartman, whose thorough study of the New York custom house and politics from mid-century to 1902 has no account of indictments or trials. See Hartman, "Politics and Patronage: The New York Custom House, 1852–1902" (Ph.D. diss., Columbia Univ., 1952); S. P. Chase to Fessenden, 4 Feb. 1863, DNA-RG46.

    21. Arthur Harry Rice, "Henry B. Stanton as a Political Abolitionist" (Ph.D. diss., Columbia Univ., 1968), 427; see also Edward Jordan to Chase, 27 Oct. 1863, DLC-Chase. Henry B. Stanton to Chase, 1 Nov. 1863, DLC-Chase; S. P. Chase to Stanton, 2 Nov. 1863, PHi-Chase.

    22. New York *Tribune*, 6 Nov. 1863.

    23. S. P. Chase to Barney, 22 Dec. 1863, PHi-Chase.

    24. John A. Stevens to Chase, 15 Sept. 1863, PHi-Chase; see also Oran Follett to Chase, 30 Nov. 1863; James W. White to Chase, 11 Nov. 1863, DLC-Chase.

    25. S. P. Chase to Barney, 21 Oct. 1863, DLC-Chase.

    26. Edward Jordan to Chase, 27 Oct. 1863, DLC-Chase.

    27. Hiram Barney to Chase, no date, 1863; S. P. Chase to Barney, 7 Nov. 1863; William Orton to Chase, 14 Dec. 1863; Rufus F. Andrews to Chase, 15 Dec. 1863, DLC-Chase.

    28. Palmer was also found to have received substantial bribes from New York merchants and others doing business with the custom house. He was arrested, and during the continuing congressional investigation of the custom house he not only testified to his own peculations but implicated Barney and others in unsavory practices; John F. Bailey to Chase, 13, 26. Dec. 1863, DLC-Chase.

    29. Basler, ed., *Works*, VII: 181.

    30. Jonathan Wills to Chase, 13 Aug. 1863, DLC-Chase.

    31. See, for instance, S. P. Chase to Cooke, 24 Oct. 1862, PHi-Chase.

    32. S. P. Chase to Cisco, 13 July 1863, PHi-Chase.

    33. *House Exec. Docs.* 255, 43rd Cong., 1st sess., passim. The principal speculator was Captain F. W. Hurtt, who was tried by court-martial during January and February 1864. Hurtt was found guilty and cashiered from the service. Secretary of War Stanton, however, kept the record secret and it was not published in congressional documents until 1874.

    34. Warden, *Chase*, 517–23.

    35. Oberholtzer, *Jay Cooke*, I: 299.

    36. See remarks of John Sherman in *Cong. Globe*, 38th Cong., 1st sess., 1046; S. P. Chase to Fessenden, 27 Aug. 1864, Chase-Manhattan.

    37. House Exec. Doc. 42nd Cong., 1st sess., 255, 324, 327; William P. Mellen to Chase, 29 Oct., 5, 15 Nov. 1863, PHi-Chase.

    38. C. Breyfogle to Chase, 14 May 1863, DLC-Chase.

    39. Thomas Heaton, one of Chase's agents in the Midwest, related that he had spent three days with Mellen helping him with his cotton agency and attending a group meeting of special agents, surveyors, and collectors "as to the practical working of [his] regulations." They also discussed Chase's campaign strategy. Thomas Heaton to Chase, 17 Aug. 1863, DLC-Chase.

    40. William P. Mellen to Chase, 4 Oct., 15 Nov. 1863, PHi-Chase.

    41. S. P. Chase to Parsons, 13 May 1863, PHi-Chase.

    42. Joseph H. Geiger to Chase, 21 April 1863, DLC-Chase; see William P. Mellen to Chase, 6 Nov. 1863, PHi-Chase.

Chapter 27. "It Is a Big Fish"

1. William D. Gallagher to Chase, 22 June 1863; S. P. Chase to Gallagher, 23 June 1863, PHi-Chase.

2. S. P. Chase to Rush R. Sloane, 27 Jan. 1862, DLC-Chase; Warden, *Chase*, I: 408, 409; S. P. Chase to Monroe, 3 March 1862, PHi-Chase; James Monroe to Chase, 7 March 1862, DLC-Chase; S. P. Chase to Homer Plantz, 14 July 1862, OCHP-Chase.

3. Donnal V. Smith, *Chase and Civil War Politics* (Columbus, 1931), 57–60.

4. S. P. Chase to Robert C. Kirk, 6 Oct. 1862; to Wade, 2 Nov. 1862; to William Upham, 1 Dec. 1862, PHi-Chase; P. Odlin to Chase, 14 Jan. 1863, DLC-Chase; S. P. Chase to Odlin, 19 Jan. 1863, PHi-Chase.

5. S. P. Chase to Wade, 2 Dec. 1862; see also Lucius Bierce to Chase, 31 Dec. 1862; S. P. Chase to Lucius Bierce, 2 Jan. 1863; to Richard Parsons, 16 Feb. 1863, PHi-Chase.

6. Joshua Giddings to Chase, 13 Jan. 1863, PHi-Chase.

7. P. Odlin to Chase, 14 Jan. 1863, DLC-Chase; S. P. Chase to Odlin, 19 Jan. 1863, PHi-Chase.

8. S. P. Chase to Joseph Geiger, 20 Jan. 1863, PHi-Chase; Joseph Geiger to Chase, 24 Jan. 1863, DLC-Chase; Roseboom, *Civil War Era*, 394, 395.

9. S. P. Chase to Stanley Matthews, 16 April 1863, in *American Hist. Rev.* 34 (1929): 554; Joseph H. Geiger to Chase, 10 May 1863; J. M. Ashley to Chase, 23 June 1863, DLC-Chase; Thomas Heaton to Chase, 23 June 1863; S. P. Chase to Geiger, 23 June 1863; David Tod to Chase, 5 July 1863, PHi-Chase.

10. David Tod to Chase, 5 July 1863, PHi-Chase; see S. P. Chase to Joseph Geiger, 18 June 1863; to John Brough, 20 June 1863, DLC-Chase.

11. Laura Stedman and George M. Gould, eds., *Life and Letters of Edmund Clarence Stedman,* 2 vols. (New York, 1910), I: 207, 208.

12. *New York Tribune,* 23 Dec. 1863.

13. Richard C. Parsons to Chase, 9 Dec. 1863, DLC-Chase; see also S. P. Chase to Frederick Pike, 10 Dec. 1863, PHi-Chase.

14. Dennett, ed., *Hay Diaries,* 130, 143.

15. Ibid., 138.

16. For Pomeroy's career in Kansas see Edger Langsdorf, "S. C. Pomeroy and the New England Emigrant Aid Company 1854–58," *Kansas Historical Quarterly* 7 (Aug. 1938): 229, 232; for Pomeroy's physical appearance, see Martha B. Caldwell, "Pomeroy's 'Ross Letter' Genuine or Forgery," ibid., 13 (1944–45): 465.

17. See, for example, Chase to Dear sir, 10 July 1853, DLC-Chase; S. P. Chase to John P. Bigelow, 22 Sept. 1854, MH-H; S. P. Chase to Christian Melz, 23 Nov. 1863, PHi-Chase.

18. Oberholtzer, *Jay Cooke,* I: 364.

19. William Orton to Chase, 5 Dec. 1863, PHi-Chase; New York *Tribune,* New York *Times,* 23 April 1878.

20. William Orton to Chase, 5 Dec. 1863, PHi-Chase.

21. S. P. Chase to Lincoln, 13 Jan. 1864, DLC-Lincoln.

22. Dennett, ed., *Hay Diaries,* 152.

23. Homer Plantz to Chase, 13 Nov. 1862, DLC-Chase; Stedman, *Life and Letters,* I: 327, 328.

24. Dennett, ed., *Hay Diaries,* 152.

25. Beale, ed., *Bates Diary,* 241, 247, 260.

26. William R. Petrowski, "The Kansas-Pacific: A Study in Railroad Promotion" (Ph.D diss., Univ. of Wisconsin, 1966), 64–89; Charles Edgar Ames, *Pioneering the Union Pacific*

(New York, 1969), 28, 29; Maury Klein, *Union Pacific, Birth of a Railroad 1862–1893* (New York, 1987), 27–29, 34, 36, 37. It would appear that the $640,000 in bonds issued to the Kansas-Pacific promoters was used as collateral for a series of equity transactions. The bonds had a mysterious life of their own. There is no mention of this sum in a statement from the Secretary of the Treasury on January 23, 1871, for the year ending July 1, 1865. But for the year ending January 1, 1866, it is so listed in dollar amounts. See *Letter from the Secretary of the Treasury House,* Misc. Docs. No. 60, 41st. Cong., 3rd sess. The Secretary of Treasury reported on July 1, 1870, that the government had paid over $1 million in interest alone on U.S. bonds the railroad held. Edward McPherson, ed., *The Political History of the United States During the Period of Reconstruction* (3rd ed., Washington, D.C., 1880), 630; Samuel Hallett to Stedman, 10 Dec. 1863, E. C. Stedman Papers, Columbia Univ., New York. Samuel Hallett to Stedman (telegraph), 20 Dec. 1864, E. C. Stedman Papers, Columbia Univ., New York. Hallett had said, "Telegraph me and Perry instance you get official acknowledgement. Get all you can." Perry was an officer of the Union Pacific Railroad.

27. J. W. Schuckers to Stedman in Stedman, *Life and Letters,* I: 323.
28. Beale, ed., *Bates Diary,* 336, 337.
29. Ibid., 337, 338.
30. Ibid.; Stedman, *Life and Letters,* I: 323.
31. *New York Tribune,* New York *Evening Post,* Cincinnati *Enquirer,* 10 Feb. 1864; *Daily National Intelligencer,* 22 Feb. 1864.
32. Richard C. Parsons to Chase, 9 Dec. 1863, DLC-Chase.
33. New York *Tribune,* 10 Feb. 1864; New York *Independent,* 18 Feb. 1864; J. W. Schuckers to Stedman, 12 Feb. 1864, E. C. Stedman Papers, Columbia Univ., New York. *Wilkes Spirit of the Times,* 19 Feb. 1864.
34. James A. Winchell, "The Pomeroy Circular," *New York Times,* 15 Sept. 1874.
35. Helen Nicolay, *Lincoln's Secretary,* 188.
36. Roseboom, *Civil War Era,* 429, 430.
37. Ibid.
38. George Denison to Chase, 19 Feb., 1 April 1964, DLC-Chase; Blue, *Chase,* 220, 221; S. P. Chase to Ball, 25 Feb. 1864, DLC-Chase; Niven, *Welles,* 478–82.
39. Basler, ed., *Works,* VII: 200.
40. Abraham Lincoln to Chase, 23 Feb. 1864, DLC-Lincoln.
41. Beale and Brownsword, eds., *Welles Diary,* I: 525. Basler, ed., *Works,* VII: 212, 213.
42. Lyman D. Stickney, to Chase, 11 Dec. 1863, 7 Jan. 1864, PHi-Chase; George Denison to Chase, 5 March 1864, DLC-Chase; S. P. Chase to Denison, 16 March 1864, DLC-Denison.
43. Nicolay and Hay, *Lincoln,* IX: 79; S. P. Chase to James C. Hall, 5 March 1864, PHi-Chase; to A. G. Riddle, 2 March 1864, DLC-Chase.
44. Beale, ed., *Bates Diary,* 333, 334.
45. Basler, ed., *Works,* VII: 120.
46. Ibid., 181.
47. Ibid.; Miers, *Lincoln Day by Day,* III, 239, 241.
48. When Gideon Welles learned of Chase's denial of King he said, "Gracious Heavens! A man who, if in a legal point of view not the equal, is the superior of Chase in administrative ability, better qualified in some respects to fill any administration position in the government than Mr. Chase"; Beale and Brownsword, eds., *Welles Diary,* II: 137.
49. Nicolay and Hay, *Lincoln,* VII: 86, 87.
50. John G. Nicolay, "Memorandum," 6 April 1864; Nicolay to the President, 30 March 1864, DLC-Nicolay.

51. Nicolay, "Memorandum," 6 April 1864, DLC-Nicolay.

52. S. P. Chase to Simeon DeWitt Bloodgood, 26 April 1864, DLC-Chase; to Jay Cooke, 21 June 1864, PHi-Chase.

53. S. P. Chase to Duer, 20 June 1864, PHi-Chase.

54. S. P. Chase to Stewart, 25 June 1864, PHi-Chase.

55. S. P. Chase, "Diary," 27 June 1864, DLC-Chase.

56. Basler, ed., *Works*, VII: 412–14, 414n.

57. S. P. Chase to Cisco, 28 June 1864; "Diary," 28 June 1864, DLC-Chase.

58. S. P. Chase to Lincoln, 29 June 1864, DLC-Lincoln.

59. Nicolay and Hay, *Lincoln*, IX: 94, 95; Dennett, ed., *Hay Diaries*, 199.

60. Dennett, ed., *Hay Diaries*, 199.

61. Ibid., 198.

62. S. P. Chase, "Diary," 30 June, 4 July 1864, DLC-Chase.

Chapter 28. "So Help Me God"

1. *U.S. Statutes at Large*, vol. 13, p. 404.

2. *New York Times*, 29 March 1864; New York *Tribune*, 16 April 1864; Mitchell, *Greenbacks*, 226, 227, 232–34.

3. Mitchell, *Greenbacks*, 228; New York *Times*, 20 May 1864.

4. S. P. Chase to Simeon D. Bloodgood, 26 April 1864, DLC-Chase; to Lincoln, 15 April 1864, DLC-Lincoln. S. P. Chase to Greeley, 16 April 1864, in Warden, *Chase*, 603. See also S. P. Chase to Fessenden, 12 April 1864, DLC-Lincoln. New York *Tribune*, 23 June 1864.

5. S. P. Chase to Fessenden, 27 Aug. 1864, Chase-Manhattan.

6. Mitchell, *Greenbacks*, 123.

7. *U.S. Statutes at Large*, vol. 13, sec. 2. Congress did pass and the President approved an income tax bill, but it failed to raise much revenue; S. P. Chase, "Diary," 4 July 1864, DLC-Chase.

8. Dennet, ed., *Hay Diaries*, 198.

9. Ibid., 198–201.

10. Ibid.

11. S. P. Chase, "Diary," 4 July 1864, DLC-Chase.

12. Ibid.

13. Ibid.

14. Beale and Brownsword, eds., *Welles Diary*, II: 120, 121.

15. Henry Winter Davis, very active in the effort to remove Lincoln from the race, was certain that Chase would "declare war against him." Henry Winter Davis to DuPont, 18 Aug. 1864, in John D. Hayes, ed., *Samuel Francis DuPont: A Selection from His Civil War Letters*, 3 vols. (Ithaca, N.Y., 1969), III: 369.

16. S. P. Chase to Opdyke, 19 Aug. 1864, NHi-Stevens; S. P. Chase, "Diary," 19 Aug. 1864, DLC-Chase.

17. See, for instance, the brief comment in his diary of a conversation with Governor Joseph A. Gilmore of New Hampshire. S. P. Chase, "Diary," 30 Aug. 1864, DLC-Chase.

18. S. P. Chase, "Diary," 3, 4 Sept. 1864, DLC-Chase.

19. Ibid., 9, 10 Sept. 1864.

20. S. P. Chase to Emerson, 24 Aug. 1864, DLC-Chase.

21. S. P. Chase, "Diary," 24 July, 2, 4, 6, 19, 26 Aug. 1864, PHi-Chase.

22. S. P. Chase to Fessenden, 2 Aug. 1864, NjP; W. P. Fessenden to Chase, 4 Aug. 1864, PHi-Chase.

23. S. P. Chase, "Diary," 17 Aug. 1864, DLC-Chase. Probably Minister to France.

24. S. P. Chase, "Diary," 3 Aug. 1864, DLC-Chase.

25. S. P. Chase to Mellen, 13 Aug. 1864, PHi-Chase.

26. Hiram Barney to Chase, 5 Sept. 1864, PHi-Chase. See a scorching appraisal of Draper in Beale and Brownsword, eds., *Welles Diary*, II: 137, 138.

27. W. P. Fessenden to Chase, 6 Sept. 1864, PHi-Chase. See also S. P. Chase to Barney, 9 Sept. 1864, CSmH-Barney.

28. S. P. Chase to Cooke, 8 Sept. 1864, PHi-Chase. S. P. Chase, "Diary," 13 Sept. 1864, PHi-Chase.

29. S. P. Chase, "Diary," 14 Sept. 1864, PHi-Chase.

30. S. P. Chase to Leavitt, 18 Oct. 1864; S. P. Chase to McCulloch, 10 Nov. 1864; Schuyler Colfax to Chase, 5 Dec. 1864, PHi-Chase.

31. There is an exhaustive study of all candidates in Charles Fairman, *Reconstruction and Reunion*, vol. VI: *History of the Supreme Court* (New York, 1971), 5–31.

32. S. P. Chase to Kate, 17 Sept. 1864; to Samuel Hooper, 15, 16 Sept. 1864, PHi-Chase; "Diary," 17 Sept. 1864, PHi-Chase.

33. S. P. Chase, "Diary," 17–21 Oct. 1864, PHi-Chase.

34. Chase of course took a hand in pressing his case upon others of influence with Lincoln. See especially, S. P. Chase to Stanton, 13 Oct. 1864, DLC-Stanton; to Greeley, 21 Oct. 1864, NN-Greeley.

35. Ward Hill Lamon, "Memo of Lincoln's Explanation of the Appt. of Salmon P. Chase in October 1864." Page torn from a pocket note book, Oct. 1864, CSmH-Lamon.

36. Quoted in Blue, *Chase*, 244, 245; Schuyler Colfax to Chase, 5 Dec. 1864, PHi-Chase. The author is grateful to Prof. Michael Burlingame, who supplied the Foster material gleaned from the Nicolay Papers; John G. Nicolay, "Interview with Foster," 23 Oct. 1878, DLC-Nicolay.

37. Basler, ed., *Works*, VIII: 154, 154n.

38. John G. Nicolay to Therena Bates Nicolay, 8 Dec. 1864, DLC-Nicolay.

39. Basler, ed., *Works*, VIII: 126, 126n.

40. Beale, ed., *Bates Diary*, 482, 483; Charles Fairman, *Mr. Justice Miller and the Supreme Court. 1862–1890* (Cambridge, Mass., 1939), 118.

41. Noah Brooks, *Washington in Lincoln's Time* (New York, 1895), 193, 194.

42. Ibid., 194.

43. Ibid., 195.

44. S. P. Chase to Dear friend, March 1865, PHi-Chase.

45. S. P. Chase, "Diary," 20 Jan. 1865, NHi-Chase; to Dear Friend, March 1865. PHi-Chase.

46. S. P. Chase, "Diary," 16, 20 Jan. 1865, NHi-Chase.

47. A brief discussion of this case is in Fairman, *Reconstruction*, 36, 37. It is reported in 2 Wallace, 135, (1865); see also S. P. Chase to Lincoln, 6 March 1865, DLC-Lincoln.

48. S. P. Chase, "Diary," 2, 12, 13 Jan. 1865, NhHi-Chase; Fairman, *Reconstruction*, 38.

49. S. P. Chase to Dear friend, March 1865, PHi-Chase.

50. Fairman, *Reconstruction*, 60n, 75; Alexander A. Lawrence, *James Moore Wayne, Southern Unionist* (Chapel Hill, 1943), 194.

51. Fairman, *Reconstruction*, 3.

52. Swisher, *Taney Period*, 229–30, 837.

53. Beale, ed., *Bates Diary*, 340; see also Swisher, *Taney Period*, 837.

54. Fehrenbacher, *Dred Scott Case*, 234; Swisher, *Taney Period*, 559.

55. King, *Lincoln's Manager David Davis*, 2–19, 307–12.

56. Fairman, *Reconstruction*, 136–38, 518n; S. P. Chase to Davis, 24 June 1867, DLC-Chase; S. P. Chase, "Diary," 7 Jan. 1865, NhHi-Chase.

57. Fairman, *Reconstruction*, 518n; S. P. Chase, "Diary," 7, 8 Jan. 1865, NHi-Chase.

58. David Davis to Julius Rockwell, 12 Dec. 1864, Davis Papers, Illinois State Historical Society, Springfield.

59. S. P. Chase, "Diary," 1, 2 Jan. 1865, NHi-Chase.

60. S. P. Chase, "Diary," 13, 17 Jan. 1865, NhHi-Chase.

61. S. P. Chase, "Diary," 15 March 1865, NHi-Chase.

62. Niven, *Welles*, 489, 490.

63. Brooks, *Washington*, 239. Mrs. Lincoln attended the ceremonies accompanied by Tad and Senators Harlan and Foster before joining the President and riding with him to the White House; Washington *Chronicle*, 5 March 1865.

64. S. P. Chase to My Dear Friend, March 1865, PHi-Chase.

65. Ibid., 241; S. P. Chase to Dear Madam, 4 March 1865, DLC-Lincoln.

66. S. P. Chase, "Diary," 17 March 1865, NHi-Chase.

67. Basler, ed., *Works*, VIII: 393, 393n; Charles Sumner to Chase, 12 April 1865, DLC-Chase.

68. S. P. Chase to the President, 11 April 1865, DLC-Lincoln.

69. Basler, ed., *Works*, VIII: 402, 403.

70. S. P. Chase, "Diary," 12, 13 April 1865, PHi-Chase; to Lincoln, 12 April 1865, DLC-Lincoln.

71. S. P. Chase to Lincoln, 12 April 1865, DLC-Lincoln.

72. S. P. Chase to Stanley Matthews, 14 April 1865, WHi-Chase; "Diary," 14 April 1865, NhHi-Chase.

73. S. P. Chase, "Diary," 14 April 1865, NhHi-Chase.

74. Ibid., 15 April 1865, PHi-Chase.

75. Flower, *Stanton*, 282; S. P. Chase, "Diary," 15 April 1865, NHi-Chase.

76. S. P. Chase, "Diary," 15 April 1865, PHi-Chase.

77. S. P. Chase, "Diary," 15 April 1865, PHi-Chase; Beale and Brownsword, eds., *Welles Diary*, II: 287, 288.

78. S. P. Chase, "Diary," 15 April 1865, PHi-Chase.

79. See Brownsword and Beale, eds., *Welles Diary*, II: 290–93, for many of the details.

80. S. P. Chase, "Diary," 17 April 1865, PHi-Chase.

81. Beverly Palmer, ed., *The Selected Letters of Charles Sumner*, 2 vols. (Boston, 1990), II: 299–304.

82. S. P. Chase to Schuckers, 4 April 1865, PHi-Chase.

83. S. P. Chase to Theodore Tilton, 1 May 1865, NHi.

84. S. P. Chase to Johnson, 18 April 1865, DLC-Johnson.

85. S. P. Chase, "Diary," 29 April 1865, PHi-Chase.

86. Charles Sumner to John Bright, 24 April 1865; to Wendell Phillips, 1 May 1865; to Francis Lieber, 2 May 1865, in Palmer, ed., *Sumner*, I: 297–303.

87. S. P. Chase to Sherman, 5 May 1865, DLC-Sherman; Michael Les Benedict, *A Compromise of Principle* (New York, 1974), 103–5; Relying on Sumner's letters to Bright and Phillips and Chase's letter to Sherman, Professor Benedict says that Johnson "authorized" Chase privately "to urge negro suffrage in the President's name."

Chapter 29. A Trip South

1. S. P. Chase, "Diary," 13 March 1862, DLC-Chase; ibid., 4, 7 April 1865, DLC-Chase.

2. Whitelaw Reid, *After the War, a Southern Tour* (Cincinnati 1866), 12, 13; for letters of introduction see Andrew Johnson to Officers et al., 29 April 1865, DLC-Johnson; Edwin M. Stanton to Department Commanders, 29 April 1865, DLC-Stanton; S. P. Chase, "Diary," 1, 2 May 1865, NhHi-Chase.

3. Reid, *After the War*, 24, 25; Brooks D. Simpson et al., eds., *Advice after Appomatox, Letters to Andrew Johnson* (Knoxville, 1987), 8, 9, 17, 18.

4. Simpson et al., eds., *Letters to Johnson*, 26, 27.

5. S. P. Chase to Johnson, 24 May 1865, DLC-Johnson; S. P. Chase, "Diary," 4 May 1865, NhHi-Chase.

6. Reid, *After the War*, 23–27.

7. S. P. Chase to Sherman, 5 May 1865, DLC-W.Sherman.

8. W. T. Sherman to Chase, 6 May 1865, NHi-Chase.

9. Ibid., 6 May 1865, *O.R.* Ser. I, vol., 47, part 3.

10. S. P. Chase to Johnson, 17 May 1865, DLC-Johnson.

11. James C. Sefton, *The United States Army and Reconstruction* (Baton Rouge, 1967), 14, 15.

12. Reid, *After the War*, 35; S. P. Chase, "Diary," 8 May 1865, PHi-Chase.

13. S. P. Chase to Johnson, 12 May 1865, DLC-Johnson.

14. Reid, *After the War*, 53.

15. S. P. Chase to Johnson, 12 May 1865, DLC-Johnson.

16. S. P. Chase, "Diary," 10 May 1865, NhHi-Chase.

17. Reid, *After the War*, 79–83, Appendix A, 585.

18. Ibid., 79.

19. Ibid., 83.

20. Ibid., Appendix A, 586.

21. Ibid.

22. S. P. Chase, "Diary," 14 May 1865, NhHi-Chase; Reid, *After the War*, 99–111.

23. David Herbert Donald, *Charles Sumner and the Rights of Men* (New York, 1970), 299.

24. See a brief discussion of these points in Simpson et al., eds., *Letters to Johnson*, 14–16.

25. Reid, *After the War*, 117.

26. Ibid., 146, 147.

27. S. P. Chase to Johnson, 17 May 1865, DLC-Johnson.

28. Reid, *After the War*, 160, 161; S. P. Chase, "Diary," 20 May 1865, PHi-Chase.

29. Simpson et al., eds., *Letters to Johnson*, 15.

30. Jerrell H. Shafner, *Nor Is It Over Yet: Florida in the Era of Reconstruction, 1863–1877* (Gainesville, Fla., 1974), 15. See also William W. Davis, *The Civil War and Reconstruction in Florida* (New York, 1913), 272, 273, 351–53.

31. S. P. Chase, "Diary," 20, 21 May 1865, NhHi-Chase; Shafner, *Florida in the Era of Reconstruction*, 15.

32. His proposals also bore a close resemblance to those Stanton had submitted to Lincoln on the Reconstruction of North Carolina; see Niven, *Welles*, 505, 508.

33. S. P. Chase to Johnson, 17 May 1865, DLC-Johnson; Niven, *Welles*, 266, 267; Beale and Brownsword, eds., *Welles Diary*, II: 455.

34. Ibid., 18 May 1865.

35. S. P. Chase, "Diary," 25–28 May 1865, NhHi-Chase.

36. Alice E. Andrews, ed., *Christopher C. Andrews, Recollections 1829–1922* (Cleveland, 1928), 200, 201.

37. S. P. Chase to Johnson, 21, 23, May 1865, DLC-Johnson.

38. S. P. Chase to Stanton, 5 May 1865, DLC-Stanton.

39. S. P. Chase, "Diary," 1, 5 June 1865, NhHi-Chase.

40. Ibid., 8, 10, 11 June 1865.

41. Ibid., 10 June 1865; Reid, "Diary," 10 June 1865, DLC-Reid; Reid, *After the War*, 274.

42. S. P. Chase, "Diary," 17 June 1865, NhHi-Chase.

43. Ibid., 19 June 1865.

44. S. P. Chase, "Diary," 23 June 1865, NhHi-Chase.

45. Ibid., 24, 25, 27–30 June, 1–3 July 1865.

46. Ibid., 4–6 July 1865; S. P. Chase to Kate Chase Sprague, 24 June 1865, DLC-Chase.

47. S. P. Chase, "Diary," 6 July 1865, NhHi-Chase; Thomas G. and Marva R. Belden, *So Fell the Angels* (Boston, 1956), 162.

48. S. P. Chase to Sumner, 25 June 1865, DLC-Chase.

49. Palmer, ed., *Sumner Letters*, II: 313, 319; S. P. Chase to Sumner, 20 May 1865, Carson Collection, Free Library of Philadelphia; to Sumner, 25 June 1865, PHi-Chase.

50. S. P. Chase, "Diary," 7, 8 July 1865, NhHi-Chase; Beale and Brownsword, eds., *Welles Diary*, I: 432–34.

51. Andrew Johnson to Chase, 11 Aug. 1865, DLC-Johnson.

52. S. P. Chase to Johnson, 12 Aug. 1865, DLC-Johnson; to Jay Cooke, 12 Aug. 1865, PHi-Cooke.

53. S. P. Chase to Kate Chase Sprague, 17 Aug. 1865, PHi-Chase.

54. S. P. Chase to Sumner, 20 Aug. 1865, DLC-Chase.

55. Legislation on circuit court allotments would confirm Chase's opinion. See an able discussion of these points in Harold M. and Ferne B. Hyman's Introduction to Bradley T. Johnson, *Reports of Cases Decided by Chief Justice Chase in the Circuit Court of the United States Fourth Circuit 1865–1869* (rev. ed., New York, 1972), xxi-xxii.

Chapter 30. Universal Suffrage, Universal Amnesty

1. James A. Pollard, ed., *The Journal of Jay Cooke or the Gibraltar Records 1865–1905* (Columbus, 1935), 116–25.

2. S. P. Chase to Kate Chase Sprague, 17 Aug. 1865, PHi-Chase; S. P. Chase to Ball, 15 May 1866, DLC-Chase.

3. See, for instance, S. P. Chase, "Diary," 7 Jan. 1866, PHi-Chase.

4. Fairman, *Mr. Justice Miller*, 251–52.

5. S. P. Chase, "Diary," 2 Dec. 1865, NhHi-Chase. See John Niven et al. eds., *The Salmon P. Chase Papers*, Vol I: *Journals 1829–1872*. (Kent, Ohio, 1993), 597n for a brief discussion of Chase's draft.

6. George Bancroft, a leading expounder of Jefferson-Jackson ideology, was the author.

7. James D. Richardson, comp., *A Compilation of the Messages and State Papers of the Presidents*, 20 vols. (New York, 1911–16), VIII: 3558.

8. Hans L. Trefousse, *Andrew Johnson, a Biography* (New York, 1989), 238, 241.

9. Sefton, *Army and Reconstruction*, 42, 43; George R. Bentley, *A History of the Freedman's Bureau* (Philadelphia, 1955), 104, 105; Eric McKitrick, *Andrew Johnson and Reconstruction* (Chicago, 1960), 11, 12.

10. S. P. Chase, "Diary," 7 Jan. 1866, PHi-Chase.
11. Ibid.
12. S. P. Chase, "Diary," 22 March 1866, PHi-Chase.
13. Swisher, *Taney Period*, 833.
14. S. P. Chase, "Diary," 7 Jan. 1866, PHi-Chase.
15. S. P. Chase to Schuckers, 15 May 1866, DLC-Chase.
16. Trefousse, *Johnson*, 244, 245; Samuel Klaus, ed., *The Milligan Case* (London, 1929), 39.
17. S. P. Chase to Elizabeth Pike, 20 March 1866, MeU-Pike.
18. See Eric McKitrick's learned and detailed account of the evolution of the Fourteenth Amendment in his *Johnson and Reconstruction*, 326–63.
19. 4 Wallace 2; Fairman, *Reconstruction*, 196; Philip B. Kurland and Gerhard Casper, eds., *Landmark Briefs and Arguments of the Supreme Court of the United States*, 216 vols. (Washington, D.C. 1978–), IV: 247–55.
20. John M. Taylor, *Garfield of Ohio, the Available Man* (New York, 1970), 118.
21. Klaus, ed., *Milligan*, 93–120; Kurland and Casper, eds. *Landmark Briefs*, IV: 274–99.
22. Kurland and Casper, *Landmark Briefs*, IV: 301–13, 323–27; Fairman, *Reconstruction*, 227.
23. Klaus, ed. *Milligan*, 121–47; Pease and Randall, eds., *Browning Diary*, II: 65, 66; Fairman, *Reconstruction*, 200–207.
24. Klaus, ed., *Milligan*, 91; Kurland and Casper, eds., *Landmark Briefs*, IV: 456–62.
25. Pease and Randall, eds., *Browning Diary*, II: 65.
26. Ibid. Klaus presents only a digest of Stanbery's argument as taken from 4 Wallace 2, 142.
27. Pease and Randall, eds., *Browning Diary*, II: 66.
28. Fairman, *Mr. Justice Miller*, 118; Thomas Ewing amplified Miller's comment: "Mr. Speed is not a competent legal advisor especially on the present critical condition of affairs— and I know that the court does not rely on him. . . ." Thomas Ewing, Sr., to Johnson, 15 March 1866, DLC-Johnson.
29. In making allowances for Speed, one must consider the fact that he had drifted into radical circles, and, except for Miller, his critics were conservatives.
30. Fairman, *Reconstruction*, 207; Klaus, ed., *Milligan*, 144–208; Kurland and Casper, eds., *Landmark Briefs*, IV: 387, 388.
31. 4 Wallace 2, 110; Fairman, *Reconstruction*, 143, 144.
32. See a succinct discussion of the iron-clad oath in Harold M. Hyman, *To Try Men's Souls* (Berkeley and Los Angeles, 1959), 164.
33. Harold M. Hyman, *Era of the Oath* (rpt., Philadelphia, 1978), 107; 4 Wallace, 377, 381.
34. Hyman, *Era of the Oath*, 110–11; Kurland and Casper, eds., *Landmark Briefs*, IV: 475–90; 4 Wallace, 328–31.
35. Stephen J. Field to Chase, 30 June 1866, DLC-Chase.
36. S. P. Chase to the Proprietors of the *Commercial*, draft ms, 1865, PHi-Chase.
37. Stephen J. Field, *Personal Reminiscences of Early Days in California* (rpt., New York, 1968), 164.
38. Stephen J. Field to Chase, 30 June 1866, DLC-Chase.
39. S. P. Chase to Miller, 9 June 1866, PHi-Chase.
40. Pease and Randall, eds., *Browning Diary*, II: 69.
41. For the Cummings Case, see 4 Wallace 277; for Garland, see 4 Wallace 333. Fairman, *Reconstruction*, 208; Kraus, ed., *Milligan*, 255–50; 4 Wallace 2, 120.

42. Klaus, ed., *Milligan*, 248, 245; 4 Wallace 2, 120.

43. 4 Wallace 2, 120.

44. The Union label had been used alternately with Republican. As party lines became more sharply defined during Reconstruction, that label was dropped in favor of Republican. McKitrick, *Johnson*, 4, 4n, 42–46.

45. S. P. Chase to Schuckers, 8 Sept. 1866, DLC-Chase; "Diary," 3 Sept. 1866, PHi-Chase.

46. S. P. Chase to Schuckers, 8 Sept. 1866, DLC-Chase; "Diary," 3 Sept. 1866, PHi-Chase; Treffouse, *Johnson*, 263, 264.

47. S. P. Chase to Schuckers, 15 May 1866, DLC-Chase; S. P. Chase to Wendell Phillips, 1 May 1866, MH-H-Phillips.

48. S. P. Chase to Lyman D. Stickney, 6 Nov. 1866, PHi-Chase.

49. S. P. Chase to Horace Greeley, 21 Nov. 1866. DLC-Greeley.

50. Ibid.

51. S. P. Chase to Schuckers, 15 May 1866, DLC-Chase.

52. S. P. Chase to Nettie, 19 May 1866; S. P. Chase to Flamen Ball, 12 May 1866, DLC-Chase.

53. Richardson, *State Papers*, IX: 3632–36.

54. S. P. Chase to John C. Underwood, 22 Oct. 1867, DLC-Chase; William C. Davis, *Jefferson Davis, the Man and His Hour* (New York, 1991), 635–67; William P. Miller to Chase, 11 July 1867, DLC-Chase. Chase outlined his position on Davis in a letter he wrote in 1868. It was published in the *Albany Law Journal*, 24 Sept. 1870.

55. Stanley I. Kutler, *Judicial Power and Reconstruction Politics* (Chicago, 1968), 53–55; *Cong. Globe*, 39th Cong., 1st sess., 2387, 3134, 3697-3699, 3909; *U.S. Statutes at Large*, vol. 14, p. 309; Fairman claims that Chase did not confer with his colleagues on his proposed amendment. But see *Cong. Globe*, 34th Cong., 1st sess., 1259; S. P. Chase to Miller, 9, 15 June 1866, PHi-Chase; Samuel Miller to Chase, 26 June 1866, DLC-Chase.

56. *U.S. Statutes at Large*, vol. 14, p. 433.

57. Wager Swayne to Chase, 10 Dec. 1868, DLC-Chase. Telegrams of Lewis E. Parsons to Johnson and Andrew Johnson to Parsons are in Edward McPherson, *The Political History of the United States During the Period of Reconstruction* (rpt., New York, 1969), 352, 353n.

58. S. P. Chase to Wager Swayne, 4 Dec. 1866. PHi-Chase.

59. McKitrick, *Johnson*, 476–82.

60. Ibid., 482.

61. S. P. Chase to Reuben Fenton, 14 March 1867; see also S. P. Chase to Rufus P. Spalding, 24 June 1867, DLC-Chase.

62. *Cong. Globe*, 39th Cong., 2nd sess., 616, 646, 685; Cincinnati *Gazette*, 23 Jan. 1867; New York *Tribune*, 15 Jan. 1867.

63. David Hughes, "Salmon P. Chase; Chief Justice," *Vanderbilt Law Review* 18 (March 1965): 584–88, argues that Chase led a conservative Court away from a direct confrontation with Congress on Reconstruction. But working informally with Congress and formally with his colleagues on the court, Chase sought always to uphold his interpretation of a federal system of government. He would not needlessly antagonize Congress or the President. But when he thought one or the other branch was out of line, he did not give way. See, for instance, S. P. Chase to John D. Van Buren, 5 May 1868, PHi-Chase. See also *Mississippi v. Johnson*, 4 Wallace 50. Fairman discusses these cases fully and presents a convincing interpretation. Chase delivered the opinion of the Court in the Mississippi case, Nelson in the Georgia case. Fairman, *Reconstruction*, 378–96.

64. S. P. Chase to Young, 26 June 1867, DLC-Chase.

Chapter 31. Impeachment

1. S. P. Chase, "Diary," 26 Feb. 1868, PHi-Chase.
2. *Trial of Andrew Johnson, President of the United States on Impeachment for High Crimes and Misdemeanors*, 3 vols. (Washington, D.C., 1868), I: 2–6.
3. S. P. Chase, "Diary," 26 Feb. 1868, PHi-Chase.
4. S. P. Chase to Rufus P. Spalding, 24 June 1867, DLC-Chase.
5. B. F. Wade to Oran Follett, 4 April 1868, OCHP-Follett.
6. S. P. Chase to Tilton, 9 July 1867, DLC-Chase.
7. Georgia v. Stanton, 6 Wallace 50; Mississippi v. Johnson, 4 Wallace 475.
8. That old Democratic politician and Buchanan intimate, J. Glancy Jones, did compliment Chase on the Georgia case. He was one of the few Democrats who did so. J. Glancy Jones to Chase, 17 May 1867, DLC-Chase.
9. *U.S. Statutes at Large*, vol. 14, 385.
10. *Ex parte* McCardle, 6 Wallace 318; see also report of Supreme Court Conference, undated, 1868, DLC-Butler.
11. S. P. Chase to John D. Van Buren, 5 April 1868, PHi-Chase.
12. "Agate," in the Cincinnati *Gazette*, 24 March 1868.
13. Niven, *Welles*, 553; Pease and Randall, eds., *Browning Diary*, II: 156.
14. S. P. Chase to John D. Van Buren, 5 April 1868, PHi-Chase.
15. For extended and fruitful discussion of these events see McKitrick, *Johnson*, Chap. 15; Hans L. Trefousse, *Impeachment of a President: Andrew Johnson, the Blacks and Reconstruction* (Knoxville, 1975), Chaps. 5, 6, 8; Eric Foner, *A Short History of Reconstruction 1863–1877* (New York, 1990); Michael Les Benedict, *A Compromise of Principle* (New York, 1974), 294–314; Benjamin Thomas and Harold Hyman, *Stanton, the Life and Times of Lincoln's Secretary of War* (New York, 1962), 581–613; S. P. Chase to Garfield, 7 Aug. 1867, DLC-Garfield; see also S. P. Chase to Flanders, 3 Sept. 1867, NhD; to Tilton, 9 July 1867, DLC-Chase.
16. S. P. Chase, "Diary," 27 Feb. 1868, PHi-Chase.
17. Ibid., 26 Feb. 1868.
18. Gideon Welles noted that Chase's letter "disturbed the Radicals." Beale and Brownsword, eds., *Welles Diary*, III: 301; S. P. Chase to the Senate of the United States, 4 March 1868, in *New York Times*, 4 March 1868; to S. C. Pomeroy, 5 March 1868, PHi-Chase; and again in opening remarks to the Senate, *Johnson Trial*, I: 12, 13.
19. *Johnson Trial*, I: 451.
20. Ibid., III 360–96.
21. Roseboom, *Civil War Era*, 460–64.
22. Georges Clemenceau, *American Reconstruction, 1865–1870* (rpt., New York, 1969), 113–18, 133, 134; McPherson, *Reconstruction*, 353, 354.
23. S. P. Chase to Gerrit Smith, 2 April 1868, DLC-Chase.
24. *Johnson Trial*, I: 10.
25. S. P. Chase to Gerrit Smith, 19 April 1868, DLC-Chase.
26. S. P. Chase to John D. Van Buren, 25 March 1868, DLC-Chase.
27. *Johnson Trial*, I: 13, 176, 179, 185.
28. Schuckers, *Chase*, 557; *Trial of Johnson*, I: 185, 186.
29. S. P. Chase to Gerrit Smith, 2 April 1868, DLC-Chase.
30. *Johnson Trial*, I: 676–97; S. P. Chase to Alexander Long, 19 April 1868, OCHP-Long.
31. *Johnson Trial*, I: 25–31, 164, 165, 169, 176, 177.
32. Ibid., 674, 675, 676, 693, 700–704; see also Trefousse, *Impeachment*, 154, 155.

33. S. P. Chase to James S. Pike, 28 April 1868, MeU-Pike.

34. Peter G. Van Winkle to Chase, 26 May 1868, DLC-Chase.

35. Washington *Chronicle*, 18 May 1868.

36. Georges Clemenceau, the visiting French journalist, was certain that Chase was attempting to secure acquittal; Clemenceau, *Reconstruction*, 182–84; S. P. Chase, "Memo," 18 May 1868; S. P. Chase to Horace Greeley, 5 May 1868, DLC-Chase.

37. S. P. Chase to Barney, 13 May 1868, CSnH-Barney.

38. Quoted in M. R. and T. G. Belden, *So Fell the Angels* (Boston, 1956), 190; Trefousse, *Impeachment*, 168, 169, 177.

39. Senate Exec. Doc., no. 10, part 3, 41st Cong., 3rd sess., 2, 3, 15, 20, 22-26, 48, 59; John A. Dix to Stanton, 22, 23 March 1865, in DNA, RG, 393 part I, 134, 135, 262, 291.

40. S. P. Chase to Kate, 10 May 1868, DLC-Chase.

41. *Johnson Trial*, II: 189, 219, 478, 479.

42. Ibid., 246, 248.

43. Trefousse, *Johnson*, 322–25; Trefousse, *Benjamin Franklin Wade, Radical Republican from Ohio* (New York, 1963), 281–89.

44. *U.S. Statutes at Large*, vol. I, chap. 8, sec., 9, 240, 241.

45. S. P. Chase to Clark Williams, 16 May 1868, DLC-Chase.

46. S. P. Chase, "Memo," 27 May 1868, PHi-Chase.

47. *Johnson Trial*, II: 486, 487.

48. *Johnson Trial*, II: 482–98.

49. Ibid.; S. P. Chase, "Memo," 18 May 1868, DLC-Chase; "Memo" of meetings with W. B. Thomas and Senator Ross, 19 May 1868, DLC-Schuckers.

50. S. P. Chase to Alexander Long, 8, 19 April 1868, OCHP-Long; to Henry W. Hilliard, 27 April 1868, DLC-Chase; to William S. Rosecrans, 16 Aug. 1869, CLU-SC.

51. S. P. Chase to Halstead, 22 May 1868, NHi. See also S. P. Chase to John D. Van Buren, 25 June 1868, PHi-Chase.

52. S. P. Chase to Belmont, 30 May 1868; to Manton Marble, 30 May 1868, DLC-Marble.

53. Edward Perzel, "Alexander Long, Salmon P. Chase and the Election of 1868," *Bulletin of the Cincinnati Historical Society* 23, no. 1 (Jan. 1965): 4, 6-8, 10, 11.

54. John D. Van Buren to Seymour, 19 June 1868, NHi-Seymour.

55. John J. Cisco to Chase, 1 June 1868, DLC-Chase.

56. S. P. Chase to Milton Sutliff, 3 June 1868, OCIWHi-Norton.

57. Charles H. Coleman, *The Election of 1868* (rpt. New York, 1971), 132.

58. William Cullen Bryant to Chase, 13 June 1868, PHi-Chase; ibid., 23 June 1868, DLC-Chase.

59. J. Prentice Tucker to Chase, 15 June 1868, DLC-Chase.

60. S. P. Chase to Smith, 17 June 1868, DLC-Chase.

61. Alexander C. Flick, *Samuel Jones Tilden, a Study in Political Sagacity* (New York, 1939), 172, 173.

62. Frederick A. Aiken to Chase, 25, 26 June 1868, PHi-Chase.

63. John D. Van Buren to Chase, 25 June 1868, PHi-Chase; Samuel Ward to Chase, 26 June 1868, DLC-Chase.

64. Cincinnati *Commercial*, 8 June 1868; Alexander Long to Chase, 17 June 1868, OCHP-Chase; Dwight Bannister to Chase, 18 June 1868, DLC-Chase; Frederick A. Aiken to Chase, 3 July 1868, PHi-Chase; Frank Clement, *The Limits of Dissent* (Lexington, Ky., 1970), 306, 307.

65. Montgomery Blair to Frank Blair, 4 June 1868, DLC-Blair; Montgomery Blair to Barlow, 10 June 1868, CSmH-Barlow.

66. James A. Bryant to S. L. M. Barlow, 3, 10, 16 June 1868, CSmH-Barlow; see also William Brown to Chase, 22 June 1868, DLC-Chase.

67. Oberholtzer, *Jay Cooke*, II: 68. Chase was being read out of the Republican party, whose birth he had overseen and whose dominance he had nurtured. See Theodore Tilton, "Folded Banners," in New York *Independent*, 16 April 1868; S. P. Chase to Tilton, 16 April 1868, DLC-Chase.

68. The full text is in Schuckers, *Chase*, 567–70; *New York Times*, 1 July 1868; Alexander Long to Chase, 3 July 1868, PHi-Chase; S. P. Chase to Long, 4 July 1868, OCHP-Long.

69. S. P. Chase to Long, 1 July 1868, OCHP-Long.

70. S. P. Chase to Van Buren, 2 July 1868, PHi-Chase.

71. *New York Times*, 1 July 1868; S. P. Chase to Long, 1 July 1868, PHi-Chase; ibid., 4 July 1868, OCHP-Long.

72. Frederick A. Aiken to Chase, 3 July 1868; Flick, *Tilden*, 175.

73. Flick, *Tilden*, 172, 173; Samuel Ward to Chase, 26 June 1868, DLC-Chase.

74. John D. Van Buren to Chase, 24 July 1868, DLC-Chase.

75. Kate Chase Sprague to Chase, 5 July 1868, PHi-Chase.

76. James E. Kennedy to Chase, 3 July 1868, PHi-Chase.

77. Ibid.

78. Beale and Brownsword, eds., *Welles Diary*, III: 306, 381.

79. Alexander Long to Chase, 3 July 1868; Jacob Schuckers to Chase, 3 July 1868; S. P. Chase to Van Buren, 5 July 1868, PHi-Chase. See also Beale and Brownsword, eds., *Welles Diary*, III: 390, 391. Sanford Church, Tilden's close friend and political confident, wrote him on the eve of the convention that "Chase is out of the question . . . we will use him well, but must not think of nominating him." Sanford Church to Tilden, 10 June 1868, NN-Tilden.

80. Charles H. Coleman, *The Election of 1868* (rpt. New York 1971), 210, 211.

81. John D. Van Buren to Chase, 24 July 1868, DLC-Chase.

82. Beale and Brownsword, eds., *Welles Diary*, III: 379, 381.

83. Kate Chase Sprague to Chase, 7 July 1868; S. P. Chase to Kate, 7 July 1868, PHi-Chase.

84. Warden, *Chase*, II: 705, quoting the *National Republican*.

Chapter 32. One Clear Call

1. Fairman, *Reconstruction*, 601–4.

2. Johnson, ed., *Reports of Cases*, passim.

3. S. P. Chase to John Dash Van Buren, 20 March 1868, DLC-Chase.

4. See Ferne B. Hyman and Harold M. Hyman, "Introduction," v–xxvii. See ibid.; *Shortridge & Co. v. Macon*, 136–43, and *Caesar Griffin's Case*, 410–26, in Johnson, ed., *Reports of Cases*.

5. See, for instance, "Agate" in the Cincinnati *Gazette*, 24 March 1868.

6. *Ex parte* McCardle, 6 Wallace 1869, 318. Fairman has an exhaustive analysis of the case in *Reconstruction*, 437–86; S. P. Chase to John D. Van Buren, 5 April 1868, PHi-Chase.

7. *Ex parte* Yerger, 8 Wallace 85, Fairman, *Reconstruction*, 564, 565.

8. James M. Carlisle to Chase, 21 June 1869, PHi-Chase.

9. S. P. Chase to Clifford, 22, 23 June 1869; Nathan Clifford to Chase, 6 July 1869, PHi-Chase.

10. *Ex parte* Yerger, 8 Wallace 85.

11. *Cong. Globe*, 41st Cong., 2nd sess., 41, 42, 86–93, 2895, 2896.

12. S. P. Chase to Murat Halstead "draft," 1865, PHi-Chase.

13. *Shortridge & Co. v. Macon*, in Johnson *Reports of Cases*, 132–50.

14. See *Texas v. White*, 7 *Wallace*, 700–743; 10 Wallace 68–91.

15. Ibid. They were Justices Grier, Swayne, and Miller.

16. S. P. Chase to Elizabeth Pike, 27 April 1870, MeU-Pike; to Dr. Perry, 10 Dec. 1870, DLC-Chase.

17. Fairman, *Reconstruction*, 728–30.

18. S. P. Chase to Richard C. Parsons, 30 Dec. 1869, PHi-Chase; S. P. Chase to Stephen J. Field, 24 Dec. 1869, Cu-BANC-Field.

19. King, *Lincoln's Manager, David Davis*, 272.

20. S. P. Chase to Horace Greeley, 17 May 1866, NN-Greeley. New York businessman J. C. Minturn wrote Chase that "one of the most favorable features in the prosperity and growth of the United States has been the inflation of the currency. It was not asked for, but has been forced on us as a necessity; but do not now take from us suddenly that which we have been taught to be the legal tender of the commerce and trade of the country. . . ." J. C. Minturn to Chase, 12 Feb. 1870, DLC-Chase. *Hepburn v. Griswold*, 8 Wallace 603.

21. Fairman, *Reconstruction*, 724.

22. Ibid.

23. *Latham v. United States* and *Deming v. United States*, 9 Wallace, 145, 146.

24. S. P. Chase, "Diary," 14, 24, 26 March 1870, DLC-Chase.

25. Quoted in Fairman, *Miller*, 170.

26. Ibid.

27. "It has been fearful," said Miller, "and my own position as leader in marshaling my forces, and keeping up their courage, against a domineering Chief, and a party in court . . . has been such a strain on my brain and nervous system as I never wish to encounter again"; ibid., 171. See also Schuckers, *Chase*, 263–67.

28. Schuckers, *Chase*, 265; S. P. Chase to Edward D. Mansfield, 24 April 1871, WM-Mansfield.

29. *Veazie Bank v. Fenno*, 8 Wallace 533, S. P. Chase to James S. Pike, 24 Dec. 1869, MeU-Pike.

30. *Knox v. Lee*, 12 Wallace 457; *Parker v. Davis*, 12 Wallace 457.

31. S. P. Chase, *Diary*, 15 Jan. 1872, PHi-Chase. In a letter to John R. Tucker, Chase wrote that the dissenting Justices, himself included, had relied on "the doctrine of Mr. Madison that the government might constitutionally issue its promises to pay but could not constitutionally make them legal tender, or in other words compel citizens to accept them as money." S. P. Chase to John R. Tucker, 1 May 1871, NcU-Tucker; John R. Tucker to Chase, 27 April 1871, DLC-Chase.

32. James E. Pollard, ed., *The Journal of Jay Cooke or the Gibralter Records, 1865–1905* (Columbus, 1935), 116–25, 226. See also S. P. Chase to Cooke, 7 July 1870, PHi-Cooke.

33. Warden, *Chase*, II: 705.

34. Guy S. Rix, *History and Genealogy of the Eastman Family in America* (Concord, N.H., 1901), 453.

35. S. P. Chase, "Diary," 13 Aug. 1866, PHi-Chase.

36. Ibid., 14–15 Aug. 1866.

37. See, for instance, long draft letter to Charlotte Eastman, undated, 1867 or 1868, PHi-Chase.

38. S. P. Chase to James W. Ward, 15 May 1870, NhD-Chase.

39. S. P. Chase to J. R. Thompson, 30 Jan. 1870, PHi-Chase.

40. Occasionally there were reminders from Henry Cooke that Chase make an effort to reduce his indebtedness by giving a promissory note for a part of the amount owed. See, for instance, Jay Cooke to Chase, 6 March 1872, DLC-Chase, in which he puts Chase's overdraft at $14,867.53. "We don't like to carry overdrawn accounts on our ledgers and therefore request that you give us your note for this amount, or say $1,500.00 payable on demand or at such date as may suit you."

41. R. C. Parsons to Chase, 16 Feb. 1871, DLC-Chase; *U.S. Statutes at Large*, vol. 10, p. 655; vol. 16, p. 499.

42. McPherson, ed., *Reconstruction*, 394, 403.

43. S. P. Chase to My dear child, 26 April 1869, PHi-Chase.

44. S. P. Chase to My dearest Katie, 15 Sept. 1869, PHi-Chase.

45. Ibid.

46. S. P. Chase to My darling child, 1 Oct. 1869, PHi-Chase.

47. S. P. Chase to Flamen Ball, 4 Oct. 1869, OCHP-Chase; S. P. Chase to My darling child, 7 Nov. 1869, DLC-Chase.

48. S. P. Chase to Ball, 4 Oct. 1869, OCHP-Chase.

49. S. P. Chase to P. E. Jones, 8 Feb. 1871, DLC-Chase; S. P. Chase, "Diary," 3 Jan. 1872, PHi-Chase.

50. S. P. Chase, "Diary," 27 April 1872, PHi-Chase.

51. On his way west, he had stopped in New York City, where at William M. Evarts's suggestion he consulted Dr. Alonzo Clark, a noted physiologist. S. P. Chase, "Diary," 10, 13 June 1870, DLC-Chase.

52. S. P. Chase to Parsons, 26 Sept. 1870. All was not well between them. Throughout Chase's convalescence, Sprague was attentive but only when Kate was away from Canonchet. S. P. Chase to Nettie, 15 Oct. 1870, DLC-Chase.

53. S. P. Chase to W. H. Reardon, 26 Oct. 1870; to Schuckers, 22 Sept. 1870, DLC-Chase.

54. S. P. Chase to Parsons, 26 Sept. 1870, PHi-Chase.

55. Ibid.

56. S. P. Chase to Dr. John G. Perry, 28 Sept., 5, 10, 15 Oct., 12 Nov., 12 Dec. 1870; to Hamilton Smith, 26 Dec. 1870; "Diary," 13–18 Dec. 1870, DLC-Chase.

57. S. P. Chase to Schuckers, 26 Oct. 1870, DLC-Chase; to Sprague, 10 Feb. 1871, NNC-Sprague; S. P. Chase to William H. Reardon, 4 Aug. 1871, DLC-Chase.

58. S. P. Chase to Parsons, 9 Dec. 1870, DLC-Chase; to Barney, 12 Dec. 1870, CSmH-Barney.

59. S. P. Chase to Parsons, 9 Dec. 1870, DLC-Chase; *Lane County v. Oregon*, 7 Wallace 76; *The Collector v. Day*, 11 Wallace 113.

60. S. P. Chase to Henry D. Cooke, 31 Jan. 1871, DLC-Chase.

61. Ibid.; to Parsons, 1 Feb. 1871, DLC-Chase.

62. Salaries were finally raised to $10,000 for the Associate Justices and $10,500 for the Chief Justice by an Act of Congress passed on March 3, 1873, and approved by President Grant. *U.S. Statutes at Large*, vol. 17, pp. 485, 486.

63. S. P. Chase to Henry Clark, 22 March 1871, DLC-Chase.

64. S. P. Chase to Thomas H. Yeatman, 19 Oct. 1869, 12 Jan. 1871, OCHP-Chase; to Peter H. Clark et al, 2 March 1870, PHi-Chase; "Diary," 8 Jan. 1870, DLC-Chase; Cincinnati

Commercial, 21–24 Jan. 1870. Chase's approach to women's suffrage was not so enlightened. Though not opposed to it in principle, he thought Susan B. Anthony was "a little too fast" in her demands to eliminate sex as a standard for voting. S. P. Chase to Gerrit Smith, 13 Feb. 1873, DLC-Chase.

65. S. P. Chase to D. W. Bliss, 10 Aug. 1871, DLC-Chase.

66. S. P. Chase, "Diary," 1, 14, 16 Jan. 1872, PHi-Chase.

67. S. P. Chase to Parsons, 8 Aug. 1871, DLC-Chase.

68. Ben Perley Poore, *Reminiscences of Sixty Years in the National Metropolis,* 2 vols. (Philadelphia, 1886), II: 244.

69. Schuckers, *Chase,* 622.

70. *Tarble's Case;* 13 Wallace 397, 423 (1872); Warden, *Chase,* II: 799.

71. 16 Wallace 36 (1873). See also Charles A. Lofgren, *The Plessy Case* (New York, 1987), 67–70, a clear, convincing, and succinct account of the Slaughter House cases. See also the somewhat biased account in Fairman, *Reconstruction,* 1349–63.

72. For his busy social life in Washington, see S. P. Chase, "Diary," 17, 23, 30 Jan. 1872, PHi-Chase; Chase to Nettie, 16 Feb. 1872, DLC-Chase.

73. S. P. Chase, "Diary," 14 Jan. 1872, PHi-Chase.

74. Ibid., 14, 16 Jan., 11 Feb. 1872.

75. Hamilton Smith to Chase, 1 April 1872, DLC-Chase.

76. S. P. Chase to Flamen Ball, 8 April 1872, DLC-Chase; Washington *Evening Star,* 19 April 1872; Alexander Long to Chase, 22 April 1872; S. P. Chase to Alexander Long, 15 April 1872, OCHP-Long; S. P. Chase to D. Lloyd, 14 Aug. 1872, PHi-Chase.

77. Carl Schurz, *Reminiscences,* II: 187.

78. S. P. Chase to Murat Halstead, 20 May 1872, DLC-Chase.

79. Poore, *Perley's Reminiscences,* II: 244.

80. S. P. Chase to William P. Mellen, 6 March 1873, MeB-Mellen.

81. *Osborne v. Mobile,* 16 Wallace 279, 280 (1873).

82. Schuckers, *Chase,* 622.

83. S. P. Chase to Blair, 28 April 1873, DLC-Chase.

84. Warden, *Chase,* II: 767–70.

85. Alice Skinner Stebbins to Chase, 26 May 1873, DLC-Chase.

86. S. P. Chase to My dear Doctor, 1 May 1873, PHi-Chase; Schuckers, *Chase,* 623.

87. Schuckers, *Chase,* 623.

88. Ibid.

89. See, for instance, Beale and Brownsword, eds., *Welles Diary,* I: 413; S. P. Chase, "Diary," 12 Sept. 1862, DLC-Chase; Gabor Boritt, *Lincoln and the Economics of the American Dream* (Memphis, Tenn., 1978), 200–202.

90. See, for instance, George S. Boutwell, *Reminiscences of Sixty Years in Public Affairs,* 2 vols. (rpt., New York, 1968), I: 304, 305; Bray Hammond, *Sovereignty and an Empty Purse: Banks and Politics in the Civil War* (Princeton, N.J., 1970), 348, 349; Robert P. Sharkey, *Money, Class and Party: An Economic Study of the Civil War and Reconstruction* (Baltimore, Md., 1959), 25, 52; and Margaret G. Myers, *A Financial History of the United States* (New York, 1970), 162, 171–73.

91. S. P. Chase, "Diary," 1 Dec. 1872, PHi-Chase.

92. Schuckers, *Chase,* 623; New York *Tribune,* 6 May 1873.

Index